Jesus and the Holy City

New Testament Perspectives on Jerusalem

Peter W. L. Walker

WILLIAM B. EERDMANS PUBLISHING COMPANY
GRAND RAPIDS, MICHIGAN / CAMBRIDGE, U.K.

© 1996 Wm. B. Eerdmans Publishing Co.
255 Jefferson Ave. S.E., Grand Rapids, Michigan 49503 /
P.O. Box 163, Cambridge CB3 9PU U.K.

Printed in the United States of America

00 99 98 97 96   5 4 3 2 1

Library of Congress Cataloging-in-Publication Data

Walker, P. W. L. (Peter W. L.)
Jesus and the Holy City : New Testament perspectives on Jerusalem
/ by Peter W. L. Walker.
p.   cm.
Includes bibliographical references and indexes.
ISBN 0-8028-4287-9 (pbk. : alk. paper)
1. Jerusalem in the Bible.   2. Bible. N.T. — Criticism,
interpretation, etc.   3. Jesus Christ — Views on Jerusalem.
4. Jerusalem in Christianity— History of
doctrines — Early church, ca. 30-600.
5. Jerusalem — History — Religious aspects.   I. Title.
BS2545.J4W35   1996
263′.042569442 — dc21   96-39120
CIP

CONTENTS

91314

Part II: Jesus and the Church

Acknowledgements

This book had its genesis in a lecture given in Nazareth in 1984, presenting a
New Testament understanding of Jerusalem. The reaction this provoked in
some, who questioned whether the New Testament had anything coherent to
contribute to this subject, provided an incentive to look more deeply at this issue when the opportunity arose. That opportunity eventually came after further training and four years in parochial ministry when Dr. Bruce Winter
encouraged me to pursue this subject as a post-doctoral Research Fellow at
Tyndale House, Cambridge. I am grateful to him for his overseeing the entire
project and to the Academic Committee of the Tyndale House Council who
sponsored me for more than two years. Financial support was also received
from Corpus Christi College and the Cambridge Divinity Faculty, as well as
from several personal friends who gave generously and sacrificially. Without
such kindness the completion of this project would have been impossible.

It has been a privilege to work in Jerusalem on several occasions in the
last three years, and especially to enjoy the facilities of the Ecole Biblique. I
am grateful to those who made such visits possible and also for the various
speaking engagements when I have been able to present my ideas—both in Jerusalem and this country, as well as in Cyprus. Many of the principal issues
received a friendly critique at the monthly meeting of the *Cambridge Papers*.
I also greatly valued being in contact with a number of the scholars whose
writings are listed in the bibliography. In the midst of busy academic sched-
ules they gave time to read individual chapters of this study in its earlier stag-
es. Their encouragement and advice was much appreciated, though I alone am
responsible for the end-result. Finally, a word of thanks to the friends and col-
leagues who gave so much practical help—especially in recent weeks.

Throughout the entire project my wife, Georgie, has been wonderfully
supportive. I owe her and the family a great debt. May Hannah and Jonathan,
to whom this book is dedicated, one day understand why they were privileged
to live in Cambridge and to visit Jerusalem at this formative time in their lives.

30th July 1996   *Tyndale House, Cambridge*

vii

Introduction

For the past three thousand years Jerusalem has ignited passions and excited controversies—not just between people of different faiths, but also between those within a particular faith-tradition. In a previous volume it was shown how two leading Christian bishops in the Holy Land of the fourth century reached quite different conclusions about the status of Jerusalem.[1] Writing around AD 330, Eusebius of Caesarea remarked that 'to think that Jerusalem is the city of God is the mark of exceedingly base and petty thinking';[2] twenty years later, Cyril of Jerusalem retorted that 'the "holy city" is quite clearly this city in which we are now'.[3] In this present volume we return to study the significance of Jerusalem in the earliest years of the Christian Church.

Ever since the time of David, Jerusalem has exerted an influence on people's imagination and aspirations out of all proportion to its physical size or its political significance. Psalmists described it as the 'city of God' (Ps. 48.1-2), pilgrims longed to stand within its gates (*cf.* Ps. 122:2), Crusaders spilt blood to gain it, and in our own day its political future is a subject of intense debate. It is still a city about which the different 'children of Abraham' cannot easily agree.

Within Jerusalem's long history, the era known as the Second Temple Period must mark one of those times when the city's capacity to excite strong religious and political emotion was at its greatest.[4] After the bitter experience of the exile in the sixth century BC, the hope of the Jewish nation had been

---

[1] *Holy City, Holy Places?* (Oxford: OUP, 1990a). As its title suggests, this volume also examined the attitudes of Eusebius and Cyril towards the 'holy places' associated with the Gospels. For two shorter articles which summarize their contrasting attitudes to Jerusalem, see my (1990b) and (1995).
[2] Eusebius, *Commentary on the Psalms* [LXX 86.3], *PG*. 23:1044.
[3] Cyril, *Catechetical Lectures* 14:16, discussing Matt. 27:53.
[4] On first-century Jewish attitudes to Jerusalem, see *e.g.* Barrett (1956) and Safrai (1974). It was considered to be the 'navel of the earth' (Ezek. 38:12[LXX]; Jub. 8:12, 19; 1 Enoch 26; *cf.* later Num.R. 12:4; Lam.R. 3:58-64; Pesik.R. 10:2); Philo could claim that Jerusalem was 'not only the mother city of the land of Judaea, but also of many other countries' (*Legatio,* 281); *cf. e.g.* J.M. Scott (1994) 497-9.

nurtured by the conviction, drawn from the prophetic writers within the Hebrew scriptures, that God would one day restore Jerusalem's fortunes.[5] For
this reason the days of the Hasmonean kingdom in the second century BC,
when at last the Jewish nation experienced a measure of political independence, were fraught with meaning and expectancy. Yet they proved to be short-
lived. Once again, from 63 BC onwards, Jerusalem was subjected to pagan
rule—this time under the alien civilisation of Rome. Hopes once raised were
now cruelly thwarted. How would the glaring discrepancy between prophetic
hope and political reality be resolved? Where would it all end?

The task of describing what eventually took place in Jerusalem fell to
Josephus, whose *History of the Jewish War* is an invaluable source of historical information, written not long after the events it describes. Yet on this
question of Jerusalem there is another, somewhat neglected source. For it was
in this period and against this backdrop of simmering frustration and ferment-
ing hope, that twenty-seven short documents were composed, known to us
now collectively as the New Testament. Perhaps because of the Christian conviction that these writings contain truths that have timeless and eternal validity, it can sometimes be forgotten that they were originally written in an age
of great upheaval, and that the events which it describes took place on a stage
that was far from dull. In proclaiming that the long-awaited Messiah had come
to Jerusalem, the New Testament writers could not but evoke and re-awaken
all the religious and political expectations that had for so long been associated
with Jerusalem—what one scholar has helpfully termed 'restoration eschatology'.[6] To sense its original flavour, we must therefore approach the New Testament with this background in mind; its authors could not have been unaware
of Jerusalem's history or of its longed-for future. How did the brief story of
Jesus fit into the much longer story of Jerusalem?

In the light of the above, the importance of enquiring into New Testament attitudes towards Jerusalem may seem obvious. Despite the vast amount
of literature that has been produced in the scholarly quest to understand these
twenty-seven documents, there have been surprisingly few studies which have
sought to answer this question in any systematic way. J.C. de Young published a short M.Th thesis on the subject in 1961,[7] and W.D. Davies touched
on the issue thirteen years later, when investigating New Testament approaches to the issue of the Land.[8] While there have also been numerous books and

---

[5]   See *e.g.* Isa. 2:2-4; 35:8-10; 41:1ff; 52:1-12; 62; Jer. 30-31; Mic. 4:1-4; Ezek. 36; 40-
48; Zech. 8, 14. Jerusalem would be the place where the restored people of God would
gather from all the corners of the earth; *cf.* also 4 Ezra 13:12-13, 39-40; Ps. Sol. 11.5-7;
4QpPs. 37. 3:10-11.
[6]   See Sanders (1985) 61-119; *cf.* also *e.g.* Meyer (1979), Wright (1992) 268-338.
[7]   *Jerusalem in the New Testament* (University of Amsterdam: Kok, 1961) 150pp.

articles which *en passant* have noted the approach to Jerusalem of a single New Testament author, no systematic treatment has been produced in the history of modern scholarship. This present work is a sustained analysis of New Testament attitudes to Jerusalem—thus filling an important gap within New Testament studies.

The overall thesis is that the New Testament authors were indeed aware of this Jerusalem-issue and that they each came to view the city in a new way. In some shape or form it can be sensed within all the major documents of the New Testament with the possible exception of some of the shortest letters (*e.g.* James, Jude and 2 Peter).[9] Moreover, in almost every instance there is evidence of some re-evaluation of Jerusalem's significance in the light of the coming of him whom they believed was the Messiah.

On the one hand, the New Testament writers clearly shared in full measure the Old Testament assumptions concerning the distinctive identity and role of Jerusalem as the city uniquely chosen by God for his good purposes. This is only to be expected from writers who, apart from Luke, were themselves Jewish, loyal to the Old Testament tradition, and who shared the sentiments of their fellow-Jews towards Jerusalem. As if to complete the picture, Luke (who before his conversion may have been a 'God-fearer' familiar with the synagogue)[10] demonstrates that his knowledge of, and commitment to, the scriptural tradition was no less strong. They were thus united in their conviction concerning the unique role of Jerusalem in the past.

On the other hand, in the light of recent events the New Testament writers began to see Jerusalem in new ways. They had a new vision of the city—both of its present significance and of its future role—and this new vision had not a little to do with Jesus. To put it simply, any passion which they might have had for Jerusalem had been transformed by reflecting on a different kind of 'passion'—Jesus' death outside the city's wall. The concept of a crucified Messiah not only undid any previous notions of Messiahship, it also affected their understanding of Jerusalem. When they then reflected further on Jesus' prophetic statements in the Gospels about the city and his claims in relation to the Temple, it became clear that their attitudes towards Jerusalem had to be re-evaluated. The events associated with this teacher, prophet and professed Messiah cast Jerusalem in a new light. In so thinking they were not being anti-

---

[8]   *The Gospel and the Land* (Berkeley: California Press, 1974): see esp. pp. 131-150; 195-208, 252-260; *cf.* also the brief overview in Beagley (1987) 151-180. The works of W.D. Davies and also of N.T. Wright are quoted frequently; although other authors are referred to who share the same surname, the reader may assume that any references to 'Davies' and 'Wright', which do not specify initials, always refer to W.D. Davies or N.T. Wright.

[9]   On this, see below ch. 9, n. 1.

[10] See below ch. 3, n. 13.

Jewish; rather, being convinced that they lived in an era of eschatological fulfilment, they were seeking to show how the long story of the Old Testament
had reached an unexpected conclusion.

These shock-waves emanating from Jesus' involvement with Jerusalem
are reflected in the various New Testament writings, which are here studied in
detail. Given their varying circumstances (whether in time or place) each writer stands in a slightly different relationship to this 'epicentre'. Not unnaturally
their different vantage-points result in our being presented with different
'landscapes' of the city. One of the fruits of our study is therefore a new ap-
preciation of the rich diversity of the New Testament writings as each author
sketches Jerusalem from his own distinctive angle. In the midst of this diversity, however, there is also a profound unity.

The book is divided into two parts. In the first part (chapters 1-7) seven
major contributors to the New Testament are cross-examined for their attitude
towards the physical city of Jerusalem.[11] In the Judaism of their day there
were three interconnected entities (the Land, Jerusalem and the Temple)
which formed, as it were, a concentric pattern of geographical *realia* which
were theologically significant.[12] Whilst the focus of our investigation is the
city of Jerusalem (the second of these three), it has been important in each
chapter to discuss their attitude to the Temple, because of its inextricable link
with the city, and in some cases (where there is sufficient evidence: *e.g.* Paul,
John and Hebrews) their attitude to the Land; these discussions provide confirming evidence as to how they would have approached Jerusalem, which in
many ways was seen as the embodiment of the Land. Each of these chapters
then concludes with a section in which suggestions are made as to how the authors came to see Jerusalem in the way they did: in other words, having looked
at the 'landscape' of Jerusalem which they present, we suggest a possible
'vantage-point' for that presentation.

Some New Testament documents, we conclude, were written before the
fall of Jerusalem in the year AD 70, others after. However, the order of the
chapters in this book does not reflect a chronological order (nor indeed a canonical one). In part this was because it seemed more appropriate to begin
with the Synoptic Gospels, rather than with Paul, and instead to look at Paul
immediately after an investigation of Luke-Acts. Yet it also reflected a conviction at the inception of the project that it was important, as much as possible, to investigate each document on its own merits without prejudicing the
conclusions that might be reached. The present order therefore allows the

---

[11] The important contribution of 1 Peter is discussed at the beginning of ch. 10.

[12] See *e.g.* m.Kelim 1:6-9, with its presentation of the ten degrees of holiness focusing
down onto the 'holy of holies' in the Jerusalem Temple; *cf.* similarly Josephus, *War* 1:26;
5:227.

reader to sense some of the variety of approaches, as the relevant chapters alternate (roughly) between those documents written before 70 and those which were written subsequently.

It also gives scope for chapter 9 ('A New Theology') to draw the threads together more chronologically; this chapter therefore acts as a convenient summary of the material discussed in more detail in Part 1. The other chapters in Part 2 address two important questions which our study inevitably raises: First, if the New Testament writers came to understand Jerusalem in some new and unexpected ways, how much of this can be traced back to Jesus himself (ch. 8)? Secondly, how might this new understanding of the city be integrated into an overall 'biblical theology' of Jerusalem and its relevance for today (ch.10)? Attitudes to Jerusalem in any generation are frequently based on a particular interpretation of the Bible. This question of a 'biblical' approach to Jerusalem has therefore been important ever since in Jerusalem's history—in our own day as much as in the past—and may be seen as a determining motivation both for this present work and for my earlier study (1990a). How *is* Jerusalem to be viewed within a fully-orbed biblical theology?

The subject of Jerusalem has occupied my attention for many years. My training as a classicist prepared me to study the period of late antiquity and to focus on the different views towards Jerusalem in the early Byzantine period. The experience of organizing a conference on the theme of Christian attitudes to Jerusalem in 1991 (followed by that of editing the papers for publication)[13] heightened my interest in the New Testament period, which has become the field of my present endeavours. Inevitably, a training in classics and ancient history has been formative and has determined the level of criticism which is deemed appropriate to bring to a classical text (be it from the fourth century or the first).

It is hoped then that this present study will be of interest to New Testament specialists and students of late antiquity, as well as to all those who are concerned with issues relating to the Bible or the Holy Land today.

---

[13] *Jerusalem Past and Present in the Purposes of God* (Cambridge: Tyndale House, 1992; revd. ed., Carlisle/Grand Rapids: Paternoster/Baker, 1994a) 226pp.

PART I

LANDSCAPES OF JERUSALEM

1

A NEW TEACHING
Mark

'We heard him say, "I will destroy this Temple that is made with hands, and in three days I will build another, not made with hands"' (Mark 14:58).

Although Mark's central theme is the identity of Jesus, the role of Jerusalem in the story means that his brief Gospel introduces important themes: the contrast between Jesus' teaching and the political hopes of his day, the drama of Jerusalem missing the secret of Jesus' Messianic identity, and most importantly that the Risen Jesus now constitutes the new Temple. If Mark was writing just before the Temple's destruction in AD 70, his critique of Jerusalem has an even more poignant significance.

From the beginning of Mark's Gospel it is clear that Jesus and Jerusalem are inextricably linked. The opening events of the Gospel are located in the desert to the east of Jerusalem, and will have important repercussions for the city:

The beginning of the good news of Jesus Christ, the Son of God.

As it is written in the prophet Isaiah, 'See, I am sending my messenger ahead of you, who will prepare your way'; the voice of one crying out in the wilderness: "Prepare the way of the Lord, make his paths straight"',

John the baptizer appeared in the wilderness, proclaiming a baptism of repentance for the forgiveness of sins. And people from the whole Judean countryside and all the people of Jerusalem were going out to him (1:1-5).

This is an arresting opening. Mark focuses immediately on the central issue of Jesus' identity, with his composite quotation from both Malachi (3:1) and Isaiah (40:3) indicating that Jesus must in a startling way be identified with 'the Lord' himself.[1] The intriguing point, however, is that both these Old Testament texts come from passages concerned with Jerusalem: the 'Lord' of whom they speak is depicted as one who is coming to Jerusalem. The next sentence in Malachi is a prediction that the 'Lord whom you seek will come to his Temple' (Mal. 3:1b). In Isaiah the prophet had been speaking 'tenderly to Jerusalem' (v. 2) and had portrayed Jerusalem as the 'herald of good tidings' saying to the cities of Judah, 'Here is your God!' (v. 9). What Mark is about to relate is the fulfilment of this long-awaited prophetic hope—the surprising story of the Lord himself coming to Jerusalem.[2] These opening events in the desert may seem marginal and peripheral, something the size of a 'mustard-seed' (cf. 4:31), but they will prove to have significant implications for the very centre of Israel's life.

From the outset the reader is being prepared for Jesus' entrance into Jerusalem. Mark's description of Jesus' baptism a few verses later makes the same point. For when the divine voice declares, 'You are my Son' (v. 11), this echoes Psalm 2:7 ('He said to me, "You are my Son; today I have become your Father"').[3] The immediately preceding verses of that psalm had been concerned with the theme of the Davidic kingship in Jerusalem:

> The kings of the earth take their stand and the rulers gather together against the Lord and against his Anointed One. . . . The Lord scoffs at them . . . , saying, "I have installed my King on Zion, my holy hill." (vv. 2, 4, 6).

Although it took place in the River Jordan, Mark indicates that Jesus' baptism was his enthronement as the true Davidic King over Jerusalem. The King has been anointed in the desert, but one day he will approach his capital. Will his kingship be recognized, and what kind of throne will he receive? When Mark later recounts the actual arrival of Jesus in Jerusalem, these themes return to the surface—of Jesus as the true Davidic 'King' (10:47-8; 11:10; 12:35) and as the 'Lord' (11:3). For now the reader is let into a secret, unseen by most of the actors in the drama: Jerusalem will soon be presented with her rightful King. It will be a strategic and unparalleled moment in the city's history. How will it respond?

---

[1] See Marcus (1993) 37-41; cf. Mauser (1963) 80; Matera (1988); Gundry (1993) 36.
[2] Cf. Marcus (1993) 35.
[3] There may also be allusions to Gen. 22:1 and Isa. 42:1. On the importance of Ps. 2:7, however, see Steichele (1980) and Matera (1987) 31-37; contra Kazmierski (1979).

From the desert Jesus goes to Galilee (1:14). Mark's narrative remains there and in the surrounding territories until the final journey to Jerusalem. This dramatic movement from Galilee to Jerusalem is the structural backbone of the Gospel. From the moment Peter confesses Jesus to be the Messiah (8:29), there begin the three-fold predictions of Jesus' death in Jerusalem; Jesus and his disciples from then onwards are 'on the road'. The last five chapters are all located in the immediate vicinity of Jerusalem—though there are two hints of a post-resurrection appearance in Galilee, which is never actually described (14:28; 16:7).

To a greater or lesser extent the other synoptic Gospels are also structured on this pattern of a single journey to Jerusalem from Galilee, and it may be that Mark is responsible for this schema. This would certainly indicate Mark's desire to heighten the dramatic moment of Jesus' arrival in Jerusalem. In Mark's Gospel (unlike the others) there is not a single episode that takes place within Jerusalem or its environs until Jesus' 'triumphal entry' into the city (11:1ff). This structure clearly emphasizes Jerusalem's pivotal role in the story of Jesus. The episodes in Galilee are important, but the dénouement will be in Jerusalem.[4] How then did Mark view this city at the centre of his story?

1. The Temple

As will be seen in subsequent chapters, an author's attitude towards Jerusalem can often be detected most clearly through noting his evaluation of the Temple. For, in terms both of its religious significance and of its physical size, the Temple constituted a major part of the city.[5] How did Mark view the Temple in the light of Jesus' coming? There are various sayings in the Gospel which need to be evaluated, but of particular importance is the so-called 'cleansing of the Temple'. Does Mark give any clues as to how he interpreted this event?

---

[4]   Lohmeyer (1936), Lightfoot (1938), and Marxsen (1969) made much of the contrast in Mark between Galilee and Jerusalem. Lightfoot concluded that 'Galilee and Jerusalem stand in opposition to each other; Galilee is the sphere of revelation, Jerusalem is the scene only of rejection' (p. 124ff); *cf.* more recently Myers (1988) 432 (Jerusalem as a 'negative pole' in comparison with Galilee), and Kelber (1974) 64 (the 'Gospel's anti-Jerusalem bias'). This has been well criticized by *e.g.* Burkill (1963) 252-7, Stemberger (1974) and Davies (1974) 236-9; *cf.* also Freyne (1992). Galilee is not all-good (6:1-6), nor Jerusalem all-evil (1:5; 3:7; 11:18; 12:12, 37; 14:2); Jerusalem is the place where the hostility *already experienced in Galilee* finds a more concentrated focus. Mark may be critical of Jerusalem, but it cannot be demonstrated that he used this Galilee-motif as a means to this end.
[5]   On the importance of the Temple in first-century Judaism, see *e.g.* Bauckham (1993c) 142, and the comment of E.P. Sanders (1993) 262: 'it is amost impossible to make too much of the Temple in first-century Jewish Palestine'.

a) The Coming of the Lord

The first clue has already been identified. At the outset of his Gospel Mark quotes Malachi 3:1, a verse which continues, 'the Lord whom you seek will suddenly come *to his Temple*'. For Mark Jesus' arrival in the Temple is a visitation from the Lord himself (*cf.* the use of κύριος in 11:3). Mark may therefore have given particular weight to Jesus' description of the Temple as '*my house*' (11:17). This was, of course, a quotation of divine speech (Isa. 56:7); yet some identification between Jesus and the divine speaker may well have been within Mark's intention.[6]

In the light of this passage from Malachi, Jesus' 'cleansing' action was also to be expected. For the following verses described this coming of the Lord as a time of cleansing judgement:

> But who can endure the day of his coming? For he is like a refiner's fire. Then I will draw near to you for judgement. I will be swift to bear witness against . . . those who oppress the widows and the orphan, against those who thrust aside the alien, and do not fear me. . . . You are cursed with a curse, for you are robbing me—the whole nation of you! Bring the full tithe into the storehouse, so that there may be food in my house (Mal. 3:2-5, 9-10).

This whole passage sheds important light on Mark 11-12.[7] As a result, Jesus' coming to the Temple must be seen as a 'divine inspection'—the Lord coming to that which was his own to see what was being done in his name, the Lord coming to see in what ways he was being 'robbed'. This 'divine inspection' may be in Mark's mind when, unlike the other evangelists, he describes how Jesus, having entered Jerusalem and the Temple, simply 'looked around at everything' (11:11).

b) The search for fruit

Mark's 'sandwiching' of the Temple cleansing (vv. 15-17) between the two parts of the story of the withered fig-tree (vv. 12-14, 20 ff) is his second clue.[8]

---

[6] See *e.g.* Best (1981) 218.

[7] Thus Hooker (1991) 272, suggests that for Mark this may underlie Jesus' appealing to the authority of John the Baptist when questioned about his action in the Temple. 'It is possible that Mark would have understood the link between Jesus and the Baptist, who is the 'messenger' of Mal. 3:1, to indicate that Jesus must be the Lord who 'comes suddenly to his Temple' (Mal. 3:1-4): those who accept the messenger will accept the Lord who follows'.

[8] On the function of such 'sandwiches' in Mark, see *e.g.* Edwards (1989).

Jesus first inspects the tree 'to find out if it had any fruit' and then on finding it fruitless declares, 'May no one ever eat fruit from you again'—an invocation which Peter subsequently describes as a 'curse' (v. 21). Most probably the fig-tree would have been understood as a symbol for Israel.[9] Passages such as Jeremiah 8:13 ('when I would gather them, says the Lord, . . . there are no figs on the fig-tree') would have helped to make the symbolic function of this strange act quite clear.[10] In the coming of Jesus to Jerusalem God was looking for fruit from his people. Through setting Jesus' action in the Temple in this context Mark portrays the Temple as the centre of Israel's national life and Jesus' 'cleansing' as an act which announces the absence of the fruit which God requires. The Temple is barren.

Mark is less specific as to the particular manifestations of this barrenness. In his Temple protest was Jesus indicating the lack of prayer in the Temple, or criticising its financial arrangements (the necessity of exchanging currency into the Tyrian shekel), or highlighting the way the Temple was becoming the focus for an exclusive nationalism (in denial of the vision in Isa. 56:7, that the Temple become a 'house of prayer for all the nations': Mark 11:17)? It is possible that all of these would have played a part in Mark's diagnosis, though he might have seen it principally in terms of the nation not being ready to welcome its Messiah when the Messianic age finally arrived.[11]

c) A Portent of Destruction

The fig-tree episode has further significance. Without it Jesus' action might be interpreted simply as an act of 'cleansing' that had as its goal the continuance of the Temple's worship (though now 'purified' and reordered according to the strictures indicated here by Jesus). The fact that the fig-tree is 'cursed' and 'withers', however, strongly suggests that Jesus' action must be taken as revealing a more thorough-going critique of the Temple; Jesus' 'overturning of the tables' is an enacted parable of God's judgement, with the probable corollary that the Temple will soon be destroyed. Jesus does not perform a miracle whereby the fig-tree begins to blossom; he pronounces a curse which causes it to die.

> Who then would doubt the extraordinary impact upon the Markan reader of Jesus' cursing of the fig-tree? The Lord whom they had sought had suddenly come to his Temple (*cf.* Mal. 3:1 and Mark 1:2) but had condemned rather

---

[9]   So Telford (1980) 193f, in his extended study of this episode.
[10] See Hooker (1991) 262.
[11] *Cf.* Telford (1980) 196; see further discussion in ch. 8.

than restored it! For the Markan reader the cursing of the fig-tree was an es-chatological sign prefiguring the destruction of Jerusalem and its Temple.[12]

Mark's understanding of the Temple cleansing is therefore plain. Jesus' action had been a pronouncement of judgement upon the Temple. It had pin-pointed certain failings which were symptomatic of its lack of fruit, but this diagnosis was not with a view to a cure, but an announcement that such a cure was no longer possible. The days of God's patience were drawing to a close. The 'cleansing' in Mark is thus a 'prophetic act symbolising God's imminent judgemental destruction, not just of the building, but of the Temple system';[13] it is a 'prophetic anticipation of the impending destruction of the Temple'.[14]

This interpretation would be confirmed by the fact that in Mark's pres-entation of the incident the final note struck is that of Jesus' quoting from the famous Temple-speech of Jeremiah (Mark 11:17, quoting Jer. 7:11). In that speech the prophet, standing 'at the gate of the Lord's house', had pronounced God's threat to destroy the Temple if the people did not reform their ways: 'What I did to Shiloh I will now do to the house that bears my Name, the Tem-ple you trust in, the place I gave to you and your fathers' (v. 14). The Temple would suffer because of the moral and religious failures of the people (vv. 5-6), but also because of the way in which the people had twisted God's purpose for the Temple: 'Has this house, which bears my Name become a den of rob-bers to you? But I have been watching!' (v. 11).[15] Through alluding to this fa-mous passage Jesus serves notice that a similar twisting of God's purposes has again taken place and a similar divine judgement now rests upon the Temple. The Markan Jesus could have quoted other Old Testament passages which spoke of God's desire to 'reform' the Temple, but this one spoke ominously of its destruction as the only solution. To have dared to describe the Temple as a 'den of robbers' was offensive enough—comparable, perhaps, to calling Jerusalem Israel's 'high place';[16] yet the underlying implication of divine judgement and destruction would have made it far worse. The angry response of 'the chief priests and the teachers of the law' was not surprising (v. 18).

Geddert's analysis of Mark is helpful here.[17] He sees the 'cleansing' in-cident as an effective 'disqualification' of the Temple (which leads on subse-quently to its destruction), and that the basis for this is that Israel's *leaders* are

---

[12] Telford (1980) 163.

[13] Horsley (1987) 300; *cf.* similarly *e.g.* Hammerton-Kelly (1994) 18.

[14] Juel (1977) 198; *cf.* E.P. Sanders (1985) 75-6; *contra e.g.* Bauckham (1988a).

[15] This divine 'watching' endorses our argument above concerning Jesus' enacting a 'divine inspection': see also Geddert (1989) 129.

[16] As suggested by Geddert (1989) 288, n. 34.

[17] Geddert (1989) 117-130.

effectively 'robbing God'—precisely the charge that was made in the passage in Malachi. This was the root disease beneath all the other symptoms. This is based on the parable of the tenants (12:1-11) which, he suggests, needs to be taken as Jesus' explanation and *apologia* for his action in the Temple. Jesus side-steps the direct question concerning his 'authority' to have performed this 'cleansing' (11:28-33), but he answers instead with a parable. This not only includes the strongest claim so far of Jesus' identity as the 'beloved son' (12:6, *cf.* 1:11), but also the declaration that God's desire is to receive 'the fruit of the vineyard' (12:2). The parable thus parallels closely the 'enacted parable' of the fig-tree. In both, God shows his desire to receive 'fruit' from his people Israel—indicated, respectively, by the fig and the vineyard.

The vineyard parable makes the additional point, however, that it is the leaders of Israel who bear the chief responsibility; it is they who are the 'tenants' of the vineyard (which represents Israel as whole) and it is they who 'rob God' by preventing God from receiving the fruit that he might otherwise have gained from his people.[18] While the Temple sermon of Jeremiah was a judgement upon the whole nation, Jesus' parable narrows the focus down more specifically to Israel's leaders. Nevertheless, though the failing is to be attributed to the nation's leaders, the Temple will itself be involved in the judgement.

d) The Destruction Predicted

When, therefore, at the beginning of the Apocalyptic Discourse (ch. 13), Jesus predicts the forthcoming destruction of the Temple, the reader has been well prepared; it is the 'expected sequel'.[19] Jesus reveals privately to four of his disciples the inner significance of his earlier public action. This is a confirmation that, whilst his 'cleansing' and subsequent teaching might have consequences at other levels, they cannot be properly understood without the realisation that Jesus is indeed announcing the end of the Temple. The Apocalyptic Discourse serves to prepare his disciples for that time when the Temple will be destroyed and will be no more. Jesus' physical location—sitting 'on the Mount of Olives opposite (κατέναντι) the Temple (v. 3)—matches his theological stance of opposition to the Temple, a major theme of the Discourse.[20] Moreover Mark's portrayal of the disciples as they comment admiringly on the Temple's 'massive stones' and then ask Jesus concernedly when

---

[18] Jesus' call to 'give to God the things that are God's' (12:17) is thus a challenge to see that the real danger is not 'giving to Caesar' but 'robbing God'; *cf.* Geddert (1989) 122.
[19] Lane (1974) 452.
[20] *Cf. e.g.* Kelber (1974) 104, Geddert (1989) 146, and Struthers Malbon (1991) 161.

this destruction will take place conveys sufficiently the shock they would have felt at hearing such a negative stance towards the Temple. Jesus is overturning all their preconceptions and dashing many of their former hopes.

Mark is careful to ensure, however, that his portrayal of Jesus' negative attitude towards the Temple is not thought to be based on a complete disrespect for the institution *per se*. Hence Jesus speaks of the 'abomination of desolation standing *where it does not belong*' (13:14). Whatever the precise reference of this saying, it clearly concerns a reference to a forthcoming event in the Temple. Jesus upholds a sense of the Temple's prior holiness and shares the perspective of his fellow-Jews which would see the presence of such an 'abomination' as a desecration. Despite his prediction of judgement, Jesus is evidently working on the assumption of the Temple's previous significance. Indeed it was precisely because the Temple was so significant that its judgement became necessary. God had purposes for the Temple, but they had been overturned. Jesus affirms that from God's perspective the Temple was, as Isaiah had said, "*my* house"; but it was now a 'den of robbers' (11:17). The Temple was judged, not because it was not special, but precisely because it was.

e) The Temple's Replacement

A new theme, however, is introduced at this point. If this Herodian Temple is to be destroyed, what will replace it? For many Jews of that time, the destruction of this Temple could only have meant one thing: that God was inaugurating the promised 'end times', the time when he would finally establish his own true Temple in Jerusalem.[21] As a result, when the disciples asked about the Temple's destruction, they might have been working with the assumption that this calamitous event would mark the inauguration of the long-promised 'end times'. It is therefore highly significant that, in Mark, Jesus never gives any hint that there will be a physical replacement for this Temple. There is no suggestion, either in the Apocalyptic Discourse or elsewhere, that this destruction will be but a preliminary stage in some glorious 'restoration' of the Temple.

Yet the question still presses: what, then, *will* replace it? Geddert helpfully suggests that Mark is already preparing his readers for his answer at the end of chapter 12. He notes how the Apocalyptic Discourse (ch. 13) which itself concerns the Temple's destruction, is surrounded by two stories that hint at the Temple's replacement: the widow's offering (12:41-44) and the anointing of Jesus by the woman in Bethany (14:1-9). Both are stories of female religious devotion, but the object of devotion is different. The widow gives

---

[21] See *e.g.* 1 Enoch 90:28ff; Jub. 1:17, 27-9. *Cf.* Juel (1977), *passim*.

generously to the Temple and its treasury, the woman gives generously to Jesus and anoints his body. Jesus commends them both. Yet, given that immediately after his commendation of the widow he predicts the destruction of the institution to which she has just given 'all that she had to live on' (12:44), there is a certain irony here.[22] Was her gift wasted? By contrast, when the accusation is made in Bethany that the woman has 'wasted the perfume' (14:4), Jesus makes it clear that it was not. Contrary to appearances, therefore, it was the gift to the physical Temple that was wasted, not the gift to Jesus. This is Mark's way of beginning to teach that Jesus is himself the true Temple. The two passages 'prefigure the replacement of temples, a theme which Mark seems to have woven through his narrative'.[23]

This then means that chapter 13 is not simply about the Temple's destruction; it also concerns its replacement. For example, the Jerusalem Temple to which the nations were meant to come (*cf.* 11:17) is contrasted with the Christian gospel that is able to reach out to the world (13:10, *cf.* 14:9). A centripetal dynamic is going to be replaced by a centrifugal one: 'Mark 13 is fundamentally concerned with the issue of breaking free from Jerusalem-centredness into world mission'.[24] Secondly, there is the contrast between the necessity for 'flight' from the old Temple (13:14) and the '*gathering* of the elect from the ends of the earth' (13:27).[25] There is certainly a complete inversion of values: the 'infinitely valuable Temple' proves in Jesus' teaching to be 'nothing of the sort';[26] indeed the Temple's destruction might be seen as a moment of vindication for the Son of Man and his people.[27] In any event, the central spiritual reality (and that to which God's people are 'gathered') proves to be not the Temple, but the 'Son of Man' (v. 26). Jesus himself as the Son of Man becomes the 'renewed centre and focus for the people of God as they will be in the future'.[28]

This replacement-theme is confirmed in chapter 14 both in the anointing at Bethany (interpreted above) and supremely in the accusation made against Jesus at his trial: 'We heard him say, "I will destroy this Temple made with hands and in three days I will build another"' (14:58; *cf.* 15:29). Although this is described as a 'false' accusation, there is no doubt that Mark be-

---

[22] See A.G. Wright (1982) 256.

[23] Geddert (1989) 137; *cf.* p. 147.

[24] Geddert (1989) 138. This could equally well be applied to the Gospel as a whole.

[25] This runs counter to the normal expectation of the elect being gathered to the Temple in Jerusalem.

[26] Geddert (1989) 139.

[27] See further below n. 66.

[28] Geddert (1989) 121. *Cf.* Myers (1988) 323: 'Jesus now offers a vision of the end of the Temple-based world'.

lieved it contained a vital truth. Given Mark's ironic style, it would be fitting
if profound truth was actually spoken unwittingly by those who in the narrative are described as 'false'.[29] This irony is certainly present when Mark has
this accusation repeated at the foot of the cross (15:29), along with the chief
priests' sarcastic description of Jesus as the 'Christ, the King of Israel'
(15:32). All these accusations are truer than the speakers know. The falsehood
of the charge lies most probably in the accusation that Jesus *himself* would destroy the Jerusalem Temple, whereas in Mark's text Jesus simply pronounces
that 'not one stone will be left upon another' (13:2), leaving it unspecified as
to who will accomplish this deed.[30]

Two aspects of this statement are important for this study. First, the description of the Jerusalem Temple as 'made with hands' (χειροποίητος) is a
strong means of playing down its significance. This had been a way of belit-
tling the pagan idols (*e.g.* Ps. 115:4; *cf.* Isa. 46:6); to describe the Temple in
such a fashion was potentially incendiary.[31] Yet in this context the point of the
phrase lies rather in its contrast with the description of the alternative Temple
that was '*not* made with hands' (ἀχειροποίητος).[32] The Jerusalem Temple
had been ordained of God, but Jesus predicted the appearance of a new kind
of Temple, originating with God—in comparison with which the physical
Temple would appear as merely human, 'made with hands'.

Secondly, there is little doubt that Mark saw the fulfilment of this prediction in the resurrection of Jesus.[33] The phrase 'in three days' (διὰ τριῶν
ἡμερῶν) was too close to the normal way of referring to Jesus' being raised
'after three days' (μετὰ τρεῖς ἡμέρας) for the connection not to have been
made. For Mark, therefore, the resurrection of Jesus brought into existence a
new kind of Temple. This could be identified with Jesus himself, or, alternatively, with the Christian community. It is perhaps for this reason that Mark
uses διά rather than μετά, thereby ensuring some connection to the Risen Jesus without requiring a total identification.

> The phrase is ideally suited if Mark's point is to tie the building of the new
> Temple very closely to that event [the resurrection], yet to suggest that the
> whole Christian community is part of that Temple with Jesus.[34]

---

[29] This is well argued in Juel (1977) 57, 169, 206.
[30] *Cf.* Geddert (1989) 131. It is not impossible that some interpreted Jesus' cleansing of
the Temple as a claim to be *himself* the agent of the Temple's forthcoming destruction.
[31] *Cf.* Geddert (1989) 132.
[32] See Juel (1977) 149, 155-6.
[33] See *e.g.* Juel (1977) 144.
[34] Geddert (1989) 133.

Taken as a whole the sentence suggests that Jesus through his resurrection will establish a new Temple, focused upon himself and in his people, and that this in turn will be in some way connected with the destruction of the Jerusalem Temple. It is as though the emergence of the new Temple automatically entails the removal of the old one.[35]

Further detail on this connection between the resurrection and the destruction of the Jerusalem Temple is not found in Mark—except perhaps in the imagery of the 'rejected stone' in 12:9-11. At the end of the vineyard parable Jesus spoke of the punishment of the tenants and then of the 'rejected stone' becoming the 'capstone'. If Mark saw this imagery from Psalm 118 as a reference to Jesus' vindication by God in the resurrection,[36] then these verses reveal this same combination of judgement and resurrection. Again no precise connection is made between them, but it can be deduced that Jesus' vindication actually consists of two events: his own resurrection on the one hand, and the punishment of the tenants on the other. Without the latter his vindication is only half-complete.

In the light of 14:58 it becomes possible to suggest that for Mark the resurrection inherently entailed the consequent destruction of the Temple; the two events were inter-connected. The resurrection was a vindication, but with a warning. 'Jesus' resurrection and the destruction of the Temple are legitimately considered two sides of the same coin'.[37] The connection could be seen (as in 12:9-11) in terms of Jesus' vindication over his enemies; alternatively (as in 14:58) it could be seen in terms of a new 'order' within the divine economy as the new Temple effectively relativized the old.

There is thus a great drama in Mark's narrative as the tension between the two 'temples' is played out. Mark portrays Jesus as the one who, having predicted the overthrow of the physical Temple in Jerusalem, promises to establish a new Temple in his own person. But will this happen? 'The fate of the two temples is about to be decided. The custodians of each have pronounced the doom of the other'.[38] At the time of the crucifixion it seems clear that Jesus is wrong: the *new* Temple, not the old, is on the point of being destroyed, and the bystanders mock the one who promised 'to destroy the Temple' (15:29). At precisely this moment in Mark's narrative, however, we are taken from the

---

[35] Schnellbächer (1983) 102, makes the further important observation: 'Jesus as the only credible representative of Israel's sonship has taken upon himself his own curse of the Temple: in himself, the Temple is being broken down, and at the same time, rebuilt afresh, albeit "not made with hands", within "three days"'.

[36] As in *e.g.* Juel (1977) 54.

[37] Juel (1977) 212; 'when the Temple falls discerning believers can be sure that Jesus has been vindicated at the expense of his enemies, and the transaction completed' (p. 213).

[38] Geddert (1989) 140.

hill of Golgotha to the opposite hill, the Temple Mount, to witness a mysterious event: 'the curtain of the Temple was torn in two from top to bottom' (15:38). For all its different possible meanings, Mark is clearly drawing a close connection between Jesus' death and the Temple, and most probably suggesting that the great reversals that have been prophesied have now been set in motion. 'With the killing of Jesus the die is cast; the prophecies of Jesus will be fulfilled'.[39] In some mysterious way 'the result of Jesus' death will prove to be the end of the Jewish Temple'.[40]

> The rending of the veil is a public sign that the rejection of the Messiah discoses a failure in sensitivity to the divine purposes so serious that it seals the disaster of AD 70. Jesus death and the destruction of the formal structures of Judaism are inseparaby bound together.[41]

For Mark therefore the Temple's fate was sealed, not simply with the resurrection, but in the moment of the crucifixion; the resurrection merely confirms this. The Jerusalem Temple 'dies' in the death of Jesus; and the underlying rationale for this is that Jesus himself is the new Temple 'not made with hands'. The destruction of the one Temple (the crucifixion) leads inevitably to the destruction of the other. As a result, the charge levelled against Jesus at his trial that he would 'destroy the Temple', though 'false' at one level, proves true at a deeper level. 'Jesus is the destroyer of the Temple in a figurative and ironic sense: its destruction is the result of his death, brought about by those in charge of the Temple worship.'[42] This then involves the irony that those who tried to protect the Temple 'merely hastened the end of the Temple, because the very death of Jesus constitutes a prolepsis of the Temple's end'.[43]

f) Conclusion

Mark's Gospel reveals a significant re-evaluation of Jerusalem's Temple. Although Jesus affirms the significance of the Temple within God's purposes (hence his quoting Isaiah's reference to it as 'my house'), he declares in word

---

[39] Geddert (1989) 145. Geddert lists no less than 35 possible interpretations of the 'rending of the veil' (pp. 141-3); underlying most of them is this theme of a promised reversal. The argument of Bailey (1990-1) 104, that the unveiling of the Temple parallels the earlier stripping naked or 'unveiling' of Jesus is speculative, yet it would similarly confirm that Mark saw Jesus as the new Temple: 'the new holy of holies is a *dying saviour*'.

[40] Juel (1977) 142.

[41] Lane (1974) 575.

[42] Juel (1977) 206.

[43] Kelber (1976) 179.

and deed that it now stands under judgement. Jesus enters the Temple as the Lord himself inspecting his own property and judging it for its lack of fruit. In due course, it will be destroyed. Its destruction, however, is also integrally linked to the person of Jesus, whom Mark portrays as God's appointed replacement for the Temple. Now that the new has come, the old must pass away. Unlike some of his Jewish contemporaries who would soon fight for the Temple's continuance (or had recently done so) Mark openly accepts the Temple's demise; for the Temple had been awaiting this fate, he claims, from the moment of Jesus' death. His focus instead is upon the centrality of Jesus: 'over against the historic importance of Temple worship within Jewish religious life Mark wants to emphasize . . . the importance of Jesus'.[44] The coming of Jesus has profoundly affected the subsequent destiny of the Temple.

2. The City of Jerusalem

The Temple was the central heart-beat of Jerusalem. Mark's new understanding of the Temple will therefore, almost inevitably, have involved a new approach towards the city of Jerusalem, considered apart from the Temple. Inasmuch as it is possible to distinguish them, are there any further indications as to Mark's attitude to the *city*?

In his narrative Jerusalem is a place where there is some popular support for Jesus (11:8-10, 18; 12:12, 37; 14:2), but where such support ebbs away (15:11, 29); a place where Jesus' Messianic identity is increasingly revealed (11:3, 17; 12:6, 37; 13:26; 14:62), but where that identity is denied, leading to controversy (11:18; 11:27-12:40; 14:1-2; 43 ff; 15:1 ff); the place of the crucifixion and the resurrection. For all this activity within the narrative, however, there is little in the text that gives any theological reflection on what these events signify for the city itself.

In Matthew and Luke there are statements on the lips of Jesus addressed to 'Jerusalem' (*e.g.* Matt. 23:37; Luke 13:34; 19:41-4). None of these appear in Mark. In Luke the Apocalyptic Discourse contains explicit references to Jerusalem (21:20, 24). In Mark's version (ch. 13) these are absent, and even the reference to the Temple in 13:14 is couched in enigmatic terms (where the desolating sacrilege 'ought not to be'). Mark's understanding of Jerusalem, therefore, is less explicit than that found in the other Gospels.

Conceivably some of the geographical movements within the Gospel narrative reflect Mark's view of Jerusalem. First, there is the way he describes Jesus' movements in and out of the city. Some interpretations read far too

---

[44] Achtemeier (1975) 26.

much into Mark's text at this point.[45] As already noted, however, Mark may have seen it as appropriate for Jesus to have delivered the Apocalyptic Discourse when sitting 'opposite the Temple' (13:3). Jesus thereby distanced himself from the city and encouraged his disciples to view the city in a similar way. Inasmuch as he warns them here to be prepared to 'flee to the mountains' (v. 14), Jesus' own departure at this juncture to the Mount of Olives could be taken as a proleptic 'fleeing' from the city—a dominical sanction for making this difficult decision when it subsequently became necessary.

Then again, Jesus' resolution to celebrate the Passover within the city (despite the apparent need for security measures and secrecy: 14:13-16) might also have been significant for Mark. In one sense this was simply in accordance with the general custom of celebrating the Passover within the city.[46] However, Jesus' institution of a 'new' Passover in the heart of Jerusalem was deeply ironic: for this effectively implied that *even in Jerusalem* the people of Israel were still in Egypt and in 'slavery'. If this might seem fanciful, there is some corroboration, in that he uses the Greek word ἐξάγω to describe Jesus' being 'led out' of the city to be crucified (15:20)—a word which elsewhere in the New Testament is regularly used to describe the 'leading out' of the Israelites from Egypt under Moses.[47] Was this Mark's way of suggesting that the *via dolorosa* was a paradoxical re-enactment of the exodus, and that through his crucifixion and resurrection Jesus had accomplished a deeper liberation from slavery than the political one desired by his contemporaries? Again Jerusalem was being cast in the role of Egypt: for this was the place from which Jesus needed to be 'led out'.

Secondly, some significance for Jerusalem lies in Mark's two references which speak of a post-resurrection appearance in Galilee (14:28; 16:7). Plainly Jerusalem is not the only place which is privileged to witness the resurrection (*cf.* Matthew and John). Indeed in Mark's text as it stands there is no resurrection-appearance as such in Jerusalem. This may indicate that, although the resurrection had taken place in Jerusalem, Mark's focus lay elsewhere. At the least, these references to Galilee ensure that the narrative 'opens out' at the end, and that Jerusalem is not depicted as the end-point or goal of the Gospel story. Mark thereby teaches that Jesus' disciples must not 'mistake

---

[45] See *e.g.* Myers (1988) 350: 'Jesus was not visiting the heart of the world as a devoted pilgrim, but mounting guerilla-like raids on the heart of oppressive power from a base in a nearby village'.

[46] See Jeremias (1969) 61, 101 n. 4; m.Zebahin 5:7-8; m.Pesahim 7:9.

[47] See Acts 7:36, 40; 13:17; Heb. 8:9. This would then tie in with Mark's presentation of Jesus' death as a 'ransom for many' (10:45) where the word for 'ransom' (λύτρον) picks up the theme of God's 'redemption' of Israel from Egypt: see Hooker (1991) 248-9. In Jesus' 'going out' from Jerusalem he is effecting a new act of redemption for God's people.

Jerusalem for the goal of the way'.[48] He also opens the door for his readers, for Jesus' going to Galilee is proleptic of the disciples' subsequently leaving Jerusalem with the gospel message for all people. God's purposes have become universal, being restricted neither geographically to Jerusalem, nor nationally to the Jewish people.[49] This universalism and the flow of the narrative away from Jerusalem at the very end suggest that Mark played down the theological significance of Jerusalem in the era inaugurated by the resurrection.

Such thoughts remain speculative; for Mark has not given us any explicit statement concerning Jerusalem, the city. Some further indication of how Mark viewed Jerusalem comes to light, however, when due attention is paid to two important themes within the whole Gospel: the theme of Jesus' hidden identity, and of Jesus' ministry as the fulfilment of prophetic hope.

a) Jesus' Mysterious Identity

The Gospel is often seen as a sustained presentation of Jesus' identity, being designed to answer the question posed to the disciples: 'Who do you say that I am?' (8:29). If this was one of Mark's primary purposes, Mark would almost certainly, in reflecting on Jerusalem, have thought first and foremost about the way in which the city had wrestled with Jesus' identity: who did *Jerusalem* say that he was? The theme of Jesus' identity has been pressed upon the reader throughout the Gospel. In the conflict stories at the outset (2:1-3:6) Mark's account of Jesus had been deliberately provocative. Who is this that claims the extra-ordinary precedent of David as a justification for his disciples' picking corn on a leisurely Sabbath walk? Is he really one greater than David? 'Who can forgive sins but God alone?' (2:7). When Jesus finally comes to Jerusalem this question of identity is still of paramount importance. It is the question which underlies the triumphal entry, the Temple cleansing (11:1-26), the subsequent theological disputes (11:27-12:4), and the interview with the High

---

[48] Kelber (1974) 146. *Cf. e.g.* Struthers Malbon (1991) 34: 'Jerusalem is not the final geopolitical reference of Mark. . . . Jerusalem cannot confine Jesus of Nazareth—not spatially, not theologically'.

[49] Some see these references to Galilee as indicating Jesus' call to his disciples to go exclusively to the *Gentiles*: see *e.g.* Boobyer (1952) and Evans (1954). This goes too far. Mark noted that, by being in Galilee, Jesus had an access to the Gentile world that would have been denied him if he had been confined to Jerusalem (see *e.g.* 5:1-20; 7:24-30; *cf.* 3:8 and 7:31). Yet none of this can deny the predominantly Jewish nature of Galilee in Jesus' day. If Mark saw Jesus' ministry in Galilee as proleptic of the subsequent mission of the Church, it would indicate instead that this too should have a two-fold focus—towards both Gentiles and Jews. This two-fold focus may be conveyed through Mark's 'doublet' of the two miraculous feedings: see *e.g.* Richardson (1941) 97f., and Struthers Malbon (1991).

Priest: '*are* you the Messiah?' (14:61). Yet if Mark' emphasis on Jesus' identity was because he wanted his readers to answer this question in the affirmative, the tragic fact was that Jerusalem, the city so long associated with God's
purposes, had largely answered this question negatively. When Jesus first approached the city, the over-riding question raised by the narrative thus far was
inevitably: would Jerusalem perceive Jesus' real identity? Would the city be
party to the 'Messianic secret'?

By the end of the Gospel it is clear that this was not to be. Jerusalem
misses her Messiah. Her true King, although anointed by God in baptism,[50] is
not given a throne but rather a cross where he is crucified as the 'King of the
Jews' (15:26).[51]

> Jerusalem, the capital of Israel, the place where God dwells in the Temple, is
> the place where Jesus is rejected and killed. Yet here in this place, his death
> is also his enthronement as God's King.[52]

In Markan terminology, the city is 'ever seeing but never perceiving'; the disciples and a few others may have been given 'the secret of the kingdom of
God', but Jerusalem as a whole remains 'on the outside' (*cf.* 4:11-12). The
very place which could claim to have been on the 'inside' of God's purposes,
proves instead to be 'outside' them. As a result of Jesus, Jerusalem was
'turned *inside out*'. The city that had cherished the memory of God's revelation in the past now misses *this* revelation. The place that should have been at
the centre of God's purposes plays a central role in those purposes by being
blind to them. Jerusalem was not 'given the secret'.

When this is placed alongside the important theme within the Gospel,
that in Jesus God had been opening the door to those previously 'outside', a
powerful contrast emerges. In his ministry Jesus had not only welcomed the
marginalized within Israel (*e.g.* 2:13-17) but had also challenged those exclu-
sivist 'boundary-markers' of Israel (such as the Sabbath, the food-laws) which
had set apart Israel as God's people. He had implicitly been redrawing the
lines around the 'people of God'. For Mark, therefore, one of the main characteristics of Jesus' ministry was precisely its inclusion of the 'outsider', his
bringing the 'outside in'.[53]

The kingdom of God announced by Jesus overturns the traditional order
of things: what had been presumed to be on the inside (Jerusalem) had proven

---

[50] *Cf.* above at n. 3.

[51] On the importance of this 'royal' christology, see *e.g.* Kingsbury (1983), Juel (1977)
and Matera (1987), though the significance of this for Jerusalem is not explored.

[52] Rhoads and Michie (1982) 71.

[53] Not surprisingly, one of the climaxes of the Gospel is the faith of the Gentile Roman
centurion (15:39).

to be on the outside, whilst those who had been on the outside (the outcasts within Israel, the Gentiles) had been brought within. What had been on the margins had been brought into the centre, whilst the centre had seemingly been cast out to the periphery.[54] Jerusalem's failing to grasp Jesus' true identity inevitably had important repercussions for the city; she was no longer at the centre, no longer 'on the inside'.

b) Jerusalem's Prophetic Future

A second theme within the Gospels that reveals something of Mark's understanding of Jerusalem is that of Jesus as the one who fulfils the prophetic hopes of the Old Testament. This may be less prominent in Mark than, say in Matthew, but Mark's opening verses indicate clearly that he saw the ministry of Jesus against this prophetic background. Hence there are allusions not just to the prophecies of Isaiah and Malachi (1:2-3; cf. also 11:17; 12:1; 13: 5, 8), but also to Daniel (13:4, 13-19, 30; 14:62) and Zechariah (11:17; 13:27; 14:27).[55] What is significant is that these prophetic passages were not simply passages that could serve Mark's christology (endorsing the notion of Jesus as the Messiah, the Son of Man, the Lord, etc), but more pointedly were passages which formed the basis for a whole expectation of what God would do one day *for Jerusalem.*

Thus around the time that Mark was composing his Gospel, some involved in the Jewish War (from AD 66) saw these same passages as endorsing their religious and political convictions about God's purposes for Jerusalem— in particular that God would bring liberation to the city from the hands of Rome.[56] For example, passages in Zechariah may well have inspired those defending Jerusalem against the Roman armies 'to hope with unshakable certainty for a miraculous intervention from God'.[57] Daniel's visions encouraged a belief that Israel would be vindicated through the ungodly being condemned. Meanwhile, the prophecy of Isaiah 40 (with its theme of God's 'good tidings for Jerusalem' being proclaimed 'in the desert') not only inspired the community at Qumran to locate itself in the desert and to expect an 'eschatological

---

[54] There is a parallel here to the way that Mark (in the terminology of Struthers Malbon [1991] 263) portrays Jerusalem as the formerly sacred place which has now become the place of chaos. Thus Hammerton-Kelly (1994) 120, writes: 'Chaos inheres in the sacred; order is found in the presence of Jesus. . . . Jesus replaces the Temple, but not at the centre. He is eccentric.'

[55] These and other scriptural allusions are all listed in Kee (1975).

[56] See Marcus (1993) 199ff.

[57] Hengel (1989b) 242.

victory following a divine march through the wilderness',[58] but also played an integral part in determining the programme of various revolutionary leaders, all of whom led their followers out into the wilderness with the promise that this would be the prelude to God's redemptive action.[59]

Mark's interpretation of these Old Testament prophecies is quite different. The Messiah had come, but the Messianic age had turned out to be different from what was expected. His was a radically new teaching. In the process, however, he necessarily came up with a quite different vision of Jerusalem and its political future. This has been highlighted in a recent study by Joel Marcus. Important themes in Deutero-Isaiah (such as God's 'holy war' and his 'return to Zion') have been refashioned in the light of his convictions about Jesus as Messiah; so too have the themes of apocalyptic war in Daniel, the vision of Jerusalem and the Mount of Olives in Zechariah, and the concept of God's Kingdom in the 'suffering servant' passages in Isaiah and the Psalms.

> Nothing could be more antithetical to conventional notions of victory than Jesus' prophecy of his own betrayal and execution. Yet this prophecy is not a *denial* of the Deutero-Isaian hope for a holy war victory; it is, rather, a radical cross-centred *adaptation* of it. The fearful trek of the befuddled, bedraggled little band of disciples *is* the return of Israel to Zion, and Jesus' suffering and death *are* the prophesied apocalyptic victory of the divine warrior'.[60]

> Instead of seeing the arrival of the kingdom of God in the appearance of a triumphant Messiah figure on the Mount of Olives, a miraculous deliverance of Jerusalem from the Gentile armies that surround it, and a resanctification of the Temple through its cleansing from pagan influence, Mark would see the arrival of the kingdom of God, paradoxically, in the deliverance of Jesus to his Jewish enemies on the Mount of Olives, his humiliating death at the hands of Gentiles in Jerusalem, and the proleptic act of Temple destruction that accompanies that death (15:38).[61]

---

[58] Marcus (1993) 200, based on the evidence of 1QS 8:12-16; see also Brooke (1992) 132.

[59] Marcus (1993) 23; *cf.* Schwartz (1992a).

[60] Marcus (1993) 36 (italics original). 'For Mark, Jesus *is* a warrior, and his entrance into Jerusalem is a decisive campaign in God's holy war of eschatological liberation; in his entrance into the holy city the Lord returns to Zion to redeem it from alien rule' (p. 149). He suggests (p. 148) that Mark may have seen Jesus' 'triumphal entry' as a direct contrast to the false Davidic claims and entrance into Jerusalem made by Menachem and Simon bar Giora in the years immediately preceding AD 70 (see Josephus, *War* 2.17.8; 4.529-34; *cf.* Geddert [1989] 148). He also sees the frequent references to Jesus' disciples being on the 'way' (9:33, 34; 10:17, 32, 52; 11:8) as highlighting this theme of the Lord's coming to Zion, which had started in the desert. Mark is thus vitally concerned with the whole theme of the future 'exodus', predicted by Isaiah and now fulfilled in Jesus—that is, 'the triumphant march of the holy warrior, Yahweh, leading his people through the wilderness to their true homeland in a mighty demonstration of saving power' (p. 29).

In colourful fashion he therefore concludes that Mark 'takes the raw ore of Jewish apocalyptic conceptions and subjects them to a christological neutron bombardment'.[62]

> [Jesus] fills the Old Testament molds in surprising ways that threaten to break the molds themselves. . . . The Old Testament patterns and themes used by Mark have thus suffered an alchemical transformation based on a logically prior belief, the good news of the arrival of the eschaton in the event of Jesus Christ.[63]

Such an analysis of Mark's presentation helpfully places it within its own contemporary context, reminding us that he was not writing in a vacuum. On the contrary, the first-century Palestine of which he was writing was an apocalyptically-charged tinderbox in the process of being ignited—fuelled precisely by Old Testament texts such as those to which Mark himself was referring.[64] Mark's understanding can then be seen to be quite distinctive. He completely disavows any approach which would see God's purposes as integrally bound up with the status of Jerusalem—its political independence and the restoration of its former religious glory. Instead, by focusing on the way Jesus had fulfilled those Old Testament scriptures in an unexpected way he effectively turned this whole prophetic hope of Israel 'upside down'.

Mark's message concerning Jerusalem was consciously subversive. Jesus' identity as Messiah had not led him to base his mission on a supposition of Jerusalem's forthcoming 'restoration'; on the contrary, the prophecies of the Old Testament needed to be re-examined and re-understood in the light of his identity as Israel's Messiah. Mark's Jesus was a Messiah on his own terms; it was he who determined the meaning of the prophecies, not *vice versa*.

---

[61] Marcus (1993) 160-161. Kelber (1974) 106, sees a similar reversal of the imagery of Zechariah in Mark 11:23 ('if you say to this mountain, "Be taken up and thrown into the sea"'), which he understands as referring to the Temple mount. In Zech. 14 Jerusalem and the Temple Mount were to be elevated, but now they are to be cast down; by contrast, the Mount of Olives was meant to be split apart. Now, however, in a 'deliberate violation of Zion mythology' 'Mark reverses the traditional role of the two mountains'. *Cf.* also Telford (1980) 119, Schnellbächer (1983), and Myers (1988) 304. If this understanding of the 'mountain' could be confirmed, then it would indeed indicate Mark's radical critique of the Temple. It is unlikely, however, (*contra* Schnellbächer) that Mark saw the mountain of Transfiguration as Mount Zion's rival and replacement.

[62] Marcus (1993) 41.

[63] Marcus (1993) 202-3.

[64] Even if Mark was writing for a predominantly Gentile audience, this Jewish matrix of ideas would still be an essential backdrop for his presentation of Jesus as 'Messiah'. He could scarcely avoid some reflection on how the Jesus, whom he presented as Israel's Messiah, related to the Messianic expectations held within the Judaism of Jesus' day.

This awareness of the contemporary Jewish context enables us to see Mark's text in a new light. For example, we may give more significance to Mark's version of the Triumphal entry in which (unlike Matthew and Luke) the crowd cries out, 'Blessed is the coming *kingdom* of our father David!' (11:10). Mark emphasizes the longing for the restoration of an independent political kingdom for Israel similar to that experienced in David's time. This also explains why the Markan Jesus has to be so 'secretive' and careful about his messiahship, in case that messiahship be mis-understood. The 'kingdom of God' of which Jesus speaks is going to be of quite a different kind. The crowds may want a restored 'kingdom of David'; but Jesus is introducing the 'kingdom of *God*'. At the time the crowds may have confused the two, but Mark's readers are not to make the same mistake.

Even though Jesus' ministry was not 'political' (in the commonly accepted sense of the word), it had profound political repercussions for the city. For Jerusalem's true King has come, unrecognized, and established his kingdom—a kingdom which is of such a different order that it leaves the expressly political aspirations of Jerusalem in tatters.

c) Jerusalem after Jesus

What then will befall the city? First, important consequences flow from the clear hints in Mark's narrative that God's raising of Jesus must be seen as God's *over-turning of Jerusalem's verdict on Jesus*. Mark 8:31-9:1 presents a strong contrast between the fate awaiting the Son of Man in Jerusalem, and the verdict of the Danielic court where that same Son of Man will be vindicated: two very different verdicts on Jesus are going to be pronounced—death or vindication, crucifixion or resurrection. Jerusalem will be involved only in the former, God alone in the latter. In effect the city will siding with those who were 'ashamed' of Jesus; presumably, therefore, the Son of Man in due course will be 'ashamed' of Jerusalem (*cf.* 8:38). This is then sensed even more strongly in the trial-scene where Jesus again uses the Danielic language concerning his future vindication, even as he is denounced by the religious authorities of Jerusalem (14:62-5).[65] As a result, although the resurrection takes place just outside Jerusalem, the city strictly has no part in it, and cannot claim it to her credit. In vindicating Jesus through raising him from the dead, God is pronouncing not his blessing upon the city, but rather his opposition to it. This has significant implications.

---

[65]   See Juel (1977) 41-115, esp. 54-55.

Secondly, given the way in which he understood Old Testament prophecy, Mark plainly gave little encouragement to the idea that Jerusalem would experience a form of 'restoration'. Those prophecies had been fulfilled decisively in the coming of Jesus. If this revealed that the expectations of his fellow Jews had been mistaken, then it also warned against any of Mark's Christian readers making the same mistake. On the contrary, when Mark gives any indication as to the future of Jerusalem, the emphasis is on a forthcoming calamity. Thus the Apocalyptic Discourse (ch. 13) predicts the Temple's destruction (13:2; *cf.* 14:58; 15:29) and also contains Jesus' warning to 'flee to the mountains' (13:14). In this way Jesus warns that, contrary to the expectations of his disciples (who no doubt would have been open to the more positive prophetic hopes of their time), the future of Jerusalem was bleak. The city which had witnessed the ministry of Jesus would soon be engulfed in a period of suffering unparalleled since 'the beginning of creation' (13:19).[66]

d) *Conclusion*

Close inspection of Mark's text thus reveals the essential contours of a distinctive approach towards Jerusalem. Although he did not especially compare it unfavourably with Galilee, this was nevertheless the place where the paradoxes of Jesus' ministry had come to a head. It was the place where the secret of his Messianic claim had been revealed but rejected, the city which had crucified its king and whose Temple had been found wanting by its Lord; the place where Jesus had predicted the forthcoming destruction of the Temple and hinted at its replacement in his own person and amongst his followers; the place in which, nevertheless, God had acted in accordance with his long-revealed purposes in order to bless not just Israel but the entire world.

Wright's conclusions concerning Mark can thus be taken as a fair statement of the case:

> The coming of the kingdom does not mean the great vindication of Jerusalem, the glorification of the Temple. . . . It means, rather, the desolation of

---

[66] Some scholars argue further that when Jesus then speaks about the 'Son of Man coming with great power and glory' (13:24-27), this is not a reference to Jesus' second coming, but rather a symbolic way of referring to Jesus' vindication—both in his resurrection, and also in the fall of Jerusalem; see *e.g.* Wright (1996) ch. 8; *cf.* France (1971) 227-239. If so, the reader would be required to understand that the opposition between Jesus and Jerusalem was total, such that the fall of the latter was the vindication of the former: only when Jerusalem was destroyed was Jesus truly vindicated. If Mark was wishing to convey this startling (and no doubt unpopular) message, then his use of the coded and discreet language of apocalyptic symbolism in chapter 13 would only be natural; *cf.* Geddert (1989) chs. 7-9.

Jerusalem, the destruction of the Temple and the vindication of Jesus and his people. . . . The prophecies of rescue from the tyrant have come true in and for Jesus and in his people. When this city falls they must get out and run; this is their moment of rescue, salvation, vindication.[67]

3. Mark and Jerusalem

People were all so amazed that they asked each other: 'What is this? A new teaching—and with authority (Mark 1:27).

Mark was introducing his readers to an authoritative, new message, which was full of surprises. The story was focused on Jesus, but it included Jerusalem as well. The themes we have noted (*e.g.* Jesus' prophetic teaching about the Temple and its replacement, and the issue of 'restoration') will recur in other New Testament writings. It will be sensed, however, that Mark's focus on this theme is less persistent than theirs.

This probably reflects the brevity of his Gospel and his single-minded purpose in presenting his readers with the challenge of Jesus's person. It may also suggests that this Gospel was not written in the geographical region of Palestine or Syria but rather (as traditionally held) in Rome[68]—and probably in the period immediately before AD 70, rather than in the years after Jerusalem's fall. Compared with, say, the issue of discipleship amidst persecution (which would have been particularly relevant in Rome in the wake of Nero), there is a certain distance from this issue of Jerusalem; it is not a matter of life and death.[69] On the other hand, the urgent and apocalyptic feel to the Gospel would fit in well with those uncertain years immediately before AD 70. There is much therefore to commend in Hengel's conclusion:

> [Mark's Gospel] was written in a time of severe affliction in Rome after the persecution of Nero and before the destruction of Jerusalem, probably during AD 69, the 'year of revolution'.[70]

---

[67] Wright (1992a) 395-6. Gaston's conclusion is similar, though perhaps overstated: 'Jesus is presented [by Mark] as being completely in opposition to Jerusalem and Jerusalem as being completely doomed': Gaston (1970) 474. *Cf.* Beagley (1987) 157: 'Mark is indicating that Jerusalem loses its status as the Holy City'.

[68] The traditional Roman audience has been defended recently by Gundry (1993); Syria is suggested by Kee (1977); Galilee by Marxsen (1969) and Kelber (1974); Pella by Marcus (1992).

[69] This would be contested by *e.g.* Myers (1988) 329, and Marcus (1992), who see Mark's understanding of Jerusalem as consciously rebutting the political position of those locally involved in the Jewish war.

Hengel also endorses the traditional understanding that Mark was himself a 'Jewish Graeco-Palestinian' 'presumably from Jerusalem', and that although through being in Rome he lacked 'firm information about events in Judea, [he] was directly interested in [Jerusalem] as the place where Jesus died'.[71] It would therefore not be unreasonable to imagine that the author of this Gospel, although now living far away, was writing about a place which meant much to him and about which he was keenly concerned. In earlier days it had been his 'home city'.[72] His views concerning Jerusalem cannot therefore be easily dismissed, but instead reveal the quite new understanding of Jerusalem which the events associated with Jesus produced—even in those who had been its former residents.

Hence the city and Temple about which he spoke were places which he knew well. Yet, 'with an intuition that the city's destruction was at hand',[73] he now realized that that Temple was approaching its final hour, and that this was integrally connected with the claims and identity of the Jesus in whom he had come to believe. The political climate in Rome where he was writing may have made it unwise to make overtly political statements about the fate of Jerusalem at the hands of the Romans. Nevertheless he had a responsibility to make plain that, concerning the Temple at least, there was a distinctive Christian viewpoint. The political implications (of the kind that we ourselves have noted) could then be drawn out by his readers on their own.

In any case, this emphasis on the Temple tied in neatly with Mark's express intention to focus on the identity of Jesus.[74] An important part of the

---

[70] Hengel (1985) 30. His arguments include: the predicting of the Temple's destruction (as by Jesus) was not uncommon; the references to it are not *vaticinia ex eventu*, and in several instances appear to be at variance with what actually transpired in AD 70; the *Nero redivivus* myth may have fuelled Mark's understanding of imminent events. For others who endorse a Roman provenance before AD 70, even if with different reasoning, see *e.g.* Cranfield (1959), Lane (1974), Best (1983), Standaert (1983), Matera (1987), Guelich (1989), Gundry (1993). *Cf.* too *e.g.* Myers (1988) 417: 'if the destruction of the Temple-state was a *fait accompli*, why did Mark need to launch his polemic against it?' If the Gospel was written from Rome, this would also make it less likely that Mark was consciously contending against the theology of the Jerusalem church. This was argued by Brandon (1967), Kelber (1974) and Trocmé (1975), but has been countered by *e.g.* Burkill (1972), Best (1981), Tannehill (1977) and Matera (1987) 42-55. Mark's critique was of the place, not of the church which had worshipped there.

[71] Hengel (1985), xi, 29, 46. *Cf.* Guelich (1989). D.W. Chapman (1993) argues that the Gospel was originally written in Jerusalem around the year AD 50.

[72] Hengel (1985) 46.

[73] Matera (1987) 16.

[74] *Cf.* similarly Bailey (1990-1) 104, who notes how Mark 'shifts the focus from the *city* to the *person*'. He argues that the parallels between Mark 15:29-32 and Lam. 2:15-16 ('all who pass by clap their hands at you, they hiss and wag their heads at the Daughter of Jerusalem') show how a text originally referring to Jerusalem is reapplied to Jesus.

claim for this Messiah was that the significance that previously had been located in the Temple had now been transferred to him. *He* was the new Temple.

If, therefore, in accordance with Jesus' prediction the physical Temple was about to be removed, his readers were not to be unduly disturbed. For that which should be touching them most deeply was not what was going on in Jerusalem in their own day but something which had taken place in that same city, though on a different hill, over thirty years previously:

> Mark and his friends will weep on mount Golgotha, not mount Zion: 'we will not despair over the loss of the Temple in Jerusalem because our loyalty has shifted to a *new Temple*—a Temple that was *destroyed*, and then *rebuilt* in *three days*. The new Temple *is already rebuilt*! The old one is obsolete!'[75]

---

[75] Bailey (1990-1) 105 (italics original, used to indicate scriptural allusions).

2

A NEW ZION
Matthew

'O Jerusalem, Jerusalem' (Matt. 23:37).

Matthew, probably writing after AD 70, contains both the most positive and the most negative statements concerning Jerusalem in the New Testament. He is the Evangelist most indebted to Judaism, but he also has to relate Jesus' warnings of judgement to the city. This raises the issue as to whether Jerusalem will subsequently be 'restored'. Matthew responds that Jesus is the one in whom the hopes associated with Mount Zion have come to fulfilment. There is some evidence that Matthew only reached this conclusion after abandoning his earlier hopes that Jerusalem would respond to the gospel message.

Matthew's concern with Jerusalem is clear. His Gospel reads as the work of one who has wrestled deeply with this whole question of Jerusalem's significance in the light of Jesus. He has a 'general fascination with Jerusalem' and 'reveals a marked awareness of Jerusalem and its fate'.[1]

This should not surprise us. It is almost universally agreed that this Gospel is written by a Jewish author, keenly concerned to show how the message of Jesus was to be understood against its Old Testament and Jewish background.[2] For such a person, committed to all the Jewish convictions concerning Jerusalem's unique significance, the belief that Israel's Messiah had been

---

[1]   Senior (1982) 317, and Davies (1964) 299. Gundry (1994) 602, speaks of Matthew's 'preoccupation with Jerusalem'.
[2]   Those who stand out against the scholarly consensus that Matthew was Jewish include Clark (1947), Strecker (1971), van Tilborg (1972) and Meier (1979) 55.

crucified outside the gates of that city would necessarily have spurred some such reflection.

However, one of the frequently observed paradoxes in Matthean studies is that this Gospel, which at one level can rightly be seen as the most Jewish one, is at another level the most severely '*anti*-Jewish'.[3] Matthew's attitude towards Jerusalem and its Temple reflects exactly the same tension.

There are several indications of a far more positive attitude towards Jerusalem than is found in Mark. For example, Matthew alone of the Evangelists uses both the concept of a 'holy place' (the Temple, 24:15) and a 'holy city' (4:5; 27:53). Similarly, Jerusalem is described as the 'city of the Great King' (5:35), and the Temple as the place in which God truly 'dwells' (23:21).

On the other hand, there are many indications of a more negative attitude. First, Matthew alone has Jesus describing himself as 'something greater than the Temple' (12:6) and as threatening within the parable of the wedding-banquet that the king would burn the murderers' 'city' (22:7). There is also an incisive attack on the murderous capacity of Jerusalem and its religious leaders which culminates in Jesus' prediction that their 'house' will be 'left desolate' (23:29-24:2).[4]

Secondly, there is Matthew's increasing emphasis on the universal nature of the Christian mission. If the original focus within the Gospel is upon the 'lost sheep of Israel' (10:6; 15:24), this gradually gives way to a more universal outlook which reaches its climax in the final appeal to 'go to all nations' (28:18-20). The 'earlier hints become a clarion call';[5] Matthew's story gradually breaks out beyond the confines of Judaism 'into the wide world of the Gentiles.'[6] Such a universal emphasis will have some repercussions of a negative kind for Jerusalem.

---

[3]   *Cf.* 5:17 with 23:1-39. On Matthew's 'anti-Judaism', see McKnight (1993), who argues that the polemical intensity reflects 'in-house' criticism; *cf.* Stanton (1992) 253, 280.

[4]   Much of this is 'Q' material and therefore paralleled in Luke (chs. 11 and 13).

[5]   Stanton (1992) 379, speaks of Matthew's 'sustained defence of open and full acceptance of Gentiles'. The 'hints' he notes include: the reference to the four women (considered to be non-Jews?) in the opening genealogy (1:3, 5, 6), the Magi (2:1ff), the disciples as 'salt of the earth' (5:13), the Gentile centurion (8:10), the two citations of scripture in connection with the Gentiles (4:15; 12:18-21) and the reference to 'all nations' (24:14). On his attitude to Christian mission amongst Jews, see below n. 92.

[6]   Gundry (1994) 9. This pattern, moving out to the universal, may underlie his references to 'land' or 'earth' (γῆ). In chs. 1-4 he uses γῆ in a restricted sense to refer to the 'land of Judah' (2:6), the 'land of Israel' (2:20, 21) and the 'land of Zebulon' (4:15). A transition occurs in 5:5 ('the meek . . . shall inherit the earth'); against the background of Ps. 37:11 this could be a reference to the 'land' of Israel, but a more 'universal' interpretation is also likely. Thereafter, Matthew uses γῆ almost entirely in this wider, more universalistic sense (*e.g.* 5:13, 18, 35; 6:10, 19; 9:6, etc).

Thirdly, in comparison with Mark, Matthew has developed further the contrast between Jerusalem and Galilee. Like Mark he does not present a 'Galilean idyll',[7] but he boosts Galilee's prophetic significance (quoting Isa. 9:1-2 in 4:15-16) and emphasizes Jerusalem's role as the place of hostility (*e.g.* by referring to the city in the first passion-prediction: 16:21). The fact that the Gospel then concludes with a resurrection encounter on a Galilean mountain (28:16-20) gives the impression that Jerusalem has been left behind in favour of Galilee.[8] This emphasis on God doing significant work in places other than Jerusalem is paralleled at the outset of the Gospel (ch. 2), where he makes a virtue out of Jesus' associations with marginal places such as Bethlehem and Nazareth (2:23).[9] Jerusalem, by contrast, is depicted as being 'frightened' by the rumour of a new 'king of the Jews' (2:2-3).

As a result, there are those who, noting this negative strand, refer to Matthew's 'anti-Temple stance', his 'bias' against Jerusalem, and his 'tendency throughout to emphasize Galilee as the place where light dawns, as opposed to Jerusalem, the city where Jesus meets rejection and death, and over which Jesus can only lament as he predicts its violent fate'.[10] Another scholar concluded that Matthew 2 'indicates the rejection of Jerusalem's centrality by comparing the city unfavourably with locations despised because of their distance from the center'.[11]

How are these positive and negative strands within Matthew's Gospel to be explained? Is there an inherent contradiction, or is some reconciliation possible? It is suggested here that both these strands must be given their due emphasis, and that this apparent tension is a creative one which takes us to the heart of Matthew's concerns for his people and for Jerusalem. In regard to his long-cherished commitments to Israel, the Temple and Jerusalem, Matthew pursued a policy both of affirmation and denial simultaneously, or (in his own terms) of seeking to balance the 'new' and the 'old' (*cf.* 13:52).

This will be sensed in examining his approach to the Temple (1) and Jerusalem (2); this then raises the major issue of judgement and 'restoration' (3). Finally, some suggestions will be made as to Matthew's own personal involvement with these issues (4) and the possible circumstances in which he was writing (5).[12]

---

[7] As phrased by Davies (1974) 241.
[8] See further below in 2(d).
[9] This explanation of Matthew's motivation in ch. 2 has been suggested by *e.g.* Stendahl (1960) and France (1980-1). Even though in Micah 5:2 Bethlehem was the expected scene of the Messiah's birth, Matthew quotes it in such a way as to emphasize that this 'little town' was '*by no means* least among the rulers of Judah' (2:6): see *e.g.* Hagner (1993/5) 29.
[10] France (1985) 407; 378.
[11] Levine (1988) 100.

1. The Temple

a) Positive References

Examples of Matthew's positive descriptions of the Temple have been noted: Jesus referred to it as a 'holy place', and its sanctuary as the place where God 'dwelt' (24:15; 23:21). There is further evidence of this positive attitude. Jesus' teaching on reconciliation is set against the background of 'offering gifts at the altar' (5:23-4), and the episode of the two-drachma tax makes it plain that Jesus was loyal in his payment of this tax for the Temple (17:24-27).

More significantly, Matthew's presentation of the Temple 'cleansing' (21:12ff) emphasizes not the Temple's forthcoming destruction (as in Mark) but rather Jesus' special Messianic authority. This is seen in three ways. First, because Matthew has already presented Jesus as the one 'greater than the Temple' (12:6), the prime issue when Jesus at last arrives in the Temple is inevitably his authority over this institution.[13] Secondly, immediately after the cleansing Matthew describes Jesus' healing in the Temple precincts and his being praised by children as the 'Son of David' (21:14-16); this, together with the way Jesus draws a parallel between the children's praise of him and the praise of *God* in Psalm 8:2, serves to emphasize Jesus' Messianic authority.[14] Thirdly, Matthew pieces together the episode of the fig-tree (21:18-19). This diminishes the integral connection with the cleansing which Mark had established with his 'sandwich' technique, and thereby weakens the link between the cursing of the tree and the Temple's destruction. Jesus' teaching about the fig-tree is focused instead on the power of prayer (21:21-22).

In these ways Matthew presents the cleansing in a more positive light. Clearly Jesus' action had also involved a critique of the Temple, and Jesus later pronounced a judgement upon it (24:2). At this stage in the narrative, however, the emphasis was on Jesus' desire that the Temple be restored to its true purpose as a 'house of prayer' (21:13). It could not be thought that Jesus was somehow dismissing the Temple *tout court*.

Finally, Matthew recounts the charge made against Jesus at his trial in such a way as to preserve Jesus' positive affirmation of the physical Temple as having been truly 'of God' (26:61). Mark's version had spoken instead of

---

[12] As with Mark the intention is to examine Matthew's Gospel in its final form. Where Matthew would have endorsed Mark's viewpoint, this has not been repeated—for reasons of space. The focus is on those areas where Matthew's presentation is distinctive.

[13] *Cf.* above ch. 1 (n. 6) on the christological significance of Jesus' quoting Isa. 56:7 (*'my house'*).

[14] *Cf. e.g.* Hagner (1993/5) 601-2.

'this Temple that is made with hands' (14:58), which might have been taken as a denial of God's endorsement of the Temple.[15] Matthew ensures that this negative inference is not drawn.

A Jewish reader of this Gospel would thus have found no grounds on which to accuse its author of having denied the basic Jewish assumptions concerning the sanctity of the Jerusalem Temple. This was probably Matthew's intention. Over against Hellenizing or Gentile Christians who might have been tempted to deny these Old Testament assumptions, Matthew showed how Jesus had endorsed them. Even if, as a Christian, there were further points which Matthew wished to make concerning the Temple, his Jewish readers could be assured that the true starting-point of such Christian thinking was thoroughly Jewish. The Temple had truly been ordained by God, and Jesus' actions and words revealed his true concern for this 'holy place'.[16]

b) Negative References

Matthew also includes within his Gospel, however, a string of more negative comments about the Temple.

Twice he quotes Hosea 6:6 ('I require mercy, not sacrifice', 9:13; 12:7). Whatever its precise meaning, the verse clearly drew on a strand within the Old Testament prophetic tradition that criticized Temple practice. In the episode of the Temple-tax, whilst Jesus' loyalty to the current system is evident, Jesus also indicates that strictly he as the 'Son' (and his disciples as 'sons') should be 'exempt' from payment (17:26); outward loyalty is combined with a radical inner subversion. As in Mark, Jesus denounces the Temple authorities for having allowed the Temple to become a 'den of robbers' (21:13). His condemnation of the Pharisees takes place within the Temple precincts and concludes with the accusation that the Temple itself has been a place polluted by murder (23:35) and would soon be destroyed: 'not one stone will be left here upon another' (24:2). Finally, Matthew presents the charge made against Jesus at his trial as a true one,[17] and focuses on Jesus' claim to have authority over the Temple. According to Matthew, Jesus was charged with saying, "I *am able* to destroy the Temple of God and to build it in three days" (26:61). That Matthew (like Mark) has this accusation repeated at the foot of the cross suggests that he too wished his readers to sense the irony of this insult and that

---

[15]   See above ch. 1 (1e), where it is suggested that Mark would not himself have drawn this radical conclusion.

[16]   *Cf.* similarly, de Young (1961) 51ff.

[17]   In contrast to Mark (14:57) the 'two' who bring this charge are not expressly described at 'false witnesses', though the previous witnesses are (26:60).

he saw in it a reference to Jesus' resurrection 'on the third day'. The resurrected Jesus *was* the 'rebuilt' 'Temple of God'.

In outline, therefore, Matthew's presentation is similar to Mark's,
though a little more detailed. It contains a critique of the Temple, a warning
of judgement upon it and an indication that something different is being inaugurated in the person of Jesus.[18]

Nevertheless, there are differences—particularly on the issue of Jesus
as a new or replacement Temple. In his version of the charge at Jesus' trial Jesus is accused not of having threatened to 'build *another*' Temple but rather
of being able to 'build it' (*i.e.* again). This in itself is indicative of a mind-set
that thought more in terms of continuity, rather than of radical disjunction or
replacement. If the Jesus who was raised 'on the third day' was the true Temple, this had to be seen as a continuation of the Temple's function (though in
a new mode) rather than as an effective denial of the previous Temple. More
significantly still, Matthew has a quite distinctive way, unparalleled in Mark,
of teaching this truth about Jesus as the new Temple: Jesus is himself the
'*shekinah*' presence of God.

c) Jesus, the Presence of God

One of the over-arching themes of Matthew's Gospel is that of 'Immanuel'—
'God with us' (μεθ ἡμῶν ὁ θεός: 1:23). Jesus is the one who in his own person
is a manifestation of the presence of God, and who at the end of the Gospel
promises to be '*with*' his disciples (μεθ ὑμῶν) 'to the end of the age' (28:20).
This is a development of theological ideas previously associated with the Jerusalem Temple. Just as God, though 'in heaven', was able mysteriously to
'dwell' in the Temple, so Jesus, though about to depart from this earth, could
promise to be 'with' his disciples.

This theme is highlighted on at least two other occasions. In 18:20 Jesus
promises that 'where two or three are gathered in my name, I am there among
them (ἐν μέσῳ αὐτῶν);' Jesus 'has simply been substituted for the *shekinah*'.[19] Matthew 23:38ff then makes it plain that the absence of God from the
Temple (which Jesus declares in pronouncing that 'your house is left to you
desolate') is to be identified with the absence from now on *of Jesus*: 'For I tell
you, you will not see *me* again . . .'[20] Jesus then 'came out of the Temple' for

---

[18] Matthew would therefore have endorsed the points made above in our discusson of
Mark concerning the nature of Jesus' critique and the causes of its eventual destruction.

[19] Davies and Allison (1988/91) 790, who also note the rabbinic parallels for those studying Torah (m.Abot 3:2, 3, 6). For the importance of the Temple and Zion as the background of this saying, see *e.g.* Ezek. 43:7, Zech. 2:10-11, and 11QTemple 46:12.

the last time (24:1). In doing so he took the presence of God with him, confiscating it from the Temple.[21]

By these means Matthew asserts in a distinctive way that Jesus as 'God with us' was the embodiment in his own person of that which previously had been signified by the *shekinah* in the Jerusalem Temple. 'Matthew's concern is to present Jesus as the *substitute* for Christians of all that the Temple stands for'.[22] If Jesus was something 'greater than the Temple' (12:6), then 'God was present in Jesus to a greater extent than in the Temple'[23] and there was now 'no continuing need for the Temple'.[24]

This realisation throws new light on the dramatic structure of chapter 23. At the beginning is that positive statement, confirming that the Temple was the place in which God 'dwelt' (23:21). By the end of the chapter all has changed. The Temple as God's dwelling-place is now described by Jesus simply as '*your* house', implying that it is no longer God's.[25] Through Matthew's careful arrangement the point is made that Jesus himself must be identified personally with the 'one who dwells in it'—an incredible claim—and then Jesus takes that divine presence away with him!

---

[20] Matthew is drawing on 'Q' material here: his insertion of 'for' (γάρ), as compared with Luke 13:35, makes this logical connection between vv. 38 and 39 that much stronger.

[21] *Cf.* Meier (1979) 166: the Temple is left 'desolate'—'visibly so in AD 70, but even now, proleptically, as Jesus leaves the Temple for the last time.' Jesus' dismissive departure is reminiscent of his command to his disciples on leaving an unresponsive place to 'shake the dust off their feet' (10:14). Wright (1994a) 60, sees in Jesus' teaching about the 'unoccupied house' (12:43-45) a reference to the Temple (the 'house') and to the Maccabean cleansing of the Temple in the second century BC: Jesus was then saying that the divine spirit had not returned to the Temple, and that it would be overcome by a final desecration (the 'seven evil spirits'). This would tie in with an ongoing debate (*e.g.* 11QTemple 29:7-10, m.Sukkah 5:4; b.Yoma 53b; p.Ta'an 65a; Targ. Hag. 1:8) as to whether the *shekinah* presence of God had *ever* truly returned to the Temple after 587 BC (Ezek. 11:23); see further G.I. Davies (1991). Even so, Matthew's substantial point, can remain (*cf.* Stanton [1992] 129): whether or not the *shekinah* had truly been present, God's protective presence was now definitively withdrawn and the house 'left desolate'. *Cf.* also 4:5, where the Temple is the place of the devil's working.

[22] Robinson (1976) 104 (italics original).

[23] Schlatter (1963) 396; *cf.* Stanton (1992) 130.

[24] Donaldson (1985) 200. In the light of the significance attributed to the foundation rock (the *eben setiyya*) beneath the Temple (which was believed to be the centre of the world: see Davies [1974] 8) there might also be some significance in Matthew's description both of Jesus' words (7:24) and of Peter (16:18) as 'rock'. That which had been focused on the Temple in Jerusalem was now to be found in Jesus and his new community.

[25] This inference, noted by Eusebius in the fourth century (see my [1990a] 387) is noted among modern commentators by *e.g.* Gundry (1994) 473.

d) *Conclusion*

This last point has important consequences. It shows that the positive references to the Temple in Matthew's Gospel must be read in the light of the
whole. In this instance (ch. 23) the positive statement in verse 21 only serves
to make a more important point about the person of Jesus, and certainly gives
no warrant for concluding that the situation that pertained in that verse must,
in Matthew's understanding, have continued without alteration into the future.
Matthew could make positive statements about the validity of the Temple up
till the time of Jesus, but that did not necessarily mean that this had continued
unchanged thereafter. If instead Matthew was convinced that the coming of
Jesus had led to significant changes for the Temple, then the only way he
could relay the enormity of this change was to affirm the previous status of the
Temple and then to show how this status was lost.

This important transition would be missed entirely by any interpretation which did not allow the Evangelist to record things that from his perspective *had* been true but which no longer pertained at the time of writing.[26] Such
an interpretation would then have to conclude that Matthew's positive and
negative statements about the Temple were inconsistent. On our reading,
however, space is given for the telling of a dramatic story concerning the Temple: despite its greatness and its true theological status in the past, God's presence was removed from it through the appearance of Jesus. Only by referring
to the Temple as 'sacred' (the 'holy place', 24:15) could Matthew convey the
horror of its *de*secration and destruction. Only by affirming its role as the
place of the divine dwelling (23:21) could he convey the drama of Jesus' pronouncing that it would now be 'left desolate' (23:38). The decisive moment
for the Temple, that great institution which Matthew valued so highly as a
Jew, had now arrived in the coming of Jesus.

2. The City of Jerusalem

This is an essential point if we are correctly to understand Matthew's comments concerning the *city* of Jerusalem. Again the positive references should
be understood within the developing dynamic of the whole Gospel.

---

[26] On this important point see Carson (1984) 354, and Stanton (1992) 380; *cf.* Lemcio
(1991) 49-73.

a) The 'City of the Great King'?

This principle is seen most clearly in connection with Jesus' statement that his followers should not swear 'by Jerusalem' because it was the 'city of the Great King' (5:35). By using this phrase Jesus affirms that Jerusalem is a city with which God, the Great King, has been pleased to identify himself. This is a positive reference indeed.

In the overall context of the Gospel's story, however, it looks rather different. For by the end of the Gospel we know that this 'city of the Great *King*' has not welcomed the one who in Matthew's understanding was not only 'born King of the Jews' (2:2) but also the true king of Zion/Jerusalem: 'Tell the Daughter of Zion, "Look, *your king* is coming to you, humble and mounted on a donkey"' (Zech. 9.9 quoted in Matt. 21:5).[27] This a powerful theme in itself, but Matthew has made it sharper by his earlier reference to Jerusalem as the 'city of the Great King'. In so doing he helps the reader to see the great ironies that are at work beneath the surface of Jesus' arrival in Jerusalem.[28]

The 'city of the Great King', the city which should rejoice in God's sovereignty, is now about to receive into her midst the 'king' whom the prophets have foretold, the one who for Matthew embodies God's kingly rule in his own person. It is a dramatic moment. Jerusalem's response will be the ultimate test of whether the city deserves this title. When therefore a few chapters later Jesus is rejected by the city's authorities, the reader realizes the great tragedy that has occurred. The 'city of the Great King' has rejected that King.

Taken out of its context within the whole Gospel, Matthew's use of this phrase might have conveyed the impression that he had an unreservedly high opinion of the city. In fact, it proves to be deeply ironic, emphasizing the city's privileged calling and revealing the standard by which she would be judged.

b) Jerusalem's Response to Jesus

That Matthew was interested in showing his readers how Jerusalem had responded to Jesus is clear. For example, he is the only Evangelist who, in describing the 'triumphal entry', pauses to remark on the reaction of the city to this event. 'When he entered Jerusalem, *the whole city* was in turmoil, asking

---

[27] Mark and Luke omit this quotation from Zech. 9. It fits in well with Matthew's concerns who (especially in his parables, see *e.g.* 18:23; 22:2) emphasizes the concept of God as 'king' and then effectively identifies Jesus with this 'king' (in the parable of the sheep and goats: 25:31, 34; *cf.* 27:37, 42).

[28] On these ironies, see further Kingsbury (1988) 80ff.

"who is this?"' (21:10). This in turn echoes his description of the city's reaction to the Magi's innocent question about the birthplace of the 'king of the
Jews': 'when King Herod heard this, he was frightened, and *all Jerusalem*
with him' (2:3). From the very outset of the Gospel, therefore, Jerusalem is
portrayed as potentially negative towards Jesus.[29] While the Gentile Magi are
preparing to 'worship' him (2:2), Jerusalem, which is supposed to be 'city of
the Great King' (but which in practice is under the rule of King Herod), joins
forces with those who would kill him (2:16).[30]

Jerusalem's unwelcoming response to God's servants is seen again in
chapter 3. In contrast to Mark who had spoken of 'all Jerusalem' going out to
be baptized by John (Mark 1:5), Matthew presents this episode more negatively as an occasion when the Pharisees and Sadducees (3:7) came out to inspect
John critically. By talking simply of 'Jerusalem' going out to John (3:5) Matthew gives the impression that this word 'Jerusalem' refers to the city's *religious leadership*. Though there were, no doubt, Jerusalem inhabitants who
responded positively to John's message, 'Jerusalem' in this sense is portrayed
as the prime source of his opposition (*cf.* Matt. 21:23-27).

Thus although there is some initial interest shown by 'Jerusalem' in Jesus (4:25), Matthew is building up the picture that Jerusalem will be the place
which rejects Jesus. In the midst of the temptation narrative Matthew may follow the customary Jewish usage and refer to Jerusalem as the 'holy city' (4:5)
but already the story is suggesting that this may be something of an ironic mis-
nomer. Will this 'holy city', the place which houses the Temple, live up to its
name, or not?[31]

The theme of Jerusalem's response to Jesus naturally comes to the fore
once Jesus arrives in the city (21:12ff). At this point the distinction between
the city's religious authorities and its inhabitants becomes quite clear. The
crowds and the children give Jesus a warm welcome as a 'prophet' (21:9-11,
15-17, 46). The religious leaders, however, question Jesus' authority (21:23-
27; 22:15ff), and begin to plot his death (26:4), all the time being fearful of the
'people' (26:5).[32] Only in the pressurized circumstances of Jesus' trial before

---

[29] It could be argued that Jerusalem's fear was of *Herod*, but Matthew's phraseology ('all
Jerusalem *with* him') suggests that Jerusalem shared *with* Herod a common fear of this
infant 'king': *e.g.* Hagner (1993/5) 28, and Luz (1989) 135.
[30] *Cf.* Knowles (1993) 44, 79, 154, who also argues that the lament of Rachel portends a
dire fate for Jerusalem and the nation. Similarly, Meier (1979) 53, sees the infancy narrative as a 'proleptic passion narrative'; *cf.* Senior (1982) 226.
[31] The fact that this reference to the 'holy city' comes in a description of the *devil* at work
in the city may be intended to highlight this irony.
[32] Is there any significance in the fact that in Matthew's version of the Beelzebub controversy Jesus talks not just about a 'house' being 'divided against itself', but also of any
'*city*' (12:25)? Jerusalem was a city divided in its response to Jesus.

Pilate does this distinction between the leaders and the people break down, with the latter being persuaded by the 'chief priests and the elders' to have Jesus crucified (27:20, 22, 25).

The passage which deals most expressly with Jerusalem's negative response comes at the end of chapter 23 (vv. 33-39). Again the responsibility for this response is shared by the city as a whole, but also focused particularly on its religious leaders. When Jesus outlines the response which can be expected to any 'prophets, sages and scribes' (v. 33ff), he is addressing the Pharisees. The focus then shifts to the city as a whole: 'O Jerusalem, Jerusalem, the city that kills the prophets and stones those that are sent to it' (v. 37ff).[33] Thus again, though wanting to emphasize the particular responsibility of Jerusalem's leadership, Matthew also sees the whole city as being implicated in this tragedy. There is something endemic within Jerusalem itself that makes it the place that rejects 'those sent' to her.

Matthew's reflection on Jerusalem's negative response to Jesus may be seen, finally, in two parables (the vineyard and the wedding banquet: 21:33-22:14) which expressly deal with the issue of the way God's servants are received. Matthew's telling of both parables suggests an intended application to Jesus and Jerusalem. In the former parable Matthew's version of the maltreatment of the 'son' reads: 'so they seized him, threw him out of the vineyard, and killed him' (21:39).[34] Mark's version had the son being killed first and *then* thrown out (Mark 12:8). Was Matthew wanting the reader to see the close parallel with Jesus' being led outside the city and then crucified?[35] Even if the 'vineyard' should be identified more widely with Israel (*cf.* Isa. 5:1-7), there would then be a certain parallelism between the vineyard and Jerusalem (as an appropriate focus for Israel). As a result Jerusalem would inevitably share in a fate similar to that of the 'vineyard' which was given over 'to other tenants' (21:41). Similarly, in the second parable, in response to the hostile reception given to his messengers, the king 'destroyed those murderers and burned *their city*' (22:7). Whether or not this is a *post-eventum* allusion to the events of AD 70,[36] Matthew is highlighting what it means for a city to respond negatively to God's message.

Matthew's text therefore emphasizes the negative response which Jerusalem made to Jesus. With great irony he shows how the 'city of the great King', had denounced her rightful King. The 'holy city', in whose Temple

---

[33] Matthew has brought together here passages which were probably separate in 'Q' (as in Luke 11 and 13).

[34] *Cf.* similarly Luke 20:15.

[35] See *e.g.* Gundry (1994) 427, who suggests that Matthew has reversed the original order found in Mark.

[36] On this and other questions of dating see below section 5.

God had truly dwelt, had now in an unholy way rejected him who embodied that presence.

> Matthew's narrative underscores the contrast between [Jesus'] identity as the Christ, on the one hand, and the response of many who persecute him, on the other—together with the grave responsibility such rejection entails in the eyes of the Evangelist.[37]

c) Consequences and Causes

This was a dramatic state of affairs, and Matthew indicates that it would not be without consequences. Both the parables just discussed, though using quite different imagery, teach that the maltreatment of God's messengers would inevitably have severe repercussions for those places which were the base of their enemies' operations: their vineyard would be leased 'to other tenants' or, alternatively, their city 'burned' (21:41; 22:7).

In this regard Matthew substantially repeats all the Markan material which had implied that Jesus' death would result in the destruction of the Temple.[38] He also has extra material. Not only are there numerous passages which warn in general terms of a judgement on this generation,[39] there are also some which are more specifically tied to Jerusalem. For example, there is the dire warning in 23:35 (that 'upon you may come all the righteous blood') which, through its close proximity to the indictment of 'Jerusalem' for its negative response to Jesus (23:37), strongly suggests that the warning is intended not just for the religious leaders but for Jerusalem itself. There is also the (much abused) text, 'his blood be on us and on our children' (27:25), which may be taken as Matthew's way of referring to forthcoming judgement upon the city of Jerusalem.[40]

Caution, however, is required here. For these passages reveal that it is not just the rejection of *Jesus* that has brought about this fateful situation; rather, it is Jerusalem's response to *all* those messengers 'sent to her'. The parable of the banquet speaks simply of a succession of 'servants', and in the key passage (23:33-39) there is no explicit reference to *Jesus'* death. Jesus is speaking more generally about Jerusalem's history of shedding 'innocent blood' and her unwelcoming response to any 'prophets, sages and scribes'. His own death

---

[37] Knowles (1993) 80.
[38] See above ch. 1 (1e-f).
[39] Wright (1996) ch. 8, cites Matt. 3:7-12; 5:20, 25-6; 7:13-14, 19; 8:11-12; 10:14-15; 11:20-24; 13:24-30, 36-43; 25:14-30; 26:52. See further below ch. 8 (1-2).
[40] See most recently the helpful comments in Hagner (1993/5) 827-8.

would be another instance. If, therefore, Matthew linked Jesus' death to the subsequent divine judgement upon the city, he would have set this against a broader canvas of Jerusalem's long-standing reputation for rejecting those sent to her in God's name. An act of judgement was coming, but the city's response to Jesus was only one of several causes.

Are there any other indications in Matthew of the causes of this judgement? It is significant that in this Gospel Jesus is expressly compared to Jeremiah (16:14); for Jeremiah, though not killed in Jerusalem, was the prophet *par excellence* whose message the city rejected. He was also the prophet who had most clearly spoken of the consequences for Jerusalem if it did not mend its ways. Judgement was brought about through lack of repentance. Jesus is also compared to Jonah (12:39ff; 16:4), another famous Old Testament prophet who similarly preached that judgement would come if there were no repentance. Jonah's preaching had been to a Gentile city, but Nineveh had repented, resulting in the aversion of the threatened judgement. Jeremiah, however, had preached to Jerusalem and the people of God, but to no avail. Matthew presents Jesus as warning his own contemporaries that they were following the precedent of their forebears in the time of Jeremiah, not the repentant example of Nineveh (12:41). One of the principal causes of judgement was the lack of repentance.

Matthew may have diagnosed two other ingredients in Jerusalem's condition. When Jesus had condemned Capernaum, Bethsaida and Chorazin for this same lack of repentance (11:20-24), he had also detected an inordinate pride: 'and you, Capernaum, will you be exalted to heaven? (v. 23). In an extraordinary way this little Jewish village was manifesting a pride similar to that of Gentile Babylon as described in Isaiah:

> You said in your heart, 'I will *ascend to heaven*, I will raise my throne above the stars of God. . .' But you are brought down to Sheol, to the depths of the Pit (Isa. 14:13-15).

And Jesus warned it would suffer the same fate: 'you will be brought down to Hades' (v. 23). If this had been true of Capernaum, what about Jerusalem?

Secondly, the very passage which spoke of Jerusalem as the 'city of the great King' (5:33-37) warned how this concept might lead to a false reliance on the city's 'holiness'. Jesus implied that, by invoking the name of 'Jerusalem', all those who made such oaths were appropriating to themselves something of the holiness that properly pertained only to the city (*cf.* also 23:16-22); they were invoking 'Jerusalem' as a kind of divine talisman. This was an abuse. The holiness of Jerusalem could not be used to bolster a statement which was 'unholy'. This might then be the beginnings of a Matthean critique

of what had happened to Jerusalem. God had graciously blessed the city, but
this divine association or holiness had been abused. Just as centuries before
Jeremiah had criticized Jerusalem's inhabitants for depending on the Temple's sanctity (Jer. 7), so now the holiness of Jerusalem had become a cloak
for that which was unholy and had worked against the purposes of God.

Matthew might therefore have seen behind Jerusalem's rejection of
God's messengers and of Jesus a false reliance on the city's holiness and an
unrepentant pride—a pride that, despite the divine association of the city, led
to the development of a mind-set that, as with Babylon, had become deeply
opposed to the real purposes of God. It was then this discrepancy between the
theory and the practice that Jesus' coming brought glaringly to light, with fatal
results for both parties. Jesus' coming was the 'last straw'.

Matthew thus presents us with a Jesus who solemnly warned the people
of his day about what lay in store. At the outset John the Baptist had spoken
of the 'wrath to come' (3:7), and Jesus offers no correction to this. Yet if
judgement was coming, Jerusalem would inevitably be affected. Jesus predicts that the Temple would be abandoned by God (23:38) and destroyed
(24:2) with its 'holy place' desecrated (24:15); the 'holy city' too would experience divine judgement. The 'city of the great King' would learn the painful lesson of what it meant to have as its King one who, as so clearly seen in
Jesus' parables, required obedience (cf. 18:23; 22:2; 25:34).

d) The Resolution

How is the issue of Jerusalem resolved within Matthew's Gospel?[41] For this
we naturally turn to his final chapter (ch. 28). Much of the preceding chapters
was similar to Mark's. Mark's final chapter, however, had come to an abrupt
end, hinting at a post-resurrection appearance in Galilee (14:28; 16:7) but never describing it. This Matthew now gives. The result is a Gospel which ends
not in Jerusalem, but in Galilee.

Matthew gives this geographical shift some emphasis. The narrative
rushes forward from events associated with the resurrection in Jerusalem
(which one might have expected to be given the greatest weight) towards what
turns out to be a greater climax—Jesus' commissioning of the disciples on the
mountain in Galilee. Twice (vv. 7, 10) the greatness of what has happened at
the tomb in Jerusalem is eclipsed by the insistence that Galilee is the place to
which the disciples must direct their steps. There is one brief resurrection-ap-

---

[41] On how Matthew integrates this theme of judgement with that of 'restoration', see
section 3.

pearance in Jerusalem (vv. 9-11),[42] but this only provides the second opportunity to emphasize the forthcoming reunion in Galilee, which then becomes
the supreme resurrection-appearance in the Gospel. At the end of the Gospel,
the reader is left, not in Jerusalem, but with the Risen Lord in Galilee.

As argued in relation to Mark, this does not reflect any particular affiliation in Matthew towards the Galilee of his own day, and certainly no exalted
belief in Galilee as a '*terra Christiana*'.[43] If, however, Matthew was playing
upon a long-standing pre-Christian tension between 'northerners' and 'south-
erners',[44] he was evidently siding with the place which Jerusalem might have
been tempted to dismiss. Just as Jesus' association with Nazareth had called
for comment, so Matthew emphasized Jesus' association with Galilee in contrast to Jerusalem.[45]

Matthew's concluding reference to 'all nations' (v. 19) indicates that
this centrifugal dynamism (going out from Jerusalem to Galilee) was designed
to show the out-going nature of the gospel message.[46] The resurrection-story,
although originating in Jerusalem, was a message for the world. Jesus' emphasis upon Galilee in the post-resurrection period thus speaks of the gospel's going from Jerusalem to Galilee and from there 'to all nations'.

This emphasis on God's universal purposes inevitably places Jerusalem
in a much wider context than had previously pertained. This may have been
Matthew's intention; for it may be no coincidence that the one reference to Jerusalem within this chapter casts the city in a negative light: 'some of the
guard went *into the city* and told the chief priests everything that had happened' (v. 11). There follows the description of the attempts to deny the resurrection message on the part of the Jewish authorities. Matthew's final
portrait of Jerusalem is of a place full of intrigue, counterfeit and bribery. It is
the dark 'foil' compared to the light of the new Christian community gathered
round its Risen Lord. The city is darkness, Galilee the place of light.

---

[42]   So Matthew saw nothing inconsistent between his own emphasis on Galilee and the
existence of other traditions concerning resurrection-appearances in Jerusalem; see *e.g.*
Stonehouse (1944) 166.

[43]   See again Davies (1974) 241, 243, and Stemberger's appendix.

[44]   As suggested by Davies (1974) 243; *cf.* (1964) 300.

[45]   On Nazareth, see below n. 103. This critique of Jerusalem's disdainful attitude may
underlie Matthew's emphasis on Jesus' ministry in 'Galilee of the Gentiles' (4:12ff) and
the responses to Jesus 'from Nazareth in Galilee' (21:10) and to Peter in 26:69-73 (where,
in Matthew, there is a Galilean reference in each of the three questions).

[46]   Matthew uses the verb 'to go' (πορεύομαι) no less than five times in this chapter (vv.
7, 9, 11, 16, 20). The first four describe the disciples going away from Jerusalem to Galilee;
the last, their going 'to all nations'. The 'going out' from Jerusalem is therefore tied closely
to the 'going out' into the wider world.

So Matthew's ultimate focus is upon the disciples' encounter with Jesus in Galilee on the 'mountain to which Jesus had directed them' (v.16). Is this a comparison with Mount Sinai (Jesus as the New Moses) or indeed with Mount Nebo (Jesus as Moses giving instructions to his followers concerning their entrance into a new 'promised land'; *cf.* Deut. 34:1ff)?[47] This would endorse the argument that the particularistic Jewish emphasis on the 'land' was now being eclipsed by an emphasis on the whole world: the 'land to be possessed' was not the 'land of Israel' (*cf.* 2:20, 21), but rather the peoples of 'all nations'.[48] The particularities of the Jewish world-view were being relativized by Matthew's emphasis on the universal.

Donaldson, however, argues convincingly that these carefully-crafted verses need also to be understood against the backdrop of Mount Zion. According to Psalm 2:6-8, Zion was the place where the Messianic King was to be enthroned as God's 'son' with the 'nations' and the 'ends of the earth' being given to him as his 'possession'; now Jesus 'the Son' (v. 19) declares that 'all authority in heaven and on earth' has been given to him and gives his disciples a message for 'all nations' (vv. 18-19).[49] If Mount Zion was the place where Gentiles would be gathered to experience eschatological blessings,[50] disciples of 'all nations' (v. 19) are now called to experience 'mountain fellowship' with the Risen Lord. Zion had been the place where the Lord had dwelt 'with' his people;[51] now Jesus promises, 'I am *with* you always' (v. 20), indicating that the 'presence of God' was no longer confined to Jerusalem.[52]

Seen against this background Matthew's final verses make a significant point about Jerusalem. Once again the city is being eclipsed as Matthew focuses his readers' attention upon the Risen Lord. That focus is clearly upon Jesus himself, rather than, say, on the anonymous mountain in Galilee:

> For Matthew, Christian experience is not merely a matter of replacing one mountain in Jerusalem with another mountain in Galilee. It is *Christ* who has replaced Zion as the centre of eschatological fulfilment, and the mountain

---

[47] The emphasis on Sinai is suggested by *e.g.* Gundry (1994) 594, and Allison (1993) 262ff; Nebo by Wright (1992a) 388-389. Davies (1974) 241, sees here a contrast with the increasing emphasis on the 'land' as promoted by the Jamnian rabbis.

[48] *Cf.* Wright (1992a) 389.

[49] Donaldson (1985) 101-2, compares this attainment of world-authority by Jesus with that worldwide dominion falsely promised to him on the mount of temptation (4:8-10). A comparison might also be drawn with Israel's quest for such hegemony over the Gentile nations. Jesus, the true embodiment of Israel, gains this in his own person, but it is not shared with Israel, nor the disciples: 'all authority has been given to *me*'.

[50] See *e.g.* Isa. 2:2ff; 25:6-10; 56:6-8; Mic. 4.1f; Zech. 8:20-23.

[51] *E.g.* Pss. 43:3; 68:16; 74:21; 35:21; Isa. 8:18; Joel 3:17.

[52] These three main points about the Zion background are made by Donaldson in (1985) 180-188.

motif in Matthew acts as a vehicle by which Zion expectations are transferred to *Christ*.[53]

If there is a 'new Zion', therefore, it must be identified no longer with a place, but rather with a person.[54] '*Jesus replaces Zion* as the centre of the gathered people of God' and 'as the centre of eschatological fulfilment'.[55]

The final resolution of the Jerusalem-theme in Matthew's Gospel is therefore found in the Risen Jesus himself. The Jerusalem that had played a central role in the life of God's people has been left to one side because of a more permanent revelation. The 'holy city', not least because of its unholy response to Jesus, has been eclipsed by the one whom God has vindicated. The 'city of the Great King', having rejected its king, experiences judgement. The Jerusalem that 'stones those who are sent to it', is rebuked for its rebellion and pride. Meanwhile the 'Son' is revealed in his kingly glory not in Zion but in Galilee, and the God who once 'dwelt' in the Jerusalem Temple now promises to be 'with' his people in the person of Jesus, Immanuel—whenever they 'gather together in his name'. In all these senses Jerusalem has effectively, through the coming of Jesus, been left behind. Jesus is the new Zion.

3. Judgement and Restoration

The issue of Jerusalem thus finds a fitting resolution in Matthew's final chapter. Matthew's emphasis on Jerusalem's forthcoming judgement, however, would have provoked in its first-century context a whole set of further questions. One of the key convictions within the Judaism of this period was that God would restore his people's fortunes and that this restoration would include a new future for Jerusalem. These hopes were fuelled by the many passages in the scriptures which spoke of a glorious future for Zion.[56] Matthew was indicating that God's purposes for Jerusalem focused on judgement, not on restoration. What had happened to those scriptural promises of restoration?

Matthew's comparison of Jesus to Jeremiah (16:14) is particularly illustrative at this point. The chief likeness between the two was that both were prophets who spoke words of judgement against Jerusalem and suffered in the

---

[53] Donaldson (1985) 184 (italics mine).

[54] *Cf.* Matt. 2:1-12, when the Magi, reflecting the Gentiles' pilgrimage to Zion as pictured in Isa. 60 (esp. v. 14), bring their gifts not to *Zion* or Jerusalem but rather to Jesus himself. *Cf.* Donaldson (1985) 185.

[55] Donaldson (1985) 185 (italics mine). *Cf.* similarly Levine (1988) 100: 'Jerusalem cannot be replaced by an alternative physical centre', but by 'the abiding presence of Jesus in the community. Sacred space is anywhere the disciples gather.'

[56] See *e.g.* Isa. 2:2-4; 62; Mic. 4:1-4; Zech. 8; Ps. 2:6-8.

process.[57] Jeremiah, however, had also expressly spoken of a restoration which would follow the period of judgement and exile, especially in the 'Book of Consolation' (chs. 30-33). Matthew's likening Jesus to Jeremiah raises two important questions. First, did Matthew believe that Jesus had similarly predicted a subsequent restoration of Jerusalem's fortunes? Secondly, since Jeremiah was but one of many Old Testament prophets who had promised such a restoration, how did Matthew reconcile Jesus' teaching about Jerusalem's judgement with those many scriptural promises?

The answer to the first question is clear. There is nothing in Jesus' teaching in this Gospel which suggests that *after* this period of judgement there will be a restoration; the 'seven evil spirits enter and live there' (12:45), the 'vineyard is leased to others' (21:41), the city is 'burnt' (22:7), the Temple is 'abandoned' (23:38); the Apocalyptic Discourse (ch. 24) moves away from Jerusalem to focus on the coming of the Son of Man. The only possible hint of such a restoration is in Jesus' statement addressed to Jerusalem: 'you will not see me again until you say, "Blessed is the one who comes in the name of the Lord"' (23:39). Coming at the end of a chapter of unrelenting critique, this almost certainly refers to Jerusalem's unwilling acknowledgement of Jesus' true status at the eschatological judgement. On that day, which will be like a 'second Triumphal Entry, Jerusalem will be forced to acknowledge and hail the coming one'.[58]

> There is in this passage no expression of the thought that this judgement on the Temple, and hence on Jerusalem as the religious centre of God's people, will ever be reversed; that God will ever return to this Temple in Jerusalem and once again make it the place where he exercises his redemptive revelational relation with his people.[59]

---

[57] See Carmignac (1971), Winkle (1986), Vesco (1988), and now the extended study of Knowles (1993). The comparison between Jesus and Jeremiah is based on several reasons (pp. 80, 161, 222, 264). First, Jesus, like Jeremiah would 'suffer rejection at the hands of his own people even as he predicted the fall of Jerusalem'. Secondly, Jeremiah had warned of dire consequences for the city if his 'innocent blood' was shed (Jer. 26:15); this then comes to pass when Jesus' 'innocent blood' is shed (27:4). Thirdly, Jeremiah had predicted the 'new covenant' which Jesus inaugurated on the basis of that innocent 'blood' (26:28).

[58] Meier (1979) 166, following an interpretation favoured by Calvin and *e.g.* T.W. Manson; *cf.* Garland (1979). The best alternative interpretation, advocated by Allison (1983), takes the 'until' as a conditional which could equally be translated 'unless'; on this reading the verse only makes a conditional promise to Jerusalem, not a sure prediction of 'restoration'. For a contrary view, see Stanton (1992) 247ff.

[59] De Young (1961) 89.

The comparison of Jesus with Jeremiah reveals a sharp truth: *this* 'Jeremiah' had not held forth a message of hope for the period beyond the judgement. This time the judgement on Jerusalem was final.

What then about those promises of restoration? Were they now null and void? The answer for Matthew lies in correctly understanding Jesus. Once it was grasped who Jesus really was and what he had done, it became clear that those scriptural promises, far from being redundant, had been fulfilled. The 'restoration' that had long been an ingredient within Jewish hope had now come to pass, but in an unexpected way.

That Matthew would have been inclined to see Jesus as the fulfillment of this important prophetic schema is almost certain in the light of his characteristic and all-pervasive emphasis on Jesus as the one in whom, more generally, Old Testament prophecy is fulfilled.[60] It can safely be assumed that the Matthew who found fulfilments of prophecy in places which required a certain charitable 'stretch' of the imagination (*e.g.* 2:17) would have also been concerned to show how Jesus fulfilled *this* prophetic expectation as well.

This assumption is confirmed in the one passage within the Gospel where this issue of 'restoration' is raised explicitly:

> 'Elijah is indeed coming and will restore [ἀποκαταστήσει] all things; but I tell you that Elijah has already come, and they did not recognize him, but they did to him whatever they pleased. So also the Son of Man is about to suffer at their hands'. Then the disciples understood that he was speaking to them about John the Baptist (17:11-13).

Jesus' identification of John the Baptist with Elijah, the one who was popularly expected to usher in the time of restoration, made clear that the longed-for age of 'restoration' was now in the process of being effected—but paradoxically though the 'suffering' of the Son of Man'.

That Matthew was pointing to Jesus as the one who fulfilled these restoration-hopes is confirmed by noting several other features in his Gospel.

a) The End of the Exile

The fact that these hopes of restoration existed in Jesus' day was itself an admission that Israel was still effectively in a period of exile. The longing for 'restoration' arose precisely because, although several prophecies concerning the 'restoration' or 'return from exile' had evidently been fulfilled in the time

---

[60] Hence his frequent 'fulfilment-quotations' (*e.g.* 2:5, 15, 17, 23; 3:3; 4:15-16; 8:17; 12:17; 21:5, etc). *Cf.* also 5:17 and 13:16-17. See *e.g.* Blomberg (1992) 30.

of Cyrus, there were others that seemed to be awaiting fulfilment. To this extent and by reference to *these* prophecies, Israel was still in exile and awaiting deliverance. Some of her people might have returned to the Land, but surely God had promised much more? A study of Jewish literature in the centuries prior to the New Testament confirms this sense that Israel was still in 'exile':

> Despite many differences in presentation [these] writings all seem to share the view that *Israel remained in a state of exile* long after the sixth century, and that the exile would only be brought to an end when God intervened in this world order to establish his rule.[61]

Against this background of ideas Matthew's opening chapters take on a new meaning. It has recently been observed that this theme of the exile is an important one throughout chapters 1 to 4.[62] For example, Matthew sees in the massacre of the innocents a fulfilment of Rachel weeping for her children' (Jer. 31:15 in 2:18)—a phrase from Jeremiah's 'Book of Consolation' which had been surrounded by prophecies of restoration.[63] Matthew uses this verse to suggest that despite this tragedy in Bethlehem, the hope which Jeremiah had expressed in the surrounding verses was about to be fulfilled. Through Jesus, God was at work to bring his people's 'exile' to an end.

A similar deduction can be made from examining the opening genealogy (1:1-17), which Matthew has divided into sections, the last of which is marked by the exile:

> Most Jews of the second-temple period regarded themselves as still in exile, still suffering the effects of Israel's age-old sin. Until the great day of redemption dawned, Israel was 'still in her sins', still in need of rescue. The genealogy then says to Matthew's careful reader that the long story of Abraham's people will come to its fulfilment, its seventh seven, with a new David, who will rescue his people from their exile, that is, 'save his people from their sins'. When Matthew says precisely this in 1:18-21 we should not be surprised.[64]

Matthew was indicating that these prophetic hopes of restoration were now on the point of being fulfilled in Jesus, the Messiah. The 'exile' would soon be over.

---

[61] Knibb (1976) 271-2 (italics mine).

[62] See Head (1994).

[63] Jeremiah's speaking of a 'voice heard in Ramah' links this verse to the tragedy of the exile, since Ramah was the place where the captives gathered before they were led into exile (Jer. 40:1).

[64] Wright (1992a) 386.

b) Jesus, the True Israel

Matthew also presents Jesus as the true embodiment of Israel.[65] Again this is seen at the outset of the Gospel. First, the infant Jesus re-enacts the earlier history of Israel, going down into Egypt before returning to the 'land of Israel' (2:14, 19-21). Matthew highlights this parallelism by quoting Hosea 11:1 ('out of Egypt I called my son'), a text which originally applied to Israel as a people, but which now, according to Matthew, speaks of Jesus the Son. If Jesus is to be termed the 'Son', it is because he fulfils and embodies in his own person the role of Israel, God's 'Son'. This identification is confirmed in Matthew's Temptation narrative, where Jesus demonstrates his sonship by entering into the historic experience of Israel in the wilderness but, instead of failing as had Israel, he offers perfect filial obedience (4:1-11).[66]

If Matthew defined the true people of 'Israel' in relation to Jesus, the same would apply to Israel's 'restoration'. There can be no restoration of Israel without Jesus. Indeed, if Jesus' own life encapsulates the history of Israel, then a whole new way of understanding restoration becomes possible. When this Jesus is 'restored' to life and raised by God from the dead, this event may itself be the 'restoration' of Israel, the true revelation of Israel's glory before the world. In the light of the resurrection Jesus himself was 'the *restored* Son Israel'.[67] In Matthew, therefore, the resurrection was not just a rebuilding of the Temple (26:61),[68] but also the moment when the 'true Israel' was 'restored'.[69]

c) The Mountain-motif

A final indication of Matthew's concern with the issue of restoration is his otherwise puzzling emphasis on 'mountains'.[70] As noted above, a strong ar-

---

[65] See *e.g.* Meier (1979) 55 and Donaldson (1985) 200, and most fully Kynes (1991), who discusses well (pp. 199-203) the more controversial issue of whether Matthew would have identified the *Church* with the 'new' or 'true Israel'; this was argued by Trilling (1964), but countered by *e.g.* P. Richardson (1969), Meier (1979) 55, and Hare (1967) 152-161.

[66] Hence the parallelism of the 'forty days' to Israel's 'forty years', and the three significant quotations from Deuteromony (6.13, 16; 8:3); see *e.g.* Gerhardsson (1966).

[67] Donaldson (1985) 200 (italics mine); *cf.* p. 210.

[68] *Cf.* above at n. 17.

[69] A key theme in Jeremiah's original 'restoration theology' had been his prophecy of a 'new covenant' (Jer. 31:31). Jesus' speaking of his 'blood of the covenant' (26:28) may indicate that the way to restoration is now through identifying with him who will soon pass through the judgement of death into resurrection life.

[70] See 4:8; 5:1, 14; 14:23; 15:29; 17:1; 21:1; 28:16.

gument can be made for the assertion that, although the associations with
Mount Sinai cannot be denied, the mountain that is chiefly in Matthew's mind
is Mount Zion.[71] Our argument that in his final chapter Matthew has presented
Jesus as the 'new Zion' can now be seen as an answer to this question of restoration. In the light of various Old Testament passages,[72] Zion was seen as
the place where God's Messianic King would be enthroned and where the
scattered people of God would be gathered; once 'restored' in this way, the
Gentile nations too would be gathered in.[73] Now, however, Jesus had been revealed as God's Son, the anointed King, and the one whose new community
of Jew and Gentile constituted the new eschatological people of God, gathered
from 'all nations'.[74] The hopes associated with Jerusalem's restoration had
therefore been fulfilled in Jesus, and in his people. So Donaldson concludes:

> Matthew is declaring that this long-anticipated promise has come to fulfil-
> ment *not with the restoration of Zion*, but with the resurrection and exaltation
> of Jesus. God is with his eschatological people, not when they gather to Zion,
> but when they gather to Jesus, who is himself called Immanuel (1:23). . . .
> The mountain-motif is a device used by the evangelist to make the christo-
> logical statement that Christ has replaced Zion as the centre of God's deal-
> ings with his people; in him *all the hopes associated with Zion* have come to
> fruition and fulfilment. [75]

d) Conclusion

Matthew's text thus reveals that the Evangelist possessed a clear theology of
restoration.[76] This is not surprising. Many of his fellow-Jews would have contested Jesus' Messiahship precisely because Israel had not been 'restored' in

---

[71] See Donaldson (1985); *cf*. n. 49. This playing down of Sinai is criticized by Allison
(1993) 324-5. Levenson (1985), however, argues that Sinai themes have been *absorbed*
into Zion-theology.
[72] See n. 50ff.
[73] See Donaldson (1985) 210: 'In contemporary Jewish thought, it was expected that the
salvation of the Gentiles would be a by-product of the restoration of Israel. When Israel was
gathered to God's holy mountain and reconstituted there as his people, the Gentiles would
be invited to share in eschatological blessings'. Matthew's frequent use (12:30; 13:2;
18:20; 25:32, etc) of the word συνάγω, a verb which had 'become virtually a technical term
for the eschatological gathering of the scattered people of God' (p. 185), may indicate that
Jesus, not Zion, was the new 'gathering-point' of God's people: see esp. 25:32 ('all nations
will be gathered (συναχθήσονται) before him').
[74] This throws new light on several Matthean texts: for example, as argued by Campbell
(1978), the 'city set on a hill' (5:14) may be an allusion to Zion.
[75] Donaldson (1985) 187-8, 200 (italics mine); *cf*. p. 202, 210.

2. A NEW ZION: MATTHEW

the way they were hoping.[77] If, as is likely, Matthew was still 'struggling for the hearts and minds of his fellow-Jews',[78] he needed an answer.

Yet the answer was unexpected and paradoxical. Matthew's readers were not to hanker after a restoration of Jerusalem, a resumption of the previous *status quo* (or even something far better). Instead they were to focus upon Jesus, the one who through his death and resurrection had brought about the restoration predicted by Jeremiah and the prophets. God had now transferred onto Jesus the future restoration promises which previously had related to Jerusalem; no physical restoration of the city was therefore to be expected.

If in Jesus' message and as a result of its treatment of him the 'holy city' of Jerusalem was under divine judgement, this was not a denial of God's restoration promises. Nor was a subsequent restoration to be expected. Those promises had already been fulfilled in the one whom Jerusalem rejected—the one who came to 'fulfil the prophets', who was himself the 'true Israel', whose coming spelt the long-awaited end of Israel's exile, and who though being himself 'restored' and 'raised' drew onto himself the cherished traditions associated with Mount Zion, inviting 'all nations' to share in its blessings. Jerusalem had proved faithless, but God had remained faithful.

4. Matthew's Reflections: from Hope to Judgement

Matthew's message was powerful. The Jerusalem that had the calling to be the 'joy of the whole earth' (Ps. 48:2, *cf.* Isa. 62:7) had lost its vocation. God's purposes would be fulfilled elsewhere—in Jesus and the people gathered to him. Yet Matthew did not convey this message in a spirit of indignant judgementalism, gloating over Jerusalem's fate.[79]

First, judgement for Matthew was an awesome reality that awaited *all* people. This may explain his characteristic focus on Christ's return and *parou-*

---

[76] There would be a further example of Matthew's theology of restoration in 21:15 if it could be proved that in replacing Zechariah's 'rejoice' with 'say to' he was consciously alluding to Isa. 62:11, a verse set in the midst of restoration hopes for Jerusalem (*e.g.* v. 7); *cf.* Niedner (1989) 44. Jesus' entry into Jerusalem would then be the catalyst for that restoration, though in unexpected ways.

[77] Compare the modern arguments in Freudmann (1994) 37: Jesus 'neither established universal peace nor did he redeem Israel. . . . For [the Messiah's] coming, according to prophetic promises, will usher in the redemption of Israel from exile . . . and herald Zion as the acknowledged religious, moral and political centre of all nations'.

[78] Saldarini (1994) 196; see below at n. 92.

[79] As suggested of all the Evangelists by Freudmann (1994) 310. S.C. Barton (1992) 29-33, says the 'moral horizon of Matthew's Gospel has become seriously clouded at this point' and 'his own application of the love commandment tragically blinkered'.

sia (e.g. 11:49; 25:1, 31).[80] This in turn ensured that a judgemental attitude towards Jerusalem was not possible, for the judgement awaiting Jerusalem awaited everyone. Hence the focus in the Apocalyptic Discourse was not just on the fate of Jerusalem and its Temple but also upon Jesus' *parousia* and the signs of the 'end of the age' (24:3ff). Jerusalem's fate was important, but Matthew's primary concern was with the fate of all people as they awaited the 'coming of the Son of Man' (24:30). This was the opposite of judgementalism. It was a desire that all, both Jew and Gentile, should heed the imperatives of Jesus' message. Matthew spoke out against complacency wherever it was found, and much of his Gospel has rightly been read as a warning to Christians. 'The lamentable story of Israel serves the didactic purpose of warning those within the Church that the same reversal which had befallen so many in Israel *may also befall them*'.[81]

Secondly, although Matthew had come to a decidedly negative conclusion about Jerusalem, this may not always have been the case. Matthew's conclusions, though now clear-cut, were not born out of dismissive disdain, but rather out of a passionate concern that had been forced to acknowledge the futility of its former hopefulness.[82] Some further evidence that points in this direction is now noted in more detail: Matthew's positive hopes for Jerusalem, his own personal concern for and involvement with the city, and the fact that his conviction of its inevitable judgement may have developed only gradually.

a) Matthew's Positive Hope

Matthew's positive references to Jerusalem and its Temple have already been discussed.[83] They reflect Matthew's Jewish heart-beat for Jerusalem: this had been 'the holy city', the 'city of the Great King', and its Temple truly the 'Temple of God', the place where God had 'dwelt'. These descriptions could

---

[80] Amongst other causes for this eschatological focus, Stanton (1992) 185-191, has argued that it was a means of countering Jewish charges as to the 'incompleteness' of Jesus' first coming (as for the apologists in the second century). Robinson (1957) 74-78, 98-100, observed how the 'language of Jesus is increasingly referred not to the historical crisis and climax of his ministry, but to a point beyond it' and that this process 'reaches its climax in the Gospel of Matthew' (p. 98).

[81] Charette (1992) 163 (italics mine); it applies, however, not only to those 'within the Church'. *Cf.* similarly Légasse (1972) and Garland (1979), arguing that Matthew's critique of Jewish leaders was also a warning to Christians, and that Christians too could be termed 'hypocrites' (7:5 etc); *cf.* Stanton (1995) 20.

[82] For a powerful statement of this loss of hope in Matthew (though in connection with the mission towards Israel), see Hare (1967) 148.

[83] Above pp. 26, 28-29.

then have become the basis for the hope that, despite the tragedy of the city's treatment of Jesus, Jerusalem and her Temple might again discover their true vocation and join in the joyful worship of him who was their true King. If these descriptions serve an ironic function in Matthew's narrative (showing the height from which these institutions have fallen), they may originally have been the seed-bed of the author's fervent hope.

The way he emphasizes the distinction between Jerusalem's inhabitants and its religious authorities also reflects Matthew's desire to be as positive as possible about Jerusalem *itself*.[84] Focusing his critique on the city's religious leadership enabled him not only to view its inhabitants more favourably, but also the city *per se*. In principle the city itself could be distinguished from that leadership: as such, it might still serve some useful role within God's purposes. As it turned out, in Matthew's experience, 'Jerusalem' continued to be thoroughly identified with its leaders. Yet his making this distinction indicates a mind-set which was prepared to give Jerusalem a chance.

Matthew's open-hearted and hopeful disposition towards Jerusalem can best be discerned in his relating the story (unparalleled in the other Gospels) about the resurrected saints: 'they came out of the tombs, and after Jesus' resurrection they went into *the holy city* and appeared to many people' (27:52-3).[85] Matthew asserted that a miraculous resurrection-event had been witnessed in the 'holy city'.[86] Although this highlighted the irony of the holy city's unholy treatment of Jesus, it also indicated that despite this the door had not been closed on it for ever. There were resurrection-possibilities, and Jerusalem was given the first opportunity to respond. Even if the message of the Risen Lord was ultimately for 'all nations' (28:19), it was certainly for Jerusalem as well.

---

[84] For this distinction, see above section 2b. Matthew's distinctive material on this theme includes 21:14-16, 46; 22:33 and the whole of ch. 23. Saldarini (1994) 43 and 195, notes this distinction and uses it in his argument that Matthew was still seeking to 'recruit' converts from amongst the Jewish populace; though see Stanton (1994) 14 and Carter (1993). Donaldson (1985) 207-8, likewise argues that the 'eschatological status of the crowds remains open to the end', as Matthew continues to hope that 'they will even yet join the ranks of the disciples'. Davies (1974) 242, may still be right that the 'crowds' in Matthew are depicted less sympathetically than in Luke (*e.g.* Luke 23:27).

[85] For discussion on the meaning of this difficult text, see *e.g.* Wenham (1981) and Witherup (1987).

[86] Although Benoit (1950) 231, revived the early patristic suggestion of Origen and Eusebius that the 'holy city' refers to the heavenly Jerusalem (see my [1990a] 358ff), this was not Matthew's original intention; see *e.g.* Senior (1982) 317 and Sabourin (1978) 383. Stonehouse (1944) 185 saw the 'holy city' as describing for Matthew the continuing reality of Jerusalem's specialness, not just its past associations; our position is more nuanced, focusing on the potential which the 'holy city' had because of those past associations—a potential, however, which Matthew now knew would not be realized.

In this way Matthew showed that there had been no outright dismissal of Jerusalem. His heart remained open to the city. Despite the tragedy of the crucifixion Jerusalem was to be invited to share in the resurrection-message. The 'city of the great King' had not been passed over.

b) Matthew's Own Concern for Jerusalem

Matthew may then have had an ongoing, personal concern for the way Jerusalem was responding to the resurrection-message. There are indications of this in the key passage concerning Jerusalem's response to Jesus (23:29-39):

> Therefore I send you prophets, sages and scribes, some of whom you will kill and crucify, and some you will flog in your synagogues and pursue from town to town (23:34).

Although Jesus may be speaking *divina voce* concerning God's sending of such 'prophets' in the past, Matthew probably records it as a description of Jesus' ongoing ministry to the Jewish leaders and to Jerusalem in the *future*—in the period after the resurrection.[87] It is a lament that the hostile response which Jerusalem has previously shown to God's messengers (vv. 35, 37) will continue unabated when it is challenged by Jesus' own 'prophets and sages'.

This is precisely *Matthew's* lament. Jerusalem has continued to oppose Jesus' messengers. Matthew is 'under-writing' Jesus' words from personal experience. A strong indication of this personal touch is his inclusion of the reference to Christian 'scribes' (γραμματεῖς), which echoes his earlier reference to the γραμματεύς 'instructed in the kingdom of heaven' (13:52). This has often been taken as Matthew's 'self-portrait'.[88] The reference in 23:34 serves the same function. Matthew is one of Jesus' 'scribes', called to testify about him to the Jewish nation and to Jerusalem. What has been the response? 'Flogging in synagogues' and being 'pursued from town to town'.[89] The extended opportunity for repentance in the period after Jesus' death has not been taken; on the contrary, the negative response to God's messengers and to Jesus in particular has simply been ratified in the way Jesus' messengers have been treated; the 'measure' has continued to be 'filled up' (*cf.* v. 32).[90]

---

[87] See *e.g.* Gundry (1994) 469-70.

[88] See *e.g.* Davies and Allison (1988/91) 445-6.

[89] This might be a useful context within which to explain Matthew's inclusion of the puzzling *logion* in 10:23 ('you will not have gone through all the towns of Israel before the Son of Man comes'). This would be particularly relevant if Matthew saw himself as still engaged personally in a mission to the 'towns of Israel'. See n. 92 below.

When Jesus then brings the issue to a pointed climax, speaking of 'Jerusalem, Jerusalem, the city that kills the prophets' (v. 37a), these are Matthew's words too, and the 'prophets' he has in mind include his fellow Christian missionaries who have suffered in the task of bringing the gospel message to their own nation. Jesus' mother-like longing for Jerusalem ('how often I have longed to gather your children together': v. 37b) also speaks of Matthew's *own* longing for the city. Yet, as for Jesus, so for Matthew, it is an unrequited love: 'you were not willing' (v. 37c).

'O Jerusalem, Jerusalem' is therefore Matthew's own *cri de cœur*. Jerusalem was the centre of his Jewish world, but now it was rejecting and effectively excluding Jesus' followers, such as Matthew. Those with no prior love for Jerusalem might be little concerned at this, but for Matthew it was extremely painful.[91] 'O Jerusalem' was the cry of someone who dearly loved the city and wistfully hoped that her inherent nature might be changed. It also expressed the awareness that this great city despite all her potential had now abandoned her calling and thus had itself been abandoned by him who once 'dwelt' within her.

That Matthew saw himself as closely involved with the ongoing Christian witness to Jerusalem can also be detected in the following chapter (the Apocalyptic Discourse: ch. 24). In Mark and Luke, apart from the opening 'when you see' (Mark 13:14 and paras), this traumatic period in Jerusalem's history was described in the third person. Matthew instead has Jesus speak of '*your* flight' (24:20), emphasizing that some of Jesus' followers will inexorably be caught up in Jerusalem's 'great distress' (v. 21). So the judgement pronounced upon Jerusalem in this chapter was not conveyed from a perspective of judgemental distance but as a matter of acute and proximate concern. The city's plight was not something far removed from Matthew's world, but rather

---

[90] This gives extra force to the message in the parable of the sheep and goats (25:31-46) that people's destiny will depend on their *response to Jesus' followers*, who in this life often find themselves to be 'strangers and in prison'; *cf.* Stanton (1992) 163-4, 207ff.

[91] For Stanton (1992) 162ff, this might explain his emphasis on eschatology, which served to 'generate a symbolic universe opposed to that of the dominant society', centred on Jerusalem. This sense of exclusion might also explain Matthew's attraction to material in Jesus' teaching that spoke of being 'shut out' (*e.g.* 7:21-23; 22:11-13; 25:11-12; *cf.* 25:41ff); for Matthew had himself been excluded from that which he loved. Saldarini, (1994) 63ff, agrees, but suggests that Matthew still felt that he 'belonged'; Hare (1967) 74, Bornkamm (1970) 104, and Stanton (1995), all argue that Matthew now accepts that he no longer belongs to the main-stream Jewish community. Jerusalem, the centre of his world had dismissed him to the margins; but at the all-important assize this would be reversed. So the casting of the son 'out of the vineyard' (21:39) might have a secondary reference— not just to Jesus' crucifixion (n. 35), but also to his followers (such as Matthew) being ostracized from the community of Israel.

something in which Matthew was integrally involved—at an emotional level, even if not at a directly physical one. He considers himself very much within the geographical and emotional orbit of Jerusalem.

This evidence indicates that Matthew was concerned about the response of his fellow-Jews to the gospel and probably involved still in a continuing mission amongst them.[92] It also suggests that the Jerusalem-issue was close to his heart and that he had hopes for Jerusalem which he now knew would never be fulfilled. The Jerusalem which had been given a further window of opportunity with the sending of Jesus' messengers had failed to respond. The 'holy city' which had been privileged to experience the resurrection of the saints, had not heeded that 'sign'.[93] If Matthew's conclusions about Jerusalem were forthright, it was not for lack of love.

c) Judgement: From Conditional to Inevitable

This raises the issue of just how inevitable Matthew construed the judgement upon Jerusalem to be. For on this interpretation he would have hoped that Jerusalem's judgement would be averted if the city's attitude towards the message of Jesus changed. We have seen that Matthew had presented Jesus' departure from the Temple (23:39-24:2) as a proleptic prophetic act symbolizing the judgement he has just pronounced. He thereby gave the impression that the Temple was doomed from then on—irreversibly.

There are, however, at least two suggestions of a more conditional approach embedded in his narrative. The reference to the repentance of the people of Nineveh (12:41) draws attention to the whole biblical concept that a

---

[92]   Hare (1967) 147, argued that Matthew was opposed to any continuing mission to Jews—perhaps precisely because of the way his hopes had been dashed in the recent past. That might be correct, but we prefer the argument that Matthew was still open to this task: see *e.g.* Gundry (1994) 605, who argues that his clear support for the Gentile mission (above n. 5) is consistent with concern for Jewish mission as well. See also Stanton (1992) 157ff, and Meier (1977); *contra* Hare and Harrington (1975). As noted above (n. 89), such an ongoing mission to 'Israel' gives extra point to the missionary discourse (ch. 10). The debate as to whether Matthew maintained that ethnic Israel had any continuing role within God's purposes is strictly a separate issue; in the same way as he now saw Jerusalem in a new light, he could have answered this question in the negative (as suggested in McKnight [1993] 68) and still believed in the importance of mission amongst his fellow-Jews.

[93]   Witherup (1987) sees the verbs in 27:52-3 (ἠγέρθησαν and ἐνεφανίσθησαν) as having the notion of testifying *against* Jerusalem: 'the purpose of the saints' rising is to testify against Jerusalem for the rejection of Jesus' (p. 582). This negative approach, however, needs to be balanced with the positive one gained from his reference to the 'holy city'. This ambivalence reflects precisely Matthew's attitude towards Jerusalem—originally hopeful, yet now abandoning that hope.

prophecy may achieve its desired intention by not actually coming into effect: Nineveh repented and the prophesied judgement was averted (Jonah 3: 4, 10). Christians in Matthew's circle, even if aware of Jesus' warning of a judgement upon Jerusalem, could nevertheless have prayed earnestly that this would not come to pass. For prophecy was never simple prediction, and was always intended to spur people to action, rather than merely to give advance details.[94]

Secondly, as noted already, Matthew's account of the 'cleansing of the Temple' (21:12-16) differs in emphasis from Mark's: it is not presented as a 'portent of destruction'.[95] Later in his narrative Matthew accepts the charge that Jesus was '*able* to destroy the Temple' (26:61) and includes his prediction that it would be destroyed (24:2). At this stage, however, his emphasis is on Jesus' authority. The one who was Lord over the Temple, indeed 'something greater than the Temple' (12:6), did not necessarily have to destroy it.

These hints of conditionality give way to a sense of inevitability. As the narrative of Jesus moves inexorably to its fateful conclusion, so too the 'superimposed' theme of Jerusalem's consequent fate moves into a mode of inevitability. Matthew's Jesus is clear how the city will treat him and his followers (23:34). By then placing the prediction concerning the house being 'left desolate' immediately prior to Jesus' physical departure from the Temple, Matthew artfully expresses the view which he *now* upholds at the time of writing—namely that from that moment onwards the Temple's destruction *had* been inevitable. This had not always been his view. Jerusalem's inevitable judgement was a truth which he *now* recognized. If he expressed this with great force, this was precisely because he had hoped it might be otherwise.

In this sense Matthew may have been more positive about Jerusalem than the Jesus he sought to follow. The one who predicted the Temple's destruction may have known that this was inevitable. It was his followers who hoped otherwise. They then learnt the unpalatable truth the hard way; and they needed to learn it for themselves—not only because Jesus had told them.

d) Conclusion

The above suggests that some of the ambiguities and tensions within Matthew's Gospel reflect his own profound wrestling with the enormities of that which he was now required to convey. His narrative has a three-dimensional quality: positive and negative voices about Jerusalem jostle for position; the theme of conditionality gives way ultimately to the theme of inevitability.

---

94 See further below in ch. 9 (2).
95 Above section 1a.

This means that an analysis of chapter 28 is particularly important. For this—unlike anything previous in the Gospel relating to Jerusalem—is Matthew's last word. This is where the issues raised in the Gospel are resolved. The fact that this chapter emphasizes Galilee at the expense of Jerusalem and presents Jesus as the 'new Zion' is thus of extra significance. It speaks of the conclusions Matthew himself has reached on this issue of Jerusalem.

So Matthew, the Evangelist who affirmed the significance of Jerusalem so clearly, who loved Jerusalem so passionately and for that reason grieved over it most keenly, concluded that the city's significance had now been relocated in Jesus. This was a conclusion not easily reached, for he would have loved, if possible, a theological *rapprochement* between Jesus and Jerusalem. He now perceived that to be a forlorn hope, and that the Jerusalem which had rejected Jesus in the historical circumstances of the Gospel was also in the *theological realm* to be seen as in essential conflict with Jesus. It was a hard choice, a costly sacrifice, and one that he would rather not have been forced to make; but when a decision was called for, there was no doubt where his new loyalties lay. If it could not be Jesus *and* Jerusalem, it had to be Jesus *without* Jerusalem. Matthew, as Davies concluded, had been forced to learn a hard lesson: 'there is in Matthew the awareness that the geographic dimensions of Jewish expectation . . . have been *shattered*'.[96]

5. Matthew's Situation

Does this help in any way to determine when and where Matthew may have composed his Gospel? Concerning its location, there is some scholarly consensus that somewhere in 'Syria' (*cf.* 4:24) is most likely.[97] Nothing in the above contradicts this—though the suggestion that Matthew considered himself intimately involved with the Jerusalem-issue (and that Jesus' prophecies concerning the 'flight' from Jerusalem have a personal ring to them) might favour a location in southern, rather than northern Syria. This would rule out the popular option of Antioch and give credence to the suggestion that somewhere in northern 'Palestine' (itself part of the province of 'Syria-Palestina'), should be strongly considered—perhaps Caesarea Maritima or Galilee.[98]

---

[96] Davies (1974) 242 (italics mine).
[97] See Davies and Allison (1988/91) 138ff; Luz (1989) 92. The wording of 4:15 and 19:1 might suggest the far side of the Jordan: see Slingerland (1979); *cf.* Stanton (1980) 1941-2.
[98] For Caesarea, see Viviano (1979); for Galilee, see Overman (1990). Segal (1991) 26, urges that 'Galilee and Syria should be considered as a single geographical area'; *cf.* Stanton (1994) 11.

As to the Gospel's date, the fact that the resolution of this Jerusalem-issue may have taken time to crystallize in Matthew's mind favours a date after AD 70. This is not *strictly* necessary. Mark was probably writing before 70, reaching similar negative conclusions about Jerusalem, and there is no need to see the predictions against the Temple as *post-eventum* creations after 70.[99] Nevertheless, in Matthew's case the issue probably took longer to become clear. His Jewish convictions ran more deeply than Mark's, and his prior commitment to Jerusalem was that much stronger. The 'penny dropped' more slowly because it was more painful. One in his position, therefore, might well have needed the tragic events of AD 66-70 to establish beyond reasonable doubt that the glory of Jerusalem was something that now lay in the past.

This painful process of being 'weaned off' Jerusalem did not, however, begin in AD 70; there were already indications that this might be the way things were going. What the events of 70 provided was the confirmation of this direction, and the conviction that something final and (probably) irreversible had now taken place.[100] The fall of Jerusalem gave Matthew the necessary critical stimulus to reflect more deeply on the implications of the gospel for Jerusalem. The comprehensive relocation of Zion-hopes onto the person of Jesus, as indicated by his mountain-motif, would then be one example of how Matthew responded creatively to the questions raised by AD 70.

Donaldson, however, sees Matthew's revised Zion-theology as resulting from an ecclesiological debate. If a Jewish-Christian such as Matthew, he argues, had held to the popular Jewish assumption that the 'ingathering of the nations' would only take place after Israel had itself been 'restored', then his acceptance of the Gentile mission must have been on the basis that Israel was now in the process of being 'restored' and returning to faith in Israel's Messiah, Jesus. As time wore on, and Israel showed no signs of a positive response to the gospel, this schema was 'stretched to breaking-point' and a new basis for the Gentile mission needed to be found. Thus

---

[99] See below in ch. 3 (6) and ch. 8 (1). Most see the references in Matt. 21:41 and 22:7 as referring back to AD 70: *e.g.* Saldarini (1994) 63; this is contested by Rengstorf (1960), Filson (1960), Pedersen (1965), Robinson (1976) 20, and Gundry (1994) 436-7, 600. It is striking that the imagery in both 21:41 and 22:7 does not fit precisely the events of 70 and is in itself mutually incompatible; so these verses may reflect pre-70 tradition. If Matthew *is* writing after 70 he may have intended his readers to detect their pointed significance.

[100] Knowles (1993) 287-8, concludes: 'the question of the Temple's significance' did not first arise 'in response to the fall of Jerusalem. Such issues were already implicit to some degree in the acclamation of Jesus as Israel's Messiah. Matthew's contribution was simply to reiterate the relevance of these themes to the concerns of his community in the aftermath of Jerusalem's fall in AD 70, precisely because the destruction of the city and its Temple had posed anew this series of theological concerns.' *Cf.* the conclusion of Stanton (1992) 381, that Matthew's concerns shaped his sources but did not cause *de novo* creations.

in place of the anticipated fulfilment of eschatological hopes on Zion Matthew proposed the realized fulfilment of every Zion expectation in Christ.
The mission to the Gentiles was to be carried out not as an anticipatory consequence of the restoration of Israel on Mount Zion, but on the basis of the
vindication of Christ announced on the mountain in Galilee.[101]

On such a reading, the fall of Jerusalem/Zion in AD 70 played little or no part
in shaping Matthew's theology, and a date before 70 might be advocated. Although this helpfully warns us not to assume too readily that what we have discovered in Matthew must be seen as a response to 70, the events of that year
remain as the most likely final impetus for his theology of a 'new Zion'.

Matthew may have considered himself, and not just Jesus (cf. 16:14), to
be in a similar situation to that of Jeremiah.[102] Jeremiah had warned of a forthcoming calamity for Jerusalem and had himself lived to see his words come
true. Six centuries later it was Jesus who had given the prophetic warning, but
Matthew who lived in the time of its fulfilment. Jeremiah's final years had reluctantly been spent in Egypt, away from Jerusalem. Matthew too may have
been physically more removed from Jerusalem than he would have liked.
Could he or some of his fellow Christians have been amongst those who fled
the city when the troubles began to loom on the horizon?[103] Certainly, just as
Jeremiah before him, he was one who, even if now at a distance from Jerusalem, still loved the city and longed for her best.

Unlike Jeremiah, however, he could not announce a message of Jerusalem's future restoration. Something more final had occurred. The city's restoration was not to be found in the future promises of God, but rather in her
people's repentance. No doubt his contemporaries longed for Zion's restoration and questioned God's promises in the light of events of AD 70, but Matthew claimed that Jerusalem's true hope lay in a recent past event. God's
promises had been fulfilled, and Jerusalem's fall did not deny his faithfulness.
For just outside the city that now lay in ruins God had recently 'restored' and
'raised' his Son, the true Israel. Jerusalem's hopes thus lay not in its political
future, but in its past—in Jesus, the one who himself was the New Zion.

---

[101] Donaldson (1985) 213.

[102] Cf. also Allison (1993) 290. It is worth noting that Josephus also likened himself to a
second Jeremiah (War 5:392-3); see Knowles (1993) 251-2.

[103] Stanton (1992) 281, suggests that he may have 'moved from Palestine to Syria as the
result of Jewish hostility.' Although some suggest that Mark fled from Jerusalem to Pella
(cf. ch. 1, n. 68), this is far more likely to have been the fate of Matthew than of Mark.
Murray (1982) 203, sees Matthew as representing 'the church which took root in Jerusalem'. According to Luz (1989) 151, Matthew's explanation of Jesus' 'Nazarene' origins
(2:23) might then reflect his identification with the 'Nazarene' Christians who, according
to later sources, lived in this region: see e.g. Pritz (1988).

3

A NEW ERA
Luke-Acts

As he approached Jerusalem and saw the city,
Jesus wept over it (Luke 19:41).

The structure of Luke's two-volume work shows how salvation-history has moved towards and then from Jerusalem. He also includes four major oracles of Jesus concerning the city's future. After the positive descriptions of the Temple and the city there is a dramatic change: Jesus predicts judgement, and the city's response to Jesus and his followers is negative. Stephen's speech illustrates Luke's attitudes, and by the end of Acts the fulfilment of Jesus' prophetic words against the city can no longer be delayed. The presence of the early church in Jerusalem endorses Christianity's claim to be authentically Jewish, but also indicates that through Jesus and the Spirit both Jerusalem and Israel have been 'restored'. A subsequent 'political' restoration of Jerusalem is denied, and the overall dynamic of the gospel message moves away from Jerusalem 'to the ends of the earth'.

Mark and Matthew were concerned about the issue of Jerusalem, Luke even more so. 'The city of Jerusalem haunts his Gospel'.[1] 'Behind Jesus' passion, the shadow of another passion stands out: the passion of Jerusalem'.[2] A 'central theme' in the Gospel is 'the clash of Jesus and Jerusalem'.[3]

---

[1]   Davies (1974) 253.
[2]   Simson (1965) 234.
[3]   Hastings (1958) 98. *Cf.* Rosner (1993) 80: 'Luke has a 'preoccupation with Jerusalem'; similarly, O'Neill (1970) 72: 'in the whole of Luke-Acts it is Jerusalem that controls the history'.

Luke's emphasis on Jerusalem is seen both in his Gospel and in its sequel, the book of Acts.[4] The structure of this two-volume work centres on Jerusalem, with the city acting as the pivot around which the narrative turns.[5] In
the Gospel the story begins and ends in the Temple (1:8-22; 24:53).[6] Luke
alone records the accounts of the young Jesus in the Temple (2:22-24, 41-51).
Unlike Matthew he places Jesus' temptation on the 'highest point of the Temple' last, thereby giving it a special emphasis (4:9-12).[7] After only five chapters dealing with the Galilean ministry Jesus 'sets his face towards Jerusalem'
(9:51). Throughout the ensuing 'travel narrative', Jerusalem is frequently
mentioned as the goal of Jesus' journey (13:33-5; 17:11; 18:31; 19:28). His
eventual arrival in Jerusalem is therefore a climactic moment, 'bringing together the two participants in the drama of the passion, Jesus and Jerusalem'.[8]
Yet in the midst of the crowds' joy Jesus weeps at the thought of what lies in
store for the city (19:37-44). After 'cleansing' the Temple Jesus teaches there
'every day' (19:47ff.; 21:37), including the 'Apocalyptic Discourse' (21:1-
38). Luke's version of this discourse focuses more explicitly than the other
Gospels on the fate of Jerusalem (21:20-24). There are no resurrection appearances in Galilee but only in the environs of Jerusalem.[9]

In these ways Luke's narrative has a concentration on Jerusalem without parallel in Matthew and Mark.[10] His interest in Jerusalem is seen most
clearly in the inclusion of four 'oracles' about Jerusalem (all but the first of
which are not found in the other Gospels): 13:32-35 (A), 19:41-44 (B), 21:20-
24 (C), and 23:27-31 (D). These are labelled to assist our detailed discussion.

This focus on Jerusalem and the Temple continues in the book of Acts.
Apart from the Ascension on the Mount of Olives (1:6-12), chapters 1-7 are
set entirely within Jerusalem. The disciples, though commanded initially not
to 'leave Jerusalem' (1:4), are also called to be Jesus' witnesses in 'Judea, Samaria, and to the ends of the earth' (1:8). This centrifugal movement begins
in chapter 8 and culminates in the arrival of Paul in Rome (28:16), but
throughout these chapters there are frequent returns to Jerusalem.[11] Although

---

[4]   In keeping with the scholarly consensus we shall be assuming the common authorship
of Luke-Acts: see *e.g.* Talbert (1974); Maddox (1982) 3-6, 24; O'Toole (1984); Tannehill
(1986/90); Marshall (1993).
[5]   In the Gospel the narrative moves towards Jerusalem, in Acts it moves away. Jerusalem
is the 'central bearings on which the double work swivels': S.G. Wilson (1973) 95; *cf.* Fitzmyer (1981/5) 168; Drury (1987) 425; Rosner (1993) 70.
[6]   *Cf.* Fitzmyer (1981/5) 165.
[7]   See Hastings (1958) 122; Davies (1974) 253; Fitzmyer (1981/5) 165; Baltzer (1965).
[8]   Hastings (1958) 120.
[9]   This need not imply Luke's ignorance of the Galilean traditions: see Davies (1974) 254.
[10]   Sixty percent of the references to 'Jerusalem' in the Synoptics are found in Luke: see
Lohse (1971) 330; *cf.* Walaskay (1983) 45.

in Acts there are no discussions (as there are in the Gospel) concerning the fate of Jerusalem as a *city*, the Temple is critiqued by Stephen (7:48-50), and it is in the Temple that Paul is charged with desecrating 'this holy place' (21:27ff). Paul is then removed from the city under cover of night, never to return.

What is to be made of all these references to Jerusalem? Some sense Luke has a 'Jerusalem bias', others that he is seeking to 'marginalize' the city.[12] In this chapter the following questions will be discussed: How does Luke view the Temple (section 1)? What is his attitude towards Jerusalem in his Gospel (2) and in Acts (3)? Did Luke believe the city would experience a 'restoration' after the period of judgement pronounced by Jesus (4)? Finally, was he writing before or after the fall of Jerusalem in AD 70?

Luke's emphasis on Jerusalem is intriguing. It is generally agreed that he was a Gentile—though most likely a well-informed 'God-fearer' on the fringe of the Jewish synagogue at the time of his conversion.[13] His interest in Jerusalem was therefore more 'acquired' than 'natural'; unlike Matthew, he could approach this city with the detachment of an 'outsider'.[14] This did not lead, however, to his being indifferent or dismissive. Another Gentile writing around this time described Jerusalem as 'by far the most famous of the cities of the East'.[15] Luke too shows a keen interest in this fascinating city. He also shows real sympathy for the way it has been affected by the coming of Jesus.

This sympathetic note is sounded most clearly in the opening chapters (Luke 1-2) when he sets the scene for his Gospel against the backdrop of the prayerful hopes that ordinary Palestinian Jews had for their nation, subjected as it was to Roman rule. Mary envisages God 'bringing down rulers from their thrones and lifting up the humble' (1:52); Zechariah speaks of God's coming to 'redeem his people', giving them 'salvation from their enemies' (1:68, 71); Simeon and Anna long for the 'consolation of Israel' and the 'redemption of Jerusalem' (2:25, 38). In this way Luke's readership, which included Gentiles,[16] is introduced immediately into another, quite alien world, and invited to sympathize with the hopes which first-century Jews had for Jerusalem's 'redemption' and their liberation as a people from the hand of Rome.

---

[11] See 8:25; 9:26; 11:2, 22, 30; 15:2; 18:22; 19:21; 21:17.

[12] These two alternatives are noted in Bauckham (1995a) 417.

[13] So Franklin (1975), Esler (1987) and Tyson (1995). Fitzmyer (1981/5) 42, suggests he was a Semite but not Jewish. Jervell (1972), Ellis (1974) 52, and Tiede (1980) argue for his being Jewish. For references to God-fearers see Acts 13:43, 50; 16:14; 17:4, 13; 18:7, 13.

[14] So *e.g.* Davies (1974) 260.

[15] Pliny the Elder, *Hist. Nat.* 5.70.

[16] Though disputed by *e.g.* Jervell (1972), there is a consensus that Luke was writing either for mixed Jewish/Gentile congregations, or for Gentiles; see *e.g.* Haenchen (1971) and summary in Moscato (1976). Whether Luke was writing to a particular community is more doubtful: see *e.g.* Chance (1988) 144ff, and now Bauckham (1997).

Luke is not portraying these characters as misguided.[17] On the contrary, he affirms the goodness of these people and the godliness of their hopes. But what happens to these great expectations? This question gives dramatic power to Luke's story. In his narrative these godly hopes turn out *not* to be fulfilled in any straightforward way. Jesus pronounces precisely the opposite outcome for Jerusalem: rather than experiencing a 'rescue from the hands of her enemies' (1:74), her 'enemies hem her in on every side' (19:43). What is God doing? What has happened and how will Jerusalem be affected?

This is our central question. For now we note that by presenting these hopes sympathetically, Luke's narrative is founded on a note of tragedy, rather than of dismissive judgement. These 'great expectations' are introduced 'so that readers will feel the tragic loss more vividly'.[18] Luke invites his readers to enter into this Jewish story, placing themselves imaginatively within its frame of reference, and to sense the fate of the city 'from the inside'.[19] For Luke the story of Jesus is also a story about Jerusalem. Jesus' coming has had major repercussions for the world (*cf. e.g.* Acts 17:6; 26:26), but also for the city which hosted these remarkable events. The coming of Jesus to Jerusalem was its most critical 'hour' (*cf.* 19:44). Will the city ever be the same again?

1. The Temple in Luke-Acts

Again the Temple can be considered separately from the city. This is appropriate, since Luke himself draws this distinction.[20] The overview of Luke-Acts above indicates the Temple's importance for Luke: approximately one sixth of his narrative is located in the Temple or is concerned with its fate. What was his attitude to the Temple both before and after the coming of Jesus?

---

[17] Hence the positive descriptions of them (1:45, 67; 2:25, 37). See Tannehill (1985) 72, Chance (1988) 137; *contra* Davies (1974) 261-3. Whether Luke would have agreed with such nationalistic hopes unaltered in his *own* day is a quite different matter. Nevertheless, Davies correctly notes Luke's awareness that the gospel had its origins amidst a 'boiling cauldron of eschatological anticipations' (p. 255). Flusser (1996) 156, notes how 'the redemption of Zion' was a slogan imprinted on the coins of the first revolt.'

[18] Tannehill (1986/90) i, 37; *cf.* also pp. 160, 165.

[19] Salmon in Tyson (1988) 76-82, that Luke perceived himself as an 'insider' to Judaism. On anti-Semitism in Acts, see Weatherly (1989) and (1994), Tyson (1988) and (1992), Tiede (1993), Evans and Sanders (1993) ch. 12. Luke's own wording in Acts (16:20f, 18:12-17; 19:34) shows his awareness of anti-Semitism and his clear opposition to it.

[20] See *e.g.* Fitzmyer (1981/5) 56. Although there is some 'over-lap', noting this distinction aids the interpretation of Luke 13, 19 and 21 (A, B, C). Luke's use of it reflects his own 'urban' context within the Greco-Roman world and his general interest in 'cities' (see *e.g.* the article by R.L. Rohrbaugh in Neyrey [1991]). That the city and Temple eventually share the same fate does not deny the validity of this distinction: *contra* Bachmann (1980) 13-66.

a) The Temple's Previous Status

The sympathetic tone in his opening two chapters shows that Luke affirmed the traditional Jewish convictions concerning the Temple's significance. There is no suggestion that the close association with the Temple of characters such as Zechariah, Simeon and Anna (and Jesus himself as a boy) was erroneous. After his classically-styled prologue Luke introduces his readers without any apology or explanation to an old man serving as a 'priest before God' in the 'sanctuary *of the Lord*' (1:9). When Jesus is presented in the Temple, Luke's phraseology similarly indicates his conviction as to the Temple's status: 'they brought him up to Jerusalem to present him *to the Lord*' (2:22). Later Jesus affirms the Temple as 'his Father's house' (2:49).[21]

These opening, positive statements about the Temple play an important part within the story-line and must be borne in mind when Luke subsequently reports some radical critique of the Temple. What will happen to this significant institution during the course of the unfolding narrative?[22]

b) The Challenge to the Temple: Jesus

In the light of Jesus' positive reference to the Temple as 'his Father's house' (2:49), the next two references to the Temple come as a dramatic surprise. First, in the temptation narrative the Temple pinnacle is the scene for the final encounter between Jesus and Satan; Satan apparently has an *entrée* into this holy institution.[23] Then Jesus solemnly pronounces in 13:35 (A): 'see, your house is left to you [desolate] (ἰδοὺ ἀφίεται ὑμιν ὁ οἶκος ὑμῶν)'.[24] In the light of the preceding verses with their emphasis on Jerusalem (vv. 33-34) this 'house' clearly includes the Temple.[25] The use of the word ἀφίεται speaks of

---

[21] This is the normal translation of ἐν τοῖς τοῦ πατρός μου, though the absence of a noun might suggest the more general, 'about my Father's *interests*' (see NRSV margin). Though less explicit, a positive understanding of the Temple would still be implied.

[22] Gaston (1970) 365f, and Giblin (1985) argue that Luke plays down the Temple's religious significance. Although the emphasis later falls on the Temple as the place for prayer (18:10; Acts 3:1) and teaching (Luke 19:47-21:38 and Acts 3-5), this opening presentation of the Temple is distinctly religious, focusing on 'prayer', 'incense' and 'sacrifice' (1:9-11; 2:24; *cf.* also 18:13). Green (1995) 4-6, notes how Luke 'side-steps' its function as an 'economic and political force', but focuses on it as a cultural centre' 'where leading ideas come together'; yet he also 'portrays the Temple as the locus of God's presence'.

[23] See further below at n. 50.

[24] The best manuscripts do not have the additional ἔρημος ('desolate'), but the verb ἀφίεται contains within itself the notion of being 'abandoned' or 'left desolate': see *e.g.* Fitzmyer (1981/5) 1033.

an 'abandonment', which in turn suggests a reference to the Temple, the peculiar place of the divine 'dwelling'. Normally one might expect a reference to '*his* house' (*i.e.* God's house) rather than '*your* house', but this is precisely the point at issue: it is no longer '*God's* house'. The Temple will be 'abandoned' by God and his protective presence removed: in effect, 'your house will become yours, and will be left to you'.

This is a solemn first pronouncement intended to shock. The story takes a violent twist, rudely disrupting the placid atmosphere created in the opening chapters. The one who as a boy affirmed the Temple as having a particular relationship to God (his 'Father') now as a man speaks of God's abandonment of that 'house'. The place of 'sacrifice' and 'prayer' is caught up in the judgement which Jesus pronounces against Jerusalem as a whole (vv. 33-35).

Luke's placing these words at what is often seen as the middle-point of the 'travel narrative' endorses their importance;[26] and the fact that Jesus is still so far from Jerusalem sets up in advance the inevitability of what lies in store. In contrast to Matthew's version of this same teaching (23:37-9), Luke leaves unspecified the precise timing of this divine abandonment (though it is closely associated with Jesus' prophetic visit to the city: *cf.* vv. 33-34). Already, however, the 'cloud' of divine displeasure rests on the Temple .

This is important. For subsequent references do not so obviously emphasize this note of judgement. From this, false deductions can be made about Luke's supposedly neutral attitude to the Temple.[27] Instead Luke's placing this solemn pronouncement early in his narrative (and at some 'detached' distance from Jerusalem) can be seen as providing the reader with a key insight into what is really at stake in Jesus' encounter with the Temple, and an ironic awareness of what will eventually happen once he arrives in the city.

Jesus' long-awaited entrance into the Temple occurs in 19:45-6:

> Then he entered the Temple and began to drive out those who were selling things there; and he said, 'It is written, "My house shall be a house of prayer"; but you have made it a den of robbers' (19:45-46).[28]

---

[25] So, de Young (1961) 89, Baltzer (1965), Ellis (1974) 191, and Keathley (1990); *contra e.g.* Weinert (1982). Fitzmyer (1981/5) 1035, rightly notes that 'whether "house" is understood as the Jerusalem Temple or in a broader sense of God's people resident there, the message of judgement is ominously the same'. The precise reference may be wider than just the Temple (so Nolland [1989/93], following Jer. 22:1-8), but there is no likelihood of the term *excluding* the Temple; see Caird (1963).

[26] Egelkraut (1976) 194, sees this as the thematic centre of the travel narrative.

[27] This would be based on the less judgemental Temple 'cleansing' (19:41-44), the absence of reference to the 'abomination of desolation' in the Apocalyptic Discourse (ch. 21) and the apostles' use of the Temple in Acts (3-5; 21ff.). See *e.g.* Weinert (1981), Larsson (1993).

This account is much briefer than the other three Gospels,[29] but it is not anti-climactic. After the suspense of his extended journeying to Jerusalem (9:51-19:44), Jesus' first actions upon arrival necessarily have a climactic importance. Unlike Mark, however, Luke does not at first sight present this as a 'portent of destruction',[30] but rather as a radical act of 'cleansing', designed to show how the Temple had departed from its true vocation. Having announced the inevitability of divine judgement in 13:35, Luke takes the alternative tack and shows the responsibility that the Temple had for this on the human level. The divine 'abandonment' has already been announced, but for the reader it has yet to be deserved. From now on Luke fills in the picture to show that the judgement, though already announced, is truly legitimate.

Nevertheless, the note of judgement is not entirely missing. In stating that 'you *have made it* a den of robbers' Jesus speaks with a sense of finality. Has the Temple's vocation already been lost irretrievably? Similarly, his use of 'my house' (ὁ οἶκός μου, quoting Isa. 56:7) picks up the reference in 13:35 to 'your house' (ὁ οἶκος ὑμῶν) confirming our interpretation above: 'this is really God's house, but it has become yours; look what *you have made* of it!' Finally, the 'cleansing' comes immediately after Jesus' critique and judgement of the *city* of Jerusalem in 19:41-44 (B). Jesus' action in the Temple therefore appears as an outworking of his judgement upon the city: just as the enemies of Jerusalem would lay violent hands on her in the future (vv. 43-44), so Jesus lays violent hands upon the Temple as a sign of this forthcoming judgement. The city's blindness (v. 42) is manifested most acutely in the Temple which is blind to its true purpose and which, just like the city, fails to 'recognize the time of God's coming' (v. 44).[31] In the light of 13:35 Jesus' entering into the Temple is not just a divine 'visitation' but also an announcement of a forthcoming divine *departure*.

That the city and Temple are inter-connected and will share the same fate is made clear in the Apocalyptic Discourse:

---

[28] Davies (1974) 257, rightly sees the suggestion in Conzelmann (1960) 75, that Jesus entered the Temple but not the city as over-subtle. The absence of Mark's phrase 'for all nations' (11:17), whilst initially surprising in the light of Luke's universal emphasis, might reflect his desire that no reader misunderstand Jesus' words as a prediction that in the future the Jerusalem Temple might adopt this new role.

[29] For Flusser (1996) and others associated with the 'Jerusalem school', this brevity is an indication of Lukan priority.

[30] See *e.g.* Davies (1974) 257; Chance (1988) 56; Conzelmann (1960) 77.

[31] 'The Temple is destroyed because of the blindness of those who reject Jesus': Tannehill (1986/90) ii, 94. Putting vv. 42 and 46 together produces a syllogism: 'if the Temple were truly a 'house of prayer', the city would have known the 'peace terms'; but because 'you have made it a den of robbers', Jerusalem is 'blinded'.

> When some were speaking about the Temple . . , he said, 'As for these things
> that you see, the days will come when not one stone will be left upon another;
> all will be thrown down' (21:5-6).

In 19:44 Jesus had predicted the same outcome for the city: 'they will not
leave within you one stone upon another'. In chapter 20 some reasons for this
judgement had surfaced, not least the reaction of the 'tenants' to the one
claiming to be the owner's 'son' (20:13).[32] Evidently the Temple is infected
with the same disease as the surrounding city and will be judged in a similar
way (cf. 20:21-4; C).[33] The rending of the Temple curtain at the time of Jesus'
death (23:45-46) was a proleptic warning.[34] With the coming of Jesus, the
Temple—the city's inner heart—had entered upon a time of judgement.

The final verse of Luke's Gospel, in which the apostles are 'continually
in the Temple blessing God' (24:53), is therefore paradoxical.[35] Luke intends
this to form an *inclusio* with the opening scene of the Gospel in the same Temple (1:5 ff); everything has come 'full circle' and outwardly all has returned
to normal. Since those halcyon days, however, there has been a dramatic twist
in the story. The child in whom the faithful invested their hopes has been crucified, and the Temple in which he once debated has become the object of his
critique. The inner reality is at odds with outer appearances. The apostles may
be in the Temple praising God, but what is going to happen to the Temple? Its
judgement has been pronounced. Will the apostles' presence somehow cause
this to be averted? Will Jesus be proved right or wrong?[36]

b) The Challenge to the Temple: the Apostles, Stephen and Paul

The apostles' involvement in the Temple, begun in Luke 24:53, then continues in Acts 3-5. Nothing negative is said here against the Temple. Instead it is

---

[32] See above in ch. 1 (1c) and ch. 2 (2b).

[33] In Luke 13 and 19 Jesus had first spoken of the city's failures and then focused on the
Temple; in Luke 21 the order is reversed. Would Luke have seen this as an example of the
Temple's sanctity being 'secularized' by the city?

[34] So Chance (1988) 119-20, Green (1991); *contra* Sylva (1986). *Cf.* Green (1995) 6: 'at
Jesus' death, Luke narrates in proleptic fashion the eventual and thoroughgoing theological
critique of the Temple to follow in Acts 7'.

[35] In contrast to Parsons (1987), who sees the Temple as now a 'cleansed house', Hastings
(1958) 124, rightly suggests the Temple was 'God's house no more'.

[36] *Cf.* Drury (1987) 425: 'the satisfyingly symmetrical return of the apostles to the
Temple, where the whole gospel began, is an expedient too temporary to amount to an
ending'; *cf.* also Tannehill (1986/90) i, 298-301, on the combination of closure and yet
openness.

the meeting-point for the disciples, and the natural place for the apostles to present their claim to Jerusalem's religious leadership that Jesus, though crucified, is Israel's Messiah. It is a 'natural strategic objective'.[37]

Luke presents the apostles as effectively giving the Temple authorities, and the people as a whole, another chance (2:37-40; 3:17-21). He also makes it plain that there was no inherent contradiction between the apostles' frequenting the Temple and Jesus' prophetic words about its future (Luke 21:6). Jesus had continued to use it for his teaching, so would they. Involvement with the Temple was still possible, even if they believed it might in due course be destroyed.[38]

This necessary ambivalence towards the Temple comes to a head with the charges brought against Stephen:

> They set up false witnesses who said, 'This man never stops saying things against this holy place and the law; for we have heard him say that this Jesus of Nazareth will destroy this place . . .' (Acts 6:13-14).

This is an allusion to the 'false' charge which, according to Mark (14:58) and Matthew (26:61), was actually made at Jesus' trial: 'we heard him say, "I will destroy this Temple"'. Luke's omission of this in the trial scene reflects neither a pro-Temple theology nor a desire to present Jesus in a politically innocuous light; if this was the case, he would not give the issue the coverage which he does here (6:13-7:60).[39] On the contrary, he defers the matter until now so that he can 'place it in a context where there is room for theological comment'.[40] The reader needs some guidance as to how the Temple, the high status of which Luke has himself affirmed so clearly, can be the object of Jesus' fierce denunciation. Stephen is presented as an example of the inevitable reflection that the first believers must have had on this ambivalent and paradoxical situation.

There is nothing to indicate that Luke distanced himself from the sentiments which Stephen expresses—as though they were the mark of an overly

---

[37] Munck (1959) 242.

[38] On this important point, see below ch. 4 (2d); on the historical issues as to what the first Christians in Jerusalem believed about the Temple in this ambiguous period, see ch. 9 (2).

[39] Nor would he have included Luke 13:35, 21:6. As in Matthew and Mark, the 'falsehood' of the charge lay in asserting that Jesus *himself* would be the agent of the Temple's destruction (Acts 6:14): see *e.g.* Tannehill (1986/90) ii, 94. The charge may also be false in its exaggeration: 'this fellow *never stops speaking* against this holy place . . .' (6:13).

[40] Tannehill (1986/90) ii, 94. He thereby avoids unnecessary repetition. Moreover, in the light of all that has happened since Jesus' trial, Jesus' prophetic critique of the Temple and its authorities can now be seen as more deserved.

negative strand within the earliest Church.[41] So Luke endorses Stephen's
most radical statement:

> the Most High does not live in houses made by human hands (ἐν χειροποιήτ-
> οις); as the prophet says, 'Heaven is my throne, and the earth is my footstool'
> (7:48-9, quoting Isa. 66:1-2).

This gives the initial impression that Stephen is denying God's past sanction-
ing of the Temple, seeing it as a human mistake with no true place in Israel's
history. From his positive presentation of the Temple in Luke 1-2, however,
the reader knows that this was not Luke's opinion. How can this be explained?

First, Stephen's brief statement is not a total denial of the Temple's past
validity.[42] Stephen has just spoken positively about David and Solomon and
their desire to 'provide a dwelling-place for the God of Jacob' (vv. 46-7).
What Stephen does is simply to remind his hearers of the truth expressed by
Solomon at the Temple's dedication: 'But will God indeed dwell on the earth?
Even heaven and the highest heaven cannot contain you, much less this Temple that I have built!' (1 Kings 8:27). From that moment there was an unresolved paradox of God's simultaneous ability and *in*ability to 'dwell' within
it—a theme which recurs frequently in the biblical tradition in passages such
as Isaiah 66:1-2. Without denying God's real involvement in the Old Testament Temple, Stephen was criticizing those who overlooked this paradox and
who were then prone to restricting God to the Temple. He was 'opposing the
notion that God had, without further qualifications, permanently bound himself to Jerusalem and its Temple'.[43] Although his statement could be misheard
(both then and now), it was not in itself a denial of the Temple's past validity.

Nevertheless, the polemical tone (and especially the description of the
Temple as χειροποίητος, a word which was regularly used to describe pagan
shrines)[44] *does* reveal Stephen's critique of his accusers: despite the Temple's
true status in God's sight, it has effectively become *for them* an idol. More

---

[41] See O'Neill (1961) 74. Hence the positive descriptions of Stephen in 6:8, 10; 7:55-6;
contra Bruce (1985) 648, Scharlemann (1968) 56, 179. According to Maddox (1982) 54,
Stephen's theology was for Luke a 'fair statement of the case', but he interprets this
theology in a Marcionite direction. However, even if Luke himself agrees with Stephen's
theology, it does not follow that all Jerusalem Christians in the apostolic era would have
done so (see below ch. 9 [2]). Stephen's attitude is often taken as expressing the naturally
dismissive thought of a Hellenistic or Diaspora Jew. Esler (1987) 146, suggests, however,
that Diaspora Jews living in Jerusalem might, if anything, have been *more* enthusiastic
about the Temple than the indigenous population.
[42] So, O'Neill (1961) 74; Chance (1988) 126; Tannehill (1986/90) ii, 93; Brawley (1987)
121; Larsson (1993); *contra e.g.* Simon (1951) 127, Esler (1987) 163, Barrett (1991) 364.
[43] De Young (1961) 53.
[44] *Cf.* Acts 17:24, and comments on Mark 14.58 in ch. 1 (1e).

startling still, perhaps the Temple has actually become an idol, not just *subjectively* in the hearts of his audience, but *objectively* in the sight of God. Their subjective idolatry of the Temple (seeking to preserve the 'holy place' against every criticism) has been an instrumental factor in causing them to dismiss Israel's true Messiah when he dared to speak against it (Acts 6:14). This is so serious that God has allowed that idolatry to become objective as well. The Temple has lost its former status and is now *in his sight too* merely a human construct (χειροποίητος), void of significance. Even if he did so in the past, God no longer continues to live in 'houses made by human hands'. 'Although God had dwelt with Israel in the Temple he no longer continues that redemptive-revelational relationship with Israel'.[45]

There is then no difficulty in Luke's fully endorsing this—so long as it is remembered that Luke is drawing attention to a major, unexpected transition which has taken place with regard to the Temple. In Luke 1-2 he endorsed a view of the Temple's sanctity; now in Acts 7, without any personal inconsistency, he can endorse the conviction that the Temple may be reduced to an idol within God's sight. The coming of Jesus has introduced a time of great upheaval—which is precisely what Luke intends to convey to his readers.

Within the narrative it is clear that, unless there is a radical change of heart, the Temple and its authorities have become the emblematic focus of opposition to God (*cf.* 5:39). In the light of Jesus' solemn words in the Gospel, the reader is aware that Temple is now in a vulnerable situation: it is 'abandoned' (Luke 13:35), it has become a mere idol (Acts 7:48), it is under threat of destruction (Luke 21:6; Acts 6:14).

The narrative then moves away from the Temple and the issue is left pending, only to resurface in Paul's final journey to Jerusalem. What will happen when this messenger of the gospel enters the Temple?

Paul is arrested in the Temple, and led away from its precincts, the Temple doors shutting behind him (21:30). The whole episode provides for Luke the perfect final comment upon what the Temple has become. Again the sensitivities of those zealous for 'this holy place' (21:28) have resulted in actions which are far from holy (though Paul, unlike Stephen, survives). The messenger of Israel's Messiah is expelled from Israel's 'holy place', and in shutting the doors behind him the Temple effectively shuts out the God who once had dwelt there. It is left as the place devoid of God's presence and ripe for his judgement: 'as a direct result of the mob's violent seizure of Paul, the Temple faces destruction'.[46] As Bruce concludes,

---

[45] De Young (1961) 56, emphasizing the continuous sense of the present tense (κατοικεῖ).

[46] Chance (1988) 122, noting the parallel with the rending of the veil (Luke 23:45) and also with Josephus (*War* 6:293, 295-6).

Paul and his creed are forced from their proper home. On it as well as him the Temple doors are shut. . . The Temple ceased to fill the honourable role hitherto allotted to it in his two-fold history. The exclusion of God's message and messenger from the house formerly called by his name sealed its doom: it was now ripe for destruction. . . The exclusion from the Temple courts betokened the divine abandonment of the city and Temple as surely as the departure of the *shekinah* from the first Temple in Ezekiel's vision was the prelude to its desolation. . . The destructive events of the summer of AD 70 served only to set the seal on what had happened at the Pentecostal season of AD 57.

The reader of [Luke's] narrative may have found it difficult to reconcile the two attitudes toward the Temple which it documents—Jesus' proclamation of the Temple' doom and the apostle's continuing respect for the building and its services. But here the tension between the two attitudes is resolved.[47]

d) Conclusion

Luke tells a story, therefore, in which a tragic fate has beset the Temple. In order to do this he had to introduce the Temple in a positive way at the outset of his narrative, so that the reader could observe its subsequent 'fall'. Without this, much of the dramatic power and theological interest of the story would evaporate. This is vitally important. For analyses of Luke's thinking which fail to take into account this dramatic flow of his narrative radically distort the picture, suggesting either that he never believed in the Temple's sanctity, or at the other extreme that he taught the enduring specialness of the Temple into the foreseeable future. Neither is the case. Luke both affirms and denies the Temple, affirming its past status, but denying its future—an attitude which reflects his own presentation of a Jesus who similarly had both affirmed the Temple and pronounced its destruction.

---

[47]   Bruce (1990) 16, 450. For similar conclusions, see van der Waal (1973). The argument in Chance (1988) 83, 112, 127, 143, 151, that Luke's failure to develop a 'replacement' theology (with Jesus or the Church as the new Temple) indicates an ongoing positive attitude towards the Temple, is weak. Luke's presentation is necessarily more 'horizontal', a story told along the continuum of history, and seeks to show the responsibility of the Temple on the human level for its demise. Whilst not contradictory, if he had emphasized this note of 'spiritual replacement', this might well have undercut his emphasis on the historical responsibility of the Temple for its fate. Even so, there are some indications of Jesus as the 'new Temple': hence the 'cloud' of the divine presence around Jesus in Luke 9:35 and Acts 1:9, and Jesus' going to the Mount of Olives for the Ascension, reflecting the departure of the *shekinah* glory from the Temple in Ezekiel's vision (Ezek. 11:22ff). *Cf. e.g.* Hastings (1958) 151: 'the glory of God was revealed in the Temple in Jerusalem; it is now revealed in the person of Jesus'.

2. Jerusalem in Luke's Gospel

The same pattern holds true for Luke's assessment of the *city* of Jerusalem. There is little doubt that he would have affirmed the unique significance of Jerusalem in the past,[48] but how has this been affected by the coming of Jesus?

a) Jerusalem, the Focus of Opposition

As in Mark and Matthew, Jerusalem in Luke's Gospel is the focus of opposition to Jesus. Not that there is none in Galilee,[49] but Jerusalem is the place where it becomes most intense.

Luke emphasizes this in several ways. In his version of Jesus' healing of the paralytic (5:17ff) those who complained at Jesus' action had come 'from every village of Galilee and from Judea *and from Jerusalem*' (*cf.* Matt. 9:1ff; Mark 2:1ff); Jerusalem is included straightaway in the incipient hostility towards Jesus. Secondly, by placing the Temple Temptation last (4:9-13), Luke, as it were, leaves the Devil *in Jerusalem* (v. 9) waiting 'until an opportune time' (v. 13). Though this cannot be pressed too far,[50] it does suggest that Jerusalem is the place where the power of evil will reach its climax, and that, for all its specialness, this city is not immune to Satan's influence.[51] Thirdly, his speaking of Jesus' 'setting his face to go to Jerusalem' (9:51) reveals the

---

[48] See *e.g.* Luke 2:38 and 19:41 ('if you, even *you*, had known . . .'). As a Gentile Luke's convictions might have been weaker than Matthew's (there are no references to the 'holy city', as in Matt. 4:5; 27:53; *cf.* 5:35); but as a 'God-fearer' he was evidently indebted to the Old Testament (*e.g.* Clarke [1922], Rosner [1993]). For Luke to deny Jerusalem's status would have set him radically at odds with the characters in his story, not least with Jesus himself. Note too Luke's using for 'Jerusalem' the term Ἰερουσαλήμ which, in contrast to the more secular term Ἰεροσόλυμα evoked Jerusalem's religious and theological significance: see *e.g.* Davies (1974) 256, Hastings (1958) 103ff, de Young (1961) 1-27, de la Potterie (1982); *contra* J.K. Elliott (1977), Sylva (1983), Ross (1992). That Luke uses Ἰερουσαλήμ at all (when Mark never uses it, and even Matthew only once—in the 'Q' passage paralleled in Luke 13:33) indicates his endorsement of the way Jewish people saw the city as different from others. Yet Luke could still be critical of the way this concept had been abused, and contend that things had changed with the coming of Jesus.

[49] Hence, for example, the programmatic episode in Nazareth (4:16-30), indicating at the outset the rejection which Jesus was to experience *throughout* his ministry: see *e.g.* Egelkraut (1976) 224.

[50] As perhaps by Conzelmann (1960) 27ff, rightly criticized by Davies (1974) 250. It is possible that Luke's order is the original (compared to Matt. 4:1-11), and therefore less significant for determining Luke's redactional interests.

[51] The two references to Satan after Jesus' arrival in Jerusalem (22:3, 31: unique to Luke) may not be coincidental.

perception that Jerusalem is the place where Jesus could expect his fiercest opposition.[52] It will certainly be the 'city of destiny'.[53]

This emphasis is seen most clearly in the next reference to Jerusalem,
the first of the four main oracles concerning the city (A):

> A. 'Go and tell that fox for me, "Listen, I am casting out demons and per-
> forming cures today and tomorrow, and on the third day I finish my work.
> Yet today, tomorrow, and the next day I must be on my way, because it is
> impossible for a prophet to be killed away from Jerusalem." Jerusalem, Jeru-
> salem, the city that kills the prophets and stones those who are sent to it! How
> often have I desired to gather your children together, as a hen gathers her
> brood under her wings, and you were not willing! See, your house is left to
> you. And I tell you, you will not see me again until the time comes when you
> say, "Blessed is the one who comes in the name of the Lord"' (13:32-35).

This is an extraordinary passage. Verses 34 and 35 are paralleled in Matthew
(23:37-39), but by placing them in his version when Jesus is still some distance from Jerusalem, Luke gives the impression that Jesus' 'longing' for the
city represents a more eternal perspective—that of the God of Israel who has
longed for Jerusalem throughout its wayward history.[54] Jesus is articulating
the divine case against Jerusalem. The first two verses (unique to Luke) indicate that Herod will not be able to kill Jesus in Galilee since that prerogative
has been reserved for Jerusalem; for, paraphrasing verse 33, 'it would never
do for a prophet to die outside Jerusalem!' Jerusalem has an inherent characteristic of opposition to those whom God sends to her. This city will inevitably
be the supreme place of opposition to Jesus.

b) The Reasons for Jerusalem's Opposition

Why is this? The more obvious reasons, associated with the challenge of Jesus' message and identity, will become clear once Jesus arrives in the city
(19:45ff); at this stage a more 'abstract' explanation is offered (vv. 34-35).

Fundamentally, Jerusalem's opposition to Jesus is rooted in its prior opposition to God himself, as manifested in its previous treatment of 'those sent
to it' in his name (v. 34a). Though associated with God and given a special
destiny, Jerusalem has developed a hostility towards him. The city called to
be *for* God has turned *against* him. If in Luke's understanding Jesus represent-

---

[52] See *e.g.* C.A. Evans (1982) and (1987); *cf.* also Maddox (1982) 46.
[53] Peterson (1993) 90; Fitzmyer (1981/5) 168.
[54] Caird (1963). Jesus speaks like 'God's Wisdom' (*cf.* 11:49): Fitzmyer (1981/5) 1034.

ed this God in a unique way, then plainly the opposition to Jesus was going to
be intense. The city that welcomed Jesus at the outset (chs. 1-2) has a startling
problem. That welcome towards Jesus will evaporate.

Jesus then uses the imagery of the hen and her chicks (v. 34b). This indicates the gentle nature of his approach, rendering Jerusalem's rejection of
Jesus all the more perverse. It also causes a distinction to be drawn between
'Jerusalem' and her 'children'. Since in the Greek 'Jerusalem' is personified
in the feminine ('Ιερουσαλὴμ, ἡ ἀποκτείνουσα . . . τοὺς ἀπεσταλμένους πρὸς αυ-
'τήν), Jesus is portraying Jerusalem as being like a mother to her 'children'.
Seen in this light, the imagery takes on a different hue; for it is as though Jesus
is wanting to take Jerusalem's children away from her and to place them safely under *his* control. Jerusalem will be robbed of her charges! By implication
Jerusalem is acting towards her children as a false mother and in such a way
that they are in danger and in need of the protection which alone can be found
with Jesus, the 'true mother'.[55]

One reason, therefore, for Jerusalem's rejection of Jesus was that he
dared to confront the city with her failings, and to identify her as a false mother that was taking in a wrong and dangerous direction those who were her
'children' (that is, the city's inhabitants and those devoted to her as *metropolis*/'mother-city'). He named the idolatrous power. The Old Testament prophets had likened Jerusalem to an adulterous young bride (*e.g.* Jer. 2:20-25, 32f;
3:1-14; Ezek. 16:1ff), but Jesus spoke to a mature Jerusalem which had children of her own and which was acting as a rival parent, taking those children
away from their true father, God himself. By contrast, Jesus offered to be a
true 'mother', but the false, usurping parent did not react kindly to the arrival
of the true.

As a result of this 'false mothering', Jerusalem's inhabitants were in a
perilous situation, though the precise nature of this peril is not specified. Jesus,
however, announced that, if those children would turn to him, they would find
in *him* the needed protection. He was essential for the city's welfare. It is an
grandiose claim, which for Luke must have confirmed that Jesus was here
speaking *divina voce*.[56] It also reveals that a vital distinction could be drawn

---

[55] If this interpretation is correct, Jesus' application to himself of the feminine imagery of
the 'hen' is determined not so much by the 'maternal' care of God in the abstract, but rather
as a deliberate divine 'foil' to the false mothering by Jerusalem.

[56] The reference in v. 35 (discussed above) to the 'house' being 'left desolate' speaks
therefore of the Temple not only being deprived of God's presence (as emphasized in Matt.
23:37-39) but also of his protection. This strongly suggests that Luke identified the protection of Jesus (v. 34) with the God who protected the Temple (v. 35); in the Old Testament
the imagery of the 'wings' is applied to God (see Deut. 32:11; Pss. 17:8; 36:7; Ruth 2:12).
Note too how the one who himself in 4:10 had refused the comforting protection of the
divine 'wings' of Ps. 91, now offers those divine wings to the children of Jerusalem.

between 'Jerusalem' herself, for which Jesus only had stern words, and her helpless 'children', for whom he was full of compassion. The problem lay not so much with the children, as with the false mother.

c) The City Exposed to Judgement

Further detail on what lies in store for Jerusalem is given in the next two oracles (B, C). The first of these is remarkable for its emotional passion:[57]

> B. As he came near and saw the city, he wept over it, saying, 'If you, even you, had only recognized on this day the things that make for peace! But now they are hidden from your eyes. Indeed, the days will come upon you, when your enemies will set up ramparts around you and surround you, and hem you in on every side. They will crush you to the ground, you and your children within you, and they will not leave within you one stone upon another; because you did not recognize the time of your visitation from God' (19:41-44).

> C. When you see Jerusalem surrounded by armies, then know that its desolation has come near. Then those in Judea must flee to the mountains, and those inside the city must leave it, and those out in the country must not enter it; for these are the days of vengeance, as a fulfilment of all that is written. Woe to those who are pregnant and to those who are nursing infants in those days! For there will be great distress on the earth and wrath against this people; they will fall by the edge of the sword and be taken away as captives among all nations; and Jerusalem will be trampled on by the Gentiles until the times of the Gentiles are fulfilled' (21:20-24).[58]

Fateful consequences await the city: Jesus warns that 'the days are coming' (19:43; 21:29; cf. also 23:29). 'What Jesus anticipates is a replay of the experience of the Babylonian period.'[59] These oracles are part of a much larger threat-tradition which begins with the Baptist's warning of a 'coming wrath' (3:7-9) and become prevalent in the 'travel narrative'.[60] Concerning Jerusalem and the Temple, these two oracles (B, C) when combined with the other

---

[57] Its fractured syntax and repetition of the sibilant συ/σε ('you') powerfully conveys Jesus' weeping: see Tiede (1980) 86.

[58] On some of the issues of how this oracle relates to the events of AD 70, see section 6.

[59] Nolland (1989/93) 933.

[60] See Egelkraut (1976) 193, 196. 'This wicked generation' (11:29) would be 'held responsible for the blood of all the prophets' (11:50-51). Pilate's execution of the Galileans was an example in miniature of what would happen to them all at the hands of Rome (13:1-6); cf. Walaskay (1983) 24. The unfruitful fig-tree would eventually be 'cut down' (13:8). See also 11:32; 12:8, 35, 56; 17:22ff. See further Wright (1996) ch. 8.

two (A, D) present a formidable picture. The coming judgement is expressed
in different ways: as God's abandonment of the Temple and a withdrawal of
Jesus' presence (A: 13:35), as the coming of Jerusalem's 'enemies' to 'crush
it to the ground', not leaving 'one stone upon another' (B: 19:42-3), as the
'desolation' of Jerusalem when it is 'trampled on by the Gentiles' (C: 21:20,
24) and as a dreadful event when people would invite the mountains to fall on
them (D: 23:30). The third oracle (C) establishes that these events are associated with God's 'vengeance' and 'wrath' (21: 22, 23). As a result, Jesus' followers are to be ready to put Jerusalem behind them, and to 'flee' (21:21).

The shocking force of these statements needs to be heeded. At the outset there had been a longing for Jerusalem's 'redemption' (2:38); now that
hope is repeatedly dashed—not once, but four times. The one who prevented
the disciples from calling down fire on a Samaritan village (9:55), nevertheless announces that the fire of God's judgement will fall on Jerusalem. Those
who might have first heard Jesus' solemn prediction about the Temple being
destroyed (21:6-7) as an indication that the longed-for Messianic era was
about to dawn, would learn that this was the prelude not to Jerusalem's restoration, but to its 'desolation' (21:20). Contrary to expectation, Jerusalem
would not be a safe haven from calamity and judgement; and, contrary to the
disciples' present hopes, the 'desolation' of Jerusalem, when it finally came,
would be a sign that their own 'redemption' was drawing near (21:28). The
'enemies' from whom Zechariah and others longed to be free (*cf.* 1:71, 74),
far from being themselves overthrown, would be used by God as the agents of
his 'wrath' against his own 'people' (21:23). The divine 'visitation' (1:68, 78)
would bring the opposite of the expected blessings (19:44); and Zechariah's
longing that Israel find the 'way of peace' (1:79) would not be realized.
'Zechariah's joy is replaced by Jesus' mourning'.[61]

Luke 19:41-44 (B) picks up the imagery of 13:34-35 (A). Jesus again
refers to 'you [Jerusalem] and your children' (v. 44). Placing these two oracles
together, we see the enormity of Jesus' claim: if Jerusalem's children had
looked to him, they would have found protection from this imminent danger.
If the city had allowed herself to be surrounded by the protective 'wings' of
Jesus (13:34), she would not have found herself surrounded by the encircling
armies of Rome (19:43).[62]

Were these consequences now inevitable? Although some references
(*e.g.* 13:5) suggest that they might be averted through repentance (as with Nineveh, 11:32), the four oracles relating to Jerusalem are noticeably void of any

---

[61] Tannehill (1986/90) i, 336. He helpfully lists the contrasts between Zechariah's expectations (1:67-79) and Jesus' words (19:41-44). There may also be a play on Jerusalem's
name, with the 'city of peace' ironically being blind to 'peace': Fitzmyer (1981/5) 1256.

such conditions. The final three (B, C, D) are presented as solemn pronouncements of what will occur. It is not that Jerusalem might now have its eyes opened; these things already 'are hidden from your eyes' and the city's ignorance of Jesus' identity is spoken of in the past tense ('you did not recognize'). For Luke the fate of both Jesus and Jerusalem is clear. The city's' destruction is already 'sealed with Jesus' entry into Jerusalem'.[63] The 'doom of the nation is now scheduled on the divine calendar'.[64]

This adds poignancy to Luke's version of the passion, for the reader senses that in deciding Jesus' fate Jerusalem was also deciding her own; behind the one tragedy, there loomed a second. In Acts, however, there is a note of conditionality, with Jerusalem being given a second chance.[65] As in Matthew,[66] the way these two (seemingly contradictory) themes of conditionality and inevitability are woven together provides one of the puzzles of the narrative. It also gives the plot a vital intrigue, with the reader simultaneously knowing, and yet not knowing, what will eventually occur.

d) The Reasons for Judgement

Luke's Jesus reverses the expectations of his contemporaries—expectations which Luke initially had implied were quite valid. What has happened to bring about this dramatic reversal? In the Old Testament there was a prophetic tradition in which God himself came in judgement against his own city (see *e.g.* Isa. 29:3; Ezek. 4:1-3; 21:27; Jer. 52:4-5); why was this happening again?[67]

As in Matthew, Jesus' cursing of the three Galilean towns (10:13-15) may serve also as a partial explanation of Jerusalem's fate: it pinpoints the danger of pride and a lack of repentance.[68] Luke, however, emphasizes a more political factor: at the level of *Realpolitik*, Jerusalem's fate is the inevitable re-

---

[62] Note too the imagery of the 'eagles' in 17:37. Jesus used the 'hen' imagery to say that he wanted to gather together (ἐπισυνάξαι) Jerusalem's children; in 17:37, however, it is the predatory eagles (of Rome?) who are gathered together' (ἐπισυναχθήσονται) around a corpse—a chilling alternative. The challenges associated with Jesus' arrival in Jerusalem would be far preferable to those associated with the arrival of the Roman armies. The references to 'children' pick up the motifs of Old Testament passages that spoke of Israel's enemies (*e.g.* Nah. 3:10 and Ps. 137:9); now they apply to Jerusalem.

[63] Egelkraut (1976) 133.

[64] Walaskay (1983) 24.

[65] See below section 3d.

[66] Above ch. 2 (4c).

[67] Tiede (1980) 81-2, emphasizes the Old Testament background to all these oracles, thus endorsing his argument against any supposed anti-Semitism in Luke.

[68] See fuller discussion above in ch. 2 (2c).

sult of the city's wrong attitude towards Rome. Luke highlights the exclusive attitudes towards Gentiles (and also the Samaritans) that were current within the Judaism of his day—attitudes which Jesus consistently corrected, as he talked positively about Naaman the Syrian (4:27), the faith-filled Roman centurion (7:1-10), the 'good Samaritan' (10:25 ff), and those in the 'roads and country lanes' (14:23). The hostile attitude towards the Roman occupiers was but an extension of this; yet Jesus said, 'love your enemies' (6:27). Jerusalem was thus set on a path that made for war, not knowing the 'things that make for peace' (19:42). Since the Greek phrase for this (τὰ πρὸς εἰρήνην) can be translated 'peace terms' (as in 14:32), Luke may be indicating that, on the purely political level, Jerusalem's fate would be the result of a foolishly hostile attitude towards Rome, not knowing the true 'peace terms'.

The chief cause of Jerusalem's judgement according to Luke has to do with its response to Jesus and to his followers. This was already seen in 13:33-35 (A): Jerusalem's being unwilling to accept Jesus' caring protection, and her preparedness to kill prophets like Jesus, resulted in her 'house being left desolate'. It is clearest, however, in Luke 19:41-44 (B). Here the cause of the city's destruction is not simply her blindness to the 'peace terms', but also her not recognizing 'the time of her visitation from God' (οὐκ ἔγνως τὸν καιρὸν τῆς ἐπισκοπῆς σου). For Luke, Jesus' arrival was its most significant hour (its καιρός), when it received a 'visitation' from God in the person of Jesus.

The logic of these verses is centred around the notion of 'rejection': since Jerusalem has rejected God's ultimate representative, Jesus, she herself will be rejected by God. This is explained further in the following chapter: the reader sees the critical response to Jesus' teaching on the part of the Jerusalem authorities, and hears the parable of the vineyard (20:9-19), in which the tenants' killing of the owner's 'beloved son' leads to the vineyard being given to others.[69] Jesus' reference to the 'stone rejected by the builders' (20:17ff) makes the theme of rejection explicit. In rejecting the 'stone' Jerusalem will itself experience rejection, with 'not one stone being left upon another' (21:6).

Chapter 21 introduces a further reason for Jerusalem's fate. At first Luke's Apocalyptic Discourse appears to give little explanation for the prophesied destruction of the Temple (21:6) and the 'desolation' of Jerusalem (21:20)—except that these events will be in 'fulfilment of all that is written' (v. 22). They are in some ways connected with the 'end', but for what reason? A clue is found in noting the way in which Jesus does not immediately answer the disciples' question about the Temple's destruction. Instead he talks about other forthcoming phenomena—especially that his followers will be persecuted. This persecution will come from many different quarters ('you will be hat-

---

[69] For fuller discussion of the parallel passages in ch. 1 (1c) and ch. 2 (2b).

ed by *all*': v 17), but especially from their own people, their 'parents, brothers, relatives and friends' (v. 16), and those in the 'synagogues' (v. 12).[70]

This delayed answer achieves several things. First, it enables the disciples to see Jerusalem in a different light: Jerusalem will become for them, as for Jesus, the chief focus of their opposition. They are therefore to distance themselves from Jerusalem, and to see their destiny no longer bound up with Jerusalem but rather quite distinct: Jerusalem will be 'surrounded by armies', 'but not a hair of *your* head will perish' (vv. 20, 18); if the 'desolation' of Jerusalem is near' (v. 20), so too is *their* 'redemption' (v. 28).[71] They are to abandon any of their own more political aspirations for the city.

Secondly, it provides a deeper rationale for the destruction of Jerusalem: for, according to these verses, there is every indication that Jerusalem will play a major part in the persecution of Jesus' disciples. Jerusalem experiences the *opposite* destiny to that of Jesus' disciples ('desolation', rather than the longed-for 'redemption') because she chooses to oppose those disciples. In the fall of Jerusalem, the divine verdict falls against her: it is Jesus and his followers whom God vindicates. In this way, 'the fall of Jerusalem is not only linked' with the rejection of Jesus, but the rejection of his disciples as well'.[72]

e) The Final Oracle

> D. A great number of the people followed him, and among them were women who were beating their breasts and wailing for him. But Jesus turned to them and said, 'Daughters of Jerusalem, do not weep for me, but weep for yourselves and for your children. For the days are surely coming when they will say, "Blessed are the barren, and the wombs that never bore, and the breasts that never nursed." Then they will begin to say to the mountains, "Fall on us"; and to the hills, "Cover us." For if they do this when the wood is green, what will happen when it is dry?' (23:27-31).

This final prophecy links the fate of Jerusalem to Jesus' crucifixion.[73] As Jesus goes to his death, he warns of what lies in store for Jerusalem. He is on the

---

[70] His inclusion of the term συγγενεῖς (translated as 'relatives') suggests that persecution will especially come from people of their own race (γένος). This focus on Israel may in part explain the omission here of the reference to the gospel going out 'to all nations' (Mark. 13:10); *cf.* Tiede (1980) 93.

[71] Scholars note how the *parousia* is no longer linked chronologically to the fall of Jerusalem: see Conzelmann (1960) 74; Braumann (1963); Davies (1974) 258-60; Egelkraut (1976) 220; Flusser (1996) 153.

[72] Chance (1988) 120.

[73] *Cf.* Walaskay (1983) 47; Hastings (1958) 106.

via dolorosa at the end of which stands the cross; but Jerusalem is on a similar path that will lead just as inexorably to tragedy. Her 'fate could be no less certain than his'.[74] Although a positive attitude to Jesus is shown by the weeping 'daughters of Jerusalem' (those who, like Jerusalem's 'children' in Luke 13:34, are under the sway of 'Jerusalem'), at this late stage no amount of sorrow can avert the judgement which is inevitable.

The passage echoes Jeremiah 9:17-21 (concerning the judgement on Jerusalem in 587 BC) and contains a quotation from Hosea 10:8 (a passage originally referring to the fall of Samaria): these famous acts of divine judgement in the past will soon be repeated against Jerusalem. Luke is 'immersed' in these biblical 'precedents'.[75] The reader is to see both the repeated pattern within God's dealings, and the integral connection between Jesus' death and Jerusalem's subsequent fate: the latter event is the assured *future backdrop* against which the former event needs to be seen and interpreted. All of this is a 'tragic reversal of the oracles of salvation for Jerusalem' which are to be found in other parts of the Old Testament.[76]

After pronouncing a paradoxical 'blessing' on women who are barren, Jesus asks the enigmatic question: 'for if they do this (ταῦτα ποιοῦσιν) when the wood is green, what will happen when it is dry?' (v. 31). Of the many possible interpretations,[77] preference should be given to those which understand the unspecified subject of the verb ποιοῦσιν as a reference to the Romans.[78] For example, 'if the Romans treat in such a way one whom they admit to be innocent, what will they do to the guilty?' A close parallel is sensed between Jesus' fate and that of Jerusalem: both suffer at the hands of Rome. According to Luke, Jesus (unlike Barabbas: 23:18-19) was innocent of the charge of being anti-Roman, but Jerusalem patently was not; in this sense Jesus was 'green', but Jerusalem was 'dry'. Despite this important distinction between Jesus and Jerusalem, there is also a note of similarity: *both are identified with the 'wood'* (ξύλον). In a profound way Jesus, though pronouncing judgement on Jerusalem (which is guilty of that of which he is innocent), identifies with that city and sees his sufferings as being part of the sufferings which he has

---

[74] Hastings (1958) 115.

[75] Tiede (1980) 82; *cf.* Rosner (1993).

[76] Tannehill (1986/90) i, 166, focusing on Isa. 40-66.

[77] There is no need for only one to be valid. For a good list, see Morris (1988) 355.

[78] If instead the subject is identified with the Jewish leaders or people, then in the second half of the verse these need to be seen as the implied *object* of the verb; this transition is more clumsy.

foreseen for her.[79] Jesus' death is a foretaste of what lies in store for Jerusalem, and Jesus is prepared to suffer it in his own person for her sake.

This yields important insights into Luke's approach to the judgement pronounced in his Gospel upon Jerusalem. If Jesus' death is not just the result of Jerusalem's sin, but also at the same time a foretaste of her punishment, then the link between the respective fates of Jesus and Jerusalem is not a simple one of 'cause and effect'. Luke presents this model of 'cause and effect' (with Jerusalem's judgement being partly the result of her treatment of Jesus) in the previous oracles (A and B). Now it needs to be balanced with the insight that Jesus' death is not just the *cause* of Jerusalem's judgement, but also the foretaste of it.

Several things follow from this: first, Jesus' *via dolorosa* becomes a 'prophetic action' in which he portrayed in a vignette what lay in store for Jerusalem. Just as some prophets had acted out in advance the fate which they predicted (*e.g.* Jer. 19:10 and Ezek. 4:4ff), so Jesus in going to his death acted out in a graphic way the judgement which he foresaw for Jerusalem.

Secondly, Luke's Jesus is not just one who judges Jerusalem; he also suffers that judgement himself and identifies with the city in its death. His words are not distantly critical, but are backed up by costly identification.[80]

Thirdly, the close connection between Jesus' death and Jerusalem's fate invites the question: would Luke have seen any parallel for Jerusalem comparable to Jesus' resurrection? One tragedy (Jesus' death) was followed by a divine reversal; would the same hold true for the other tragedy (Jerusalem's destruction)? Or was that precisely the point of contrast between the two?[81]

Luke leaves the issue of Jerusalem's fate with an unanswered question on the lips of Jesus: 'what will happen when the wood is dry?' Partly this is because it was not for him as a Gentile writer to touch upon this issue in his own right. It also leaves Luke's readers with a question which they need to answer for themselves: 'what *will* happen?'

Finally, this episode ensures that Luke's readers are not left with any distant or dismissive attitude to Jerusalem. They sense Jesus' loving identification with Jerusalem. He also tells the women to 'weep for yourselves' (v. 28) and implicitly for the city which can expect this violent fate. The Jesus who had wept over Jerusalem indicates that such weeping is the appropriate

---

[79] *Cf.* Caird (1963) 250: 'Jesus is already carrying on his heart the cross of Israel's condemnation'. Nolland (1989/93) 1138: Jesus 'goes to the cross as [God's] destined more of participation in that wider impending disaster'.

[80] See further below in ch. 8 (4). At a different level, Flusser (1996) 162, notes how Luke's portrait of Jesus as a 'prophet of doom' has also 'preserved the true historical picture of Jesus' solidarity with his people'.

[81] See section 4 below.

response of all who consider her fate. If Mark encouraged his readers not to weep for Jerusalem but for Jesus,[82] the *Gentile* Luke encourages us to do the opposite—to weep not for Jesus, but for Jerusalem.

f) Conclusion

The great hopes for Israel and Jerusalem adumbrated at the beginning of Luke's Gospel do not materialize. Jesus' coming to Jerusalem, which should have been the city's finest hour (*cf.* 19:44), has proved to be its undoing. Moreover, the concluding event in the Gospel, the resurrection of Jesus, only compounds the irony of the situation: 'it increases the tension, for by it God has affirmed as Messiah the one who was denied by Jerusalem'.[83]

For this reason, Luke would not have seen the fact that Jesus' death and resurrection had taken place in Jerusalem as being to the city's 'glory'. Not insignificantly Luke refers to these salvific events in terms of the 'exodus': '[Moses and Elijah] were speaking of his departure (ἔξοδος) which he was about to accomplish at Jerusalem' (9:31). This effectively cast Jerusalem in the role of Egypt, the place from which the first 'exodus' had been required.[84]a Even in Jerusalem God's people were still in need of liberation.

The exodus theme is also present in the last verses of the Gospel (24:44-53). First, Jesus' words to the disciples ('this is what I told you . . .': v. 44) are remarkably similar to the opening words of Deuteronomy (1:1), where Moses addressed the people of Israel.[85] Secondly, in describing Jesus' going out to Bethany, Luke uses a word which was commonly used of the exodus under Moses (ἐξήγαγεν: 'he led out', v. 50).[86] This is further evidence that there is a parallel between Jesus' work of redemption in Jerusalem and Moses' work of redemption from Egypt.[87] Again this cast Jerusalem in the role of Egypt, as the place from which the 'exodus' was necessary. The location of these events in Jerusalem did not elevate its importance, but only revealed its true nature.

---

[82]   Above ch. 1 at n. 75.

[83]   Tannehill (1986/90) i, 295.

[84]   So, Mánek (1957) 13, who stresses the importance of the 'exodus' theme throughout Luke's writings.

[85]   Compare the Greek of Luke 24:44 (οὗτοι οἱ λόγοι μου οὓς ἐλάλησα πρὸς ὑμᾶς) with the Septuagint for Deut.1:1 (οὗτοι οἱ λόγοι οὓς ἐλάλησεν). I owe this point to a personal conversation with Prof. C.H. Giblin (Jerusalem, March, 1994). This parallel with Moses is confirmed by Luke's portrait of Jesus as a 'prophet like Moses in Acts 3:22; 7:37 (*cf.* Luke 9:35). This has been fully developed by C.F. Evans (1955) and Moessner (1989).

[86]   So, Mánek (1957) 20.

Secondly, although (for reasons of 'closure') the Gospel narrative ends with the disciples returning to Jerusalem (where the Gospel had begun), Jesus' 'leading out' the disciples is a proleptic sign that they too will need to go forth from Jerusalem. In contrast to the first 'exodus', which had involved a movement into the Land, this second exodus required a movement *away from* Jerusalem. Jesus' going to the Mount of Olives 'shows symbolically what direction to follow'.[88] For the time being they are to 'stay in the city' (v. 49), but there will come a time when, if they are to fulfil God's true purposes, they will need to leave the city behind.

Luke's Gospel thus ends in suspense. The narrative closes in the same Jerusalem where it had started, but much has happened in the meantime, and Jerusalem, though outwardly unchanged, has undergone a major transformation.[89] Great hopes have been expressed, but so too have great oracles of a judgement which is seemingly inevitable.

In the course of this surprising new story there has appeared in Israel one who has issued an awesome challenge to Jerusalem—both in his words and with his person. 'One greater than Solomon' had appeared (11:31). What will that mean for Jerusalem, the city which rejects him? A new 'exodus' has been accomplished in Jerusalem, but few in the city are aware of it. In the resurrection a divine reversal of Jerusalem's judgement upon Jesus has taken place, but what will be the repercussions of that for the city? Is it a sign of Jerusalem's forthcoming 'restoration' in accordance with the hopes expressed at the outset, or is it in itself the fulfilment of those hopes? Has Jerusalem in rejecting Jesus destroyed its own promised destiny? The reader is invited to read Luke's sequel, the book of Acts.[90]

---

[87] In both instances the substantial 'work' has been accomplished, but the people of God are now told what *they* will have to do to implement its full implications: the Israelites were to enter the Promised Land, the disciples must preach in Jesus' name 'to all nations, beginning from Jerusalem' (v. 47). Luke might then have seen the Old Testament emphasis on Land as now reapplied to the Church's mission throughout the world; *cf.* below ch. 9, n. 10. On Luke and the Land, see Davies (1974) 266-274.

[88] Mánek (1957) 14. Bethany (Luke 24:50) on the Mount of Olives serves a similar proleptic purpose to that of 'Galilee' in Mark and Matthew. Luke's account can ignore the Galilean appearances, because his second volume will illustrate the gospel's going out from Jerusalem; the departure to the Mount of Olives sufficiently adumbrates this theme.

[89] *Cf.* Simson (1965) 227: 'Luke begins and ends in Jerusalem—as if she is unaware that she is now no longer the city of God'.

[90] On this 'incomplete closure', see Parsons (1987) 113: 'the fate of Israel is still undecided by the end of Luke. Many prophecies and predictions do not find fulfilment within the narrative time of the Gospel.'

3. Jerusalem in the Book of Acts

The book of Acts begins where Luke's Gospel left off—or not quite. Luke repeats the account of the Ascension on the Mount of Olives (1:9-12). It is this
event which acts as the centre of Luke's two volumes.[91]

    This is significant for our purposes: the Mount of Olives, not Jerusalem,
is the geographical 'hinge' of Luke-Acts. If (as argued above) Jesus' departure
to the Mount of Olives was theologically significant for Luke, then the fact
that Luke-Acts is 'centred' on an event just *outside* Jerusalem's walls may
also be important.[92] The Christian gospel has a close connection to Jerusalem,
but its centre is fractionally, but significantly, different—not least because Jesus (the true centre of the Christian message) had himself been rejected by Jerusalem. Jerusalem itself could never be the true centre.

    This ambivalence, whereby the Christian message is simultaneously
rooted *in* Jerusalem but not *of* Jerusalem, will recur throughout this study of
Jerusalem in the book of Acts. We note, first, how Jerusalem for Luke was the
all-important starting-point for the gospel, but not its final goal.

a) Source, but not Goal

At the outset of Acts, before any details are given of the Pentecost events, the
reader is alerted to what will be happening *away* from Jerusalem: 'you will be
my witnesses in Jerusalem, *and* to the ends of the earth' (1:8; *cf.* Luke
24:47).[93] Of all the potential accolades for Jerusalem, Luke considers this the
most important. The city is the source of the gospel message for the world.

    However, this role for Jerusalem was double-edged. It gave Jerusalem
an unparalleled position within salvation-history, but it also highlighted the
fact that the gospel was no longer tied to Jerusalem. As the 'source' of the gospel, Jerusalem's importance was at the same time both affirmed and denied.

    This latter point comes to the fore as the narrative moves towards its fi-
nale in Rome. There are frequent returns to Jerusalem, but these become few-
er,[94] and give way to Paul's extended journey away from Jerusalem towards

---

[91] On the Ascension in Luke's theology, see *e.g.* Franklin (1975) and Maile (1986).
[92] *Contra* Hengel (1995) 46. Looked at from a slightly different point of view, one might
say: if the Mount of Olives is deemed to be part of Jerusalem, then the Christian gospel can
claim to be *for* Jerusalem; if it is deemed to be outside Jerusalem, this indicates that the
gospel must go out *from* Jerusalem.
[93] The suggestion in Schwartz (1986) and (1992b) 127, that 'earth' (τῆς γῆς) should be
translated 'land', plainly conflicts with Luke's wider intention: see *e.g.* Wright (1994a) 68.

Rome. There is a gradual severance from Jerusalem, with the city becoming increasingly 'dispensable'.[95]

This is seen, for example, in a neat parallelism between Acts 28 and Luke 24. Paul does in Rome precisely what Jesus had himself done in Jerusalem, arguing from 'Moses and the Prophets' that Jesus was the 'Christ' (Acts 28:23; *cf.* Luke 24:44). Although Luke was not particularly emphasizing Rome's significance,[96] he *was* making a point about Jerusalem. What was done in Jerusalem could be done elsewhere, and what had occurred there had worldwide consequences. The gospel's universal implications meant that the prime movement of the 'Way' must be from, not towards, Jerusalem. Seen in this light Jesus' journey to Jerusalem had been the 'first step in a mission which ultimately leads to the ends of the earth'.[97]

Jerusalem is therefore important, but only in a temporary sense. This is seen elsewhere in Acts. Stephen argued that God blessed his people when they were outside the Land, but that through focusing on the Temple's uniqueness they were falling into idolatry (7:2-53).[98] Such ideas presented at just this point within the narrative neatly prepare the way for the gospel's going out beyond the confines of Jerusalem (8:1ff). God is not tied to Jerusalem, and those holding such ideas may make Jerusalem and even God's Temple into an idol.

Similarly the Ethiopian eunuch, having visited Jerusalem on pilgrimage, finds the liberating gospel message in the desert on his way *from* Jerusalem (8:26-28); 'the Ethiopian had *not* received the Spirit at Jerusalem'.[99] He 'went on his way rejoicing'—to Ethiopia, not back to Jerusalem![100] The indebtedness to Jerusalem which fuelled Diaspora pilgrimage was thus reduced.

---

[94] Listed above at n. 11. This may explain Luke's rather oblique reference to Paul's visit to Jerusalem in 18:22; for completeness he needed to include this visit to Jerusalem, but in terms of the overall pattern of Acts, he wanted a more extended 'absence' from Jerusalem between the Council in Acts 15 and Paul's climactic 'going up' to Jerusalem in Acts 21. That this *is* a reference to Jerusalem, see *e.g.* Bruce (1985) 656, and R.N. Longenecker (1990), xxiv; *contra e.g.* Haenchen (1971) 544, and N. Taylor (1992) 56-7.

[95] See Filson (1970) 73-5; *contra* Chance (1988) 101.

[96] As argued by *e.g.* Chadwick (1966) and O'Neill (1961) 170-1; see rather Davies (1974) 274ff. For Luke, Rome did not replace Jerusalem. Paul's coming to Rome speaks of the gospel penetrating the capital of the Gentile empire—a key part, but only a part, of the story of the gospel's reaching to the 'ends of the earth: see *e.g.* Davies (1974) 276; Tannehill (1986/90) ii, 16-18; Hengel (1995) 36; Bauckham (1995a) 422.

[97] Gill (1970) 215. This ties in with Luke's general emphasis on the universal nature of the gospel, seen in his Gospel (*e.g.* 4:25-8) and in Peter's opening speeches in Acts (2:39; 3:25-6); see Tannehill (1986/90) ii, 134.

[98] See Munck (1959) 22; Cullmann (1959-60) 41; Scharlemann (1968) 96; Davies (1974) 270; Kilgallen (1976) 17-21; Schwartz (1992b) 119. See above at n. 44.

[99] Davies (1974) 273 (italics original).

This theme of the *centrifugal* going-out of the gospel from Jerusalem needs to be contrasted with the more predominant *centripetal* notions that were current at the time, as expressed both in the phenomenon of pilgrimage, and also in the belief in the eschatological 'ingathering of the Gentiles' to Jerusalem.[101] Such notions kept Jerusalem very much at the centre. Now they were inverted: the message of Christ 'turned the prophetic hopes into a new direction'.[102]

The biblical justification for this unexpected inversion was almost certainly Isaiah's prophecy that 'out of Zion shall go forth instruction, and the *word* of the Lord *from Jerusalem*' (Isa. 2:3).[103] Luke does not quote this verse explicitly.[104] Yet an over-arching theme in Acts, as commonly noted, is the 'triumphant progress of the word of God',[105] and Isaiah was evidently an important influence—not least because of its charter for universal mission in Isaiah 49:6 (Acts 13:47; *cf.* 1:8).[106] With the coming of Jesus this prophecy from Isaiah 2:3 could at last be fulfilled.[107] The significance of Jerusalem within the Old Testament could readily be affirmed, if it was seen in terms of a dynamic potential for the blessing of 'all nations', which was now brought about in Christ. Jerusalem had fulfilled its long-awaited prophetic destiny, but in so doing its own privileged distinctiveness was necessarily under-cut.[108]

In other words, Luke emphasizes that Jerusalem fulfils its eschatological destiny as a 'source', but not as a goal. The book of Acts

---

[100] R. Porter (1988-89) 54, speculates whether the eunuch's scroll also included the promises made to 'eunuchs' in Isa. 56:5 to 'give them within my Temple a memorial and a name'. If in some measure 'excluded' during his visit to Jerusalem, he now experienced the longed-for inclusivity of the gospel promise.

[101] See further below p. 100.

[102] Franklin (1975) 122.

[103] Suggested in Fitzmyer (1981/5) 168; *cf.* Franklin (1975) 122. The phrase 'to the ends of the earth' (Acts 1:8) reflects other passages in Isaiah such as Isa. 8:9; 48:20; 49:6; 62:11.

[104] Though he may be alluding to it in 2:17 when he commences his quotation from Joel with the phrase 'in the last days' (*cf.* Joel 2:17).

[105] Marshall (1980) 29; *cf.* Davies (1974) 286; Kodell (1974). Hence Luke punctuates his narrative with the summary that the 'word of the Lord grew and spread' (6:7; 12:24; 13:49; 19:20). In three of these instances, there is a reference to Jerusalem within the immediate context, which might further indicate Luke's being influenced by Isa. 2:3.

[106] Quoted in full below at n. 159. On Isaiah and Luke, see *e.g.* Seccombe (1980-1). Tannehill (1986/90) ii, 348, observes how much of the narrative tension in Acts is caused by the clash between the positive promises concerning Israel in Isa. 40-66 and the indictment of the nation in Isa. 6 (as quoted in Acts 28:26-7).

[107] Note how the centrifugal vision of this prophecy is balanced in the surrounding verses by a centripetal emphasis: 'all nations will stream to [the Lord's house]. Many peoples shall come and say, "Come, let us go up to the mountain of the Lord"' (Isa. 2:2-3). Luke's account shows how this 'ingathering' was now taking place: yet, instead of the Gentiles' being required to go up to Jerusalem, the gospel was coming out to *them*.

portrays Jerusalem emphatically as the source of the movement that brings
salvation to the ends of the earth, but hardly as the eschatological goal of this
movement. . . For Luke Jerusalem was central as the centre from which the
centrifugal movement of the gospel went out to the ends of the earth, but not
as the centre to which, in a corresponding centripetal movement, the eschatological people of God must constantly look back.[109]

b) A Source of Validation

The opposite truth is also important. If the concept of Jerusalem as the gospel's 'source' relativized its significance, it was also a frank acknowledgement that the city had played a unique role in the history of salvation. Luke's
focus on Jerusalem both in his Gospel and in the early chapters of Acts indicates that he would have gladly affirmed this. The fact that the gospel had
originated in Jerusalem (and nowhere else) was vitally important.

This fact substantiated the claim that the Christian message was an authentic version of Judaism. If this new message had originated anywhere else
within the empire, even within Galilee (as opposed to Jerusalem), then its
claim to be an authentic Judaism would have been open to criticism. The
Christian message had to be proclaimed in Jerusalem, before it spread elsewhere. The importance of this for Luke is seen in several ways: the repeated
insistence of Jesus that the disciples must 'stay in the city' (Luke 24:49; Acts
1:4); the omission of any resurrection-appearances in Galilee; the concentration exclusively on the city of Jerusalem throughout Acts 1-7. So the ministry
of Jesus and the apostolic mission had not taken place 'in a corner' (Acts
26:26), but publicly within the very heart of Judaism's mother-city. Christians
did not see themselves as inherently 'marginal'; on the contrary, throughout
Acts they claimed that Jesus was the true fulfilment of the Old Testament.

Luke's emphasis on this may reveal that the Christian message *was* vulnerable to this charge—precisely because it had been rejected by Jerusalem's
religious leadership. Jerusalem's rejection of Jesus and the apostles was not
just a tragedy to be heeded but also an embarrassment to be explained. Inevitably Luke's account had to include Jerusalem's ultimate rejection of the gospel, but that only provided a greater incentive to emphasize the initially
favourable response to the gospel within the city, and the fact that Jesus commanded the apostles to proclaim the message first of all in Jerusalem. This

---

[108] *Cf. e.g.* Munck (159) 272, who, commenting on Jerusalem's integral relationship to the
world in Jewish thought, describes its focus on Jerusalem as 'apparently particularist, but
really universalist'.
[109] Bauckham (1995a) 426, 480.

needed to be emphasized before it was forgotten. If Jerusalem chose eventually to reject the message, that was not what the apostles would have wished.

But why was Luke, himself probably a Gentile, so keen to assert this inherent link between the apostolic message and Judaism? Was it, as some have argued, a pragmatic desire that the Church should inherit the privileged status of Judaism as a *religio licita* within the Roman Empire?[110] More probably his motivation was theological: the continuity of the gospel with the Old Testament faith was a non-negotiable part of its very essence, and Christians needed to assert that they were the valid heirs of Judaism and had a right to the 'legacy of Israel as the people of God'.[111] This was vital for any Christian apologetics in relation to Judaism. It was also important for any Gentile Christians who were either tempted to be dismissive of their Old Testament heritage or, at the other extreme, uncertain of their position in God's purposes:

> Luke writes to reassure the Christians of his day that their faith in Jesus is no aberration, but the authentic goal towards which God's ancient dealings with Israel were driving. The full stream of God's saving action in history had not passed them by.[112]

For these reasons (both apologetic and pastoral), the Jewish roots of the faith must not be allowed to be either forgotten or denied; Christianity was unashamedly a faith which had been nurtured in Jewish soil, and Christians would only find their true identity as they recognized this.

So the source of this essentially Jewish message had to be Jerusalem. 'Jerusalem was the symbol of the continuity of Christianity with Judaism, and of the fulfilment of Judaism in the Church',[113] and though 'Gentile Christians might be free from Judaism, they remained debtors to Zion'.[114] In this way Jerusalem functioned as the 'bridge between Israel and the Church'.[115] It was vitally important that Jerusalem had been the source of the gospel, the place in which it was first proclaimed and from which it spread.

---

[110] *E.g.* Conzelmann (1960) 137-44; Davies (1974) 276, 280; Haenchen (1971) 100-102.

[111] Brawley (1987) 159; *cf. e.g.* Esler (1987) 16-23, 46-70.

[112] Maddox (1982) 187; *cf.* 91-97, 184. Munck (1959) 318, emphasizes how Christians saw themselves as authentically Jewish, though this was denied by non-Christian Jews (*cf.* also Hastings [1958] 130). On Luke's indebtedness to Judaism, see *e.g.* Marshall (1992) 46 ('throughout Acts Luke seizes the opportunity to show that the Christian faith is not contrary to Judaism') and Chance (1988) 101ff, citing numerous authors. For Luke to affirm Jewish roots, however, was clearly not identical with his affirming non-Christian Judaism, nor did it prevent him from looking at Jerusalem in a new light.

[113] J. Knox (1987) 13.

[114] Chadwick (1966) 25; *cf.* also Conzelmann (1960) 209-13.

[115] Gasque (1988) 121.

Underlying such reasoning there is the notion that on the human level Jerusalem had a special role as the place which could *validate* the truth of the gospel. A similar motivation may be discerned in Luke's description of the Jerusalem *church* and the way in which its apostles could give validation to branches of the church that originated elsewhere. So the Jerusalem apostles were involved in assessing the validity of Philip's mission to Samaria (8:14ff), the genuineness of Paul's conversion (9:27), and the reality of the Spirit's coming upon the Gentiles in Caesarea (11:1ff). Above all, for Luke, the Jerusalem church had validated the Gentile churches associated with Paul at the apostolic Council (Acts 15).[116] Whether this validation was being denied by Paul's opponents in Luke's own day (or, conversely, dismissed by Paul's followers as unimportant) cannot be known. Clearly it was important to Luke, who sought to retrieve from the historical record as much as possible of this validation. Since the Jerusalem church uniquely provided the historic link back to Jesus and the apostles, it was vital that the Gentile mission had been affirmed by this, the original church.

The importance of this for Luke was that Paul's Gentile mission, to which (most probably) Luke himself was indebted, was rooted in Jerusalem. If in Luke's day some Jewish Christians were less favourable to the Gentile wing of the Church,[117] this all-important Council in Jerusalem *had* endorsed Paul's Gentile mission. Luke's own standing as a Gentile Christian had been affirmed by the founding church.[118] This relationship between the Gentiles and Jerusalem thus 'secured their incorporation into the renewed people of God'.[119]

When this validation of the Jerusalem church is put alongside that from Jerusalem (*qua* the centre of Judaism), a balanced picture emerges. From Jerusalem itself Luke gained the validation of Christianity's Jewishness; from the Jerusalem *church* he gained the validation of his right to be a Christian Gentile. Luke's own position becomes clear: a Gentile who maintained the essentially Jewish nature of the gospel, and yet also his right to be a Christian without first becoming a Jew. Jerusalem thus plays a vital role within his nar-

---

[116] *Cf.* also Acts 9:26-30. In Gal.1-2 Paul may have wanted to deny his need of such 'human' validation. Luke, we suggest, sensed that, even if Paul preferred to claim a 'divine' authority, he *had* nevertheless received this human validation as well.

[117] Though Bauckham (1995a) 471ff, argues that this may not have been the case, there being little evidence after the Jerusalem Council that Jewish Christians still pressed for the circumcision of Gentiles.

[118] Brawley (1984) 156, notes how Paul's *Jewishness* also paradoxically served to validate the Gentile mission.

[119] Franklin (1975) 128.

rative, because it is integrally related to Luke's perception of his own identity and the identity of the Christian Church.[120]

Luke's emphasis on Jerusalem must, therefore, be placed in its proper perspective. Is it intended to preserve the ongoing centrality of Jerusalem in his own day? Or, was he only highlighting the central role which Jerusalem had had *in the past*? The emphasis in his Gospel on the city's judgement strongly suggests the latter. Jerusalem's significance is transitional, rather than permanent. Conzelmann concluded that 'these factors' (of the Church's relationship with Jerusalem) 'belong to the initial period, but *are not of eternal validity*.'[121]

In Acts Luke draws attention to Jerusalem's centrality for the early church (and its integral involvement in the gospel's going out to 'all nations') not primarily in order to make a point about Jerusalem, but rather to make a point about the Christian message which first started there. It is not that Jerusalem must be seen as forever central in Christian understanding; it is rather that the Christian gospel must not be dismissed as marginal. The Christian message is authentically Jewish, and the Church a legitimate heir of Judaism. Luke emphasizes Jerusalem, not for its ongoing theological significance in the present, but for its capacity to offer validation in the past.

c) The Place of the Spirit's Work

To sustain this contention that the Christian message was not marginal to Judaism, it was important for Luke to establish not only that Jerusalem had been the source of the gospel but also that some of the gospel's blessings had been experienced by Jewish people within their own 'mother-city'. Not only had the gospel been openly proclaimed there, it had also produced a significant response; Luke wished this to be put on record for posterity. The Spirit had been powerfully at work in the city (chs. 2-7). Even if subsequently the Jerusalem church found itself in a difficult situation,[122] Luke's portrait of the earliest days was bright (2:41, 47; 4:4; 5:13-16; 6:7). There had been a 'Jerusalem spring-time'.[123]

Would Luke, however, have seen this outpouring of the Spirit in Jerusalem as of greater significance than the Spirit's similar work elsewhere (*e.g.*

---

[120] Our interpretation would endorse the conclusion in Tannehill (1985) 81, as to Luke's three main purposes: to explain Jewish rejection, to validate the Gentile Church, and to show the continuity of redemption history.

[121] Conzelmann (1960) 212 (italics mine).

[122] See further below section 6.

[123] Maddox (1982) 52.

in Samaria, Caesarea, Antioch or Ephesus)? Did Luke see the Spirit-filled
community in Jerusalem as a fulfilment of eschatological prophecies particularly related to Jerusalem?

One such prophecy comes in Joel, immediately after the section that Peter quotes at Pentecost.[124] Peter's quotation breaks off at precisely the point
where the prophet had declared:

> for in Mount Zion and in Jerusalem there shall be those who escape, as the
> Lord has said, and among the survivors shall be those whom the Lord calls.
> For then, in those days and *at that time, when I restore the fortunes of Judah
> and Jerusalem*, I will gather all the nations and bring them down to the valley
> of Jehoshaphat, and I will enter into judgement with them there, on account
> of my people and my heritage Israel, because they have scattered them
> among the nations (Joel 2:32b-3:2).[125]

Was Luke avoiding these issues, or was this Jerusalem-connection within Joel
an integral part of what he believed had come to pass within Jerusalem during
the days of the apostles? Was the outpouring of the Spirit a sign of Jerusalem's
'restoration'?

The precise issue of 'restoration' will be discussed in the next section.
That these verses *were* in Luke's mind is indicated by the echo of the phrase
'whom the Lord calls' in Acts 2:39b. There are also indications in these chapters that Luke saw Jesus' identity as peculiarly relevant for Jerusalem.[126] He
may therefore have seen the coming of the Spirit in the same way—as a significant moment of fulfilment for Jerusalem, a defining moment in the city's
history. Just as the coming of Jesus to Jerusalem was its 'hour' of 'visitation'
(Luke 19:44), so the coming of the Spirit was perhaps its 'hour' of 'restoration'. Luke's purpose in emphasizing the Spirit's work in Jerusalem was not
simply to extract from Jerusalem its validation of the Christian message, but
also to show God's faithfulness to his promises to Jerusalem itself.[127]

This means that the Spirit-filled community in Jerusalem may have
been an eschatological fulfilment. 'In the city of Jerusalem there was realized
a "restoration of the people" who enjoyed the blessings given by the Spirit'.[128]

---

[124] *Cf.* Tiede (1980) 90.

[125] *Cf.* also Joel 3:17.

[126] Jesus is compared with Jerusalem's greatest king, David (2:25ff), identified as David's
'Lord' (Ps. 110:1 in 2:34-5) and called the 'Christ', the anointed one (2:36); the reference
to the 'anointed one' in 4:26 comes from Ps. 2 where a few verses later he is identified with
God's appointed 'King on Zion' (Ps. 2:6). Jesus is therefore Jerusalem's 'Davidic king'; *cf.*
Wright (1992a) 380. So Chance (1988) 63, sees the Ascension as Jesus' enthronement on
the 'throne of David' (*cf.* Luke 1:32). *Cf.* also Bruce (1988) 53 and now Turner (1996).

[127] According to Chance (1988) 'Jerusalem and the Temple *began* to play their eschatological roles' (p. 127), and the apostles were the rulers of Israel in the 'new age' (p. 83).

Nevertheless, Luke does not really make this explicit. Instead, the Joel passage had expressly spoken of the Spirit being 'poured out on *all* flesh' (Acts 2:17, quoting Joel 2:28), and the Spirit would soon be breaking free from the confines of Jerusalem (8:2ff). So for Luke the true eschatological community was not so much the Jerusalem church as the church *throughout the world*. God had blessed Jerusalem (according to his promises), but he had also blessed other places far removed from Jerusalem. In this way Jerusalem's uniqueness was significantly under-cut, its moment of glory shared.

There is good evidence that the Jerusalem church *did* see itself in terms of eschatological fulfilment—more precisely, as the eschatological Temple.[129] Luke, however, 'does not give much impression of the eschatological ideas of the early community', perhaps because by the time of writing they appeared 'rather antiquated'.[130] His playing down of this theme may have been influenced as well by his instinctively more 'universal' approach. God had fulfilled his purposes for Jerusalem, but in so doing he had also unleashed his wider purposes for the world. Not just the church in Jerusalem, but believers everywhere, constituted the true fulfilment of these promises.

d) The City of Repeated Rejection

The coming of Jesus and of the Spirit presented Jerusalem with two distinct opportunities. The theme of Acts, however, is that, although the city was given a second opportunity to assess its verdict upon Jesus, it failed to do so. Despite God's fulfilling of his purposes in the sending of his Spirit, it is a 'story of a tragic turn away from fulfilment when it was readily available.'[131]

In the opening chapters of Acts, Luke draws attention to the way in which the crucifixion was to be seen in terms of Jerusalem's rejection of Jesus. Whether speaking to the religious leaders or to the unsuspecting crowd gathered on the city's streets, Peter repeatedly charges that 'you crucified him' (2:36; *cf.* 2:23; 3:13-15, 17; 4:10). The believers' prayer (4:24ff) reflects on the paradox that it was 'in *this city*' that the 'peoples of Israel' had 'gathered together with the Gentiles against your holy servant Jesus' (4:27): the 'holy

---

[128] Johnson (1992) 63, who, noting the significance of this passage in Joel, also suggests that the early chapters of Acts are a fulfilment of Jesus' words in Luke 22:30, that the apostles would 'sit on thrones judging the twelve tribes of Israel' (pp. 74, 80ff). *Cf.* also Jervell (1972) who sees Jewish-Christians, more generally, as 'restored Israel'.

[129] See Bauckham (1995a) 442ff; *cf.* also Grappe (1992). On the self-perception of the Jerusalem church, see further below ch. 9 (2).

[130] Bauckham (1995a) 439.

[131] Tannehill (1986/90) ii, 16.

city' had rejected God's 'holy servant'. Paul later comments, 'the residents of
Jerusalem and their leaders did not recognize Jesus' (13:27).

Despite this there was an offer of forgiveness:

> Repent . . . so that your sins may be forgiven; and you will receive the gift of
> the Holy Spirit. For the promise is for *you* (2:38-9). . . . I know you acted in
> ignorance, as did also your rulers. . . Repent therefore, and turn to God so that
> your sins may be wiped out (3:17, 19).[132]

Would Jerusalem take the second opportunity being offered? Many individu-
als did (2:41, 47; 4:4), including 'a large number of priests' (6:7) and 'thousands (μυριάδες) of those zealous for the law' (21:20), but at an institutional
level the religious leadership clearly did not (4:5-21; 5:17-40). From the time
of Stephen, Jerusalem becomes a perilous place for Jesus' followers (6:9ff;
7:54-8:3; 9:2; 12:1-19). When Paul is arrested in Acts 21 it is clear that, despite the valiant presence of the Jerusalem church, Jerusalem as a whole wants
nothing further to do with this new 'way': '*all* the city' was 'aroused . . . and
dragged him out of the Temple'; '*all* Jerusalem was in an uproar' (21:30-31;
cf. Luke 23:1, 18, 25). Effectively Jesus had been rejected once again by Jerusalem.

Luke conveys this theme of Jerusalem's repeated rejection in various
ways. First, it is a sub-theme within Stephen's speech. Moses, having been rejected by the Israelites at the age of forty (7:26-28, 35) was eventually rejected
again after the great events of the exodus in the episode of the 'golden calf'
(7:39f); in the same way the Jerusalem authorities were in danger of rejecting
Jesus a second time now that he has 'returned' after his resurrection.[133]

Secondly, a close connection is drawn between Jesus and his messengers, such that to reject the apostles is to reject Jesus. Saul, the persecutor of
Christians is asked by the Risen Jesus 'why do you persecute *me*?' (9:4). The
wording of Acts 1:1 (the Gospel account of Jesus' ministry being a description
of the things he '*began* to do') suggests that the 'acts of the apostles' must be
seen as the action of *Jesus*; so Luke draws attention to striking parallelisms between the experience of Jesus' followers and that of Jesus himself.[134] To reject Jesus' followers is thus to reject Jesus himself a second time.

---

[132] To use the language of the other Synoptic writers, it is clear that the sin 'against the Son
of Man' (even crucifying him) 'may be forgiven', not so the sin 'against the Holy Spirit'
(Matt. 12:32; *cf.* Mark 3:28-9).

[133] See *e.g.* Johnson (1992) 136-7. The same word (ἀρνέομαι) is used for Moses' being
rejected (7:35) as for Jesus' being rejected by Jerusalem (3:13): Tannehill (1986/90) ii, 91.

[134] See *e.g.* Radl (1975), Praeder (1984), O'Toole (1984), Moessner (1986). Tannehill
(1986/90) ii, 69ff, argues convincingly that repetition is not to be equated with redundancy.

Luke's description of Paul's final journey to Jerusalem is particularly instructive. By highlighting its similarities to Jesus' earlier journey he indicates that, just as Jesus' arrival in Jerusalem had been a vital moment for the city, so too Paul's arrival was far more significant than it realized. 'Jerusalem should know that it is about to lose what could have been a second opportunity to hear the good news'.[135] In evicting Paul from the Temple and the city, the city was endorsing its earlier response to Jesus. At Jesus' trial the crowds had cried 'away with this fellow!' (Luke 23:18); they used the same words of Paul (Acts 22:22). Jerusalem and Jesus were fundamentally incompatible. The city had been given a second opportunity, but its response was unchanged.

In his Gospel Luke portrays the forthcoming judgement upon Jerusalem as inevitable. This second opportunity for the city is therefore undeserved, and suggests that the judgement may have been conditional after all. Yet Jerusalem only endorsed its previous rejection of Jesus. The day of extended opportunity had drawn to a close. Having rejected Jesus again, the city was now vulnerable to the judgement of which he had spoken.

e) The City under Judgement

Is this correct? In comparison with the Gospel, the theme of Jerusalem as a city under judgement is scarcely mentioned in the book of Acts. There are no unambiguous prophecies predicted against the city by Peter, Stephen or Paul. Peter's urgent call to his hearers to 'save yourselves from this corrupt generation' (2:40; *cf.* 3:23) may suggest that those who had rejected the appointed Messiah were in particular danger; there is no explicit indication, however, that this involved a specific judgement upon Jerusalem. The issue of the *city* as opposed to the Temple is at first sight markedly absent. In the Gospel there was an express focus on the city in each of the four oracles (A-D). In Acts the focus is rather upon the Temple, as the scene for much of the apostolic action (Acts 3-7; 21:26-22:29) and the subject of the most extended theological discussion (Stephen's speech: 7:1-53). Has Luke abandoned his earlier presentation of the *city* resting under a cloud of judgement?

Luke-Acts is to be read as a narrative whole, and Jesus' prophetic words are not to be forgotten. Instead they provide a rich reservoir of dramatic irony; the reader knows the authorial (and divine) verdict, of which many participants in the drama are unaware. Jerusalem's response to the apostles, to Stephen and to Paul, may from the city's perspective be minor matters; but in the light of Jesus' solemn words it is clear that they are all-important.

---

[135] Tannehill (1986/90) ii, 279.

Jesus' words also result in Luke's own authorial touches being imbued with a new significance. As already noted, the phrase indicating that after Paul's arrest the Temple doors were 'shut' (21:30) speaks ominously of the forthcoming judgement upon the Temple and city which Jesus had earlier predicted. Luke's more frequent use of Ἱεροσόλυμα, the 'secular' name for the city, may indicate to the well-tuned reader a devaluation of Jerusalem's previous religious significance as the gospel goes out into the Greco-Roman world.[136] The whole pattern within Acts of the gospel leaving Jerusalem behind can now be seen as Luke's way of indicating the divine movement away from the city. Thus there is an increasing 'spiral' effect as the return journeys to Jerusalem become less frequent, culminating with Paul's journey away from Jerusalem to Rome. It is not said that this has implications for Jerusalem; yet in the light of Jesus' words (and through reflecting on the parallelism between Jerusalem's rejection of Paul and of Jesus), a message of judgement *is* conveyed. It is as though Paul, acting on God's behalf, has 'shaken the dust' of Jerusalem off his feet and turned elsewhere.

In the light of this the final episode of Acts, when Paul addresses the Jewish leaders in Rome, may also have repercussions for Jerusalem. There is much scholarly debate as to whether Luke intended Paul's third and final statement about turning 'to the Gentiles' (28:28; *cf.* 13:46f; 18:6) to indicate a final end to Christian evangelism amongst Jewish people.[137] A resolution is possible if a vitally important distinction is drawn between individual people of Jewish birth and 'official Judaism'. As Polhill observes,

> There is no reason to believe that individual Jews have been excluded in this instance. Yet there is a sense in which the Jewish rejection is seen to be definitive. It had become clear that 'official Judaism', the Jewish people as a whole, would not embrace Christ.[138]

By the end of Luke's narrative it is clear that official Judaism has rejected the gospel. This inevitably has repercussions for Jerusalem, the institutional centre of that Judaism. Not only has the city itself rejected the Christian message, but so too has its dependent Diaspora (as symbolized by Paul's being rejected by the synagogue leaders in the capital, Rome). No further respite for Jerusalem can be found. All that Jesus has said concerning the city, which has mercifully been held at bay throughout Acts, is now ready to come fully into force.

---

[136] *Cf.* above at n. 48.

[137] See discussion in Tyson (1988). Those who see the Church's mission to Jewish people continuing include Franklin (1975), Brawley (1984) and (1987), Chance (1988), and Tannehill (1986/90) ii, 328, 344ff.

[138] Polhill (1992) 544-5; *cf.* Tannehill (1986/90) ii, 347, noting the contrast between individual Jews and Judaism as a 'social entity'.

The cloud, poised for so long, is ready to burst. God's purposes in the gospel for Jewish people have not changed, but the time has come for their institutional centre to be removed.[139]

On this reading, the fact that the question of Jerusalem is not resolved within Acts, is part of the narrative's dramatic power.[140] The emphasis given to the city's judgement in the first volume had established this as a major issue. Jerusalem was 'under a cloud' throughout Acts, despite its comparative silence. The brighter days of the gospel's initial success in Jerusalem are set against this awesome backdrop of impending judgement. Will this work of God's Spirit be sufficient to hold back the already-upraised hand of God? In Acts Luke focuses on the Temple, the religious centre of the city.[141] How will it respond? When the Temple closes its doors on Paul, the answer is clear—but so too is its fate, and that of the city as well. Now that the Temple, the city's inner heart, has confirmed its response to Jesus' message, all that Jesus said about the wider city can come into effect. Time had been needed for the objective cause of that judgement to be 'filled out' and proved irretrievably valid. That process has now taken place.

Some may consider this interpretation false, precisely because Luke does not refer to Jerusalem's fate at the end of Acts. Was it really still in his mind? Throughout his two volumes, however, Luke has shown his great concern with the fulfilment of prophecy;[142] it would be exceedingly strange if he were quite unconcerned as to whether the prophecies of *Jesus* himself would be fulfilled.

> It is hard to imagine that [Luke], for whom the fulfilment of scriptural prophecy was a central article of faith, would ever admit that a primary aspect of prophecy, emphasized in his own work, was finally void.[143]

Jesus had been presented as the one who fulfilled the hope of a 'prophet like Moses' (Deut. 18:15).[144] Was Luke unconcerned as to whether Jesus' predictions about Jerusalem were true? This is most unlikely. Luke fully underwrites the prophecies he attributes to Jesus.

---

[139] Hence the distinction, noted above (2b), between 'Jerusalem' and her 'children' in Luke 13:34 (A).

[140] *Cf.* Tannehill (1986/90) ii, 354, on the 'openness' of the narrative to the threat of subsequent judgement.

[141] One wonders if Luke deliberately focused on the Temple in Acts in order to show that his concerns were strictly religious; it was tactful to avoid becoming embroiled in the more overtly 'political' considerations raised by the *city* of Jerusalem.

[142] See *e.g.* Bock (1987).

[143] Tannehill (1985) 83 (though concerning the issue of 'restoration': see below section 4).

[144] On this important theme, see Moessner (1989).

There was also a good reason for his not raising the question of Jerusalem's fate at the end of Acts. This was a solemn matter, and, as a Gentile, he
could scarcely raise the issue without being accused of anti-Semitic prejudice.
There was only one way that such a subject could be raised appropriately—on
the lips of Jesus alone. It was better for Luke to keep silence. This explains
what has been termed his 'remarkable reticence' on this delicate issue.[145]

So Jerusalem's future judgement is left exclusively on Jesus' lips. The
way in which Jesus had pronounced this judgement—in tears—was to be the
model, both for Luke himself and for his readers (Luke 19:41-44). There was
to be no gloating over Jerusalem, only weeping. If Jesus had wept over the
city, 'it was appropriate for others also to weep for Jerusalem'.[146]

Luke saw Jerusalem's tragic story as an integral part of the gospel message. This conviction stemmed from no anti-Semitic grudge or distant judgementalism, but rather from a profound reflecting on the traditions about Jesus
as he had received them. The matter had to be raised, but it had to be treated
in the most sensitive way possible. This was a matter for the master alone.

4. Luke and 'Restoration'

Was Luke entirely negative about Jerusalem's future? Or did he believe that
after the predicted judgement the city would be re-established in God's sight?
Might such a future event be identified, in whole or in part, with the longed-
for 'restoration' of Jerusalem and of Israel?

Luke's opening chapters highlighted this issue, setting forth the longing
that God should 'redeem his people', granting them 'salvation from their enemies', and bringing about the 'consolation of Israel' and the 'redemption of
Jerusalem' (1:68, 71; 2:25, 38). If this issue was important when the Temple
was still standing, how much more so if it was soon to be destroyed? In the
Gospel these hopes are seemingly turned on their heads as Jesus repeatedly
predicts the downfall of Jerusalem. Is this all that Luke wishes to convey? If
they were not misguided hopes, how are they to be understood?

The issue is hotly debated.[147] Have these hopes been fulfilled in Jesus'
resurrection and the spread of the gospel (Luke 24:21ff), or has a more obvious fulfilment been deferred into the unknown future (Luke 21:24)? Or would

---

[145] Tiede (1980) 86.

[146] Tannehill (1985) 75; cf. Tiede (1980) 82ff.

[147] Those who argue that Luke was countering any hopes of a physical 'restoration'
include Conzelmann (1960) 165, O'Neill (1970), Davies (1974) 263-66, Giblin (1985);
contra Franklin (1975) 128-30, Wainwright (1977-8), Tiede (1980) 89, Merkel (1994),
Ravens (1995), Fusco (1996) and Chance (1988) 127ff. Cf. also Helyer (1993).

Luke have combined the two perspectives, emphasizing the work of Jesus and the Spirit as the principal fulfilment, without dismissing a subsequent more straightforward fulfilment? Certainty eludes us, but there is more evidence than perhaps has been realized for the conclusion that Luke saw these hopes as already fulfilled in Christ.

First, the very fact that Luke highlighted this theme in his opening chapters makes it probable that *within* the course of his narrative there will be some answers to his own questions, and some measure of fulfilment. Certainly the reader receives the distinct impression that the infant Jesus will fulfil Israel's hope (*e.g.* 1:32, 54-55; 2:32). When Anna speaks 'about *the child* to all who were looking for the redemption of Jerusalem' (2:38) we expect this child to be the agent of that redemption.

These hopes, however, included a 'political' element ('salvation from enemies': 1:68) which sounds paradoxical in the light of later developments in the narrative. Whatever happened to this political 'salvation' for Israel? Luke's emphasis on Jesus indicates that *this* aspect will need to be radically reunderstood in the light of what Jesus actually achieves for Israel. At the end of Acts Paul's wording makes plain that the gospel must still be seen as 'the salvation of God' for Israel (28:28), but it is not as expected: this 'salvation' is also to be released to Gentiles.

This unexpected fulfilment through Jesus is an important theme in the two central chapters of Luke-Acts (*i.e.* Luke 24 and Acts 1). The Emmaus disciples re-echo the hopes expressed about the infant Jesus: 'we had hoped that he was the one to redeem Israel' (24:21). The dramatic irony of this is intentional: Jesus *has* 'redeemed Israel'. The redemption accomplished by Jesus, however, is quite different from that expected by the disciples—not only in its means (Jesus' sufferings) but also in its end (not a political liberation for Israel but 'repentance and forgiveness of sins' for 'all nations': 24:47). Luke's first volume closes with a resolution to the questions raised at the outset: the hopes of Simeon and Anna have been fulfilled, but also transformed.

In Acts 1, unlike the Emmaus disciples, the apostles know of Jesus' resurrection and are taught about the 'kingdom of God' and the forthcoming 'baptism in the Holy Spirit' (1:3-5). However, they do not see these events as having fulfilled their hopes of redemption; 'the resurrection has revived the hope .. but has not fulfilled it'.[148] When Jesus shows signs of departing without having accomplished all that they expect, they have an urgent question: 'Lord, are you at this time going to restore the kingdom to Israel?' (1:6).

---

[148] Tannehill (1985) 76.

> 'It is not for you to know the times or periods that the Father has set by his
> own authority. But you will receive power when the Holy Spirit has come on
> you; and you will be my witnesses in Jerusalem . . . and to the ends of the
> earth' (1:7-8).

Although this could be simply a correction of their 'time-tabling' (this 'restoration' *would* take place, but not now), the background in Luke 24 suggests
that Jesus is criticizing their very concept of 'restoration'. He reaffirms the expectation, but alters the interpretation'.[149] His emphasis is on the 'kingdom of
God' (v. 3), not Israel's political kingdom; the Spirit will be given (vv.4-5),
not for the 'restoration of the kingdom to Israel', but to enable them to witness
far beyond the borders of Israel. They had 'not yet realized that Jesus had
transformed the Jewish hope of the kingdom of God by purging it of its nationalistic political elements'.[150] In Luke 24 the disciples were invited to see
Jesus' work of redemption by looking *back* to his crucifixion, now they are
invited to look *forwards* to their mission 'to the ends of the earth' (Acts 1:8).
The 'redemption' of Israel' is a two-fold entity—inaugurated through Jesus'
death and resurrection, but implemented through the disciples' mission .

The concept of restoration reappears in Acts 3:

> Repent and turn to God, so that your sins may be wiped out, so that times of
> refreshing may come from the presence of the Lord, and that he may send the
> Messiah appointed for you, that is, Jesus, who must remain in heaven until
> the time of universal restoration that God announced long ago (3:19-21).

The intervening episode of Pentecost has revealed the nature of the 'restoration' that is available through Jesus, and Peter invites his hearers to experience
these 'times of refreshing'. Hope of a more widespread or 'universal' restoration has now, in contrast to Acts 1, been deferred to the period of Jesus' return;
and at that time God's purpose will be to restore 'everything', not just the
'kingdom of Israel'.[151]

Then in Acts 15 James justifies the Pauline Gentile mission by appealing to a 'restoration' text from Amos (9:11-12):

---

[149] Wright (1992a) 374; *cf.* Tiede (1986) 286. The same questions are raised in Luke 19
when the 'people thought that the kingdom of God was going to appear at once' (v. 11).
Have they a wrong view of the nature of the 'kingdom', or is it simply their timing which
is in error?

[150] Marshall (1980) 60.

[151] On these two senses of 'restoration', see Johnson (1992) 74; *cf.* Bayer (1994). Bruce
(1988) thinks Luke would have disagreed with Peter here; Tannehill (1986/90) ii, 15,
rightly affirms that Luke portrays Peter as a reliable source. See further Moule (1980),
Marshall (1980) 93-4, and Barrett (1985).

> After this I will return, and I will rebuild the dwelling of David, which has fallen; from its ruins I will rebuild it, and I will set it up, so that all other peoples may seek the Lord—even all the Gentiles over whom my name has been called (Acts 15:16-17).[152]

A convincing explanation of why James uses this text (apart from the important concept of Gentiles 'bearing God's name') is as follows.[153] In accordance with Acts 1:8, the apostles may have come to see evangelism amongst their fellow Jews as their part in the 'restoration' of Israel. They abandoned a political hope for Israel, but believed God would implement the restoration he had inaugurated in Jesus' death and resurrection through bringing Israel to repentance and faith in their Messiah (cf. 3:19-21). According to a common eschatological timetable, there would then occur (and only then) the 'ingathering of the Gentiles'. Having modified their beliefs once, however, they were forced to modify them even further. The mission to Israel was not as successful as they might have wished and now God appeared to be doing a powerful work amongst the Gentiles in advance of his visibly restoring Israel (in this already redefined sense). The initial reluctance to endorse a Gentile mission was based primarily on the conviction that this was not according to their expected timetable: surely Israel had to be restored first?[154]

James' quotation of Amos is therefore very significant. The text suggests there must indeed be a 'restoration' before the Gentiles can come in ('I will restore it, that . . . the Gentiles'). James' using it to affirm the validity of Gentile mission must indicate an acceptance that Israel had *already* been restored. 'The Scripture has been fulfilled because the Davidic heir has been installed as reigning Lord at God's right hand'.[155] There was no point in waiting for the repentance of ethnic Israel before evangelizing the Gentiles, because (contrary to appearances) the 'restoration' of Israel had already occurred—principally in Jesus' death and resurrection, but also in the number of Jewish people (however small) who had turned to their Messiah.[156] Israel's 'restoration' was a present reality.[157]

---

[152] On the other scriptural allusions and the seeming discrepancy between the LXX and the Masoretic text, see Bauckham (1995a) 452 ff; cf. also Kaiser (1977) and Braun (1977).

[153] See C.J.H. Wright (1994) 16, and further discussion below in ch. 9 (1).

[154] So e.g. Tiede (1980) 91.

[155] Tannehill (1986/90) ii, 189.

[156] This is the merit of the emphasis in Jervell (1972) 41-74, on the importance in Acts of Jewish-Christians, showing the fulfilment of God's purposes towards Israel and depicting Gentile converts as being drafted into this 'restored Israel'. It is unlikely that Luke would have seen the mission to the Jews as successful: see Tannehill (1985) 83, and (1986/90) ii, 272. There was a response to the gospel amongst Jewish people (and this *was* sufficient to be identified with Israel's restoration), but it was not what might have been hoped.

This is confirmed by the importance Luke places on Isaiah 49:6, part of which he quotes in 13:47 and to which there are allusions elsewhere.[158]

> It is too light a thing that you should be my servant to raise up the tribes of Jacob and to *restore* the survivors of Israel. I will give you as a light to the nations, that my salvation may reach to the ends of the earth' (Isa. 49:6).

Luke's indebtedness to Isaiah[159] makes it probable that he knew the detail of this verse and was aware of the way it linked Israel's restoration with God's call of the Gentiles, with the latter as a consequence (or part) of the former. Again the Gentiles' being reached with the gospel was the sign that the longed-for moment of Israel's restoration had arrived.

A final piece of evidence that for Luke the restoration had already been inaugurated through Jesus comes in Paul's repeated declarations that the resurrection was to be seen in terms of the 'hope of Israel' (23:6; 24:15; 26:6-7; 28:20). Just as the disciples had earlier expressed their hope in the forthcoming restoration of the kingdom to Israel (1:6), so Paul describes his fellow Jews as hoping to 'attain the promise made by God to our ancestors, as they earnestly worship day and night' (26:7)—a promise which Paul now identifies with the resurrection of the dead (v. 8). To the extent that this remains a future hope in the final resurrection of the righteous, such thinking corrects the more political aspirations associated with 'restoration'. Nevertheless Paul also links this 'hope' with an event that has already occurred, *Jesus'* resurrection. This implies that Jesus' resurrection was the fulfilment of Israel's hope, or at least its first instalment.

This emphasis on Israel's hope in the closing chapters of Acts resonates fittingly with the opening chapters of Luke, which emphasized the Jewish hopes prevalent when Jesus was born.[160] Now Paul is convinced that in some ways the 'hope of Israel' has been realized in the resurrection of Jesus (even if the ultimate fulfilment of that hope must wait until the End). Those hopes had not been in vain. God has not been unfaithful—through raising Jesus from the dead he has fulfilled his promises to Israel.

---

[157] Alternatively, the Amos quotation could indicate that the Gentiles' ingathering was *itself a part* of Israel's restoration (*cf.* 1:8). Our analysis above (3c) suggests that Luke himself might have preferred this, seeing the conversion of both Jewish people *and* Gentiles as indicative of Israel's restoration and constituting the *locus* of eschatological fulfilment. On this reading, this 'restoration' would still be substantially a past and present reality, not a future hope.

[158] See Luke 2:32 ('light to the Gentiles') and Acts 1:8 ('the ends of the earth').

[159] *Cf.* above n.106.

[160] So Tannehill (1986/90) ii, 320, who emphasizes the 'tragic nature' of this fulfilment being missed by the Jewish people: 'the very hope so eagerly sought is rejected when it appears' (p. 345).

In the concluding paragraphs of Luke-Acts Paul speaks of his being in chains 'because of the hope of Israel' (28:20)—a reference both to Jesus' resurrection in the past and the End in the future. As for the 'restoration' of Israel in the present, the narrative portrays the substantial turning away from the gospel by the Jewish leaders in Rome. *This* aspect of 'restoration' appears hope-less (hence the quotation of Isa. 6:9-10 in 28:26-29). Though the gospel remains open for 'all' who come (v. 30), there is no hope held out of a future 'restoration' of the Jewish people in *this* sense.

Luke thus presents us with a set of Jewish hopes (restoration, redemption, resurrection) which in their essence are entirely valid, but which have been fulfilled in ways that would not have been expected: through the death and resurrection of Jesus, through the acceptance of Jesus' Messiahship by Jewish people (and by Gentiles), and ultimately in the End-time resurrection of the righteous when God will 'judge the world' (17:31) and 'restore all things' (3:21). All of these are valid fulfilments, but at different points in his narrative the focus falls first on one, then on another. In one sense Israel is 're-stored' in the resurrection of Jesus; in another sense, Israel is 'restored' when Jewish people respond to Jesus' message and the Gentiles are 'gathered in'; in a final sense Israel is 'restored' only at the Last Day. The political hopes associated with the 'kingdom of Israel' that had originally been the disciples' concern are eclipsed as the prime issue becomes instead the 'kingdom of God'. Not coincidentally, in the last verse of Acts (28:31, echoing Acts 1:3), the subject of Paul's preaching is the 'kingdom of God'.[161]

There are two verses in his Gospel, however, which might suggest that Luke still linked the concept of 'restoration' to the *future of the physical Jerusalem* (Luke 13:35 [A]; 21:24 [C]). In the former Jesus says: 'See, your house is left to you. And I tell you, you will not see me until the time comes when you say, "Blessed is the one who comes in the name of the Lord."' Does this indicate a future restoration of Jerusalem when the city will joyfully acknowledge Jesus' identity? It would be hard to prove what Luke made of this enigmatic *logion*. Matthew, we suggested, understood this as a solemn warning that at the *parousia* Jerusalem would reluctantly acknowledge Jesus to have been truly sent from God.[162] The solemn context of this saying in Luke (with its indictment of Jerusalem: vv. 33-4)[163] suggests that the note of judgement is also uppermost here. 'The metropolis of the people of God . . . will turn out to be the city which refuses him . . . and will one day rue his coming in another capacity'.[164] It is not, therefore, a promise of restoration.

---

[161] *Cf.* also 8:12; 14:22; 19:8; 20:23, 28:23.
[162] See above p. 42.
[163] See above section 1 and the discussion of this oracle (A) in section 2.
[164] Fitzmyer (1981/5) 1035.

If, however, the verse were understood to speak of Jerusalem's *joyful* welcoming of Jesus, and this in turn was understood as the moment of the city's 'restoration', then Luke would clearly have connected this restoration with the confession of Jesus' lordship.[165] Jerusalem could not be 'restored' apart from him. Moreover, if this is the moment when Jerusalem 'sees' Jesus again, this must still be understood as a reference to the *parousia* (*cf.* Acts 3:21). Jerusalem would not be 'restored' till then. Even on this interpretation the verse does not speak of a political restoration of Jerusalem within the ordinary course of history.

Such a restoration might, however, be deduced from Luke 21:24: 'Jerusalem will be trampled on by the Gentiles until the times of the Gentiles are fulfilled'. This suggests that after the 'times of the Gentiles' Jerusalem will revert to Jewish hands. Is this the time of the city's long-deferred 'restoration'?

There are two problems with this. The 'times of the Gentiles' is often interpreted by referring to Paul's argument in Romans 11 (esp. v. 25: 'Israel has experienced a hardening in part *until* the full number of the Gentiles has come in') such that the phrase refers to the time of the Gentile mission of the Church. But is this correct? Reicke suggests that the phrase simply refers to that short period in military history when the Roman armies were 'occupied with the subjugation of Jerusalem'.[166] Jesus was promising that, although Jerusalem would be 'trampled upon', the duration of this painful process would be limited: the Gentiles would only have an allotted time in which to do this deed. When the 'times of the Gentiles were fulfilled', the 'trampling' would come to an end. Confirmation of this interpretation comes from Mark and Matthew who at the parallel point in their versions of the Apocalyptic Discourse have a verse which expresses the same truth in different words:

> 'If the Lord had not cut short those days, no one would be saved; but for the sake of the elect, whom he chose, he has cut short those days' (Mark 13:20; *cf.* Matt. 24:22).

The duration of this humbling and painful experience for Jerusalem will not be endless, but of a fixed, comparatively short duration.[167]

Secondly, even if the 'times of the Gentiles' does refer to a more extended era within the Church's history, there is nothing in the text to suggest

---

[165] Tannehill (1986/90) i, 156, accepts this second interpretation in principle, but says 'there is no indication when or *even if* Jerusalem will finally accept Jesus as Messiah' (italics mine).

[166] Reicke (1972) 127. Fitzmyer (1981/5) 1347, similarly understands it to mean 'until the triumph of the Romans over Jerusalem is complete' (though seeing this in a more open-ended way of Roman rule over Judea after AD 70 as well); *cf.* Gaston (1970) 361: 'a time of Gentile oppression in retribution for the sins of Jerusalem'.

that these times will be followed by the 'times of the Jews'. In the light of the following verses which talk of the *parousia*, it would be far more natural to understand that the moment when the 'times of the Gentiles' are fulfilled will be the time of the 'coming' of the 'Son of Man' (v. 27). As with Luke 13 the future 'restoration' would then be simultaneous with the *parousia*.[168]

These two verses provide the most slender of foundations on which to build a Lukan doctrine of Jerusalem's subsequent 'restoration'. In both, the interpretation is partly dependent on what is meant by the ambiguous words translated 'until' (ἕως in 13:35; ἄχρι οὗ in 21:24);[169] and neither text explicitly invokes the concept of 'restoration' or similar ideas. A few verses later Jesus speaks to his followers of '*your* redemption' (21:28) in apparent contradistinction to any supposed 'redemption' of Jerusalem. Above all, the over-riding context of both these verses is the judgement that awaits the city.

Rather than expressly holding out a hope for Jerusalem's restoration, Luke's reference to the 'times of the Gentiles' may therefore be designed instead to convey a message to those of his readers who were themselves Gentiles. This phrase contains a thinly-disguised warning that there will be a future judgement for the Gentiles. Any temptation to gloat over the judgement upon Jewish Jerusalem must be dismissed, since there will come a time when this apparent Gentile ascendancy will also come to an end. God alone will have the final word.

> The fate of Jerusalem is an anticipation of the last judgement. The same fate which befell Jerusalem will, on a much vaster cosmic scale, embracing the whole world, overtake the Gentiles—when their time is fulfilled.[170]

If Luke did not hold out great hopes for Jerusalem, this did not arise from any Gentile triumphalism or anti-Semitism. Rather it reflected a humility before the overwhelming purposes of God and an awareness that through the coming of Jesus, God's purposes had moved forward into a new era.

Luke's text not only reveals that this issue of 'restoration' was a topical one in the time of Jesus, but also that Luke himself had come to some definite

---

[167] The 'trampling' then refers to the physical acts involved in laying waste the city. The graphic nature of the phrase suggests something far more painful than the possibly benign rule of an absent Gentile overlord. The alternative suggestion in Giblin (1985) 90, and Nolland (1989/93) 1002f, that the 'times of the Gentiles' is the era when the Gentiles (and Jerusalem's enemies) are *judged* would only confirm Luke's lack of Gentile triumphalism.

[168] To argue that because in the Old Testament Jerusalem experienced restoration after being 'trampled' is to assume what needs to be proved: *contra* Tiede (1980) 92, Brawley (1987) 126, Chance (1988) 134.

[169] See *e.g.* Giblin (1985) 90-91.

[170] Flender (1967) 113; *cf.* also p. 165: 'the fallen world is under divine judgement already proleptically executed on Jerusalem'.

conclusions as to how it was to be understood. As Davies concluded, 'he deliberately opposed hopes for the restoration of Israel'.[171] In contrast to the political aspirations of his day, Jesus had not come to establish a physical
'kingdom' in Jerusalem in the here and now (Luke 19:12ff). Instead Jerusalem
was to experience judgement as a result of its response to Jesus and his followers (oracles A-D). Above all through his death and resurrection Jesus had
brought about a 'redemption' that was both unexpected and yet in full accord
with the essence of the Old Testament prophecies (Luke 24:21 ff). Through
this act Israel was 'restored' and 'redeemed', and those in Israel who responded to this good news and acknowledged the Messiahship of Jesus (now enthroned as Israel's Davidic King) became themselves a tangible sign of this
restoration. As a result the long-awaited 'ingathering of the Gentiles' could
begin. As for the future of Jerusalem, the Apocalyptic Discourse revealed that
at the End the central focus would not be upon Jerusalem, but rather upon the
Son of Man. The nature of that End was such that, if there *was* any connection
with Jerusalem, it consisted in the fact that the End would be modelled typologically upon Jerusalem's *destruction*. No 'restoration' of a more physical or
political kind was therefore to be expected. The 'restoration' was of Jesus, not
of Jerusalem.[172]

5. Luke's Conclusions

So the theme of Jerusalem was of central importance for Luke. Although his
primary purpose was to present the claims of Jesus, the issue of Jerusalem was
a major theme within this story.

Did Luke have other purposes as well? Was he intending to demonstrate the validity of the Christian message despite its being largely rejected
by the Jewish people, the reality of God's sovereignty and his faithfulness to
Israel despite that rejection, or the enormity of recent events as God's salvation at last became available to the Gentiles? All of these, together with others,
are possible.[173] Jerusalem is integrally linked to them all—not so much because the city had been the scene of the gospel events, but because it was so

---

[171] Davies (1974) 286. If, contrary to our argument, Luke does not finally close the door
on this possibility of 'restoration', this would only manifest again Luke's Gentile reticence
(*cf.* above n. 145). According to Chance (1988) 5-34, he would be the only New Testament
writer who holds out this hope for Israel. So Tannehill (1986/90) concludes that, 'in spite
of much negative experience', Luke 'holds open this possibility'; 'hope does not die easily'
(i, 156; ii, 95).

[172] On this whole theme, see further below in ch. 8 (3c) and ch. 9 (1).

closely bound up with the people of Israel. In order to establish any of these points Luke had to focus on Jerusalem, the symbolic centre of Israel.

Luke's concern with Jerusalem (even though a sub-plot) has frequently invited comparison with the Jewish historian, Josephus, whose *Jewish War* expressly focuses on Jerusalem.[174] Both writers were seeking to help Gentiles to understand this strange Jewish story. Further interesting parallels emerge:

> In both cases, the writer claims that this is the true reading of scriptural prophecy. In both cases, the new story radically subverts the old one. Neither Josephus nor Luke suggests that there will be a fulfilment along the lines expected by militant Jews. In both cases, Israel's God is responsible for a royal progress from Jerusalem to Rome. Vespasian, and Jesus, are proclaimed king, first in Judea, then in Rome. In each case, Jerusalem is left in ruins.
>
> Josephus claims that Israel's history has had a strange, dark, unlooked-for ending: Israel's God has gone over to the Romans. The providence that has watched over Israel throughout her history has finally abandoned her, because of her sin, leaving the Temple desolate.[175]

Josephus' conclusions were strikingly similar to Luke's. They only lacked the distinctively Christian explanation that Luke offered.

Luke too was telling a 'new story' which could only be understood in the light of the old. This explains the way he so carefully established in his opening chapters some of the key ingredients in that old story (the significance of the Temple and Jerusalem, the longing for 'redemption'), each of which underwent a surprising transformation in the unfolding of this new story.

In sum, Luke presented Jerusalem as a city which had mysteriously lost its destiny. The place which had been at the centre of God's purposes had missed its 'hour'. 'The very Jerusalem that, according to the Jewish scriptures and later Jewish expectation, was to function as the magnetic pole of salvation' had become the 'hub, indeed the very bastion of unbelief'.[176] Jesus'

---

[173] Powell (1991) 13-20, helpfully summarizes the many different possibilities as to Luke's purposes (eirenic, polemical, apologetic, evangelistic, pastoral, theological), rightly concluding that no single explanation can (nor need be) sufficient. Luke's work does, however, appear primarily as apologetical (whether to Jews, Romans or 'God-fearers', or simply for the edification of Christians); but this *apologia* was necessarily evangelistic as well. Given his pervasively eirenic tone, the suggestion that Luke's purpose was 'polemical' is the least likely. See further Maddox (1982), Walaskay (1983) and Brawley (1987).

[174]See discussion in Hemer (1989) 63-100, 371-3; Mason (1992) 185-229; Wright (1992a) 373-84, sees Luke and Josephus, not as dependent on each other, but as 'literary cousins' (p. 378). The parallel reflections of Josephus on Jerusalem are a useful comparison throughout our study, though they are most pertinent when studying Luke.

[175] Wright (1992a) 375, 374. However, the concept of 'God going over to Rome' (Josephus, *War* 3:354) was probably not in Luke's mind, *contra* Walaskay (1983) 62.

coming had brought to light the truth about Jerusalem's intrinsic nature (noted by prophets in times past)—its opposition to God's messengers. This now had to be seen as a profound opposition to God himself—because in Luke's understanding, Jesus represented Israel's God in a unique way. This Jesus had pronounced judgement on the city, while simultaneously offering an alternative; but Jerusalem's response (culminating in Jesus' death) made the judgement all but inevitable. In Acts the issue became focused upon the Temple, the inner heart of the city; but when that institution endorsed its rejection of Jesus' apostles (thereby effectively rejecting Jesus a second time), all hope for both city and Temple finally disappeared.

In all of this the enormity of Luke's claim for Jesus' person is clear. The 'rejected stone' had become the 'capstone' (Luke 20:17); the illustrious city of Jerusalem had become an awesome example of the dictum: 'Everyone who falls on that stone will be broken to pieces, but he on whom it falls will be crushed' (Luke 20:18). In Jesus Jerusalem had been presented with someone who, despite appearances, had truly held the city's destiny in his hands. In Jesus' encounter with Jerusalem there had been a 'clash of the Titans', and it was Jesus whom God declared to be the victor.

Any more positive aspects in Luke's portrayal of Jerusalem need to be seen in this light. Jerusalem was the unique source of the gospel, but in the light of Jerusalem's own response to the gospel, this was not an accolade for the city; 'it becomes the centre of the mission to the Gentiles, but it rejects the gospel for itself'.[177] Instead the out-going, universal nature of the gospel only served to undercut Jerusalem's particular status. On the human level Jerusalem had validated the legitimacy of the gospel as an essentially Jewish message (an important point both for Gentile Christians and for non-Christian Jews), but that validation, once given, was no longer necessary.

Jerusalem and the land are important as the scene of the beginning and they continue important to preserve the historical roots of the gospel and its continuity with the ministry of Jesus. But the gospel is not tied to them.[178] Finally, Luke's portrayal of the Spirit's work in Jerusalem and of the number of converts resident in the city was not to Jerusalem's credit; for this was clearly not representative of Jerusalem as a whole. On the contrary, the existence of these Jewish-Christians in Jerusalem only made it easier for Luke to suggest that the 'restoration' of Jerusalem was to be found not in any political sense, but in this small Messianic community—the first-fruits of a restored people of

---

[176] Georgi (1992) 119-20.

[177] O'Neill (1970) 73.

[178] Davies (1974) 266.

God, both Jew and Gentile. Though smaller and different from what had been hoped, there *had* been a work of restoration nonetheless.

Jerusalem, therefore, had been 'stripped of its divine perquisites'.[179] Previous judgements upon the city had been severe but temporary; this one was final. None of this denied the validity of the Old Testament (in its time): 'Jerusalem was rejected, but not the Old Testament.'[180] Nor was it a sign of Luke's being inherently anti-Semitic, any more than was Josephus.[181] The last chapter of Acts, though tragic in tone and realistic about the response of institutional Judaism to the gospel, in no way indicated a withdrawing of the gospel's availability from the Jewish people *per se*.[182] Moreover, Luke's reference to the 'times of the Gentiles' was an implicit warning to Gentiles of the judgement which they too faced; Jerusalem's judgement was a warning to all. There was in Luke no triumphalism, but a profound concern to offer a warning based on Jerusalem's solemn fate.

The following assessments of Jerusalem's final role in Luke-Acts put the matter well.

> Acts is the story of the church set free from its moorings at Jerusalem and led by the winds of God's Spirit to the ends of the earth. It is the story of how the Temple surrendered its redemptive significance to Jesus and his church.[183]

> The deepest tragedy of the third Gospel is not that of the crucified Messiah, but that of the city that failed to recognize its Lord. Luke was trying to wean [his readers] from their psychological centredness on the earthly Jerusalem. With Christianity the old loves had to be rejected. Jerusalem could no more be the holy city, nor the centre of religious life for God's chosen people.[184]

> Luke fully recognizes Jerusalem as the geographic centre of Christian beginnings; he also knows its mystique. But he deliberately and clinically transcends this spatial dimension. Christianity is a Way which began at Jerusalem, but passes through it. . . In the coming of Jesus, God had decisively visited Jerusalem, but it was in judgement.[185]

---

[179] Walaskay (1983) 47.

[180] Hastings (1958) 184, who helpfully shows how Luke's position (affirming the Old Testament, but denying Jerusalem) was vital in the second century for steering a middle path between the opposite extremes of the Marcionites and the Ebionites.

[181] Tiede (1980) 123, contrasts Luke's approach with the 'obscenity' of Josephus' appeal to the Jerusalemites to repent (*War*. 3:375-419). This is not to say that Luke-Acts could not later be used in an anti-Semitic way: see Tiede (1980) 128; Donaldson (1981) 44-5.

[182] See above n. 137.

[183] McKelvey (1969) 91.

[184] Hastings (1958) 106, 176, 178. *Cf.* O'Neill (1961) 71: 'Luke means to show that the Church comes of age when it finally left Jerusalem behind'.

[185] Davies (1974) 260.

Jerusalem ceases to be the bearer and guardian of the divine promises and becomes no different from the rest of the world. The judgement over the city
becomes a typical example of what will happen to the rest of this old, transi-
tory world. Jerusalem is thus reduced to a purely secular significance. Yet at
the same time it acquires a universal significance.[186]

According to Luke, therefore, God's purposes for Jerusalem had moved into
a new mode, precisely because his purposes for the world had similarly moved
into a new era:

The history that has come to a close with the death and resurrection of Jesus
is the history of one vital phase in the purposes of the creator God. Precisely
because that phase has been successfully concluded, world history now becomes the theatre of the final act of the drama.[187]

6. Luke's Situation

Was Luke like Josephus, writing after the actual fall of Jerusalem in AD 70?
If there could be a final resolution to this important question (frequently discussed in the commentaries) it would certainly affect our understanding of
the text.[188] If we could be assured that Luke knew what had recently happened
to Jerusalem, this would provide a vital element of dramatic irony to the narrative. Even before Jesus pronounces judgement on the city, his readers would
know that there is a glaring disparity between the prayerful hopes expressed
in Luke 1-2 and what will actually take place; they would 'read these happy
words in a historical context which gives them a tinge of pathos'.[189] Moreover, Luke's opening sentence about the 'events that have been fulfilled among
us' (1:1), whilst chiefly referring to the events of Jesus, might also refer to the
known tragedy of Jerusalem. Luke would then be explaining the fall of this
great city: it was no coincidence that Christianity's founder had lived but a
generation previously, for there was a profound link between the coming of
Jesus and the fall of Jerusalem. 'One could read Luke's entire second volume
as his answer to the problem of the loss of the Holy City and its Temple'.[190]

---

[186] Flender (1967) 114.
[187] Wright (1992a) 383.
[188] For a helpful list of dates suggested by scholars for Luke-Acts, see Hemer (1989) 367-
70. The balance, as he argues, is more evenly spread between pre- and post-70 datings, than
is often supposed. He argues at length for a pre-70 date (pp. 365-410).
[189] Tannehill (1986/90) i, 34; cf. ibid. ii, 95, n. 45. If written before AD 70, it would only
be a matter of years before all Luke's readers would have sensed this, though this would
then be subsequent to Luke's original intention.

The issue turns, chiefly, on whether the wording of Jesus' oracles concerning Jerusalem (A-D) betrays Luke's knowledge of AD 70. Dodd's conclusions that they do not (and that the primary influences on Luke's language are the Old Testament descriptions of the fall of Jerusalem in 587 BC) has been influential.[191] For others, however, Luke's reference to 'Jerusalem being surrounded by armies', sounds like a post-70 adaptation of the enigmatic phrase in Mark 13:14 about the 'abomination of desolation'.[192] Bruce concluded that, though the predictions about Jerusalem's fate (B, C, D) are not *vaticinia ex eventu*, their form does seem to 'presuppose their fulfilment'.[193]

It cannot be ruled out that Luke's compilation has been influenced by the events of AD 70. It is incorrect, however, to see this event as a major inspiration to his theology. The essential outlines of his understanding of Jerusalem were already in place well before that date, and the events of AD 70 only confirmed that this prior understanding had been correct.[194]

The basis for this is simply that according to a natural reading of the so-called 'we-passages' in Acts,[195] Luke himself had been to Jerusalem in the

---

[190] Walaskay (1983) 46. Luke therefore writes to orientate a Church no longer dominated by Jerusalem. *Cf.* Drury (1987) 426: 'behind the gradual abandonment of Jerusalem which occupies the whole of Luke's *oeuvre* stands the catastrophe of 70'; the Church thus needed to find a new urban centre 'instead of Jerusalem which was, in happier days, its home'.

[191] Dodd (1947) 79 (quoted below in ch.8, n. 10). *Cf. e.g.* Caird (1963) 231; Reicke (1972); Borg (1992). Luke's description is striking for its being cast in non-specific, general terms (so Fitzmyer [1981/5] 1255).

[192] Walaskay (1983) 48, however, suggests Luke is avoiding what might sound like an anti-Roman allusion to the previous emperor, Caligula.

[193] Bruce (1990) 16. Against the notion of these oracles as *post-eventum* creations see also Tiede (1980) 67, Borg (1984). See further below in ch. 8 (1).

[194] See *e.g.* Hastings (1958) 185: 'it is difficult to imagine that the outlook of Paul's Gentile friend and companion was radically altered by the event [of AD 70]; to deny that the general character of Luke's writings could belong to the earlier period is to deny that Paul could have existed at all.' He argues that, though there was the 'painful process of discovering over the years all the implications of their new allegiance' (p. 178), Luke's emphasis on Jerusalem is but an 'unusual stress on something which was common and primitive doctrine' (p. 131), as seen in the example of Stephen.

[195] The authenticity of these 'we-passages' has been frequently criticized: see esp. Vielhauer (1980) 48. Was Luke using a well-known device to give a sense of dramatic involvement, an anonymous 'focalizing character' (so Tannehill [1986/9]) ii, 246)? Or was the real author of Luke-Acts himself merely using a source-document which he has preserved in its first-person form (as *e.g.* S.E. Porter [1994])? Those who accept the traditional view that these are the reflections of Luke himself, include Cadbury (1956-7), Marshall (1980) 39, Fitzmyer (1989) 22, Hemer (1989) 321-334, and Hengel (1995) 27-78 (showing Luke's familiarity with the geography of Caesarea and Jerusalem). Edmundson (1913) 87, noted, 'there are few passages in ancient historical literature more clearly the work not merely of a contemporary writer but of an observant eye-witness than is the narrative contained in the last seven chapters of Acts'.

late 50's—a visit which would have given him ample opportunity to reflect on the nature of Jerusalem.[196] It was this memorable visit, we suggest, that alerted Luke to the city's enigma, and which then provided the framework for his two-volume work. The following are some suggestions as to how that personal experience could have brought about the theological convictions concerning Jerusalem that are presented above.[197]

Irrespective of his place of origin, the evidence of the 'we-passages' suggests that Luke may have resided in Philippi in the period between Paul's 'second' and 'third' missionary journeys (c. AD 49-57).[198] There he might have remained, had not Paul changed his travel plans at the last moment (20:3) and come back through Macedonia, inviting him to join him on this vital mission to Jerusalem.

It was a risky journey. Soon after Luke's joining the expedition, Paul explained to the Ephesian elders at Miletus that he had already been warned 'in every city' to expect 'prison and hardships' (20:22-3). By the time they reached the shores of Palestine, Luke himself was amongst those who tried to dissuade Paul from making the final journey up to Jerusalem (21:12). Were Paul's Gentile companions fearful only for Paul's life, or for their own as well? In either case, Luke found himself going up to Jerusalem as an anxious 'pilgrim', and probably a reluctant one: how would they fare in Jerusalem?

Luke arrived in Jerusalem in an alert mood, already disposed to find Jerusalem a difficult place for Jesus' followers, and perhaps asking how this sorry state of affairs had come to pass. The hospitality of Mnason and the warmth of the initial 'welcoming party' made their first day in the city a positive one (21:16-17). The next day, they made their official visit to 'James and all the elders', where they received a positive welcome (21:18-20). Yet James mentions the problem caused by a sizeable number (μυριάδες) within the Jerusalem church who had heard negative rumours about Paul. Luke sensed

---

[196] Concerning dating, this assumption would suggest that Luke researched his work whilst in Palestine in 57-59 (e.g. Caird [1963]), Morton and MacGregor [1964]), though perhaps only producing a final version after the fall of Jerusalem: so Williams (1952-3); Russell (1955); Parker (1965). Whether Luke-Acts was published in toto before AD 70 (and only briefly modified by Luke afterwards) or in a much-different proto-Luke is beyond the scope of this enquiry.

[197] Because of the scepticism about the 'we-passages', few, if any, of those who have examined Luke's attitude to Jerusalem have noted this possibility of Luke's own first-hand acquaintance with the city.

[198] E.g. Munck (1959) 294, who suggests that Luke was the representative of the Philippian church for the 'collection'. The 'we-passages', which break off when Paul and his companions reach Philippi (16:17), are resumed as Paul travels back through that city (20:6).

straightaway the divisions amongst the local Christian community and the stresses caused by living in the Jewish capital.[199]

He could not but be aware that Paul's precarious position had been brought about through his involvement in mission to Gentiles such as himself. In all of what follows (as Paul went along with James' stipulations, making himself vulnerable to attack in the Temple and eventually being arrested) Luke knew that Paul was in this situation because of his commitment to Luke and his fellow-Gentile companions (and the distant Christian communities whom they represented). Luke insisted that he and his fellow-Gentiles were warmly welcomed by 'James and the elders', but their presence there *had* caused the local church some embarrassment. It was an awkward situation. Despite their protestations to the contrary, he may not have *felt* so welcome after all.

Into this scenario it is important to introduce what Luke himself studiously failed to mention: Paul's 'collection'. Luke did allude to it later (24:17), though Paul there spoke more loosely of bringing 'alms to my nation', not expressly for the Jewish *believers*; here, however, it was omitted. Why? Various solutions have been proposed.[200] One of the most likely is that the gift was not received as warmly as Paul had hoped.[201] Luke was not blatantly distorting the facts when he described the welcome they were given. Because of the sizeable minority within the church who were anxious about Paul's reputation, the gift was probably not received straightforwardly.[202] James' suggestions become an implicit condition: if Paul obliged, then James would be able to re-

---

[199] On the Jerusalem church in this period, see *e.g.* J.J. Scott (1975), Bruce (1985), Bauckham (1995a), and below ch. 4 (4). It is generally agreed (*contra* Munck [1959] 240f) that the μυριάδες (21:20) refers not to non-Christian Jews, but to Christian Jews: see *e.g.* Bruce (1985) 658. The church was therefore not tiny, but under increasing pressure (culminating in the martyrdom of James in AD 62).

[200] Nickle (1966) 150, suggests Paul's availing himself of the official protection associated with the collection of the *Temple tax*, may now have been deemed illegal by the Roman authorities; *cf.* Bruce (1985) 657. For Tannehill (1986/90) ii, 266, the omission of any reference to the collection minimizes the human motivation for the journey, focusing attention instead on its divine purpose. For Bauckham (1995a) 479f, it is a sign of Luke's distancing himself from any earlier ideas of the 'eschatological centrality of Jerusalem in God's purposes'.

[201] So Haenchen (1971) 613-4; Dunn (1977) 256-7; Holmberg (1978) 42; Martin (1986) 258; Achtemeier (1986), and now Bruce (1986) 123; *contra* Munck (1959) and Nickle (1966) 70-72. See further below ch. 4 (4-5).

[202] Georgi (1992) 125-6, helpfully surmises: 'Luke must have been taken aback by the lack of undivided joy on the part of the church in Jerusalem over the arrival of the delegation and the rich offering they brought with them. The collection, which had started with such great hopes . . . was received as if 'on the side', accompanied by whispers; quite a blow to the delegation'. However, to say, as does Holmberg (1978), 43, that 'the collection was a diplomatic catastrophe' is to go too far.

ceive the gift officially. Paul, however, was never able to fulfil this condition. So was the gift ever received? Did Luke and his Gentile companions insist that the Jerusalem church keep the money all the same, or did an extreme element within the church prevent James from accepting it?[203] Not everything went as smoothly as they had hoped. Paul had asked for prayers that 'his ministry to Jerusalem might be acceptable to the saints' (Rom. 15:31). Were those prayers answered, or did his fears come true?

Paul had also asked for prayers that he might be 'rescued from the unbelievers in Judea' (15:31). *This* prayer was clearly not answered—except inasmuch as he escaped with his life. Paul's being arrested in the Temple would have made Luke keenly aware of Jerusalem's hostility towards this new Messianic movement. It highlighted how the Temple could become a fierce hotbed of nationalistic enthusiasm and illustrated the paradoxical principle that God's agents could be rejected by God's people even in God's sanctuary;[204] the desire to preserve the Temple's sanctity could lead to the flouting of God's purposes. Throughout Luke-Acts two issues recur which are of particular sensitivity within Judaism: the sanctity of the Temple and the appropriate attitude to the Gentiles.[205] Luke may have become particularly conscious of these two issues as he reflected on Paul's experience in the Temple— accused of 'defiling this holy place' by bringing a Gentile into the court of Israel (21:28).

In the light of Paul's theology (in which the distinction between Jew and Gentile had been removed in Christ)[206] this whole episode was full of paradoxes, of which Luke himself will have been aware. As a Gentile he was not himself able to accompany Paul beyond the *soreg* wall into the inner sanctuary; he would have defiled it (κεκοίνωκεν: 21:28). Paul's whole missionary enterprise, however, and his purpose in bringing some of his Gentile converts to Jerusalem, were designed to show that Gentiles *were* genuinely included in God's people, and (just as Cornelius) were not now 'unclean' in God's sight (κοινός: Acts 10:15; 11:9). Now in Jerusalem Paul was required to act in an exclusive way, which temporarily re-erected the Jew-Gentile barrier between himself and Luke. This must have raised questions about the nature of the Temple in the light of the coming of Jesus. Was there not here an inherent incompatibility between the two visions of reality? If Paul's gospel for the Gentiles was the truth, how could the Temple continue in its present form?

---

[203] Festus' later hoping to receive a bribe from Paul (24:26) may possibly be an indication that Paul still had the funds on him.

[204] Petersen (1978) 83, sees this as a basic plot-device in the narrative of Luke-Acts.

[205] On the Temple, see Luke 19:45ff; Acts 6:13ff; on Gentiles, see above 2d.

[206] Gal. 3.28; *cf.* Eph. 2:14. See further below in ch. 4 (2c) on how this will have affected Paul's attitude towards the Temple.

Luke may have stayed in Jerusalem after Paul's departure (perhaps returning there occasionally during Paul's two years in Caesarea?). Even if not, that short week in Jerusalem would have given Luke ample food for thought, raising many questions—about the nature of Jerusalem, the future of the Temple, the relationship between Paul and the Jerusalem church, and Luke's own standing as a Gentile in relation to this Jewish city. Conceivably they were issues which Luke and Paul discussed together while Paul was in prison. What would become of the city? Why had she rejected her own Messiah? Was Jerusalem's rejection of the Christian message something which could ever serve God's purposes? How could one explain to critics that both Jesus and Paul, who had been rejected decisively by Jerusalem, were the true spokesmen of God's intention for Judaism? What would happen to the Jerusalem church?

All of these can then be seen to fuel Luke's concerns in his writing: his fascination with Jerusalem, but his comparative detachment from it; his presentation of the gospel as a story with repercussions for Jerusalem; his affirmation of the city and its Temple in time past, but his questioning that for the future; his interest in anything Jesus was reported to have said concerning the city; his awareness that somehow there was an irreconcilable clash between Jesus and Jerusalem; his conviction that the city was now under a 'cloud' of judgement and Jesus had warned his followers to be ready to abandon it; his concern to show that the Christian message *had* met with some positive response in Jerusalem initially; his awareness that the Christian message was weaker in the land of its origin than elsewhere ('no prophet is acceptable in his home country', Luke 4:24); his contention that Paul's mission to the Gentiles had been validated by the apostles in Jerusalem at the Council (Acts 15); his defence of Jesus and Paul as God's messengers, though rejected by Jerusalem; his near silence concerning the collection; his description of the Jerusalem church, indicating some of the tensions which it experienced as a result of the Gentile mission (Acts 21); his distancing Jesus and the apostles from any 'nationalism' and showing how the Christian message offered a valid and yet non-political fulfilment to the Jewish 'hope';[207] his desire to show how Old Testament truths had been moved forward into a new era of fulfilment.

Eventually Paul and Luke found themselves on a boat leaving the shores of Palestine, with no expectation that they would ever return. In their own experience, and in their theology, Jerusalem was a thing of the past. They had 'faced up' to Jerusalem, but it had rejected them. At some point Luke may have begun to realize that their experience in Jerusalem was a reflection of Je-

---

[207] Davies (1974) sees Luke as consciously opposing Jewish nationalism in the Palestinian *church*: he 'desired to check Messianic fervour amongst the earliest Christians for the restoration of Israel' (p. 266) and used Stephen's words to keep them away from a 'Christianity too narrowly bound to Judaism, the Temple, Jerusalem, and the land' (p. 272).

sus'. And so the structural contours of his writing-project began to form: Jesus' going up *to Jerusalem* would be a foundational theme in the Gospel (the dominical precedent for Paul's); but the story of the Church would be a movement *away from Jerusalem*, a movement which then was enacted both symbolically and in reality as Luke and Paul left Jerusalem for Rome.

The pattern of Luke-Acts (up to Jerusalem, away from Jerusalem) was something which *Luke himself* had experienced in microcosm. He knew both the centripetal pull of Jerusalem and its centrifugal expulsion. As a follower of Jesus and as a companion of Paul he had been called to go up to Jerusalem on a mission fraught with uncertainty, but now he had left that place for good. The time he had spent in Jerusalem (though what he encountered was mild by comparison with that endured by Jesus and Paul) was pivotal and crucial. Luke too had had a Jerusalem-experience, and it was not a happy one.

Much of this had been caused by his own status as a Gentile, and it would have been easy for him to adopt a dismissively judgemental tone on this Jewish city. Yet in the traditions uncovered during his research he learnt that Jesus, whilst pronouncing judgement upon the city, had been moved to tears at the sight of Jerusalem from the Mount of Olives. This was the attitude which Luke as a follower of Jesus must emulate himself and encourage in his readers. The tone of Luke-Acts reflects this: Luke wished to follow faithfully in the steps of Jesus. It is tempting to suggest that this desire to follow in his master's steps might have then caused him on at least one occasion to walk himself to that same Mount of Olives. From there he could contemplate the city below—the city that had been central to Jesus and his apostles, and which would therefore be central in his own two-volumed work

4

A NEW CENTRE
Paul

> *The present Jerusalem is in slavery with her children. But the Jerusalem above is free, and she is our mother (Gal. 4:25, 26).*

Paul's critique of Jerusalem, voiced expressly in Gal. 4:25, is matched by his new theology of both the Land and the Temple as a result of the coming of Christ and the Spirit. His teaching in Rom. 11 does not imply a significant future role for Jerusalem; instead there is evidence (1 Thess. 2) that he saw the city as entering a period of judgement and that the days of the Temple were numbered. This gave his mission its urgency and his involvement with the Temple (as recounted in Acts) a necessarily 'interim' quality. Paul could be critical of the Jerusalem church and did not readily acknowledge its natural authority over him, but his collection for the 'saints' expressed the essential unity between them.

Luke's understanding of Jerusalem, we have argued, was influenced by Paul. Before turning to the Fourth Gospel, it is therefore appropriate, to focus on Paul's letters. These are the earliest documents within the New Testament, all written well before AD 70.[1]

Each of the three evangelists considered so far may have had to differing extents some personal contact with Jerusalem. With Paul this is certain. According to Acts, Jerusalem was the scene of his education (22:3), of his ac-

---

[1] The argument here is confined almost entirely to those letters of which the authenticity is little in doubt (Romans, 1 & 2 Corinthians, Galatians and 1 Thessalonians). Evidence from the other Pauline letters is normally referred to simply by way of comparison (though many accept their authenticity).

tive persecution of Christians (8:1, 3; 22:4-5), of his occasional meeting with
the apostles (9:26-30, 11:30; 15:2-30; 18:22), and of his final ill-fated visit and
arrest (21:17-23:31). Although some might question Luke's information,
none would deny that Paul knew the city at first-hand (Gal. 1-2). This gives
his reflections concerning Jerusalem particular weight. It also makes it possible to examine not only his written statements, but also his practical involvement with the city—both his theology and his practice.

The picture that emerges can be interpreted in different ways. On the
one hand, there are aspects of Paul's theology and practice which suggest a
positive evaluation of Jerusalem: his studying there under Gamaliel; his (reasonably) frequent visits despite working elsewhere; his risky decision to bring
the 'collection' in person (Rom. 15:25-8; *cf.* 1 Cor. 16:4); his loving commitment to the people of Israel (Rom. 9-11); his describing the Temple worship
as God's gift to the Jewish people (Rom. 9:4); and his implicit acknowledgement that Jerusalem had been the unique source of the gospel message (Rom.
15:19; 1 Cor. 14:36). One commentator has concluded that 'Paul saw Jerusalem as the holy city, which had played—and would continue to play—a central role in the unfolding drama of salvation'.[2]

On the other hand, there is a negative strand: his ambivalent attitude towards the Jerusalem church leaders (Gal. 1-2); his polemical description of Jerusalem as being 'in slavery with her children' (Gal. 4:25); his conviction that
through the Spirit's indwelling Christian believers now constituted the 'Temple of God' (1 Cor. 3:17; 6:19; 2 Cor. 6:16); his understanding that his fellow-
Jews were experiencing a measure of God's divine judgement (1 Thess. 2:14-
16; Rom. 9-11); the universal emphasis of his teaching (that the gospel has an
equal claim upon both Jews and Gentiles throughout the world);[3] his 'spiritual' focus, calling believers not to set their minds 'on things that are on earth'
(Col. 3:1-2); and his apparent disregard for the geographical locations associated with Christ's life.[4]

---

[2]   Gerhardsson (1961) 274.

[3]   See further *e.g.* 2 Cor. 5:19 (God 'reconciling the *world* to himself'), Rom. 4-5 (God's
call to Abraham set against the backdrop of the fall of Adam), Gal 3:8 ('all the Gentiles
shall be blessed in you.'), Eph. 2:14ff. On the spiritual equality of Jews and Gentiles, see
e.g., Rom. 5:2; Gal. 3:26; Col. 2:10 (*cf.* Eph. 2:18; 3:12, 19). Because of Christ's risen life,
the benefits of the Cross (which had occurred in Jerusalem) could be appropriated by
baptism anywhere in the world (Rom. 6:4; *cf.* Col. 2:20).

[4]   When referring to Christ's life he nowhere comments on this having occurred in Jerusalem or Palestine (Rom. 10:6-7; 15:8; 2 Cor. 8:9; Eph. 4:9-10; Phil. 2:7-8). The institution
of the Lord's supper is located in time, not in space ('on the night when he was betrayed':
1 Cor. 11:23); the resurrection appearances are described without any reference to the
'tomb' (1 Cor. 15:4).

Can these different aspects be reconciled? Possibly this is evidence of an unresolved polarity in Paul's thought. After all, if he could affirm that there was 'no longer Jew or Greek' (Gal. 3:28) and yet there was a certain priority accorded to Jewish people ('the Jew first and also to the Greek': Rom. 1:16; 2:10), might not the same paradox hold true in the case of Jerusalem?[5] As an 'apostle to the Gentiles' (Rom. 11:13) his principal tendency might be to look away from Jerusalem (placing all peoples and places on an equal footing), but he could also without contradiction have preserved a more focused interest in Jerusalem. A universal emphasis could be combined with an emphasis on the particular.

An alternative model, however, must also be borne in mind. Paul indicates that when necessary he practised as an observant Jew even though he no longer saw the Jewish law as ultimately binding ('to the weak I became weak': 1 Cor. 9:19-23).[6] Beneath this principle lies the conviction that certain things, which still had a prevalent force in the minds of his contemporaries, had neither a universal nor a lasting significance. This might also be applicable to Paul's approach to Jerusalem. His involvement in the Temple (Acts 21:23ff), for example, could be seen as a conciliatory gesture—necessary in the interim, but not fully reflecting his own 'strong' convictions in Christ.[7]

Primary consideration would then need to be given to Paul's own express statements on the issue, rather than to his practice (as related in Acts), which may have been determined by questions of pragmatism.[8] If his 'practice' is put aside for the time being, do Paul's writings reveal a coherent understanding of Jerusalem's present significance (3)? What about the parallel issues of the Land (1) and the Temple (2)?

These questions are part of the larger question, as to how much Paul reevaluated his own native Judaism. How radical was the break? Although Paul himself would have always claimed to be authentically Jewish, he had come to some startlingly new convictions. According to Paul, God's purposes towards humankind had moved into an unprecedented epoch: the first Christians were those 'on whom the end of the ages have come' (1 Cor. 10:11).[9] Paul therefore had a new 'understanding of where he stood in the divine timetable'.[10] Some things which were valid before Christ (εἰς Χριστόν in Gal. 3:24) were so no longer. Certain long-cherished notions then had to be reevaluated (e.g. the necessity of circumcision and the Jewish food laws).[11] The

---

5   As suggested in Davies (1974) 184.
6   On this principle, see e.g. Chadwick (1954-5), Carson (1986) and Barton (1996).
7   So R.N. Longenecker (1964); see below at n. 154.
8   We return to the description of Paul in Acts in sections 4 and 5 below.
9   Cf. also Gal. 4:4; Rom. 5:6; also Eph. 3:9, 1 Tim. 2:6.
10 Rubinstein (1972) 40.

boundary-marker of the 'people of God' was no longer circumcision but faith in Israel's Messiah, Jesus (Rom. 2-5). These were radical conclusions, going to the very heart of Jewish identity. Would his understanding of Jerusalem and the Temple (the central *geographical* identities of his people) fall into this same category? Would he retain his pre-Christian convictions about Jerusalem, or would these too be refashioned in the light of Jesus?

1. The Land

Paul's attitude towards the Land of Israel provides an instructive parallel. Since the Land constituted the third of three concentric *realia* within Judaism (of which the inner two were Jerusalem and the Temple),[12] Paul's evaluation of it will give some indication as to how he may have approached Jerusalem.

Paul's attitudes to the Land have been extensively studied by Davies. He begins with the observation that these issues would have been important for Paul: 'Paul would have felt the full force of the doctrine of the land, Jerusalem and the Temple; few would be likely to deal with it more emphatically, even passionately, than he'.[13] His conclusions are striking:

> Paul ignores completely the territorial aspect of the promise.... In the christological logic of Paul, the Land (like the law, particular and provisional) had become irrelevant.... The people of Israel living in the Land had been replaced as the people of God by a universal community which had no special territorial attachment.... The Land has for him been 'christified'. It is not the promised land (much as he had loved it) that became his 'inheritance', but the Living Lord, in whom was a 'new creation'.... To be 'in Christ'... has replaced being 'in the Land' as the ideal life.... Once Paul had made the Living Lord rather than the Torah the centre, he had in principle broken with the Land. 'In Christ' Paul was free from the Law and, therefore, from the Land.[14]

This is based on the observation that Paul rarely, if at all, speaks of the Land, and that other theological motifs have taken its place.

Davies builds his argument upon two initial observations. First, that in Romans 9:4 (when listing Israel's privileges) there is no mention of the 'promise' of a Land for Israel, but only a catch-all reference at the end to 'the prom-

---

[11]   Circumcision: 1 Cor. 7:19; Gal. 5:6; 6:15; Rom. 2:28-9; Phil. 3:3; *cf.* Col. 2:11. Food laws: 1 Cor. 10:25-6.

[12]   *Cf. e.g.* Wright (1994a) 70.

[13]   Davies (1974) 166.

[14]   Davies (1974) 178-79, 182, 213, 217, 219, 220. Giving Paul's frequent phrase 'in Christ' this 'locative' sense gives new meaning to texts such as Phil. 1:1; Eph. 1:1, 11; 2:13.

ises'. Secondly, that in all Paul's discussions concerning the Abrahamic promise (*e.g.* in Rom. 4 and Gal. 3) he omits one of its central themes—namely God's promise to give to Abraham and his 'offspring for ever' 'all *the land* that you see' (Gen. 13:15; *cf.* 17:8, 21:17); Paul concentrates on the promise that in Abraham 'all the families of the earth shall be blessed' (Gen. 12:3; *cf.* 17:5, 21:18; see Gal. 3:8). This is especially noteworthy in Galatians, where much of the argument turns on the use in Genesis of the word 'offspring' (σπέρμα), which does not occur in this 'universal' promise, but *does* appear in each of the three promises relating to the Land. Paul can hardly, therefore, have been unaware of this question. In Romans there might be tactical reasons why Paul omitted this more 'political' issue of the Land, but in Galatians it would have been particularly apposite.[15] Concerning this 'territorial aspect of the promise', Davies therefore concludes: 'his silence points not to the absence of a conscious concern with it, but to his deliberate rejection of it. His interpretation of the promise is a-territorial'.[16] This was a remarkable attitude, which ran quite contrary to the increasing Jewish nationalism of Paul's day.

The following observations confirm Davies' conclusions:

1) Paul passes over the issue of the Land again in Romans 15:8-9 ('Christ has become a servant of the circumcised in order that he might confirm the promises given to the patriarchs, and in order that the Gentiles might glorify God for his mercy').[17] The original inclusion of the Land within the patriarchal promises has either been ignored, or radically redefined.

2) Paul's statement in 2 Corinthians 1:20, gives some indication that the latter is the case. If Paul believed that Christ's coming had brought about the fulfilment of all God's promises ('for in [Christ] every one of God's promises is a 'Yes'), then this would necessarily include those in Genesis concerning the Land. The fulfilment had come about not in the expected, territorial way.

3) The nature of this unexpected fulfilment can then be inferred from Paul's use of the imagery of exodus, passover and 'redemption'. These Old Testament motifs had their origin in God's act of bringing Israel from Egypt into the 'promised land'. Paul now applied them to the Cross and resurrection. The logical development of this was that through Christ's work believers had now been ushered into the 'promised land'—though a quite different one. This is probably in Paul's mind in 1 Corinthians when he speaks of Christ as the 'passover lamb' (5:7) and of the similarity of the believers' experience in conversion to that of Israel under Moses (10:1 ff); as a result the Corinthians will 'inherit the kingdom of God' (6:9; *cf.* 3:21). In other words, through Christ's

---

[15] On the possible nationalistic assumptions of the Judaizers in Galatians, see n. 54.
[16] Davies (1974) 179.
[17] *Cf.* also the use of ἐπαγγελία in 2 Cor. 7:1; Eph. 1:13; 2:12; 3:6. In none of these instances is there any reference to the 'land'.

act of redemption (*cf.* also 1:30; 6:20) they had been brought into all that the 'promised land' had been intended to signify—the 'kingdom of God'.[18]

4) The word for 'gospel' (εὐαγγέλιον) is derived from Isaiah's proclamation of 'good news' to Israel that Jerusalem had been 'redeemed' (Isa: 52:7-9).[19] Again this would suggest that Paul (together with later New Testament writers) was applying to the salvation experienced in Christ terminology which originally had applied to Jerusalem and the Land. The physical Land needed to be seen in a new light.

5) The Land-concept is not just given a spiritual reference; it is also made universal. This results from Paul's conviction that Christ is Lord over the whole world. He is Israel's Messiah, but his rule also extends far beyond the borders of the original 'promised land' (see *e.g.* Phil. 2:10; *cf.* 1 Cor. 3:22-23; Eph. 1:10). The ethical commands that previously pertained to Israel's life in the Land are therefore applicable to all who seek to live under Christ's rule. Hence when the fourth commandment is quoted (Eph. 6:3), the phrase 'that the Lord your God is giving you' is omitted; this then leaves the reference to 'land' (τῆς γῆς) un-defined, such that it comes to refer to the 'earth' in general. God's rule over the 'promised land' now extends through Christ to the whole world, and his true 'people' are a worldwide community—not an ethnic group associated with a particular land.

6) Finally, Romans 4:13 speaks of Abraham's receiving 'the promise that he would inherit the *world*'. In Genesis the promised 'inheritance' was only of the 'promised land'. Contemporary Jews may have aggrandized the promise in their belief that Israel would indeed inherit the 'world'.[20] Paul, however, gives the promise a different twist. He asserts that behind God's promise of a particular land to Abraham, his prior purpose had been to use that particularity as a means of ultimately blessing 'all the nations of the earth'. That divine purpose had come to pass in Christ—the one who as Abraham's 'seed' (or 'offsrping': Gal. 3:16), was indeed the 'heir of the world'.

The Land, like the Torah, was a temporary stage in the long purpose of the God of Abraham. It is as though the Land were a great advance metaphor for

---

[18] *Cf.* also the use of 'redemption' in Eph. 1:7 (leading to blessing in the 'heavenly places', 1:3) and in Col. 1:14 (resulting in being rescued from the 'power of darkness' and transferred into the kingdom of his beloved Son': 1:13). The concept of 'kingdom' was clearly universal (though not 'other-worldly') and no longer related exclusively to the people of Israel in Palestine: see *e.g.* 1 Cor. 15:24; Gal. 5:21; Col. 1:13; 4:11; 1 Thess. 2:12; 2 Thess. 1:5; Eph. 5:5. Note too his similar understanding of the Christian's 'inheritance' and 'hope' (Gal. 3:29; 4:7; 1 Cor. 6:9-10; Col. 1:5, 12; 3:24; *cf.* Eph. 1:3, 14, 18; 5:5).

[19] Wright (1994b) 223ff; *cf.* Bruce (1982b) 81-2.

[20] So Dunn (1988) 213, with references: see *e.g.* 4 Ezra 6:59 ('if the world had indeed been created for us, why do we not possess our world as an inheritance?').

the design of God that his people should eventually bring the whole world into submission to his healing reign. God's whole purpose now goes beyond Jerusalem and the Land to the whole world.[21]

Davies' analysis is confirmed. There is good evidence that Paul saw the Land and the promises associated with it in a new way. 'The real centre of his interest has moved from the Land, concentrated in Jerusalem, to the communities in Christ'.[22]

2. The Temple

Paul rarely refers to the physical Temple in Jerusalem, but when he does he makes it plain that he saw this institution as truly ordained by God in times past. In Romans 9:4 he includes 'Temple worship' in his list of the Jews' special privileges,[23] and in 2 Thessalonians 2:4 he describes it as the 'Temple of God'.[24] Both texts presuppose his positive attitude towards the Temple in principle. In other letters he supports his arguments by drawing on Temple-based material—even though writing to Gentile converts, who might not have shared this initial presupposition (1 Cor. 9:13; 10:18). Important spiritual truths were enshrined in the Jerusalem Temple, because it had been based on godly principles.

Was that the end of the matter? There are several indications that Paul's theology now looked at the Temple in a new light. This can be discerned by noting how he understood concepts such as 'dwelling' and 'sacrifice'—concepts that owed their meaning to the Temple.

a) The New Divine 'Dwelling'

First, he made the bold assertion that the Christian Church was truly the 'Temple of God':

> Do you not know that you are God's Temple [ναὸς θεοῦ] and that God's Spirit dwells in you? If anyone destroys God's Temple, God will destroy that person; for God's Temple is holy, and you are that Temple (1 Cor. 3:16-17).

---

[21] Wright (1994a) 67.
[22] Davies (1974) 217.
[23] The Greek for 'Temple worship' is simply λατρεία, but this clearly refers to the Temple cult: see e.g. Dunn (1988) 534.
[24] See further below, n. 80 and 109.

> What agreement has the Temple of God with idols? For we are the Temple
> of the living God; as God said: 'I will live in them and walk among them, and
> I will be their God, and they shall be my people' (2 Cor. 6:16).[25]

Not only does this powerful imagery suggest that Paul saw the full weight of
God's purposes now invested in the Church (God would 'destroy' any who
'destroyed' this new Temple); it also raises important questions about the status of the Jerusalem Temple.

> To Western Christians, thinking anachronistically of the Temple as simply
> the Jewish equivalent of a cathedral, the image is simply one metaphor
> among many and without much apparent significance. For a first-century
> Jew, however, the Temple had an enormous significance; as a result, when
> Paul uses such an image within twenty-five years of the crucifixion (with the
> actual Temple still standing), it is a striking index of the immense change that
> has taken place in his thought. The Temple had been superseded by the
> Church.[26]

The Christian community is identified with the Temple, because it is
the 'dwelling-place' of God; as such it is 'holy', and those who threaten the
community's life are duly warned. Each of these sentiments, however, can be
paralleled in the literature of the Qumran community.[27] Were Paul's comments so radical after all? Despite their conviction that they were the embodiment of the true Temple, the sectarians at Qumran seem to have believed that
the physical Temple in Jerusalem would return to its previous place within
God's purposes—once it was properly purified.[28] If *they* did not see them
selves as a complete replacement for the Jerusalem Temple, is it likely that
Paul believed this of the Christian Church?

This parallelism with Qumran may tell in the opposite direction. First,
if the ideas at Qumran were developed in conscious reaction to the Jerusalem
Temple, this can be true of Paul as well; his terminology would then be far
from haphazard, but include a consciously critical evaluation of the existing
Temple in Jerusalem. Secondly, whilst there is a formal parallelism between
Paul and Qumran in their notion of the community as the 'dwelling-place' of
God, the basis for this assertion is quite different.

---

[25]   The phrase 'do you not know?' in 1 Cor 3:16 (and 9:13) suggests that this teaching had
been part of Paul's earlier catechesis (*cf.* Gärtner [1965] 57). For a thorough discussion of
these passages, see McKelvey (1969) ch. 7.
[26]   Wright (1994a) 70. Davies (1974) 190, notes that Paul's use of ναός, rather than ἱερόν,
indicates his concern to 'replace the very heart of the Temple with a new shrine'.
[27]   See Gärtner (1965) 49-60, with references.
[28]   See Gärtner (1965) 21; Brooke (1985) 19; *cf.* 11QTemple 15ff.

Paul's argument is based on two factors, without parallel in Qumran. First, Jews and Gentiles in Christ constitute a new 'people of God'. Paul's conflation of Old Testament texts in the second passage quoted above ('and they shall be my people': 2 Cor. 6:16) is remarkable. Texts which originally applied to physical Israel (Lev. 26:12; Jer. 32:38; Ezek. 37:27) are now applied to those born *outside* the boundaries of ethnic Israel—something unthinkable for the Qumran community who saw themselves as the true remnant *within* God's people. For Paul something new and irreversible has taken place: the formation of a new 'people of God' in and through Israel's Messiah. Through understanding themselves as the true Temple,

> both communities [were able to] redefine the covenant people, but whereas the Qumran sect did so by taking to an extreme the emphasis on purity and differentiation from Gentiles, the Christian community did so in a way quite opposite to this emphasis.[29]

Secondly, the Church is God's 'dwelling-place'—not (as at Qumran) because its worship and lifestyle is cultically pure, but because of the active presence of the Holy Spirit. This is made clear in the former passage (1 Cor. 3:16-17), but also a few chapters later, when Paul uses the same imagery of the individual Christian believer:

> Or do you not know that your body is a Temple [ναὸς] of the Holy Spirit, within you, which you have from God, and that you are not your own? For you were bought with a price' (1 Cor. 6:19-20).

Here again is an argument unparalleled in Qumran—the individual believer being identified with God's Temple because of a dramatic redemptive act ('you were bought with a price'). The Spirit had become available in a new way, and this was directly linked to a once-off event (the Cross) which was now the high-point in God's purposes—never to be reversed.

Paul's doctrine of the Church (and its members) as the true *locus* of God's Temple was therefore founded on distinctively Christian assumptions: the reality of the Holy Spirit, and also the person of Christ himself. Elsewhere Paul writes of Christ:

> For in him all the fullness of God was pleased to dwell [κατοικῆσαι] (Col. 1:19). . . . For in him the whole fullness of Deity dwells [κατοικεῖ] bodily and you have come to fullness in him (Col. 2:9-10).

---

[29] Bauckham (1993c) 147.

In using such language, Paul was drawing upon the Temple-motif of God's name 'dwelling' in the sanctuary. Just the presence of God was believed to have 'dwelt' in the Temple (e.g. 1 Kings 8:27; Ps. 132:14), so God's 'fulness' had dwelt in Christ. Because of this divine indwelling in Christ, there was then an ontological basis for the early Christians' experience that those who were themselves 'in Christ' became the dwelling-place of the Spirit (cf. Rom. 8:9-11; Eph. 3:16-17). That which the Temple had adumbrated was now substantiated in Christ's own person, who made it possible for those identified with him to be indwelt by the Spirit.[30] The end-result was something that looked superficially similar to Qumran, but its bases were quite different.

Paul's understanding that the 'substance' had been truly revealed in Christ would then cast the Temple in an altogether new light. Whereas at Qumran the commitment to the maintenance of the Temple's ideology meant that the application of Temple-imagery to its community was self-consciously metaphorical, in the emerging Christian communities the reverse was the case. The Spirit's manifest presence and God's work in Christ *were* the reality, to which the Temple-imagery had but pointed. There could be no 'return' to the Temple after this. From Paul's vantage-point, as opposed to that from Qumran, the Jerusalem Temple could appear as redundant and unnecessary.

> The decisive difference between the Temple symbolism of Qumran and that of the New Testament is based on the New Testament's attitude to the person and work of Jesus. . . . This, it was believed, had replaced the Temple and its sacrifices once and for all.[31]

b) The New Nature of Worship

After referring to the λατρεία/'Temple worship' of the Jewish people (Rom. 9:4), Paul uses the same word to begin his description of how Christians should respond to the gospel:

> I appeal to you therefore, brothers and sisters, by the mercies of God, to present your bodies as a living sacrifices, holy and acceptable to God, which is your spiritual worship (τὴν λογικὴν λατρείαν: Rom. 12:1).

---

[30] Cf. 2 Tim. 1:14: 'the Holy Spirit living in us'. Note also 2 Cor. 12:9 and Paul's 'bold metaphor' (Plummer [1915], 355), drawn from the imagery of the tabernacle and Temple: 'that the power of Christ may dwell in me (ἐπισκηνώσῃ)'.

[31] Gärtner (1965) 104. Cf. Bauckham (1993c), who similarly concludes that the Christians' approach to the Temple was ultimately more radical than that of Qumran—even though, unlike those at Qumran, they continued to frequent it.

The adjective λογικὴ ('spiritual') may have several possible meanings, but in part it serves to contrast *this* form of worship from that offered in the Temple (as in Rom. 9:4).[32] Having spoken in the previous chapter of the largely un-believing Jewish nation, Paul now indicated to the Roman Christians what kind of worship was required of *them*.[33] It was to be an offering of their whole lives to God in response to his mercy. No indication is given, either here or elsewhere in his letters, that the Temple worship in Jerusalem should form a part of their new Christian identity. Nor is it ever suggested that worship in the Diaspora should be seen as an extension of the true worship being offered in the 'centre', in Jerusalem.[34] Those ways of thinking, with which Paul might have been familiar before his conversion, no longer had any place.

Secondly, Paul emphasized in this verse that Christian worship was es-sentially a response to God's 'mercies' as already accomplished in Christ; it was dependent upon a 'sacrifice' that had already been offered. Although Paul does not use sacrificial language here, his use of 'mercies' picks up his whole exposition of God's redemptive work in Christ and in particular his cultic lan-guage in 3:23ff. Christ's death is there described as a 'sacrifice of atonement' (ἱλαστήριον)—a word which, though metaphorical in this context, was de-pendent upon the imagery of the 'mercy-seat' in the Temple, and which was particularly associated with the Day of Atonement.[35] When this is combined with Paul's references elsewhere to Christ's 'blood'[36] and his description of Christ as 'our paschal lamb' (1 Cor. 5:7),[37] it is evident that Paul saw Christ's work as integrally connected to the two chief festivals associated with the Temple: Passover and Yom Kippur. Given his emphasis on its unique effica-cy, however, Paul will have seen the Cross as the *fulfilment* of these Temple rituals—not simply as something which could helpfully be compared to them. 'Jesus' death is seen in cultic terms, and it is clear that it replaces what would otherwise have been the function of the Temple and its sacrifices'.[38]

If Temple worship had been a hallmark of the people of God in a pre-vious era, it was not so now. That worship had been centred upon the concept of sacrificial death as a means of gaining access into God's presence. There

---

[32] So Ziesler (1989) 293; Dunn (1988) 711-2.

[33] It may be no coincidence that the reference to λατρεία comes at the outset of both discussions, the former (Rom. 9-11) discussing the Jewish people, the latter (Rom. 12-16) discussing the new 'people of God'.

[34] That this was assumed within the Diaspora can be seen by 'the assiduity and enthu-siasm with which Diaspora Jews paid their Temple tax; this was the means by which the sacrifices offered in the Temple enabled their own access to God': Bauckham (1993c) 142.

[35] So Dunn (1988) 171.

[36] See Rom. 3:25; 5:9; 1 Cor. 11:25; Col. 1:14, 20; *cf.* Eph. 1:7; 2:13.

[37] *Cf.* Eph. 5:1: 'Christ gave himself up for us as a fragrant offering and sacrifice to God'.

[38] Gaston (1984) 70.

was a new centre, Christ himself. It was he who had secured this 'access' for believers (Rom. 5:1-2) which could be appropriated directly through exercising 'faith' in his 'blood' (Rom. 3:25; *cf.* Eph. 2:13; 3:12). The Temple's role in the past had been vital, not so in the future.

c) The New 'Dividing-line'

Finally, Paul's theology was based on the conviction that in Christ there was no longer 'Jew or Greek' (Gal. 3:28). The Jerusalem Temple, however, was

> the greatest boundary-marker between Jew and Gentile. However fluid the distinction between Jew and Gentile might seem in a Diaspora synagogue, in the Temple the distinction was dramatically absolute. . . . The Temple, embodied, as the principle of its sanctity, the exclusion of Gentiles.[39]

Standing between the outer and inner courts was the *soreg* wall on which was fixed a notice with a stern warning:

> no man of another race is to enter within the fence and enclosure around the Temple. Whoever is caught will have only himself to thank for the death which follows.[40]

Paul's message ran counter to the message of the Temple at this point. Even though its authenticity is open to question, the passage in Ephesians 2:14 expresses his conviction succinctly: through the Cross Christ has 'made both groups [Jew and Gentile] into one and has broken down the *dividing wall*, that is, the hostility between us'. Christ's death had dealt a mortal blow to the vision of humanity that was encapsulated in the Temple.[41]

> Whereas the Gentiles could not enter God's presence in the old Temple without becoming Jews, in the new Temple of the messianic age, the Christian community, they could do so as Gentiles.[42]

It would not then have been easy for Paul to incorporate the Temple as it stood into his new-found convictions.

---

[39] Bauckham (1993c) 143, 146.

[40] As translated in Lincoln (1990) 141.

[41] If the Temple was increasingly being used as a symbol of the nationalistic cause, Paul's critique of the Temple's 'exclusiveness' would also have included this. Moreover, the Paul who criticized his fellow-Jews for their trust in the 'external' act of circumcision (Rom. 2:25ff) might easily have seen the same danger in Jewish attitudes towards the Temple.

[42] Bauckham (1995a) 458.

Three passages in Romans are significant in this connection. First, when Paul indicates that he now regards no food as 'unclean' (Rom. 14:14), his removal of the 'clean'/'unclean' categories might equally apply to *people*—if not more so: Gentile believers, it could be inferred, are not in themselves 'unclean' merely through being born as Gentiles.

Secondly, was this in Paul's mind when he described his forthcoming visit to Jerusalem (15:25ff)? He has just talked of his ministry in unusually cultic terms: as 'a minister [λειτουργός] of Christ Jesus to the Gentiles in the priestly service of the gospel of God so that the offering of the Gentiles may be acceptable, sanctified by the Holy Spirit' (15:16).[43] In taking the Gentile believers to Jerusalem with their gifts of money, Paul challenged people in Jerusalem to recognize that these Gentiles, together with their gifts, were indeed 'acceptable'. They were not 'unclean'. In fact the Jerusalem church needed to accept gratefully that it was on the receiving end of a ministry (λειτουργῆσαι: 15:27) performed by Gentiles!

Thirdly, Paul may have had the Temple specifically in mind in his earlier quotation of Hosea 1:10 (Rom. 9:26): 'in the very place where it was said to them, "you are not my people", there they shall be called "children of the living God."' Some see this as a reference to Jerusalem and to his forthcoming visit there.[44] This might betray a hope that one day Jerusalem would become a place where Gentiles, instead of being made to feel unwelcome ('you are not my people'), would be able to enjoy the truth that they were truly part of the 'people of God'. So long as the Temple remained, however, that truth would be denied in Jerusalem's very stones: for the 'dividing-wall' made it quite clear that they were not 'God's people'. The Temple in its present form denied a fundamental part of Paul's theology.

d) Conclusion

Paul's Christian convictions militated against the Temple. Inasmuch as the Temple endorsed the notion of the prior claim upon God of the Jewish people, it was countered by the teaching that there was now 'no longer Jew or Greek' (Gal. 3:28). Inasmuch as it symbolized the reality of God's presence on earth, it was countered by the teaching that God had been 'in Christ' (2 Cor. 5:19), fully 'dwelling' in him (Col. 1:19; 2:9), and that the Spirit of God now dwelt in Christ's people (Rom. 8:11). Inasmuch as it spoke of the need for sacrifice, it was countered by the teaching that Christ on the Cross was the 'sacrifice of

---

[43] For other instances of this cultic metaphor, see *e.g.* 1 Cor. 9:13-14; Phil. 2:17.

[44] See Munck (1959) 306-7, and Ziesler (1989) 248.

atonement' which God had now 'put forward' (Rom. 3:25), and which gave
Christians immediate 'access' into God's presence (Rom. 5:1ff). As far as
Paul was concerned,

> although Christians might choose to continue to approach God cultically in
> Jerusalem, as a whole they were aware of the fact that through Jesus they had
> such a close relationship to God that it was not necessary.[45]

Scholars note the 'remarkable displacement of the Jerusalem Temple in
Paul's theology well before the events of AD 70',[46] and that for him the Temple had 'lost its significance in view of the person and work of Jesus Christ'.[47]
All of this stands irrespective of whether Paul knew of the traditions found in
the Gospels of Jesus pronouncing the Temple's forthcoming destruction.[48] If
he did know of such traditions, then this would only have provided a dominical incentive to re-evaluate the Temple along such lines; it would also have
given Paul a sense of urgency to ensure that the Christian Church established
its essential independence from the Temple as soon as possible.

Nevertheless, it has to be admitted that Paul did not explicitly draw out
these conclusions about the Temple in his letters. This may be because it had
already been covered in his catechetical instruction, or (perhaps more likely)
because this Temple-issue was not a burning one for those to whom he was
writing. His converts consisted of Diaspora Jews and Gentiles, for whom the
troublesome issues were far more likely to be those related to the 'boundary-
markers' of Israel, namely the food laws and circumcision. If Paul had been
writing to people who were keenly concerned about the Jerusalem Temple,
our analysis suggests that his central theses would have turned out to be very
similar to those found in Hebrews.[49] The fact that he does not give this issue
a systematic treatment does not indicate that Paul had not drawn out the logical corollaries of his own position. In other areas he showed a remarkable ca-

---

[45] P. Richardson (1969) 198.

[46] D. Wenham (1995) 210.

[47] R.N. Longenecker (1964) 250. Davies (1974) 193, acknowledges that Paul 'had substituted for [the Temple] the new shrine of the Church', but suggests he could still have been
'able to recognize the Temple in Jerusalem'. The argument here is that Paul, even if
perforce he had to 'recognize' its continuance from a pragmatic and conciliatory point of
view (and was happy to do so: see Acts 21:26ff), would not have 'recognized' it in the sense
of according it a continuing theological status and validity.

[48] See further below n. 60 and 72.

[49] On the similarities between Paul's theology and that of Hebrews, see *e.g.* Witherington
(1991) and literature there cited; *cf.* also below ch. 9, n. 39.

pacity to see the far-reaching implications of the Cross.[50] The same would have been true in this case.

To have this theology was one thing, but so long as the present Temple stood, there was little that could be done in practice. Indeed the continuance of the Temple might have been seen as the single greatest argument against the veracity of this position. An expectant silence was therefore quite appropriate. If Paul was called to undermine the enduring validity of circumcision and the food laws, then this could be tackled on the human level. The end of the Temple was a matter that lay on another level altogether. As Paul said in another context, it was often necessary to 'leave room for the wrath of God' and not to take matters into one's own hands (Rom. 12:19). If Jesus had predicted its destruction, all one could do was wait. What Paul *could* do in the meantime was to assert the explosive truths analysed above, while for the sake of peace showing a certain deference to the Temple so long as it still stood (hence his visit in Acts 21:26ff).[51] In so doing Paul was laying a secure foundation for the Church should it ever need to exist in a Temple-less age, ensuring that the centre of its life was no longer the Temple, but Christ himself. This was part of the perspicacity and foresight of the 'apostle to the Gentiles'.

3. The City of Jerusalem

The way Paul has re-evaluated both the Land and the Temple suggests that the same may have occurred in his reflections concerning Jerusalem.

On several occasions in his letters Paul quotes Old Testament references to Zion, comments on his contemporary fellow-Jews, or gives some explanation of the rationale behind his taking the 'collection' to Jerusalem. Only once does he expressly make some theological comment about 'Jerusalem' *per se*—in Galatians 4.

a) Galatians 4

> Now Hagar is Mount Sinai in Arabia and corresponds to the present Jerusalem [τῇ νῦν Ἰερουσαλήμ], for she is in slavery with her children. But the other woman corresponds to the Jerusalem above; she is free, and she is our mother (Gal. 4:25-6).

---

[50] *E.g.* in Gal. 2:11-21 and 6:12-15, where his vision of the Cross forms the basis of his understanding of table-fellowship and circumcision.

[51] See below at n.154.

Galatians is often reckoned to be Paul's first extant letter (AD 47-9); alternatively it is dated to c. 55.[52] This startling statement, which completely reverses and overturns normal Jewish assumptions, is therefore made within fifteen or twenty years of Paul's conversion.

According to many scholars, Paul in Galatians is combatting the arguments of those 'Judaizing' Christians who, while originally based in Jerusalem, had visited Paul's converts in Galatia and insisted on their circumcision.[53] A prime motivation in this activity was the rising tide of Jewish nationalism at this time in Palestine.[54] This meant that the Jerusalem church was fearful of being associated with Paul's Gentile mission, since his dismissal of the need for circumcision could be seen as destroying the national and ethnic cohesiveness of Judaism. For fear of persecution back in Jerusalem (cf. Gal. 2:12; 6:12) and to 'thwart any Zealot purification campaign against the church back home',[55] the Judaizers had come to Galatia to bring Paul's converts safely 'into line' (though possibly concealing this, the real personal purpose of their activity). Barrett reconstructs their argument as follows:

> The true descendents of Abraham are the Jews, who inhabit Jerusalem. Here are the true people of God and it will follow that Jerusalem is the authoritative centre of the renewed people of God, now called the Church. Those who are not prepared to attach themselves to this community by the approved means (circumcision) must be cast out; they cannot hope to inherit promises made to Abraham and his seed.[56]

---

[52] Following the careful arguments of R.N. Longenecker (1990) lxi-c, we here assume that Galatians was written by Paul to the churches of south Galatia before the Jerusalem council (AD 49), and that his visit to Jerusalem in Gal. 2:1 is to be identified with the visit recorded in Acts 11:30; cf. e.g. Hemer (1989) 261-70; D. Wenham (1993) 234-43; Morgado (1994); and Bauckham (1995a). This entails the corollary, not noted by Longenecker, that therefore the Galatians were only converted after the Jerusalem meeting of Gal. 2:1-10, though probably before the Antioch incident (2:11-21). Paul was thus defending the 'truth of the gospel' for all Gentiles in principle, and experiencing difficulties for their sakes even before they knew of him. It was for 'you' (2:5).

[53] For a good summary of viewpoints, most of which assert the link with Jerusalem, see R.N. Longenecker (1990) lxxxix-xcvi; cf. e.g. Howard (1979) 19; N. Taylor (1992) 174.

[54] See the important article by Jewett (1970-1). This is followed by e.g. R.N. Longenecker (1990) xcv; George (1994) 60; Hansen (1994) 15.

[55] R.N. Longenecker (1990) xcvi.

[56] Barrett (1976) 10; the summary of the Judaizers' position offered by Bruce (1982b) 26, is similar, though focusing more on Paul's relationship with the Jerusalem church authorities. In similar vein, Longenecker (1990) 218, sees the extended allegory of Hagar and Sarah as Paul's ad hominem inversion of what the Judaizers had been arguing: as Jewish Christians in Jerusalem they considered themselves to be in true continuity both with Sarah and also with Sinai and Jerusalem, but Paul links these two latter entities with Hagar.

The important point is that Paul is dealing here not merely with non-Christian Judaism, but also with a Jewish-*Christian* theology of Jerusalem. His opponents are Judaizing Christians. When Paul talks of 'the present city of Jerusalem' this is not simply an abstract metaphor for unbelieving Judaism;[57] he is also thinking about the whole understanding of Jerusalem which is currently influencing some members of the Christian Church in that city. Thus when Jerusalem is described as being 'in slavery', he is not simply referring to non-Christian Jews apart from Christ; nor is the reference to 'slavery' brought about merely by the need to identify Jerusalem with Hagar, the slave-woman. Rather, it is a way of acknowledging that Jerusalem has the power to bring again into spiritual 'bondage' those who are in principle liberated and 'set free' in Christ (5:1).

Paul is reflecting critically on the Jerusalem of his own day ('the *present* Jerusalem'). Jerusalem was the religious centre of non-Christian Judaism;[58] it was also the place which was causing Christian believers to be blinded to the full implications of the gospel—and to interfere with his Gentile converts. Although Galatians reads as Paul's defence of himself (of his apostleship and his gospel), it is more truly a defence of his converts against those who would make them feel 'second-class' Christians. Paul was defending his own 'children' in the gospel (4:19) against those who would have them to be 'children' of Jerusalem (4:25).

Behind the presenting-issue of circumcision there was the issue of Jerusalem. The Judaizers' insistence on circumcision was part of a theological framework and ecclesiastical policy that sought (as in Barrett's summary above) to inculcate a sense of *Jerusalem-dependency*. Paul's converts were not fully in the family, they claimed, until they had been duly linked to Jerusalem through the outward sign of circumcision and had also acknowledged the authoritative and primary role of Jerusalem within the Church.[59]

It was this Jerusalem-dependency which Paul criticized when he talked of Jerusalem and 'her children' (4:25).[60] Jerusalem's 'children' were those who looked to her, who were dependent upon her in some way for their sense of identity—whether Christians or non-Christian Jews. Christian believers, Paul argued, were not to look to that Jerusalem, but rather to the 'Jerusalem that is above'. It was *she* who was 'our mother' (4:26).[61] Those who confi-

---

[57] As suggested by Bruce (1968) 4, and Guthrie (1974) 125.

[58] Even if Paul's chief target is the Judaizers, it is impossible to suggest that these verses do not also contain an implicit critique of Judaism; so Lincoln (1981) 17.

[59] *Cf.* also Lincoln (1981) 18.

[60] De Young (1961) 107, rightly suggests that Paul's reference to Jerusalem's 'children' has been influenced by his knowledge of pre-synoptic tradition (*cf.* the statements attributed to Jesus in Luke 13:34, 19:44 and Matt. 23:37). *Cf.* below n. 72.

dently asserted that Abraham was their 'father' (3:6-4:7) and Jerusalem their 'mother' based their identity in an insecure place. Rather Christian identity was found 'in Christ' and Christian hope focused upon the 'Jerusalem above'. In other words, believers in Christ, be they Jewish or Gentile, be they in Jerusalem or in Galatia, had a radically new identity—an identity not based on Jerusalem. Jerusalem had to be seen for what it was in the light of Christ—a place 'in slavery', bound up with Sinai and the law, the law which needed to give place to faith (3:23-25). 'The community which belongs to the heavenly Jerusalem must be kept free from the enslaving influence of the present Jerusalem'.[62] Those Christians who failed to see Jerusalem in this way, were in danger of being burdened again by a further 'yoke of slavery' (5:1).

If Paul was responding to a situation caused in part by a resurgent Jewish nationalism,[63] his emphasis on freedom may have been particularly apposite. The greatest act of liberation had already been accomplished in Christ ('for freedom Christ has set us free': 5:1); and this had taken place in Jerusalem itself! When Jerusalem's 'children' failed to acknowledge this true freedom, they would be tempted to look elsewhere, and those Jewish Christians who shared these concerns for political freedom (or instead let their thinking be unduly coloured by fear of them) were looking in the wrong direction. The 'Jerusalem' which was at the centre of their aspirations was manifestly still 'in slavery' (and under Roman rule); their focus should not be on this 'present' Jerusalem, but rather on the 'Jerusalem above'.

Irrespective of this latter point, Paul was plainly critical of his contemporary Jerusalem. Moreover, this criticism was expressly made in the light of all the traditional religious meaning ascribed to the city. For, although he could have used the more secular Greek name for Jerusalem (Ἱεροσόλυμα), he used the more religiously significant term, Ἱερουσαλήμ.[64] It was *this* Jerusalem, the one which God had invested with such special privileges, that was now 'in slavery'. It was spiritually 'in Arabia'.[65]

---

[61] Lincoln (1981) 17, plausibly suggests that Paul is reversing a slogan used by the Judaizers—that the physical Jerusalem which had always been the mother-city for Jews was to be the mother-city for Christians as well, even for Gentile converts. On the prehistory of this concept of the 'Jerusalem above', see *e.g.* Longenecker (1990) 214.

[62] Lincoln (1981) 29.

[63] See above at n. 54. Although the 'Zealot' political party may not finally have been formed until the 60's, is it purely coincidence that in this very chapter Paul speaks of the Judaizers as being 'zealous' (4:17), and then defines when zeal is appropriate (4:18). *Cf.* also Gal. 1:14; Phil. 3:6. See *e.g.* J. Taylor (1996).

[64] On this distinction, see above ch. 3, n. 48. Paul had used Ἱεροσόλυμα when referring earlier to the city in simple, geographical terms (1:18; 2:1).

[65] *Cf.* Lincoln (1981) 17: 'the association of Jerusalem with Arab territory . . . would have enraged a patriotic Jew'.

In developing this critique, Paul not only applied to the *heavenly* Jerusalem an Old Testament text (Isa. 54:1 in Gal. 4:27) which had originally applied to the *earthly* Jerusalem; he also denied that the latter was in any way connected to the 'Jerusalem above'. In contemporary Jewish thinking there was a spiritual link between the two: the heavenly Jerusalem was the prototype of the earthly (*cf.* 2 Baruch 4:1f) and the earthly city was the gateway to the heavenly.[66] Paul now denied this. Access to the 'Jerusalem above' had nothing to do with the Jerusalem below—contrary to any suggestions made by the Judaizers. Paul's Galatian converts did not need a link with the earthly Jerusalem and did not gain access, as it were, to the heavenly Jerusalem *via* the earthly one. They already had the highest possible status, being God's 'children' (3:26) and 'heirs' (4:7). Any who sought (consciously or unconsciously) to undermine this were identifying themselves with Hagar and needed to be 'driven out' (4:30, quoting Gen. 21:10).

> Gal. 4:21ff represents, perhaps, the sharpest polemic against Jerusalem in the New Testament. . . . Far from being pre-occupied with hopes for a glorification of the earthly Jerusalem, Paul's thought represents a most emphatic repudiation of any eschatological hopes concerning the earthly city.[67]

These were powerful ideas, fuelled by Paul's concern to defend his converts' liberty and fired by indignation at how the Judaizers had 'confused' them (5:10). The particularity of this context, however, does not mean that Paul would necessarily have retracted these comments on another, more eirenic, occasion. Nor does it suggest that Paul's comments here were an outburst, based on little previous reflection.[68] Rather the making of such radical comments, which at a stroke undermined many of the beliefs of his fellow-Jews, is more likely to have been the result of serious thought—despite the polemical tone with which they are expressed. They are to be seen as an integral part of his whole new approach to his inherited tradition.

For all his Jewish affiliation, Paul was convinced that Christian identity was markedly different; it was not bound up with the physical Jerusalem, but rather with the 'Jerusalem above'. Only when Christians, especially Jewish Christians such as himself, saw how their belief in the Messiah called into question the previously accepted norms (of the law, circumcision, *and* Jerusalem) would they experience the full freedom that was theirs in Christ. The Christian gospel did not offer a new validation for Jerusalem; on the contrary,

---

[66] See *e.g.* the string of texts collected in Buchanan (1978) 526-8, 550-553.

[67] De Young (1961) 106.

[68] In Gal. 1-2 he describes two visits to the city after his conversion, both of which could have occasioned some such reflection on Jerusalem.

the Christian Church needed to be set free from the 'slavery' that was inherent in the 'present Jerusalem'. The Cross of Christ had had profound repercussions, leading to the death of many things (*cf.* Gal. 6:12-15); one of these, paradoxically, was Jerusalem itself.

b) 1 Thessalonians 2

> For you, brothers and sisters, became imitators of the churches of God in Christ Jesus that are in Judea, for you suffered the same things from your own compatriots as they did from the Jews, who killed both the Lord Jesus and the prophets, and drove us out; they displease God and oppose everyone by hindering us from speaking to the Gentiles that they may be saved. Thus they have constantly been filling up the measure of their sins; but God's wrath has overtaken them at last [ἔφθασεν εἰς τέλος] (1 Thess. 2:14-16).

This is a difficult passage.[69] Although it contains no explicit reference to Jerusalem, it is important for our study. In contrast to Galatians 4, there is no criticism here of fellow-Christians;[70] Paul's focus is on the Jews in Judea (the 'Judeans'),[71] and on the experience of Christians who suffered under them.

Paul's purpose is to encourage his readers to know that they are not the only ones who have suffered, and to realize that the first Jewish-Christians, far from having an easy time because of their Jewish background, had suffered far worse things than they. This leads on to a reflection on how the local Jewish population in Judea had so far responded to the message about 'the Lord Jesus'. Here we have a glimpse into Paul's thoughts on how his own people and especially Jerusalem had rejected both Jesus himself and his messengers.

That it is fair to read these verses with Jerusalem in mind is confirmed by noting how Paul's wording closely resembles that found in the 'Q' passages in Matthew (23:37) and Luke (13:34): 'Jerusalem, Jerusalem, the city that

---

[69] Because of its polemical tone, the authenticity of this passage has been questioned by several scholars who see it as a later non-Pauline interpolation: see *e.g.* Pearson (1971), Schmidt (1983) and Bruce (1982a) 51. Its authenticity is defended by *e.g.* Davies (1978), Okeke (1980-81), Donfried (1984), Simpson (1990), Wanamaker (1990), Weatherly (1991), N. Taylor (1992) 152, D. Wenham (1995) 319-26. For a defence of this passage against the charge of anti-Semitism, see *e.g.* Hagner (1993) and Schlueter (1994).

[70] Instead the Jewish-Christian 'churches in Judea' are held forth as a pattern for emulation; see *e.g.* Holmberg (1978) 50. This is a good example of how Paul can be positive about the Christians in Jerusalem and Judea, even while he is critical of the Judaizers who come from there to interfere with his own work. *Cf.* N. Taylor (1992) 154, and below 4b.

[71] That Paul's use of Ἰουδαῖοι may here have this more local sense of 'Judean' is argued by Weatherly (1991) and D.J. Harrington (1992) 23-24.

kills the prophets and stones those who are sent to it! How often have I desired to gather your children together. See, your house is left to you, desolate.' Paul was probably indebted to this saying about Jerusalem in an earlier phase of its tradition-history.[72] His discussing the anomaly of the Jews' rejection of their Messiah would then necessarily involve some reflection on the paradox of Jesus being rejected by *Jerusalem*. When Paul spoke of God's 'wrath' (1 Thess. 2:16), he may have associated this especially with Jerusalem—the cen tral 'heart' of Judea, and the place in which Paul himself (according to Acts 9:29) had experienced threats upon his own life.

It is important to remember that Paul writes these words as one who *himself* had been a persecutor of the church in Jerusalem and in Judea, and is writing about those amongst whom he too would have been numbered before his conversion. His own response to the gospel message had been wrong, so he believed, and would have led to *his* experiencing God's judgement. Therefore he could not have seen this 'wrath' as an 'irrevocable retribution',[73] since he himself had been rescued. The same could be true of anyone else—but only through 'Jesus, who rescues us from the coming wrath' (1:10). This earlier reference to the 'wrath' in store for *all* people (Jew and Gentile) makes it clear that the 'wrath' which he now associates with the 'Judeans' (2:16) is only a focused example of the general judgement awaiting the entire world.[74]

This is the closest Paul comes to expressing a belief that Jerusalem (as a result of its response to Jesus and his messengers) has laid itself open to judgement. Not surprisingly some of those who see these verses as an interpolation see them as referring *post-eventum* to the tragedy of AD 70. If they are Pauline, however, they may indicate Paul's prophetic understanding (influenced by pre-synoptic traditions?) that some such event was in store for Jerusalem. Paul could see where history was going.

> There is a bifurcation within the destiny of the Jews, as seen from a Pauline standpoint: either they must come the way of the cross, finding the new covenant, the Spirit and faith, or they will head down the road whose τέλος is AD 70. 1 Thessalonians 2:15ff then shows that Israel *as a whole* is heading on this latter course, rejecting the call of God to the new covenant.[75]

---

[72] The parallels with the synoptic material are noted by many; see *e.g.* Wanamaker (1990) 116. For the argument that this shows Pauline dependence on pre-Synoptic tradition, see *e.g.* Donfried (1984); D. Wenham (1995) 319-26. There are also echoes of the Gospels in his talking of 'heaping up their sins' and God's 'wrath' (*cf.* Matt. 23:32 and Luke 21:23).

[73] Bruce's words in (1982a) 48, countered in *e.g.* Marshall (1983) 82.

[74] *Cf.* above ch. 3, n.170 and below ch. 10.

[75] Wright (1991) 156, n. 61 (italics original). He continues helpfully: 'The Israel of 1 Thessalonians is the 'Israel in principle', which does not mean that individual Jews are as it were *automatically*, still less irrevocably, destined this way or that'.

Paul's precise wording in the final sentence is difficult. Although the past tense of the verb (ἔφθασεν) might refer back to the judgement associated with the Cross, it is more likely that it reflects a prophetic assurance about the future: 'divine wrath has drawn very near and will fall upon them once the measure of their sins is complete'.[76] This suggests that Paul saw Jerusalem as being under imminent threat of divine judgement. Is this right? If he had lived to witness the events of AD 70, would Paul have agreed with those of his fellow-Jews (such as the authors of 2 Baruch and 4 Ezra) who interpreted this event in terms of judgement? But, unlike them, had he seen it coming?

Certainly Paul would have rebuked any Gentiles who took such a tragedy as an excuse for triumphalism. His writing Romans 9-11 was designed precisely to 'nip in the bud' any such eventuality, warning Gentiles that the 'severity' God had shown to the unbelieving Jewish people might, if they were not careful, lead one day to *their* being 'cut off' (Rom. 11:22). If Paul had been prepared to see Jerusalem's fall as an act of judgement, he would clearly also have wanted to see it as a severe warning to *all people* of the 'wrath that is coming' (1 Thess. 1:10).[77]

Paul, however, also reveals his willingness to invoke the category of God's judgement. 'The wrath of God is revealed' (Rom. 1:18ff) against humankind, and the Jewish people are not exempt (2:1ff); indeed there will be 'distress' 'for the Jew first and also the Greek' (2:9). For Jews and Gentiles are alike 'under the power of sin' (3:9). In Romans 9-11 he speaks more precisely about contemporary Israel. Apart from the remnant of believing Israelites, Israel as a whole has 'stumbled' (9:32), 'fallen' (11:22), and been 'broken off' from God's people (11:17). Such language suggests that Paul viewed his fellow-Jews as experiencing God's judgement.

---

[76] Marshall (1983) 81. The past tense might also refer to some well-known recent past events which Paul saw as indicating what now awaited Jerusalem—for example, the expulsion of the Jews from Rome in AD 49 (so Bammel [1959]), or (more probably) the massacre at Passover during that same year of over 20,000 Jews in Jerusalem during the procuratorship of Cumanus (Josephus, *Ant.* 20:112; *War* 2:224-7): see Jewett (1970-71). Paul 'could well have seen in the recent actions of the Romans against the Jews the beginnings of the disasters predicted for the Jews and Jerusalem in the [apocalyptic] discourse': D. Wenham (1995) 322. In these events Paul saw a sign of the future. Such an understanding would then explain the 'present crisis' (ἀνάγκη) in 1 Cor. 7:26. The only other use of this word in this unusual sense is in Luke 21:23 which expressly refers to the fate of *Jerusalem*. The 'present crisis' might therefore reflect troubles in Jerusalem. If (from at least the time of 1 Thess. onwards) Paul was expecting a calamitous event in Jerusalem, news of any disturbances in Jerusalem might be taken as a sign that this event was imminent (*cf.* also Eph. 5:16, 'the days are evil').

[77] *Cf.* 2 Thess. 1:3-10, where Old Testament language of God's judgement upon Israel is now applied to all who 'do not obey the gospel'. Again Israel's judgement functions as a pre-cursor for the judgement of the world (*cf.* Rom. 2:9).

Was the 'hardening' that had come upon them (11:25) the sole sign of judgement? Or would God at some future point demonstrate the reality of this judgement in a more visible form? Would there be any indication of God's 'severity towards those who have fallen' (11:22)? Did Paul see himself as living in an era when God was showing his patience (*cf.* 9:22: μακροθυμία)—a window of opportunity, however, that would not last forever?[78]

It has been argued recently that this urgency was indeed part of Paul's message, and that he saw himself as a 'preacher of eschatological repentance to Israel'.[79] If so, regardless of his *ultimate* hope and belief in God's goodness to Israel (Rom. 11:25ff), he was a *proximate* pessimist concerning the imminent future of the Israel of his own day (Rom. 9-11:12).[80] Paul believed a great divide had appeared within God's people and that God had acted decisively towards the world in Christ. At some point in the near future God might act to demonstrate that this was so. Had he lived, Paul might not have been altogether surprised at what happened in Jerusalem a few years after his death.

Seen in this light, the passage in 1 Thessalonians makes sense and can be integrated into Paul's overall thought. Within its brief scope Paul does not reveal his passionate longing for his own people as he does in Romans 9-11 (this was not required by the context), but he does reveal his conviction that contemporary Israel is in a perilous place—which for Paul, as suggested, would have been focused in the future fate of Jerusalem. Again this is an early text in the Pauline corpus, revealing the radical break which had already occurred in Paul's thinking. Would this be changed in subsequent writings?

---

[78] Paul's earlier comments in Rom. 2:3-5 read quite differently if he was not speaking only in general terms but also had in mind a particular 'day of wrath'.

[79] Moessner (1988), citing in support Acts 13:40-46, 18:6, 28:25-28; *cf.* J. Taylor (1996).

[80] For those living before AD 70 Jerusalem's fate could not easily be separated from speculation about the *parousia*: would the two events coincide? An over-literal interpretation of 2 Thess. 2:4 might be taken as evidence that Paul at this stage connected the two events in his mind, and that only later were they separated, opening up the possibility of a brighter future for Israel in the period *after* this judgement. However, the references to the 'Temple' in 2. Thess. 2:4 can be taken as symbolic, (so Bruce [1982a] 169; Marshall [1983] 191-2), with Caligula's recent attempts to defile the Temple being taken as emblematic of the ultimate opposition to God. Wright (1994a) 64, argues quite differently that the phrase 'the day of the Lord (2 Thess. 2:2) refers not to the *parousia*, but to God's awaited judgement upon Jerusalem; this would explain both Paul's use of imagery that relates to the Temple and also why the Thessalonians might hear of this 'day' by 'letter' (hardly appropriate for the *parousia*!). This approach would need to explain why Paul begins 2 Thess. 2 by referring to the 'coming of our Lord Jesus Christ and our being gathered to him' (v. 1); for it would be natural to identify this with the subsequent reference to the 'day of the Lord'. Possibly Paul has brought together two distinct events (the judgement on Jerusalem and the *parousia*) in order to argue that the latter cannot take place until the former has occurred.

c) *Romans 11*

The letter to the Romans touches on the Jerusalem-issue at several points. Does it give evidence of Paul's attitude to Jerusalem becoming more positive?

Inasmuch as he was writing on the eve of his departure to Jerusalem (Rom. 15:25ff) it is quite possible that Jerusalem was not far from his thoughts as he composed it.[81] Though formally presenting his gospel to the Romans he might have seen how his arguments here could also serve as the basis for any defence of his ministry required in the coming months in Jerusalem. For example, his stating that he had a continuing passionate concern for ethnic Israel (Rom. 9:1-3; 10:1) would be important if he wished to allay any fears to the contrary in Jerusalem.[82] Even if Paul *was* giving a more well-rounded presentation, however, and correcting any false inferences drawn from his earlier statements, the tone of the letter is still one of careful rearticulation, rather than a recantation. He was not changing his tune for Jerusalem's consumption.

The argument that his 'collection' (Rom. 15:25ff) shows a more positive attitude to Jerusalem than previously is also too superficial. Even in Galatians Paul had declared his 'eagerness' to 'remember the poor' (2:10)—a phrase which was probably understood as a reference to the 'poor' of the Christian community in Jerusalem and Judea.[83] This text in Galatians makes it clear that Paul could have an open-hearted attitude towards the Jewish-Christian members of the Jerusalem church, even though he was critical of them in certain respects. This can also be detected in Romans. By the time Paul wrote Romans there is a possibility that Judaizers from Jerusalem had caused further unrest in Corinth (2 Cor. 10-11);[84] yet he was still committed to collecting funds for the Jerusalem church. Paul's attitude towards the Jerusalem church had not altered.

---

[81]   So Munck (1959) 300; Jervell and Stuhlmacher in Donfried (1991) 53-64, 236; Ziesler (1989) 11.

[82]Seen in this light it would be interesting to compare Galatians and Romans as documents which were both written before an *imminent visit to Jerusalem*; *cf.* Holmberg (1978) 55-6, and below n. 147. An important contrast, however, is that Galatians is written to prevent Jewish Christians from absorbing Gentile Christianity, whereas in Romans Paul is facing the opposite danger—a Gentile dismissal of Jewish-Christians.

[83]   See *e.g.* R.N. Longenecker (1990) 60, and further below at n. 117.

[84]   The identification of Paul's opponents in 2 Corinthians is notably complex. For their possible connection with Jerusalem, see Barrett (1971) and (1986) 29-30, 276; Bruce (1968) 15; Holmberg (1978) 46-7; *cf.* also Theissen (1982) 50; Martin (1986) 336ff, and Georgi (1986) 46. This is disputed, however, by *e.g.* Sumney (1990), Hill (1992) 158-73, and N. Taylor (1992) 214. Our presentation below would suggest that if they *were* connected with Jerusalem, they were representative of the position neither of Peter nor of James (*cf.* n. 110).

Despite its more eirenic tone, Romans proves on closer inspection to be anything but a recantation. The critique of circumcision and of the food laws is maintained,[85] and after the description of paganism in the first chapter (1:18ff) there is a sustained critique of Judaism's 'national righteousness' (esp. Rom. 2-4). As just noted, Paul states plainly in Romans 9-11 that contemporary Israel is currently under God's judgement—perhaps with some particular manifestation of that judgement being imminent.[86] Yet, throughout this section (and this is a note that perhaps *was* insufficiently sounded in his previous letters) Paul is anxious that his own love for Israel be understood; the door of his heart was always open. He was also concerned that the increasing numbers of Gentiles (especially when they heard a Jewish apostle talking about his own race in terms of judgement) should not fall into any form of triumphalism.[87] If there was to be 'distress' 'first for the Jew', it would be 'for the Gentile' as well (Rom. 2:9).

All this needs to be borne in mind when reading the key passage relating to this theme:

> Brothers and sisters, I want you to understand this mystery: a hardening has come upon part of Israel, until the full number of the Gentiles has come in. And so (καὶ οὕτως) all Israel will be saved, as it is written: 'Out of Zion will come the Deliverer; he will banish ungodliness from Jacob. And this is my covenant with them when (ὅταν) I take away their sins' (Rom. 11:25-27).

It is a passage which has raised countless questions. For example, what precisely does Paul mean by 'all Israel'[88] and by his use of οὕτως?[89] Was Paul thinking of a mass conversion of Jewish people to Christ at the time of his second coming? For our purposes the important questions focus more narrowly on Paul's reference to 'Zion' in the middle of his conflated quotation from the

---

[85] On circumcision, see Rom. 2:25ff in the light of the whole of ch. 2-3; concerning food, see the discussion in Rom. 14, which whilst applicable to wider issues certainly embraces the narrower question of Jewish food laws (esp. v.14).

[86] Paul's strategy in writing Romans and planning his missionary work in Spain (Rom. 15:24) might then have been motivated by an urgent awareness of Jerusalem's forthcoming fate and the need to plant as many Jew-cum-Gentile congregations as possible before that cataclysmic event: see Wright (1994a) 64-5 (quoted below at n. 168). This does not deny that Paul might also have seen Romans as a provisional 'last will and testament' (*cf.* Bornkamm in Donfried [1991] 27)—in case he did not leave Jerusalem alive.

[87] On the dangers of anti-Semitism in Rome, and the possible vulnerability of *Jewish*-Christians returning to Rome after their expulsion from the city (in AD 49), see *e.g.* Wievel in Donfried (1991) 92-101. This need for Christian humility before God's judgement *had* been present in, for example, his warning the Corinthians to avoid the Israelites' fate under Moses (1 Cor. 10:1-13) and to see their present condition as partly a result of God's judgement upon *them* for their abuse of the eucharist (1 Cor. 11:30). To be the new 'people of God' meant they inherited the Old Testament judgements as well as its blessings.

Old Testament. Is this a reference to the physical Jerusalem, or does it now refer to the 'heavenly' Zion/Jerusalem?[90] Is the event predicted in the Old Testament still future to Paul, or has it already begun to take place? Thirdly, why has Paul not retained the original wording of Isaiah 59:20 (which in the Masoretic text had read, 'the Deliverer will come *to* Zion')? Finally, did Paul believe that Jerusalem would play a central role in God's *ultimate* future, perhaps at the time of the *parousia*? Did he believe that Jerusalem was to be the 'place from which the crowning phase of the salvation of mankind would be displayed'?[91]

The following points need to be noted to answer these questions.

i) Paul's Understanding of 'Zion'

Are there any indications from Paul's writings elsewhere as to how he understood the theme of 'Zion' in the Old Testament scriptures? Given that his only other reference to 'Zion' comes in Rom. 9:33 (when quoting Isa. 28:26), it might be thought initially that this was a part of Old Testament theology upon which Paul had seldom reflected. Many of Paul's quotations from the Old Testament, however, are verses which in their original context were very much involved with Zion/Jerusalem—even if the actual verses he quotes fail to mention 'Zion' explicitly. Attention to this wider context reveals more than might have appeared possible at first sight.

The Old Testament book which Paul cites most often is Isaiah, the prophetic book which in its three sections is held together by the theme of Jerusalem—judged (1-39), redeemed (40-55) and glorified (56-66). He quotes much from First Isaiah[92], but also, more significantly for the purposes of this study, from Second Isaiah. In 2 Corinthians 6 he quotes it twice:[93]

---

[88]   Against Wright (1991) 251, it is more natural to take 'Israel' and 'Jacob' in an ethnically restricted sense and not as a reference to the Church, including Gentiles: so *e.g.* Watson (1986) 229, n. 38; Dahl (1977) 138. Thus Paul *is* focused in these verses on the question of ethnic Israel and is not polemically redefining 'Israel' to include Gentiles—though it is likely he *did* do so in Gal. 6:16, following R.N. Longenecker (1990) 299, and George (1994) 440; *contra* Dunn (1993a) 345, and P. Richardson (1969) 82ff. 'All Israel' will be saved, not in the sense of 'all without remainder', but all those whom God intends—including many who currently have been 'broken off' from the vine. *Cf.* B. Longenecker (1989) 97: 'Paul draws out the disparate courses of two groups, believing and unbelieving, within ethnic Israel. By the inclusive 'all' in 11:26, he joins both groups together. He has in mind an ethnic group whose members at present are schismatically divided'.

[89]   It is far more likely to be modal ('in this way'), rather than temporal ('in the end')? *Cf.* B. Longenecker (1989) 118, n. 35.

[90]   As suggested in *e.g.* Dunn (1988) 682; Davies (1974) 197; Cranfield (1985) 283.

[91]   As claimed by Bruce (1968) 25. *Cf.* his comments in Donfried (1991) 190: 'Jerusalem would be the scene of the [gospel's] consummation'.

> At an acceptable time I have listened to you, and on a day of salvation I have
> helped you (Isa. 49:8, in v. 2). . . . Therefore come out from them . . . (Isa.
> 52:11 in v. 17).

In Isaiah the former of these two verses had continued by defining 'the day of
salvation' as the time when God would 'restore the land'; Zion would no longer be 'forsaken' (49:14ff), and the Gentiles would help to bring God's people
to the land (49:22ff).[94] Similarly, Paul's second quotation is from a passage
where God tells his people to 'depart' from Babylon (Isa. 52:11), because the
exile is over and the Lord 'has redeemed Jerusalem' (52:9); as a result, 'all the
ends of the earth shall see the salvation of our God' (52:10). Paul applied these
prophecies without explanation to the Corinthians!

He could only do so with integrity if he believed these prophecies *had
now been fulfilled*. This universal salvation 'before the eyes of all nations'
(Isa. 52:10) *had* now come to pass; 'Jerusalem' therefore had been 'redeemed'—in the sense that the exile which had *partly* ended in the time of
Isaiah had now been *fully* brought to an end in the work of Jesus.[95]

In keeping with this is the section in Romans 10 where he again quoted
from Isaiah 52 (v. 7 in Rom. 10:15), thereby identifying the Christian 'good
news' (εὐαγγέλιον) with the 'good news' proclaimed by Isaiah of the exile's
end.[96] In 10:13 he had also quoted part of Joel 2:32 which in its entirety reads:
'Then everyone who calls on the name of the Lord shall be saved; for *in Mount
Zion and in Jerusalem* there shall be those who escape'.[97]

In all these instances Paul was taking verses which originally had spoken of a specific work of God in and for Jerusalem and was applying them to
God's work in the gospel.[98] He believed that God's act in Christ was a fulfilment of these Zion-prophecies; it was something which had been accom-

---

[92] Isa. 22:3 (1 Cor. 15:32); 25:8 (1 Cor. 15:54); 28:16 (Rom. 9:33; *cf.* Eph. 2:20); 29:14
(1 Cor. 19). The last of these is especially interesting, since it occurs in an oracle expressly
delivered against Jerusalem.

[93] Paul also quotes this section of Isaiah in 1 Cor. 2:16 (Isa. 40:13). On the question of the
authenticity of 2 Cor. 6:14-7:1, see the discussion in Martin (1986) 191-6.

[94] The theme of 'restoration' also appears two verses earlier in Isa. 49:6, which (as argued
above in ch. 3) was an important verse for Luke and probably for Paul (see Acts 13:47).

[95] See further below at n. 122.

[96] *Cf.* above n. 19.

[97] Note the parallels here between Paul and Luke (in Acts 2:16-40); see above ch. 3 (3c).

[98] His allusion in 1 Cor. 15:54 to Isa. 25:7-8 is of a piece with this. In Isaiah God would
'swallow up death for ever' '*on this mountain*', but this Jerusalem-reference is omitted by
Paul. From this bare quotation Paul's readers could not be expected (by a process of inter-
textual understanding and *metalepsis*) to deduce this Zion-theology: see the discussion of
Hays (1989) in Evans and Sanders (1993). Paul *himself*, however, must have been through
this process in order that he could use these quotations in this transformed way.

plished on Zion's behalf, and it was only therefore appropriate that the Cross and resurrection had taken place in Jerusalem.[99]

This sheds light on Paul's reference to 'Zion' in Romans 9:

> They have stumbled over the 'stumbling-stone', as it is written, 'See, I am laying in Zion a stone that will make people to stumble, a rock that will make them fall, and whoever believes in him will not be put to shame (9:32-33, conflating Isa. 28:6 and 8:14).

From the context it is clear that Paul is seeking to explain the 'stumbling' that had occurred in his own generation in the response of his fellow-Jews to the gospel: the 'stone' is Jesus, whilst God's act of 'laying in Zion' refers to his sending Jesus to Israel, but especially to Zion/Jerusalem, the very heart of Israel's life.[100]

Paul saw Jesus' historic involvement with Zion/Jerusalem as very significant. Not only had he accomplished there the 'redemption' of Zion; his ministry in the city had also been used by God to bring Israel to a crucial and decisive moment in her national and spiritual life. The events associated with Jesus could not have taken place elsewhere.[101]

This analysis of Paul's understanding of the Zion-theme in the scriptures proves valuable when we approach the key verses in Romans 11:26. In keeping with this earlier usage of 'Zion' (Rom. 9:33), there is an increased likelihood that 'Zion' is associated in Paul's mind, not with some future event, but chiefly with Jesus' recent work accomplished in Zion/Jerusalem.

ii) Isaiah's Prophecy

At first glance, this appears unlikely. Paul seems to be looking towards some future event; the wording of the prophecy in Isaiah is in the future ('out of Zion *will* come the Deliverer'). But the important question is this: future to whom? What was future to Isaiah might now be in the past for Paul.

Paul took this prophecy as referring to Christ's first coming. Although this event lay in the recent past, he quoted Isaiah's words with their original future tense. This was not unreasonable; indeed if Paul was wanting to quote

---

[99] If God had fulfilled these prophecies in a surprising way, this also called into question whether any more overtly political 'redemption' of Jerusalem could now be expected. Paul does not develop this in Romans. Borg (1972-3), however, suggests that this background of Jewish political nationalism may explain Paul's emphasis (Rom. 13:1-7) on Christians being seen to be submissive to the state.

[100] Paul clearly interprets the 'stone' christologically as a reference to Jesus: see Dunn (1988) 584-5.

[101] *Cf.* again Rom. 15:8: only by becoming a 'servant of the circumcised' could Jesus confirm 'the truth of God' and his 'promises'.

an Old Testament prophecy concerning Christ's first coming, how else might he have done so? Isaiah had predicted that 'a Deliverer will come'; so Paul retains the prophet's syntax, in order to show that this had now been fulfilled. The first part of the quotation can thus refer quite plausibly to the incarnation ('the Deliverer will come') and to the consequent going out of the gospel ('from Zion'). 'Paul understands the future tense of the Isaiah prophecy as fulfilled in the first coming of Christ'.[102]

Paul's reason for quoting this verse is to indicate that when the Deliverer finally comes (and he now has), the sure result of that coming will be his turning 'godlessness away from Jacob'. In other words, the promise which Paul looks forward to being fulfilled does not lie in the first half of the quotation, but in the second: because he believes that Jesus was truly the Deliverer sent by God (v. 26b) he has faith that the divinely intended consequences will follow: 'he *will* banish ungodliness from Jacob' (v. 26c). In this way (οὕτως) 'all Israel will be saved' (v. 26a). Paul is not predicting a 'large-scale, last-minute salvation of Jews' but speaking of an ongoing process which has now begun through the gospel.[103]

Paul's replacing '*to* Zion' with '*out of* Zion' also makes sense according to this interpretation. Even on other interpretations, this word-change has been noted to be Paul's way of playing down the role of Jerusalem.[104] This proves to be the case. If 'Zion' refers here to the city visited by Jesus, Paul would clearly not be wishing to deny that Jesus as the Deliverer had come *to* Zion. Nevertheless, his own preference was to focus on what happened next—the out-going effects of this gospel *from* Zion.

The phrase 'out of Zion' may have been inspired by Old Testament passages such as the prayer in the psalms that 'salvation for Israel would come

[102] Holwerda (1995) 173; *cf.* Motyer (1989) 154; Wright (1991) 250 and (1994) 66.
[103] 'So Wright (1991) 251; *cf.* also Holwerda (1995) 172-5. When Paul referred to the covenant' (Isa. 59:21, Jer. 31:33-4) he was speaking of something which he believed *had already come into existence* for believers in Christ. Secondly, the word translated 'when' (ὅταν) might equally be translated 'when*ever*', indicating an ongoing process, not a once-off dramatic event. Thirdly, according to the more probable Greek text, v. 31 should be translated 'that they too may *now* receive mercy', indicating a present, not a future event. Finally, Paul's conviction that 'jealousy' will provoke Israel's response sits uneasily with the notion of an end-time event. On this view Paul was looking forward to his fellow-Jews finding their Messiah throughout history as a result of the message of that Messiah coming out 'from Zion'.
[104] See *e.g.* Davies (1974) 198. *Cf.* Dunn (1988) 682: 'he does not wish to rekindle the idea of Israel's national primacy in the last days; he is in process of transforming—not merely taking up—the expectation of an eschatological pilgrimage of Gentiles to Zion'. Paul will probably have been influenced by the LXX, which offered a mediating position between these two readings (namely, ἕνεκεν: 'for the sake of'). Stanley (1992) 166-168, argues that the substitution had already occurred in Paul's *Vorlage*.

out of Zion' (Pss. 14:7; 53:6)[105] or, more probably, the prophecy at the outset of Isaiah, that 'out of Zion shall go forth instruction' (Isa. 2:3).[106] As this verse is often thought to have inspired Paul's own evangelistic ministry,[107] it would not be surprising if it was influential here, for it was through the spread of the gospel and the 'word of the Lord' going forth 'from Jerusalem' that the Deliverer had effectively come forth 'out of Zion'. Not least because he had already spoken of Jesus' coming *to* 'Zion' (Rom. 9:33), it was now entirely appropriate for him to note the consequences of that coming for those far removed *from* Zion.

The making of this substitution is significant. It reveals Paul's conviction that Zion's principal role in God's economy was that of being the channel of divine blessing to the nations. The over-riding dynamic was to be 'centrifugal' ('out of Zion') not centripetal ('to Zion'). Although in the gospel God had acted specifically in Zion and for Zion, through the resurrection and the gift of the Spirit he had now unleashed Zion's potential to be the place from which the 'word of the Lord' could 'go forth'. Paul saw himself as an agent in the 'ingathering of the Gentiles'; this was taking place, not in the Gentiles' going to Jerusalem but rather in the gospel's coming out to them. Paul's own focus was not so much on what Zion might continue to be in the future but rather on what God had done there in the recent past in order to move his purposes forward onto a world-wide canvas.

iii) Conclusion

As a result, this much-examined verse does not readily support the idea that Paul believed Zion/Jerusalem would play a pivotal and central role in God's future purposes.

> The reference to 'Zion' has nothing to do with a renewed physical Jerusalem; rather, it picks up the Zion-tradition according to which Zion was to be the source of blessing for the world, and claims that this has now come true in Jesus.[108]

> Neither Jerusalem nor the Temple located there retained in the thought of Paul any significance in the realization of God's eschatological promises.[109]

---

[105] So Bruce (1968) 21 and in Donfried (1991) 190.

[106] See *e.g.* Wright (1991) 251.

[107] This verse possibly underlies both 1 Cor. 14:36 ('did the word of God originate with you'?) and Rom. 15:19 ('from Jerusalem and as far round as Illyricum I have fully proclaimed the good news of Christ'): Bruce (1968) 3 and in Donfried (1991) 189-90; Gerhardsson (1961) 214, 274, and Bauckham (1995a) 426. This would confirm the importance to Paul of Jerusalem being the appropriate 'source' of the gospel; *cf.* above ch. 3 (3a).

[108] Wright (1994a) 64; *contra e.g.* Horbury (1996) 220.

This coheres with our earlier findings. He looked back to what God had done for Israel and the world in Christ, and prayed that his fellow-Jews would come to experience this salvation.

Despite its dangers Paul did not hold back from using the category of judgement in relation to Israel. Nor did his love for Israel cause him to compromise his essential convictions about the radical changes with which Israel now had to come to terms. Despite his love for his fellow-Jews and the strength of his own Jewish presuppositions he did not relax his contention that circumcision, the food laws, Jewish 'national righteousness' *and the role of Jerusalem* all needed to be seen quite differently in the light of Christ's coming. To renege on these issues would naturally have been far easier if he was seeking a peaceful *rapprochement* with non-Christian Judaism, but Romans suggests that this was far from his purpose, and that he *was* concerned to outline a completely new basis on which the members of the 'people of God' should orientate their lives—a basis which, he claimed, was a true fulfilment of that which had been operative in the time before Christ.

Concerning Jerusalem this meant that the new 'people of God' were forever to acknowledge their debt to 'Zion'—the focus of Israel's life, the place where the Messiah had for their sakes died and been raised, the place from which the gospel had gone forth; they were not, however, to depend on it in the present or build their hopes on it for the future. Even in far-away Rome they could 'rejoice in the hope of the glory of God' (5:2) and in the mean-time offer the all-important 'worship' (λατρεία) through the offering of their whole selves to God (12:1). One of the glories of the gospel was precisely that they no longer needed to go 'to Zion'; instead 'the Deliverer' had come forth 'out of Zion' to them (11:26). Christ had enabled Jerusalem to fulfil its long-awaited role. Its role for the future would inevitably be quite different.

---

[109] Chance (1988) 24. If, contrary to the present argument, Rom. 11:25ff. is taken as referring to the *parousia*, Paul may still have understood 'Zion' as a reference to the heavenly Jerusalem. R.N. Longenecker (1990) 214, describes this as an 'established Christian tradition' (*cf. e.g.* the use of Ps. 68:18 in Eph. 4:8). Only when this possibility has been excluded could one conclude that this was a reference to Jerusalem in the future. Our interpretation has the advantage of showing Paul's eschatology to be more uniform, for elsewhere his thought is marked by a consistent 'universal' emphasis. Apart from 2 Thess. 2:4 (see above n. 80), Paul nowhere links the *parousia* with Jerusalem; instead Christ's coming will be 'from heaven' (1 Thess. 1:10; 4:16; 2 Thess. 1:7; Phil. 3:20; *cf.* also Col. 3:4). If, as argued by *e.g.* Wanamaker (1990) 2 Thess. chronologically preceded 1 Thess., then Paul's universal emphasis in 1. Thess. might be his way of correcting any misunderstanding of his words in 2 Thess. 2:4. They had been meant symbolically, but the Thessalonians had taken them literally and, because of their geographical distance from Jerusalem, had feared that they (and those who had died) would miss out on that great event. Paul then writes 1 Thess. 4-5 to assure them that none of Christ's people (alive or dead) will miss out on that day.

4. Paul and the Jerusalem Church

This new approach to Jerusalem would naturally set Paul at odds with some of his fellow Jewish Christians, not least those living in or near Jerusalem itself, for whom the city continued to exert its appeal. The final part of this enquiry must examine the relationship between Paul and the Jerusalem church.

This is a topic which has raised many questions, both historical and theological, which cannot be discussed in detail.[110] Our focus will be on the single question: do Paul's statements and actions in relation to the Jerusalem church confirm our argument about Paul's underlying, critical attitude towards the physical city of Jerusalem itself?

Scholars working in the 'Tübingen' tradition following Baur in the last century have tended to maximize the contrast between Paul and the Jerusalem church, portraying Paul as 'held back' by Jerusalem. Such a view would naturally be favourable to the suggestion that Paul was critical of 'Jerusalem' itself. There has, however, been an understandable and necessary reaction to this interpretation. Munck has argued that Paul and the Jerusalem church were in agreement on all matters except their understanding of the strategic order of appropriate mission (should the Gentiles be evangelized in advance of the people of Israel?).[111] In keeping with this, Munck emphasized Paul's unaltered commitment to the priority of Jerusalem in God's purposes. Beneath the question of Paul's relationship with the Jerusalem church there lurks our own question about his attitude towards the city itself.

---

[110] For a useful discussion, see *e.g* R.N. Longenecker (1964) 211-29, 271-88. That the Judaizers did not come to Paul's churches with the full backing of James, but were acting *ultra vires*, see *e.g.* N. Taylor (1992) 173, Bauckham (1995a) 471. On the essential unity of Paul and James, see *e.g.* Schmithals (1965), Gaston (1984) 64, 72; Howard (1979) 80-81; Hill (1992) 183-191; *contra* Goulder (1994). Bauckham (1995a) argues that the differences between Paul and James are often over-stated, and that even the 'right-wing' of the church may have approved of Paul's Gentile mission, only being concerned that *Jewish* Christians should observe the Law. Although for simplicity reference is made in the following to the 'Jerusalem church', in reality there may have been a federation of house groups with a wide variety of opinions. J.J. Scott (1975) distinguishes between 'moderate Hebrew Christians' and 'Pharisaic Hebrew Christians', arguing that James belonged to the former, Paul's opponents to the latter: it then becomes 'quite understandable how Paul might have been accepted by and maintained good relations with one group and at the same time been bitterly opposed by another segment of the same church' (p. 226).

[111] Munck (1959). In the light of our discussion about Isa. 49 (above n. 94) it might be more accurate to say that Paul and the Jerusalem church agreed about the proper order of salvation (Israel's restoration, followed by the ingathering of the Gentiles), but disagreed as to whether one could legitimately claim that Israel had already been 'restored' in Jesus.

a) *The 'Collection'*

Much of the debate turns on the interpretation of Paul's 'collection' of money for the Jerusalem church (Rom 15:25ff; 1 Cor. 16:1-4; 2 Cor. 8-9). This was clearly more than just a begrudging act of compliance with a dictate from an imperious mother-church;[112] but, going to the other extreme, can it be taken as indicating his whole-hearted endorsement of a 'Zion-theology'?[113]

Some argue that Paul believed his personal visit to Jerusalem would kick into action the process whereby Israel, envious of the Gentiles' Christian experience, would be moved towards faith in Jesus as their Messiah.[114] Even if this 'provocative' purpose to the collection be denied, Paul may still have seen it in a prophetic light, pointing to the truth that the 'ingathering of the Gentiles to Zion' (Isa. 66:19-21) had been inaugurated; the 'wealth of the nations' was pouring into Jerusalem (*cf.* Isa. 45:14; 60:5-17; Mic. 4:13).[115]

These ideas are worth exploring, but there is no clear evidence within Paul's own statements that he was thinking in such terms.[116] What he does say is found chiefly in Romans 15:

> At present, however, I am going to Jerusalem in a ministry to the saints; for Macedonia and Achaia have been pleased to share their resources with the poor among the saints at Jerusalem. They were pleased to do this, and indeed they owe it to them.; for if the Gentiles have come to share in their spiritual blessings, they ought also to be of service to them in material things. So when I have completed this, and have delivered to them what has been collected, I will set out by way of you to Spain. (Rom. 15:25-8).

---

[112] There is nothing in Paul's letters to indicate that this was a binding requirement made upon him; it was a 'generous gift' (2 Cor. 8:20). So Georgi (1992) 49ff, Davies (1974) 199, Cranfield (1985) 371, R.N. Longenecker (1964) 228; *contra* Holl (1928) and W.L. Knox (1925) 298. Bruce (1968) 10, suggests that, although *Paul* saw it as voluntary, the Jerusalem church may have seen it as a fitting 'tribute'.

[113] Davies (1974) 202, summarizes Munck's view that for Paul Jerusalem was the 'centre of the world', and that 'the geographic centre of Jewish eschatology remained significant for him'.

[114] *E.g.* Munck himself in (1959) 303; P. Richardson (1969) 202; Dahl (1977) 157; Aus (1979b) 24; Martin (1986) 258; Hill (1992) 177. 'As an instrumental event, intended to prod the unbelieving Jews to profess faith in Christ, Paul's project was a crushing failure': Nickle (1966) 138. Davies (1974) 202, helpfully points out that this view of Paul's failure to bring about an eschatological event, is directly parallel to Schweitzer's presentation of Jesus, who likewise went to Jerusalem to force God's hand and without success.

[115] See *e.g.* Bruce (1968) 22ff.

[116] The presentation in Nickle (1966) 140, and Aus (1979b) of Paul deliberately concealing this eschatological significance is unconvincing, and suggests Paul used the Corinthians as pawns within his own secret purposes.

Paul's first concern is at the physical level, that the Jerusalem 'saints' who were financially 'poor'[117] should benefit from Paul's converts. This is also made clear in 2 Corinthians where his focus is almost entirely on material issues, concerning the nature of Christian giving and the importance that there should be material 'equality' between the different parts of the Church (8:13). If in addition to this very pragmatic concern, the collection also served a symbolic function, then Romans 15 suggests that this resided in the notion of Gentiles showing their indebtedness for what they had received from Jerusalem.

As in the references to 'Zion' in Romans 9 and 11, the focus is not forwards, but backwards. Paul is not motivated by some scheme in which Zion will play a key role in the future, but rather by the desire that his Gentile converts should acknowledge the great blessings they have received in the gospel's having come to them 'from Zion'. It is an appropriate way of saying 'thank-you' for God's 'indescribable gift' (2 Cor. 9:15). Paul's desire is that this theme of 'thanksgiving' should then be reciprocated by the Christians in Jerusalem (2 Cor. 9:12) as they witness this token of the Gentiles' 'service'.

The primary purpose of the collection was therefore 'ecumenical'. It was a gesture designed to ensure peace and good-will between two strands in the Church that potentially could fall apart; it demonstrated the fundamental unity of Jew and Gentile in Christ, and sought to instil within Gentile believers a sense of their debt to their Jewish brothers and sisters. The gospel had come out to the Gentiles from Jerusalem; the collection now 'symbolized the complementary movement back to the centre'.[118]

The more 'eschatological' interpretation (that it was designed to provoke a reaction from Jews in Jerusalem) not only seems far-fetched, but goes beyond the evidence. Despite the impression of some translations,[119] Paul's

---

[117] It matters little whether the Jerusalem church saw themselves as the 'poor' in a more eschatological sense as well (see esp. Holl [1928] but countered by Keck [1965]). Clearly Paul was convinced that they were financially poor and it was on this basis alone that he sought to persuade his congregations to be generous towards them. Paul's use of the word 'saints' may reflect some deference to the idea that the Jerusalem Christians were the original 'saints' (as Bruce [1968] 4), but clearly his usage elsewhere shows that he believes his Gentile converts are equally worthy of this title (see *e.g.*1 Cor. 1:2; 2 Cor. 1:1; Phil. 1:1; *cf.* Eph. 1:1, 15, 18, etc). Paul's description of Peter, James and John as 'pillars' (Gal. 2:9) probably reflects some of the self-perception of the Jerusalem church, but the context suggests Paul might not himself have favoured this kind of terminology. For different explanations of this phraseology, see Barrett (1953), Aus (1979a), Wenham and Moses (1994), Bauckham (1995a) 441-50.

[118] Bauckham (1995a) 426.

[119] The NIV inserts the 'Jews' twice into v. 27. The NRSV rightly understands those who shared their 'spiritual blessings' as the 'saints in Jerusalem' (v. 26). Any Gentile debt to Judaism in general was focused through support of the Jewish-*Christians* in Jerusalem.

focus was entirely on the church in Jerusalem (the 'saints') and not on the majority Jewish population of Jerusalem. This was strictly an 'in-house' affair.

In part this eschatological schema is thought likely on the basis of the interpretation of Romans 11:25-26 that has been rejected above (that there would be a mass conversion of Jewish people when Jesus appeared 'from Zion' at the time of the *parousia*). Even if that alternative interpretation were granted, Paul does not make this link explicit.[120] Moreover, the tone of Romans 15, with its urgent request for prayer support, is far more pessimistic; if there were any hopes for Jerusalem contained in Romans 11, they were certainly not for the immediate future. What is more credible is that Paul wanted his 'service' in Jerusalem to be seen as a practical example of the grateful attitude which he hoped the Roman Christians would have towards their Jewish origins—precisely his concern in Romans 9-11. Since Christ had himself 'become a servant of the circumcised' (Rom. 15:8), it was fitting for his followers to have a similar attitude. As he said to the Corinthians (2 Cor. 8:9), they would be acknowledging how they had 'become rich' through the 'grace of the Lord Jesus Christ' who for their sakes 'had become poor' in Jerusalem.

Nevertheless, the more nuanced suggestion—that the collection might have been connected in Paul's mind with the scriptural theme of the 'ingathering of the Gentiles', even if it did not have a provocative purpose—remains attractive. Though Paul nowhere makes this explicit, the one who saw himself as a 'minister to the Gentiles' (Rom. 15:8) would almost of necessity have had to reflect on how this ministry conformed to God's purposes revealed in the Old Testament. The theme found there of the Gentiles 'ingathering' would come to the fore as a important explanation of what was occurring through his own preaching of the gospel.[121] To take to Jerusalem some Gentile converts (albeit only a handful, but bearing gifts from much larger Gentile churches) could hardly fail to make the point that this prophesied 'ingathering' had now begun to materialize. Paul's Gentile mission was a fulfilment of this scriptural hope, and his Gentile companions were a token testimony to its success.

The important point is precisely that the manner of fulfilment was contrary to that expected.[122] The Gentiles had not been 'ingathered' physically to a restored Jerusalem. The arrival of Paul's six companions only pointed to the fact that the overwhelming majority of Gentiles had *not* come to Jerusalem! The gospel had gone out *to them* 'from Zion', and the 'restoration' had been accomplished through the death and resurrection of Israel's Messiah. If Paul's

---

[120] The more extreme interpretations whereby Paul saw his Jerusalem visit as ushering in the *parousia* (on this view, outlined in Rom. 11:25 ff) read a little strangely in the light of Paul's plans to visit Spain after Jerusalem and Rome (Rom. 15:23-24): Davies (1974) 202.

[121] *Cf.* above n. 94 on the influence of Isa. 49 on Paul's thought.

[122] See above n. 95 and Dunn's quotation in n. 104.

collection signified anything about Jerusalem, it was this startling paradox that, without its being aware, the longed-for restoration had already occurred in Jesus, resulting in Gentiles being able to experience salvation.

> Paul made an audacious alteration in the prevalent Jewish conception of the eschatological role of Jerusalem. The Gentile Christians . . . were coming to proclaim the salvation of God instead of to receive salvation through the mediation of Israel.[123]

This act of pragmatic support clearly had deeper symbolic functions. It spoke of the importance of unity between Jewish and Gentile Christians, and it witnessed to God's activity through the gospel. To claim, however, that it spoke of Jerusalem's future importance would be to claim too much. It spoke only of what God had already done in Jerusalem for the sake of the world.

b) Paul's Attitude to the Jerusalem Church

These passages relating to the collection reveal that Paul bore no malice towards the members of the Jerusalem church. The very fact that he saw the collection as so important, however, might be taken as an indication that such a gesture was required, and that some in the Jerusalem church may have doubted his good-will. Moreover, if some of their number are to be identified with the 'Judaizers' who had interfered with Paul's congregations in Galatia,[124] then the Jerusalem church would know that the actions of its own members might have provoked Paul into an attitude of hostility towards them. If those who were now troubling the Corinthian church (one of the very congregations from whom he was gathering funds for Jerusalem) also had some connection with Jerusalem,[125] the fact that Paul carries through with this project would have to be seen as a sign of a magnanimous and generous spirit.

Yet does it show more? Did Paul's persistence in seeking to bless the Jerusalem church stem from a conviction that the Jerusalem church possessed a special status as the 'mother-church'? At a practical level, the Jerusalem church was undeniably the original church, and it made sense that it should hold a certain sway in ecclesiastical matters. Would Paul have gone further and ascribed to the Jerusalem church not just a pragmatic pre-eminence, but also a theological one—based not on its proximity to the original gospel

---

[123] Nickle (1966) 139; cf. Beagley (1987) 174, and Wright (1992b) 207 (quoted below in ch. 9, at n. 9).

[124] See above at n. 54.

[125] See above at n. 84.

events, but on the continuing centrality of Jerusalem in the new Christian era? If the Jerusalem church understood its special significance as deriving from the fact that it was *in Jerusalem*, would Paul have agreed with them?

The only place where Paul deals explicitly with his attitude to the Jerusalem church and its leaders is in Galatians (chs. 1-2). One puzzling feature is often noted: the way in which Paul values his good standing with the leaders in Jerusalem whilst at the same time asserting that his message and apostleship were ultimately independent.[126] In all likelihood this is caused by the nature of the Judaizers' criticism to which he is responding: Paul, they were saying, should in principle have seen himself as an emissary of the Jerusalem church and under the authority of the apostles located in Jerusalem, but he was preaching an incomplete gospel because of his scanty connections with Jerusalem.[127] Against this charge of official dependence but practical independence, Paul retorts that the truth is quite the opposite. His gospel ministry is ultimately and 'officially' independent of Jerusalem, inasmuch as he was commissioned by God himself. On the other hand, from a practical point of view it was necessary for him to show a proper deference to Jerusalem: it was only sensible to have consulted with Peter and to keep in good standing with this important church (1:18, 2:2).

Paul was ascribing to the Jerusalem church a pragmatic role, but denying it a theological one. He acknowledged that on the human level there was great value in his being in good standing with Christians in Jerusalem; if they had denied the validity of Paul's gospel, then his subsequent ministry would have been hampered and he would have been 'running in vain' (2:2). On the other hand, simply because of its location and its founding prestige, the Jerusalem church did not have the right to deny the authenticity of his commissioning by Christ. His gospel did not come from Jerusalem but rather from Christ himself; Jesus, not Jerusalem, was the ultimate authority.[128]

Given the deft balance which was needed for the cogency of his argument, Paul might well have found this distinction useful—seeing the significance of the Jerusalem church as pragmatic, but not theological. Paul would then have denied that it had its authority because of its location in Jerusalem; for the underlying assumption of such a view was that Jerusalem itself re-

---

[126] See *e.g.* Bruce (1968) 4; Holmberg (1978) 55-6; Dunn (1982); N. Taylor (1992) 155ff.

[127] See above 3a. Holmberg (1978) 55, writes concerning Paul's conversion near Damascus (rather than in Jerusalem): 'for this monstrous begetting he paid the price all his life long'. Bornkamm (1974) similarly notes that Damascus lies between Jerusalem and Antioch 'not only in a geographical but also in a deeply symbolical sense'. N. Taylor (1992) 67-85, notes Paul's non-integration with church life in Jerusalem.

[128] See Bruce (1968) 9, noting how the Jerusalem church recognized Paul's ministry, but did not confer on him the right to exercise it.

tained a special theological significance. This was precisely what he denied: 'the present Jerusalem' was 'in slavery' (4:25). The fact that this clear statement appears two chapters later is no coincidence; for Paul's argument for his independence from the Jerusalem church (chs.1-2) was integrally connected to his critique of Jerusalem itself (4:25). If Paul had retained a 'Zion-theology', this would have undermined his own argument, for it could then be argued that he should be subservient to, not independent of, Jerusalem. His blunt words in chapter 4 make it plain that this was not Paul's position.

Was this Paul's final and settled opinion on the matter? According to the dating favoured here, Paul subsequently received the endorsement of the Jerusalem church at the Apostolic Council (Acts 15); might he not then have changed his tune? The fact that Paul continues to show his independence from Jerusalem (*e.g.* by not using the Apostolic Decree as an authoritative starting-point in his debates about 'food offered to idols' in 1 Cor. 8-10),[129] and also that he may have continued to experience interference from people claiming some association with the Jerusalem church (2 Cor. 10-11), makes it most unlikely that Paul would ever have resorted to a simplistic affirmation of the Jerusalem church on the basis of the city's significance.

Paul's refusal to make this affirmation may have been one of the bones of contention between himself and some in the Jerusalem church who appealed to Jerusalem's role as a 'mother-city' in support of their claim to ecclesiastical authority; yet this was precisely what Paul denied. From the time of Galatians onwards, Paul's dealings with the Jerusalem church were purely pragmatic, recognizing that it had a natural ecclesiastical pre-eminence but denying that this pre-eminence was either intrinsic or necessary.

This comports with our argument above that Paul's collection was primarily pragmatic, and that any of its attendant symbolism did not serve especially to elevate the role of Jerusalem in the present or in the future. This is not to deny that some in the Jerusalem church might have interpreted this charitable gesture to mean things that Paul himself never intended; that was part of the risk he took.[130] That Paul himself accorded to Jerusalem this significance runs contrary to the evidence.

Paul's refusal to acknowledge this theological primacy of Jerusalem may have been quite galling for the Jerusalem church (indeed, if he had been desiring a quiet life, it would have been troublesome for Paul himself!). Yet the verdict of history was on Paul's side. Just over a decade after Paul's last visit to Jerusalem the days of Jerusalem's hegemony in church affairs came to an end. 'The theology of the Jerusalem church had no future, while the theol-

---

[129] See *e.g.* Bruce (1968) 14, and Bauckham (1995a) 470; though see Witherington (1993).
[130] As suggested by *e.g.* Bruce (1968) 10; Hurtado (1979); Holmberg (1978) 41-3.

ogy of Paul triumphed'.[131] Paul's refusal to tie the Christian gospel to a Jeru-salem-dependent theology (in matters eschatological or ecclesiastical) would prove a valuable legacy for the Church of the next generation as it sought to come to terms with Jerusalem's fall and the loss of its former 'centre'.

The truth therefore lies between the extremes of Baur and Munck. Munck was right to emphasize Paul's continuing concern for Jerusalem and Israel and his seeing his own Gentile mission as integrally related to the whole issue of the mission to the Jews. Yet Paul disagreed with the Jerusalem church on issues other than eschatological chronology. Without looking at the level of agreement over such issues as circumcision and the food laws,[132] we can assume that Paul's attitude to the Land, the Temple, and Jerusalem itself would have been controversial, to say the least, for those living in Jerusalem and Judea. Contrary to those in the Tübingen school, however, Paul's attitude to the Jerusalem church, for all these various disagreements, was never antag-onistic or dismissive. Inasmuch as they were fellow-believers in Christ, they were fundamentally united, and it was in order to express that deepest level of unity that Paul was prepared to risk his life, bringing to these Jerusalem 'saints' the love-offering of their fellow-saints who, though they lived in dis-tant lands, were also 'in Christ'.

A consistent picture emerges: Paul's attitude towards Jerusalem (like his attitude towards the Land and the Temple) had been radically affected by his conversion. Just as he developed a whole new approach to the Law, so he understood Jerusalem in a new light. In Galatians he reveals his negative as-sessment of the city, and in 1 Thessalonians his fears for its future. In Romans he balances this by seeking to inculcate an appropriate sense of indebtedness towards the city, for all that God has done there—an indebtedness that is then expressed in a concrete way through the collection. As for the future, his new understanding of how in Christ God has fulfilled the scriptural promises relat-ing to 'restoration' and the 'ingathering of the Gentiles', precluded his espous-ing the positive attitude that many in his generation, both Jewish and Jewish-Christian, might have preferred. Within his own life-time God had done some-thing unexpected in Jerusalem, something which he had initially dismissed as impossible—perhaps precisely because it undermined all those fond imagin-ings. It became Paul's life-work to draw people away from speculating about the political future and to make them understand the solid reality of what had recently taken place in Zion—the death and resurrection of Israel's Messiah.

---

[131] Gaston (1984) 72.

[132] See R.N. Longenecker (1964) 281, on reasons for the Jerusalem church's conservatism.

5. Paul in Jerusalem

The relevant material in Acts has, for the reasons given at the outset, been left till now. How do our conclusions tally with Luke's portrait of Paul, and does a consistent pattern emerge of Paul's attitude to Jerusalem amidst the situations which he faced?[133]

Paul was 'born in Tarsus, but brought up' in Jerusalem (Acts 22:3). Traditionally this has been understood to indicate that Paul's childhood years were spent in the Diaspora and that he only came to Jerusalem for training under Gamaliel at a later date. One could then explore how Jerusalem might have been viewed from such a Diaspora-perspective and ask if Paul's pursuing his further education in the city revealed a strong conviction as to Jerusalem's importance. If, however, Paul's family moved to Jerusalem much earlier,[134] Paul's approach to Jerusalem would then be more that of a resident or 'insider'. Of particular interest is the recent suggestion that Paul's parents may have been deported to Tarsus because of involvement in the Jewish uprising under Varus in 4 BC.[135] Paul's coming to Jerusalem would then be particularly significant—a return from exile. In any case, in his pre-Christian days Paul would almost certainly have been affected by Jerusalem's religious importance; in a spiritual sense he was a child of Jerusalem.[136]

Life changed on the road to Damascus (Acts 9:3ff; *cf.* 22:6ff, 26:12ff). It is unclear how many of the gospel's implications (as later expounded by Paul) were immediately clear in that life-changing encounter,[137] or how much of Paul's subsequent 'three years' in Arabia and then Damascus (Gal. 1:18) was spent in quiet reflection.[138] A host of questions, however, might have

---

[133] As above in ch. 3 (6), assumptions will be made here about the general veracity of Acts which some will find unpersuasive.

[134] As argued by van Unnik (1962); see discussion in Hengel (1991) 18-39. The presence in Jerusalem of Paul's nephew (Acts 23:16) might indicate that Paul came to Jerusalem as part of a family move in his childhood.

[135] See J. Taylor (1996). This would explain the tradition found later in Jerome that Paul's parents came from Gischala in northern Palestine, and also suggest that he was more 'Hebraic' than 'Hellenist'. Paul's Roman citizenship might then derive from his father having been manumitted from slavery. Taylor suggests that before his conversion Paul belonged to the religious nationalists who later became the Zealots.

[136] If (as on the traditional reading) Paul came from a long-standing Diaspora family, he could still have been especially attached to Jerusalem. Those who relocate themselves in order to have what others have by accident of birth are often more enthusiastic than the local residents; *cf.* similarly, R.N. Longenecker (1964) 275; Esler (1987) 146.

[137] On what Paul learnt in his conversion experience, see *e.g.* Kim (1984); Barclay (1988) 238; Dunn (1990) 100-101; Furnish (1993) 12-13.

[138] Murphy O'Connor (1993) argues for Paul spending some of this time in evangelism to the Nabataeans. See discussion in N. Taylor (1992) 67-70.

come to his mind concerning Jerusalem—the city to which he should have re-turned (Acts 9:1-2).[139]

What would he say once back in Jerusalem, and what did his conviction that Jesus was Israel's Messiah (the one crucified and therefore 'cursed' out-side its walls: *cf.* Gal 3:13) say about the the city? Why had its authorities missed their Messiah? Was it because Jesus had not been a political Messiah and 'had not driven the Romans out of Palestine'?[140] Such nationalistic self-absorption, to which Paul himself might have been prone, could now be seen as a mistake.[141] Jerusalem had been a central part of Paul's 'world', but that world and all its aspirations had been crucified to him, and he to that world (*cf.* Gal. 6:14). Jerusalem looked very different from the perspective of Arabia.

Such reflections could date to Paul's earliest years as a Christian; after all, the Paul who persecuted the church knew how powerful were the forces at work in Jerusalem against the message of Jesus. Alternatively, this critique of Jerusalem may have developed more slowly—perhaps in response to his dif-ficult time in the city as a new Christian (Acts 9:26-30) and after the Temple-vision of Christ calling him to leave the city to work among the Gentiles (Acts 22:17-21).[142] Certainly his subsequent absence from Jerusalem for 'fourteen years' (Gal. 2:1)[143] suggests a significant detachment from Jerusalem—as well as in itself increasing his theological independence from the city.

Paul says that his eventual return to Jerusalem (for an important meet-ing with other apostles) was 'in response to a revelation' (Gal. 2:2)—a phrase which betrays some reluctance, as if only a sense of God's call caused him to abandon his self-imposed exile from the city. According to his own account

---

[139] Paul's spending time in Arabia was probably motivated not simply by the need for reflection or even for evangelism, but also by the need to 'lie low' until the time was ripe to return to Jerusalem: so Peake (1929) 36.

[140] Wright (1991) 40.

[141] This desire for a nationalistic Messiah may lie behind Paul's statement (2 Cor. 5:16) that he 'no longer regarded Christ from a worldly point of view [κατὰ σάρκα]': so Wright (1992) 408. If authentic, Luke's description of Paul's conversion as including the call to preach to the Gentiles (Acts 22:15; 26:17) would confirm that for Paul this restricted, nationalistic focus (which had played its part in Israel's missing her Messiah) was replaced from the outset by a universal concern.

[142] *Contra* Blair (1965), we take this to refer to an event during the 'fifteen days' (Gal. 1:18) of Paul's first return to Jerusalem after his conversion (Acts 9:26-30); so also Haenchen (1971) 627. The need to leave Jerusalem to avoid persecution (as in Acts 9) can easily be blended with Paul being given a personal vision that to leave Jerusalem was indeed the right thing to do (as in Acts 22). On Paul's reasons for making this first visit as a Christian to Jerusalem, see N. Taylor (1992) 75-8.

[143] If these fourteen years are reckoned from his conversion (1:15), not from his previous visit to Jerusalem (Gal. 1:18),the interval between his two visits to Jerusalem would be eleven years. On these 'silent years' in Paul's life, see *e.g.* Osborne (1965).

that meeting went well (Gal. 2:2-10), though it made clear that some in the Jerusalem church continued to oppose his Gentile ministry.

His letter to the Galatians shows the fruit of this extended reflection. In declaring that 'Jerusalem was in slavery with her children' (Gal. 4:25) he had several things in mind: his own repudiation of the Law, to which his fellow-Jews were 'enslaved'; Jerusalem's blindness to God's purposes in Jesus, revealed both in the crucifixion and in its subsequent hostility towards his followers; his own involvement in Jerusalem as a persecutor of the believers; and the way Jerusalem and the pressures of being a Christian believer there (including the rising tide of nationalism) had caused the Judaizers to be blind to God's saving purposes towards the Gentiles. In all these ways Jerusalem proved itself to be out of touch with God's purposes. There was something about Jerusalem that worked against the gospel.

The controversy in Antioch (Gal. 2:11ff) made it obvious that another meeting was necessary to settle the issue of circumcision and also the question of 'table-fellowship' between Jewish and Gentile believers.[144] Since the issue was provoked by the concerns of those who had come to Antioch from Jerusalem (Gal. 2:12) and since those concerns were (probably) caused by the pressures of living in Jerusalem surrounded by a rising nationalism, it was only appropriate that this meeting should be convened in Jerusalem. Those who debated the issue had to realize the consequences of their decision for the local believers in the city. So Paul goes to Jerusalem for the third time as a Christian (Acts 15). Would this council endorse the previous agreement (Gal. 2:9-10), or would Paul's opponents cause his gospel ministry to be denied?

Despite the potentially unpleasant consequences for the local church, James comes out clearly in support of Paul's mission. This showed 'astounding magnanimity'.[145] There were clearly those in the Jerusalem church who might have hoped (or even expected) that James would oppose Paul, but the success of the Gentile mission proved to be unassailable evidence of God's new world-wide purposes in Christ. The issue could so easily have gone the

---

[144] On the events of Gal. 2:1-10 preceding those of Acts 15, see above n. 52 and Bauckham (1995a) 468-9: 'Gal. 2:1-10 records an initial decision by the three "pillars", in private consultation with Barnabas and Paul. . . . But the continuing debate on this highly contentious issue soon necessitated that the whole matter be the subject of a full discussion and authoritative decision by the Jerusalem church leadership as a whole'. He adds that those who 'express surprise that the same issue should be discussed and decided by the same people on two occasions, clearly have little experience of university politics!' If the Antioch incident preceded the council of Acts 15 (where Paul was vindicated), there is then no need to wonder if Paul ultimately 'lost' the argument at Antioch, as is commonly supposed: see e.g. Catchpole (1977); Achtemeier (1986); Dunn (1990) 160; Hill (1992) 126-47; N. Taylor (1992) 144.

[145] Hengel (1975) 87.

other way, but Jerusalem decisively endorsed Paul's gospel—though the extreme right-wing in the Jerusalem church (precisely because it had now been
officially defeated) would presumably continue to give James a tough time.[146]
Paul could never again be assured of a unanimous welcome in Jerusalem.

In the next five years or so Paul's missionary base expanded impres-
sively around the Aegean. In that sense the long-term success and viability of
the Gentile mission was increasingly assured.[147] At the same time the pressures in Jerusalem were increasing, causing more and more Christian believers (μυριάδες in Acts 21:20) to take a hard line on questions relating to the
Jewish Law.[148] During this period Paul may have paid a quick 'reporting' visit to 'the church' in Jerusalem (Acts 18:22),[149] but clearly the tension was
mounting as Paul prepared to take his collection to Jerusalem. How would the
city respond this time?

Initially Paul considered not accompanying the collection in person (1
Cor. 16:1-4), but then decided to go. Not surprisingly he asked for prayers
(Rom. 15:30-32). He feared the reactions of the Jewish population in Jerusalem (by now Paul had achieved some notoriety); he also suspected that the
Christian believers might not respond as warmly as he hoped. It was intended
as a gesture of good-will, but with the increasing tensions, there was every
likelihood that this time many in the local Jerusalem church would chose to
reject him—not least in the absence of a conciliatory figure such as Peter.

Paul took at least six Gentile companions with him (Acts 20:4), not only
to protect the money, but also that the Jerusalem church might be brought face
to face with Gentiles who were fellow-believers in Christ; this would force
them to acknowledge the growing strength of the Gentile church, as well as
making it more difficult for them to reject their love-gift.[150] Furthermore, in
taking with him these Gentiles, who as 'delegates' represented all the major

---

[146] Bruce (1968) 13: 'Paul himself had no more delicate situation to hold in hand than
James had in Jerusalem. *Cf.* Bruce (1988) 122: 'to the Jewish-Christians it seemed that the
'pillars' had sold the pass'. R.N. Longenecker (1964) 218, 276, suggests the defeated party
at the council in reaction then became stronger in the following years; though see
Bauckham (1995a).

[147] This may be reflected in the more confident tone of Romans when compared with Galatians (*cf.* above 3c). Paul again faced a visit to Jerusalem; this time, however, although a
rejection in Jerusalem would be bitterly disappointing, it would not be devastating. Paul
already had the official support of the 'council'; moreover, power was already perhaps slip-
ping away from the the Jerusalem church.

[148] See Reicke (1984).

[149] See above ch. 3 at n. 94.

[150] Paul's earlier taking Titus to Jerusalem (Gal. 2:3) may have been inspired by a similar
desire for the Gentile converts to be represented *in person*. Although Paul's gift was
outwardly 'disarming', it did function as a 'test': would the response of the Jerusalem
church be motivated by pride, envy or fear (of their fellow-Jews)?

areas of Paul's mission-field, Paul may also have been reflecting on that call
which he had received in the Temple to 'go to the Gentiles' (Acts 22:21); now
he was returning to Jerusalem with a visible token of his 'mission accomplished' for the Lord.[151] Thus the journey to Jerusalem also functioned at the
personal level as a means of authenticating the validity of Paul's 'apostleship'.

Paul set off for Jerusalem, hoping that this gesture of Christian love and
unity would be accepted, but aware that the result might be the opposite. Luke
records that the journey was marked by a sense of foreboding (Acts 20:23) and
that Paul's companions wanted to abandon it (Acts 21:12). Why did Paul press
on? Because he was not going to surrender his vision of Christian unity without properly trying? Because he did not wish it to be thought that the 'apostle
to the Gentiles' could not face the pressures of Jerusalem? Because he now
sensed that God was calling him to go to Jerusalem as Jesus had done and to
be prepared to face the consequences?[152] Because he feared for the future of
Jerusalem and wanted to do what he could to forestall that 'day'?'

We will never know which of these personal issues was at stake. Nor
can we know precisely what happened to the collection. It was probably not
received straightforwardly.[153] Instead the proposal of the Nazirite vow became a tacit condition before it could be accepted—a condition which Paul
never succeeded in fufilling. The fact that Paul obliged with this request
(when it involved the risks which subsequently materialized) should be taken
as a sign of his real desire to support his fellow Jewish-Christians, even though
he disagreed with them in many areas. It was also a prime example of his own
stated principle of flexibility (1 Cor. 9:19-23).[154] Even though he maintained
his own pessimistic views concerning the long-term future of the Temple, it
was important in the meantime to show a proper deference to the Temple.
Once in the Temple, however, he would have been acutely conscious that his
Gentile companions could not join him there.[155] By its very structure the
Temple conveyed a view of Jew-Gentile relations that Paul's gospel saw as
superseded, but as long as it stood, he needed to abide by its stipulations.

Then calamity fell. He was accused of flouting those stipulations—taking a Gentile into the inner courts (Acts 21:28).[156] For a short while he had

---

[151]Hence perhaps his talk of 'sealing' the gift (Rom. 15:28)—not just ensuring its safe
arrival, but also marking the appropriate end of this particular mission.

[152] As developed e.g. by Hastings (1958) 136-38: 'it was not for him, any more than it had
been for his master, to reject Jerusalem, but to be rejected by Jerusalem. . . . Paul bore his
witness to Jesus in Jerusalem; and he bore witness especially by the very similarity between
his treatment and that inflicted on his master'; cf. e.g. Songer (1974) and Stagg (1990).

[153] Cf. above ch. 3 at n. 202.

[154] Cf. above at n. 6; cf. Blair (1965) 27.

[155] So Bruce (1968) 24 and in Donfried (1991) 191; R.N. Longenecker (1990) lxxvii. See
further above ch3 (6).

the opportunity to proclaim publicly in Jerusalem something of the Christian gospel (Acts 22:1-21). In doing so he may have fulfilled a long-cherished desire to witness again (*cf.* Acts 9:26) to his Lord in Jerusalem, the place where Jesus had died for him, but also the place where he, Paul, had been involved in the death of some of Jesus' followers (Acts 8:1). Was this a factor that had driven him on to Jerusalem—to repay a form of debt which he owed to Christ? Or, being aware of the great pressures that James and the other believers were under in Jerusalem, did he wish to prove both to himself and to them that he was prepared to uphold even in Jerusalem the uncompromising line that he had developed in the comparative 'comfort' of the Diaspora?[157]

Even if these latter suggestions are incorrect, the narrative in Acts 22 makes it probable that this desire to witness to Christ in Jerusalem was something that had been on Paul's heart since his earliest days as a Christian—only he had been called elsewhere. One senses that the call he had earlier received in the Temple to go the Gentiles (vv. 17-21) was one that had gone against his own preferences. His protestations (vv. 19-20) indicate his belief that, having been a persecutor, his testimony might be especially powerful in Jerusalem; they may also reveal his preparedness to undergo the sufferings which he had once inflicted on others in that city. Yet it was not to be.[158]

This is important. Even if Paul had already developed a critical approach to Jerusalem, he was still deeply concerned about the city. His own preference had been to stay in Jerusalem.[159] Just as his fellow-countrymen were always on his heart even when pursuing his mission amongst the Gen-

---

[156] Ironically, Paul is banished from Jerusalem for his inclusive attitude towards Gentiles precisely on the one occasion when, in keeping with the stipulations of the Temple, he had been forced to act in an *exclusive* way. Nevertheless, Paul's Jewish opponents may have been right to assume that the logic of his position was that his 'Gentile converts should be admitted to the Temple': Bauckham (1993c) 146.

[157] Tannehill (1988/90) ii, 266, helpfully speaks of Paul needing to 'face the cultural consequences of his previous ministry. . . . Paul's decision to go to Jerusalem and to Rome is a decision to face that crisis. Jerusalem and Rome are the centres of the two powers that Paul has disturbed and to whom he must give a reckoning'. To 'boast' in the Cross alone (Gal. 6:14) was perhaps more difficult when in Jerusalem than when elsewhere. Some of the force of Paul's appeal to his *stigmata* in Gal. 6:17 might be that, even though (unlike the Judaizers) he is not having to maintain his views concerning circumcision in the face of active Jewish opposition *in Jerusalem*, he *has* suffered for his beliefs and is prepared to do so again; he is not acting out of fear of being 'persecuted for the cross of Christ' (6:12).

[158] Neither the fact that Paul had a desire to witness in Jerusalem nor his being called again to 'go to the Gentiles' need necessarily deny the fact that at his conversion he had already received a special call to work amongst the Gentiles; *contra* Blair (1965). Dunn (1990) 100-101, is in favour of seeing Paul's call to work amongst the Gentiles as an authentic part of his conversion experience. Even so, his early years of mission may have been focused on his fellow-Jews, as suggested by *e.g.* Watson (1986) 177.

tiles (Rom. 9:1ff), so too was Jerusalem even when working in lands far away.
Just as his critical words concerning Israel were spoken in love, so too with
his critique of Jerusalem. For all his denial of its ultimate significance, he never lost his hope and longing for the city—an attitude that would have remained
unchanged until the end of his life (cf. again Rom. 9:1; 10:1).

It was precisely this reference to his being called to 'the Gentiles'
(22:21) that provoked the crowd and brought his speech to an abrupt end. This
only illustrated that Jerusalem's nationalism was particularly hostile towards
God's wider purposes. In a short while he found himself in Caesarea, never to
return again; for it was clear that to return to Jerusalem would mean an almost
certain death (23:15; 25:3).

Some of the ways in which Paul may have reflected on this episode during his Caesarean confinement have been outlined above in our discussion of
Luke's experience.[160] As far as the Jerusalem church was concerned, he had
to accept that not all the believers could readily offer him their support. This
was a personal blow, but not ultimately devastating: the Gentile mission
would continue, regardless of how it was viewed by some in the 'mother-
church'.[161] As for Jerusalem itself he had done all that he could. He had not
naively hoped for a grand conversion of its population.[162] His witnessing in
Jerusalem had been a 'testimony' against the city, proving what had long been
expected—that it was still opposed to the message of Christ. 'Official Jerusalem emerged in the eyes of the Jewish prophet Paul as the hub of unbelief.'[163]The future was in God's hands.

So Paul's attention turned to other things. The Jerusalem which had absorbed much of his attention in the previous year (preparing for the collection)
lay behind him—though still on his heart. There is little in the 'captivity epistles' (if written by Paul and dated to this later period) that relates to Jerusalem.
The Temple-imagery in Ephesians and the reference to the 'dividing-wall'
(2:14; 20-22) might indicate Paul's reflection on his fateful visit to the Jerusalem Temple.[164] New light would be shed on Philippians if Paul's recent experience in Jerusalem is seen as a factor in his thought; did his wanting to know
'the sharing of [Christ's] sufferings, by becoming like him in his death' (Phil.

---

[159] This might be sensed in his talking of having preached 'from Jerusalem all the way
round to Illyricum' (Rom. 15:19), thereby reflecting his desire to preach Christ not just in
the Diaspora but also in Jerusalem. See Hengel (1991) 24; N. Taylor (1992) 80.

[160] Above p. 110.

[161] Cf. above n. 147.

[162] Cf. above n. 114.

[163] Georgi (1992) 119-20.

[164] Reicke (1970) 281-2, notes that three themes in Eph. 2 may have been coloured by
Paul's experiences in Jerusalem and then Caesarea (the 'dividing-wall', the tension
between Jew and Greek, and the issue of 'citizenship').

3:10-11) reflect some of his earlier motivation in going up to Jerusalem?[165] Overall, Paul's focus has moved elsewhere. Personally, there was a deepening awareness of the all-sufficiency of Christ (Phil. 1:21-26; 3:7-11) and corporately there was a growing awareness that the Christian Church would need to develop its own identity in the world apart from institutional Judaism (cf. Eph. 2:11 ff). The focus on ecclesiastical issues, on the Church and its administration, becomes intelligible, not as the sign of the loss of 'charismatic' spiritual life, but as reflecting the conviction that that spiritual life must be channelled and conserved for future generations. As his own life drew to a close, Paul needed to prepare the Church for the day when he (and perhaps Jerusalem, as they then knew it) would be no more.

Paul had indicated that judgement upon Jerusalem was a possibility[166]—a conviction which would only have grown as a result of his own experience there. Any neutral observer could reckon that a clash of some kind with Rome was not many years away. Some Christians may have identified it with the *parousia*. Paul, however, had separated these two events in his mind and was expecting a prior judgement upon Jerusalem which, whilst enormously significant, would not spell the end of the world.[167] If he had lived to witness AD 70 and the end of the Temple, he would not have been surprised, for these events vindicated his theology.

That theology might well have been shaped by the conviction of the imminence of this coming event. For example, his calling Gentiles (Rom. 9-11) to eschew any triumphalism in their attitude towards the Jews might have been written with this in mind: when judgement came, they were to heed Paul's warning that this was a foretaste of God's judgement upon *all* people. This conviction about Jerusalem's future would give his involvement with the city (both in the collection and in his visit to the Temple) a consciously 'interim'

---

[165]These verses would then confirm that when Luke presents Paul's journey up to Jerusalem as parallel to Jesus', he was reflecting Paul's own convictions. It was his *via dolorosa*, his *imitatio Christi*. As it was, the pattern of death and resurrection was played out in his Jerusalem visit in a more spiritual sense, with Paul's imprisonment (death) and then journey to Rome (resurrection). If Philippians were written from Caesarea, as argued by Hawthorne (1987), several verses would have extra resonance in the light of Paul's recent experience in Jerusalem: 1:17 (referring to Palestinian Jewish-Christians?); 3:2ff (referring not to the Judaizers but to his fellow Jews?: *cf.* Hawthorne, p. xlii); 3:4ff (his sense of the 'loss' of Jerusalem which, though it meant much to him, had been surrendered 'because of Christ'); 3:5-6 (remembering his 'zeal' as a 'Pharisee' in Jerusalem); 3:13-14 ('forgetting what lies behind' [Jerusalem] and 'straining forward to what lies ahead' [Rome, and eventually martyrdom]); 3:19-20 (a Christian's true 'citizenship' being in heaven, from where [not Jerusalem] Christians were to await Christ's return). Some of these factors might still be operative if Paul was instead writing from Rome, though to a lesser extent.

[166] Above pp. 133-36.

[167] *Cf.* above n. 80.

nature; such things were necessary for the time being, but this would not always be so. Above all, it gave an impetus to ensure that the Christian Church established an unassailable viability, putting down strong roots in lands far from Palestine, and with a theology independent of Jerusalem.

> It is this awareness of an imminent end to the way the Jewish world had looked for so long . . . that drove Paul on his mission with such urgency. From his own point of view he lived in an odd interim period: judgment had been passed on Jerusalem, but not yet executed. There was a breathing space, a 'little time' in which people could repent, and in which the message of Jesus could spread to Gentiles as well as Jews. This explains both the urgency of his mission and the language in which he expressed that urgency.[168]

All this had to be done in faith, while the Temple and Jerusalem were very much in operation, and in the face of real opposition from some in the Jerusalem church. Paul could see where the future lay, and it was not in Jerusalem.

And so Paul 'came to Rome' (Acts 28:14), perhaps convinced that his own movement away from Jerusalem was a prophetic adumbration of the pattern which God was also intending for his Church. Jerusalem would not forever be the 'centre' of the Christian movement. Perhaps Paul had already sensed in writing to the Romans that, if a human, institutional 'centre' were necessary, Rome would be an obvious candidate (though his chief concern was simply that he should have a base for his subsequent mission). Yet in another sense the 'centre' of the Christian Church could never be a physical place. Paul's conversion-experience (which not coincidentally occurred away from Jerusalem) had instilled within him a whole new sense of what constituted the heart of God's purposes. Those purposes were focused on Christ—the One who called those who were 'in him' to have a foretaste even now of the 'Jerusalem that is above'. The physical city of Jerusalem, for all its previous significance, could no longer serve as the centre of God's people. There was now a new centre—not Jerusalem, but Jesus.

---

[168] Wright (1994a) 64-5.

5

A NEW TEMPLE
John

'The hour is coming when you will worship the Father, neither
on this mountain nor in Jerusalem; those who worship him must
worship the Father in spirit and truth' (John 4:21, 23).

Probably writing after the fall of Jerusalem, John highlights the theme of Jesus as a new
Tabernacle and Temple, the true locus of God's presence; he is the one in whom the Temple
festivals find their fulfilment. He also portrays Jesus' followers as constituting a Temple.
John sees Jerusalem not so much as a 'holy city' from the past, but rather as the central
city of Jesus' 'own' people; in the light of John's universal concerns it then becomes the
place which embodies the 'world' in its opposition to God and where God in Jesus has act-
ed to redeem that world. John also plays down any particular focus on the Land, be it as
the 'promised land' or as the place which witnessed the Incarnation.

The writings of John, when compared to the passionate intensity of Paul, have
a more reflective tone—an indication that John's writings may belong to a later period within the first century.[1] Having studied in Paul the earliest New

---

[1] On dating, see below section 4. Following the arguments of *e.g.* Marshall (1978) 31-
42, the present author understands the 'catholic epistles' which bear John's name (1, 2 and
3 John) to emanate from the same author as the Gospel. Because this is disputed, our
concentration will be on John's Gospel with only passing reference to the epistles. The
precise identity of 'John' need not detain us here (though see at n. 130), nor the details of
the process by which the Gospel came to be written (its use of sources etc). As in previous
chapters the intention is to treat the canonical Gospel as a coherent whole and offer a
reading of the text as it now stands.

Testament documents we turn to what may be the latest. John's Gospel reveals the mature fruit of extended reflection on the issue of Jerusalem.

It could be questioned, however, whether John would have shown any interest in this matter. Is this so-called 'spiritual gospel' concerned with such physical entities?[2] Is not Christ's coming presented on a much wider canvas— as a divine entrance into the 'world'?[3] Is John concerned with these more particular issues concerning Jerusalem and its Temple?

John's interest in such Jewish ideas would have been dismissed more easily in the days when scholarship tended to depict John as deeply imbued with the spirit of Hellenism. Increasingly the Jewish nature of John's Gospel is now recognized, and its proximity, more particularly, to *Palestinian* Judaism.[4] Recent studies have drawn attention to the precise knowledge of Palestinian geography which is evidenced in John's Gospel,[5] and to the way that the Evangelist invests his geographical comments with theological significance.[6] Moreover, Jerusalem and the Temple feature more prominently than in the Synoptic Gospels, with approximately 80% of the narrative being located in Jerusalem, compared with 30% in Matthew.[7] It is therefore quite valid to ask how this author would have evaluated the city of Jerusalem in the light of Christ (section 2).[8]

Again there is a preliminary examination of the author's attitude to the Temple (1). A subsequent section (3) asks how John viewed the wider land of Palestine in its capacity both as the 'promised land' and as the general *locus* of the Incarnation. Possible influences upon the author at the time of writing are addressed in the final section (4).

---

[2]   The phrase 'spiritual Gospel' goes back to Clement of Alexandria in the early third century (Eusebius, *EH* 6.14.7). Schnackenburg (1980/2) i, 436, comments on John's 'aloofness'.

[3]   See the references in n.78 below.

[4]   'The world of the fourth Gospel is the Jewish world': Fortna (1988) 310. *Cf.* J.B Lightfoot (1893) 135; Dodd (1963) 423-432; Carson (1991) 59-60. On Palestinian Judaism, see Hengel (1989a) 109-114; Cullmann (1976) 43-56; Schillebeeckx (1980) 320.

[5]   See Schein (1980); Robinson (1985) 45-67. Streeter (1936) 418, had spoken of John's first-hand knowledge of the topography of Palestine, and especially of Jerusalem'.

[6]   So Fortna (1974) 82: John's 'topography is neither incidental nor merely factual, but is schematic and everywhere has theological significance'. *Cf.* also Mollat (1959), Davies (1974) 289ff.

[7]   The narrative is located away from Jerusalem only in the following passages: 1:1-2:12; 4:4-54; 6:1-7:9; 10:40-11:16; 11:54-57; 21. Hoskyns (1940) 64, noted that all the Galilean episodes are linked to Jerusalem in some way. Dodd (1963) 426, speaks of John's 'interest in the capital' and his 'metropolitan outlook'.

[8]   Hence the recent study by Therath (1994).

1. The Temple

a) Jesus, a New Temple

> The Passover of the Jews was near, and Jesus went up to Jerusalem. In the
> Temple he found people selling cattle, sheep, and doves, and the money-
> changers seated at their tables. . . . He told those who were selling the doves,
> 'Take these things out of here! Stop making my Father's house [τὸν οἶκον
> τοῦ πατρός] a market-place!' His disciples remembered that it was written,
> 'Zeal for your house will consume me'. The Jews then said to him, 'What
> sign can you show us for doing this?' Jesus answered them, 'Destroy this
> Temple [λύσατε τὸν ναὸν τοῦτον], and in three days I will raise it up.' . . .
> But he was speaking of the Temple of his body. After he was raised from the
> dead, his disciples remembered that he had said this (2:13-14, 16-19, 21-22).

The issue of the Temple is raised straightaway. In contrast to the other Gospels, the Johannine Jesus 'cleanses the Temple' at the outset of his ministry.
Setting aside the historical questions that this raises,[9] John focused immediately on the tension between Jesus and the Temple—a tension which looms
large throughout the ensuing narrative.

As with the Synoptic accounts, it is not entirely clear what the author
saw as Jesus' motivation for this action. But John's own purpose is clear—to
show what this incident reveals about Jesus' identity. Jesus affirms the prior
validity of the Temple, but in a manner which points to his own unique relationship to God: it is his 'Father's house' (v. 16). More importantly, his cryptic logion, 'destroy this Temple, and in three days I will raise it up' (v. 19),
becomes the basis for John's claim that 'he was speaking of the Temple of his
body' (v. 21). In the light of the resurrection (v. 22) John was convinced that
Jesus himself, in his own body, was a new 'Temple'. He was not only the 'son'
of the God of Israel whose Temple this was (v. 16); he also embodied in himself the meaning of the Temple and all that it had previously signified.

The reader of John's prologue might have surmised that some such incident would eventually occur. Jesus is described there as the agent of God's
creation who came to his own (εἰς τὰ ἴδια), but encountered rejection (1:10-
11). When it becomes clear that this God is the God of Israel and that Jesus is
himself a Jew, the question is inevitably raised: what will happen when Jesus

---

9   Some argue that there may have been two such incidents in Jesus' ministry, one at the
beginning and one at the end: see Morris (1971) 188-191 and Carson (1991) 177-80. The
majority would favour the Synoptics' presentation and see John's order as resulting from
theological concerns: see further below 1e.

comes to Jerusalem?[10] Not only was Jerusalem the central city of his 'own' people; within the terms of the prologue, Jerusalem and its Temple might also claim to be peculiarly God's 'own'. In entering the Temple Jesus was coming in a vivid sense to 'his own':[11] 'the Temple belongs to Jesus in a special way'.[12] What will be the response?

There is a second way in which the Prologue had prepared for this episode—its description of Jesus as the Word which became flesh and 'lived among us' (ἐσκήνωσεν ἐν ἡμῖν: 1:14). Through using the verb ἐσκήνωσεν John presented Jesus' coming as being comparable to the 'tabernacling' of Israel's God in the wilderness. That 'tabernacle' (σκηνή), which powerfully symbolized God's presence with his people in the desert (Exod. 26ff), had subsequently been absorbed into the understanding of the Jerusalem Temple, as the place where God tabernacled or 'dwelt' (e.g. 1 Kings 6:13). The moment Jesus entered that Jerusalem Temple would inevitably be a moment fraught with meaning. This happens almost immediately: Jesus comes to the Temple, and through his deeds and words he points to these deeper truths concerning his identity. He serves notice that something new has dawned, that he has an unrivalled authority in that place, and that if people wish to fathom his identity, they must understand him against the backdrop of the beliefs associated with the Temple: 'he was speaking of the Temple of his body' (v. 21).

For John, therefore, 'Jesus is the new Tabernacle and the new Temple',[13] drawing onto himself all that these entities had previously signified. Jesus' coming affirmed the rich meaning of the Jerusalem Temple in times past. There was no denial of its previous theological status, but that status was now appropriated by Jesus. In particular, if the Temple/Tabernacle had been understood as the place of the focused presence of the God of Israel amongst his people, Jesus himself was now that divine presence. This claim contrasted markedly with the assumptions in other Jewish literature where it was claimed

> that Jerusalem and the Torah were the focal points of the entire cosmos, the place where the creator's own Wisdom had come, uniquely, to dwell. *John claims exactly this for Jesus.*[14]

---

[10] Not coincidentally, 'Jerusalem' is mentioned in the very first verse after the Prologue (1:19). Schnackenburg (1980/2) i, 343, comments how the narrative here now 'presses on to the self-revelation which is to be made in the city of God'.

[11] *Cf.* Mollat (1959) 324, who intriguingly links this with John's understanding that Isaiah had seen the 'glory' of *Jesus* (John 12:41); was this during his vision in the Temple (Isa. 6:1ff)? As with the other Gospels, the prophecy in Mal. 3:1 (of the 'Lord coming to *his* Temple') may not be far from the evangelist's mind.

[12] Moloney (1990) 442.

[13] Brown (1966/70) 411.

The episode in the Temple discloses in narrative form what John had previously stated in more allusive terms in the Prologue. Though the idea of Israel's God coming in person to visit his created world was startlingly novel, John found in the imagery of the Tabernacle and in the theological understanding of the Temple a clear, biblical precedent for explaining the paradox of God's coming to 'dwell' in his world. Rightly understood they could be seen as God's preparation of his people for the eventual coming of Jesus. 'Tabernacle imagery was uniquely able to capture the idea that people encountered God's Word and glory in the person of Jesus'.[15]

b) The Future of the Temple

What did this manifestation of a 'new' Temple mean for the 'old'? Could the two co-exist?

At this point the deeper meaning of Jesus' statement becomes apparent: 'destroy this Temple and in three days I will raise it up'. John's subsequent identification of this with Jesus' body (vv. 21-22) might initially suggest that it refers without remainder to Jesus' death and resurrection. To its original hearers within the narrative it was plainly understood as a threat to the Jerusalem Temple, pointing allusively to its destruction (v. 20). 'It is clearly intended by John that the primary (though not the only) reference of this verse should be to the destruction of the Temple buildings'.[16] Jesus had performed a violent act which had brought proceedings to a temporary halt. When he then said, 'destroy this Temple', the presumption must be that these words offer some kind of explanation for that action. They suggest that Jesus' cleansing of the Temple was an enacted parable, a sign of its forthcoming destruction.[17]

According to John, therefore, Jesus had been warning in this cryptic statement that the Jerusalem Temple was heading towards destruction, and that this tragic event was integrally connected to the emergence of a new Temple in the person of Jesus, and more particularly to the destruction of that new Temple in Jesus' death. As argued by Wead, the implication of this 'ironic imperative' is effectively: "'Destroy this body (in which I live) and you shall de-

---

[14] Wright (1992a) 416 (italics mine), noting the significant parallels and contrasts between John's prologue (1:1-18) and the passage in Sirach (24:1-28) about the manifestation of Wisdom.
[15] C.R. Koester (1989) 115.
[16] Barrett (1978) 199.
[17] *Cf.* above in ch. 1 (1c) for the similar emphasis in Mark; see further below ch. 8 (2). See also Nereparampil (1972-3), Derrett (1977), Hartman (1989), C.R. Koester (1995) 83.

stroy this Temple (in which we stand)'".[18] The Temple would be profoundly affected by the coming of Jesus, and especially by his death.

This conclusion is confirmed in two subsequent passages. First, Jesus teaches in John 4:21-3: 'the hour is coming when you will worship the Father neither on this mountain nor in Jerusalem'. Despite appearances, this is a statement not about the city of Jerusalem in general but rather about its Temple; for the contrast is between the Samaritan Temple on Mount Gerizim and the Jewish Temple on Mount Zion. Jesus was predicting that these locations would soon become irrelevant. Conceivably this might mean that the Jerusalem Temple would continue in existence but be deprived of its exclusive claim to be the place of the worship of the one, true God. Given that the Samaritan Temple had already been destroyed 150 years previously,[19] however, Jesus' words 'neither in Jerusalem' contain a harsh prediction that the Jerusalem Temple would soon experience the same fate as its Samaritan counter-part. That this would come about because of Jesus is made clear in the otherwise repetitive verse 23: 'a time is coming and *has now come* when the true worshippers will worship the Father in spirit and in truth.' It was through Jesus that a new day had dawned, and though its outward manifestations might take some time to become clear, the old order would eventually yield to the new. The coming of Jesus spelt the end of the Jerusalem Temple: 'another Gerizim or Jerusalem will not come to the fore'.[20]

Secondly, there is the passage in John 11:48-53 in which Caiaphas debates with the members of the Sanhedrin, who fear that 'the Romans will come and destroy both our holy place (τόπον) and our nation (v. 48)'. Τόπος here almost certainly refers to the Temple[21] which they feared the Romans would destroy if the Jesus-movement showed signs of becoming a popular uprising. Caiaphas confidently asserts that this will not occur so long as 'one man dies for the people' (v. 50). Given the multiple irony of this passage, John probably understands Caiaphas' confidence to have been misplaced. Just as Jesus' death would prove to be 'for the Jewish nation' (and 'also for the scattered children of God') in quite a different sense from that which Caiaphas had intended, so too the result of that death would not be as expected—not the Temple's reprieve, but its doom. Jesus would be involved mysteriously in the

---

[18] Wead (1970) 65. *Cf.* Guilding (1960) 171-2 ('to destroy the Temple of his body was to doom their own Temple') and Ellul (1970) 138: 'The Temple in question is both that of the city, which once destroyed will never rise again, and that of his body, which will be resurrected after three days. This double destruction, followed by a single reconstruction, is an indication of the substitution of the Temple of Christ's body for the Jerusalem Temple'.

[19] See Josephus, *Ant.* 13: 255f.

[20] Burge (1987) 195.

[21] As indicated in the NRSV translation ('holy place'): see also *e.g.* Acts 6:13; 21:28.

Temple's destruction—though not in the way the Sanhedrin feared. As in 2:19, the implication is not drawn out and the whole incident involves an un-quantifiable dose of irony; yet the link is there. The death of Jesus will have unsought-for consequences for the Temple in Jerusalem.

c) *Jesus' Subsequent Involvement: Fulfilment and Eclipse*

John's locating the 'Temple cleansing' early in the Gospel has important con-sequences. On the one hand, it places Jesus' subsequent involvement with the Temple 'under a cloud' (7:14-8:59; 10:22-39).[22] John's readers know that Je-sus' frequenting of the Temple (for the festival of Tabernacles and for Hannu-kah) does not imply his total approval of that institution; he was simply using it as the most suitable place for a teaching ministry in Jerusalem.

On the other hand, it reveals the appropriateness of Jesus' returning to the Temple for these occasions. For if Jesus *was* a new 'Temple' (2:19ff), then that claim could not be made from a 'safe distance'; rather it had to be forged in close association with the physical Temple. If Jesus was the new Tabernac-le (1:14) it was appropriate for him to be in in Jerusalem for the festival of Tabernacles (7:2ff). A return visit was inevitable. In accordance with this ex-pectation John presents Jesus, not only as returning to the Temple, but also as deliberately taking the opportunity to reveal his identity through comparing himself with the Temple and its rituals. He does this in at least three ways.

Tabernacles was the feast in which God's people looked back to their wilderness experience under Moses and looked forward to that day when God would do a similar work of blessing for his people. Each day water was brought from the Siloam pool and poured out on the altar; this was a reminder of Moses' producing water in the desert through striking the rock (Exod. 17:1-7; Num. 20:8-13) and also a symbol of God's promises that one day water would flow out from Jerusalem and its Temple, despite its natural barrenness (*e.g.* Ezek. 47:1ff; Zech. 14:8).[23] Jesus' first identity-claim takes up this im-agery:

> 'Let anyone who is thirsty come to me, and let the one who believes in me drink. As the scripture has said, "Out of the believer's heart shall flow rivers of living water"' (7:37-8).

---

[22] The episode concerning the woman caught in adultery (7:53-8:11), whatever its own authenticity, is almost universally seen as a later interpolation, not originally belonging to the narrative in this place. See *e.g.* Brown (1966/70) 335-6.

[23] See *e.g.* Beasley-Murray (1987) 113-114.

Although there is much debate about the correct translation of this saying (should the 'christological' reading be preferred, where the water flows not from the believer but from Jesus himself?)[24] John's point is clear: this Temple ritual (of the water being poured out on the altar) points to Jesus. The longed-for 'day' has arrived. Instead of the water flowing from Jerusalem or its Temple, it flows from Jesus (and/or those who believe in him).[25]

Secondly, Jesus responds to the lighting during Tabernacles of the four great candelabra by declaring that he is the 'light of the world' (8:12). These lights were so vast that, according to other accounts, they illumined not just the Temple but the whole of Jerusalem;[26] Jesus claims to be the light 'not only of Jerusalem, but of the whole world'.[27]

Thirdly, the heated debate that follows (8:13-59) culminates in Jesus' explosive revelation that 'before Abraham was, I am' (8:58). If this divine Name ('I am') was recited as part of the Tabernacles liturgy,[28] then Jesus was again using the Temple's ritual as a pointer to his identity. In this case what Jesus was appropriating to himself was not just some particular ritual within the Temple, but the whole essence of the Temple as being the dwelling-place of the divine Name. Speaking in the Temple, the place of the divine presence, he claimed identity with that presence. Jesus was a new Tabernacle (1:14) and a new Temple (2:19), so John asserted, precisely because he embodied the presence of Israel's God.

The Johannine Jesus uses this 'I am' formula' at other times to make a similar point.[29] On this occasion (which is the first such claim made in Jerusalem, and the only one made in the Temple) John points out the repercussions of this for the Temple—the place which previously had been the *locus* of that divine Name. He presents us with a new *locus*—not a place but a person. In Jesus God has brought into the world him who embodies all that the Temple stood for. The physical Temple 'must decrease; he must increase' (*cf.* 3:30). The time of fulfilment has come: the Temple is to be replaced—by a person.

The response to Jesus' use of the divine Name is hostile and necessitates Jesus' departure from the Temple (8:59). The conflict between Jesus and

---

[24] Those commentators who favour the 'traditional' reading include Barrett (1978) 327, and Lindars (1972) 299; for the 'christological' reading see *e.g.* Haenchen (1984) 17; Schnackenburg (1980/2) ii, 154, Beasley-Murray (1987) 114f; *cf.* also Pryor (1992) 39.

[25] Some would see the 'flow of blood and water' from Jesus' side after his crucifixion (19:34) as the initial fulfilment of this prophecy: see *e.g.* Brown (1966/70) 949f.

[26] See m.Sukk. 5:1.

[27] Brown (1966/70) 344.

[28] As argued by Davies (1974) 295, quoting m.Sukk. 4.5.

[29] See *e.g.* 6:35; 8:12; 10:7, 9, 11, 14; 11:25; 14:6; 15:1, 5; 18:5-8. In all but the last instance it is used in the predicative sense. The 'absolute' use of 'I am' in 8:58 is therefore very significant.

his opponents, however, reflects a deeper conflict between Jesus and the Temple; for both are making mutually incompatible claims—to be the supreme focus of God's presence. Having made this claim within the Temple, Jesus leaves—an action which John may have seen as indicative of this fundamental tension.[30] Henceforth these two 'temples' will be in essential conflict.

Jesus' claims in relation to the Temple have reached their climax; Jesus gradually withdraws from the Temple. Chapter 9 is located not in the Temple, but elsewhere in Jerusalem: when the blind man 'worships' Jesus (9:38), this is an example of 'true worship' (*cf.* 4:21-24), but it is offered to the one who has been cast out of the Temple. In 10:22-39 Jesus returns to the Temple, but compared to the extended episode in 7:14-8:59, this is but a brief return, and Jesus' location 'in Solomon's Colonnade' indicates his comparative 'disengagement' from the festival proceedings.[31] In any event, this proves to be Jesus' last recorded visit to the Temple in John's Gospel.[32]

John has made his point. Jesus' identity as the new Tabernacle and Temple has been made at the outset (1:14; 2:19). Jesus' claim to fulfil the rituals of Tabernacles has been adequately covered (7:37-8; 8:12). Clear hints have also been given that Jesus fulfils the theological ideas associated both with Passover (1:29, 36; 6:4)[33] and with Hannukah, the Feast of Dedication (10:36).[34] Above all, Jesus' claim to be the divine presence has been made within the Temple (8:59). The subsequent setting aside of the Temple within John's narrative indicates how it has also been set aside within the purposes of God. The Temple has been eclipsed.

---

[30] *Cf.* Matthew's similar treatment in Matt. 23:38-24:1, where Jesus' departure signals the removal of the divine presence from the Temple: see above ch. 2 (1c). Since John has Jesus 'in the Temple' again in 10:23, this departure is not a final one, and therefore does not have the full significance suggested in Davies (1974) 291: he saw it as connoting the 'turning away of Jesus from Judaism'.

[31] So Davies (1974) 292 (though Jesus was not *outside* the Temple, as he claims). Davies' general point about Jesus' 'disengagement', however, is confirmed by Motyer (1992) 154-5, who observes that even at the earlier feast of Tabernacles (7:14ff) Jesus appears to be 'distancing himself from the Jerusalem celebrations'.

[32] In 18:20 Jesus refers to his having taught publicly 'in the Temple' and 'not in secret'. Within John's own presentation, this can only refer to what has already been recorded in chs. 2, 7, 8 and 10. After the reference in 11:48, the Temple thus disappears entirely from view. *Cf.* below n. 86.

[33] *Cf.* 13:1; 18:28; 19:14, 36; see *e.g.* Beasley-Murray (1989) 71-76.

[34] In 10:36 Jesus is described as 'the one whom the Father has *sanctified*'; this word (ἡγίασεν) picks up the Festival's theme of Dedication. See just below at n. 42. Thus Brown (1966/70) 411: 'At Passover (ch. 6) Jesus replaced the manna of the Passover-Exodus story; now at the feast of Dedication . . . Jesus proclaims that he is the one who has truly been consecrated by God'; *cf.* similarly Carson (1991) 399.

John's over-riding message is that the Temple has been *replaced* by Jesus. Brown notes the 'importance given to the theme of Jesus' replacement of Jewish institutions'.[35] The same point is made by Davies:

> 10:37 is the culmination of a series of replacements associated with the feasts of Judaism in John. . . . In chapter 6 the manna of the passover story is replaced by the multiplying of bread. . . . At Tabernacles, in chapters 7-8, the water and light are replaced by Jesus, the true source of living waters and the light of the world. And, finally, at the Feast of Dedication the old tabernacle and Temple are replaced by the consecrated Christ.[36]

In similar vein Cullmann concluded:

> Opposition to the Temple worship, or rather, the spiritualization of the Temple worship is an essential idea for the Fourth Gospel. The divine Presence, which had until now been bound to the Temple of Jerusalem, is from now on visible in the Person of Jesus Christ, in the Word made flesh. The Evangelist sees the idea that Christ takes the place of the Temple to be realized *in the events of the life of Jesus*. This question of worship is one of his principal preoccupations. He tries to show through the life of the incarnate Jesus that from now on the question of worship must be asked differently. . . . The Divine glory, in Hebrew *shekinah*, previously limited to the Temple is visible in Jesus Christ. . . . For every Jew the *shekinah*, the Divine glory, is limited to the Temple. But from now on it is separated from the Temple, because it is bound to the *Logos* become flesh.[37]

The Temple has been eclipsed and replaced by the advent of a new Temple—namely, Jesus himself.

d) The Temple of Believers

These conclusions are widely recognized. Another strand of John's thought, however, has been noted less frequently—his understanding that Christian *believers* (both individually and corporately) also constitute a new Temple. Although the new Temple *par excellence* was Jesus himself, in a derivative sense that status was passed on to those who believed in him.

---

[35] Brown (1966/70) lxx: he then lists, 'ritual purification, the Temple, and worship in Jerusalem', and 'Jewish feasts like the Sabbath, Passover, Tabernacles, and Dedication'.

[36] Davies (1974) 296. Commenting on John chs. 1-4, Guilding (1960) 172, writes: 'the contrast between the old order and the new, the Temple at Jerusalem and the Temple of Jesus' body, is the theme of the whole section'.

[37] Cullmann (1959-60) 12, 41-2.

The evidence for this comes chiefly in chapter 14, but also in the whole of the narrative in the 'upper room' (chs. 13-17). Speaking to his disciples, Jesus assures them that in his *'Father's house*, there are many rooms' (monai: 14:2). The majority of commentators rightly see this as a reference to heaven.[38] Earlier Jesus had used the same phrase to describe the Jerusalem Temple ('my Father's house': 2:16). Here then is an allusion to Temple motifs as well. If both 'heaven' and the Temple can be described as the 'Father's house', then that Temple in Jerusalem must (amongst other things) be a symbol of heaven and of God's dwelling there amongst his people in a heavenly Temple.[39] The disciples, though currently separated from this heavenly Temple, look forward to dwelling within it in the future. On that day 'the distance between heaven and earth will be levelled out in the New Temple of the Risen Jesus'.[40]

Later in this chapter another truth emerges. Initially the ensuing discussion is focused on the issue of how disciples may 'know the way' (v. 5) and safely 'come *to the Father*' (v. 6). From verse 15 onwards the thought flows in the opposite direction. Drawing on Jesus' hitherto unexplained promise that he would 'come back' (v. 3), Jesus speaks of the coming of the Holy Spirit *to the disciples*. He then says, 'My Father will love them, and we will come to them and make our home (μονὴν) with them' (14:23). The use here of μονή clearly evokes a memory of verse 2, but in such a way as to show a whole new dimension of truth. In that earlier verse, the disciples had been looking forward to a future 'dwelling' with God in heaven; now they are promised in the interim God's 'dwelling' with them through the agency of the Holy Spirit. And if it was right to discern Temple resonances in that earlier reference, they are legitimate here too. Whilst the disciples must still await their coming to that heavenly Temple, they can in the meantime know what it is to be a 'Temple' themselves, the place where God makes his 'dwelling'.

John's frequent use of the idea of 'abiding/dwelling' (μονή, μένω) should be understood against the backdrop of the Temple. Jesus had publicly claimed to be a new Temple; now he discloses to his disciples that this is because he was truly 'in the Father' (v. 20). He then promises (v. 23) that this distinctive relationship with God will in a derivative way be the disciples' ex-

---

[38] As suggested by the context of Jesus' now 'going to his Father' (13:1; *cf.* 14:28); so Brown (1966/70) 620; Lindars (1972) 470; Barrett (1978) 456.

[39] It is unlikely, however, that because Jesus identifies himself with the Temple in 2:19 we should see this second reference to 'my Father's house' as a reference to Jesus himself (*contra* Gundry [1967]). This make nonsense of the imagery in 14:2-3 (where Jesus is taking people to his 'Father's house'). In the light of ch. 14 the Jerusalem Temple should rather be seen in two different ways: as the 'Father's house' which typifies 'heaven', and the place of God's 'dwelling' on earth, which then typifies Jesus. These two aspects should not be confused.

[40] The concluding words of the extended study of these verses in McCaffrey (1988) 255.

perience as well. If he was the Temple because God truly dwelt in him, so his
disciples through the presence of the Holy Spirit could be 'temples' too.[41]

Such thinking brings John close to Paul who had stated that Christian
believers were the 'Temple of the Holy Spirit' (1 Cor. 6:19). Unlike Paul, John
makes it clear that this status is dependent on the prior truth that Jesus himself
is a new Temple (ch. 2 ff). Seen in this light, a pattern emerges within the
structure of John's Gospel. In the first half of the Gospel John established the
identity of Jesus as the Temple; only later did he proceed to draw out the essentially derivative truth that Jesus' disciples were also 'temples'.

There are further ways in which John draws attention to this. For example, his use of the verb ἁγιάζω in 10:36 (where Jesus was described as 'the
one whom the Father has *sanctified*') had indicated that Jesus' eternal 'consecration' to the Father was of greater significance than the Temple's 'consecration' remembered in the Festival of the Dedication.[42] In the second half of the
Gospel, the same word occurs in Jesus' prayer: '*Sanctify* them in the truth;
and for their sakes I *sanctify* myself, so that they also may be *sanctified* in truth
(17:17, 19). The 'consecration' associated with Jesus alone in the first passage
is extended to include the disciples in the second.

There is evidence that John presents the whole episode in the 'upper
room' (chs. 13-17) as a 'Temple-experience'. The foot-washing (13:3ff)
serves as a form of initiation. All those who entered the Jerusalem Temple had
first to make themselves ritually clean; now Jesus offers that cleansing to his
disciples.[43] Once initiated and brought within this new Temple, they are
taught about the heavenly Temple to which they are going (14:2) and encouraged to see themselves as places in which God himself will 'dwell' by his
Spirit (14:17, 20, 23). They are to be holy and set apart from the 'world' outside (15:10, 18ff; 16:8-11, 33; 17:18), and unlike their enemies who see the
persecuting of the disciples as an act of 'worship' (16:2), it will be they who
offer the true worship. In imagery that may reflect the great 'vine' placed over
the doorway to the Temple sanctuary,[44] they are taught that Jesus is the vine
and that they are its branches (15:1, 5). Just as Solomon had prayed for God
to hear prayers focused on the Temple (1 Kings 8:29-30), so now they are assured that they may 'ask for anything in [Jesus'] name' (14:14; 15:16; 16:24).

---

[41] The fact that John does not use the verb he used of Jesus in 1:14 (ἐσκήνωσεν) does not
contradict this. Not only is it proper to reserve this allusion to the *Shekinah* for Jesus, but
this verb also indicated the temporary nature of Jesus' dwelling upon the earth; the use of
μένω instead suggests the notion of the permanency of God's dwelling amongst his people.
[42] See above at n. 34.
[43] So Thomas (1991) 27-31.
[44] Josephus, *War*, 5:210; as suggested by *e.g.* Westcott (1908) ii, 197, and W. Temple
(1943) 253.

All this comes to a climax when Jesus prays for them in what is frequently referred to as his 'high-priestly prayer' (17:1-26). In this prayer Temple themes are frequent: 'glory' (vv. 1, 4, 5, 10, 22, 24), holiness and consecration (vv. 11, 19, 25), the revelation of God's Name (vv. 6, 11, 26), and divine indwelling (vv. 21-3). There is also an implicit contrast drawn with the Jerusalem Temple: whereas that Temple had excluded Gentiles, now Jesus prays that all those who believe will be 'one even as we are one' (vv. 20-23).[45]

Jesus effectively functions as the high priest of an alternative Temple— a Temple focused upon himself, and which brings his disciples into intimate knowledge of the Father (cf. 17:3) and an experience of God's presence through the Holy Spirit. In one sense the individual believer functions as the Temple (14:23); in another sense it is the community of disciples gathered together in the upper room. In either case, the Temple is constituted as such by the presence of Jesus, who through the Holy Spirit makes God himself to be present. The meeting of the Risen Jesus with his disciples (20:19ff) then resumes this Temple-experience and demonstrates that through the resurrection this experience will now be universally available. Within the city of Jerusalem and not far from the Herodian Temple, an alternative Temple has been established. As a result, when Jesus refers to the 'Temple, where all the Jews come together' (18:20), John may be drawing a note of contrast: Jesus' disciples now gather in a quite different Temple.

Unlike that original Temple, however, this Temple is not bound by geographical space. Since the Temple motifs have been relocated in a living person (Jesus) and transferred to his disciples, this new Temple comes into existence wherever his Spirit is present; and that Spirit is no respecter of place, but 'blows where it chooses' (3:8; cf. 4:23). The 'Temple-experience' of those first disciples is essentially repeatable and can be relocated anywhere.

The inherent 'mobility' of this new Temple is indicated by the fact that John never specifies the location of these episodes in chapters 13-17 and 20;[46] he also depicts Jesus and his disciples as being 'on the move' throughout chapters 15 to 17.[47] This anonymity and flexibility as to physical location only

---

[45] Brown (1966/70) 781, sees these as covenantal themes, indicating the establishment of a new covenant. This need not deny the prominence of the Temple theme as well. More speculatively, the abundance of Temple allusions in ch. 17 might stem from the way John presents this discourse (chs. 15-17) as if it had been delivered 'on the move' (14:31: 'rise, let us be on our way'). If the reference in 18:1 to Jesus 'going out' (ἐξῆλθεν) refers not to the room, but rather to the city walls (cf. 19:17; 20:3), John may imagine the disciples wandering from the upper room through the city. The predominance of Temple themes in ch. 17 might then reflect their increasing proximity to the Temple.

[46] Our referring to the 'upper room' is simply for convenience and by assimilation to the Synoptics, but is nowhere present in John's text.

[47] See above n. 45.

serves to endorse the truth that this experience is not place-bound, but can be
known wherever Jesus is present through his Spirit. Though fittingly inaugurated within Jerusalem, this new Temple of Jesus will become a reality in places far removed from Jerusalem: the time was coming when true worship
would be offered in places other than Jerusalem (*cf.* 4:21).

e) Conclusion

Jesus' coming had profoundly affected the Jerusalem Temple. Although in
calling it his 'Father's house' Jesus had affirmed its previous status, he himself now fulfilled its essential meaning: he was a new Tabernacle, a new Temple, the one in whom the Temple festivals found their true significance, the
one who, through the gift of the Spirit, enabled his disciples to become 'temples' of God's presence in the world. If asked whether the Jerusalem Temple
had any continuing function, John's answer would have been negative; for to
emphasize the importance of the physical Temple detracted from the significance of Jesus. John indicates that there had been an inevitable clash between
Jesus and the Temple, with both claiming to focus God's presence on earth.
John therefore reveals his own 'opposition to the Jerusalem Temple'.[48]

John's reasons for placing the 'Temple cleansing' so early in his Gospel
now become clear. First, there was no better way within a Jewish context to
teach that Jesus was the presence of God on earth than through comparing him
with the Temple; in the light of the prologue (1:14) the encounter in the Temple is only to be expected. Secondly, establishing the truth of Jesus as a new
Temple at the outset, provided an important key for interpreting Jesus' subsequent involvement with the Temple. Thirdly, it made it possible for John to
develop in later chapters the derivative theme of the disciples as sharing in this
Temple-status. Fourthly, it meant that the Temple could fade from view in the
second half of the Gospel, thereby symbolizing the eclipse of its importance.

There may have been one further reason. This arrangement meant that
Christian critique of the Temple was focused primarily on the way in which
Jesus' own person replaced the Temple. The issue therefore concerned God's
eternal purposes as revealed in Jesus, not so much the faults of the Temple or
its administering authorities. To be sure, there are the ingredients of such a
Temple critique within John's narrative. Jesus criticized the commercial practice in the Temple courts (2:14ff). His criticism of those who put their trust in
their physical ancestry (8:33ff) could have been developed into a critique of
those who trusted in the physical Temple. Similarly his critique of the way in

---

[48]   Barrett (1978) 201.

which God's scriptures had been twisted (10:35, 17:17) could have been paralleled by a critique of the way in which the good gift of God's Temple had
been corrupted—not least because it was a love of the Temple and the desire
for its preservation that played some part in his opponents' conspiring for his
death (11:48). Yet John did not especially draw attention to these factors. He
did not seek to apportion blame, but simply emphasized the unique significance of Jesus. Such an approach (which focused on the positive rather than
the negative) would be especially valuable, if, as seems likely, his audience
included Jewish people considering Jesus' claims.[49] Ultimately, however, for
this most positive of reasons, his teaching about the Jerusalem Temple was
negative. Its significance could never be the same—because of Jesus.

> Jesus' death, followed by the resurrection, creates the new Temple and the
> new worship, and the life-giving stream for the renewal of the world. The old
> order is displaced by the new, not so much because the old is essentially
> bad—for salvation is of the Jews—but because Christ fulfils what it stands
> for so magnificently that it is necessary for it to have a quite new form.[50]

2. The City of Jerusalem

What of John's attitude towards the city of Jerusalem, as opposed to its Temple? If John saw the Temple in a new way, did the same hold true of the city?

There is an important distinction between the city and the Temple.
John's chief means of demoting the latter was to emphasize Jesus' *replacing*
the Temple as the focus of God's 'dwelling'; it is hard to see how this category
of replacement could be applied to the *city*. The only indication of such thinking is in 7:38, where the 'rivers of living water' probably allude to Zechariah
14:8 ('on that day living waters shall flow out from *Jerusalem*'). If so, John
saw Jesus as fulfilling the role which Zechariah had given to Jerusalem. Noting this, scholars have concluded that 'in John, as Jesus takes the place of the
Temple (2:19ff), so . . he takes the place of the City (7:37f)';[51] alternatively,
that 'Jesus is the true Zion'.[52] Apart from this the category of fulfilment or replacement is scarcely applicable to the city. If John were to develop a critique
of the city it would have to be based on quite different grounds.

---

[49] On John's intended audience, see further below 4a.
[50] McKelvey (1969) 84.
[51] C.W.F. Smith (1962-3) 143.
[52] Pryor (1992) 39. Lindars (1972) 300, notes that 'this equation with Jerusalem remains
unexplained' but suggests that the reference to 'belly (κοιλιας) may indeed reflect the
belief that Jerusalem was the 'navel' of the earth' (*cf.* Ezek. 38:12); *cf.* R.H. Lightfoot
(1956) 183 and Schnackenburg (1980/2) ii, 155.

a) *The City's Previous Status*

It is necessary first to ascertain how John viewed Jerusalem before the coming of Jesus. The presumption must be that he shared the understanding of his fellow-Jews as to its importance. However, it is harder to find solid evidence for this in John's Gospel than in others. There are no unambiguous references to it as a 'holy city' (as in Matt. 4:5; 27:53). Nor is there anything comparable to John's own positive presentation of the *Temple* in times past (John 2:16). The discussion about 'Jerusalem' in 4:21-24 speaks more properly about the Temple;[53] and the fact that in all his twelve references to 'Jerusalem' John always uses ʹΙεροσόλυμα (the more 'secular' name for the city) might indicate that he was distancing the city somewhat from its theological heritage within the Old Testament.[54] The only possible sign of a positive attitude towards Jerusalem in the Old Testament era is his quotation of Zechariah 9:9 ('do not be afraid, *daughter of Zion*': 12:15).[55] This acknowledges Jerusalem's history, but again John appears to play this down; for the original had contained a Hebraic parallelism with a reference to the 'daughter of Jerusalem', which John omits.[56] For whatever reason, John's text does not include the plain statement concerning Jerusalem's previous significance that might be expected.

John may have subscribed to this conviction about Jerusalem's previous significance, however, but used a different set of concepts to express this—a distinctively 'Johannine' category, not paralleled in the other Gospels. In his prologue he had commenced with a profound irony: the Word 'came to what was his own (εἰς τὰ ἴδια), and his own people (οἱ ἴδιοι) did not accept him' (1:11). Was this how John saw the tragedy of Jerusalem—the rejection of Jesus by 'his own' city?

Primarily this verse refers to the people of Israel, Jesus' own race—a theme which recurs throughout the Gospel with its many references to the 'Jews'.[57] Nevertheless, in using the neuter plural (τὰ ἴδια) John may also be indicating that Jesus would come, not just to people, but to places. This is confirmed by noting John's speaking later of Judea and Galilee as Jesus' '*own* country' (τῇ ἰδίᾳ πατρίδι: 4:44).[58] Thus both Brown and Davies see 'his own' (in 1:11) as including a reference to 'his own land'.[59] 'The Logos came to his native land'.[60]

---

53 See above 1b.

54 *Cf.* above ch. 3, n. 48. For John's references to Jerusalem, see 1:19; 2:13, 23; 4.20, 21, 45; 5:1, 2; 10:22, 11:18, 55; 12:12.

55 John's quotation is a conflation of Zech. 9:9 with some other text, possibly Isa. 40:9.

56 For a further, possible reason, see below at n. 86.

57 On this major issue of John's use of Ἰουδαῖοι, see Lowe (1976), von Wahlde (1982), Ashton (1985), Fortna (1988) 295, Kysar (1993), Motyer (1992) 61-73; and below n. 80.

The word ἴδιος, however, is inherently ambiguous. At one level, to think of Jerusalem as Jesus' 'own city' simply indicates that Jesus as a Jew could look upon this city, even if not his place of residence, as his 'own'—because it was the mother-city of Judaism. At another level, the phrase can be invested with a full christological significance: Jerusalem was peculiarly Jesus' 'own', because of his unique relationship with the God of Israel, the God who could claim this city as his 'own'.[61] This latter perspective may have been present in John's description of Jesus' coming to the Temple—as its rightful owner;[62] on the other hand, it certainly would not apply to Judea and Galilee, 'his own country' (4:44). Where on a sliding scale between these two would John have placed Jerusalem? Would he have seen Jerusalem in such terms—as God's 'own' city being encountered by God's 'own' Son?

The suggestion is attractive, but the only possible indication of this is John's quotation from Zechariah 9:9, where Jesus is described as Zion's 'king' (12:15)—a point which John does not develop. The matter must therefore be left open and undecided.

A straightforward endorsement of Jerusalem's distinctive status is lacking within the Gospel. This is not to say that John would have denied this status to the city. It may have more to do with presentation. His presentation is not of a city which experienced a 'great fall'.[63] If John developed a negative portrait of Jerusalem, he has cast it in different terms. His focus lies elsewhere.

---

[58] 'For Jesus himself had testified that a prophet has no honour in the prophet's own country'. In agreement with Pryor (1987), Carson (1991) 234-8, and Motyer (1992) 63, we understand πατρίς to refer to Judea and Galilee together (*cf.* 1:44ff, 7:41ff); *cf.* also Ashton (1985) 73. Many scholars have wanted to refer it to Judea/Jerusalem in contradistinction to Galilee; often this is tied in with a desire to portray Jerusalem as the place of Jesus' rejection and Galilee as the place of acceptance: see *e.g.* Lindars (1972) 201, R.H. Lightfoot (1938), Meeks (1966), Schillebeeckx (1980) 317, Bassler (1981), Fortna (1988) 294ff, Brodie (1993) 28-9, C.R. Koester (1995) 119. Although Galilee was a place of initial acceptance, this neat distinction breaks down in ch. 6. John casts Jerusalem in a negative light (as *e.g.* Lindars), but this shadow also falls over Galilee. In its context, despite a certain awkwardness, the *logion* at 4:44 must refer to the positive reception which Jesus has just received in Samaria, and is designed to contrast this with the negative response which Jesus will receive from his fellow-Jews who dwell not just in Judea *but also in Galilee*. Since at this stage, the response to Jesus in Jerusalem has included some positive elements (2:23; 3:2), the verse indicates what can be expected *in the future*. The Galilean welcome (4:45) will prove as fickle as that of the believers in Jerusalem (8:31; 12:37).

[59] Brown (1966/70) 414 (*cf.* below at n. 66); Davies (1974) 333. This had been suggested by *e.g.* Westcott (1908) 15. Hence the NRSV margin: 'to his own home'.

[60] Pryor (1992) 54

[61] Following Brown (1966/70) 30; *contra* Pryor (1990) 210.

[62] *Cf.* above at n. 11.

[63] As suggested above for Matthew and Luke.

b) *The City of his Own People*

The evidence for John's investing Jerusalem with a strong theological status remains ambiguous. The clearest category with which to understand the city in John's Gospel is this: it is simply the focal point of Jesus' 'own homeland' (ἰδία πατρίς: 4:49). Regardless of its theological status, on the human level Jerusalem is the city at the centre of Jewry—Jesus' 'own people'. This is the place where *par excellence* 'his own kinsmen' gather (*cf.* 18:20; 7:1ff). It is here that Jesus as a Jewish prophet and messianic claimant must speak his message and forge his claims. In the light of the prologue (1:11), the question is: how will 'his own people' receive him?

The story proves to be one of increasing rejection. In one sense the whole of Galilee and Judea constitute Jesus' 'own homeland' and are therefore the places where he experiences rejection. In another, precisely because it is the centre of that πατρίς, Jerusalem is the place where that rejection reaches its height. Galilee is the place where, according to his brothers, Jesus could well remain 'in secret', but Judea and Jerusalem are the places where, according to John, there were people 'looking for an opportunity to kill him' (7:1-3). Likewise, when on hearing about Lazarus Jesus invites his disciples to return with him to 'Judea', Thomas equates this with danger: 'let us also go, that we may die with him' (11:7; 16). Judea and Jerusalem are the places of greatest risk, the place 'where danger threatens'.[64]

They also prove to be the places where Jesus meets with the fewest responses of faith. It is not that there is no response at all: John records on several occasions that people in Jerusalem did believe in Jesus (2:23; 7:40-41; 8:31; 9:36-8; 11:45; 12:11). Yet only with the blind man whom Jesus healed does John promote this as a good paradigm (9:36-41); in all the other instances, there are indications that this faith was of the wrong kind (2:24; 8:31ff), did not go far enough (7:40-41) or was ultimately fickle (11:45; 12:11). With the exception of Nicodemus (3:1ff; 7:50-52) and some 'leaders' (12:42), such support as there is comes entirely from among the populace; Jerusalem's religious authorities are in the main implacably opposed (7:13, 25, 32, 45-52; 8:13; 9:13ff; 11:47ff; 12:10, etc). When John finishes his account of Jesus' public ministry in Jerusalem, he therefore included a brief reflection on the nature of this unbelief in terms of Isaiah 6:10 and 53:1 (12:37-41).

In this light John's comments in 10:40-42 are especially revealing. Jesus leaves Jerusalem and returns to the 'place across the Jordan where John had been baptizing earlier; . . . and many believed in him *there*.'[65] 'He now leaves the hostile land and people of Palestine to cross the Jordan. There he

---

[64] Schnackenburg (1980/2) i, 341.

finds the faith that was lacking in his own land'.[66] It is as though it is easier
for people to believe in Jesus the farther removed they are from Jerusalem, and
that once Jesus enters again into 'Judea', the darkness descends. The most unambiguously positive response to Jesus in the Gospel (beyond the range of the
immediate disciples) proves to be amongst the Samaritans: 'we know that this
is truly the Saviour of the world' (4:42).[67]

John does not especially explain this phenomenon. There are hints that
the political nature of Jerusalem causes people to misconstrue Jesus' message
(2:23; 7:40-41; 12:13-15; 18:36ff); but that had been a problem in Galilee too
(6:15).[68] Jerusalem's dismissive attitude towards 'things Galilean' may also
have been a factor (7:52).[69] John probably sees Jerusalem, being the guardian
of Jewish life and symbols, as particularly threatened by one who claimed that
its institutions pointed to him (2:19; 7:37-9; 8:12; 10:36) and who through his
healing on the Sabbath (5:9; 9:14) showed a seeming disrespect for the Law
(7:19ff). If Jesus was Israel's true Messiah, Jerusalem stood to lose the most.

Jerusalem becomes in this Gospel the place where the dramatic theme
in his Prologue is seen most clearly: 'Jerusalem, the religious centre of Judaism, was "his own home", but "his own people did not receive him"' (1:11).[70]
It is the capital city of Israel, the 'very center of Jewry'.[71] Confirmation of this
is found in those references to 'Judea' where a simple reference to 'Jerusalem'
might be expected (7:1-3; 11:7).[72] At a mundane level Jerusalem was located
in 'Judea' as opposed to Galilee. In another sense this Johannine usage serves
to show that this is how we are best to understand Jerusalem: it is the centre
of 'Judea', the city of his fellow Jews.

c) *The City of the World*

This is not John's last word. If it were, he might legitimately be charged with
mercilessly highlighting the failure of the Jewish people in Jerusalem. Subsequent interpretations have skewed the evidence in that direction, but to do so

---

[65] In the Greek the word translated 'there' (ἐκεῖ) is given emphasis through being placed
last (hence the italics).

[66] Brown (1966/70) 414.

[67] *Cf.* C.R. Koester (1990).

[68] McHugh (1992) 133, suggests that Jesus openly declared his Messiahship in Samaria
because there was no danger of a nationalistic misinterpretation.

[69]If Nathaniel from Bethsaida looked down upon Nazareth (1:46), how much more would
the residents of Jerusalem!

[70] Lindars (1972) 201.

[71] Fortna (1974) 93.

[72] The references to 'Judea' in 3:22; 4:3, 47, 54, however, refer to the wider area of Judea.

is to lose sight of other important inter-connections within the Gospel. The author is himself Jewish; in speaking of Jesus' coming to 'his own people', John is speaking of *his* 'own people' too. More striking still, is the way in which he has depicted Jerusalem's story in a way that leaves non-Jews with nothing to take pride in. Jerusalem is portrayed as the focal point of the whole 'world'.

One of the paradoxes of John's Gospel is that it is focused almost exclusively upon Israel, and yet its tone and its concerns are so clearly universal.[73] There is little explicit teaching on how this message about Jesus will go out to the Gentiles. The 'Gentiles' are not mentioned as such,[74] though the arrival of 'some Greeks' (12:20) is probably a foretaste of the gospel going out to 'all people' (12:32).[75] Jesus speaks of 'other sheep' (10:16; *cf.* 17:20ff) and John refers enigmatically to the 'scattered children of God' (11:52), but apart from chapter 4 (where the response of the Samaritans may be taken as paradigmatic of other non-Jewish responses to Jesus) and chapter 21 (which may be beginning to look outward to the world-wide mission of the Church), the focus is resolutely upon Jesus' interaction with Judaism. Within this confine, however, what is happening in Israel has truly world-wide implications.

> Just when the narrative seems to concentrate on a small focal point, it contains the seeds of the larger picture which make John the book it is. The prologue, and hints at various points all through, indicate how this story of Jesus-and-the-Judeans is to be read. It is the microcosm, the focal point, of the story of the creator god and the world. The question of the creator and the *kosmos*, the world, becomes the question of Jesus and Israel. And when that question is resolved, with the full paradox and irony of the crucifixion of the King of the Jews, then at once the world can become the beneficiary.[76]

John achieves this by his frequent use of the word 'world'.[77] 'God so loved the world' (3:18; *cf. e.g.* 1:29; 6:33; 8:12) and Jesus is the 'Saviour of the world' (4:42); his coming to Israel is really a divine visitation of the 'world' as a whole.[78] Lying behind the events in Judea, Galilee and Samaria, is a divine entrance into the world. This Land merely happens to be the place where this cosmic event has taken place.

---

[73] See *e.g.* Brown (1966/70) lxxvii; Fortna (1974) 92; C.R. Koester (1995) 234 ('images with strong roots in Judaism are expanded and universalized').

[74] Though Pancaro (1969-70) argues that John would have understood them to be included in the 'scattered children of God' (11:52); this is criticized by Pryor (1992) 49.

[75] There may also be some intentional irony in the misunderstanding that Jesus might 'go to the Dispersion among the Greeks and teach the Greeks' (7:35).

[76] Wright (1992a) 412.

[77] There are 78 occurrences, compared with only 3 in each of Mark and Luke.

[78] See also 9:5, 39; 12:46; 13:1; 16:28; 17:18; 18:37.

It is especially interesting that John on occasions uses the word 'world' where a reference to Jerusalem might be expected. Encouraging him to go up to the Feast of Tabernacles in Jerusalem, his brothers tease him: 'show yourself to the world' (7:4). The brief positive response of the Jerusalem crowds to Jesus at the Triumphal Entry evoke the Pharisees' response: 'look, the world has gone after him!' (12:19). In his teaching ministry in Jerusalem Jesus declares God's truth to the 'world' (8:26); 'I have spoken openly to the world in synagogues and in the Temple' (18:20). Thus what Jesus did in Jerusalem, he did in and for the world.

This has positive and negative consequences. Positively, John's readers (both Jews and Gentiles) who did not witness these events personally can sense that Jesus had been present in their world and had come to achieve things for them. Negatively, Israel and Jerusalem have proved to be no different from the world. Jerusalem has become but a city of the world, like any other city; and Israel, though called to be different from the world, has all too easily become a representative of the world. Given the fact that in so many other instances John uses the word 'world' in a highly negative sense (of the world in its opposition to God), his identifying Jerusalem/Israel with the world, is quite a startling indictment.

This was precisely John's point. In speaking to his *Jewish* interrogators, Jesus states, 'you are of this world' (8:23). In preparing his disciples for the 'hatred' which they will receive from the 'world', he warns them that 'they will put you out of the *synagogues*' (16:2); their fellow-Jews are evidently to be identified as representatives of the 'world'. For John, Israel and Jerusalem have become representative of the world in this negative sense, and Jerusalem has become the place where the 'prince of this world' has sought to exert his power, though ultimately without success (12:31; 14:30; 16:11).

> Israel, though acknowledged as the πατρίς of Jesus, his own people by race, have been shown by their rejection of him to belong totally to the world.[79]

> For John, the Jews belong to 'the world', that is they are part of that division of men who are in dualistic opposition to Jesus. . . . John is not anti-Semitic; the evangelist is condemning not race or people but opposition to Jesus.[80]

Non-Jews and those living in cities other than Jerusalem cannot turn this to their own pride. For if Israel/Jerusalem is no better than the world, then equally the world is no better than Israel/Jerusalem. All alike have been reduced to the same level.[81] This was precisely the point of John's prologue: be-

---

[79] Pryor (1990) 218. *Cf.* too his comments on ch. 13 in (1992) 54: Israel is not distinct from the world, but embodies its values. From now on the behaviour of the Jews will increasingly be spoken of as the activity of the world'.

fore speaking of Jesus' being rejected by 'his own people' Israel (1:11), he spoke of Jesus' coming to the 'world'; yet the world did not know him' (1:10). Jesus' being rejected by 'his own' people in Jerusalem was but a pointed manifestation of the way in which, as Jesus said, 'the world hates me' (7:7; cf. 15:18; 7:14). Jerusalem's response to Jesus was the response of the world to Jesus, the response of all John's readers, both Jew and Gentile.

It may be for this reason that John focuses in the Passion narrative on the role of Pontius Pilate (18:28-19:22). Although John seemingly clears him of responsibility for Jesus' death, his complicity in the event is evidently culpable and betokens the involvement of the non-Jewish 'world' in Jesus' crucifixion. His extended exchanges with Jesus placed Jerusalem against the background of the wider Roman Empire; what is about to take place will have repercussions throughout that empire and beyond. The declaration of the Jews to Pilate that 'we have no king but the emperor' (19:15) gives ultimate expression to the truth that Jerusalem is no different from any other city in the empire. When Pilate hands Jesus over 'to be crucified' (19:16), however, the converse truth is seen: the Gentile world too has little of which it may boast.

In reducing Jerusalem to the level of a 'worldly' city, John thus stripped it of its theological privileges, revealing what lay at its naked heart. In so doing he gave expression to a deeper hope—that the world, for all its opposition to God and to Jesus, 'might be saved' (cf. 3:17). For it was into this 'world' that Jesus came and in the immediate vicinity of this world-city (in the form of Jerusalem) that he gave his life in order to bring 'life to the world' (cf. 6:33, 51). For the sake of the world, Jesus had to come to the sinful world at its deepest point; for the sake of that wider world that deepest point had to be Jerusalem.

Lightfoot concluded in similar vein:

> If Jerusalem is the scene of God's mightiest working and of mankind's supreme deliverance, it is also the sphere of the bitterest, intensest conflict. . . . In John's Gospel there falls on Jerusalem, as on the cross itself, not only light but shadow, and Jerusalem holds the chief place in St John's Gospel because the cross stood there.[82]

---

[80] Brown (1966) lxxii. Cf. Ashton (1985) 68, who follows Bultmann over against Lowe (1976) and von Wahlde (1982), in seeing the 'Jews' as a symbol of the 'sinfulness of mankind'. He distinguishes between the *reference* of the term Ἰουδαῖοι (the Jews as Jesus' opponents) and its *symbolic* function (humanity). Fortna (1988) 312 ff, agreeing that the 'Jews' 'stand for the whole of humanity', notes that in later times the Jews 'no longer stand for the world, but are viewed as scarcely belonging to humanity'. From our discussion here, it should be clear that this would have been a total distortion of John's intention: because of the mutual interchangeablity of the 'world' and the 'Jews' in John's thought, the 'world' cannot claim any higher standing than the 'Jews', for both are equal.

[81] This brings John's thought close to Paul's (see esp. Rom. 3:9, 23).

d) The City for the World

Jerusalem is identified with the world so that the 'world can become the beneficiary'.[83] This awareness of worldwide implications comes to the fore in
chapter 12, especially when some 'Greeks' request to see Jesus (12:20ff). Jesus replies: 'Unless a grain of wheat falls into the earth and dies, it remains
just a single grain; but if it dies, it bears much fruit' (12:24). As his 'hour' approaches (v. 23) Jesus sees his death in Jerusalem as being the means whereby
there will come blessing to the wider world.[84] Developing this imagery, it
might be concluded that the soil or 'earth' in which that seed would be placed
(Jerusalem) would prove to be no different from the soil of the world, and that
this lack of distinctiveness (which might otherwise have been culpable) will
become the very source of its fruitfulness. Irrespective of this, Jesus proceeds
(in this his last public appearance before the Passion) to speak of the moment
when 'lifted up from the earth' he would 'draw all people' to himself (v. 32).
The forthcoming events, though tied in a particular way to Jerusalem, will
have universal consequences.

There is a similar focus on the 'universal' in the Triumphal Entry, recounted just before this (11:12-19).[85] This confirms our conclusion that John
may not have been especially interested in the poignancy of Jesus' being welcomed into Jerusalem as her rightful 'king' (12:15). Instead he presented this
episode as a picture of the welcome to be given to Jesus by the world at large.
'Look', say the Pharisees, 'the *world* has gone after him!' (v. 19).[86]

The focus of John's Gospel is clearly at a moment of transition.[87] Until
this point John's focus was upon Jerusalem and the nature of the city's response to Jesus. Now, despite the fact that he still has to narrate the most important specific event that took place in Jerusalem, the universal theme begins
to predominate. The 'upper room' discourse (chs. 13-17) is presented in a
timeless and spaceless fashion, with its central themes being concerned with
the disciples' mission in the future—far away from Jerusalem. At the end of

---

[82] R.H Lightfoot (1938) 153.
[83] From the quotation at n. 76 above.
[84] *Cf.* Wright (1992a) 413. Here at last there is some resolution to the paradox (noted
above) that the Jesus who almost totally concentrated his ministry on the people of Israel
was yet the 'Saviour of the world' (4:42). Further resolution will come with the teaching
about the Spirit (chs. 14-16).
[85] Brown (1966/70) 462; Menken (1992) 576.
[86] If John's focus is not on Jerusalem *per se*, this certainly might help to explain why, in
striking contrast to the Synoptics, John has failed to mention that Jesus entered the city (let
alone the Temple!).
[87] As argued by *e.g.* Schillebeeckx (1980) 350-1. The 'universal' theme was present
before (see above at n. 76ff), but it now receives greater emphasis.

the Gospel is the resurrection itself (20:1ff)—a particular event, but with universal implications (20:21, 31; 21:18ff). The dynamic of the Gospel's second half is therefore away from Jerusalem. Having entered the world (1:9-10), the time has come for Jesus to 'depart from this world and go to the Father' (13:1). Meanwhile, the disciples are prepared for their forthcoming mission to the world: 'as you have sent me into the world, so I have sent them into the world' (17:18; *cf.* 20:21). All the actors in the drama are preparing to make their departure, whether *from* the world (Jesus) or *into* the world (the disciples).

As an indication of this, 'Jerusalem' is never again mentioned by name in the Gospel after the reference in 12:12. After twelve appearances in the first half of the Gospel it now disappears altogether.[88] Thus, as Brodie observes,

> [There is] ambiguity about Jerusalem. At one level it comes more and more to the fore. . . . Yet at another level it appears to recede. . . . In chapters 13-21, even though most of the action is set in Jerusalem, the name is never again mentioned. . . . Jerusalem is being left behind. . . . At one level the story moves towards Jerusalem; but at another it moves steadily away.[89]

Even if a subsequent editorial addition, the Galilean episode in chapter 21 continues a trend that is already well developed. The Gospel ends with Jerusalem seemingly far away. Instead the focus is *outwards* (to the worldwide mission of the Church, parabolically enacted in the great number of fish 'drawn' in (21:11; *cf.* 12:32), *forwards* ('follow me': v. 19) and *upwards* ('until I return': v. 23). John's final words concern the 'world', but this time in a neutral sense—the world that had been visited by God and which through the events in Jerusalem would never be the same again. If all that Jesus had done were written down, 'I suppose that the world itself could not contain the books that would be written' (21:25).

In this way the particularity of Jerusalem is steadily eclipsed, as it becomes the mere backdrop for that action by which God will save the world. There is nothing in the 'upper room' which cannot be experienced elsewhere, and through the reality of the Risen Jesus the effects of the Passion can be multiplied throughout the world. Jerusalem has proved a fruitful soil, but this hardly redounds to its credit. The city *of* the world has become the means of salvation *for* the world.

---

[88] For references, see above at n. 54. This may explain the three occasions where John uses the verb to 'go out' (ἐξέρχομαι) without specifying that the point of departure was Jerusalem (18:1; 19:17; 20:3): see above at n. 45.

[89] Brodie (1993) 28-9, who explains this universalizing strand by noting that John has to achieve in one volume what Luke could present in two. However, because of the possibility that John 21 is a later addition to the Gospel's structure (though possibly by the same hand: below n.129), it is unwise to say that the Gospel is consciously 'focused on Galilee' (p. 28).

e) *Conclusion*

The emphasis in the second half of the Gospel is therefore different from that in the first. Just as the initial concentration on Jesus as the Temple gave way to a focus on Christian believers as 'temples', so the initial concentration upon Jerusalem gives way to an emphasis on the implications of these Jerusalem-events for the wider world.

John's greater concentration on Jesus' association with Jerusalem, when compared with the Synoptics, is not to be misconstrued. Within the terms of his ministry there was a certain necessity in Jesus' involvement with Jerusalem. John may have wanted to offset any false inference from the Synoptics that Jesus was distant from Jerusalem or marginal to the centralities of Jewish life. He could only be understood as being the one who challenged those centralities by claiming himself to be the new centre of Judaism—a claim which had to be made in and to Jerusalem. The necessary role which this gave to Jerusalem in Jesus' ministry, however, did not continue to pertain in the period thereafter. The disciples' focus, even while they were located within Jerusalem, was drawn away from Jerusalem to the world beyond.

In contrast to his treatment of the Temple, John did not draw attention to the city's theological status within the Old Testament period. On the evidence available, it was unclear whether John himself would have accepted this notion, or challenged it. In either case there was no emphasis on Jerusalem's previous significance within the narrative itself. As a result, Jerusalem was depicted not in strictly theological categories, but rather in human terms—as the focal centre of 'Judea', the city of the Judeans. Jerusalem became for John a window into the heart of Judaism. This in turn, through the identification of Israel with the world, enabled Jerusalem to become a window into the world at large. Jerusalem was seen to be 'in the world', and the world in Jerusalem.

The great events which Jerusalem had witnessed did not serve to elevate the city's status. After the resurrection the Risen Jesus appeared only to his disciples who were in 'fear of the Jews' (20:19); it was not an appearance to Jerusalem as a whole. This was a first indication of Jesus' intention to 're-veal himself' to his own followers, but 'not to the world' (14:22). Jerusalem was the location of the resurrection, but not strictly its witness or beneficiary. It was simply the place through which Jesus had necessarily to 'pass through' on his return to the Father.[90]

---

[90] Hence John sees Jesus' 'going up' (ἀναβαίνω) to Jerusalem in 7:8-10 as part of the much larger drama in which Jesus 'goes up' or 'ascends' to the Father (*cf.* 20:17): so Brown (1966/70) 308; on this theme of 'ascent/descent', see Schillebeeckx (1980) 321-331.

John would not have accorded any ongoing significance to the Jerusalem of his own day. Not only had he played down Jerusalem's significance in the past; he had also given ample indication that Jesus' concentration on Jerusalem, while necessary in its time, was now eclipsed by the universal nature of his message. The Temple had been replaced and Jerusalem eclipsed.

3. The Land of Palestine

The issues of the Temple and City were necessarily interconnected with the issue of the Land. What were John's reflections on the significance of Palestine as a whole? In the Christian era the 'Holy Land' can be given a theological significance for two quite different reasons—its role in the Hebrew scriptures as the 'promised land', and its unique role as the location of the Incarnation. Is there anything within John's writing to suggest how he would have responded to these two (very different) ways of thinking?

a) The 'Promised Land'

Was it right for Christians still to think of Palestine as the 'promised land'? Initially there appears to be little in John on this theme. However, some factors emerge which may have been key ingredients in his assessment of this issue.

First, what would be the consequences of John's portrait of Jesus as a latter-day Moses?[91] There was an expectation that God would send a 'prophet like Moses' (Deut. 18:15ff).[92] John responds by showing how the three gifts given by God in the time of Moses (manna, water from the rock, the fiery pillar) were now available in Jesus (chs. 6-8).[93] Moses was heralded as the great 'shepherd/leader of Israel; Jesus was the 'good shepherd' (10:11ff). Jesus' death was compared to Moses' action with the bronze snake (3:14) and John's terminology concerning those crucified with Jesus (literally, 'on either side one') reflects the description of Moses' arms being supported on either side (Exod. 17:12).[94] For John the 'time of Moses had returned'.[95]

---

[91]   See the illuminating brief study by Glasson (1963) and the extended study by Meeks (1967); cf. also Enz (1957), R.H. Smith (1962), and Schillebeeckx (1980) 312-321.

[92]   See e.g. Motyer (1992) 157ff.

[93]   Glasson (1963) 10-11; Motyer (1992) chs. 5-6.

[94]   Glasson (1963) 40-44. John's Greek (ἐντεῦθεν καὶ ἐντεῦθεν: 19:18), which contrasts with the Synoptics, is close to the LXX translation of Exod. 17:12: ἐντεῦθεν εἷς καὶ ἐντεῦθεν εἷς.

[95]   Jansen (1985) 136.

John saw Jesus not just as a 'new' or 'second Moses'; 'he regarded Jesus as greater than Moses.[96] In 1:17 there is clearly an element of contrast in
favour of Jesus: 'the law was given through Moses; grace and truth came
through Jesus Christ'. Even though Moses had conversed with God 'face to
face' (Num. 12:18), John asserts that '*no one* has ever seen God'; instead only
he who 'is close to the Father's heart' 'has made him known' (1:18).[97] If God
had sent to Israel another (or greater) Moses, this must have led Christians to
ask about the 'promised land' to which he had brought them.

> It is inconceivable that the discussion of the figure of Moses who led Israel
> on the way to the promised land should not have led to discussion of the land
> among the earliest Christians.[98]

A similar question would arise from noting the way John also presents Jesus
as the Passover Lamb:[99] what is the new 'exodus' that has been achieved?

Again the second half of the Gospel, and in particular the Farewell Discourse, provides an answer. Here there are clear allusions to Moses' 'farewell
discourse' to Israel (as in the book of Deuteronomy).[100] Unlike Moses, Jesus
will return after his death to be with his disciples, but what is the 'promised
land' that they are about to enter? Is it 'heaven', as portrayed in 14:1-3?

> The disciples, no less than the Israelites have a home promised to them, the
> possession of which is imminent.[101]

Is it the whole experience of being 'in the truth'?

> What Jesus surveyed on the eve of his death was a domain which, in the eyes
> of the Evangelist, held out more promise than the land of Canaan did to the
> Israelites: it was 'the truth', a territory whose boundaries had already been
> clearly defined as the revelation of Jesus, but the extent of whose riches had
> yet to be discovered—under the guidance of the Paraclete.[102]

---

[96] Meeks (1967) 319; *cf.* Ashton (1991) 470ff; Pryor (1992) 120-1. This is comparable to
the implication that Jesus is 'greater than Jacob' (4:12) and Abraham (8:56-58).
[97] *Cf.* also 6:32ff, which contrasts the manna of Moses' era with Jesus who is *himself* the
'bread of life'.
[98] Davies (1974) 333-4.
[99] *Cf.* above at n. 35.
[100] This is worked through in detail by Lacomara (1974). Brown (1966/70) 625, also notes
the parallels with Deut. 1:29, 33, where God tells his people not to be afraid because he
himself will go ahead to search out the places, showing them the way (*cf.* John 14:1-3).
[101] Lacomara (1974) 78.
[102] Ashton (1991) 476.

Or is it the forthcoming responsibility of being 'sent into the world' as Jesus' disciples (17:18)?

> The Israelites are about to enter Canaan . . . ; the disciples of Jesus are about to become his definitive community.[103]

This Moses-Jesus parallelism strongly suggests that John saw the theme of the 'promised land' as typologically fulfilled in Christ—in a way that no longer related to the physical land of Palestine. There could be little doubt that Christians, although not yet reunited with Jesus (14:1-3), were in some profound sense already in the 'promised land'—wherever they were living in the world. If the Johannine Jesus emphasized not the slavery of Israel in Egypt but the slavery (even of his contemporary Israel) 'to sin' (8:34-5), then those who were 'set free' by 'the Son' were even now in the 'promised land'. Jesus offered 'a new exodus from sin and death'.[104]

This conclusion is confirmed, secondly, in John's presentation of Jesus as the fulfilment of the ceremonies associated with Tabernacles (7:37-9; 8:12). This festival not only looked back to the first 'exodus' but also became a vehicle for channelling Jewish hopes for a second 'exodus' (when the many prophecies relating to the Jerusalem of the new age would come to fulfilment).[105] Jesus' words would have challenged many contemporary messianic ideas. Those hopes, implies John, were to be focused not on God's doing a new thing for Jerusalem in the 'promised land', but upon what God was doing for them in Jesus.[106]

The prophecies associated with Tabernacles fuelled the expectation that there would be an 'ingathering' of Jewish exiles (or even Gentiles?) to Jerusalem and the 'promised land'.[107] John's language in 11:52 clearly indicates that this gathering process did not involve any geographical relocation. Rather, it came about when people responded to the message of Jesus and were brought into his one 'people'; Jesus was 'about to die . . . to gather into one

---

[103] Lacomara (1974) 66.

[104] Motyer (1992) 229 (cf. pp. 160, 196). Cf. Morgan (1957) 159: 'as Moses, the shepherd of God's flock, led the nation out of slavery into the 'promised land', so Jesus leads the new Israel out of the bondage of sin into the pastures of new life and freedom'. Cf. also Beasley-Murray (1989) 76: 'through his sacrificial death and risen life he enacts the Second Exodus and opens for all mankind the promised kingdom of God'.

[105] Brown (1966/70) 326; cf. above at n. 36.

[106] Some further confirmation of this would be found in John 21, if the '153 fish' (21:11) were an indication (by the process of numeral *gematria*) of the fulfilment of the prophecy in Ezek. 47:10. This is argued for by Emerton (1958) and Grigsby (1993-4), but is necessarily highly speculative.

[107] So C.W.F. Smith (1962-3) 143, following the ideas of R. H. Lightfoot: Tabernacles looked forward to the 'ingathering or harvest of the nations in the days of the Messiah'.

the dispersed children of God (τὰ τέκνα τοῦ θεοῦ τὰ διεσκορπισμένα συνα-
γάγῃ εἰς ἕν: 11:51-52). Jesus was also the 'good shepherd' who promised to
'bring others also' into his flock (10:14-16). In the light of Ezekiel 34, where
God himself is the 'shepherd' who restores the 'scattered' flock of Israel from
their exile, John's presentation suggests that the promised 'restoration' and ingathering was now coming to pass in Jesus. Thus,

> those who recognize their blindness and are 'found' by Jesus and come to
> 'worship him' are caught up in a restoration of exile on the Ezekiel 34 model,
> with Jesus as the Shepherd of Israel.[108]

Jesus, not the 'promised land', is now the focus of this long-awaited 'ingathering'.[109] 'The 'promised land has been reached'.[110]

This suggests, thirdly, that John's Gospel acts as a corrective to any
Jewish nationalism. Such nationalism, with its convictions about the role of
the 'promised land' within God's purposes, sought a political freedom. Instead the Johannine Jesus talks about a different kind of 'freedom' (8:32-36)
and a different kind of 'kingdom' (3:3-5). Though presented to Pilate as a political activist, claiming to be the 'king of the Jews' (18:33), Jesus says that his
'kingdom is not from this world' (18:36). Thus when the crowds wish to
'make him king', he withdraws (6:15), and when they hail him as the 'King of
Israel' he deliberately takes a donkey to counter any false notions of what that
kingship means (12:14).[111] Jesus is indeed the 'king of Israel' and 'king of the
Jews', but, precisely because he is rejected as king by his own people (19:15),
his kingdom proves to be of a quite different kind. The Messianic kingdom,
which was popularly associated with the freedom of the 'promised land', has
been manifested in a most unexpected way. The hermeneutic that led to that
way of thinking was profoundly wrong: Israel's notion of kingship 'belongs
to the realm of the world' (cf. 18:36).[112]

Fourthly, John's identification of Jesus with the 'true vine' (15:1ff)
points in a similar direction. Burge argues that in the light of its use in the Old
Testament (e.g. Isa. 5:1ff), the vine was understood as the 'people of Israel'
and the vineyard as Israel's Land.[113] Thus,

---

[108] Motyer (1992) 163.
[109] Cf. also Giesbrecht (1986); cf. possibly 17:24 (Jesus' prayer that his followers might be
'with me where I am, to see my glory').
[110] C.W.F. Smith (1962-3) 144.
[111] Brown (1966/70) 462, sees the openings words of 12:14 (εὑρὼν δὲ) as adversative, a
response to the misunderstanding which is implicit within the crowd's greeting.
[112] Pryor (1992) 77.
[113] Burge (1994) 393.

> the crux of John 15 is that *Jesus is changing the place of rootedness for Israel*. The commonplace prophetic metaphor (the Land as vineyard, the people of Israel as vines) now undergoes a dramatic shift. God's vineyard, the Land of Israel, now has only one vine, Jesus. . . . And the only means of attachment to the Land is through this one vine, Jesus Christ. He offers what attachment to the Land once promised: rootedness and life and hope. . . . The Fourth Gospel is transferring spatial, earthbound gifts from God and connecting them to a living person, Jesus Christ.[114]

In a Gospel that has been replete with the motif of Jesus as the replacement of central Jewish symbols, this final 'I am' saying suggests that the 'promised land' too needs to be seen as fulfilled in Christ. As a result,

> the Land, as holy territory should now recede from the concerns of God's people. The vineyard is no longer an object of religious desire as it once had been.[115]

There are clearly features in John's presentation of Jesus which led him to re-evaluate the concept of the 'promised land'. Jesus is the one who is greater than Moses; he is the 'true vine', the true fulfilment of the festival of Tabernacles, and the one in whom God's 'scattered' people are truly 'gathered' to himself. If John's readers included those who still wished to emphasize the importance of the 'promised land', John's message would be plain.

b) The Places of the Incarnation

John's emphasis on the unique significance of Jesus caused him to play down Palestine's role as the 'promised land'. That same emphasis, however, might be thought to give Palestine a new significance—as the 'holy land' which alone had witnessed this saving event. This was where the 'Word became flesh' (1:14). Are there any signs in John of such a 'geographical mysticism'?

Some positive indications are gleaned from the concern shown in the Johannine epistles with the errors of docetism (1 John 4:2-3; 2 John 7); in this context an emphasis on the geographical *realia* of Jesus' life would be a useful

---

[114] Burge (1994) 393-4.

[115] Burge (1994) 395. There is little in John's understanding of eschatology to suggest that Palestine will feature prominently in the future. The predominant note of the Gospel is one of 'realized eschatology', by which John indicates that many of the blessings associated with the future are already the Christian's possession—again through their union with Christ, not through their physical location. When a more 'traditional' understanding of Christ's return comes to the fore (*e.g.* 21:22-23), however, there is nothing to suggest that this is to be linked to the land of Palestine—though the evidence is admittedly slight.

corrective to any gnostic tendencies to 'over-spiritualize' the gospel. Alternatively, some might see this tying in with John's 'sacramental' approach.[116] John's 'sacramentalism' is quite ambiguous, however, such that some interpreters see John not as advocating such an approach, but denouncing it.[117] John would then have been critical of any geographical sacramentalism.

A more useful question to ask is: are there any signs in John's Gospel of his approach towards *Jewish* 'holy places'; for his attitude towards these would, if he was consistent, spill over into his understanding of the appropriate Christian approach towards a 'holy land' or 'holy places'.

Davies' analysis again proves valuable. He has argued convincingly that the Gospel's opening chapters are consciously designed to promote this issue of Jewish 'holy places' with their references to Bethel (1:51), the Jerusalem Temple (2:19-21), Mount Gerizim (4:20-26), the pool of Bethesda (5:2ff) and finally the pool of Siloam (9:7).[118] In each case John presents Jesus as fulfilling or replacing the significance of these places. Since the pool of Bethesda may well have had pagan associations, an impressive picture is developed of Jesus as the answer to all that was previously invested in 'holy places' by Jews, Samaritans, and pagans. This is all part of John's 'deliberate presentation of the replacement of "holy places" by the Person of Jesus'.[119] 'Holy space' has been 'christified', and the category of Place replaced by that of Person.[120]

> In the Fourth Gospel the Person of Jesus Christ replaces "holy places". In the light of this, it is, therefore, not a gospel likely to ascribe theological significance to geographic entities. To do so, it would seem, would be to contradict much of its concern.[121]

Any Christian attempt to invest the places associated with Jesus in Palestine with a new spiritual significance should be ruled out—Jesus himself was the only true 'holy place'.

Such ideas are countered, secondly, by John's presentation of the Spirit. The mystique of 'holy places' is nourished by the belief that certain physical locations associated with the divine may enable the faithful to draw closer to God; they help to span the gulf between God and humanity. For John, that gulf

---

[116] On John's sacramentalism, see the overview in Kysar (1985) 2460ff.

[117] So, Dunn (1977) 171; Carson (1991) 298.

[118] Davies (1974) 289-318.

[119] Davies (1974) 334.

[120] Davies (1974) 290; *cf.* 368.

[121] Davies (1974) 318. *Cf.* similarly Betz (1981) 65; Burge (1987) 195-7; Schillebeeckx (1980) 318: God's final revelation is no longer bound up with a country or place, but *with the movements of the person of Jesus*' (italics original).

is spanned by the Spirit. God is not absent, because he is fully present through the gift of the Spirit of Jesus.

Again the second half of the Gospel develops what has been established in the first. John's focusing 'holy space' exclusively onto Jesus in the opening chapters inevitably raises the question: what will happen when the time approaches for that 'holy space' to be removed from this world? How does one gain access to that 'place' when it has disappeared? The answer is given in the Farewell Discourse, and focuses on the Holy Spirit.

Jesus is the unique 'way' to God (14:6) and a true window into God's character (14:9). Although he is about to leave his disciples, this is to their advantage (14:28; 16:7); for only then can he send the Spirit of truth who is described as 'another Paraclete' (ἄλλον παράκλητον: 14:16). The use of ἄλλος ('another of the same kind') indicates that the Spirit is to be understood as essentially 'another Jesus'—the 'presence of Jesus when Jesus is absent'.[122] The Spirit will be the 'continuing presence of Jesus in their midst'.[123] This Spirit will also be the means whereby Jesus and the Father will make their 'dwelling' (μονὴν) in the believer (14:23). As a result, believers are not left 'orphaned' (14:18): Jesus is not absent, but present through his Spirit.

This cuts at the root any attempts to invest with significance the particular places associated with Jesus' life. They have no ability to compensate for Jesus' departure. That ability resides with the Spirit. Nor is a believer disadvantaged if far removed from the scenes of the Incarnation. The Spirit is fully available, regardless of location; for (in contrast to the Jesus of the Gospel) the Spirit of Jesus is not restricted by space but 'blows where it chooses' (3:8).

Physical place is, therefore, no longer important—because of the Spirit's presence. This is why John never specifies the location of the 'upper room'. If there was any physical place within his Gospel which might legitimately become a 'holy place' at a later date amongst Jesus' followers, it was this—the place where Jesus poignantly shared with his closest followers his final hours before the Cross.[124] John pointedly leaves its location unspecified—focusing on Jesus' person and his teaching, and indicating that the disciple's intimate experience of Jesus was essentially possible for all believers, even if far removed in space and time. Jesus' earlier teaching, in which he had dismissed the importance of the Temple 'in Jerusalem' (4:21), applied equally to any subsequent Christian attachment to physical space: with the coming of Jesus and the Spirit, the hour had come at last when believers could and should 'worship the Father in spirit and truth' (4:24).

---

[122] Brown (1966/70) 1141.

[123] Pryor (1992) 62-3.

[124] For further possible reasons, see above at n. 45ff.

Through this emphasis on the Spirit, John taught that, although Christians might be distant in time or space from the events recounted in the Gospel, they were not disadvantaged.[125] The physicality of the Gospel events could not be denied, and John himself mentioned many different locations in Palestine which are not found in the Synoptics.[126] These places, however, were not invested with any long-term significance beyond their role within the actual narrative. John's tendency to emphasize the universal implications of Jesus' 'coming into the *world*',[127] which affected his approach to Jerusalem, similarly diffused any particularistic emphasis on Palestine.

> The Fourth Gospel is not especially concerned with the particular relation of Jesus of Nazareth to his own geographical land. . . . It does not lend itself easily to geographical concern so much as to the personal confrontation with the One from above, whose Spirit bloweth where it listeth and is not subject to geographical dimensions that had been dear to Judaism.[128]

John did not then give an enduring significance to the 'holy land'—despite the events that had taken place there. Instead he focused on Jesus, who drew onto himself all notions of 'holy space', precisely because he was the meeting-point between God and humankind (*cf.* 1:51; 12:32); believers could trust that this Jesus through the Spirit was as available to them as he had once been in Palestine. In this way John held together two major themes—the specificity and historicity of the *Incarnation*, and the ubiquity and availability throughout time and space of the *Spirit*. History was important (indeed his writing of the Gospel played a part in ensuring that that historical anchor was not lost) and the Incarnation a vital fact; but the Incarnation did not encourage a renewed focus on 'holy places', because Jesus' resurrection and the gift of his Spirit rendered unnecessary all such attachment to physical space.

John's Gospel would have corrected all those who elevated Palestine—whether as the 'promised land' of the Old Testament or as the unique scene of the Incarnation. But who would think in this way? The former notion suggests an audience with a Jewish background, the latter a readership that already shared John's Christian conviction about the Incarnation. Who was John writing for? How have the circumstances of the author and those of his intended audience affected his attitude towards Jerusalem?

---

[125] The unbelief of many of those who encountered Jesus (*cf.* above 2b) would only confirm that proximity in time and space was no advantage.

[126] *E.g.* Bethany beyond the Jordan (1:28), Cana (2:1; 4:46), Aenon near Salim (3:23), Sychar (4:5), the Sea of Tiberias (6:1; 21:1), Ephraim (11:54).

[127] 1:10; 3:17; 6:14; 9:5, 39; 10:6; 11:27; 12:46; 13:1; 16:28; 17:11, 18; 18:37; *cf.* above at n. 76. Note too 17:4: 'I have brought you glory on earth (ἐπὶ τῆς γῆς)'.

[128] Davies (1974) 333.

4. John and Jerusalem

a) Johannine Uncertainties

Who was John? When was the Gospel written, by what process, and for whom?[129] Given the scholarly uncertainty on these issues, it is hazardous to reconstruct the way in which the attitude towards Jerusalem of the Gospel's author may have been influenced by circumstances, past or present.

For example, if the 'traditional' identification of the evangelist with John the apostle, the son of Zebedee, could be firmly established, then certain reconstructions would become possible.[130] The author's experience of Jerusalem could include those experiences attributed to 'John' in the book of Acts,[131] and a strong case could be made that one of the subsidiary reasons for the writing of the Gospel was John's need to prepare his fellow-Christians for the day when he, their 'premier witness'[132] and (last surviving?) apostle, would be taken from them (21:20-24). This would explain several features of the Gospel: the author's emphasis on his own insignificance compared with Jesus,[133] the strategic importance of the Farewell Discourse,[134] the promise that the Spirit would 'dwell' in the disciples after Jesus' departure (14:23), and the dominical blessing on those 'who have not seen and yet have come to believe' (20:29). This would dove-tail neatly with the implicit critique examined

---

[129] On the question of whether John 21 was composed by a different author, Barrett (1978) 577, and Lindars (1972) 622, argue that the similarities in style with the rest of the Gospel suggest it was by the same hand; *cf.* Minear (1983). On the various layers of tradition behind the Gospel, see *e.g.* Brown (1979). On the intended audience of the Gospel, see below n. 144.

[130] This traditional interpretation is advocated by *e.g.* Robinson (1985) 93-122, Morris (1969) 139-292. For a general overview of the issue of authorship, see *e.g.* Culpepper (1994). Other identifications of the 'beloved disciple' include Lazarus (Stibbe [1993]), Thomas (Charlesworth [1995]), and a different John who was resident in Jerusalem (Hengel [1989a]).

[131] As suggested in *e.g.* Robinson (1985) 114-6.

[132] C.R. Koester (1995) 229.

[133] Jesus holds 'centre-stage' throughout the Gospel, with all others playing a very subsidiary role; *cf.* Lindars (1972) 54. The Evangelist's role as a 'witness' is not to draw attention to himself, but simply to be 'truthful' (19:35; 21:24); *cf.* his depiction of the witness of John the Baptist ('he must become greater, I must become less': 3:30). The anonymity of the 'beloved disciple' would then be in keeping with this.

[134] The Farewell Discourse would then have the extra poignancy that the apostle was himself about to leave *his* 'disciples'. By drawing his readers into this originally private episode in the 'upper room', the apostle would also be sharing his unique privilege with his readers (*cf.* 1 John 1:1-4); through the Spirit they could experience an intimacy with Jesus comparable to that experienced by the apostle himself.

above of any Christian nostalgia for the places in Palestine visited by Jesus; for John would be indicating that the link between the believer and Jesus was not dependent upon the continuing existence of either himself (as an apostolic eye-witness) or of such physical places. Jesus could be known through the presence of the Spirit, who was effectively Jesus' 'replacement' ('another Advocate': 14:16), and who unlike the historical Jesus (14:9 etc), or John himself, would be with them 'for ever' (14:16).[135]

For our purposes the more solid hypothesis, however, would be that the evangelist (regardless of his precise identity) was almost certainly writing after AD 70, probably from somewhere in the Diaspora, beyond the shores of Palestine.[136] John and his readers would then be well aware that, since the events recorded in the Gospel, the great city of Jerusalem had fallen to the Romans; above all, the Temple was no more.

b) A Response to AD 70?

Is there anything to indicate the author's attitude to this important, quite recent event? Robinson has argued convincingly that John's text does not betray any explicit reference to it.[137] This in itself would be significant. Contrary to some interpretations, John was not drawing overt attention to this tragedy and seeking to pin-point the blame.[138] John's Gospel is patently a Gospel first and foremost about Jesus, not about Jerusalem.

Nevertheless, if Jerusalem had recently been overthrown, this would give to John and his readers a shared piece of knowledge in the light of which they would understand the text. Ample scope for 'dramatic irony' would be

---

[135] So Brown (1966) lxxxvi, sees John's presentation of the Spirit as designed to combat any perceived danger of the 'severance of the human links with Jesus of Nazareth', when 'the relationship between Church life and the historical Jesus has grown dim'.

[136] Since the work of Robinson (1985) the case has been opened again on the possibility of the Gospel pre-dating AD 70. Robinson's arguments have done much to show the rootedness of the Gospel in Palestinian soil and its preservation of very early traditions. Yet the majority of commentators, including conservative ones, still argue for a later date: see *e.g.* Carson (1991) 82-7. Carson favours Ephesus (pp. 86-7), Wengst (1981) argues very specifically for Batanaea. Others see John's tradition as having been affected by local Palestinian church issues (*e.g.* Meeks [1967]); even so, the community could now have left Palestine (see *e.g.* C.R. Koester [1995] 227). The affinities between John's theology and that of the 'Hellenists' (such as Stephen) is noted by Schillebeeckx (1980) 319, and Cullmann (1976).

[137] Robinson (1976) 254ff and (1985) 70.

[138] As argued by Motyer (1992) 175, in his discussion of ch. 9. This concurs with John's primary emphasis (above n. 36ff) on the category of 'replacement' which emphasizes the positive truth (concerning Jesus' identity) rather than the negative one of judgement.

created, whereby both the author and his readers would be aware of future events unknown to the characters within the narrative.

The precise extent of this irony is hard to gauge. When might John have expected his readers to be mindful of AD 70? When Jesus speaks about 'judgement' (*e.g.* 3:17; 5:22; 8:50-51; 9:39; 12:47-48)? When Jesus speaks of false 'shepherds' fleeing when the wolf arrives (10:12) and of 'thieves' taking God's people towards destruction rather than towards safety (10:9-10)? When Jesus is presented as the 'King of the Jews' but announces that the important kingdom about which to be concerned is 'not from this world' (18:33-36)? In each of these instances an ironic allusion to AD 70 is possible, but not especially probable. There are, however, at least three places where such an allusion is far more likely: i) when Jesus' 'zealotry' (2:17) leads to his cleansing of the Temple and to his enigmatic statement beginning with the words, 'destroy this Temple' (2:19); ii) when the crowd claims it has 'no king but the emperor' (19:15); and iii), when the Sanhedrin express their fear that 'the Romans will come and destroy both our holy place and our nation' (11:48).

In this last instance, anyone aware of the events of 70 would note the irony that Caiaphas' 'solution' proved no solution at all, and that the Sanhedrin's fears became a solemn reality—though not for the expected reason: the Romans would take action in response, not to Jesus' followers, but to those who shared the Sanhedrin's concern for their 'place and nation'—only to an extreme degree. Was there was any organic connection between the eventual fate of the Temple and the way Jesus, who had already been presented as a new 'Temple' (2:22), was sacrificed so that that 'old' Temple might be preserved?[139] John does not make this connection explicit (and this is a sign of his non-vindictive approach); yet his readers have been given some clear encouragement to develop their thoughts along these lines.

Others go further and see the fall of Jerusalem as a particular 'point of sensitivity' for John. For example, a fascinating study has recently set the heated exchange between Jesus and the Jews in chapter 8 against this backdrop.[140] The discussion concerning true 'freedom' (8:33-36), the reference to the slave having no permanent place in the 'household' (οἰκία: 8:35), and the fact that the man healed of blindness comes to 'worship' Jesus outside the Temple (9:38, and beyond the circle of the synagogue: 9:22), all take on a new significance when seen in the light of AD 70.[141]

John may well, therefore, have intended to offer a Christian approach to Jerusalem's fall. What explanation did he give of this event? The predom-

---

[139] Wead (1970) 66. 'Christ is the new Temple, replacing that which the Jews destroyed by their misguided attempt to save it. In their attempt to save their holy place they crucified him who was to bring fulfilment to it'.

[140] Motyer (1992). On 'points of sensitivity', see p. 50ff.

inant note is that, in sending Jesus, God was revealing him who was the new Temple and therefore the fulfilment and replacement of what had previously been at the heart of Jerusalem. Even though the events of AD 70 took place forty years later, the manifestation of Jesus meant that in principle the time had already come when 'Jerusalem' (4:21) would lose its distinctive status: 'the time is coming and *has now come*' (4:23). Because of his unique identity, Jesus' coming had inevitable repercussions for Jerusalem; indeed there was between them an intrinsic incompatibility. John's readers were to sense the enormity of what God had done in the person of Jesus and how his coming had truly moved God's purposes forwards into a new epoch.[142]

He also saw the fall of Jerusalem as the result of God's 'own' people not 'receiving' the one whom their God had sent (*cf.* 1:11). If Jerusalem was meant to be peculiarly God's 'own' city, it had proved to be the opposite; it preferred another 'king' (19:15). If it claimed to be 'in the light', it was really in darkness and blind (*cf.* 9:41; 1 John 1:6-7). Jerusalem had become a 'worldly' city—the epitome of the 'world' in its opposition to God. It would not be surprising then if it was stripped of its previous status; for (as is made clear in the Johannine epistles) the 'world' was under God's judgement and would surely 'pass away' (1 John 2:17). This close identification between Jerusalem and the 'world' would necessarily entail that, if the fall of Jerusalem was in some sense a sign of God's judgement, it was also a sure sign of God's judgement *upon the world*; it was a foretaste of what the whole world could expect at the end of the age.[143]

As a result, if any of his readers felt bereft of the Temple and of the spiritual focus provided by Jerusalem, John would have encouraged them not to mourn the loss of the city, but rather to see what God had done for them in Jesus.[144] Thus others have concluded:

> The Evangelist, writing after the Temple's destruction, does not bemoan its loss. . . . The presence of God has not been withdrawn, for Jesus has taken the place of the Temple. Jesus gives more than the Temple had ever given.[145]

---

[141] Motyer (1992) ch. 7. Moreover, in the light of the way in which Judaism at Jamnia began to reconstitute itself around the Torah, John's presentation of Jesus as the true representative of the Torah becomes particularly pertinent. On this, see esp Pancaro (1975).

[142] Westcott (1908) lxxviii-ix, explained John's omission of Jesus' words of judgement on Jerusalem (as found in the Synoptics) as follows: 'all is changed. There are no prophecies of the siege of the Holy City; the judgement had been wrought. There was no longer any need to dwell on the outward aspects. . . . The task of the Evangelist was to unfold the essential cause of the catastrophe'.

[143] *Cf.* above 1c.

Jesus became a sanctuary that transcended and replaced other places of worship, and endured beyond the destruction of the Temple, to unite the community of those called to worship 'in spirit and in truth'.[146]

Jesus stands in the place of everything that Israel has lost.[147]

Everything previously associated with Jerusalem was now available in the person of Jesus, mediated by the Spirit. He was the new Temple and through him his disciples could have a Temple-like experience of intimacy with God. He was the 'true vine', the new centre of God's people. None of this required them to call into question their previous beliefs about the former status of Jerusalem and its Temple, or to abandon them as an aberration in the past. In Jesus these Jewish beliefs were all affirmed.[148] Now, however, they had been fully appropriated and focused upon Israel's Messiah. 'Salvation' was truly 'from the Jews' (4:22), but God had done a new thing for Jerusalem and for the world. A new allegiance was now required, and a preparedness to say good-bye to the old.

Commenting on chapter 12, Motyer concludes,

> Jesus is presented as the 'true' cultic centre of Judaism, drawing people away from the celebration of the Temple feasts. . . . He is a Pied Piper, whistling a new melody which descants the deep resonances of Law and cult, and summoning Israel to a new following which means eternal life *now*. . . . Will the reader likewise 'go away' (12:19), leaving the Jerusalem cult behind?[149]

---

[144] This would apply equally whether John was seeking to persuade non-Christian Jews or to encourage Jewish Christians; the loss of Jerusalem could have raised questions for both groups. It is not unreasonable to suggest that John's Gospel was written with both in mind: so Barrett (1978) 26; Beasley-Murray (1987) lxxxix. Although the majority would interpret 20:31 as applying to Christians (see *e.g.* Fee [1992] 2205, Pryor [1992] 91), the Gospel may also have had an evangelistic purpose towards Jews as well: see Carson (1987), Motyer (1992) 247. John's purpose may then not have been to denounce but to deter, presenting Jesus not as the answer *to* Judaism, but as the answer *for* Judaism; so *e.g.* Beasley-Murray (1989) 10-11; Balfour (1995). Brown (1966/70) lxxv, argues that John's emphasis on 'replacement' is also part of his appeal to Jewish Christians to leave the synagogue; *cf.* Pancaro (1975) 534, and Kysar (1993) 121. The argument that John's writings are 'sectarian' and isolationist in outlook is well criticized by Pryor (1992) 166-9.

[145] Hoskyns (1940) 144.

[146] C.R. Koester (1995) 85.

[147] Motyer (1992) 3. *Cf.* also R.H. Lightfoot (1956) 183: Jesus is the 'full and perfect realization of the aspirations of Judaism'; Pryor (1992) 115: 'Jesus fulfils and is superior to all that has come before in Israel. In the [Church's] experience of the Incarnate Logos is fulfilled all that was foreshadowed in Israel's redemptive experience'.

[148] So C.A. Evans (1993a) 185: 'belief in Jesus does not contradict these sacred and authoritative traditions. On the contrary, Jesus has fulfilled them'.

[149] Motyer (1992) 164.

The loss of Jerusalem, whilst painful, could therefore be endured. Just as the immediate followers of 'John' may have needed encouragement to believe that there could be life 'without John',[150] so any Jewish readers would have received the message that life was possible 'without Jerusalem'. Both groups (in different ways) were being tempted to hanker after an irretrievable past; but Jesus, through his Spirit, would be 'with them for ever' (14:16).

c) Conclusion

John's chief purpose was to present the claims of Jesus; he was 'determined that the reader should be overwhelmed by the singleness of the theme which is Jesus of Nazareth'.[151] Nevertheless, there was great value in setting those claims against the background of the questions relating to Jerusalem and its Temple. This ensured that the essential Jewishness of Jesus was not forgotten. More importantly, when properly understood, the Temple provided a window into Jesus' identity, and Jerusalem an insight into God's dealing with his people and with the 'world'.

One senses, however, that John himself now had little 'emotional attachment' to Jerusalem and Palestine;[152] he had left his homeland behind. Despite the necessary focus upon Jerusalem, the ultimate direction of his Gospel was outwards, and any particularities were subsumed in a comprehensive emphasis upon the universal implications of what had taken place in Palestine. If John was writing from Ephesus (or anywhere in the Diaspora), then this universal emphasis may in part reflect his physical departure at some earlier date from the land of Palestine: whilst not 'of the world' he was writing 'in the world' and for the world (17:15-16).

That departure from the shores of Palestine might itself have been prompted by a profound awareness of God's new purposes for the world in Christ, and a response to his commission: 'as you have sent me into the world, so I have sent them into the world' (17:18).[153] John's reflection upon Jerusalem might not be simply a response to the great events of AD 66-70; it could be an explication of things which long before that date he had discerned to be implicit in the essential gospel message about Jesus.

John teaches that, even if not apparent at the time (*cf.* 2:22), from the moment Jesus first appeared in the city the role of Jerusalem and its Temple

---

[150] *Cf.* above at n. 132ff.

[151] Hoskyns (1940) 67.

[152] So *e.g.* Davies (1974) 334.

[153] Robinson (1985) 90, presumes John will have left Palestine soon after the Apostolic Council (Acts 15) in AD 48/9.

were destined to undergo a dramatic change. These entities would no longer be necessary for any sense of proximity to God, nor in future centuries for a sense of proximity to Jesus. God was now found in Jesus, and Jesus through the Spirit. From the outset of the Gospel, the Johannine Jesus announces in word and deed the imminent end of the old order which had been centred on the Temple (2:22) and on Jerusalem (4:21). Such was the authority and significance of Jesus and his Spirit, that their entrance onto the world-stage had cast these previous entities into the shade and brought about their demise. For John it was abundantly plain that 'Jesus supplants Jerusalem and her cultus'.[154]

---

[154] Fortna (1974) 93.

6

A NEW CALLING
Hebrews

Let us then go to him outside the camp and bear the abuse he en-
dured. For here we have no lasting city, but we are looking for
the city that is to come (Heb. 13:13-14).

Much of the argument in Hebrews is concerned with the Temple. The author sees the Old
Testament 'tabernacle' as pointing forwards to Christ's sacrificial death on the Cross.
This has repercussions for the Jerusalem Temple. There is a similar re-evaluation of both
the Land (ch. 3-4, 11) and Jerusalem (chs. 11-13). In a key passage (13:9-14), there is a
three-fold critique of Jerusalem: reflecting on the Passion narrative, the author urges his
readers to follow in Jesus' footsteps and to 'leave the camp'. The letter reflects the crucial
years before AD 70 when Jewish-Christians were under increasing pressure to show soli-
darity with Jerusalem and its Temple.

The 'epistle' to the Hebrews is the New Testament document which most explicitly focuses on the Temple and its significance in the light of Christ. In
contrast to John's Gospel, written for a potentially wide readership, this is a
sermon, composed in a crisis for a specific congregation, consisting (almost
certainly) of believers from an entirely Jewish background.[1] In common with
John, however, both authors are people of Jewish birth who are convinced not
only that Jesus is Israel's Messiahship, but also God's eternal 'son' (John 1:1-
18; Heb. 1:1-14). As in John, this results in the author of Hebrews viewing the
Jerusalem Temple in a new way (section 1 below). In the light of his understanding of the Land (2), there is also a parallel re-evaluation of Jerusalem (3).

An argument could be made that the author was not concerned with Jerusalem. His 'Alexandrian' emphasis could reflect a disinterest in such practical matters.[2] Like John, rather than focusing on Palestine as the scene of the Incarnation, he reflects on the universal affects of Christ's coming 'into the world'.[3] When referring to 'Salem' (7:2), he does not indicate that a tradition identified this with Jerusalem.[4] His references to Temple ritual can appear 'bookish', owing more to Old Testament texts than to detailed knowledge of current practice.[5] Some conclude that he 'shows no interest in what was going on in Jerusalem at the time he wrote', and no 'interest in the Jerusalem Temple', 'nor is he greatly concerned with events in contemporary history'.[6]

This is incorrect. The proper approach to the earthly city of Jerusalem was an important part of the message of Hebrews. At the other extreme, some assert that Hebrews must have been written for Christians living in Jerusalem,[7] but it is more probably the product of the Diaspora.[8] Nevertheless, the issue of Jerusalem was vital. At the very least, the sermon's urgent tone suggests that the extended space given to the Temple (chs. 7-10) was hardly tangential. If it was so important to inculcate a proper understanding of the Temple, however, the same may have been true of Jerusalem.[9]

---

[1]   Hagner (1983) 12, calls it an 'exhortatory sermon' and a 'sermon-treatise', though sent to a particular community 'as a letter'; cf. Lane (1985). In this chapter we refer to it as a sermon (not 'epistle') and sometimes speak of its 'audience'. 'Hebrews' will be reserved for referring to the document (not the anonymous 'author'). The audience's Jewish background is generally agreed, following the arguments of Manson (1951), contra e.g. Moffatt (1924), Windisch (1931), and Käsemann (1984); Ellingworth (1993), however, argues for a community of mixed background. Few would doubt that the author was himself Jewish.

[2]   The similarities of Hebrews with Alexandrian thought, are frequently observed: see e.g. Montefiore (1964), Héring (1970), Thompson (1981).

[3]   See e.g. Heb. 1:6 ('when God brings the firstborn into the world') and 10:5 ('when Christ came into the world'); cf. also 9:11.

[4]   This tradition (based on e.g. Ps. 76:2) is evidenced in Josephus, Ant. 1.180, and the Palestinian Genesis Apocryphon (1QapGen. 22.13); it is likely, though not certain, that the author of Hebrews knew this: see Horton (1976) 86, 159.

[5]   See e.g. G.A. Barton (1938) 198: the author may have been 'to Jerusalem as a festal pilgrim, but he has no intimate knowledge of the Temple such as a priest would have'. Murray (1982) 205, assumes that the 'Jerusalem Temple was not an experienced reality' for the author.

[6]   Ellingworth (1991) viii; Filson (1967) 48; R.M. Wilson (1987) 140. Cf. Ellingworth (1993) 29, 710.

[7]   Buchanan (1972) 256ff, represents an extreme position here; he sees Hebrews as written to a group of disappointed Christian 'monastic Zionists' who, expecting Christ to inaugurate his kingdom in Palestine, gathered in Jerusalem (which earthly city is supposedly referred to in 12:22 as the 'heavenly Jerusalem'). See further below at n. 113.

[8]   Lindars (1991a) 19, concludes: 'the best that can be said is that nothing forbids the view that Hebrews is addressed to comparatively well-educated Jewish Christians somewhere in the Mediterranean Dispersion'.

1. The Temple

The author's attitude to the Temple is clear. He affirmed its vital role in previous generations, but asserted that this had changed. This can be deduced by examining his many references to the 'tabernacle' or 'tent' (σκηνή).[10]

a) Affirmation and Denial

The establishment of the 'tabernacle' in the wilderness was clearly in accordance with God's purposes: Moses responded to a divine command to 'make everything according to the pattern that was shown on the mountain' (8:5). There is no quasi-Marcionite dismissal of the Old Testament and its 'regulations for worship' (9:1).

> The institutions of Judaism were ordained of God, and had a positive, if limited, value in their own time. It is nowhere suggested that the Jews ought not to have observed them.[11]

'In these last days' (1:2), however, something had occurred which gave those regulations a whole new meaning. God's 'Son' (1:2 ff), who 'is worthy of more glory than Moses' (3:3) had 'come into the world' (1:6) and provided 'purification for sins' (1:3). He had done this as a priest 'according to the order of Melchizedek' (7:17)[12] and through offering 'himself' as a 'sacrifice' for sins 'once for all' (7:27; cf. 9:26). In comparison with previous 'high priests' (8:3ff) Jesus had received a 'more excellent ministry' and was the mediator of a 'better covenant' (8:6). As a result, the previous regulations for worship were part of a covenant which was now 'obsolete' and 'growing old' (8:13). A whole new way of approaching the holy God of Israel had been forged through Christ's atoning death.

. [9]   For an earlier discussion of these issues in Hebrews, see my article (1994b), some of which is reworked here.

[10]   See 8:2, 5; 9:1-3, 6, 8, 11, 21; 13:10. On why the author uses this term, see below 1c.

[11]   Barrett (1956) 392. In its context, the implication that the 'tabernacle' was 'made with hands' (χειροποίητος, 9:11) serves only to contrast it with the 'greater and perfect tent'; it does not imply that it had never been ordained by God. Cf. above ch. 1 (1e), ch. 3 (1c).

[12]   The notion of Jesus as a 'high priest' had been outlined earlier in 2:17 and 4:14-15. In chs. 7-8, however, the author argues that this is true not only at a 'metaphorical' level but literally: 'the main point in what we are saying is this: we *have* such a high priest' (8:1). See further Lindars (1991a) 1. See *e.g.* Baigent (1981) on whether this was the first time the concept was applied to Jesus. We incline to the view that the audience was familiar with this concept in general terms, but need to note its logical implications.

In the light of this it was now possible to acknowledge some of the inherent weaknesses within the previous system. The high priest's entering the 'Holy of Holies' only 'once a year' (on the Day of Atonement) 'indicates that the way into the sanctuary has not yet been disclosed' (9:8); the repetition of this ritual 'year after year' reveals that worshippers were not 'cleansed once for all', 'for it is impossible for the blood of bulls and goats to take away sins' (10:1-4; cf. 9:9). Although the coming of this new 'high priest' gave the previous rituals a greater meaning, it also showed their innate inadequacies.[13]

This led to a paradoxical position with regard to the worship patterned on the 'tabernacle': on the one hand its validity *in the past* was strongly affirmed (it had not been a mistake); on the other its enduring validity *for the future* was denied (now that Christ had come, it was no longer necessary). Its substantial value was that it explained—in a way which perhaps nothing else could—what Jesus had accomplished; it was the God-given preparation for understanding Jesus' death. It could also be seen as the earthly counterpart of the 'greater and perfect tent' that Christ had entered (9:11): at the moment of his exaltation to God's 'right hand' (1:3) he had entered the 'Holy Place' *par excellence* (*cf.* 9:24). New significance could therefore be seen in Moses' creating the tabernacle 'according to the pattern on the mountain' (8:5); this sanctuary had always been intended as only a 'sketch and shadow of the heavenly one', which had existed from eternity. It was this heavenly sanctuary that had been definitively revealed in Jesus' death and exaltation.

Worship based on the tabernacle had to be seen in a distinctively new way. It was a useful 'symbol (παραβολή) of the present time' (9:9); it was the 'old' which had to give way to the 'new' (8:13); it was the 'sketch' (or 'copy': ὑπόδειγμα) which was but a 'shadow' (8:5) of the true, heavenly sanctuary; although in accordance with God's will, it had been 'made with hands' (χειροποίητος) in contrast to that which was 'not of this creation' (9:11); it was the 'type' (ἀντίτυπον: 9:24) that had been fulfilled in Jesus. In all these ways, the author of Hebrews made clear its essential inferiority, compared with that revealed 'once and for all' through Christ.[14]

---

[13] Thus Caird could speak of the Old Testament's 'self-confessed inadequacy': quoted in Hagner (1981) 230.

[14] Lehne (1990) 111, notes how in all his comparisons between the 'new covenant' and the 'old' the author portrays the former in terms of 'correspondence, contrast, and *superiority*'. In contrast to John's Gospel, there is no room for the concept of Jesus himself as the new Temple: instead Jesus is the 'great High Priest' *within* the heavenly sanctuary (2:17; 4:14-15; 9:11-14. 24-25, 10:12, etc). That Christian believers constitute a Temple (as in John and Paul) may be suggested in 3:6 ('we are his house'); *cf.* also 10:21.

b) Implications for the Jerusalem Temple

What did this mean for the Jerusalem Temple—that same Temple which Jesus himself had visited? Did the author intend the negative corollaries of these arguments to be noted for the one place which continued to embody the principles of tabernacle-styled worship? The fact that he never refers as such to the 'Temple' (ἱερόν or ναός), but only to the 'tabernacle' (σκηνή), might initially suggest that such contemporary applications were of no interest to him (he was simply making a spiritual point about the new access to God through Jesus). A key passage in the final chapter of Hebrews, however, reveals that this distinction between principle and application did not exist.

Up to this point in the argument the author's use of σκηνή meant that the prime focus had been upon the Mosaic tabernacle. In this final reference to the 'tabernacle' or 'tent', however, he writes of something which manifestly relates to the present time:

> 'Do not be carried away by all kinds of strange teachings; for it is well for the heart to be strengthened by grace, not by regulations about food [βρώμασιν], which have not benefited those who observe them. We have (ἔχομεν) an altar from which *those who officiate in the tent* (οἱ τῇ σκηνῇ λατρεύοντες) have no right to eat. For the bodies of those animals whose blood is brought into the sanctuary by the high priest as a sacrifice for sin are burned outside the camp. Therefore Jesus also suffered outside the city gate in order to sanctify the people by his own blood. Let us then go to him outside the camp and bear the abuse he endured. For here we have no lasting city, but we are looking for the city that is to come' (13:9-10).

This passage, which has been described as one of the 'most difficult passages of the entire New Testament', is of vital importance.[15] Its urgent and challenging tone suggests that the author was referring to a current phenomenon which was of direct concern and practical relevance to his audience. Almost certainly the author wanted his audience to desist from being involved in the 'communal dinners which were held on Jewish feast days in Diaspora Judaism' in which 'Jews far away from Jerusalem maintained their *sense of solidarity with the Temple and its cultus*'.[16] He saw this practice, which affirmed the Temple's significance, as an effective denial of what they now had in Christ—described pictorially as an alternative 'altar' (v. 10). A strong contrast is established between Christian worship focused through Christ and the worship focused on the 'tabernacle'. The phrase 'those who officiate in the

---

[15] H. Koester (1962) 299. See further discussion below in 3c and 4a.

[16] Lindars (1989) 388 (quoted fully below at n. 82; italics mine); *cf.* Lane (1991) 530-6.

tent' (v. 10) must therefore be a reference (although cast in an archaic form) to those currently involved with the Jerusalem Temple, the 'adherents of that old cultus'.[17] He argued that 'there was a complete break between the levitical and Christian cultus'.[18] In practice this would mean nothing unless he was thinking about the Jerusalem Temple, since that was the only place where that levitical cultus manifested itself and continued to be a live issue. Any other interpretation reduces the author's concerns to the level of vague abstractions, which hardly provide a strong basis for his climactic appeal to 'go to [Jesus] outside the camp, and bear the abuse he endured' (v. 13). This was no academic issue; it had vital, and probably costly, consequences in the here and now.

Christian believers now had an 'altar' which was quite different from the one associated with the 'tent' (the Jerusalem Temple). Strictly, this 'altar' was not a physical one;[19] but the physical aspect of the word 'altar' suited his purpose well; for he wanted to show that his earlier theological arguments concerning Christ's sacrifice *did* have practical consequences for the contemporary 'altar' in Jerusalem. For Christians that previous 'altar' was redundant because in Christ they had an 'altar' of their very own, which offered them a sure access into God's presence. Jesus had inaugurated a new Temple-system (symbolized by the term 'altar') which stood in stark contrast to the Temple-system associated with the 'tent'. In fact the two systems were mutually exclusive: those involved in that earlier system were effectively excluded from this new system ('those who officiate in the tent have no right to eat': v.10); by implication those who now believed in Jesus were equally to regard themselves as excluded from that former system ('let us go to him *outside* the camp': v. 13).

This contrast between the Jerusalem Temple system and the new Christian dispensation was implicit throughout his argument concerning Jesus as the 'true High Priest' (7:11-10:25). There, however, the relationship between Christ and the Temple, had been portrayed in *vertical* terms. This meant that the earthly 'tabernacle' had the positive role of pointing upwards to the heavenly one; apart from some hints in 8:13 and 9:8, few questions were raised at this point about the long-term future of this earthly 'tabernacle' in the light of Christ. What is new in chapter 13, however, is that (by proceeding in the following verses to draw on the historical and geographical aspects of the cruci-

---

[17]   Lane (1991) 539.
[18]   Ellingworth (1993) 709.
[19]   Though it was based on a physical event—Jesus' sacrificial death. *Cf.* Isaacs (1992) 216: 'the altar is located neither in heaven, nor on earth at the Eucharist, but represents the sacrifice of Jesus'. The author's choice of words here is skilful: by combining the notions of the 'altar' (a physical term) and the 'tabernacle' (a more theological term) he shows that his argument, though theological in essence, is not merely theoretical in its consequences.

fixion) the relationship between Jesus and the Temple is now portrayed *horizontally*. This forces a new sense of contrast. Jesus' death had taken place 'outside the city gate' (v. 12), not (as for the sacrificial animals) in the 'sanctuary' (v. 11). A choice was therefore required—either to go to Jesus 'outside the camp' (v. 13) or remain, as it were, within the city and focused on the Temple. To use alternative 'geographical' language, were one's loyalties with the Temple mount or with 'the place of the skull'? The contrast between the two was plain. A new means of approaching God had been established; a choice had to be made.

Appropriately this teaching comes shortly after the author's appeal to his audience to 'worship God acceptably' (λατρεύωμεν εὐαρέστως: 12:28). The clear implication is that obedience to the commands given throughout chapter 13 will enable them to offer this true worship; for example, God no longer requires the 'sacrifice' of animals, but rather the 'sacrifice of praise, that is, the fruit of lips that confess his name' (13:15).[20] It is those who worship at the new Christian 'altar' who are offering acceptable worship. The worship offered by those who 'officiate at the tent' (λατρεύοντες) is no longer valid; Temple worship is a thing of the past.

c) *The Archaic Use of* σκηνή

The author's continued use of 'tabernacle' (σκηνή) may seem puzzling. If he was referring to the contemporary Jerusalem Temple, why did he not say so explicitly? This may have been caused in part by appropriate political sensitivities,[21] but fundamentally it was a strategic device which enabled him to develop his argument at a strictly theological level. There were other Jewish groups (most notably at Qumran) which were critical of the Temple and its current establishment.[22] The author of Hebrews, however, was not wanting to cast any aspersions on the contemporary Temple in practice, but rather making a far more fundamental point concerning the very essence of the Temple. By concentrating his attention on the 'tabernacle' in the wilderness, he could argue that the Tabernacle system of worship, even when considered in its most pristine and pure form under Moses (before any human sin might have twisted

---

[20] The author's non-cultic reapplication of Temple motifs may possibly be discerned in his choice of Old Testament texts here. Both Ps. 118:6 and Hag. 2:6 (quoted in 13:6 and 12:26 respectively) had originally been associated closely with the Jerusalem Temple. This focus is entirely lacking in Hebrews. See Lane (1991) 485f, who notes an allusion to Ps. 96:9 which in the Septuagint included a reference to the 'holy court'.

[21] See below 4c.

[22] On Qumran and the Temple, see above ch. 4 (2a).

the divine intention), had been declared redundant by God through Jesus. His critique of the present Temple was not bound up with any political issues or personal disenchantment, but rather with God's eternal purposes. Avoiding any contemporary references to the first century was thus a theological necessity; for else his criticism would have appeared not as revolutionary but as merely reforming. 'He is not arguing that the Temple should be reformed. His aim is far more radical'.[23] His was a criticism that went to the root: 'it was the very principle of a special cult . . . which the author wished to contest'.[24]

Nevertheless, this could never remain as a merely 'academic' theological point. It had pragmatic consequences, and the author fully intended that these should be recognized. 'Despite the archaizing, it is the service of the Second Temple that the author rejects as *passé*'.[25] The practical application to the contemporary Temple, discerned in these verses in the final chapter (13:9-14), is then the fruit of this concern. Possibly he deliberately held back from spelling out these practical consequences at an earlier stage in his argument because of his audience's sensitivities on this subject; if he had raised them earlier, he might have caused offence and lost his case. In his closing remarks, now that he had developed his argument fully and drawn out its many positive applications, the time was ripe to make this critical, more negative point. God's establishing of a new 'altar' focused on the sacrificial death of Jesus spelt the end of the Jerusalem Temple as they had known it.

d) The Future of the Jerusalem Temple

The author of Hebrews believed the Jerusalem Temple was but a 'shadow' of the reality now found in Christ (8:5). What, then, would actually happen to it? He urged Christians to disassociate themselves from it, but did he believe this paradoxical situation would go on forever, with physical sacrifices continuing to be offered in the Temple even though Christ's death had already accomplished the ultimate sacrifice 'once for all' (9:27; 10:10)?

On the one occasion when he comments on the future of those things linked to the 'old covenant', he writes (8:13) : 'In speaking of 'a new covenant, he has made the first one obsolete. And what is obsolete (τὸ παλαιούμε-vov) and growing old will soon disappear (ἐγγὺς ἀφανισμοῦ).' Strictly, having quoted Jeremiah 31:31-34, the reference here is to the 'old covenant'

---

[23] Lindars (1991b) 425.

[24] Dunn (1991a) 87. *Cf.* similarly Hagner (1983) 3: 'the new that has come in Christ replaces not simply the present manifestation of Judaism but also its ideal statement in the Torah'.

[25] Gordon (1991) 449.

in general terms, not specifically to the 'tabernacle'/Temple. Yet in the next verse he talks about the 'earthly sanctuary' (9:1), which had also been an important theme earlier in chapter 8. What other sign could there be that the 'old covenant' was 'obsolete'? So long as the Temple stood, there was nothing to suggest that the old covenant had 'disappeared'. The author is therefore clearly giving a prophetic warning that the revelation of the 'new' in Christ will have major, visible repercussions on the 'old': it 'will soon disappear'.

The author's language is instructive. τὸ παλαιούμενον (translated 'obsolete') might more literally be rendered as 'that which is being made obsolete' (referring to a process which had been inaugurated, but not yet completed); secondly, the phrase ἐγγὺς ἀφανισμοῦ could also be translated as 'close to destruction'. The consequences of this verse for dating Hebrews before 70 will be discussed below.[26] The author believed that ever since Christ had accomplished his work of 'purification' (1:3) the days of the Temple were numbered. The 'old' would give way to the 'new', the shadow to the reality—not just in theory, but in practice. Thus one commentator concluded in radical terms: 'the Temple service, though it may continue a few years more in outward splendour, is only a bed of state on which a lifeless corpse is lying.[27]

Confirmation of this comes a few verses later (9:8): 'By this the Holy Spirit indicates that the way into the sanctuary has not yet been disclosed *as long as the first tent is still standing* (ἐχούσης στάσιν).' Not only will there come a time when the system associated with the 'tent' will cease to 'stand', but there is some necessary conflict between that system's survival and God's purposes in Christ. It would not 'stand' forever. If the phrase ἐχούσης στάσιν is interpreted to mean 'having status',[28] the effective result is the same. This makes it clearer that, because the way into God's presence has been revealed in Jesus, the Temple has lost its 'status'. If that is the case, what will happen to it? Now that is has lost its 'standing', the Temple cannot stand forever.[29]

e) Conclusion

The author of Hebrews saw the significance of the Jerusalem Temple as entirely fulfilled in Christ. The 'earthly sanctuary' was affirmed and given a vital new meaning in the history of salvation—as the divinely-intended precursor

---

[26] See below 4b. On this verse being indicative of a pre-70 date, see *e.g.* Ellingworth (1993) 32.
[27] Delitzsch, quoted in Hughes (1977) 302.
[28] As in Lane (1991) 223.
[29] For the argument that this verse makes most sense if written before AD 70, see *e.g.* Lindars (1991b) 428.

of Christ's work; yet in the light of Christ, it no longer had any 'status'. It was an integral part of the 'old covenant', which had given way decisively to the 'new'. The access to God which it had promised was fully available through Christ's offering of himself 'once for all' (9:28)

This radical re-evaluation of the Temple betrayed the author's convictions not only about the enormity of Jesus's work, but also about the new era in God's purposes which had been inaugurated—what he described as 'these last days' (1:2), 'the time of the new order' (καιροῦ διορθώσεως: 9:10).[30] Jesus had been the 'agent of epochal change that had introduced a radically new situation'.[31] For a Jewish writer such a change in God's purposes could only be propounded if there was adequate scriptural testimony indicating that this was the divine intention: hence the importance of the quotations from Jeremiah 31:31-34 and Psalm 40:6-8 (8:8ff; 10:5ff). What was being unveiled, though apparently new, was in accordance with God's eternal purposes. At the end of his sermon, he spoke of 'the blood of the *eternal* covenant' (13:20). Beneath the apparent discontinuity there was a deeper continuity; God had now revealed his eternal will. The implication was that this 'new order', unlike the 'old', would last forever.

This was a sweeping conclusion for any Jewish writer.[32] Yet any note of judgement on the contemporary Temple was absent from his presentation; for his argument was entirely theological (hence his use of σκηνή) and focused on the theme of God's long-standing intention to 'replace' the Temple through Christ. Even if the Temple had been fully fulfilling God's purposes in every detail, the work of Christ would eventually have rendered it unnecessary. It was inherently provisional, pointing away from itself to Christ. Believers in Christ, the true High Priest, need not have—indeed should not have—any further involvement with it. The 'new' had come. Noting the author's description of the tabernacle as a 'symbol' or 'parable' (9:9), Barrett concludes:

> The parable itself can be understood only in the light of that which it parabolically portrays; Christians are therefore the first to perceive the true meaning of the Old Testament cultus *which they themselves have abandoned*. . . . When that which is perfect is come, that which is in part is done away.[33]

---

[30] As translated in NIV. Lane (1991) 214, translates καιρός διορθώσεως as 'time of correction'. *Cf.* Cody (1960) 133: 'the ripe time for a correction of perspectives and of the whole order of salvation'.

[31] Lane and Wall (1993) 183.

[32] The closest parallel in the New Testament canon is Stephen in Acts 7: on possible historical parallels between them, see *e.g.* W. Manson (1951), Simon (1958), Hurst (1990) 140-74, Lane (1991) cxlvi-cl.

[33] Barrett (1956) 392 (italics mine).

2. The Land

There is evidence that the author similarly re-evaluated the Land. The Temple theme chiefly appears in the sermon's central section (ch. 7-10); the theme of the Land comes to the fore in the surrounding chapters (chs. 3-4; ch. 11).

a) The True 'Rest' (3:7-4:13)

In the former passage the author applies to his audience the divine warning in Psalm 95:8 (that the rebellious Israelites would not 'enter my rest'). This divine 'rest', which had originally referred to the Israelites' entrance into the 'promised land', was capable of being applied in quite a different way—to 'sharing in God's eternal "sabbatical" repose'.[34] This implied that the entrance into the promised land under Joshua had not really been the promised 'rest', but only a pointer to that greater, heavenly reality.

This is seen in 4:8-9, where the author goes so far as to deny that the historical entrance into the promised land had given the people any 'rest' at all: 'For if Joshua had given them rest, God would not speak later about another day. So then, a sabbath-rest still remains for the people of God.' If the concept of the 'promised land' was really an advance metaphor or 'antitype' for the heavenly 'rest' enjoyed by God's people, this would necessarily affect the author's understanding of the contemporary Land. Just as the Temple would be eclipsed by the revelation of the 'heavenly sanctuary' (chs. 7-10), so too the Land might be eclipsed by a focus on the heavenly 'rest'.

b) The Patriarchs and the 'Promised Land' (11:8-40)

This impression is confirmed when the theme of the Land reappears in chapter 11. It may not be coincidental that the detailed descriptions of those who lived 'by faith' come to an end at precisely the point in the Old Testament when the Israelites took Jericho and entered the Land (vv. 30-31). Those who were 'great' in the Land are then listed briefly (v. 32), before the description of those of whom 'the world was not worthy' (v. 38). His argument is that God's people need to look beyond the present. Yet his presentation also implies a critique of any over-emphasis on the Land; for his list amply illustrates that faithful living does not depend on residence there. The greatest examples of faith were seen in those who practised it outside the Land.

---

[34] Attridge (1980) 283.

Abraham and his sons, who *did* live briefly in the Land, appear to be the exception to this. In his analysis of their faith (vv. 8-16), however, the author articulates this same ambivalent view of the promised land. In verse 9 he uses, without further specification, the actual phrase 'land of promise' (γῆν τῆς ἐπαγγελίας); this clearly is to be identified with the 'place that he was to receive as an inheritance' (v. 8). These positive descriptions of the physical Land, however, are eclipsed by his insistence that the real focus of the promise to which Abraham 'looked forward' was the 'city that has foundations, whose architect and builder is God' (v. 10). This eschatological focus is repeated in verse 16: 'They desire a better country, that is, a heavenly one. Therefore God is not ashamed to be called their God; indeed, he has prepared a city for them.'

On this interpretation, the patriarchs were looking forward, not so much to the day when their descendants would inherit the physical Land, as to the day when they themselves would inherit the heavenly country which the physical Land signified. They 'saw through' the promise of the Land, looking beyond it to a deeper, spiritual reality. The promise concerning the Land, whilst real and valid in its own terms, pointed typologically to something greater. Any subsequent focus on the Land would then be misplaced; for the faith commended by the author was one which looked beyond such things.

The author's revised conception of the significance of the 'promised land' is seen elsewhere. The notion of 'inheritance', for example, is consistently applied either to Christ as the 'heir' (1:2, 4) or to those who believe in him (1:14; 6:12, 17; 9:15; *cf.* 11:7). Similarly, the concept of 'promise', whilst including the reference to the physical Land when related to Abraham (11:8ff),[35] is used elsewhere in a more general way: he encourages his audience that they too are 'inheritors' of the divine promise, which will only come to fruition in the eschatological future (9:15; 10:36; 11:39; *cf.* 4:1; 8:6). The 'promise' is clearly focused on Christ and that which he offers to those who trust in him—regardless of their physical location. The ancient 'promise' of the Land was an indication of God's faithfulness and of his nature as a God who promises, but that divine promising was now focused on Jesus.

c) A New Exodus, a New Moses

Undergirding such thinking is the conviction that Christ has accomplished a new Exodus—leading to a different 'promised land'. It was the author's conviction on this score which enabled him to apply the theme of the wandering

---

[35] But note how in 6:13-15 the 'promise' to Abraham is described in terms of his many descendents, not in terms of the Land.

of the 'people of Israel' in the desert to his own audience (3:7ff): they had been
through a similar experience, a comparable 'exodus'. If he could claim that the
'gospel' had come to the wandering people of Israel (4:2), then by parity of
reasoning these first-century Christians, it could be deduced, had been
brought through a second exodus—by Christ.

The comparison of Jesus with Moses (3:3) points in a similar direction,
again with consequences for any theology of the Land.[36] This Moses-Jesus
parallelism can be sensed not only in the author's contrast between Sinai and
Mount Zion (12:18ff), but also in his final benediction where (translated literally) he speaks of God 'leading up (ἀναγαγών) from the dead our Lord Jesus'
(13:20). This terminology reflects the Exodus motif of God 'leading up' his
people from Egypt.[37] Jesus is then described in language reminiscent of Moses as the 'great shepherd of the sheep'.[38] The author viewed Christ's work as
comparable to the Exodus under Moses. All of this has important corollaries
for his understanding of the Land; for the 'promised land' to which Christ was
leading people was not the Land of Palestine. The place of promise was the
place to which Jesus himself had gone ahead as the 'pioneer' (12:2)—the
'heavenly Jerusalem' (12:22). This was to be their goal; this was the place
where God's promises would ultimately be fulfilled. Seen in this light, any political aspirations claiming to be based on the scriptures were to be denied. In
a climactic conclusion he fixed his audience's attention on the 'kingdom (βα-
σιλείαν) that cannot be shaken' (12:28). Other, earthly kingdoms would
prove to be part of the 'created things' that would not 'remain' (12:27).

For the author of Hebrews, therefore, the Land had been caught up into
a new understanding. Even though it was an important theme within previous
biblical faith, it had been given a quite new meaning—one which fulfilled, and
therefore eclipsed, its former role within God's purposes.

3. The City of Jerusalem

The coming of Jesus led the author to espouse a new approach to two of the
key physical components of his Jewish faith—the Temple and the Land.
Would the significance of the city of Jerusalem be similarly affected?

The issue of the 'city' only emerges in chapters 11-13. It may be a coincidence that this reveals a tri-partite pattern within the sermon, as he touches
first on the Land (chs. 3-4), then on the Temple (chs. 5-10) and finally on the

---

[36] On this Moses-Jesus parallelism, see *e.g.* Jones (1979).
[37] See *e.g.* Exod. 33:15; Num. 14:13; 16:13; 20:4-5.
[38] See Lane (1991) 561-2. *Cf.* also 11:24ff (though see further below n. 69).

City (chs. 11-13). This could be taken, however, as an indication that these
three concentric *realia* of the Jewish faith were important aspects of his overall argument. Each of them was to be understood in new ways.[39]

a) The 'City with Foundations' (11:8-16)

There is, however, some overlap. The verses in which the theme of the 'city'
is introduced are those in which the theme of the 'promised land' had returned
briefly (11:8-16). On both occasions (vv. 10, 16) the author introduces the
concept of the 'city' at the conclusion of paragraphs that initially were concerned with either the 'promised land' or the patriarch's homeland (πατρίς).

> By faith [Abraham] stayed for a time in the *land* he had been promised. . . .
> For he looked forward to the *city* that has foundations, whose architect and
> builder is God (11:9-10).

> If they had been thinking of the *land* that they had left behind, they would
> have had opportunity to return. But as it is, they desire a better country, that
> is, a heavenly one. Therefore God is not ashamed to be called their God; in-
> deed he has prepared a *city* for them (11:15-16).

This is evidence not only for the author's applying the concept of the 'promised land' to heavenly realities (as above), but also for the importance which
he attached to the notion of the 'city'.

The reference to Jerusalem is quite oblique at this stage, but the reference to the 'city with foundations' (11:10) almost certainly alludes to Psalm
87:1-2: 'He has set his foundation on the holy mountain; the Lord loves the
gates of Zion more than all the dwellings of Jacob.'[40] If so, the earthly Zion/
Jerusalem is not far from the author's thoughts. There is also an implicit re-
interpretation of Psalm 87. In identifying the 'city that has foundations' (v. 10)
with the 'heavenly' one (v. 16) he was denying that the earthly Zion could also
be truly described in such terms—even though this Psalm had given the opposite impression. The Psalm referred either to a temporary reality (which was
no longer the case) or, more likely, to the 'heavenly Zion'. In either case, he
was calling into question the divine foundation of the earthly Zion/Jerusalem.

---

[39] This order reflects not only the Temple's pivotal centrality, but also the importance of
the 'city' as an eschatological goal. Most recent analyses of Hebrews' structure are
indebted to the various studies of Vanhoye (see *e.g.* his [1989]), none of which note this
development through Land and Temple to City.

[40] As translated in the NIV. For the allusion to Ps. 87, see Moule (1966) 45; *cf.* Bruce
(1964) 297, n. 85.

b) The 'Heavenly Jerusalem' (12:22)

The sermon, which itself has been based so much on the concept of the pilgrim journey of faith, reaches its own τέλος or climax with the colourful description of his audience's proleptic arrival in the heavenly city: 'But you have come to Mount Zion and the city of the living God, the heavenly Jerusalem' (12:22). This key text has several implications for the earthly Jerusalem.

First, the author's careful word-order indicates that it is not just the cultic aspects of the Temple which have been 'relocated' in the heavenly Jerusalem. The 'heavenly Jerusalem' is described as a two-fold entity ('Mount Zion *and* the city of the living God'); not only 'Mount Zion' (*i.e.* the Temple and its cult), but also the *city* of the earthly Jerusalem was an integral part of the anti-type of the 'heavenly Jerusalem'.[41] This suggests that, although he gave greater space in his argument concerning types to the Temple cult, the author was prepared to apply a similar pattern to the city. Both cultic and civic aspects pointed beyond themselves to the greater, heavenly reality.

Secondly, Hebrews has significantly reworked the popular notion of pilgrimage. In the minds of his audience the concept of pilgrimage would have been inextricably linked to the city of Jerusalem; for this alone was the goal of a Jewish pilgrim.[42] The author of Hebrews has taken over this important concept and applied it exclusively to the heavenly Jerusalem. Seen in this light, the practice of pilgrimage to the earthly Jerusalem was at best but a picture of this more important, spiritual pilgrimage to the heavenly Jerusalem. If this practice was ever developed theologically to the point where those who were far from the earthly Jerusalem were deemed to be at some disadvantage, then the author of Hebrews insists that, regardless of their geographical location and without any need to embark on a physical journey, his audience had already 'come to Mount Zion'. If there was any belief that the earthly Jerusalem was 'the navel of the earth, because it was the point nearest to the deity', it was now the heavenly Jerusalem which was the 'navel of the universe, not realized on earth'.[43] Furthermore, 'if the recipients were being enticed . . . to look for the restoration of an earthly city', these verses were 'yet another corrective to misconceptions of this kind'.[44]

---

[41]   Following *e.g.* Westcott (1903) 413; *contra* Lane (1991) 465.

[42]   This connection with Jerusalem has not been sufficiently noted by those who have drawn attention to the pilgrimage theme in Hebrews: see *e.g.* Johnsson (1978). Barrett (1956) 380, notes that in Hebrews '*city* finds its correlative in *pilgrimage*' (italics original), but does not link this with Jerusalem.

[43]   Johnsson (1978) 245, 247.

c) 'Outside the Camp' (ch. 13)

These important ideas concerning the 'city' come to fruition in the final chapter, when he speaks of the need for Christians to identify with Jesus' suffering 'outside the city gate' and to focus their attention on the 'city that is to come' (13:12-14). The whole of this important passage (13:9-14) was quoted in full above.[45] It was noted there that this is the one place, where the author applies his theoretical teaching to the precise issue of the contemporary Temple. It also reveals most clearly his evaluation of contemporary Jerusalem.

The author demands some hard decisions. His audience was, as already noted, to maintain a distinctively Christian approach towards the Temple. There were yet choices to be made, which had to do with Jerusalem. He calls his readers to 'go to [Jesus] outside the *camp*'. What did this involve?

The imagery of the 'camp' (παρεμβολή) naturally fits in both with his earlier focus upon the people of Israel wandering in the wilderness (3:7-4:15) and his consistent use of the word 'tabernacle' (σκηνή).[46] That imagery continues here, such that the 'camp' must refer to those entities which, in this imaginative sense, are focused upon and gathered round the 'tabernacle'. It proves to have both a geographical and a personal sense. At one level it speaks of Israel—the people of God who dwelt in the camp gathered round the tabernacle. In another sense, it must refer to the city of Jerusalem, gathered around the Temple. For the phrase 'outside the camp' clearly draws upon the language in the previous verse (v. 12) which had spoken of Jesus' suffering 'outside the city gate'. Christians were called to follow him who went out to Golgotha from Jerusalem: 'let us then go to him outside the camp'. 'Camp' here is a description of Jerusalem.[47] The author is using the word in several different senses simultaneously:

---

[44] Hughes (1977) 546; this remains valid, even if one disregards his contention that the audience was influenced by ideas comparable to those at Qumran. That this reworking of 'pilgrimage' motifs also involved a new understanding of the promised 'restoration', may be confirmed if, as argued strongly by Lane (1991) 490, Jer. 31 is part of the background to this passage: see *e.g.* Jer. 31:11-12 ('for the Lord has *ransomed* Jacob; they shall come and sing aloud on the height of Zion').

[45] Above p. 205.

[46] Above 1c.

[47] This identification of Jerusalem with the 'camp' had ample precedent. It was a natural part of the symbolism associated with the celebration of the Day of Atonement: see Sipre Num. 1; b.Zebah 116b; Num.R. 7; t.b.Qam. 1:12. It was also an ingredient in the way the Qumran sect viewed Jerusalem, as seen in 4QMMT: 'We think that the Temple is the place of the tent of meeting, and Jerusalem is the camp; and outside the camp is outside Jerusalem. . . . And into the holy camp dogs should not be brought because . . . Jerusalem is the holy camp' (as translated in Martinez [1994] 77-78).

'Camp' is employed in a three-fold sense. It signified . . . the Hebrew camp in the wilderness. In v. 12, the 'camp' means Jerusalem, outside the gate of which Jesus suffered. Again in v. 13 'camp' means the Jewish community.[48]

This allusive imagery serves his purpose well. By speaking of the 'camp' he was able to widen the focus of the critique to include both Jerusalem and the Jewish community. Much of the author's argument had focused exclusively on the Temple. Now it becomes clear that in calling them to 'leave the camp' he was calling them to forego both a people and a place.[49] Despite the difficulty of this for people of Jewish stock and the evident 'abuse' or 'disgrace' (ὀνειδισμόν: v. 13) which it would incur from their Jewish contemporaries, this was Jesus' call to them. Jesus beckons from Golgotha, effectively inviting his followers (v. 13) not to be afraid to 'take up their cross and follow him' (cf. Mark 8:34).[50]

The challenge here to the recipients to 'sever their ties with the Jewish community' has often been highlighted.[51] The challenge to 'leave the camp' in the sense of Jerusalem, however, has not been noted. In referring to the crucifixion narrative the author considers the theological implications of Jesus' death against the backdrop of the physical city of Jerusalem. His encouragement to 'go outside the camp' is figurative language, but it depends for its impact on the fact that this was what Jesus had done in historic reality when he was led out from Jerusalem to Golgotha. He did not use the phrase 'leave the city' because he needed to say more than that, but his choice of 'camp' cannot be interpreted in such a way that a reference to the city of Jerusalem is totally excluded. Any doubts are removed by noting how he spoke immediately about the 'city' (v. 14). The 'city-concept' was on his mind.

---

[48] G.A. Barton (1938) 205.

[49] This interpretation makes better sense of the Jewish context than seeing this as a call to leave the 'sacred' world for the 'non-sacred' (H. Koester [1962] 315) or the earthly sphere for the heavenly world (Thompson [1978]). Similarly Attridge (1989) 399, sees the use of 'camp' as being 'evocative rather than definitive', suggesting the 'realm of security and traditional holiness, however, that is grounded or understood'. This is too vague. Instead the allusive nature of the imagery reflects the author's caution and sensitivity as he touches on this delicate subject: see Lindars (1991a) 9.

[50] Lane (1991) 543, suggests that the author may have been adapting Jesus' statement.

[51] Lane (1991) 545. Cf. e.g. Hagner (1983) 243: 'they are called to leave behind the security and comfort of Judaism and in so doing to bear "the disgrace he bore" (13:13)'. Bruce (1987) 3505, 3514: 'God had once again, in the person of Jesus, been rejected in the "camp"—the organized system of Judaism—and everyone who wished to approach him had therefore to leave that system'. The author is urging them 'to burn their boats, to leave the security of Judaism', and to make a 'final severance of their associations with the Jewish people'. De Young (1960) 109: they are 'to cut themselves loose from the former religious and ethnic ties' in the 'commonwealth of Israel'. Cf. also Filson (1967) 61-66.

i) The Critique of Jerusalem: Three Reasons

The author encourages his audience to make a break with 'Jerusalem'. This involved viewing the city in a new way in the light of the gospel events associated with Jesus. He gives three different reasons for doing so.

First, Jerusalem's previous religious significance had been integrally connected to the Temple, but Christians were now focused on a different 'altar' (v. 10). Whatever the author's precise understanding of this new 'altar', it 'certainly lies beyond the bounds of the terrestrial Jerusalem'.[52] In contrast to this new one, the 'altar' in the Temple had been rendered redundant. This would have consequences for the 'holy city' which had been built around the former 'holy of holies'.

Secondly, the fact that Jesus' death fulfilled the pattern of the Atonement ritual (vv. 11-12) has important implications for Jerusalem's 'holiness'. The author notes how the carcases of the sacrificial animals were not taken into the 'sanctuary' (τὰ ἅγια) but rather burned 'outside the camp'. This was a place of 'cultic impurity'.[53] Yet Jesus himself had now been dismissed from the holy enclosure and sent to his death. In that very place, however, he had done the great act which alone could 'sanctify the people' (v. 12). The 'unholy place' had become the source of the only true holiness.

> We are sanctified, not polluted, by leaving the sacred sanctuary.... The 'holy of holies', the place of God's presence is no longer within the sacred city; it is outside the gate.[54]

This had inevitable repercussions for the city of Jerusalem.

> In Jesus the old values had been reversed. What was formerly sacred was now unhallowed, because Jesus had been expelled from it; what was formerly unhallowed was now sacred, because Jesus was there.[55]

Since it was Jerusalem, and not the Temple, from which Jesus had been 'expelled', it follows that it was the city which was now 'unhallowed'. The city's claim to holiness could never be the same again, for Jesus' death had desecrat-

---

[52] W. Manson (1951) 151.

[53] Lane (1991) 540; see Lv. 16:26-8.

[54] Trudinger (1982) 237; cf. Hughes (1977) 579, and H. Koester (1962) 300: 'this act of sanctification marks the abolition of the necessity of holy places for sanctification'.

[55] Bruce (1964) 403. Cf. also Hagner (1983) 245: 'the true sacrifice for sin ... was accomplished not on the hallowed ground of the Temple precincts, but outside the holy city. This in itself suggests the separation between Christianity and Judaism'. Cf. Ellul (1970) 139, on the paradox of Jesus' dead body being taken outside, so that it might 'not defile the holy city', when that death indicated that the city 'was no longer holy'.

ed it. Jesus had performed a loving act which could make its *people* 'holy' (τὸν λαόν: v. 12), but the city itself was rendered 'unholy'.[56]

Given these evocative ideas, it is not hard to draw out the negative corollaries for Jerusalem to which the author was leading. It would have been most offensive to state explicitly that the Temple and city had been desecrated and polluted, yet the consequences of his picture were not hard to infer. What would happen to the holy city which had treated as unholy him who was the true source of holiness? Moreover, if the author intended a parallel here with the story of Moses who after the episode of the 'golden calf' set up an alternative sanctuary 'outside the camp' (Exod. 33:7ff), these negative consequences for Jerusalem would be confirmed. On that occasion Moses' action

> effectively emphasized that the people's sin of apostasy . . . had defiled the holy ground of the camp, with the result that it was now necessary for anyone who sought the Lord to go forth outside the camp. Thus the normal situation was at this time reversed.[57]

Just as the 'camp' had been defiled in the time of Moses, so had Jerusalem been desecrated in the time of Jesus.

Thirdly, focusing spiritually on Jerusalem was to be avoided because 'here we have no lasting city' (v. 13). Wrenched from its context this verse can easily be interpreted in very general or even Platonic terms as teaching the 'other-worldly' focus of Christian spirituality.[58] In its context, however, and especially given the Jewish background of the readers, the resonance concerning Jerusalem cannot be avoided. Here is clearly a 'veiled reference to the city of Jerusalem'.[59] The author was drawing them away from a religious interest in Jerusalem by alerting them to the impermanent (οὐ μένουσαν) and transient nature of that city. As an object of religious hope it would disappoint them; not so 'the city that is to come'. This transient, earthly city was not to be part of their fundamental identity. Instead 'the repudiation of Jesus unmasked Jerusalem as an ephemeral, transient city and made certain the coming of the future city'.[60]

---

[56] As seen in our discussion of Luke 13 and 19 in ch. 3 (2b), this distinction between the people and 'city' is vitally important. The author of Hebrews shares Luke's perception that Jesus, despite his critique of Jerusalem, continued to be concerned for its inhabitants. Hence his speaking here of Jesus' dying in order to sanctify τὸν λαόν—the regular word for the 'people' of Israel, which therefore included the residents of Jerusalem.

[57] Hughes (1977) 581. *Cf.* Bruce (1964) 403, and Lane (1991) 544: 'God has again been rejected by his people. His presence can be enjoyed only "outside the camp"'.

[58] This Platonic reading of Hebrews is seen especially in Thompson (1981). For a criticism of this position see *e.g.* Barrett (1956); *cf.* also Hagner (1983) 18.

[59] Lane (1991) 546, following *e.g.* de Young (1960) 107-8.

[60] Lane (1991) 546.

Both the previous chapters refer either to the 'city built by God' or to the 'heavenly Jerusalem' (11:10, 16; 12:22). What this meant for the earthly Jerusalem was not indicated at the time. Talking of 'the city that is to come' (13:14), however, forced an inevitable contrast with the earthly Jerusalem, which could now be seen as a city which would not 'last'. In the imagery of 12:27-8 it would be 'shaken'; the 'city that is to come' was part of the 'kingdom that cannot be shaken'.[61] Such ideas, though a natural part of the author's overall eschatological focus, also reveal an evaluation of Jerusalem. Reflecting on Jesus' death 'outside the city gate', he realized that Jerusalem could never again play the pivotal role within God's purposes that it once had.

When these arguments are put together a powerful picture emerges. The Temple at the city's heart is defunct; the city itself through Jesus' death has been defiled; the earthly Jerusalem in comparison with the heavenly has been diminished. 'Jerusalem has lost all redemptive significance because Christ has made the final sacrifice for sin outside the gates of Jerusalem. . . . Jerusalem has lost all eschatological significance, for there is no abiding city on earth'.[62]

The author offers his readers a critique of Jerusalem and its significance. The religious affection, which as native Jews they naturally felt towards their mother-city, was part of what they had to surrender if they were to follow in the steps of the crucified Jesus. Unless they were resident in Jerusalem (which is unlikely),[63] they could not literally 'leave the city', but in this spiritual sense they could. Thus, there is

> a deep sense of alienation from the present Jerusalem. Discipleship of Jesus means going 'outside the camp'; looking for the heavenly city to come means also looking away from the earthly Jerusalem.[64]

ii) The Way to the 'Heavenly Jerusalem'

This has the significant consequence that, if his audience were ever to attain to the 'heavenly Jerusalem', they first had to 'leave' or discard the earthly Jerusalem. This was a 'tale of two cities' between which a choice was required.

> The importance of the literal Jerusalem, symbolic of the Temple and the levitical sacrifices, must give way to that of the heavenly Jerusalem. But it is exactly the latter that the readers will not participate in if they remain in the Judaism of the literal Jerusalem.[65]

---

[61] This is especially significant in the light of the statements in the Old Testament that 'Mount Zion which cannot be moved (Ps. 125:1; cf. Isa. 33:20); cf. Lane (1991) 486.

[62] De Young (1960) 109, endorsed by Lane (1991) 547-8.

[63] See further below at n. 111.

[64] Dunn (1991a) 90. Cf. de Young (1960) 109: 'they are called 'to break all ties with the Judaism *centred at Jerusalem*' (italics mine).

The earthly Jerusalem was not a means to the heavenly city (as commonly assumed in Jewish thinking),[66] it was an obstacle; now that the 'heavenly Jerusalem' had been revealed (12:22-24) the earthly sign had become a barrier.

The new starting-point for the journey to the 'heavenly Jerusalem' was the shameful place where Jesus had 'suffered' (v. 12). In calling his readers to 'go out to him outside the camp' (v. 13) the author effectively portrayed Jesus as if he were still located on the cross; yet in the previous chapter Jesus had been portrayed as awaiting his followers in the 'heavenly Jerusalem' (12:24). By means of this powerful superimposition of ideas (suggesting that Jesus was simultaneously both at Golgotha and in the 'heavenly Jerusalem') he indicated that the way to the latter could only be through the former, that the route to glory began in shame (*cf.* 12:2), and that Golgotha was the surprising gateway into heaven.[67] Because Jesus was rejected at the cross but then vindicated in 'heaven', his followers had to take a similar path—which demanded both endurance in the face of 'abuse' and faith in the hope of future vindication. Following in the way of the Cross would lead to the heavenly Jerusalem.

d) Conclusion

These few verses contain some startling challenges. In the light of the previous arguments the audience might have expected a contrast between Jesus and the Temple, but now they were required to make a choice between Jesus and Jerusalem.

If they affirmed their allegiance to Jesus rather than to Jerusalem, this would be interpreted by their fellow-Jews as a denial of their Jewish heritage. 'Leaving the camp' of Jerusalem in a spiritual sense would lead inevitably to their actually 'leaving the camp' of Judaism—even if they continued to see themselves as authentically Jewish.[68] They would then experience the 'disgrace' that Jesus himself experienced when rejected by Jerusalem (13:12-13). Yet that was precisely the challenge. It had been hard for Moses to leave the 'treasures of Egypt', but he had done so, being prepared to experience 'abuse

---

[65] Hagner (1983) 243.

[66] *E.g.* R. Yohanan in Ta'anit 5a: "The holy One blessed be He said, 'I will not enter celestial Jerusalem until I enter terrestrial Jerusalem'".

[67] The observation in Barrett (1956) 391, is similar: 'When they go forth outside the camp they go out not merely into the wilderness but *unto Jesus* (13:13), and though they share his reproach they are brought near by his blood and *actually approach the heavenly Jerusalem*' (italics mine).

[68] *Cf.* Dunn (1991a) 91: 'we find a clear sense of a decisive breach with what had gone before. . . . For Hebrews and a Judaism still focussed on the Temple the ways had parted'.

for the Christ' (11:26); they too had to follow Moses' example, only now the place of Egypt had been taken by Jerusalem.[69]

This was a radical call, which might involve suffering. There was also an emotional cost. If they espoused the new pattern of worship revealed through Jesus they would never again be able to look to a city as their fellow-Jews could look to Jerusalem. In all other matters, the author claimed, Jewish-Christians, even though they might appear to be impoverished when compared with their fellow-Jews, were actually the richer.

> Hebrews' affirmations of what 'we have' are surprisingly comprehensive. We have the land, described as the 'rest' into which we have entered through Christ, in a way which even Joshua did not achieve for Israel (3:12-4:11); we have a High Priest (4:14; 8:1; 10:21) and an altar (13:10); we enter into the Holy Place, so we have the reality of tabernacle and Temple (10:19). We have come to Mt. Zion (12:22) and we are receiving a kingdom, in line with Haggai 2:6 (12:28). Indeed, according to Hebrews (13:14), the only thing which we do *not* have is an earthly, territorial city![70]

The author's strategy was generally one of encouragement, but on this issue of Jerusalem there was a definite and inevitable challenge. Although they could look forward to the 'heavenly Jerusalem', for now they had to forego their attachment to the earthly city: 'for here we have no lasting city, but we are looking for the city that is to come' (13:14).

4. The Crisis

In the light of his Christian faith the author of Hebrews saw the Land, the Temple and Jerusalem in new ways. Each of these three *realia* was a picture given by God in advance of some deeper, heavenly reality. The Land pointed towards eschatological 'rest' (4:9), the Temple illustrated the 'greater and perfect tent' in heaven (9:11), and the earthly city of Jerusalem prepared the way for the 'heavenly Jerusalem' (12:22). Moreover the three different modes of movement associated with each of these pictures (namely, wandering, worship, and pilgrimage) were all employed to make distinctively Christian points for his audience. On the one hand, when focusing on the Temple and worship, he taught that they enjoyed direct access to the 'holy of holies'; on the other,

---

[69] If this parallelism between Moses and Christian believers is intentional (as is suggested by the repeated use of ὀνειδισμός in 11:26 and 13:13), this is a striking example of the author's strategic care; for it is only with hindsight that the identification between Jerusalem and Egypt can be discerned.
[70] C.J.H. Wright (1994) 18-19; *cf.* Moule (1950) 37; Dunn (1991a) 86-91.

when using the imagery of their wandering towards the 'promised Land', he portrayed the life of faith as a wandering journey through the 'wilderness'. Putting these together the paradox emerges that believers are a 'cultic community on the move'[71]—enjoying God's presence and yet still on a journey towards him. The author then wove these two strands together in his final chapters, when focusing on the third image (of Jerusalem and pilgrimage): like Abraham they were on a journey of faith towards the 'city that has foundations' (11:10), but in another sense they had already arrived—'you *have come* to . . . the heavenly Jerusalem' (12:22).

This necessarily had repercussions of a negative kind for the actual, physical *realia*. How much was the author concerned that those corollaries should be noted? Was this theology about Jerusalem and the Temple central to his purposes in writing, or quite peripheral?

Such questions raise the problems as to the author's identity, and the date and circumstances of his writing. However, the question of authorship proves to be comparatively unimportant; it is sufficient for our purposes if, as is usually agreed, the author was someone of Jewish background who was known personally to this congregation of Jewish Christians.[72] The issues of situation and dating are more crucial, and significantly affect our understanding of his attitude towards Jerusalem.

a) The Audience's Situation

The sermon was evidently composed in the face of some crisis. What was it? The author sees the recipients in danger of 'neglecting such a great salvation' (2:3) and of 'falling away' (6:5).[73] Were they about to embrace paganism? The whole tone of the sermon suggests otherwise. The majority of commentators agree that what the author feared was the congregation's lapse back into the familiar security of their ancestral Jewish faith.[74] Having confessed Jesus as Messiah, they were in danger of not 'holding fast' to that 'confession' (4:14; 10:23)—most probably through a renewed involvement with the synagogue. Rather than retreating back within the 'camp' of Judaism, however, the author pleaded for them to 'go out' to Jesus (13:13).

Lindars' summary of the situation is particularly helpful:

---

[71] Johnsson (1978) 249; *cf.* his (1977-8). The classic work on the 'wandering' theme is Käsemann (1984).

[72] *Cf.* above n. 1. For detailed discussion, see the standard commentary introductions: *e.g.*, most recently, Ellingworth (1993) 3-21.

[73] See also 10:26ff; 12:15, 25.

The author is dealing with an extremely urgent practical situation which demands his utmost skill in the art of persuasion, if disaster is to be averted. [He] writes as a greatly respected member of a church which is torn by dissension. He writes at the instigation of the leaders. The church is a Jewish Christian group of Hellenists, probably in the Diaspora. . . . The dissident group, however, are reverting to the synagogue. . . . This, in the eyes of the leaders and the author, entails denial of Christian faith, though this is not necessarily how these people see it for themselves. But to the author they are heading for apostasy, and the purpose of the whole letter is to draw them back from the brink before it is to late. He has a difficult and delicate task to perform, because the efforts of the leaders have not been successful, and he has been approached as a last resort.[75]

He was also aware that through giving this sermon he was raising their awareness of the issues, such that if they rejected his 'word of exhortation' (13:22), they would no longer be sinning unwittingly but in conscious denial of God's final word in his Son. The stakes were already high, but in committing this sermon to paper the author was raising them yet higher. It would be a close call.[76]

Lindars then analyses the rhetorical strategy, which the author used to achieve this delicate task. Significantly he concludes that chapter 13 is crucial

---

[74]   *Cf.* above at n. 51. See *e.g.* Nairne (1913) 21; W. Manson (1951) 24, 160ff; Bruce (1964) xxiii-xxx, and (1987) 3502; Hagner (1983) 11; Lindars (1991a) 4ff. Dahms (1977) helpfully asserts that the recipients *themselves* may not have seen this involvement with Judaism as an abandoning of Christ; *cf.* W. Manson (1951) 24. This context of a 'relapse into Judaism' then explains: i) the author's portrayal of Jesus as 'greater' than Old Testament persons (3:6; 4:8; 12:24; *cf.* also 1:4; 8:6; 9:23); ii) his emphasis on Sinai, though now overshadowed by Mt Zion (12:18-24); iii) his insertion of Christian terminology into Old Testament events (4:2; 11:26), showing the continuity of the Old and the New, and that therefore a return to the Old Testament *tout simple* was now impossible; iv) his stressing the need to move forward with God's purposes and not to 'shrink back' (10:39).

This necessarily gives the sermon an anti-Judaic note, since he is expressly countering a Judaism without Christ. Yet this is not anti-Semitic. First, the author is evidently Jewish himself and fully respects God's revelation to the 'people of Israel' (indeed his Christian commitment may have given him a renewed reverence for this). Secondly, he avoids any critique of contemporary Judaism; his point is kept at a purely theological level, emphasizing instead the (very Jewish) themes of fulfilment and of Jeremiah's 'new covenant' (1:2; 8:13). His focus of criticism is upon Christians: if they claim now to be the true descendents of the 'people of Israel' in the wilderness, then they inherit not just that privileged status but also its challenging requirements: *they* may miss God's 'rest' (4:11). On this see further Klassen (1986); Lane and Wall (1993) 171-185.

[75]   Lindars (1989) 384, 390; these ideas were then developed in his book (1991a).

[76]   We will never know if he was successful, but 'the fact that Hebrews survived for posterity permits the conclusion that this passionate appeal did not fail in its effect': Lindars (1989) 406. The *captatio benevolentiae* in 6:9ff does not necessarily indicate that the author was personally confident about his audience's response.

within the author's argument and indispensable for understanding the precise issue that had occasioned the sermon;[77] for it is here (in a chapter which otherwise is more gentle and 'pastoral') that he at last becomes specific, showing his concern 'not with theory but with practice'.[78] Just when he was 'bringing down the temperature',[79] and perhaps allowing his audience to feel somewhat more relaxed, he comes to the precise issue. Reminding them that 'Jesus Christ is the same yesterday, and today and for ever' (v. 8), he then warns:

> do not be carried away by all kinds of strange teachings; for it is good for our hearts to be strengthened by grace, not by ceremonial foods (οὐ βρώμασιν), which are of no value to those who eat them (13:9).[80]

'Behind this brief instruction there lies the major issue of the whole letter'.[81] This is the passage which was central for assessing the author's attitude to the Temple and Jerusalem. If Lindars is correct in seeing these verses as dealing with the critical point at issue between the author and his recipients, then it becomes all the more likely that the issues in this passage relating to Jerusalem and the Temple were part of the audience's 'problem'. These issues were not tangential, but integral to the author's purpose.

What precisely was that problem? What was the congregation doing (or about to do) that was so serious? What was so harmful about 'foods', and why did the author see it as necessary to invoke a whole new understanding of the Temple in order to undercut this practice? What was the connection?

All becomes clear when this is understood to be a reference

> to the communal dinners which were held on Jewish feast days in Diaspora Judaism. These were one way in which Jews far away from Jerusalem maintained the sense of solidarity with the Temple and its cultus. . . . The daily sacrifices were offered there on behalf of Jews everywhere, and they could rely upon the efficacy of them, so long as they did their part. . . . The behaviour of the dissident group, which caused so much anguish to the church lead-

---

[77] Lindars (1991a) 7. This then confirms the arguments of Filson (1967) that chapter 13 is an integral part of the sermon; *contra e.g.* Buchanan (1972) 267f.

[78] Lindars (1989) 388.

[79] Lindars (1989) 402. In his book (1991) 8ff, Lindars refers to the author's use of 'understatement' and 'allusive references', his 'dropping of his severe tone', and his strategies to 'win the emotions' of his audience.

[80] As translated in NIV (see below n. 83).

[81] Lindars (1991a) 9. *Cf.* his (1989) 388: 'the single-minded drive of the epistle excludes the possibility that at this late stage the author is bringing in a new issue'. Lane (1991) lxi and 504, similarly concludes that these verses were of 'ultimate importance' and were 'crucial to the writer's pastoral strategy'.

ers, [was] the resumption of Jewish practices which expressed solidarity with the covenant people and the Temple at its heart.[82]

The presenting problem was not that the congregation were merely wanting to keep in good standing with the synagogue; they were actively wanting to be involved in these communal or 'ceremonial' meals which were bound up with a whole theology of the Temple in Jerusalem.[83] The author believed that at that point a line had been crossed which was inadmissible for believers in Jesus. The issue of 'foods' (βρώμασιν) might appear insignificant, but he feared that it would have fatal consequences—just as had that single meal (βρώσεως) for Esau (12:16-17). Hence he focuses at great length on the way the Temple cultus has effectively been rendered redundant in the light of Christ's coming; for only by such means can he undercut his audience's temptation to participate in these activities.

His earlier concentration on the Temple cultus was not, therefore, an elaborate argument conceived in a vacuum—designed simply to help people with a problem concerning forgiveness or 'assurance'. The Temple cultus was itself an integral part of the issue. Being involved in activities which affirmed the continuing validity of the Temple effectively constituted a denial of that which Christians had already received through Jesus, and certainly could offer no spiritual benefit which they did not already possess in him. They could not, and must not, go back to these practices. Showing solidarity with the Jerusalem Temple (for whatever reason, and however laudable) was no longer a Christian option.

If this was the heart of the issue, then the author's re-evaluation of the Land and Jerusalem would have served an important supportive role in the structure of his argument; for these physical entities were an inherent part of the Jewish tradition which had to be re-evaluated in the light of Jesus' coming.

---

[82] Lindars (1989) 388, 404; *cf.* his (1991a) 10. He refers to Josephus, *Ant.* 14.213-16, for a description of these communal meals (though unfortunately little evidence survives of the exact nature of such meals in the Diaspora). This interpretation of the 'foods' goes back to Bleek in 1840 and has been defended since by Westcott (1903) 436, Buchanan (1972) 233, and Hughes (1977) 572-4. Lane (1991) 530-6 agrees: 'ultimately one can thank God fully for redemption only through the thank offering and the fellowship meal in the presence of the altar in Jerusalem'; such fellowship meals in the Diaspora, however, 'recalled this thank offering' and 'evoked this eating at the altar in Jerusalem'.

[83] Though the word 'ceremonial' in NIV is strictly an addition to the text, it brings out the sense that this was no ordinary 'food' but food eaten within a specifically religious context. Yet, as Lane observes in (1991) 534, 'it is unnecessary to distinguish sharply between ordinary Jewish meals and special cultic meal times. Every Jewish meal possessed a cultic character'. Nor is the author concerned with the external trappings of 'ceremonial'; his criticism is due to the integral connection between these meals and the Temple cult.

b) Date of Composition

This analysis of the audience's problem contributes towards our understanding of the likely date of Hebrews. Apart from a couple of references which might be of assistance if one could be sure of a Roman destination for the epistle,[84] the only sure indication of dating within the text itself has to do, once again, with the Jerusalem Temple: was it still standing or not? Was Hebrews written before or after AD 70?

At this point those who advocate a pre-70 date naturally point to the numerous passages where the author alludes to the Temple services in the present tense.[85] They point to the implications of verses such as 8:13 and 9:8.[86] They also argue that the omission of any reference to the destruction of the Temple is 'almost inconceivable', if it had already taken place;[87] for 'a reference to the fall of the Temple would have clinched his argument as nothing else could have done'.[88]

> It is highly remarkable—indeed, unbelievable—that had our author written after the destruction of the Temple he could have failed to mention it, since this historical event could have been seen as the divine authentication of the author's central argument that the levitical ritual was outmoded and hence without significance (cf. 8:13). Indeed, it would have provided the perfect capstone to his attempt to persuade his readers not to return to Judaism. It is, therefore, especially the silence about the events of AD 70 that leads to the probability of an earlier date.[89]

These are strong and convincing arguments.[90] Yet, if it is argued that the issue facing the congregation concerned their desire to show solidarity with the Temple, the assumption that Hebrews was written before AD 70 becomes all

---

[84] If a Roman destination is accepted, then 10:32ff may be a reference to the expulsion of Jews under Claudius in AD 49, and 12:4 an indication that the Neronian persecution had not yet started: see e.g. Lane (1991) lxiii-lxvi. See further below n. 111.

[85] These are helpfully laid out in Hughes (1977) 31-2. He lists: 5:1-4; 7:21, 23, 27-8; 8:3ff, 13; 9:6, 9, 13, 25; 10:1, 3, 8, 11; 13:10-11.

[86] See above 1d.

[87] Lindars (1991a) 20.

[88] Bruce (1987) 3514; cf. e.g. Hughes (1977) 30; Witherington (1991) 151.

[89] Hagner (1983) 8.

[90] Advocates of a pre-70 date thus include: Lane (1991) lxii-lxvi; Lindars (1991a) 10-21; R.M. Wilson (1987) 14; Guthrie (1983) 28-31; Hughes (1977) 30-32; Robinson (1976) 200-220; Moule (1966) 44; Bruce (1964) xlii-xliv; Montefiore (1964) 9ff; Spicq (1953) 253-261; see also the commentaries by Héring (1970), Buchanan (1972) and Strobel (1991). Those who prefer a later date include: Isaacs (1992) 44, 67; H. Koester (1982) ii, 272; Kümmel (1975) 304; Klijn (1975); Fuller (1966) 147.

the stronger. They are far more likely to have been tempted to show solidarity with the Temple while it was still operational than after its destruction. 'A return to active association' with the Temple was clearly a 'live option'.[91]

Advocates of a later date naturally seek to show that the author's references to the 'tabernacle' betray his 'academic' disinterest in the contemporary Temple.[92] They also posit that the audience was suffering from a sense of bereavement at the loss of the Temple. Yet the impression gained is not that they are bereaved, but that they are tempted. None of the many passages which suggest their frame of mind indicates that they were feeling lost or bereft. On the contrary, the author constantly warned them of the dangers of 'temptation' (chs. 3-4; cf. 6:4-12; 10:23-39). Despite some notes of encouragement, the predominant atmosphere of the sermon is one of strong warning. Such language makes sense if the Jewish alternative, based on the Temple, was a viable and established system. After AD 70 Judaism would not have presented the audience with such an alluring and hard-to-resist temptation. Manson rightly concluded that the lure towards the cultic provisions of Judaism is 'more intelligible if the altar and the sacrificial worship of Judaism were still in existence, in other words, if the situation was prior to AD 70'.[93]

The most probable setting for Hebrews is therefore in the years before AD 70, when a group of Jewish Christians (against the advice of their own leaders) were tempted to return to the synagogue and, in particular, to involve themselves in activities which affirmed the validity of the Jerusalem Temple.

Some would venture to be more precise. Jews throughout the Empire might well have had extra sensitivities concerning the Temple after the outbreak of the Jewish revolt in AD 66. This led Moule (following Nairne) to see the issues facing the congregation in Hebrews as belonging to the

> tense period shortly before AD 70, when, with the outbreak of the Jewish War, a wave of patriotic nationalism may well have swept from Palestine over the whole of diaspora Judaism, constituting a sore temptation to Christian Jews to revert to Judaism.[94]

---

[91] Lindars (1991a) 6.

[92] This was countered above (1c).

[93] W. Manson (1951) 166.

[94] Moule (1950) 37; cf. Nairne (1913) 22: 'The Jewish war was beginning. Appeal was being made to all Jews to band together in defence of Jerusalem and the ancient creed'. It is not impossible, however, that the pressure to show solidarity with the Temple was growing throughout the 60's; if so, Hebrews could have been written before the actual outbreak of hostilities. Somewhat similar suggestions were made by Brandon (1951) 239ff, and Snell (1959) 21. For a recent advocate of the years AD 67-68, see Stedman (1992) 13.

This was a time for all Jewish people to show solidarity and to affirm the centrality of the Temple within their religious and political identity. If Jewish Christians then failed to attend a Jewish festival meal (or some other ceremony that drew its significance from its link to the Temple cult), this might be interpreted as an act of disloyalty, and as a refusal to show political solidarity with the Jewish cause. It was a difficult and decisive time for Jewish Christians—a tug of loyalty. Should they identify themselves with the cause of the Temple, or not?

This setting for Hebrews has much to commend it, and explains the delicate situation in which these Christians found themselves. It also explains their motivation. On this reading, they were not being tempted merely by the traditional and familiar trappings of their former religion, still less by a personal need for atonement ritual to deal with their post-baptismal sin.[95] Their chief desire was to avoid being ostracized by their fellow-Jews.[96] The problem was primarily social, not theological.[97] They were afraid of sharing in Christ's 'disgrace' (ὀνειδισμός: 11:26; 13:13).

Despite these pressures, the author insists that they must see the Jerusalem Temple for what it truly is—a 'shadow' of the real thing, a mere picture of the reality which they now possess in Christ. This reality must not be sur-

---

[95] This is Lindars' emphasis in (1991a) 10-14. On this view, the audience's consciousness of sin was paradoxically leading them (in the author's opinion) into a far deeper sin—apostasy. The sermon's strong tone suggests that the audience's problem was not primarily a tender conscience.

[96] Cf. e.g. G.A. Barton (1938) 205. Caird (1960-61) 205, endorses Nairne's position that 'the readers are being prepared not so much for martyrdom as for shame' and this may be particularly 'the shame of pacifists whose Christian commitment debars them from identifying with the struggle for liberty'. Similarly, Moule (1950) 37, sees the audience as motivated by the 'fear of being called traitors' and that the 'disgrace' and persecution which they feared was that which would be caused by 'private Jewish antagonisms', not by the secular authorities. This would then weaken the popular interpretation that they desired the protected status of Judaism as a *religio licita*. This position is adopted by German scholars such as Oepke (1950) and Loader (1981); cf. also e.g. W. Manson (1951) 87, 151, and Bruce (1987) 3514. For a critique of the *religio licita* argument as the background to the New Testament, see e.g. Maddox (1982) 91ff.

[97] The author's conscious emphasis on theology has caused interpreters to miss the 'political' context and to assume that the recipients were troubled by some 'spiritual' problem. If instead they were succumbing to *social* pressure, this would explain how the author could fear their apostasy and yet be confident that this was not what they really wanted (6:4-12; 10:26-39); for their compromise owed more to social convenience than to theological conviction; they were motivated by 'fear of persecution', not by 'mental dullness' or even conscious disobedience (cf. Hagner [1983] 4). It was then the author's delicate task to argue that their position *did* involve an unacceptable *theological* compromise. This would also explain why the emphasis in chs. 3-4 is more on circumstantial 'testing' than on moral 'temptation'.

rendered through compromise on this important issue. The author was 'well aware that this would mean breaking the relationship . . . with the local Jewish community' and that this would be very 'difficult emotionally'—not least because that community was made up of their 'friends and relations'.[98] It was hard too to 'renounce a valued past'.[99] God's purposes, however, had moved forward; they needed to press onwards, not going back to that which had been left behind (cf. e.g. 10:39; 12:2). As Moule concludes,

> He says, if you would be loyal Jews you are committed to go forward in company with the . . . Christian Church, not back to a pre-Christian stage of Judaism. Judaism itself implies Christianity. It is a very potent argument.[100]

c) Four Further Indications

A date for Hebrews in the tumultuous years before AD 70 helpfully explains several further features—for example, the author's exercising great care in his choice of words.[101] This was caused not only by the particular sensitivities of the audience, but also by the inherent sensitivity of his subject-matter in the political realm. In the light of the current tension between Jerusalem and Rome, the author's radical attitude to the Temple as a Jew might appear almost treacherous. This provides a further reason for his referring to the Temple in terms of the 'tabernacle' (σκηνή). Far from being a mark of the author's 'academic' character, this was a strategic device which prevented his becoming embroiled in the contentious issues of contemporary politics.[102] He had to avoid giving undue offence to anyone who might read his sermon. The issue of the Temple would continue to be a focus of dissent after AD 70, but such tact and caution is especially appropriate in the years before when the Temple's future hung in the balance.

Secondly, the author appeals to his audience to be prepared to 'go to [Jesus] outside the camp and bear the abuse he endured' (13:13). The primary reference in its original context must surely have been to the feared hostility of those within the 'camp' of the Jewish community. For the power of this picture lies in the fact that the author sees the closest of parallels between what Jesus suffered and what his readers may suffer in the near future. They were

---

[98] Lindars (1991a) 11.

[99] Nairne (1913) 293.

[100] Moule (1950) 37. Cf. Lane and Wall (1993) 184f: 'they could not turn back the hands of the clock and deny their Christian understanding and experience'.

[101] Above n. 49.

[102] Cf. above 1c.

fearing 'abuse' or 'disgrace' from their fellow-Jews.[103] This again suggests the pre-70 situation. After 70 not only would institutional Judaism be in a weaker position, but the negative attitude to the Temple, which the author encouraged them to adopt, would excite less opposition; for after its destruction, some of their fellow-Jews would themselves be developing a similar spiritualizing attitude towards the Temple. After 70 the viewpoint of Hebrews would appear appreciably less radical.

Thirdly, the author's emphasis on the need for 'faith' (ch. 11) makes good sense in the years before 70. Not only his critique of the Temple but also his challenge to 'leave the camp' required a faith that looked beyond the present to God's unseen future. After 70, when the Temple had been destroyed and Judaism severely weakened, both this critique and this challenge would have demanded far less faith; for there was visible circumstantial evidence to support this position. If, however, Hebrews was written *before* the Temple's destruction in 70, then to adopt its position concerning the Temple and to heed its challenge required real faith—faith in a God who could do what was as yet 'not seen' (*cf.* 11:1). It also required faith in the great significance of Jesus—that through his dying in weakness the entire Temple system had been rendered redundant. No wonder the author called his fellow Jewish-Christians to a renewed faith.

Finally, there is the author's eschatological emphasis.[104] Was some of this fuelled by living at a time when something important was brewing in and around Jerusalem?[105] Do the references in 3:9 and 3:17 to the 'forty years' in the wilderness have an extra resonance because the forty-year period since Jesus' crucifixion was 'running towards its close'?[106] If the author had a similar view to that found at Qumran that 'God's dealings with Israel, which began with a probationary period of forty years, would be rounded off at the end-time by a probationary period of like duration', this would have added a new urgency to his appeal.[107] He may have understood the 'last days' (1:1) in a particularly urgent way—looking to a further 'act of God' in the imminent future which would endorse God's purposes in Christ. His conviction that the Temple was 'close to destruction' (ἐγγὺς ἀφανισμοῦ: 8:13) would then be an important part of this.[108] Nairne concluded that he was expecting 'an imme-

---

[103] *Cf.* above n. 96.

[104] On Hebrews' eschatology in general, see esp. Barrett (1956) 363-93.

[105] *Cf.* above ch. 4 (3b) and below ch. 8 (1).

[106] W. Manson (1951) 167; see also Bruce (1964) xliv, 65; Guthrie (1983) 29; *cf.* Spicq (1953) 261.

[107] Bruce (1964) 65, citing four passages in the Qumran literature: CD 20:14f; 4QpPs. 37, frag. A, 1:6ff; 1 QM *passim*; and b.San. 99*a*.

[108] Above 1d.

diate "coming", yet a coming which would not be the "end of the world" in the old cruder sense'.[109]

If the author was assuming that something important would soon take place in Jerusalem, several passages take on a new meaning. This conviction about Jerusalem may underlie both his wording in 10:37 ('in a very little while the one who is coming will come and will not delay') and his warning about the 'removal of what can be shaken' (12:26-27). Particularly interesting is his language in 10:25 ('all the more as you *see* the Day approaching'); does this suggest that there were some visible and observable signs that some such dramatic dénouement was looming?[110] The 'Day' was clearly 'approaching'.

In each of these instances there is no need to deny the wider reference to an event more universal in scope; but the more specific application to Jerusalem may need to be acknowledged as well. Living prior to the event the author could not easily have distinguished between the particular and the universal, between the destruction of the Temple (*cf.* 8:13) and Christ's 'appearing a second time' (9:28): would these events be integrally connected, or would they be quite separate? The language of Hebrews indicates that it was written in the period before 70 when, fuelled by a conviction that the Temple would soon be destroyed, the author wrote with a sense of profound urgency—an urgency born of not knowing if this dramatic event in Jerusalem would signal the final 'coming' of Jesus or not.

Such an understanding of the author's vision for the future not only adds to the likelihood of his writing before AD 70, it also augments our contention that the Jerusalem theme is close to the heart of his concerns. For if the Temple was soon to be destroyed, that would inevitably have repercussions for the city of Jerusalem and for the whole religious polity of Judaism. It would also explain his insistence that Jesus' followers needed to make a break with their Jewish heritage; for on this reckoning 'Jerusalem' was by no means the haven of safety that they presumed it to be.

d) Conclusion

The author of Hebrews was writing a critical work at a critical time, and the issue of Jerusalem was an integral part of his concerns. Given the sensitivities of these issues both for his audience and in the public arena, he had to write

---

[109] Nairne (1913) 30.

[110] So Nairne (1913) 383; Caird (1960-61) 205; this point is argued more fully in my (1994b) 67.

with great care. Despite this tact and caution, however, the radical nature of his message was ultimately not hard to infer.

Sensing this importance which the author gives to Jerusalem, some scholars suggest that the audience was located in Jerusalem or Palestine,[111] although the arguments in favour of Rome have much to commend them.[112] Certainty on this issue is quite impossible. Was it perhaps instead the *author* who had some connection (whether past or present) with Palestine?[113]

Such geographical questions may be beside the point. In the years before 70 the issue of a proper evaluation of Jerusalem and the Temple was vitally relevant to people of Jewish background *wherever* they were. Possibly both the author and his audience sensed that something dramatic was about to take place in Jerusalem (*cf.* 10:25): 'the imminent crisis they seem to face in Hebrews could be the destruction of Jerusalem by the Romans'.[114] In these circumstances Jewish believers were pressurized by their fellow-nationals to show their solidarity with their nation and the Temple. As a result 'some' of them had ceased 'to meet together' with their fellow-Christians (10:25), and were strongly tempted to attend the synagogue's communal meals which were seen as organically connected with Jerusalem and its Temple. The author of Hebrews, however, urged that this was not the moment for siding with the Jewish people, nor with Jerusalem, but with the people of Jesus. Christian believers were to turn away from such things, and to be prepared for the opposition that would result when their allegiance was seen to lie elsewhere: 'let us go to him outside the camp and bear the abuse he endured' (13:13).

The author was giving this congregation a powerful call. It was also a personal call, because (though unknown to us) he was well-known to them. It

---

[111] Much depends on 13:24 ('those from Italy send their greetings'): is he writing *from* Italy or *to* Italy? Scholars who have favoured Palestine include Delitzsch, Westcott, Ramsay, Turner, Spicq, Hughes and Isaacs; for Jerusalem itself, see Buchanan (1972) and those in the long list given by Spicq (1953) i, 239, n. 1. If the recipients were Palestinian Jews experiencing local opposition, there would be extra poignancy in Abraham's being described as an 'alien in the promised land' (11:9). Their fear of 'disgrace' in Jewish eyes would also be more reasonable if they lived in Judea—especially in the years of the Jewish revolt. Certainly this could explain the emphasis on cult rather than Law (as in Paul's letters), though the (probable) absence of Gentiles in their number may account for this.

[112] See *e.g.* W. Manson (1951), Bruce (1964) and (1987), Lane (1985) and (1991).

[113] As a Jew by birth, his attendance at festival gatherings in Jerusalem at an earlier stage in his life is not impossible (though see above n. 5). His reapplying the pilgrimage-motif to the 'heavenly Jerusalem' (above 3b), however, suggests he would have seen such visiting to Jerusalem by Christians as unnecessary. If he had personal experience of Palestine in the 60's (or indeed at the very moment of writing) this might have been brought about through involvement with Christian work. Was he, together with 'those from Italy' (13:24), on some kind of church delegation to the mother-church in Jerusalem?

[114] Hagner (1983) 6.

was a call articulated with great care, because of the sensitivities involved and the delicacy of the situation. It was a radical call—a call to make a decisive break with the past at a time when there was much pressure to invest in the Temple and Jerusalem with a future. It was a prophetic call, based on convictions which as yet had not been fully substantiated. It was a costly call—a call that his readers might disassociate themselves from both people and traditions that meant much to them. It was call into an unknown future, for they were being 'asked to embark on a pilgrimage, confessing that in the old and well-loved traditions of Judaism they had no abiding city';[115] in another sense, however, it was a call to a certain future, for they could be 'sustained by the fact that that for which they were striving had already been achieved' (cf. 12:22).[116] Above all, it was a call to be identified with Jesus—first in his suffering (12:3; 13:13), but ultimately in his exaltation, victory and glory (12:2-3, 24); and it was very urgent, for there were important issues at stake. 'They can gain *everything* together with Jesus or they can lose *everything* without him'.[117]

How much, though, was it a call that was completely novel? No doubt the urgency of the situation forced the author to see matters with a new clarity. Yet, in invoking as the basis for his appeal the picture of Jesus going out to Golgotha and being rejected by Jerusalem, he was intimating that *even then* this conflict of loyalties (between Jesus and Jerusalem) should have been apparent. There was a necessary conflict between them which was written into the fabric of the gospel story. Now, more than ever before, that conflict needed to be recognized and acted upon. Christian believers had a new calling—to identify with Jesus, not with Jerusalem.

---

[115] Caird (1960-61) 206.

[116] Barrett (1956) 365.

[117] Lane (1991) 546 (italics original).

7

A NEW CITY
Revelation

*I will write on you the name of my God and the name of the city
of my God, the new Jerusalem that comes down from my God out
of heaven (Rev. 3:12).*

*As in John's Gospel, the true Temple is identified both with Jesus himself (Rev. 21:22) and
with the Church (Rev. 11:1-2). There is no continuing role for the physical Jerusalem, either in the millenium or at the time of the descent of the 'new Jerusalem' (Rev. 21:2); the
biblical imagery previously associated with the earthly Jerusalem is now applied to the
heavenly city. Writing almost certainly after the fall of Jerusalem, the author makes connections between 'Babylon' (Rome) and Jerusalem, seeing Jerusalem's fall both as an act
of divine judgement and as a warning to the Church and the Roman Empire.*

The book of Revelation is a document which ever since its appearance has
given rise to a bewildering variety of interpretations, many of which impinge
on our question of Jerusalem. Three aspects are in sharp contrast with the book
of Hebrews. First, we know the name of its author, John, if not his precise
identity. Secondly, we know for whom it was first written: whereas Hebrews
had been composed for a single congregation (perhaps just a part of one?),
Revelation was written in the first instance for seven churches in the Roman
province of Asia Minor: Ephesus, Smyrna, Pergamum, Thyatira, Sardis, Philadelphia and Laodicea (1:11). Thirdly, there is a greater scholarly consensus
that Revelation was written some time after the fall of Jerusalem in AD 70.[1]

---

[1]   On authorship and dating, see below 4.

There are also points of similarity. Both works were penned by Jewish writers, steeped in their knowledge of the Old Testament. Both may have been occasioned by the author's disagreement with the recipients' attendance at certain meals; in Revelation these meals were not Jewish meals associated with the Jerusalem Temple (as in Hebrews), but pagan meals associated with pagan temples and with 'food sacrificed to idols' (2:14, 20).[2] This difference in context then contributes to the different atmosphere of Revelation which, despite its indebtedness to Jewish thought-forms, is concerned with wider issues relating to the pagan world.

The seemingly insoluble complexity of Revelation's structure, combined with uncertainty regarding its date and the situation that it addressed, means that it has been subject to a number of widely varying interpretations—some quite bizarre.[3] The focus of this chapter is specific: what was John's attitude to the physical city of Jerusalem and its Temple? Did he see these physical entities as continuing to play a distinctive role in God's purposes into the future—either in his vision of the 'end-time' or in the intervening period? Was the 'earthly' Jerusalem still of central significance?

Issues relating to Jerusalem prove quite divisive when interpreting Revelation. One line of interpretation sees its author as unconcerned with Jerusalem; the references to the 'great city' and to 'Babylon'[4] are to Rome (or the 'world-city'), and any references in chapter 11 to the 'Temple', the 'holy city' and the city 'where also their Lord was crucified' (11:1, 2, 8) are not directed to Jerusalem, but are purely symbolic. Jerusalem is of little importance.[5]

Another strand sees John as vitally interested in Jerusalem—but in a negative way, focusing on its destruction in AD 70. On this view the references in chapter 11 are in the first instance to the physical Jerusalem and its Temple. Some of those who hold this position date Revelation before 70, seeing

---

[2] On the importance of this precise issue in Revelation, see *e.g.* Kiddle (1940) 39; Hemer (1986) 120-23.

[3] Not least among those (such as Hal Lindsey) who see in it a blue-print for events in the Middle East in the late twentieth century. The structural scheme adopted here is that of Garrow (1997) who argues that Revelation is organized around the presentation of the contents of the 'scroll, which reveals 'what must soon take place'. Garrow's structure focuses on 12:1-14:5, 15:6-16:21, 19:11b-21:8 as the scroll-revealing, story-telling parts of the text, with other passages foreshadowing or reviewing these vital pieces of text. He also sees this structure as influenced by a liturgical setting, with the text being read in six separate instalments, beginning at 1:1, 4:1, 8:1, 11:19, 15:5 and 19:11. For an alternative structural analysis, see *e.g.* Bauckham (1993a) 1-37.

[4] For references to the 'great city', see 11:8; 14:8; 16:19; 17:18; 18:10ff; for 'Babylon', see 14:8; 17; 18.

[5] *E.g.* Bauckham (1993a) 272, who says that 'John nowhere . . . shows any interest' in the Temple and the earthly Jerusalem.

much of it as a prediction of Jerusalem's destruction.[6] Others, accepting a post-70 date, see John as dealing with Jerusalem's destruction in the first half (chs. 1-11) but moving on in the second to describe the destruction of Babylon (chs. 12-22).[7] Yet others identify 'Babylon' (or just the 'woman' seated on the 'beast': 17:3ff) with Jerusalem, such that the whole book is concerned in one way or another with Jerusalem, both earthly and heavenly. In any event, Jerusalem has been judged.[8]

A third approach sees John as having a positive concern for Jerusalem. The millenium (20:1ff) and the 'beloved city' (20:9) refer literally to the physical Jerusalem; the earlier references to places in the Holy Land, such as those in chapter 11 as well as 'Mount Zion' (14:1) and 'Harmageddon' (16:16), are similarly taken literally. This is the stage on which God's future purposes will be played out. Irrespective of any of the negative repercussions of the destruction of the Temple and the city in AD 70, Jerusalem retains its central significance throughout history; for at the end of time it will be on centre stage. On this view, Jerusalem will return. These options will not be assessed in detail here. It is helpful to note, however, that they correspond roughly to three of the ways in which Revelation *as a whole* is interpreted (often labelled as the idealist, the preterist and the futurist).[9] The first approach to Jerusalem emphasizes the role of symbol (idealist), the second the importance of contemporary first-century events (preterist), the third the significance of the end-times (futurist). If it is true that 'more than one of these views are required for a satisfactory understanding of Revelation',[10] it should not cause surprise if a similar conclusion is reached concerning Jerusalem. In other words, all three have useful insights but none in itself has the whole picture.

Of the three, the first is nearest the mark. The third approach acts as a corrective to those who too easily spiritualize the nature of the millenium, but fails to reckon seriously with the nature and prevalence of John's symbolism. The second is right to alert us to the importance of AD 70 and how this has affected John's presentation, but fails to see the way in which John has appropriated this event in order to make a different and larger point, which relates to Rome and the wider world. In keeping with the majority of scholars it will be assumed in the following that, whilst John is writing after 70, the contemporary reference of 'Babylon' is not Jerusalem but Rome. Even on this view,

---

[6]   See *e.g.* Chilton (1987); Gentry (1989).

[7]   See *e.g.*W.J. Harrington (1969).

[8]   See *e.g.* Ford (1975), Beagley (1987), Lupieri (1993).

[9]   These are helpfully summarized in Morris (1987) 18-20, where he also mentions the 'historicist' view (which sees Revelation as an inspired forecast of the whole of human history); *cf.* Harrington (1993) 14-17.

[10]   Morris (1987) 20.

however, there are some important implications for Jerusalem which too easily can be overlooked.

The author's Christian convictions caused him to re-evaluate the role of
the Temple and of Jerusalem to such a degree that his views would have been
quite at variance with his fellow-Jews who did not share those convictions. It
is appropriate before considering John's references to the Temple (2) and the
city of Jerusalem (3), to note some points of critical disagreement between
John and the contemporary Jewish community. Are there sufficient signs of a
critique of Judaism to make it conceivable that John would also have re-evaluated the Temple and Jerusalem?

1. John and Judaism

That John's thought-forms are indebted to Judaism is not in doubt. Part of the
reason why his prophecy has often proved so difficult for subsequent Gentile
readers is precisely that it is steeped in the imagery of first-century Jewish
apocalyptic. This has caused some to go so far as to see Revelation as more
Jewish than Christian.[11] There is ample evidence, however, to show that John
was using the imagery of his contemporary Judaism to make Christian claims
with which his fellow-Jews would have significantly disagreed. If anything,
he was consciously subverting the traditional language and its symbolism.

The most obvious example is his conviction that the Jewish Messiah
has come in the person of Jesus, and that this Jesus, seated on God's throne as
the 'Lamb', is to be worshipped in a way which would be quite inappropriate
if he were merely an angel (cf. 19:10; 22:9).[12] This reveals a remarkably high
christology, with a clear intimation that Jesus is 'the one who was seated upon
the throne'.[13] The focus on the Lamb in chapter 5 thus proves to be a vital 'ful-
crum' on which the rest of the apocalypse turns.[14] Thereafter, although the
heavenly drama is described in imagery borrowed from non-Christian Jewish
apocalyptic, it clearly relates to the Lamb and the ultimate victory of *Jesus*.

---

[11] So Bultmann (1952/55) ii, 175 could say, 'The Christianity of Revelation has to be
termed a weakly christianized Judaism'.

[12] *Cf.* also the descriptions of Jesus at the start of each of the seven letters (chs. 2-3; esp.
2:18). Since the author of Revelation is so conscious of the danger of worshipping angels
(19:10; 22:9), his accepting the appropriateness of worshipping Jesus is all the more
striking: see Bauckham (1993a) 135.

[13] Rev. 21:5; *cf.* also 3:21; 5:6, 13; 7:9, 17; 12:5; 22:3. In 7:17 a paradoxical twist is given
to Psalm 23 where it is the *Lamb* who 'will be their shepherd'; in 17:14 the Lamb is identified as the 'Lord of lords and King of kings'; in 22:13 Jesus is identified as the 'Alpha and
Omega', a title used at the outset of God himself (1:8).

[14] See Beasley-Murray (1974) 25.

Similarly, those who believe in this Jesus are unashamedly the true continuation of the 'people of God'. The twelve gates of the new Jerusalem are
named after the 'twelve tribes of Israel', but the city's twelve foundations are
named after the 'twelve apostles of the Lamb' (21:12-14). John is asserting the
essential unity between Old Testament Israel and the followers of Jesus and
his apostles. Rather than being dismissive of 'Israel' in the past, there is a bold
appropriation of its status.[15] A similar point can be deduced from John's describing the 'great city' in which was 'found the blood of the prophets and of
the saints' (18:24) as 'Babylon' (14:2 etc). This latter term recalled the hostility of ancient Babylon towards Judah and Jerusalem. Its reapplication to the
city opposed to the 'saints' clearly implies that those 'saints' occupy a parallel
role to that occupied seven centuries earlier by the people of Jerusalem. Elsewhere John describes as 'saints' those who believe in Jesus (16:6). For John,
therefore, the Church could be identified with an 'inclusive eschatological Israel that comprised both Jews and Gentiles in the one people of God'.[16]

Thirdly, John's universal emphases stand in contrast to some strands in
contemporary Judaism. Not only is his prophecy set against the canvas of the
whole 'world',[17] but his attitude towards the 'nations' is radically inclusive.
In Jesus the contrast between Israel and the 'nations' has been removed. The
followers of the Lamb include those from every 'tribe and language and people and nation' (5:9; 7:9; *cf.* 14:6),[18] and they can claim to be 'priests' in the
service of Israel's God (5:10). A careful analysis of chapter 7 (in which John
juxtaposes this universal emphasis alongside more particularistic references
to the 'tribes of the people of Israel': 7:4) 'indicates not so much the replacement of the national people of God as the *abolition of its national limits*'.[19]

---

[15] The 144,000 'sealed out of every tribe of Israel' (7:4) probably represents the redefined
people of God (Christians, both Jew and Gentile), and is identical to the 'great multitude
that no one could count, from every nation' (7:9): see Caird (1966) 95 and C.R. Smith
(1990). Bauckham (1991) 106, concludes that John 'intends to reinterpret the twelve tribes
as the new international people of God'. If, however, the '144,000' describe Jewish
believers as opposed to Gentile ones, our essential point is preserved: the imagery of
'Israel' is being applied to Christians, albeit exclusively for *Jewish*-Christians.

[16] Borgen (1993) 209.

[17] Note the references to the ὀικουμένη (the inhabited 'world') in 3:10; 12:9; 16:14.
rather than to the land of Palestine. The word for 'earth' (γῆ) appears 77 times in Revelation; the references to the 'kings of the earth' (*e.g.* 1:5; 6:15; 16:14; 17:2; 18:3, 9; 19:19)
and the four corners of the earth' (7:1) make it quite implausible that John was referring to
the 'land' (γῆ) of Judea; *contra* Gentry (1989) 121.

[18] See also 10:11; 11:9; 13:7; 17:15 (significantly a total of seven times); see discussion
in Bauckham (1993a) 27f, 326-337. He notes that John may be here reinterpreting Exod.
19:5 ('you shall be my treasured possession out of all the peoples') 'in the light of the international character of the New Testament people of God' (p. 327).

[19] Bauckham (1993a) 224-5 (italics mine).

A striking indication of this universal emphasis is the way John consistently uses the terms for 'people' (λαός) and 'nation' (ἔθνος) in the plural.[20] The most significant occurrence is at the climax of the work when he declares that 'the home of God is among mortals (ἀνθρώπων), and they will be his *peoples*' (21:3).[21] A precious Old Testament promise has been reapplied in a way that is no longer tied to ethnic Israel. Jewish ethnocentricity has been broken. Chapter 21 concludes with the vision of the 'glory and the honour of the nations' being brought into the new Jerusalem (v. 26). With its strictures on anything 'unclean' being permitted in the city (v. 27), it is clear that for John there is nothing *intrinsically* unclean or 'common' (κοινόν) about the 'nations' *per se*. The universal implications of Jesus' death in Jerusalem, and the imperative that the 'eternal gospel' should be proclaimed to all 'those who live on the earth' (14:6), had dispelled any pre-suppositions concerning Gentiles that John might have inherited from his Jewish background.[22]

A further indication of this universal emphasis is the way in which he has reapplied the imagery of the 'exodus' to the situation of the Church. When recounting both the six 'trumpets' (8:6-9:21) and the six 'bowls' (16:1-14), John is plainly alluding to the ten plagues of Pharoah's Egypt (Exod. 7-11). The 'song of the Lamb' (15:3-4) is also based on the 'song of Moses' (15:3), which was sung after the crossing of the Red Sea (Exod. 15:1-18).[23] In other words, John sees the Israelites' escape from Egypt as prefiguring the deliverance accomplished in Jesus, which will be brought to full effect at the end of time. So Christians are concerned with a quite different 'promised land'.

> Moses celebrated a deliverance by the Lord which adumbrated a greater deliverance to come. The greater redemption eclipsed the former by a similar degree as the second redeemer transcended the first. Moses and the Lamb are no more to be bracketed than the promised land of Israel is to be equated with the kingdom of God.[24]

---

[20] This is the case even when in grammatical terms he uses the singular in the phrase '*every* people' (see *e.g.* 5:9; 14:6). The exception is when God's 'people' are commanded to 'come out' from Babylon (18:4) in language which clearly echoes Jer. 51:45; this Old Testament command is now applied to Christians.

[21] The plural is often omitted in modern translations (*e.g.* NIV). The Old Testament promise is found in *e.g.* Lev. 26:11-12, Jer. 31:33, Ezek. 37:27 and Zech 2:10-11. In the last of these there is the beginning of a more inclusive vision: 'many nations shall join themselves to the Lord on that day'.

[22] Beale (1988) 327-9, lists other instances where John has 'universalized' Old Testament passages which originally were focused on Israel. For example, Christians are now a 'kingdom of priests' (1:6; 5:10; *cf.* Exod. 19:6).

[23] See further Rowland (1993) 125. For an interpretation of Revelation, which sees this 'exodus' theme as central, see *e.g.* Schüssler Fiorenza (1985) and (1991).

[24] Beasley-Murray (1974) 235.

John's concerns are universal in extent, and restricted neither to the people of Israel nor to a particular 'promised land'.

Fourthly, if any of his Jewish contemporaries considered that some Old Testament prophecies and more recent apocalyptic visions justified the use of military force against the pagan foe, then John's message is quite different. John's dramatic vision of the '*Lion* of the tribe of Judah' as a '*Lamb* standing as if it had been slaughtered' (5:5-6) means that, when subsequently he uses the language of 'holy war', this must be interpreted in a metaphorical sense (*cf. e.g.* 13:10).

> The novelty of John's symbol lies in its representation of the sacrificial death of Christ as the fulfilment of Jewish hopes of the messianic conqueror. . . . Revelation makes lavish use of holy war *language* while transferring its *meaning* to non-military means of triumph over evil. . . . The distinctive feature of Revelation seems to be, not its repudiation of apocalyptic militarism, but its lavish use of militaristic language in a non-militaristic sense.[25]

These four brief observations are sufficient to confirm that John was not merely repeating ideas inherited from Judaism, nor even giving them a slightly christianized interpretation. On the contrary, he was reworking those Jewish traditions in startling new ways, which gave expression to his Christian conviction concerning Jesus' Messiahship. In writing a Christian apocalypse he was 'breaking new ground', and the raw material of his genre was inevitably Jewish.[26] He was using those raw materials, however, to build something new, appropriating them and reapplying them in fresh and creative ways. In Bauckham's terminology, it therefore becomes vitally important to distinguish John's *language* from his *meaning*. If John has given a new meaning to a concept (*e.g.* 'Lion of Judah', 'war', 'the city', 'Mount Zion') then this must be heeded. Failure to do so will lead to a total distortion of his intention.

That this conflict between 'church and synagogue' was a real one in John's day is evident from the references in two of the opening letters to 'those who say they are Jews and are not, but are a synagogue of Satan' (2:9; 3:9). Evidently John saw 'Judaism' in itself as an honourable institution; the term 'Jew' has no inherent anti-Semitic opprobrium, since it is implied that this is a title which the author would readily apply to himself.[27] Yet it does show the contrast which the author sensed between himself and those in the synagogue who were not Christian. The promise to Philadelphia is especially important:

---

[25] Bauckham (1993a) 184, 233; *cf.* 183, 214.

[26] See Morris (1987) 41, following Moffatt (1927) 492.

[27] On these verses and the whole question of anti-Semitism in Revelation, see the helpful analysis of Borgen (1993) 199ff.

> If you conquer, I will make you a pillar in the Temple of my God. . . . I will write on you the name of my God, and the name of the city of my God, the new Jerusalem that comes down from my God out of heaven, and my own new name (3:12).

This first reference to 'Jerusalem' and its 'Temple' appears in a context where John makes a sharp distinction between Christians (be they Jewish or Gentile) and non-Christian Jews, and asserts that the latter will have to acknowledge the vindication of the former (3:9). These verses have a polemical ring to them—a note which is still present when the full vision of the 'new Jerusalem' is described at the end (chs. 21-22).

Contrary to those in the synagogue who emphasized the importance of Jerusalem and its Temple (and their own close relationship to them), the Risen Christ promised these Philadelphian Christians an integral part in both. Yet the Temple in question would not be the Jerusalem Temple but a different one, the 'Temple of *my* God'; nor would the Jerusalem promised be the earthly one, but rather the 'new Jerusalem that comes down from my God out of heaven' (3:12). If the earthly Jerusalem had already been destroyed, this was a promise that these Christians would be compensated; alternatively, if they felt far removed from the 'centre' of things, they were to know that through their faith in Jesus they could not be any nearer to God. They would have a full part to play in God's purposes. Jerusalem would, as it were, come *to them*.[28]

In this passage the Risen Christ refers four times to '*my* God' and twice to the 'new' thing which he has authority to give to his followers. This reveals John's focus on Jesus' unique relationship with Israel's God and his conviction that this great truth has led to some further 'new' truths of a radical nature. It was John's task, whilst employing the conventions and traditions that were available to him, to teach those new truths. One area in which Christians needed to develop a new stance in relation to their Jewish heritage was, as already adumbrated in this letter to Philadelphia, their whole attitude to Jerusalem and its Temple.

---

[28] It is hardly surprising if a century later the Montanists in this very region would be emphasizing that the 'new Jerusalem' would descend on their little village of Pepuza (see Eusebius, *EH* 5.14ff). They were right to be encouraged, but wrong to take the imagery so literally.

2. The Temple

a) *Its Previous Status*

As with other New Testament writers, there is no suggestion that John denied the Temple's importance in the Old Testament era.

The highest compliment to the Jerusalem Temple is that John's vision of heavenly worship is so clearly modelled upon it. The opening vision of worship around the throne, with the 'four living creatures' saying 'Holy, holy, holy, the Lord God the Almighty' (4:8), reflects Isaiah's vision in the Jerusalem Temple (Isa. 6:1-7). The heavenly Temple, which is 'filled with smoke from the glory of God' (15:8) also reflects Isaiah's experience (Isa. 6:4), as well as other particular theophanic moments of revelation associated with the Jerusalem Temple (*e.g.* 2 Chron. 7:1; Ezek. 44:4). John refers to the heavenly Temple at least nine times;[29] it is described as the 'tent of witness' (15:5), and includes both the 'ark of the covenant' (11:19) and an 'altar' (6:9; 8:3, 5; 9:13; 14:18; 16:7). All this imagery is drawn from the Jerusalem Temple.

Particularly significant is the fact that at one point 'there was silence in heaven for about half an hour' (8:1). A good case can be made for asserting that this is linked with the subsequent reference to the offering of 'incense', which is identified with the 'prayers of the all the saints' (vv. 3-4). There was a Jewish tradition that God silenced the praises of the angels so that the prayers of Israel on earth might be heard during the day—and especially at dawn at the time of the offering of incense in the Temple.[30] Thus,

> what happens in vv. 3-4 is clearly the heavenly parallel, enacted by an angelic priest in the heavenly Temple, to the offering of incense in the Temple in Jerusalem. . . . Revelation portrays the heavenly reality which the earthly ceremony had symbolized. The incense in heaven accompanies the prayers of God's people and ensures that they reach the throne of God.[31]

This was a further way in which John affirmed the validity of the Jerusalem Temple and its many traditions.

---

[29] See 7:15; 11:19; 14:15, 17; 15:5, 6, 8; 16:1, 17. This imagery is combined with that of the heavenly court and throne-room (introduced in 4:1ff); not until the reference in 6:9 to the 'altar' is the reader aware of the heavenly Temple. Mounce (1977) 384, helpfully comments: John's reference to the heavenly Temple is not so as to 'describe the architecture of heaven, but to speak meaningfully to a people for whom the Temple was supremely the place of God's presence'.

[30] See b.Hag. 12b.

[31] Bauckham (1993a) 81.

b) A New Perspective

He was, however, appropriating those traditions for his own purposes. Twice he specifies that the incense represents the 'prayers of the *saints*' (8:3, 4; *cf.* also 5:8)—not those (as formerly) of ethnic Israel. For all his affirmation of the Temple in times past, he now understood God's purposes to have moved forward onto a new stage. In this new era, would there be a continuing role for the Temple?

Here Revelation proves to be a close parallel to the book of Hebrews. Both authors emphasize (to a degree not seen in other New Testament writers) the theme of Jesus' 'blood'.[32] Regardless of John's precise understanding of this sacrificial language, he clearly interprets Jesus' death against the backdrop of the cultic system associated with the Jerusalem Temple. His consistently referring to Jesus as the 'Lamb' points in a similar direction.[33] If the 'Lamb' has offered such an effective and decisive sacrifice through his 'blood', would this not have some consequences in the future for the continuance of the sacrificial system associated with the Temple?

A similar conclusion is reached through noting his emphasis at the outset that 'by his blood' Jesus has made 'us to be a kingdom and *priests* to serve his God and Father' (1:5-6; *cf.* also 5:9-10). This is cultic language borrowed from the Jerusalem Temple, but now reapplied to John and his fellow-Christians far away in the churches of Asia Minor. There is no suggestion in the ensuing letters that these Christians are in any way to be dependent upon the Temple. On the contrary, God's awesome presence is focused in the person of the Risen Christ who mediates that divine presence to them in a personal way. What could the Temple offer that was not already theirs through their response of faith to this 'Living One' (1:18)?

c) The Final Vision (ch. 21)

The notion that Jesus is the focused presence of God receives its clearest expression in the final vision of the 'new Jerusalem' when John makes the staggering claim that there was 'no Temple in the city, for its Temple is the Lord God the Almighty *and the Lamb*' (21:22). Speaking of this Jesus who some years previously had entered the Temple in the earthly Jerusalem, John boldly claims that, together with 'God the Almighty', he constitutes the essence of

---

[32] In Hebrews, see esp. 9:14; 10:19, 29; 13:12, 20. In Revelation, see 1:5; 5:9; 7:14; 12:11; 19:13.

[33] There are 29 references to the 'Lamb' in Revelation (beginning in 5:6).

the Temple in the heavenly Jerusalem. That which the Temple had signified, in terms of God's presence amongst his people, is now found in the Lamb.

This necessarily cast the Jerusalem Temple in a new light. According to the revelation given to John, history was moving towards the eschatological reality of a 'new Jerusalem', which contained no Temple. Christians were not therefore to focus on such an entity. If even the Temple in heaven (which had formed such an important backdrop for his previous visions of heavenly worship) was now eclipsed in this final vision (21:22), how much more would this hold true of the earthly Temple in Jerusalem?

There is another sense, however, in which the *whole* of the 'new Jerusalem' is portrayed as a Temple. John describes the dimensions of this city ('its length and width and height are equal': 21:16) in terms which reflect the cubic form of the 'holy of holies' in the earthly Temple (1 Kings 6.20).

> This cubic symbol of the earthly presence of God among his people has expanded before his mind's eye, so that it . . . fills the whole templeless city. The presence of God, no longer confined to a sanctuary apart, pervades the whole life and being of the city.[34]

The 'holy of holies', though formerly an empty place visited but once a year (and thereby symbolizing the ambiguous nature of God's presence), is now a place inhabited by countless thousands. The barriers between God and humankind have been removed at last: 'the home (σκηνή) of God is among mortals. He will dwell with them; . . . and God himself will be *with* them' (21:3).[35]

Much of John's imagery here is based on the vision of the Temple in the closing chapters of Ezekiel (Ezek. 40ff).[36] Those prophetic chapters easily fuel the expectation of a renewed physical Temple in Jerusalem. Here John applies them exclusively to the eschatological new Jerusalem—a Jerusalem which has *no* Temple! Ezekiel had seen a river flowing from underneath the Temple and going out from the city. In Revelation, though the indebtedness to Ezekiel is clear, the 'river of the water of life' flows instead 'from the throne of God and of the Lamb' and stays within the city going 'through the middle of the street of the city' (22:1-2). In this way the new Jerusalem becomes an

---

[34] Caird (1966) 273, 279. *Cf.* Hughes (1990) 229: 'in one respect [the holy city] is itself all sanctuary'.

[35] This vision is adumbrated in 7:15 and 13:6 where God's 'shelter' or 'dwelling' (σκηνή) is a place inhabited by his people; God's holiness no longer requires him to be separate from them. C.R. Koester (1989) 120ff, helpfully refers to the new Jerusalem as a 'tabernacle-city', which he then identifies with the 'Church in the new age' (p. 131).

[36] For a helpful analysis of Revelation's indebtedness to Ezekiel, see Vanhoye (1962). The promise of God's 'tabernacling' amongst his people occurs in Ezek. 37:27, before Ezekiel's vision of the Temple (40:1ff).

inclusive eschatological reality which has drawn upon itself imagery that originally had been associated not only with the earthly Jerusalem, but also with
the earthly Temple.

> In Old Testament terms the expectation of a new Jerusalem without the re-
> building of the Temple would have been unthinkable. Indeed it was the pres-
> ence of the Temple (cf. Ezek. 40-48), which made Jerusalem the city of God
> (cf. Ps. 46:5). . . . In brief, all aspects of the Temple symbolism have here
> come together.[37]

Clearly any expectations of a renewed physical Temple in Jerusalem were
thereby ruled out; for, according to John, these Old Testament passages concerning the Temple find their fulfilment, not in the physical Jerusalem, but instead in the new Jerusalem.

d) The 'Temple of God' (11:1)

This overall framework then helps us to interpret correctly the reference to the
Temple (and Jerusalem) in 11:1-2:

> Then I was given a measuring rod like a staff, and I was told, 'Come and
> measure the Temple of God (τὸν ναὸν τοῦ θεοῦ) and the altar, and those who
> worship there, but do not measure the court outside the Temple (τὴν αὐλὴν
> τὴν ἔξωθεν τοῦ ναοῦ); leave that out, for it is given over to the nations, and
> they will trample over the holy city for forty-two months.

At first, one might be tempted to hear this as a reference to the heavenly Temple, alluded to in 7:15. However, the reference to the 'trampling' by the 'nations' and the subsequent vision of the 'two witnesses' (11:3-13) make it clear
that John is here referring to more earthly realities.[38] In 11:19 the reversion of
the scene to heaven is then clearly indicated by John's specifying that he is
speaking of 'God's Temple in heaven' (ὁ ναὸς τοῦ θεοῦ ὁ ἐν τῷ οὐρανῷ).

Is John speaking of an earthly Temple, which can be identified directly
with the Jerusalem Temple? If he were, these verses would have to count as
an instance of false prophecy, since at the literal level they were plainly un-
true. The 'measuring' of the Temple almost certainly signifies its being divinely protected (cf. Isa. 34:1; 2 Kings 21:13; Amos 7:7)—in contrast to the

---

[37] Dumbrell (1985) 38.

[38] The shift from heaven to earth probably results from the fact that John has just eaten
'the little scroll' (10:10); chapter 11 (vv. 1-13) is then the articulation of its contents. See
further below at n. 64.

destruction of the 'outer court' and the 'holy city' (v. 2). In AD 70, however, *all* the Jerusalem Temple was destroyed, together with the surrounding city.[39]

The majority of commentators conclude that John is speaking of a different Temple, namely the Christian community. 'He understands the Temple and city as symbols of the people of God'.[40] Indeed he is consciously contrasting this new Temple with that in Jerusalem. It is as though a recollection of the destruction of that physical Temple is a springboard that prompts the realisation that there must be another Temple to which this promise of protection *does* apply. The prophecy then indicates that, even though the Church is outwardly vulnerable and prone to attack (v. 2), it can rest assured that spiritually it is under God's sure protection (v. 1).

> He is distinguishing the inner, hidden reality of the Church, as a kingdom of priests who worship God in his presence, from the outward experience of the Church as it is exposed to persecution by the kingdom of the nations. The Church will be kept safe in its hidden spiritual reality, while suffering persecution and martyrdom.[41]

On this reading, the Christian Church is the true 'Temple of God' (v. 1), the true inner sanctuary, and the sure outpost of God's presence in the world. John's *language* may refer to the Jerusalem Temple, but his *meaning* does not. The verse makes no promise concerning that Temple's future. Instead there is a contrast between these two Temples. The Church would experience divine protection, but this had *not* held true for the Jerusalem Temple. John draws attention to this truth. By using this Temple imagery he brought to the surface an issue (the destruction of Jerusalem's Temple), which if painful for some was probably significant for all. John's readers were to see that they, not ethnic Israel, had the true Temple: indeed they themselves *were* that Temple.[42]

---

[39] For this reason, it has been suggested that John was quoting a Zealot prophecy from the years preceding AD 70 which he knew had proved false. See *e.g.* Beasley-Murray (1974) 37: 'Contrary to many of his apocalyptically-minded Jewish contemporaries he did not regard the Temple of Jerusalem as impregnable'. Caird (1966) 131, declares this theory as 'improbable, useless and absurd'. Even without it, this pointed contrast between the physical Temple and the Church is plain.

[40] Bauckham (1993a) 272; *cf. e.g.* Beasley-Murray (1974) 182. Caird (1966) 131, can even say: 'it is hardly too much to say that in a book in which all things are expressed in symbols, the very last things the 'Temple' and 'holy city' could mean would be the physical Temple and the earthly Jerusalem'.

[41] Bauckham (1993a) 272; *cf. e.g.* Mounce (1977) 221, Caird (1966) 132, Beasley-Murray (1974) 42. *Cf.* the similar presentations of the Church's fate in 7:13-17 and 12:11.

[42] *Cf.* Garrow (1997) ch. 6: John transferred 'the Temple symbolism from Jerusalem, the province of the Jews, to the Church, the province of his hearers in Asia Minor'.

e) Conclusion

The attitude towards the Temple in Revelation is very close to that found in
John's Gospel. Both speak of Jesus as the 'Lamb' (*cf.* John 1:29) and assert
that he is the essence of the Temple (John 2:21; Rev. 21:22); both assert that
Christians too, by extension, may take that title upon themselves (John 14:23;
Rev. 11:1-2).[43] Both affirm the past status of the Temple, but no distinctive
role is envisaged for the Temple in the future. In Revelation an additional emphasis is given to the reality of the heavenly Temple, of which the earthly
Temple had been a valuable foretaste. At the very end of Revelation this vision of the heavenly Temple is replaced by the vision of a new Jerusalem in
which there is no longer any need for a Temple. The message of Revelation is
that the Jerusalem Temple, for all its past significance, has had its day.

3. The City of Jerusalem

Chapter 11 is a key text when considering John's attitude to the city of Jerusalem. He speaks here both of the 'holy city' (v. 2) and of the 'great city,
where also their Lord was crucified' (v. 8)—references which in their context
must in *some* way be related to Jerusalem. In addition to the references associated with Babylon the 'great city'[44] and with the new Jerusalem (21:2, 10),
there are others to an unspecified 'city' both in 14:20 ('the winepress was
trodden outside the city') and 20:9 ('the camp of the saints and the beloved
city'). Any account of John's attitude to Jerusalem needs to take all these into
account, though the references in chapter 11 prove the most revealing.

a) The New Jerusalem

The climactic vision of Revelation is of 'the holy city, the new Jerusalem,
coming down out of heaven from God' (21:2; *cf.* v. 9). The fact that this city
is called by the name 'Jerusalem' and not by some quite different name is significant. It is the purposes of Israel's God, the God associated with Jerusalem,
which are now being fulfilled; there is a golden thread of continuity from the
Old Testament into the New. This reflects John's assumption that Jerusalem
itself as a city had been peculiarly significant in God's purposes. The allusions
elsewhere to the 'holy city' (11:2) and the 'beloved city' (20:9) point in a sim-

---

43 For these two points in John, see ch. 5 (1).
44 References in n. 4 above.

ilar direction. Even if, as argued here, their precise reference is not to Jerusalem *simpliciter*, these motifs clearly draw upon the biblical concept of Jerusalem's specialness in God's purposes. John stands squarely in the biblical tradition which affirms the uniqueness of God's revelation in Jerusalem.

What is revealed, however, is decidedly a *new* Jerusalem. Any identification or connection with the earthly Jerusalem cannot be maintained. This new Jerusalem stands in deliberate contrast to the former Jerusalem. There is no encouragement to believe that the earthly Jerusalem might somehow be metamorphosed into the heavenly one, for John expressly says that this Jerusalem 'comes down *out of heaven*'. He depicts a radically new eschatological reality: 'a new heaven and a new earth, for the first heaven and the first earth had passed away' (21:1).

Ever since the promise made to the Philadelphian church (3:12), the first hearers of Revelation would have been waiting to see what this new Jerusalem was. The whole description that follows is intended as an incentive to ensure that they are among those who will be numbered in the Lamb's 'book of life' (21:27; *cf.* 17:8) and so enter this marvellous inheritance. Only moral 'impurity' (21:27) will debar them—certainly not geographical distance!

Most importantly, this new Jerusalem is the true fulfilment of the various eschatological prophecies in the Old Testament which had originally been grounded in the physical Jerusalem. Reference has already been made to the fulfilment of Ezekiel's vision concerning the Temple.[45] These chapters also draw upon the later chapters of Isaiah (40-66).[46] Jerusalem had been a major theme in Isaiah:

> The book of Isaiah moves from the perverse worship of physical Jerusalem under judgement to the worship of Yahweh in the new Jerusalem. Gradually in the course of this great book Jerusalem becomes a major biblical symbol uniting city and saved community, combining sacred space and sanctified people. . . . Isaiah is concerned with the ultimate end. His Zion is an ideal; the perfected people, the righteous people of God.[47]

The process begun within the pages of Isaiah is now affirmed by John and brought to its appropriate conclusion. Isaiah had used 'Jerusalem' as a symbol of God's ultimate purposes for his people; John does the same. The true reference of Isaiah's prophecies was therefore not the physical Jerusalem but the new Jerusalem—'the perfected people.' This was not to deny that God had

---

[45] See above at n. 36.

[46] For example, compare Rev. 21:18ff with Isa. 54:12, and Rev. 21:23-6 with Isa. 60:1-5. See further, Mouw (1983).

[47] Dumbrell (1985) 19.

truly been involved with the physical city of Jerusalem in times past, but it did mean that these prophecies from Isaiah could not be interpreted in a literal manner as if they referred to future events in Palestine. God *was* being faithful to his promises; but the *locus* of that fulfilment was the new Jerusalem.

> Unlike many of the Old Testament prophets, John prophesies no restoration of the earthly Jerusalem, but instead envisages a 'new Jerusalem' which comes down to earth from heaven.[48]

John's vision of the new Jerusalem, therefore, rather than endorsing the idea that the physical Jerusalem had some future in God's purposes, does precisely the reverse. This contrasts sharply with the Rabbinic understanding that was developing throughout this period.

> The Rabbinic literature looks forward to a restored Jerusalem under earthly conditions. The new city is described in detail in terms which are often fantastic, but the welter of imagination bestowed upon the subject does not alter the fact that what the Rabbis hoped for, and described as 'the Jerusalem of the age to come' was essentially the material capital of a material state.[49]

For John the physical Jerusalem, whilst a helpful precursor, never had the potential to become itself the perfected reality that the prophets foresaw: a *new* Jerusalem was required. The prophecies from the Old Testament applied to the heavenly Jerusalem, not to the city in Palestine.

b) The Fall of Jerusalem

The opening verses of chapter 11 read most naturally as an allusion to the events of AD 70. If John is writing after Jerusalem's fall, it then becomes important to ask if there are any indications as to how he viewed that event theologically. Was it a temporary hiatus, or did it speak of something more final in God's purposes? Was it an accident of history or, alternatively, an act of divine judgement? Did it lead to John's being hopeful for the city or dismissive?

i) A Response to AD 70?

In 2 Baruch and 4 Ezra, two Jewish apocalypses roughly contemporary with Revelation, the recent fall of Jerusalem is a major theme.[50] Is the author of Revelation similarly using the apocalyptic medium to express his understand-

---

[48] Beagley (1987) 150
[49] Barrett (1956) 374.
[50] See further B. Longenecker (1995).

ing (even if somewhat different) of this disturbing recent event? Some are convinced that this is one of John's primary purposes. They see Jerusalem to be the true reference of 'Babylon', and understand John's depiction of Babylon's fall as his comment on the fall of Jerusalem.[51] This has major repercussions for our understanding of John's approach to Jerusalem.

On this interpretation, it is Jerusalem, not Rome, that is the city which has killed the 'prophets' and the 'saints' (18:24; cf. 17:6), such that when she falls there is rejoicing amongst the 'saints and apostles and prophets' (18:20). This 'holy city' might then be identified with the 'whore', who was in an unholy alliance with the 'beast' (17:3-6);[52] it certainly could not claim to be different from any other city of the world. Its judgement would then be paradigmatic of God's end-time judgement upon the world. On such a reading, there would manifestly be no bright future for Jerusalem. The only hope would lie instead in a completely new Jerusalem.

One of the advantages of this interpretation is that it makes even tighter the connection between the fall of Babylon (18:1-19:10) and the emergence of the new Jerusalem (21:1ff). It is precisely the demise of the old Jerusalem that paves the way for the revelation of the new. Yet the overwhelming consensus of scholarly opinion is against it. The 'seven mountains' (17:9) clearly allude to the seven hills of Rome and it is hard to see how Jerusalem could really be described as the 'great city that rules over the kings of the earth' (17:18), or why her destruction would cause such concern to the 'merchants of the earth' (18:11) and to 'all shipmasters and seafarers, sailors and all whose trade is on the sea' (18:17).[53]

The primary reference of 'Babylon' is Rome. Nevertheless, John may have sensed some parallels at this point between Rome and Jerusalem, since some of the imagery which he uses in relation to 'Babylon' is drawn from Old Testament passages that had originally applied to Jerusalem. Babylon, for ex-

---

[51] See Ford (1975) and (1978) 215-18, Beagley (1987), and Lupieri (1993).

[52] So Beagley (1987) 103.

[53] The fact that sometimes (e.g. in Sib. Or. 5:154, 226, 413; Josephus, Cont. Ap. 1.197; Pliny, Nat. Hist. 5.14.70) Jerusalem is referred to as a 'great city' is beside the point: contra Ford (1975) 180. For further arguments in favour of seeing 'Babylon' as an allusion to Rome, see e.g. Bauckham (1993b) 35-40. Having granted this reference to Rome, however, it is still possible to see the 'great city' as referring more deeply to the 'world' in its opposition to God, with Rome being seen as the specific contemporary embodiment of that 'world'. So Caird (1966) 138: 'the city is Rome. . . . Yet even this cannot be said without further qualification. Rome is simply the latest embodiment of something that is a recurrent feature of human history. The great city is the spiritual home of those John dubs as the inhabitants of earth; it is the tower of Babel, the city of his world, Vanity Fair'. Similarly Morris (1987) 146, says, 'the "great city" is every city and no city. It is civilized man in organized community.'

ample, drinks a 'cup' of divine judgement (18:6) similar to that which the prophets saw being given to Jerusalem (Isa. 51:17; Jer. 25:15-8; Ezek. 23:32-34).[54] This shows his awareness that the divine judgement which he foresaw for Rome was an outworking of a judgement that in Old Testament history had been meted out upon Jerusalem. If in recent decades that self-same city of Jerusalem had once again been destroyed, together with its Temple, it would not be hard to trace the connections. The God who was now judging Rome was the one who had also judged Jerusalem. It would be exegetically legitimate to deduce from John's description of Babylon's fall some general idea as to how he might also have interpreted the fall of Jerusalem. On this reading, John was not referring to Jerusalem's fall explicitly, but he might have seen those principles which applied to Rome as applying with equal validity to Jerusalem. John's understanding of Jerusalem's fall could then be deduced *retrospectively* in the light of his understanding of the forthcoming fall of 'Babylon'.

ii) The Influence of the Synoptic Apocalypse: Jerusalem as Paradigm

It is possible, however, to go further. It has frequently been noted that the events associated with the opening of the six seals (ch. 6), which in many ways provide a 'table of contents' for the entire book, bear a striking resemblance to the Apocalyptic Discourse in the Gospels (Mark 13 and parallels).[55] The themes of world disorder and the suffering of Jesus' followers appear in both, and the language in places is very close. Nor should this be especially surprising. If the Apocalyptic Discourse (in whatever precise form) was now an established part of the Christian tradition, the writer of a Christian apocalypse such as Revelation could scarcely avoid making some allusion to it. Indeed it would almost be a requirement to show how this new apocalyptic revelation related to the words of Jesus himself.

Having noted this parallelism, some go further and wish to see the whole of Revelation (especially chs. 4-11) as John's version of the Apocalyptic Discourse.[56] Again this seems to go too far, given John's wider focus on the Roman empire. Closer to the mark would be the suggestion that John is using the Apocalyptic Discourse as the springboard for a wider application. At first glance the Apocalyptic Discourse had dealt specifically with Jerusalem; yet it also operates at a second level—the level of Jesus' *parousia* and the judgement of the entire world. John draws out that secondary application.

---

[54] *Cf.* too the 'bowls' of wrath in 16:1ff. Beagley (1987) 98, also notes that the concept of Babylon paying 'double for her deeds' (18:6), echoes the language applied to Jerusalem (Jer. 16:18; 17:18; Isa. 40:2; Hos. 10:10).

[55] See *e.g.* Beasley-Murray (1974) 42, 129, Beale (1984), Beagley (1987) 45-46, following the lead of Charles (1920) i, 158. *Cf.* D. Wenham (1984).

[56] See *e.g.*W.J. Harrington (1969) 35, 55, and Gentry (1989) 131.

In part this may have been motivated by the desire to rescue the Discourse's validity. Some of John's contemporaries, through failing to note this second level, may have seen it as largely irrelevant now that Jerusalem had fallen; others, through identifying the fall of Jerusalem too closely with the return of Christ, may have seen it as invalidated. John, however, is able to assert its abiding relevance. He sees 'that there is a real distinction between the end of Jerusalem and the end of the world'[57] and that this prophecy accordingly works on two levels—applying both to Jerusalem and to the world as whole. His own apocalypse offers, amongst many other things, a fresh presentation of the Apocalyptic Discourse for the post-70 Church.

In particular the 'sixth seal', which describes the catastrophic events associated with the imminence of the End, closely resembles Mark 13:24-25 (alluding to an earthquake, the darkening of the sun and the moon, the falling of stars, etc). In the Apocalyptic Discourse these motifs had been set within a context more closely tied to Jerusalem, but there had also been an 'imperceptible transition from type to anti-type . . . in which the fall of Jerusalem becomes in its complete fulfilment the end of the age'.[58] John now concentrates on this latter point, the application to the wider world.

This has important consequence for our study. First, it shows John's desire to take attention away from the physical Jerusalem.

> John presents a version of the Apocalyptic Discourse which excludes any mention of Judea, Jerusalem or the Temple. . . . There is a notable omission of a reference to the eschatological significance of the Jerusalem Temple.[59]

Secondly, and more importantly, if John was aware of this dual purpose within the Apocalyptic Discourse (applying both to Jerusalem and to the End), he may well have been assuming that the fall of Jerusalem acted *as a paradigm of that later event*. There would then be an inherent inter-connectedness between what happened to Jerusalem and what happened to the world as a whole (which John will subsequently term 'Babylon'). For those who were concerned to understand Jerusalem's fall, the meaning was plain. It was a sign of things to come. Jesus' words in the Apocalyptic Discourse, at one level, had been fulfilled; at another level they awaited their far greater fulfilment. As a result, it would not be simply that the fall of Babylon had led John retrospectively to an understanding of Jerusalem's fall (as above). It will also have worked in the other direction, with the fall of Jerusalem providing the inter-

---

[57] W.J. Harrington (1969) 55.
[58] Mounce (1977) 45.
[59] Garrow (1997) ch. 6.

pretative model and paradigm for the fall of Babylon. Whichever way one approached them, these two events were inter-linked.

This interpretation would then explain some of the scholarly uncertainty as to the meaning of John's references to 'Babylon' and the 'great city'. Is it either Rome or Jerusalem? Or is it somehow a combination of both, or perhaps a reference to something less specific? In the light of the Apocalyptic Discourse and its *own* blurring of the distinctions between the fall of Jerusalem and the end of the world, it becomes possible to answer as follows:

1) John's focus is on the final judgement of the world
2) Probably influenced by the Apocalyptic Discourse, this is depicted in terms of a world-*city*.
3) In John's own day the embodiment of this city was none other than Rome.
4) The inter-connectedness with Jerusalem means that allusions to this city are to be expected, since Jerusalem to some extent forms part of the base-metaphor out of which John has constructed his depiction of the 'great city'.

While the *reference* is to Rome, some of the *allusions* may be to Jerusalem. Again there is a distinction between the *meaning* (which applies to Rome) and the *language* (which may sometimes allude to Jerusalem).

iii) The 'Fall' of the Great City' (11:8, 13)
This offers a helpful framework within which to approach chapter 11. First, it explains the ambiguity of 11:8:

> Their dead bodies will lie in the street of the great city, that is prophetically called Sodom and Egypt, where also their Lord was crucified.

This latter phrase is a 'strikingly matter-of-fact, historically specific statement, quite uncharacteristic of the Apocalypse'.[60] Its reference to the Lord's 'crucifixion' makes it impossible to deny an allusion to Jerusalem. The reference to the 'great city', however, points beyond Jerusalem to the world-city. This is the first appearance of the 'great city'—a phrase which will be repeated frequently in the following chapters as a reference to 'Babylon'.[61] This is then a prime example of this distinction between allusion and reference: the verse alludes to Jerusalem, but it refers to Babylon.[62] The same is true of verse 13, which describes the 'fall' of a 'tenth of the city'; though there are probable

---

[60] Bauckham (1993a) 171. For Zahn (1909) iii, 438, the reference to 'Sodom' 'presupposes that the destruction of the former Holy City had already taken place'; see also Mounce (1977) 35.

[61] For references, see again above n. 4.

allusions to Jerusalem, the ultimate reference is to the city which John will shortly identify as 'Babylon'.[63]

Verse 8 functions as a pivotal point of transition within Revelation. Our analysis above (asserting that Jerusalem's fall acts as a pre-descriptive paradigm of Babylon's fall) opens up the possibility that the whole of this section (11:1-13) is designed as a foretaste of what lies in store for Babylon (chs. 12-19). This would be particularly appropriate if these verses reveal the contents of the 'little scroll' (10:10), with the contents of the main 'scroll' (first referred to in 5:2ff) then being revealed in 12:1ff. As its diminutive title suggests, the 'little scroll' would offer a microcosm of what is revealed in the main scroll.[64] This then explains why there are more overt allusions to the physical Jerusalem in this section than anywhere else in the entire apocalypse, for these Jerusalem-associated events act as a microcosmic window into the purposes of God for the wider world. From this point Jerusalem moves comparatively to the background, though its resonances never entirely fade away. The *double entendre* of 11:8 marks a deliberate moment of transition. On the one hand it is a reminder of Jerusalem 'where also their Lord was crucified'; on the other it moves the reader on to see the wider implications of this Jesus-event for the 'great city'—implications which will shortly be unveiled in the great scroll.

If this underlying parallelism exists in John's mind between Jerusalem and Babylon, then certain important consequences follow. First, although Je-

---

[62]   *Cf.* Bauckham (1993a) 207-8: 'if the great city has some of the characteristics of Jerusalem, it also has those of Babylon. John's purpose here is to merge rather than to distinguish the two cities'; *cf.* Beasley-Murray (1974) 229; Morris (1987) 145.

[63]   The language of 'earthquakes' echoes again the Apocalyptic Discourse, originally associated with Jerusalem, and the city's population (70,000) is far closer to Jerusalem's than to Rome: see *e.g.* Beasley-Murray (1974) 177, 187. Nevertheless Beasley-Murray (who argues that this was originally a Jewish prophecy which actually referred to Jerusalem) can conclude: 'the holy city is then to be understood as representing the city of the world in its opposition to God' (p. 179).

[64]   I am indebted here to the insights of Garrow and his forthcoming book (1997); *cf.* above n. 3. Prior to the revealing of the contents of the 'scroll' (5:1-2) in 12:1ff, there are several 'foreshadowings', one of which is 11:1-13; he interprets this as the contents of the 'little scroll' (βιβλαρίδιον: 10:2, 8-10), to be distinguished from the 'scroll' of 5:2 (βιβλίον). In the main story-text, the principal themes concern the Church's spiritual protection amidst persecution, and her ultimate vindication with the destruction of Babylon and her persecutors. The counterpart to these in 11:1-13 are the preservation despite attack of the 'Temple' (the Church in 11:1-2), the work of the two witnesses (11:3-12), and the fall of the city (11:13). The imagery of this 'little scroll' is indebted to prophecies such as Ezekiel and Daniel, thereby showing the validity of their witness, yet their incompleteness when compared with Christ's revelation about to be revealed in the great 'scroll'. Bauckham (1993a) 243ff, similarly emphasizes the importance of the 'scroll', but argues for the identity of the two 'scrolls', as does Mazzaferri (1989); nevertheless, 11:1-13 still gives the 'revelation of the scroll *in nuce*' (p. 266).

rusalem and Babylon cannot be identified with each other, in the end they prove to be not so different after all. The double reference of 11:8 makes it quite clear that Jerusalem is capable of being no different from the 'great city'; they can be 'tarred with the same brush'. Thus, if the 'great city' can be identified with 'Sodom and Egypt', so can Jerusalem. If the 'great city' is the focused epitome of human godlessness and worldliness, Jerusalem is little different. As this verse indicates, this was the very place where the 'Lord was crucified'.

> Jerusalem where the Lord was crucified, behaved in that action just as every other city in the world was to behave, and became in a sense the model for the rest. . . . The story is set in Jerusalem because Jerusalem's treatment of the prophets and especially of Jesus is paradigmatic: this is what those who bear the witness of Jesus may expect from the world.[65]

> The earthly Jerusalem already in AD 30 had joined Sodom and Egypt as one of the typical samples of the great unholy city.[66]

> The earthly Jerusalem . . . has become the symbol for the godless world. The city [is] a place of moral and spiritual degradation, opposition to God's people, and rejection of the Lord's Christ. But in so far as the world manifests these characteristics, it writes itself in the same condemnation.[67]

Secondly, the *fall* of Jerusalem needs, amongst other things, to be understood as an act of divine judgement: for John AD 70 is 'but a foretaste or prototype of the final judgement that will mark the end of the age'.[68] This is derived from seeing an allusion to the fall of Jerusalem in 11:13 ('there was a great earthquake and a tenth of the city fell'). It also can be deduced from the way John introduces the allusions to the destruction of the Temple in 11:1-2.[69] There is a matter-of-factness about John's describing the 'holy city' being 'trampled on' and 'given over to the nations' which suggests that he had no difficulty in seeing God's hand in this. It may have been a tragedy which moved him deeply, but there is little sense that he was still in mourning.

Thirdly, however, reflection on Jerusalem's judgement did not lead him in the other direction—to be vindictive or triumphant.[70] In addition to these

---

[65] Bauckham (1993a) 172.
[66] Caird (1966) 132. *Cf.* similarly, Hughes (1990) 127.
[67] Beasley-Murray (1974) 222; 185-6.
[68] Hughes (1990) 121, commenting on Rev. 11:1.
[69] Strictly, John sees the *Church* as the new 'Temple', but his language echoes the destruction of the physical Temple in AD 70 (above 2d). He could not, however, have used this language in this way (*even if now reapplied*) if he did not accept that Jerusalem's fall was as much within God's purposes as was the Church's persecution.

lessons concerning God's judgement upon a worldly Jerusalem, there were also some humbling lessons for the Christian Church. The logic of 11:1-2 was precisely that Jerusalem's fate was a paradigm of the suffering of the Church, which now claimed to be the 'Temple of God'; if the 'holy city' had been 'trampled upon for forty-two months',[71] then Christians too as the spiritual inheritors of that holy city could expect to suffer. 'If in Mark 13 it was the Temple of Jerusalem which was desecrated and devastated, in the Revelation it is the Church of Christ in the world which is ravaged'.[72] Beneath this, however, there is also a warning that if the 'holy city' of Jerusalem had been judged by God, then members of the Church needed to be careful too. There had been no special pleading for Jerusalem when it manifested its worldliness; neither would there be for those Christians in the seven churches who compromised with the world (cf. e.g. 2:14, 20; 3:1-3, 15-17). The 'holy city (11:2) had taken on the hues of the 'great city' (11:8); the Church must not do the same.

The fall of Jerusalem could thus be interpreted in two quite different ways, which might appear mutually contradictory; for it was both an act of divine judgement and *simultaneously* an act of God's enemies. Viewed in the former way, it was a paradigm of God's judgement upon the world's evil (cf. 11:13), in which the Church on occasions could be included. Viewed in the latter way, it was a paradigm of the suffering that would come upon the Church at the hands of that evil world (cf. 11:1-2).

Finally, it is worth noting that although Jerusalem was destroyed by the armies of Rome, John nowhere indicates that the fall of Babylon/Rome was the consequence of being involved in this destructive work. The very use of 'Babylon' as a term for Rome recalls the memory of that city which had proved its enmity towards God by sacking the city of Jerusalem;[73] John may therefore have used the term to express, not only his hostility to Rome's worldliness, but also his own Jewish identification with Jerusalem in opposition to its destructive enemy. Yet in contrast to the Babylon of old, there is no clear statement that this contemporary Babylon will meet its own destruction because of its hostile activity towards Jerusalem.[74] On the contrary, when rea-

---

[70]This contrasts with the saints' rejoicing over the fall of *Babylon* in 18:20.

[71]This phrase reflects the allusion to Antiochus' pagan domination over Jerusalem in Daniel (9:24-7; 12:7). Again John takes a Jerusalem-based metaphor to refer to the Church's witness in a pagan world. The siege of Jerusalem (AD 67-70) lasted 42 months: see Court (1994) 41, and Gentry (1989) 253. Was John aware of this coincidence?

[72]Beasley-Murray (1974) 42.

[73] For Yarbro Collins (1984) 58, this is an argument in favour of a post-70 date, since 'Babylon' is only truly appropriately used of the the city which has destroyed Jerusalem (cf. e.g. 4 Ezra 3:2, 28). Though probably correct, the reference to 'Babylon' in 1 Peter 5:13 suggests that this identification could have been made before 70, albeit on other grounds (i.e. as the place of 'exile').

sons are given for Babylon's fall, the focus is on its pride (18:7), its luxury (18:8, 11-17), its trade in 'human lives' (18:13), and its hostile attitude towards the 'Lamb' and his 'saints': 'in you was found the blood of prophets and of saints' (18:24; *cf.* 17:14).[75] If Rome has 'trespassed on holy ground' it was not when it sacked Jerusalem but rather when it opposed the 'witnesses to Jesus' (17:6). It is they who now constitute the true 'holy city' which cannot be 'trampled on' with impunity (*cf.* 11:1-2). Rome is judged not because of the sack of Jerusalem, but because of the martyrdom of Christians.[76]

iv) Conclusion

The fall of Jerusalem is an important factor underlying John's text. There are echoes of it in chapter 6 and in 11:1-13. This latter passage proves on closer inspection to play an important role within the book's overall structure, outlining in miniature what is to follow in the remaining chapters. John's whole vision, therefore, both in its shape and its content, presupposes that he had given some serious consideration to Jerusalem's recent fall.

Despite his natural Jewish sympathy towards Jerusalem and his opposition to 'Babylon' its enemy, John sees its destruction as an act of God—not least because of Jesus' words in the Apocalyptic Discourse. He suggests that this event was related to its having been the scene of Jesus' crucifixion (11:8), and to its proving to be no different from the worldly 'great city'. Although there are clear warnings to a worldly Church, the fall of Jerusalem speaks most powerfully of God's judgement upon the entire world. John's apocalypse therefore functions in part like those of his Jewish contemporaries (4 Ezra and 2 Baruch) as a response to AD 70; but the conclusions he reaches are quite different.

There is then in John's understanding of Jerusalem a note of finality. Jerusalem has had its day and, despite its past, has now been brought low. Its future is therefore no brighter that that of 'Babylon'. When God comes to vindicate the saints and to reveal his answer to Babylon's evil, he will draw upon

---

[74] Beasley-Murray (1974) 249, contrasts this with contemporary Jewish attitudes: 'after the destruction of Jerusalem, the Jews would have looked for just such a judgement of God upon Rome as this chapter describes'. *Cf. e.g.* the Sibylline Oracles (4 and 5) which express the hope that God would allow Nero to return to wreak vengeance on the city which had sacked Jerusalem: see Bauckham (1993a) 416-7. Charles (1920) ii, 87-95, saw ch. 18 as an actual reworking of a Jewish piece of hostility against Rome: see Mounce (1977) 321. Yet, if so, the reason for the judgement no longer includes the sacking of Jerusalem.

[75] As Bauckham observes in (1993a) 338-83, John's critique of Rome includes a severe economic critique and is not based simply on its persecution of Christians; yet that persecution brought 'the evils of Rome to a head . . . because here Rome's self-deification clashed with the lordship of the Lamb' (pp. 349-50).

[76] *Cf.* Mounce (1977) 335.

some new material. The old Jerusalem has failed; he will unveil the *'new* Jerusalem' (21:2, 9). This new Jerusalem will share the same name as the previous city, but otherwise it will be quite different—'the new Jerusalem, coming down *out of heaven from God'* (21:2). As such it will fulfil that strand of the biblical hope that Jerusalem, for all its sin and worldliness, might be purified once again (see *e.g.* Isa. 1:26). Yet this promise of renewal comes to fruition not in the earthly Jerusalem, but rather in the new Jerusalem revealed from 'heaven'. At its best, Jerusalem had functioned as a 'type' of the new, heavenly Jerusalem, the city where God dwells; at its worst it was a 'type' for 'Babylon', the city of God's enemies, the world under the judgement of God.

In all of this the reference to Jerusalem as the place 'where their Lord was crucified' proves of vital importance (11:8). In commenting on this verse scholars have drawn the following appropriate conclusions concerning John's attitude towards Jerusalem:

> in its rejection of Jesus, Jerusalem forfeited the role of holy city (11:2), which John therefore transfers to the new Jerusalem.[77]

> Jerusalem as an earthly city has no ongoing place in the purposes of God. It did not receive its long-awaited king when he came: Jerusalem was the city in which the 'Lord was crucified' (11:8). By its killing of Jesus Jerusalem proved just as hostile to God's purposes as Sodom and Egypt had been.[78]

> The historical city is under judgement.[79]

c) *The Millenium*

We have examined John's attitude both to the fall of Jerusalem (in the recent past) and to the coming of the new Jerusalem (in the ultimate future). Under neither heading does he emphasize the enduring significance of the physical Jerusalem. Any special status it possessed in the past has now been removed and transferred to the heavenly city of the future. In between these two eras, however, John has a vision of a third era: the millenium (20:1-15). Does the earthly Jerusalem have some role to play during *that* era—even if not before or after?

The scholarly and popular debate concerning the millenium is well-known. If nothing else, it makes plain that John's vision is allusive and not re-

---

[77] Bauckham (1993a) 172.
[78] Barnett (1989) 95.
[79] Borgen (1993) 205.

plete with the details that some might prefer. Since John emphasizes Jesus' 'coming' so much in the final chapter (22:7, 17, 20), there must be some point in the course of his vision which describes this event. The most likely candidate is in 19:11: 'Then I saw Heaven opened, and there was a white horse! Its rider is called Faithful and True.' The subsequent description of the Rider (vv. 11-16) clearly identifies this with the Risen Christ as described at the outset (1:12-18; 2:18, 26-7; 3:7, 14); his coming with the 'armies of heaven' (v. 14) then leads to the long-awaited demise of the Beast and (eventually) of the Dragon. This strongly favours the 'pre-millenial' interpretation: the millenium is an event which follows on from Christ's return, rather than being something which precedes it.[80]

The millenium can therefore be distinguished, not only from the final consummation of God's purposes (as symbolized by the descent of the new Jerusalem: 21:1ff), but also from the normal course of human history which precedes Christ's coming. It is in a class of its own. In contrast to 'post-millenial' interpretations, there is a disjunction between the present era and the era of the millenium—caused by Christ's return. If then the earthly Jerusalem had a significant role in the millenium, this would not necessarily be the case in the preceding era; for the coming of Christ ushers in a new age.

The evidence for the physical Jerusalem featuring in the millenium is slight. It depends on interpreting 20:9 in a literal way: 'they marched up over the breadth of the earth and surrounded the camp of the saints and the *beloved city.*' This is an allusion to the biblical motif of Jerusalem and its particular status in God's sight (Ps. 48:1; *cf. e.g.* Sirach. 24:11). Again there is a distinction to be drawn between an allusion and a reference. If John uses language that draws upon the rich heritage of the biblical world, this does not require that he actually intends or means a specific reference to Jerusalem—any more than he intends a specific reference to some 'camp' in the desert.[81] On the contrary, the 'camp' and the 'city' are two well-recognized ways of describing God's people (the 'saints'); the city 'is not a walled city but a community of the true Israel'.[82]

The two images together, which at the strictly literal level are plainly incompatible, speak of God's people as being 'on the move' and yet having 'arrived';[83] they are simultaneously vulnerable, but ultimately secure. This paradox is precisely the one that earlier had been conveyed through the image-

---

[80]   On Rev. 19:11 as John's depiction of the *parousia*, see Beasley-Murray (1974) 277f, Mounce (1977) 351f, Bauckham (1993a) 19; for an 'amillenial' interpretation (seeing this episode not on a chronological line, but as a further picture of the present era), see *e.g.* Morris (1987) 228f, and Hughes (1990) 211.

[81]   *Cf.* Hughes (1990) 217.

[82]   Mounce (1977) 363, n. 30.

ry of the Temple's inner and outer courts (11:1-2).[84] Once again Jerusalem-based imagery is being used to convey important truths—not about the physical Jerusalem, but about the 'saints', the followers of Jesus. The Christians of Asia Minor, if they remain faithful, will be viewed by God as his 'saints' and as his 'beloved city'. They can be assured that, just as Jerusalem had been central in God's purposes in the past, so now they occupied that central stage.

It is therefore invalid to interpret this reference to the 'beloved city' in a literal fashion and then to read this back into the period before the millenium. The earlier reference to 'Mount Zion' (14:1), for example, is not a reference to the earthly Jerusalem, but clearly describes something 'in heaven'.[85] As with his descriptions of the heavenly 'Temple' and its 'altar', the imagery of the earthly Jerusalem is being drawn upon to describe the *locus* of heavenly realities. Within the well-known imagery of Psalm 2, Mount Zion was the place where the Messiah was established as God's King in the face of the hostility of the 'kings of the earth' (Ps. 2:2, 6). Since he is describing the hostile influence of the 'beast' over the 'inhabitants of the earth' (13:8, 12, 14; 14:6) and the 'kings of the earth' (17:2; 18:3, 9; 19:19; *cf.* 16:14), John's referring to Mount Zion at this juncture is an encouraging reminder that God's true King has been established and that, despite the horrors of what is described, this King will ultimately be victorious.[86]

Similarly, the reference to the 'wine press outside the city' (14:20) is not a reference to the earthly Jerusalem. If John was thinking of a specific 'city', a more likely candidate is 'Babylon'—introduced for the first time a few verses previously (14:8). It may be a necessary part of the images associated with the 'wine press' (ancient wine presses tending to be located outside the city), or alternatively a literary *topos* dependent on an Old Testament text such as Joel 3:12-13.[87] However tempting it might be to sense a parallel between Jesus' suffering for sin 'outside the city gate' (*cf.* Heb. 13:12) and thereby experiencing vicariously the 'wine press of the wrath of God' (14:19),[88] John does not expressly make that connection. Even if there is a possible *allusion* here to Jerusalem, it can hardly claim to be a straightforward *reference*.

---

[83] Though paradoxical, this combination of images is paralleled in Hebrews, where God's people are presented similarly as being both on the move in the wilderness (chs. 3-4) and yet also having arrived in the 'heavenly Jerusalem' (12:22).

[84] See above at n. 41.

[85] See Bauckham (1993a) 230: 'the triumph . . . is always in Revelation in heaven, until the opening of heaven at the *parousia* (19:11)'. See also Beasley-Murray (1974) 221-2, who (concerning Harmageddon) similarly concludes: 'whatever the origin of the term, we are not to think in terms of a geographical locality in Israel' (p. 246).

[86] *Cf.* Caird (1966) 178. Morris (1987) 170, sees a reference to Joel 2:32 as well.

[87] As suggested by Bauckham (1993a) 47.

[88] See esp. Caird (1966) 192; Hughes (1990) 167.

John's vision of the millenium includes remarkably few details—
enough, no doubt, to fuel speculation (ancient and modern), but scarcely
enough to be the basis for a whole reconstruction which then colours the remainder of the text. Given that he was writing to Christians in Asia Minor, far
from Jerusalem, it is more probable that, if he conceived the millenium in geographical terms at all, he did so in universal categories.[89] His whole pastoral
strategy encouraged his audience that they were included in God's purposes.
His use of Jerusalem imagery (be it the 'Temple', 'Mount Zion', the 'beloved
city' or the 'new Jerusalem') was thus being reappropriated in their favour: the
coming of the new Jerusalem would be *their* moment of vindication, and the
inviolability of the 'beloved city' spoke of *their* security. To argue that John
was teaching about the future of the physical Jerusalem is to run entirely in the
opposite direction. For John was not drawing attention *to* Jerusalem, but drawing material *from* Jerusalem that would be of lasting importance for the congregations for whom he was writing. The significance that had pertained to
Jerusalem was now a thing of the past, but that only gave a greater incentive
to draw upon that reservoir of significance and to transfer it instead to the followers of Jesus. God was providing his people with a new city.

d) *Conclusion*

There is therefore no teaching in John's apocalypse concerning a specific future for Jerusalem. As one interpreter has observed: 'the Holy Land does not
really feature in John's prophecy'.[90] John's universal emphasis and his use of
symbolism prevents a restricted application to Palestine. The focus on the
earthly city has given way to a concentration on the eschatological new Jerusalem; this alone will prove the true fulfilment of the motifs in Old Testament
prophecy concerning Jerusalem. This eschatological focus has been strength-
ened by reflection on the recent fall of Jerusalem, revealing God's attitude to
the city and its failure to be distinct from the 'Babylons' of this world. Christians, even if like John of a Jewish background, are not to look back nostalgi-
cally to the physical Jerusalem, but instead to look forward to the revelation
of the new Jerusalem.

---

[89] Hence, for example, the reference to the 'nations' in 20:3, 8.
[90] Beasley-Murray (1974) 246.

4. John's Concerns

Although we have the advantage of knowing the identity of the original recipients of Revelation, the debates concerning authorship and date remain. Our analysis of the theme of Jerusalem contributes to those debates in two particulars. First, it confirms the likelihood of Revelation having been composed after the fall of Jerusalem in AD 70. Secondly, it raises again the possibility that the 'John' who wrote Revelation might not be so different from the person who wrote John's Gospel.

For our purposes, the precise identity of Revelation's author, though interesting, is of little consequence. However, the parallels noted on several occasions between the theology of Revelation and John's Gospel with regard to Jerusalem and the Temple are intriguing. In both works Jesus is understood to be the essence of the Temple, while (by extension) Christian believers too may appropriate that title; in both works, what Jesus experienced in Jerusalem proves that the city is a microcosm of the world in its evil opposition to God.[91] The notion that Revelation provides the apocalyptic element that is otherwise lacking within John's Gospel might not, after all, be so wide of the mark.[92]

This evidence would lend some support to the small number of scholars who, following the attestation of the early church, are inclined to believe that Revelation is the work of John the apostle.[93] If this were so, then Revelation's author would be not just an exile on Patmos, but also a refugee from Palestine. As with the Gospel of John, this would then explain his own evident interest in Jerusalem, and yet his intention that his audience should rise above such concerns.[94] John speaks with authority as one who, though himself privileged to have been in Jerusalem, does not want his hearers to feel under-privileged through their distance from Jerusalem. Jesus will make *them* to be 'pillars' in his Temple and to bear the name of the 'new Jerusalem' (3:12); all the valuable treasures of Jerusalem have come to *them*! If the author were the apostle John, this direction of thought (*away* from Jerusalem) would reflect his own geographical movement away from the city. It would also reflect the desire, seen in both John's Gospel and the Johannine epistles (see esp. 1 John 1:1-4),

---

[91] *Cf.* above ch. 5 (2c).

[92] See *e.g.* Gentry (1989) 130-131.

[93] See Morris (1987) 27-35; Smalley (1987) and (1994) 37-40; Garrow (1997) ch. 4; *cf.* also Mounce (1977) 25-31. The early attestation is found in Justin (*DT* 81.15) and Irenaeus (*AH* 4.14.1; 5.26.1). Nevertheless, since the time of Marcion (c. 160) and then Dionysius of Alexandria (c. 250), the apostolic authorship has been strongly questioned both on theological and literary grounds—a view upheld by the majority of scholars today.

[94] *Cf.* above ch. 5 (4). Hence, for example, his reworking of material from the Apocalyptic Discourse (6:1-17; above 3b) reflects his own interest in these issues, but he does not require his readers to follow through all the implications, if they do not choose to do so.

to share his apostolic privileges and to make available to all believers that which previously had been geographically circumscribed.

Such questions of authorship are necessarily speculative, and do not materially affect the validity of our presentation. Concerning dating, however, our analysis strongly suggests that the post-70 dating of Revelation must be upheld. Chapter 11 makes far more sense in this light; moreover, the fact that John so readily accepts the Temple's redundancy suggests that this was no longer an especially controversial point of view (as it had been for the author of Hebrews before AD 70).

Given the acceptance of a post-70 date it may seem most natural to affirm the 'traditional' Domitianic dating of c. AD 95, which is based on the testimony of Irenaeus that Revelation was seen 'almost in our own day, towards the end of Domitian's reign'.[95] If John's being on the island of Patmos was a punishment of some kind,[96] he might well have seen his own experience as a foretaste of what was in store for others. He needed to alert the churches on the mainland that, although persecution at the moment was only sporadic, something much worse lay around the corner.[97] Some Christians might be viewing Rome's imperial power positively; the majority, by contrast, might be viewing it more negatively—some perhaps even welcoming the mythic idea of Nero's returning 'to wreak the vengeance of the east upon the west'.[98] Both groups, however, needed to be reminded of what Nero had done to Christians in Rome and to see the ultimate issues lying hidden beneath the surface.[99] They needed to be given an authoritative vision of the future.

One of the paradoxes here is that, despite the fact that John's references to Jerusalem strongly suggest he was writing after AD 70, there is no sense

[95] Irenaeus, *AH* 5.30.1-3. Garrow (1997) ch. 4, however, argues that Irenaeus' argument gave him an incentive to narrow the gap between Revelation's composition and the lifetime of his sources, thus strengthening the likelihood that (contrary to the heretics) the name behind the number of the 'beast' had *never* been known. He therefore suggests a date during the reign of Titus; see also Sweet (1990) 256, and Court (1994) 100.

[96] As is frequently assumed from his wording in 1:9 ('because of the word of God and the testimony of Jesus)'; see *e.g.* Beasley-Murray (1974) 64.

[97] Thus Sweet (1990) 28, sees Revelation more as a warning of forthcoming trouble, than as evidence for a current, systematic persecution.

[98] Bauckham (1993a) 450.

[99] Garrow (1997) chs. 5-6, argues that this pro-Nero stance was part of the teaching of the 'false prophet' (and especially of Jezebel in the church in Thyatira). This would then explain not only the emphasis given to the letter to Thyatira (both in length and as the middle letter of the seven) but also why the 'false prophet' is judged at the same time as the 'beast' (19:20); in 19:11-21 there are several echoes of the language in the Thyatiran letter (*cf.* vv. 12, 15 with 2:18, 27), suggesting that this climactic scene is particularly pertinent to the situation of that particular church. It would explain why John emphasizes so strongly the truth of his own work of prophecy (1:3, 19; 22:16-20); *cf.* Bauckham (1993a) 89.

in Revelation that the events of that year are a great shock to the author or pose a problem that must be explained. If any recent event is uppermost in his mind, it is more probably the Neronian persecution (AD 65).[100] The author can allude to Jerusalem's fall, but does not especially concentrate upon it. This suggests John's own theological distance from Jerusalem. He was not writing as one tragically bereft to Christians uncertain of what now to believe. The fall of Jerusalem was already a matter of history. Far more urgent were the issues relating to the 'great city'.

A fine balance needs to be struck. Some interpreters, presuming that Jerusalem issues must have been central to John, see this theme throughout Revelation (and therefore either date Revelation to before AD 70 or identify Jerusalem with Babylon). Others see his focus as being exclusively on Rome (and often then date Revelation as far removed from 70 as possible). What, however, if Jerusalem was indeed of some concern to John, but not nearly as much as many presume—precisely because he had *already* accepted a more negative view of the city (even before 70) and because the real issue now quite plainly had to do with Rome? If so, it becomes plausible to posit a somewhat earlier date, perhaps around AD 80.

On this interpretation John's attitude to Jerusalem reflects a careful balance. While he is not concerned with Jerusalem as a continuing historical entity, he is keenly aware of the symbolic importance of Jerusalem's role within the Old Testament and within recent history. He was wedded to the symbol, not to the physical city. As a Jewish believer and as one committed to the teachings of Jesus, he could not help but have reflected on Jerusalem's nature and destiny. Yet it was no longer the central issue. The purposes of Israel's Messiah now encompassed the entire world and were in fierce opposition to those currently embodied in Rome. The battle had moved elsewhere, and on to a larger stage. Though still providing a rich quarry of theological truth, the physical Jerusalem now lay in the past; what now consumed the centre of his attention was the reality of evil in the Roman empire. Beyond that 'great city', however, he was able to see in the distance a new city and a new dawn—the small but ultimately all-encompassing light of the new Jerusalem.

---

[100] Garrow (1997) ch. 5.

PART II

JESUS AND THE CHURCH

8

A NEW DIRECTION
Jesus and Jerusalem

'Do you see these great buildings?' (Mark 13:2).

The New Testament's re-evaluation of Jerusalem and its Temple heightens the probability that this process was begun by Jesus himself. It is argued that Jesus, both in his prophetic critique and in his own understanding of himself and his mission, was revealing a distinctively new assessment of Jerusalem and its role within God's purposes. His arrival meant that the city was entering a crucial period in its history and revealed that the city's destiny was integrally bound up with his own. The issues of judgement and restoration, focused previously on Jerusalem and Israel, are now transformed through the lens of Jesus' own death and resurrection.

All the writers examined in Part I re-evaluated Jerusalem in the light of Jesus.[1] Looking from their different vantage-points and writing at different times, each painted a distinctive landscape of Jerusalem. Yet amidst diversity of detail, there was a common theme: Jerusalem was not what it was.

This holds true whether the relevant landscape was painted after AD 70 (as we have suggested for Matthew, John and Revelation) or before (Paul, Mark, Hebrews and possibly Luke). There are indeed developments of thought which can be traced from the earliest writings to the latest, but at a basic level there is a substantial unanimity of presentation. Thus even before 70, the Christian community was looking at Jerusalem with new eyes. When therefore the tragic events of that year took place, the majority of Christians may not have been much surprised—sad, perhaps, but not shocked. 'The cap-

269

ture of Jerusalem and the burning of the Temple seem to have made a surprisingly small impact upon the Christian communities'.[2]

For those sensitive to biblical history (then as now), this tragedy invited
comparison with the only similar precedent within Jerusalem's past: its destruction at the hands of the Babylonians in 587 BC . For this reason both 2
Baruch and 4 Ezra, Jewish writings written in the aftermath of AD 70, are set
pseudonymously back in the sixth century, and the book of Lamentations becomes the basis for further reflection within the Jewish tradition.[3] There was
no Christian equivalent of this, however. As far as can be gleaned from our
limited sources, Christians responded quite differently. With the possible exception of Matthew, there is little sense of loss or bereavement. What has
caused the predominantly Jewish authors of the New Testament to view the
city in a new way? Why was the fall of Jerusalem seen, not as a shocking challenge to their presuppositions, but rather as a confirmation of their previously-
held position?

The answer lies with Jesus of Nazareth. It is said that there is 'no smoke
without a fire'. To pursue that analogy, our previous chapters, when taken together, bear witness to an impressive amount of smoke. Can we locate the
fire? Is this new understanding of Jerusalem simply the result of Christians reflecting on Jesus' crucifixion outside Jerusalem or of their experiencing the
Spirit's outpouring on believers far removed from the city? These will have
played a part, but on their own they do not sufficiently explain the strength of
their new convictions.

Far more probably, on this issue as on others, they were taking a lead
from Jesus himself; for it is most unlikely that the apostles would have dared

---

[1]   Mention should be made here of the three remaining contributors to the New Testament: Peter, James and Jude. With the exception of 1 Peter (discussed in ch. 10) these
letters are little concerned with this issue of Jerusalem—even though each of the historical
persons to whom these letters are traditionally attributed had important associations with
Jerusalem, each having leadership responsibilities with the city's Christian community
(Acts 1:14-15; 2:14; 12:17; 15:13-21; 21:18-26; Gal. 1:19; Jude 1; Eusebius, *EH* 4.5.3-4,
5.12.1-2). This might confirm our overall argument that Jerusalem was not central in their
thought. For a discussion of the authenticity of these letters, see the various studies by
Bauckham (1983) and (1988b). He concludes that the case for the authenticity of 1 Peter is
far stronger than that for 2 Peter ([1983], 158-162; *cf.* Michaels [1988], lxvi), and that Jude
is authentic ([1983], 13-16); he sees James' letter as the earliest surviving document in the
New Testament (dating from c. AD 45) and is an important witness to the thought of the
first Christian community in Palestine (1995b). On Jude's involvement with the Jerusalem
church, see his (1990b) ch. 2.
[2]   Lampe (1984) 153; *cf.* de Young (1961) 110, following Moffatt.
[3]   Lamentations was recited annually on the anniversary of the Temple's destruction, and
the parallels between 587 BC and AD 70 were noted frequently in Lamentations Rabba
(Lam.R); see Freedman and Simon (1939) vii, and Strack and Stemberger (1991) 309-10.

to espouse this critique of Jerusalem if Jesus had never said a word against the holy city, and if his claims had in no way threatened its future identity. This is not to say that they never developed ideas beyond what Jesus had expressly said; but that they would not have ventured along this path if they had no evidence that Jesus had first embarked upon it.

Our contention, therefore, is that this new perspective on Jerusalem owes its origins to Jesus himself. In this chapter suggestions are made as to Jesus' own attitude towards Jerusalem. Although there are clearly many difficulties associated with assessing the reliability of the Gospel traditions, even a cautious reading of the Gospel material indicates that Jesus' views on this subject had a forceful 'ripple-effect' among his followers. Reverberations of those views within the New Testament are then traced in the next chapter. In the final chapter there is a brief discussion of how these New Testament findings might be drawn together into an overall 'biblical theology' of Jerusalem.

Any telling of the story of Jesus becomes inevitably a story about Jerusalem as well. Whether one follows the pattern of the synoptic Gospels which focus on Jesus' final journey to Jerusalem or instead the emphasis of John on Jesus' several visits to the city, it is clear that Jerusalem played a key part within Jesus' ministry and was the place where that ministry reached its climactic dénouement.

It is also clear that Jesus would have shared with his contemporaries a high regard for the role which Jerusalem had played within God's purposes up until that time. He described it as 'the city of the great king' (Matt. 5:35) and applied to the Herodian Temple the words in Isaiah where Yahweh describes it as '*my* house' (Isa. 56:7 in Mark 11:17; *cf.* 'my Father's house' in John 2:16). The centrality which Jerusalem had in Jesus' ministry thus reflected a real centrality which the city had had within God's whole purposes towards Israel and thereby to the world. According to John, therefore, Jesus had no hesitation in correcting the preference of the Samaritan woman for Mount Gerizim: it was Jerusalem that had truly been the place where one 'must worship' (John 4:20, 22). There was no denial of the significance of Jerusalem in the past.

Yet did Jesus see that situation as continuing without alteration into the future? In that same conversation John presents Jesus as talking of something new that was about to take place ('the hour is coming and is now here')—something which was integrally related to the arrival of his own person, but which would also have a profound effect on Jerusalem: 'you will worship the Father neither on this mountain nor in Jerusalem' (4:21). According to John, Jesus understood himself to be living in a time when dramatic changes were afoot and that his own coming would have significant consequences for Jerusalem. Does this fit with what else we know of Jesus in the synoptic Gospels?

There is certainly some evidence that Jesus saw himself as introducing something distinctively new within God's purposes; hence his talk of the need to
place 'new wine in fresh wineskins' (Mark. 2:22) and his role as an eschatological prophet announcing that , 'the time is fulfiled, and the Kingdom of
God is at hand' (Mark 1:15). But did Jesus have a critique of Jerusalem? And
did he believe that the city's role within God's purposes would be different in
the future as a result of his own mission to Israel?

A case for answering this question in the affirmative can be built on the
following considerations.[4]

1. Jesus the Prophet

There is an increasing recognition that the prophetic critique of Israel and of
Jerusalem which is found in the Gospels was an authentic part of Jesus' message. One scholar has itemized no less than thirty-four separate sayings that
warn in some way of an imminent crisis. He convincingly argues that this
'threat-tradition' must be acknowledged as an integral part of Jesus' teaching.[5] This is confirmed by the fact that, although the early church would later
favour other titles, the people of Jesus' own day (and Jesus himself) referred
to him as a 'prophet';[6] yet a characteristic of the canonical prophets was that
they warned God's people when they were departing from God's ways. Evidently, Jesus was recognised as having this 'prophetic' quality. This then suggests that his teaching included this element of prophetic critique, just as did
the teaching of John the Baptist (who likewise was termed a 'prophet').[7] The

---

[4] In the following, frequent reference is made to the work of Tom Wright. His important
book, which argues in great detail for an understanding of Jesus' ministry similar to that
offered here, will be published at the same time as this present volume: *Jesus and the
Victory of God* (London: SPCK, 1996). I am grateful for his allowing me to see portions of
the manuscript before publication, and for his instructive ideas. The present volume is,
amongst other things, an attempt to pursue some of the consequences of his thought on this
single issue of Jerusalem, as first outlined in his (1994a).

[5] Borg (1984) 201-27; 265-76. Many of these sayings have traditionally been interpreted
as *post mortem* threats of hellfire. Whilst such an application may be valid in some
instances, the original reference to Jesus' own generation must be heard. Similarly, many
of Jesus' apocalyptic sayings may be referring, not to some end-time or 'other-worldly'
events at the time of the *parousia*, but rather to forthcoming events on the human stage now
invested with theological significance: see esp. Wright (1985) 78-83 and (1992a) 280-299.
If so, then a greater proportion of the synoptic tradition is concerned with this prophetic
message of judgement upon the Israel of Jesus' day.

[6] See Matt. 21:11, 46; Mark 6:15; 8:28; Luke 24:19. For Jesus' use of this term for
himself, see *e.g.* Luke 4:24; 13:33.

[7] See *e.g.* Luke 7:26-28; 20:6. For his warnings to contemporary Israel, see Luke 3:7ff.

fact that Jesus was likened to Jeremiah (Matt. 16:14) is particularly significant. For Jeremiah was the prophet whose ministry, more than any other, focused upon warning Jerusalem of its imminent destruction at the hands of the
Babylonians.[8] Jesus stood in this tradition.

While some of Jesus' prophetic warnings are not tied specifically to Jerusalem,[9] several sayings focus expressly on Jerusalem and its Temple.

> When you see the desolating sacrilege set up where it ought not to be, . . .
> then those in Judea must flee to the mountains (Mark 13:14; *cf.* Matt. 24:15;
> Luke 21:20-21).

> We heard him say, 'I will destroy this Temple that is made with hands, and
> in three days I will build another, not made with hands' (Mark 14:58; *cf.*
> Matt. 26:61).

> See, your house is left to you, desolate (Matt. 23:38; *cf.* Luke 13:35).

> If you, even you, had only recognized on this day the things that make for
> peace! But now they are hidden from your eyes. Indeed, the days will come
> upon you, when your enemies will set up ramparts around you and surround,
> and hem you in on every side. They will crush you to the ground, you and
> your children within you, and they will not leave within you one stone upon
> another; because you did not recognize the time of your visitation from God
> (Luke 19:41-44).

> As for these things that you see, the days will come when not one stone will
> be left upon another; all will be thrown down (Luke 21:6; *cf.* Mark 13:2;
> Matt. 24:2).

> Daughters of Jerusalem, do not weep for me, but weep for yourselves and for
> your children. For the days are surely coming when they will say, 'Blessed
> are the barren, and the wombs that never bore, and the breasts that never
> nursed.' Then they will begin to say to the mountains, 'Fall on us'; and to the
> hills, 'Cover us.' For if they do this when the wood is green, what will happen
> when it is dry? (Luke 23:29-31).

Attempts to dismiss this whole strand within the synoptic tradition as
post-eventum rationalisations look too much like special pleading. The presentation of Luke has been especially subjected to this criticism. In an influential article, however, it has been argued that nothing in Luke's description of

---

[8] See above ch. 2 at n. 57ff.

[9] See *e.g.* Luke 13:6-9 (the fig-tree). Nevertheless, as argued in Wright (1996) ch. 8, this
and similar passages retain a reference in the first instance to contemporary Israel.

Jerusalem's fall (Luke 19 and 21) was indebted to memory of the actual details of what took place in AD 70.

> So far as any historical event has coloured the picture, it is not Titus' capture of Jerusalem in AD 70, but Nebuchadnezzar's capture in 586 BC. There is no single trait of the forecast which cannot be documented directly out of the Old Testament.[10]

This may have been precisely the point: people needed to be made aware that history was about to repeat itself, and for similar reasons.

Nor can this threat-tradition be dismissed as inherently anti-Semitic. Once again Jesus was standing four-square within an accepted tradition seen throughout the canonical prophets, whereby God's people and their institutions could be denounced in the name of Israel's God. Indeed within the Jewish sectarianism of Jesus' day the pronouncing of judgement upon the present regime in Jerusalem was not unusual.

> On the contrary, it was a sign of deep loyalty to Israel's true God, and of deep distress at the corruption which seemed endemic in the national life. Jesus' solemn announcements were completely in place within the world of first-century inner-Jewish polemic.[11]

It was not only thoroughly Jewish. It also made perfect sense at the level of *Realpolitik*. Without denying the possibility of Jesus' particular prophetic insight, it can be admitted that the ultimate outcome of rebellion against Rome may have been clear to many in Jesus' day.

> It did not take much political wisdom to extrapolate forwards and to suggest that, if Israel continued to provoke the giant, the giant would eventually awake from slumber and smash her to pieces.[12]

If Jerusalem became the focus for an independent Jewish nationalism, it would lose. This sombre, political reality in Jesus' lifetime only increases the possibility that he may have given some such warnings to Jerusalem. Although many longed for the over-throwing of the pagan yoke, Jesus warned that opposing Rome would not bring about the salvation that they hoped. Instead down that road lay disaster.

There are thus good reasons for accepting the Gospel tradition that presents Jesus as speaking solemnly about dramatic events which would soon

---

[10] Dodd (1968) 79.

[11] Wright (1996) ch. 8.

[12] Wright (1996) ch. 8, noting how a generation later Josephus came to a similar conclusion.

engulf the nation—and especially Jerusalem and its Temple. More disturbing still, Jesus saw in these events the hand of Israel's God. Some might have foreseen the likelihood of defeat at the hands of the Romans, but few would have dared to suggest that the Romans would need to be seen (as Assyria and Babylon before them) as God's agents in exacting judgement upon his own people. Yet the whole tenor of Jesus' pronouncements is that these forthcoming events are not historical accidents. In the words of John the Baptist, they were part of the 'wrath to come' (Matt. 3:7). Jesus was effectively turning Israel's political aspirations and religious expectations on their head. Far from regaining its political independence and being preserved in some distinctive way as God's city, Jerusalem would be 'trampled on by the Gentiles' (Luke 21:24). It was about to enter a pivotal moment in its history. The future of Jerusalem was far from what many of his contemporaries hoped it would be.

2. Jesus the Critic

So Jesus' warnings to Jerusalem, though they made eminent political sense, were based on something more than a merely pessimistic political analysis. As a prophet Jesus pronounced that Jerusalem's plight was not simply the result of Rome's military invincibility; it had also to do with God's indictment of his own people. There were spiritual reasons, which fuelled his prophetic critique. An assessment of Jesus' attitude towards Jerusalem and the Temple must go on to consider what exactly it was, according to Jesus, that was wrong.

Within the synoptic Gospels there are various suggestions as to the substance of Jesus' critique. First, Jesus labels Jerusalem as the place which 'kills the prophets and stones those who are sent to it' (Luke 13:34). He identifies as a defining characteristic of the city that it rejects God's messengers and therefore has become in itself a focus of opposition to the purposes of God. Jesus' tone is full of irony: 'it is impossible for a prophet to be killed away from Jerusalem!' (Luke 13:33). By some perverse twisting of its destiny Jerusalem has become the place where God's messengers can expect their fiercest opposition. If Jerusalem had previously had a legitimate status as the 'city *of* God', it was now at some deep and intrinsic level working *against* God.

Secondly, there is some elaboration of this point in Jesus' vivid use of maternal imagery in Luke 13:34b: 'how often have I desired to gather your children together as a hen gathers her brood under her wings, and you were not willing.' This imagery places Jesus in the role of Divine Wisdom or even as the representative of Israel's God. It also reveals Jesus' claim to be the true 'mother' of Jerusalem's inhabitants. For Jerusalem is portrayed as behaving towards her 'children' like a false mother, luring them away from the safety which Jesus said could be found under his 'wings' alone. If Jesus was claiming to represent Israel's God, then Jerusalem, in keeping its children from accepting his embrace, was effectively acting against God's purposes. It was functioning thereby as an idol.[13]

Thirdly, in keeping with this, Jesus implicitly criticized the religious authorities in Jerusalem for the way in which they were no longer working in accordance with God's wishes and under his recognized authority. The thrust of the parable of the vineyard (Mark 12:1-12 and parallels) was that the tenants desired to have the 'inheritance' for themselves (v. 7) and to gain their independence from the original owner. The 'tenants' were no longer concerned with the master's business. Jesus implied that the people of Israel (the 'vineyard', cf. Isa. 5:1-7), and especially its leaders in Jerusalem (cf. v. 12), were in fundamental opposition to God. Athough Jesus' words here focused not on Jerusalem itself but on its religious leadership, the implications of his message for the city prove to be essentially the same as that of Luke 13 (above). Rather than truly being the place which derived its existence from God, acknowledging its dependence upon his ultimate authority, Jerusalem desired its *in*dependence. It opposed God's messengers and abused its God-given status (as part of the vineyard carefully planted by God), because at root it wished to take God's place.

Fourthly, many see Jesus' cursing of the fig-tree (Mark 11:12-14 and parallels) as a prophetic action designed to teach important truths about Jerusalem and the Temple.[14] For Mark at least, this cursing was a clue given *privately* to Jesus' disciples (the 'insiders'; cf. Mark 4:11), to explain his enigmatic *public* action in the Temple. It allowed the cleansing to be seen as a warning of a forthcoming divine judgement upon the Temple, and as having something of the force of Jesus placing a curse upon it. What Jesus had done in miniature for the fig-tree, God would do for the Temple.

The reason for the curse is stated. 'Seeing a fig-tree in leaf, he went to see whether perhaps he would find anything on it. When he came to it, he found nothing but leaves' (Mark 11:13). The Temple has itself become 'barren' and is failing to produce the expected 'fruit'. Jesus' action in the Temple,

---

[13] For a more detailed discussion of Luke 13:33-35, see above ch. 3 (2b).

[14] These incidents have generated an enormous amount of comment, being discussed in most commentaries and studies of Jesus' ministry: see *e.g.* E.P. Sanders (1985) 61-76, Bauckham (1988a), Chilton (1992), C.A. Evans (1989) and (1993b). There is a spectrum of opinion between those who, at one extreme, see Jesus' action in the Temple as simply a reformative cleansing, and those, at the other, who see it as portent of the Temple's destruction. Most probably both elements should be recognized. There were specific abuses which needed to be highlighted and 'cleansed', but, because they were endemic, they served as the warrant for the Temple's forthcoming destruction; see the helpful over-view in Wright (1996) ch. 9 (3 iii), who concludes that it was an enacted parable of judgement.

whilst evidently seeking to 'cleanse' it of some specific practical abuses, must also be understood as an indictment of a much deeper malaise. It was not simply that the court of the Gentiles was being treated with contempt; nor that exorbitant exchange rates were being used for the purchase of the Tyrian shekel. It was failing to function truly as a 'house of prayer' (Mark 11:17, quoting Isa. 56:7); it was failing to provide the proper 'fruit'. Agendas other than the worship of God had infiltrated into its midst.

Jesus' quoting from Jeremiah's famous 'Temple sermon' (the 'den of robbers': v. 17; *cf.* Jer. 7:11) then gave a further clue that, as in Jeremiah's day, the inevitable result was divine judgement—and for similar reasons. Jeremiah had spoken out against the false trust which his contemporaries were placing in the 'Temple of the Lord' (Jer. 7:4), seeing this gift of God as something behind which they could hide from God's ethical concerns. Jesus' actions and words implied that there was a similar abuse of the divine gift in his own day. The Temple was being used to service god-less agendas—not least as it became increasingly the central, symbolic focus of Jewish nationalism (see esp. John 11:47-50).[15] Jesus warned that such attitudes rendered the Temple barren, and ripe for judgement. If it was being seen as a bastion of independence from Rome, it would fail—not least, paradoxically, because it was thereby proving itself to be a bastion of independence *from God himself.*

Fifthly, this opposition to the various nationalistic agendas of his day would inevitably form part of Jesus' critique of Jerusalem. That Jesus was so opposed can be demonstrated in numerous ways: for example, his attitude to the Samaritans (Luke 10:33; 17:16), to the Romans (Luke 7:1-10) and to Caesar (Mark 12:13-17). Yet much of this contemporary nationalism was fuelled by a devotion to Jerusalem and the desire for its independent sovereignty. As such, Jerusalem was playing an important part in diverting God's people from their true path. This explains why Jerusalem is personified in Jesus' teaching and portrayed as taking God's people away from him and effectively coming between God and his people: 'I have desired to gather your children together . . . and *you* were not willing!' (Luke 13:34). Jerusalem thought it knew the best 'peace terms' but in fact they were 'hidden from your eyes', such that it was cruelly misleading people (Luke 19:42). Refusing Jesus' protection and encirclement (Luke 13:34), it thought it could offer protection for its people, but in fact it would itself be 'encircled'—by its 'enemies' and by 'armies' (Luke 19:43; 21:20). Jerusalem was playing its part in leading people astray—away from God and (disastrously) straight into the arms of Rome.

Finally, Jesus criticized Jerusalem for its negative response to himself. Again this is implicit within Luke 13 and 19: the pronouncement that Jerusa-

---

[15] See Borg (1984) 170-177, and Wright (1996) ch. 9.

lem's 'house is left desolate' (13:35) flows directly from Jesus' recognition that Jerusalem will be the place where he will be killed (13:33-4); 'they will not leave one stone upon another', he says later, 'because you did not recognize the time of your visitation from God' (19:44). Though the point is not developed further, the implication is plain: Jesus' coming to Jerusalem was the city's appointed 'hour', the moment for which it had been prepared. Yet the 'hour of visitation' was not recognized, the city's true destiny not realized.

Jesus' prophetic critique of Jerusalem therefore centred upon the way in which the city and its Temple were effectively acting as a focus of opposition to God, rather than being (according to their destiny within the scriptures) the place where God's name was hallowed and God's authority over his people recognized and welcomed. It was not producing the necessary fruit; it was leading people astray; it had become the focus of agendas that left little room for God. If Jerusalem was rightly considered to have been a gracious gift from God to his people, those recipients had now 'turned the tables' on the donor. They no longer wanted him in the vineyard. When Jesus then turned the tables on them (Mark 11:15), not surprisingly it caused a commotion.

3. Jesus' Self-understanding

Underlying many of these statements concerning Jerusalem lurks the perennial issue of who precisely Jesus thought he was. Who was this that confidently announced the need for 'new wineskins', and who saw Jerusalem's forthcoming rejection of him as a key moment in its history—the 'time of its visitation'? If John the Baptist was 'more than a prophet' (Luke 7:26), the evidence suggests that Jesus saw himself too as not just 'one of the prophets' (Mark. 8:28). So he asked his disciples, 'But who do *you* say that I am?' (Mark 8:29).

The issue of Jesus' self-understanding has been copiously studied and discussed elsewhere.[16] Here we note that the higher the 'christology' that Jesus assumed for himself, the more coherent becomes the rationale that, in rejecting him, Jerusalem was exposing itself to judgement. If the 'city of God' was truly rejecting the chosen Messiah (or the vineyard owners truly plotting against the owner's '*son*': Mark 12:6), then the consequences were plain. If Jesus was indeed the representative of Israel's God, then its response to him proved in fact to be its response to God himself. The indictment (outlined above) of Jerusalem's opposition to *God* would thus be proved true and come to a focused embodiment when the city rejected *Jesus*.

---

[16] See *e.g.* the excellent recent work by Witherington (1990).

There are three particular claims attributed to Jesus within the Gospel tradition that are especially relevant. Again the material can only be touched on in summary form.[17] These can be traced back to Jesus himself with some degree of confidence—for two reasons. First, each of them can only be understood in the context of the Old Testament, involving concepts more relevant for Jesus' immediate Jewish context than for the early church as it moved into the Gentile world. Gentile readers of the Gospels would have needed some detailed explanation if they were to grasp these points; since that explanation is largely absent from the Gospels, it is most unlikely that the Evangelists created this material *ex nihilo* for their benefit. Secondly, the very audacity and originality of these claims work against the assumption that they are the invention of the early church. On the contrary, they speak of a masterly and creative mind, fully immersed in Old Testament themes, yet confidently rethinking and developing those themes in new and surprising ways—relating them unashamedly to himself. As Dodd concluded in a similar context:

> Creative thinking is rarely done by committees. . . . To account for the beginning of this most original and fruitful process of rethinking the Old Testament we need to postulate a creative one. The Gospels offer us one. Are we compelled to reject the offer?[18]

a) Jesus, Zion's True King

In all four Gospels Jesus' symbolic act in approaching Jerusalem on a donkey is interpreted in terms or royalty (Mark 11:10; Luke 19:38; Matt. 21:5; John 12:13, 15), with Matthew and John explicitly quoting the text from Zechariah that must have given the original event its unspoken meaning: 'Tell the daughter of Zion, Look, your king is coming to you, humble and mounted on a donkey' (Zech. 9:9 in Matt. 21:5; *cf.* John 12:15).

This prophetic background made it plain that Jesus was coming to Jerusalem in humility and not with political force of arms. It also revealed Jesus' claim to be the true king of Zion/Jerusalem. Yet who really was Zion's true King? When it is remembered that part of Israel's hope was precisely that, after the departure of the *shekinah* presence from Jerusalem at the time of the exile (Ezek. 11:22-3), *God himself* would again return to Zion and take up residence as her rightful 'King', the enormity of Jesus' claim becomes apparent.

---

[17] For fuller discussion of these ideas, see *e.g.* Wright (1992a) ch. 13 and (1996) ch. 13; *cf.* also *e.g.* Caird (1965) and (1982).

[18] Dodd (1952) 109-10.

The Old Testament prophets had described this glorious return of Yahweh to Zion on several occasions and in different ways:

> Speak tenderly to Jerusalem and cry to her that . . . her penalty is paid. . . . A voice cries out: 'In the wilderness prepare the way of the Lord; make straight in the desert a highway for our God'. . . . Get you up to a high mountain, O Zion, herald of good tidings; . . . say to the cities of Judah, 'Here is your God!' (Isa. 40:2-3, 9).

> How beautiful upon the mountains are the feet of the messenger who announces peace, . . . who says to Zion, 'Your God reigns'. Listen! Your sentinels lift up their voices; together they sing for joy; for in plain sight they see the return of the Lord to Zion. Break forth together into singing, you ruins of Jerusalem; for the Lord has comforted his people, he has redeemed Jerusalem (Isa. 52:7-9).

> The glory of the God of Israel was coming from the east. . . . The vision I saw was like the vision that I had seen when he came to destroy the city. . . . As the glory of the Lord entered the Temple by the gate facing east, the spirit lifted me up, . . . and the glory of the Lord filled the Temple. . . . I heard some speaking to me out of the Temple. He said to me: 'Mortal, this is the place of my throne, and the place for the soles of my feet, where I will reside among the people of Israel for ever' (Ezek. 43:2-7).

> Sing and rejoice, O daughter Zion. For lo, I will come and dwell in your midst, says the Lord. . . . Thus says the Lord: 'I will return to Zion, and will dwell in the midst of Jerusalem' (Zech 2:10; 8:3).

> The Lord whom you seek will suddenly come to his Temple (Mal. 3:1).[19]

When Jesus then, in the seemingly innocuous act of sitting on a donkey, makes a tacit claim to be Zion's King, the implications are staggering—both for Jesus' self-understanding and for the city that is greeting him. According to Luke, Jesus had also taken the opportunity of his imminent arrival in Jerusalem (Luke 19:11) to tell a mysterious parable about a king, who after a time of absence 'returns home' (Luke 19:12-27). Who is the King, and where precisely is he returning to? For Luke at least, Jesus' entering Jerusalem is clearly the 'home-coming' of the divine King.[20]

---

[19] *Cf.* also Zech. 14:4ff. According to Mal. 4:5, God would send the 'prophet Elijah before the great and terrible day of the *Lord*'. Jesus' identification of John the Baptist with Elijah (Matt. 17:12) thus says more about Jesus himself than about John.

[20] For a discussion of this parable which argues that it does not refer, as traditionally held, to the *parousia*, see Johnson (1982).

Jesus' action therefore affirms all the Old Testament tradition about Jerusalem as being peculiarly God's 'home' city, the place where his name was truly to dwell. That tradition is not denied, but rather renewed and affirmed. Indeed only when this context is affirmed can the full measure of Jesus' claim be appreciated—his claim to be the true King of Zion, the city of God. At the same time, however, the Gospel narrative indicates that there was a tragic 'sting in the tail'. Psalm 2 (an important Messianic psalm for the first Christians)[21] had spoken of God installing his chosen King on 'Zion, my holy hill' (v. 6). When Jesus came to Jerusalem, however, there was from a human point of view no such installation or 'enthronement'. The King was rejected and his only 'throne' an execution-hill outside the city, where he was crucified as the 'King of the Jews' (Mark 15:26 and parallels). What would become of Zion now that she had rejected her true King?

b) Jesus and the Temple

Just as the requisitioning of a donkey had hidden symbolic meaning, so too did Jesus' involvement with the Temple. We have already noted Jesus' predictions of its destruction and something of his critique. A host of further, important issues are raised by his cryptic statement, 'Destroy this Temple and in three days I will raise it up' (John 2:19).[22] What does this reveal of Jesus' claims for his own identity?

Given the treasured value of the Temple, such talk in public that spoke, albeit enigmatically, of its destruction would have been explosive indeed. Moreover, given some of the expectations that the Messiah would introduce a new, restored Temple, his talking of 'raising it again' would have sparked off all sorts of hopes for the future and assumptions about his identity. No wonder it featured in his trial. Yet John was convinced that Jesus was referring in a cryptic fashion to the resurrection of his own body: 'he was speaking of the Temple of his body' (John 2:21). If this was so, Jesus was evidently claiming to be the true Temple, and the expectations of a restored Messianic Temple would be fulfilled not in the construction of a future physical Temple (after this present one was destroyed), but rather in his own resurrection after 'three days': 'in three days I will raise it up'. In other words, Jesus embodied the Temple in his own person.[23]

---

[21] See Mark 1:11; Acts 4:25ff; 13:33; Heb. 1:5, etc.

[22] It is extremely likely that Jesus said some such statement (recounted in different ways in Mark 14:58; Matt. 27:61, John 2:19 and Acts 6:14).

[23] See above ch. 5 (1a-c).

Once again we are contending with Jesus' understanding of his own identity. Some may be sceptical of John's interpretation, preferring evidence from the other Gospels, but there is evidence within the Synoptics too that this claim was an integral part of Jesus' self-understanding.

As noted above, the return of Yahweh to Zion drew in part upon the imagery of the *shekinah* glory that had departed the Temple (Ezek. 11:22-3). If Jesus was claiming to be Zion's true King, this may have included the further claim to be the embodiment of that divine glory formerly associated with the Temple and its 'holy of holies'. When it is remembered that this was how God revealed his presence *with* and *among* his people, Jesus' statements take on a new ring. 'Where two or three are gathered in my name, I am there *among* them' (Matt. 18:20). 'I am *with* you always to the end of the age' (Matt. 28:20). Indeed 'something greater than the Temple is here' (Matt. 12:6). Jesus was appropriating Temple language and imagery to himself.

Reflecting on such statements in the Synoptics, Wright concludes:

> It is not enough to say, within a normal western-Christian mode of thought, that he was 'claiming to be God'. What he was claiming to do was to act as the replacement of the Temple, which was of course the dwelling-place of the *Shekinah*, the tabernacling of God with his people.

> Thus when Jesus came to Jerusalem he came embodying a counter-system. He and the city were both making claims to be the place where the living God was at work to heal, restore and regroup his people. Though many people still say that the Old Testament had no idea of incarnation, this is clearly a mistake: the Temple itself, and by extension Jerusalem, was seen as the dwelling-place of the living God. Thus it was the Temple that Jesus took as his model, and against whose claim he advanced his own.[24]

Jesus was claiming to be that presence. The Temple was also through its sacrificial system the appointed place for receiving God's forgiveness. Jesus, however, shocks the assembled scribes by declaring to the paralytic that 'the Son of Man has authority on earth to forgive sins' (Mark 2:10), and declares to the surprised crowds around Zacchaeus' house, 'today, salvation has come to this house, because he too is a son of Abraham' (Luke 19:9). The force of these remarks and their consequences for the Jerusalem Temple are too easily overlooked.

> If one was with Jesus, one did not need the restoration into covenant membership which was normally attained by going to Jerusalem and offering sacrifices in the Temple. The force of such sentences is lost unless it is realized

---

[24] Wright (1994a) 58, 66; see now (1996) chs. 9 (4 v) and 13.

that, in making such pronouncements, Jesus was implicitly claiming *to do and be what the Temple was and did*. His offering of forgiveness and restoration undercut the normal system; in modern terms, it had the force of a private individual offering a passport, thus bypassing the accredited office. Jesus was offering just such a bypass.[25]

When Jesus then came to Jerusalem, some form of clash with the Temple was inevitable. In addition to his critique of its current practice and undergirding his prophetic warning of its imminent destruction, there lay this deeper layer of causation. It was not just a matter of divine judgement; it was also that God was revealing his long-established plan, focused in Jesus' own person. For Jesus was embodying the essence of the Temple—the *locus* of the divine presence and the source of forgiveness. The symbolic functions of the Temple were incarnated in Jesus; the shadow was being presented with its own reality.

This conflict is encapsulated brilliantly in Jesus' aphorism, 'destroy this Temple and in three days I will raise it up'. It hints at both the destruction of the physical Temple and the emergence of another Temple through resurrection. It also suggests that these two events are not entirely unconnected; the appearance of Jesus, and especially his resurrection, spells the end of the Temple. Evidently, therefore, now that Jesus had come, Jerusalem could never be the same again. For the divine presence, previously associated with the city's Temple, was focused instead on the person of Jesus.

c) Jesus, the Agent of 'Restoration'

Thus Jesus' talking of 'raising' the Temple 'in three days' gave a dramatic twist to the many expectations that looked for the Temple's restoration in the Messianic age. This theme of 'restoration' included a whole cluster of hopes and expectations at the time of Jesus. This background of 'restoration eschatology' is vital if any sense is to be made of Jesus' ministry in its own time.[26] Focus on this issue will also shed light on Jesus' understanding of Jerusalem.

The Old Testament prophets had spoken in expansive terms of the glories that Israel would experience when it returned from exile and of its restored Temple.[27] Yet there was a sense in which these prophecies had only

---

[25] Wright (1994a) 58; *cf.* 1996) ch. 9: 'all that the Temple had stood for was now available through Jesus and his movement'. Note too the two quotations (Matt. 9:13; 12:7) of the dictum in Hosea 6:6: 'I desire mercy, not sacrifice'.

[26] See E.P. Sanders (1985) 77f; see also *e.g.* Meyer (1979), Wright (1985) 79, and (1992a) 268-338.

[27] See *e.g.* Isa. 40ff; Jer. 30-31; Ezek. 40-48.

been fulfilled in part. 'The ancient prophecies of a new and glorious Temple were not regarded as having been realized in the Temple built after the exile';[28] and while there had been a return from exile and many Jews lived 'in the Land', in some senses they were still 'slaves in the land' (cf. Neh. 9:36), only briefly knowing any political independence (under the Hasmoneans). Now they were under the domination of a pagan Empire. Did God not have something better in store for his people and for Jerusalem? Were not the pagan nations meant at some point to acknowledge the truth of Israel's God and the importance of Zion?[29]

The various religious groupings within the Judaism of Jesus' day sought to answer these questions, each offering a way forward for Israel to attain its promised place within God's purposes for the world. Inevitably, therefore, Jesus too had to focus on these same questions. If he had not done so, then his mission and agenda would have been unintelligible and certainly unlikely to attract a major following.

Jesus' answer was that there was a different way of being Israel. It was not the way of internal isolationism (as for the Essenes) nor of defining Israel's halachic code in such strict terms that it excluded large numbers of the 'people' (the way of the Pharisees). Nor was it a matter of preserving the Temple cultus from outside interference (as for the Sadducees) or of increasing militaristic nationalism (which led in time to the emergence of the Zealots and the Jewish Revolt). God would fulfil his promises to his people and towards Jerusalem, but it would not be by any of these means. It would be through Jesus, Israel's Messiah, and his people. More particularly it would be, paradoxically, through the suffering and death of this Messiah, and then through the message of his resurrection going out 'to the ends of the earth'.

Certainly this is how Luke understood the matter. At the beginning of his Gospel he had pointedly raised this whole issue of contemporary Jewish hope: Zechariah longed for a salvation 'from our enemies' (1:71), whilst Simeon and others in Jerusalem waited for the 'consolation of Israel' and the 'redemption of Jerusalem' (2:25, 38). In his two pivotal chapters (Luke 24 and Acts 1) Luke returns to the issue in order to help his readers see the dramatic twist that has taken place. In Acts 1:6 the disciples ask Jesus, 'is this the time when you will restore the kingdom to Israel?'—evidence that the Jewish people of Jesus' day were vitally concerned with the issue of restoration. As far as the disciples could see, this work of restoration was necessarily a top priority for anyone with Jesus' Messianic credentials: the resurrection was important, but surely it had to lead on to political 'restoration' of some kind?

---

[28] McKelvey (1969) 24.
[29] See e.g. Isa. 2:2-4; Zech. 8:20-23.

Similar questions and confusions underlie the depression of the Emmaus disciples: 'we had hoped he was the one to *redeem* Israel' (Luke 24:21). Jesus' answer is a rebuke:

> How slow of heart you are to believe all that the prophets have declared! Was it not necessary that the Messiah should suffer these things and then enter into his glory? (vv. 25-6).

The clear implication is that Jesus has redeemed or restored Israel, but in a manner contrary to their expectations. In looking for a political Messiah ushering in a political 'restoration', they had completely misunderstood those Old Testament prophecies. They were to see the restoration of Israel as having been accomplished in the resurrection of Jesus.

Confirmation of this whole argument can be found in the way in which Jesus teaches that his resurrection on 'the third day' had been 'written' within the pages of the Old Testament (Luke 24:46). Yet to what verses is he referring? Whilst it is possible that there is an allusion to the story of Jonah, the far more likely reference is Hosea 6:2 ('after two days he will revive us; on the third day he will restore us'). If so, Jesus has taken a verse which originally referred to the restoration or revival of Israel and applied it instead to himself as Israel's Messiah. Israel's destiny was integrally bound up with the destiny of her representative Messiah. As Dodd rightly concluded: 'the resurrection of Christ *is* the resurrection of Israel of which the prophets spoke'.[30]

This has important consequences for Jesus' understanding of Jerusalem and its future role. Just as he had taken the idea of the Temple's restoration and applied it to his own resurrection, so here again he takes the broader themes of Israel's restoration and applies them to himself. If as a result of the various prophecies in the Old Testament people were looking for some great and future day for Jerusalem, they were looking in the wrong direction. Instead they needed to observe what God was doing through Jesus. Thus divine vindication would not come for Jerusalem in some form of restoration or political independence. On the contrary, it had already come for Jesus himself in his resurrection. There would be an end to the exile, but it would be accomplished through the Messiah's entering into divine judgement and then emerging victorious in being raised from the dead.

> The promises to Israel had come true in Jesus; in his death he had taken the exile as far as it could go; . . . in his resurrection he had inaugurated the real return from that real exile.[31]

---

[30] Dodd (1952) 103; *cf.* Tiede (1990), for whom the resurrection is God's 'contending for Israel's restoration'.

It would then be the responsibility of the people of Israel, and of all the 'nations of the earth', to align themselves with this raised and 'restored' Messiah through faith. In this lay Israel's hope, not in the political future of Jerusalem.

The resurrection of Jesus thus had profound implications for Jerusalem. Not only was it a divine reversal of the city's negative verdict upon Jesus and a vindication of the one whom Jerusalem had rejected. It also signified that its own hopes of restoration had been effectively transferred onto Jesus. If Jerusalem longed for 'restoration' this would be found, not in the aftermath of AD 70, but in Jesus.

Jesus pointedly did not promise a restoration of Jerusalem after the forthcoming destruction.[32] As previously noted, there were significant similarities between Jesus and Jeremiah, but at this point their messages parted company: whereas Jeremiah foresaw a restoration of Jerusalem when the years of exile were over (Jer. 30-31), Jesus made no such promise. This time the matter would be final. In one sense, Jesus' teaching indicates that he saw himself as bringing the age-long exile to an end: in him, though in an unexpected way, Israel would be restored. In another sense, his coming only paved the way for Jerusalem to go into a permanent state of exile after a decisive era of judgement. For the prophecies of restoration were to be fulfilled in him and in his followers, not in the city of Jerusalem.

The eventual fall of Jerusalem was therefore something which in a mysterious way was integrally related to the person of Jesus. At one level it was an act of judgement on the basis of the prophetic critique which Jesus plainly offered; it was also the inevitable result for the Zion which rejected her King. Yet, on another level, it had to do with the fact that God was now revealing in Jesus not only the true Temple but also the one in whom Israel was 'restored' and Jerusalem's prophetic destiny truly fulfilled. Jesus was bringing into existence a new age in God's economy of salvation. As a result of his coming the role of Jerusalem and the Temple would never be the same again.

This then lends credence to those interpretations of the Apocalyptic Discourse which suggest that Jesus was teaching his disciples to see Jerusalem's fall, not as an unintelligible tragedy, but rather as one part of the vindication of the Son of Man.[33] This private teaching was given appropriately on

---

[31] Wright (1992a) 400. This involves the inter-related ideas that, as the 'Son of Man' (the true representative of Israel now embodying her destiny), Jesus took Israel down into death, thereby fulfilling her role as the 'suffering servant' and experiencing her judgement. With his resurrection, that judgement could then be removed, Israel 'restored', and the exile truly brought to an end.

[32] Contrary to popular opinion, Luke 21:24 need not bear this meaning: see above ch. 3 at n. 166ff.

[33] See *e.g.* above ch. 1, n. 66.

the Mount of Olives, where Jerusalem and its Temple could be seen with a measure of critical distance and perspective. As the disciples viewed that glorious panorama, Jesus encouraged them to see it from his quite different, prophetic perspective—as it would look to Titus and his generals in forty years time. He wanted them to know in advance that those tragic events were not outside of God's purposes. It was not an event without any explanation. It had to do with Jesus himself—the prophet who had unmasked the city's twisted identity, the King whom it had rejected, the one who was the true Temple and the central focus of God's purposes for Israel and the world. When Jerusalem fell, it would be clear at last that both the warnings that Jesus had issued to the city and also his staggering claims for his own identity had all along been true.

The fall of Jerusalem thus had important lessons for people throughout the world, not just for those disciples on the Mount of Olives. It not only vindicated Jesus as the Son of Man but also warned of what lay in store for those who opposed him. There is a prophetic merging of ideas within the Discourse, with the Fall of Jerusalem being thematically, though not chronologically, linked with the final End and the *parousia*. 'Beyond the end of Jerusalem is the end of the world; . . . the immediate event is the sign, guarantee, and mystical inauguration of the more remote one'.[34] 'The destruction of Jerusalem becomes the type or sign of the final eschatological occurrences'.[35]

Jerusalem's fall, Jesus implied, was not just an event within the history of Israel but also a paradigm of God's judgement upon the whole world—a warning to all who did not heed the seriousness of Jesus' claims. Yet if so, then Jerusalem was clearly no different from the world. It can therefore be concluded that Jesus' coming to Jerusalem 'leads to an enormous change in her character. No longer is she holy. Jesus literally desecrated Jerusalem by taking away her sacred role'.[36]

4. Conclusion

There is not only a major critique of Jerusalem within the teaching of Jesus, but also a claim that Jesus' identity can only be understood when seen in the light of Jerusalem. The location of the passion events within the city was no accident. It is not as though Jerusalem is an accidental backdrop for those events, which could in principle have occurred anywhere. Jesus had to go to Jerusalem, for this was the one place where his true identity could be revealed.

---

[34] Hastings (1958) 66; *cf.* Giblin (1985) 77f. See above ch. 3 (n. 170) and ch. 7 (n. 58ff).
[35] De Young (1961) 99.
[36] Ellul (1970) 138.

Only here, at Israel's heart, could he make good his claim to be the Messiah and Zion's true King, the true representative both of Israel and of Israel's God; only here could he with integrity make his prophetic denouncement of Jerusalem's leaders and address four-squarely the issue of Jewish nationalism and its ultimate political consequences. This was the one place where he could focus on the Temple's failings, revealing his own unique relationship to that institution, and also point his contemporaries beyond their desires for Jerusalem, demonstrating the new and unexpected work of restoration that God was doing in their midst.

The evidence suggests that Jesus saw his going to Jerusalem as revealing a fundamental clash of identities. He needed to denounce the city for its failing to live up to its scriptural and prophetic calling, while showing that that calling had now devolved upon himself. If Jerusalem had become an idol, taking God's people away from himself, it would be Jesus' task to bring them back and to reveal himself as their true King. If Jerusalem's Temple was failing to be a place where true worship could be offered to God, Jesus would need to point people to himself as the central 'place' within God's purposes, the place around which God's true people would be gathered. If devotion to Jerusalem was leading to a false understanding of God's purposes for Israel and impeding his purposes for the world, Jesus would surprise them with what God had in mind for them through their Messiah.

Jesus and Jerusalem stood for opposing things. Or perhaps more accurately, Jesus was offering in reality what Jerusalem had previously offered only in shadow, and which she was now failing to offer. This was then Jerusalem's 'hour', a defining moment in the city's history. When Jesus wept over the city he termed it the 'time of its visitation' (Luke 19:44), and his tears may in part have been caused by the solemn realisation that as a result of his own coming to the city, Jerusalem would never be the same again. Jesus and Jerusalem would become embroiled in a painful combat, and both would experience death. Jesus would then be raised from death—not so Jerusalem.

It was on his way to Golgotha that Jesus looked beyond his own fate to the *via dolorosa* which was awaiting Jerusalem: 'do not weep for me, but weep for yourselves; if they do this when the wood is green, what will happen when it is dry? (Luke 23:28, 31). In so saying he indicated that Jerusalem would experience a fate similar to his own crucifixion, and that these two fates were in some way intrinsically linked. The latter was inevitable because of the former; the former was a foretaste of the latter. The stark conflict that we have traced between Jesus and Jerusalem is now softened. For, despite all his critique and declarations of judgement upon the city, this 'prophet' was so identified with the aspirations of that city that he suffered in his own body a foretaste of that very judgement which he had pronounced upon it. Although

Jesus was strictly innocent of the charge of insurrection ('the wood is green'), unlike Jerusalem ('when it is dry'), he willingly bore the punishment of those who oppose Rome. Thus in a powerful prophetic action,

> He acted out the destruction (the death of the rebel, at the hands of the occupying forces) which he had predicted for Israel, so that his fellow-countrymen might have a way by which to avoid it. [37]

> [Jesus] goes to his death at the hands of a Roman judge on a charge of which he was innocent and his accusers, as the event proved, were guilty. And so, not only in theological truth but in historic fact, the one bore the sins of the many, confident that in him the whole Jewish nation was being nailed to the cross, only to come to life again in a better resurrection.[38]

In the mystery of the divine plan, the prophet who pronounced divine judgement upon the city was taking that judgement upon himself. Jerusalem was being warned, both in prophetic word *and in prophetic action*, of the fate that lay in store for it. The one who gave that severe warning did not do so from a comfortable distance but entered personally into the city's fate. Then, through the vindication that he would receive 'on the third day', he would be able to offer to that city and its 'children' the way through to a new dawn, a lasting 'restoration' and the new age of resurrection-life.

This is the new understanding of Jerusalem which lies at the root of all subsequent New Testament reflection. As in other areas where the New Testament takes the scriptural tradition in a surprising new direction, the culprit appears to be Jesus of Nazareth. It is he who stands at the epicentre.

---

[37] Wright (1994a) 63-4. In an earlier article (1985), he developed this in detail in the following syllogism: a) Jesus warned his contemporaries of imminent judgement; b) he identified himself with Israel; c) as Israel's representative, he then took upon himself the judgement which he had pronounced against the nation. Thus although 'he cannot preach Israel's national hope, he can die for it; . . . he now becomes a Zealot, a rebel against Rome, identifying himself with the national disease he himself had diagnosed, in order that it might be healed; . . . he takes the wrath of Rome (which is the historical embodiment of the wrath of God) upon himself so that, in his vindication, Israel may find herself brought through judgement and into the true kingdom; . . . if Israel's death could be died by her representative she might not need to die to it herself' (pp. 87, 89, 90, 93).

[38] Caird (1965) 22.

9

A NEW THEOLOGY
New Testament Reverberations

The Spirit will guide you into all the truth (John 16:13).

This chapter, which draws together material discussed in detail in chapters 1-7, examines the consequences within the New Testament of Jesus' understanding of Jerusalem under three headings: the issue of 'restoration', the Temple and the city. It shows that a consistent pattern of development can be traced amongst the various New Testament authors, even though they write from distinctive vantage-points. In each of these three areas, the New Testament offers a significantly new interpretation, pointing to an important shift within God's purposes towards Jerusalem in the era of the new covenant.

The New Testament writings bear witness to the reverberations of what took place during Jesus' ministry, culminating in Jerusalem. In previous chapters these writings were assessed in isolation, but now they are drawn together in order to show how the theology of the New Testament authors may be placed coherently within a chronological scheme of development.[1] Given the radical twist which our investigation shows Jesus to have given to the tradition, the full ramifications may have taken a little while to be understood. The repercussions were enormous. It would take some time for the ripples to settle down and for the implications to be fully grasped. This can be seen in three areas, relating to Israel's restoration, the Temple, and Jerusalem itself.

---

[1]   The material presented here summarizes the arguments of the previous chapters. For fuller discussions see the relevant sections in each chapter dealing with 'restoration', the Temple, and Jerusalem.

291

1. Restoration: From Politics to Mission

This process of gradual realization is seen most clearly in our first example. In writing Acts, Luke shows quite clearly and intentionally the 'learning-curve' of the apostles on this issue of restoration.[2]

This was a key issue, not only for Luke as he presented his material, but also for first-century Judaism in general and for the disciples in particular: 'Is this the time when you will restore the kingdom to Israel?' (Acts 1:6). Their working assumption was, not unnaturally, that the solution to Israel's problems would be observable at a socio-political level. Luke, however, had already made it clear (Luke 24:21ff) that Israel's true redemption and restoration was of a different kind. Here in Acts 1 it is as though the disciples wish to have a two-stage solution. The resurrection might legitimately be interpreted in 'restoration' categories, but surely that did not obviate the need for a more political solution—a fulfilment of Old Testament prophecy concerning Jerusalem and Israel which was more 'literal'?

Jesus' reply consists of two parts. Taken on its own, the first part ('it is not for you to know times . . : v. 7) might initially be taken as indicating Jesus' acceptance of their underlying assumptions. What was wrong?—their desire for a political fulfilment, or simply their chronology? When due consideration is given to the second part of Jesus' answer ('you will receive power . . . and you will be my witnesses . . . to the ends of the earth'), what emerges is something quite different. Not only was Jesus seeking to turn the disciples' attention away from such political concerns; he was also indicating that their forthcoming mission to the 'ends of the earth' would itself be an indication of Israel's restoration and the means whereby the truths of that restoration would be implemented upon the world-stage.[3] Israel was being restored through the resurrection of its Messiah and the forthcoming gift of the Spirit. The way in which Israel would then exert its hegemony over the world would not be through its own political independence, but rather through the rule and authority of Israel's Messiah. The chosen method of this Messiah's rule was through the apostles' proclamation of his gospel throughout the world bringing people into the 'obedience of faith' (cf. Rom. 1:5). Jesus' concern, now as before, was not for a political 'kingdom of Israel', but rather for the 'kingdom of God' (Acts 1:3).

It is by no means obvious that the actors in the drama, unlike Luke the author, understood all this immediately. It would need to be something which

---

[2] Some of the following material is discussed in more detail above in ch. 3 (4), when examining *Luke's* understanding of 'restoration'. The focus here is on the apostles themselves, as recounted in Luke's narrative.

[3] *Cf.* Wright (1994a) 68.

they learnt, somewhat painfully, in their own experience—beginning with the events associated with Pentecost. In the light of these, they may have ceased looking for a political solution and begun instead to see the potential of the gospel for bringing about a spiritual 'restoration' of God's people (though this will not have lost entirely its political overtones and implications). If Israel repented and large numbers came to faith in Jesus as their true Messiah, then would this not constitute, or usher in, the longed-for time of 'restoration'? Such thinking may lie behind Acts 3:21: '[Jesus the Messiah] must remain in heaven until the time of universal restoration that God announced long ago through his holy prophets.'

The focus here is upon a future time, when after Israel's repentance, the Messiah would return to establish his kingdom. The 'restoration' is deferred until the return of Christ—a hope that was far from invalid. Yet the interim hope, that the Jewish nation would come to faith in Jesus, proved to be unfulfilled. When the gospel began to bear unexpected fruit amongst the Gentiles, the questioning only increased.

> According to Jewish expectation, if the ingathering of the Gentiles were to take place, Israel had first to be restored. Even after the resurrection and the ascension, Israel had apparently not yet responded and experienced the 'times of refreshing' that were promised. So the ingathering of the nations could not happen yet, could it?[4]

The Jewish people were not yet 'restored' (in any sense of the term, be it political or merely spiritual). What was God doing?

These were some of the questions which precipitated and concerned the Jerusalem council (Acts 15). Important confirmation of this (and that the issue was not simply a pragmatic question concerning circumcision) comes in James' definitive ruling, where he based his decision in favour of the non-circumcision of Gentiles on a quotation from Amos 9:11-12:

> I will return, and I will rebuild the dwelling of David, which has fallen; from its ruins I will *rebuild* it, and I will *set it up*, so that all other peoples may seek the Lord—even all the Gentiles over whom my name has been called (Acts 15:16-17).

In selecting a text which justified the inclusion of the Gentiles, James chose one which fuelled the conviction that God's work amongst the Gentiles could only begin *after* he had acted on behalf of his own people ('David's fallen tent').[5] The clear implication was that this sequence of expectation (Israel's restoration, followed by the 'ingathering of the nations') was in itself quite

---

[4]   C.J.H. Wright (1994) 16.

correct. What had been wrong was the definition of Israel's 'restoration'. Any qualms or hesitations could be allayed once they grasped the truth that, regardless of the spiritual response of the Jewish people or their political status, Israel had in the most important sense already been restored—in Jesus.

> The considered apostolic interpretation of events was that the inclusion of the Gentiles was the necessary fulfilment of the prophesied restoration of Israel.[6]

> As a matter of history, it had to be recognized, however reluctantly, that the redemption of the Gentiles was not bound up with the prior establishment of the House of David in Jerusalem.[7]

James' ruling was accepted, indicating that the apostles finally laid aside any earlier belief that Israel's restoration consisted either in political independence or in its people coming *en masse* to faith in Jesus. They now realized that the inclusion of the Gentiles, being seen as the 'ingathering of the nations', signified that Israel had already been restored. Through the work of the Spirit in their midst, and against their own natural preferences and assumptions, they now understood in their own experience what Jesus had intimated to the Emmaus disciples. His resurrection was indeed the 'restoration of Israel'. That it took a little while for the 'penny to drop' is not surprising. These were long-held beliefs which were being shown to have been mistaken and in need of radical redefinition. The scriptural tradition had not been swept aside, but it had been significantly reapplied. God had been faithful to his promises, but not in the way that they had been expecting.

The result of the conference was that the apostolic community made a strategic decision which sent it out into the wider, Gentile world, proclaiming Jesus, Israel's Messiah, as Lord of all. The universal and centrifugal nature of the gospel became predominant, precisely because the home-based theological questions relating to Israel had in principle been resolved. The painful issue of the limited Jewish response to the gospel did not go away (see *e.g.* Rom. 9-11), nor the need to continue the work of evangelism amongst Jewish people (hence, for example, James' own ministry in subsequent years in Jerusalem:

---

[5]   Bauckham (1995a) 455, instead interprets the 'tent' as a reference to the 'eschatological *Temple* which God will build in the messianic age when Davidic rule is restored to Israel'; he then identifies this Temple with the Christian community (p. 457). This sees God's work of 'restoration' as evidenced in the Church, rather than (as here) in Jesus. The principle still remains, however, that it is only *after* this work of 'restoration', in whichever sense, that the Gentiles can be included.

[6]   C.J.H. Wright (1994) 16.

[7]   Davies (1974) 372.

Acts 21:18ff).[8] The Land of Israel and the political future of Judea, however, was no longer a vital issue for the Christian community.

This new understanding of 'restoration' can be seen in other New Testament writers. The way in which Mark alludes to Old Testament prophecies indicates that he interpreted them in a distinctively 'christological' way, which stood opposed to those interpretations which encouraged a more political solution to the problems of Israel. Matthew developed the idea that Jesus was the true Israel who had brought about the end of the exile. It can also be seen, much earlier in Paul's writings and ministry. Although it has been commonly assumed that Paul simply reversed the order of prophetic fulfilment (*i.e.* the 'ingathering of the Gentiles' would now precede the 'restoration') and was therefore looking to some 'restoration' of Israel in the future, this is wrong. As Wright concludes, in his discussion of Romans 11:25-7,

> for Paul the restoration of Israel *had already happened* in the resurrection of Jesus, the representative Messiah. The texts he calls upon are the very ones that speak of Gentiles hearing the word of the Lord consequent upon the restoration of Israel. He invokes . . . Isaiah 2:3 and/or Micah 4:2. When Zion is restored, the word of the Lord will flow from it to the nations: now, Zion has been restored in Jesus the Messiah, so that the word of salvation consists of Jesus himself, as Redeemer, coming from 'Zion' to bless the nations.[9]

A further result of this new understanding of restoration is the way the New Testament writers reveal little interest in issues relating to the Land—the 'inheritance' promised to Abraham, and a focal concern of Jewish desires for restoration.

Paul hardly speaks on this issue. When reflecting on God's promise to Abraham of the Land, he speaks instead of Abraham's 'inheriting the *world*' (Rom. 4:13)—a telling comment that reveals how he saw the promises as now widened and universalized in the Messiah. Luke's theme in the book of Acts is that the gospel of the Messiah's kingdom is going out to 'the ends of the earth' (Acts 1:8), and it is arguable that his structure is consciously indebted to the book of Joshua:[10] just as in the Old Covenant God's people had entered the Land, so now the gospel was to go out to the 'promised land' of the world.

---

[8] *Cf.* above ch. 3, n. 137.

[9] Wright (1992b) 207 (italics original), in contrast to E.P. Sanders (1985).

[10] Hence for example his repeated summaries about the state of the church and the 'increase' of the 'word of God' (6:7; 9:31; 12:24; 13:49; 19:20) serve a parallel function to the refrain in Joshua, 'the land had rest from war' (Josh. 11:23; *cf.* also 14:15; 21:44; 23:1). There are also interesting parallels between Acts 1:8 and Josh. 1:11 (the divine command to go into the land/the world) and the fates of Achan (Josh. 7) and Ananias and Sapphira (Acts 5:1-11). See further C. Chapman (1989) 141-2.

The author of Hebrews has also redefined the 'promised land', but in a different way—as a powerful symbol of the Christian's final 'rest' in God's kingdom (Heb. 3-4). This is part of the consistent reworking in the New Testament (as found in each chapter above) of the imagery associated with Moses and the exodus; in Jesus a new 'exodus' has been achieved, leading God's people to a different 'promised land'.[11] In a similar vein it was seen how the imagery of 'inheritance', which originally would have had a physical connotation rooted in the Land, was now applied to the Christian's heavenly hope.[12]

In concluding his comprehensive study of New Testament attitudes to the Land, Davies noted how the whole concept had been 'taken up into a non-geographic, spiritual, transcendent dimension'.[13] In explaining this he noted several factors: first, what he terms the 'cosmic awareness of primitive Christianity—its doctrines of the new creation, the new age, the cosmic Christ, the cosmic Church and the cosmic salvation'; secondly, the startling 'flood' of Gentiles into the Church which 'soon swept away for many those patterns that had governed Jewish thinking on the Land' causing Christians either to abandon or transform the 'geographic *realia* of Judaism'.[14] Finally he notes:

> Like everything else, the Land also in the New Testament drives us to ponder the mystery of Jesus, the Christ, who by his cross and resurrection broke not only the bonds of death but also the bonds of the Land. There were aspects of Judaism before his day, which anticipated that achievement, but, in the last resort, it was *his* impact that ensured that . . . [the history] of Christianity, despite the Crusades, has largely been that of detachment from it.[15]

Jesus' teaching, when combined with the subsequent work of the Spirit amongst the Gentiles, led to a new understanding of Israel's 'restoration'.

2. The Temple: From One to Another

The same combination leads to a similarly radical re-evaluation of the Temple. In the light of Jesus' teaching and example, the apostolic community in Jerusalem may initially have had ambivalent attitudes towards the Temple. On the one hand, Jesus had not stayed away from the Temple, but shown a keen

---

[11] See *e.g.* 1 Cor. 10:2; Luke 9:31; Acts 7:20-24; Heb. 3:3; Matt. 5:1; John 1:17; 6:32; Rev. 15:3.
[12] See Heb. 6:12; 9:15; Acts 20:32; 1 Pet. 1:4; Eph. 1:14, 18; Gal. 3:29ff; Col. 3:24; 1 Cor. 6:9-10; 15:50; Jas. 2:5.
[13] Davies (1974) 366.
[14] Davies (1974) 369-70, 373.
[15] Davies (1974) 375 (italics mine).

concern that its worship should be conducted in a fitting way. On the other, he had spoken clearly about its destruction, and some of his actions and sayings could be interpreted as indicating that he saw himself and his community in 'Temple' categories.[16] The former strand would fuel a 'reformist' tendency, seeking to bring the Temple more truly in line with God's requirement, the latter a 'rejectionist' approach. The evidence suggests that, to begin with, both these strands co-existed within the Christian community.

According to Luke's account in Acts (which is effectively our only source for understanding Christian *practice* as it related to the Temple), there were those who gave the Temple a prominent place within their thinking. It was the obvious place for the apostles to teach the people of Jerusalem (Acts 3:11ff; 5:12ff) and the implication is that they would have continued to be involved in the services associated with the 'hour of prayer' (Acts 3:1ff; *cf.* 2:46). Luke makes no mention of Christian involvement in the sacrificial aspect of the Temple. This may reflect his knowledge that 'for the primitive community in Jerusalem the Temple had changed from being a place of sacrifice to a place of prayer'.[17] Alternatively, they may have continued to participate in the sacrificial system;[18] in which case, Luke's silence on the matter could be interpreted as a mark of his distancing himself from this practice. Nevertheless, the final references to the Temple in Acts refer to the many believers who were 'zealous for the law' and in light of whom Paul agrees to pay for some Nazirite vows in the Temple (Acts 21:20ff). Clearly the first Christians (or at least some of them) did not dismiss the Temple out of hand. Nevertheless, the Christian community in Jerusalem, whilst continuing to participate in the Temple services,

> seems to have regarded itself as *the* eschatological Temple. . . . Such a view relativizes the Jerusalem Temple more radically than the Qumran view. Whatever the value of the Temple, it was highly provisional and soon to be replaced by that eschatological presence of God to which the Church already had access in its own fellowship.[19]

Even if still involved with the physical Temple, they now viewed it in a somewhat different light.

The rejectionist strand, however, comes to the surface early in Luke's account when he gives extended coverage to the views of Stephen, who is charged with constantly 'saying things against this holy place' (Acts 6:13).

---

[16] Above ch. 8 (3b).
[17] Hengel (1995) 42; *cf. e.g.* Gaston (1970) 97-100.
[18] Bauckham (1993c) 144.
[19] Bauckham (1993c) 144; *cf.* his (1995) 441f.

His speech of defence included the statement that 'the Most High does not dwell in houses made by human hands' and a quotation from Isaiah (66:1-2) which seemed to question the very possibility of building a house for the Lord (Acts 7:48-50). Whether this is interpreted as a plain statement denying the essence of the Temple *per se*, or instead as a more nuanced critique of the contemporary Temple and its leadership,[20] it provides evidence that there were some in the earliest Christian movement (especially from amongst the 'Hellenists') who took a more negative approach to the Temple. Not coincidentally, Luke connects this with the memory of Jesus' prophetic comment (even if misunderstood) to the effect that he would 'destroy this place' (Acts 6:14). In so doing Luke intimated that such negative stances towards the Temple were not entirely out of keeping with, and indeed could claim support from, the teaching of Jesus himself. Moreover, the prominence which he gives to the Stephen episode suggests that his own sympathies lay in that direction.

The fact that according to Acts there were Christians in Jerusalem who took a different line from Stephen, maintaining their involvement with the Temple, is frequently used as an argument for suggesting that Jesus cannot have prophesied against the Temple after all. For, if Jesus had really been so negative towards the Temple or pronounced its judgement, surely his followers would have disassociated from it and left it to its own demise? Since they did not, it is argued, Jesus' attitude towards the Temple must have been entirely positive (such that the negative strand found in the Gospels must be deemed the result of later Christian reflection). The situation is not that simple.

First, Jesus himself, despite his oracles of judgement, continued to frequent the Temple and to use it as the basis for his final public teaching ministry: 'day after day I was with you in the Temple' (Mark 14:49). If Jesus could be present in the Temple, whilst also denouncing its practice and warning of its future, then so could his followers. Even if 'the Temple's physical regime had ended', it was 'still appropriate to meet there'.[21]

Secondly, if Jesus did indeed pronounce judgement upon the Temple, it is entirely conceivable that this would have led to some quite different, but equally legitimate, responses. On the one hand, some (such as Stephen) might take this as their cue to be dismissive of the Temple straightaway—possibly because this tied in with convictions which they had held in their pre-Christian days.[22] On the other hand, others might conclude that their responsibility was by contrast to be committed to the Temple institution for as long as it was rea-

---

[20] As argued above in ch. 3 (1b).

[21] D.Wenham (1995) 207.

[22] On the suggested backgrounds to Stephen's theology and its influence on subsequent Christian thought (amongst the Hellenists, and seen possibly in Hebrews), see *e.g.* Simon (1958).

sonably possible. They would be 'in it to win it'. After all, the judgements
which Jonah had predicted for Nineveh had not been translated into solemn
reality, because the people of that city repented (Jonah 3:10). Might not this
prove true for Jerusalem? Even if many Christians believed that their calling
lay in lands further afield, Jerusalem surely needed a few Jonahs to stay within
it. Jesus had commanded them to be his 'witnesses' not only 'to the ends of
the earth', but also 'in Jerusalem' (Acts 1:8). *Some* Christians at least needed
to stay in Jerusalem and maintain their involvement with the Temple. The fact
that they pursued this course of action cannot then be used to discredit the idea
that Jesus had pronounced a judgement upon the Temple and the city. To have
deserted straightaway would have revealed a marked lack of compassion and
commitment to their own people. Instead their involvement only betrayed
their enduring commitment to their ancestral faith and their fellow-Jews. Indeed they may have seen their involvement with the Temple not just as a pragmatic choice, but as a theological duty. So long as the Temple continued, God
required them to be involved.

In the light of Jesus' prophecies and the Church's experience of the
Spirit two quite different positions concerning the Temple could therefore be
maintained with equal integrity.:

> it was possible to conclude either that Christians should (or at least could)
> continue to take part in the worship of the Jerusalem Temple while it still
> stood (until, that is, God himself removed it), or that, since the Temple was
> already superseded by the community as the new Temple, Christians should
> not participate in the Temple worship.[23]

The situation was therefore one that was inherently ambiguous and
anomalous. This was bound to be the case so long as the Temple, the destruction of which Jesus had predicted, still continued to stand. If, as argued above,
the threat-tradition was an authentic part of Jesus' teaching and formed a part
of the earliest Christian message, it was inevitable that Christians in that first
generation would see themselves as living in a strange, interim period.

> They must have viewed the Temple as a doomed institution, in which they
> participated while it lasted, but which they did not expect to last for long.[24]

Paul's teaching and example then bears witness to this ambiguity. On
the one hand, he developed a theology, especially when relating to his Gentile
converts, which left little place for the Jerusalem Temple. 'God's Temple is
holy', he says, but to what does he refer? '*You* are that Temple' (1 Cor. 3:17).
The indwelling of the Holy Spirit made every believer and congregation a

---

[23] Bauckham (1993c) 144.

'Temple of the Holy Spirit' (*cf.* 1 Cor. 6:1; 2 Cor. 6:16). As a result, the offering of 'true worship' did not require any physical sacrifices but rather a 'living sacrifice'—the offering of one's 'body' to God (Rom. 12:1). That such rethinking was taking place while the Temple was still standing is a measure of the immensity of the changes introduced by the coming of Jesus.

On the other hand, when he arrived in Jerusalem, Paul acceded gladly (so it appears) to James' request concerning the Nazirite vow. This could be defended on the grounds of his own stated principle of being 'all things to all people' (1 Cor. 9:22) and was not ultimately inconsistent. Yet it led him directly into the anomalies associated with the current Temple. In Christ, he had argued, there was no distinction between 'Jew and Greek' (Gal. 3:28) and the 'dividing-wall of hostility' had been broken down (Eph. 2:14). But the very structure of the Jerusalem Temple militated against this truth. It embodied and proclaimed something which Paul believed no longer truly pertained in God's purposes. There was something therefore bitterly ironic in Paul's being arrested on a charge of bringing a Gentile into the Court of Israel (Acts 21:28)—something which he had not done, but which strictly would have been the logical outworking of his theological position.

Our reading of Paul, and also of Luke who accompanied him on this journey, suggests that from that time onwards they turned their backs on the Temple. The resolution of the anomalies lay in God's hands alone. Their task was to continue establishing congregations which would not be surprised if the Temple as an institution were to come to an end, but which would see that the rich imagery formerly associated with the Temple had been brought into their own experience through Christ and his Spirit.

The political and religious tensions in Jerusalem deteriorated further after Paul's departure, with the position of the indigenous Christian community becoming increasingly untenable. James himself was martyred in AD 62[25] and there is a strong tradition that soon after the Jewish revolt began in AD 66 the Jerusalem church sought refuge in Pella.[26] The community that had at-

---

[24] Bauckham (1993c) 143. The evidence for Paul's awareness of this 'cloud' hanging over Jerusalem is discussed above in ch. 4 (3b). *Cf.* Moessner (1988). If this was a common Christian understanding, it would have meant, for example, that the Christian community would have watched the Caligula crisis (AD 49) particularly closely. Gaston (1970) 334-364, argues that this threat-tradition was part of the *kerygma* preached by Christians in Palestine amongst their fellow-Jews in the AD 50's. Wright (1985) 91, sees Jesus' warnings as explaining the urgent tone of the speeches in Acts: people were to 'take advantage of the breathing space . . . before the cataclysm comes in which Israel as then constituted would be swept away'.

[25] Eusebius (*EH* 2.23.18) gives the impression that this occurred immediately before the siege of the city (*i.e.* AD 66), but this is incorrect (see Josephus, *Ant.* 20:197-203: see *e.g.* Schürer (1973-87) i, 468; Murphy O'Connor (1995) 15.

tempted to hold together its dual Jewish and Christian identities could do so
no longer. By around AD 68 'they found this dual loyalty to both Jesus and
nation brought to the point of an either/or decision'.[27]

It is around this time, in the decade leading up to the final destruction
of the Temple in AD 70, that the letter to the Hebrews was written. Writing to
a group of Christians who similarly felt a great instinctive loyalty to the ways
of Judaism (though probably not in Jerusalem, but in Rome) the author warns
against apostasy and gives his understanding of how Christians should view
the Jerusalem Temple. Although the Temple is still standing, he argues that
Christ's death is the fulfilment of the Temple sacrificial system. Indeed the
whole thrust of his argument is that to be involved with rituals associated with
this Temple system is strictly now incompatible with a Christian's calling
(13:9-14). The Temple is part of the 'old covenant' which 'will soon disappear' (ἐγγὺς ἀφανισμοῦ, 8:13); Christians do not need the Temple but can approach God with 'confidence' through him who has entered the heavenly
Temple on their behalf (4:16; 10:22).

By the time this was written, it is not impossible that the inheritors of
James' stance in Jerusalem would have found themselves in tacit agreement
with such ideas. This understanding of Christ's death as the fulfilment of the
Temple's sacrificial system might not have been alien to James himself in his
day; he would only have disagreed with the conclusion that Christian involvement with the Temple was therefore contradictory.[28] The author of Hebrews,
however, was probably writing both from and to a context at some distance
from Jerusalem. From that distance, and being less embroiled in the 'pastoral'
delicacies required of the Jerusalem church, he could take a stance on theological principle. In the face of mounting pressure from non-Christian Jews to
show solidarity with the Temple, he declared with a prophetic touch that this
was now a false track. Although it was the intense climate of the times which
forced him to pen this exposition, his teaching about Christ as the 'true High
Priest' and his death as a sacrifice were far from new. The crisis of the hour

---

[26] Eusebius, *EH* 3.5.3; this testimony (dependent on Eusebius' source, Aristo of Pella) is
questioned by many (*e.g.* Lüdemann [1989] 200-211); it is defended by Hengel (1989b)
301, and Blanchetière and Pritz (1993). Murphy O'Connor (1995) 16-17, suggests the
Christian community *did* escape from the city, but not as far as Pella.

[27] R.N. Longenecker (1964) 268.

[28] The difference between the Jerusalem church, Paul and Hebrews might therefore be
stated as follows. They all agreed that the Temple had no lasting future, but whereas in
Hebrews it was concluded that Temple involvement was wrong in principle, some in the
Jerusalem church may have seen such involvement as a theological duty; Paul's position
was more pragmatic and lay in-between, permitting Temple involvement but not seeing it
as theologically necessary. *Cf.* Bauckham (1993c) 145. On the possible conections between
Hebrews and Stephen, see above ch. 6, n. 32.

did not bring to birth totally novel ideas, but rather (as so often) a clearer articulation and deeper penetration into truths that were already treasured.[29]

The concept that Christ's coming had brought to an end the significance of the Temple was thus firmly in place before its destruction in AD 70. Mark, writing possibly during the course of the Jewish war (c. AD 68) makes it plain that Christian hope is not focused on the physical Temple but rather on him who pronounced its forthcoming destruction and said he would 'in three days build another, not made with hands' (Mark 14:58). Jesus' prophetic words and actions, his self-understanding, his death and resurrection—each of these contributed to a quite fresh assessment of this central institution within Judaism, which was then confirmed by the experience of the ubiquitous availability of God's Spirit amongst the believers. When at last Jesus' words were fulfilled, there would have been little surprise for many Christians. The anomalies that its continued existence had created came to an end and the conclusions advocated in advance by Paul, Luke and the author of Hebrews were vindicated.

In the years after AD 70 Matthew emphasizes the notion of Jesus as 'something greater than the Temple', indeed as the *shekinah* presence of God (Matt. 18:20; 28:20), whose departure from the Temple signified that it had thereafter been left desolate (23:39f). John makes this theme central to his whole work: Jesus himself is the true Temple (John 2:21) who embodies in his own person the true 'tabernacle' of God's presence in the world (1:14). He places the episode of the Temple cleansing at the outset of his Gospel (2:13ff), and in subsequent chapters portrays the Jewish feasts associated with the Temple as finding their true fulfilment in Jesus.

On one of these occasions John presents Jesus as applying to himself (or to the believer) the prophetic imagery of Ezekiel's eschatological Temple: 'as the scripture has said, rivers of living water will flow from within him' (7:38). This is especially significant since in the years after AD 70 there would inevitably be some question as to whether the Temple was ever to be rebuilt, and Ezekiel's vision of the eschatological Temple might have fuelled such hope and expectation. John's Gospel indicates that this is to look in the wrong

---

[29] Although the traditional ascription of this letter to Paul cannot be upheld, there is probably little in it which Paul could not have written in his own day. Seen in this way, the letter to the Hebrews fills an important *lacuna* in Paul's extant writings. Despite his occasional use of concepts associated with the Temple, Paul never systematically tackled the issue of the Temple cult, but concentrated (as his largely Gentile congregations required) on the issue of the Law. On the parallels between these two writers, see Witherington (1991), who concludes that they 'are more similar to each other than we in the modern era have sometimes thought. Might we not have a case here of Paul broadcasting some ideas and then Apollos or some other intimate in the Pauline circle watering them?' (p. 152).

direction. A restored Temple can no longer be expected on the basis of that prophecy, because Jesus must now be seen as its true fulfilment.

The author of Revelation then makes a similar point, only he applies Ezekiel's imagery instead to the new Jerusalem (Rev. 21-22). This only complements the understanding in John's Gospel of Jesus himself as the new Temple. For the author of Revelation stresses that in this new Jerusalem there will be 'no Temple' because Jesus as the 'Lamb' *is* its Temple (21:22). Since Jesus was the embodiment of the Temple and the fulfilment of the scriptural prophecies, the Jerusalem Temple was no longer of any significance and no subsequent Temple on that site was to be expected. Having focused on the person of Jesus, Revelation (as did John's Gospel) also extends the concept of the true Temple to include, in a derivative sense, the Christian community.

The book of Revelation thus brings to a fitting conclusion a radical revision of thought that had its origins in the ministry of Jesus. The previous significance of the Temple was transferred to Jesus and his people. Whether the Temple was thought of as the place which embodied God's presence on earth or as the place of sacrifice, the New Testament writers affirmed in their different ways that both these aspects had been fulfilled in Jesus: his death was the true sacrifice and his person the true *locus* of God's dwelling upon earth. By extension Christian believers too might be seen as a 'Temple'. The inevitable consequence of this was that the Jerusalem Temple was no longer necessary, nor was any eschatological Temple of a physical kind to be expected. 'Nowhere in early Christian literature is there any trace of an expectation of an eschatological Temple still to come in the future.'[30] On the contrary, God's eternal purposes had now been revealed in Christ.

A comprehensive survey of the Temple in the New Testament therefore concluded:

> The New Testament declares that God has fulfilled his word of promise made by the prophets and erected a new and more glorious Temple. The ministry of Jesus is the divine visitation in judgement and mercy. The people of God are judged . . . and restored. The restoration, like previous ones in Israel's history, is marked by the restoration of God's dwelling-place. The new Temple is not indeed the kind of Temple that was expected but it is the long-expected Temple none the less.[31]

---

[30] Bauckham (1993c) 144.
[31] McKelvey (1969) 180.

3. Jerusalem: From the Earthly to the Heavenly

A similar process was at work as the Christians of the New Testament era re-flected more generally on the status of Jerusalem, the city. Again it would be understandable if there were initially a mix of attitudes. After all, Jerusalem was the place both of the crucifixion and of the resurrection; Jerusalem was the city which had opposed Jesus, yet it was also the place which was given the privilege of first hearing the good news of Israel's Messiah.

A note of optimism is struck in the opening chapters of Acts, but it does not last for long. In his Gospel Luke had opened his narrative with the hopes of those people associated with the births of Jesus and John the Baptist, but then showed how those hopes would not be realized in the expected way; in his sequel volume there is a similar pattern at work. The thoughtful reader was to understand that God had been working out his good purposes, but not in the way in which the participants had originally imagined. Thus before long a 'se-vere persecution began' and 'all except the apostles were scattered throughout Judea and Samaria (Acts 8:1). Luke's choice of words, with the phrase 'Judea and Samaria' picking up the words attributed to Jesus in Acts 1:8, shows that Luke saw Jerusalem's rejection of the gospel as only serving to take the Church forwards in its mission; by this means, albeit paradoxically, the gospel was going out through 'Judea and Samaria . . . to the ends of the earth' (1:8).

In due course it became reasonably clear that there was going to be no straightforward response of Jerusalem to the gospel—whether *en masse* or amongst its religious and political leadership. The goal of Jerusalem as a strong Messianic centre was not going to be realized, and those Christians who did stay in Jerusalem would need to brace themselves for being a small, minority community in an environment which, if it was not always actively hostile, was not especially sympathetic. In its attitude to Jesus' followers Je-rusalem was effectively underwriting its previous rejection of Jesus himself. It was proving to be more the city of crucifixion than the city of the resurrec-tion. Meanwhile the work of the Spirit amongst the Gentiles confirmed that God's purposes had taken a new direction and encouraged the conclusion that the old particularities associated with Jerusalem and Judaism were being eclipsed by the long-awaited emphasis on the 'universal'.

Such reflections may underlie Paul's cutting statement that 'the present Jerusalem' was 'in slavery with her children' (Gal. 4:25). In some ways 'Je-rusalem' here stands metonymically for Judaism as a whole, but such a state-ment clearly implied a negative evaluation of Jerusalem itself—presumably because of its opposition to the gospel and its 'enslavement' to the law as op-posed to the 'freedom' of Paul's gospel. The force of Paul's statement proba-bly reflects the fact that his Christian opponents in Galatia, the Judaizers, had links with Jerusalem. In which case Paul was also reflecting on the cramping effect that Jerusalem had on those who professed faith in Jesus, resulting in their not being able to welcome the full implications of the gospel as he understood it. He encourages his Galatian converts to concentrate instead upon the 'Jerusalem above' and wishes them to see that they can claim *this* city as part of their identity: 'she is our mother' (Gal. 4:26). In so saying Paul became the first Christian to open up the concept of the 'heavenly Jerusalem'—something which Jesus had seemingly not spoken of directly, but which became an important theme for subsequent New Testament writers.

Paul's attitude to Jerusalem was therefore a delicate mixture. On the one hand, it was the city at the centre of God's revelation and the place from which through the gospel the 'law of the Lord was now going forth to the ends of the earth' (Isa. 2:3). His 'collection' was designed in part to help his Gentile converts to sense their debt to this place, and towards the Jewish-Christians who remained there upholding the witness of the Messiah. It was also the continuing spiritual focus of his fellow-Jews, to whom he remained passionately committed (Rom. 9-11). On the other hand, the city's effective rejection of the gospel forced him to see it in quite a new light. His own calling as the 'apostle to the Gentiles' forced him to reflect critically on the supposed centrality of Jerusalem. Meanwhile, his somewhat difficult encounters with the Jerusalem church may have disposed him to question whether Jerusalem should continue to be the *locus* of religious authority. Although Jerusalem had been the place of his formal training under Gamaliel (his *alma mater*: Acts 22:3), the commitment to the city which that represented may have played a part in his own initial hostility to 'the Way'. If so, Paul would have known from his own experience the dangers of over-emphasizing Jerusalem and how it could cause people to be in a form of 'slavery' rather than truly free. Not surprisingly, after his visit to Jerusalem with the collection, he turns his attention elsewhere.

Luke's understanding of Jerusalem will have been influenced by Paul's. His writings exhibit a Gentile indebtedness to Jerusalem, yet also an emphasis on the ironic loss of the city's true destiny. His Gospel of Jesus proves also to be a tragedy concerning Jerusalem. What has previously been at the centre has been eclipsed by the out-going mission of the Church. By comparison, Mark's Gospel gives little emphasis to Jerusalem (as opposed to the Temple), probably reflecting its brevity and concentrated focus on the person and work of Jesus—to the exclusion of almost everything else.

The author of Hebrews, like Paul, focused on the 'heavenly Jerusalem', the place where Jesus now reigned and to which all his followers were ultimately called (Heb. 12:22-4). Writing in the years before AD 70, he exhorted his readers that it was this heavenly Jerusalem, not the earthly one, that was to be the core of their identity and the object of their hopes. He too had reflected on the irony of the earthly Jerusalem being the place which rejected Jesus and which was continuing to be dismissive of his followers. In powerful imagery based on the Passion narrative, he urged his readers to 'go to [Jesus] outside the camp and bear the abuse he bore' (Heb. 13:13). Disciples of Jesus were to accept the ostracism which Jesus had received from Jerusalem. They could do this with confidence, and with little pining for their associations with the earthly Jerusalem: 'for here we have no lasting city, but we are looking for the city that is to come' (13:14). The earthly Jerusalem would let them down; their focus was to be on the heavenly, 'enduring' city which would last for ever.

Though speaking at a more theological level, this injunction proves to be not far from that found in the very practical command within Luke's Apocalyptic Discourse: 'then those in Judea must flee to the mountains, and those inside the city must leave it' (Luke 21: 21).[32] No doubt many Christians in Jerusalem would have hoped that things would turn out more positively, and that they would not be required to make such a choice. It is probable, however, that when the moment finally came, they heeded Jesus' warning. The call in Hebrews to Jewish-Christians in the Diaspora to disassociate themselves from Jerusalem thus came to be paralleled within Jerusalem itself by the believers' obedience to this dominical command. They fled the city. If there had been some unavoidable ambiguity before, the matter was now resolved: the commitment of the Jewish-Christians to Jerusalem could never be identical to that of their fellow-Jews. In the end their new loyalties came to the fore, and Jerusalem was abandoned.

This final departure from Jerusalem, however, though forced upon the local Christians by a major political crisis, was not something unforeseen or without precursors in the apostolic generation. Reflecting on Paul's attitude to Jerusalem one scholar has written:

> Had he been there, Paul would have marched at the head of the column, as the Christians left Jerusalem that day. Indeed, he had mentally and physically left Jerusalem long before that date.[33]

This earlier 'departing' from Jerusalem at a spiritual level may also be discerned in the fact that the apostles too gradually left the city. Although they returned for the important council in Jerusalem in Acts 15, from chapter 12 onwards it was James who was leading the Jerusalem church.[34] This suggests that the apostles recognized that Jerusalem, even though undeniably the historic source-point of the gospel, was not to remain as an 'apostolic centre' or headquarters, the enduring focal-point of the new Messianic community. Re-

---

[32] This similarity is noted by *e.g.* Filson (1967) 64; *cf.* above ch. 6, n. 63.
[33] Motyer (1989) 18.

flecting the fact that the Church's mission was now a world-wide concern, the notion of apostolic authority was allowed to be dispersed. It would also indicate their lack of commitment to Jerusalem, whether politically or spiritually, and their greater concern with the worldwide implications of the gospel.

After AD 70 Matthew's reflections on Jerusalem are perhaps the most pained. He speaks of Jerusalem, the 'holy city' (4:5; 27:53) as one to whom it meant a great deal. It is not impossible that he himself had been associated with the Jerusalem church in the period before 70, and knew how its members had recently felt forced to leave the city; for there are traces in his Gospel of an earlier hope that Jerusalem might yet respond to the message of Jesus. But now the city's fate has been made clear. Against their wishes, Jewish Christians now needed to forge their identity in a situation where they were exiled from Jerusalem and also ostracized by the mainstream Jewish community. It was a traumatic time. His reflections on Jerusalem, the Jerusalem which rejected Jesus and continued to reject disciples such as himself, thus have a stinging quality to them. Luke, whilst sensitive to the issue, had been able as a Gentile to be somewhat detached; for Matthew it was very personal.

John, whatever his own personal involvement with Jerusalem, could place the issue in a larger context; he saw Jerusalem as a microcosm of the 'world'. Beyond Jerusalem's rejection of Jesus lay the mystery of the world's rejecting the *Logos*. This was his principal emphasis (John 1:10). If, however, he had touched more explicitly on Jerusalem's consequent fate, he would no doubt have seen in its destruction a dire warning of what awaited the whole world if it did not respond to the Word, through whom it had been made (1:3).

This is precisely the point that is then picked up and developed in Revelation. The fall of Jerusalem serves as a paradigm of God's judgement upon the world, an event which is depicted in the fall of the 'great city'. Although this 'great city' was no doubt intended chiefly as an allusion to Rome, its symbolic meaning owes something to Jerusalem in the past and ultimately applies to the whole world in its opposition to God. In speaking of the 'great city' where the 'Lord was crucified' (Rev. 11:8), John deliberately makes a connection between Jerusalem and that city which he will soon describe as 'Babylon' (14:8ff). The evil manifested in Jerusalem is an evil which is endemic in the world; the opposition which Jesus experienced in the one city will be matched by that which his followers will experience in the other. There is thus evidence within Revelation that John is consciously offering an interpretation of the

---

[34] See Bauckham (1995a) 427-441, who rightly notes that this departure of the apostles was probably occasioned both by the persecution under Agrippa I (AD 43 or 44) and by more pragmatic considerations: 'leadership at the centre in Jerusalem could no longer be combined with personal leadership in the missionary movement out from the centre' (p. 436). This contrasts with the earlier period when the apostles stayed in the city (Acts 8:1).

Apocalyptic Discourse which looks beyond its immediate reference to the fall of Jerusalem and sees this as speaking of the final judgement upon the world.

The physical Jerusalem provides important imagery for God's judgement; but it also provides the imagery for God's ultimate purposes of blessing. For when the 'great city' has been judged, what is revealed is the 'new Jerusalem' (21:1ff). That John speaks in this way is significant, because it affirms the underlying continuity in God's purposes. Although the physical Jerusalem has now been judged, that does not deny that God had truly been at work there in times past. On the contrary, all that was good in that city, and all that it stood for within God's purposes, can now be affirmed. The prophetic vision of Jerusalem in the Old Testament is thereby endorsed. To be sure, these prophecies had not met with the expected political fulfilment, but neither had they evaporated into thin air. The visions of prophets such as Isaiah and Ezekiel, who had foreseen Jerusalem's future glory, were not null and void. The true reference of these prophecies, however, is not the physical Jerusalem, but the 'new Jerusalem'. The author pointedly describes this city as a *'new* Jerusalem, coming down *out of heaven* from God' (21:2, 10). This is not the old, earthly Jerusalem, now elevated onto a higher plain; that city is hopelessly contaminated by the ways of the world. This is a quite 'new' city built by God himself.

Thus, despite differences in experience and expression, the New Testament witness on this theme of Jerusalem (just as on the Temple) forms an impressive unity. Taking their lead from Jesus' teaching and led by his Spirit to further reflection on the Jerusalem of their own day, the New Testament writers concur that a dramatic shift has occurred. Something unparalleled has taken place in the city's history, leaving an indelible mark for its future. Jesus pronounced judgement upon the city; the 'holy city' has proved unholy; instead its prophetic destiny has been fulfilled in Jesus' death and resurrection.

Christians' experience was now to be centred on Christ himself and their focus for the future was to be on the 'heavenly Jerusalem', not the 'Jerusalem below'. Moreover, when focusing on the return of Christ, those future expectations did not include some end-time rebuilding of the Temple or a 'restoration' of Jerusalem, precisely because in Jesus that Temple has been revealed and that restoration accomplished. Jerusalem therefore had lost its distinctively 'sacred' character—though for reasons of historical and religious association it would be forever 'special'. No other city had been so central in God's purposes, but those days were now past.[35]

---

[35] Our conclusions confirm those of others who have similarly surveyed the New Testament witness: see De Young (1961) 98, 109, 116; and Beagley (1987) 178.

10

A NEW SIGNIFICANCE
Towards a Biblical Theology

I saw the holy city, the new Jerusalem, coming down out of heaven
from God. I heard a loud voice saying, 'See, the home of God is
among mortals; he will dwell with them' (Rev. 21:2-3).

A brief examination of 1 Peter provides a first-century example of how a biblical theology
of Jerusalem might be developed. Biblical theology requires that the Old Testament mate-
rial be interpreted through the prism of the New. Although this denies to Jerusalem some
of the significance associated with it both in the Old Testament and even by some today,
the Jerusalem-theme is one of the vital interpretative keys for understanding the dynamic
flow of the scriptural revelation.

The New Testament offers a new theology of Jerusalem, reforging the biblical
tradition because of God's revelation of himself in Christ. This then raises the
important question as to how this theme of Jerusalem is to be interpreted in
the Bible as whole. What is to be made of the Old Testament witness in the
light of the New?

One of the best places to begin to answer this question is 1 Peter—a
document which till now has been omitted from our survey, but which in its
few chapters offers some significant pointers as to how the biblical theme of
Jerusalem is to be understood in the light of Christ. An integral part of the author's purposes is to encourage his readers that, even though they might consider themselves as 'exiles of the Dispersion' (1:1), living in the province of
Asia Minor and at some distance from Jerusalem, nevertheless they are at the
centre of God's purposes. Although previously they were 'not God's people',

309

now they are (2:10).[1] Jesus' death and resurrection had occurred far away in Jerusalem ('Zion': 2:6), but these events had been expressly for their benefit;[2] and even though (unlike Peter himself: 5:1) they had never 'seen' Jesus (1:8), it was important that they endure any forthcoming persecution for his sake. They might experience social alienation, but they were 'honoured' in God's sight (2:7), because of their allegiance to the one who has recently been 're-vealed at the end of the ages for your sake'.[3] As part of this pastoral strategy Peter develops a new understanding of Jerusalem and its Temple.

First, these Christian believers must consider themselves as a new Temple. There was no need for them to make a pilgrim visit to Jerusalem's Temple or to confirm their status as 'proselytes', because the important thing was to 'come' to Christ (προσερχόμενοι: 2:4), who as a *living* stone' was not tied to any one place. Indeed through their integral relationship with the Risen Christ, they themselves now constituted a 'spiritual house' and a 'holy priest-hood' (2:5)—metaphors quite clearly taken from the Jerusalem Temple.[4] Even if they were absentee Gentiles, in Christ they could be a true Temple, 'offering spiritual sacrifices' which would be 'acceptable to God'. All the blessings and spiritual import that had previously been localized in the Jeru-salem Temple were now theirs in Christ.[5]

> The presence of the covenant God in the midst of his people, which had set apart the Jerusalem sanctuary, has now become the hallmark of the assem-bling congregation of Asia Minor.[6]

This is confirmed in chapter 4, when, having used imagery reminiscent of the *shekinah* to describe the 'Spirit of glory and of God' resting upon the believers (4:14), he portrayed their present sufferings as part of God's judge-ment upon his own 'Temple': 'The time has come for judgement to begin with the house of God (τοῦ οἴκου τοῦ θεοῦ); if it begins with us, what will be the

---

[1]   Hence the wording in *e.g.* 1:18 and 2:10. 'The very language that identifies them as Gentiles at the same time confirms their identity as "Israel"': Michaels (1988) 112. He notes 'Peter's strong conviction that his Gentile Christian readers are actually Jews in God's sight' (p. 230).

[2]   Hence Peter's frequent references to the death and resurrection of Christ as the solid Jerusalem-events upon which they could rely, in many of which he emphasizes that Jesus endured the Cross for their benefit (1:18; 2:21, 24-5; 3:18).

[3]   For this translation of τιμή in 2:7 see Michaels (1988) 104; *contra* NRSV.

[4]   *Contra* J.H. Elliott (1981), Michaels (1988) 100, rightly says, 'it is difficult to imagine a house intended for priesthood as being anything other than a Temple of some sort'.

[5]   Hence Michaels (1988) 64, concludes more generally: 'one of the major concerns of 1 Peter is to claim for Christians a heritage (*i.e.* the heritage of Judaism as reinterpreted in Christ).'

[6]   Johnson (1986) 287.

end for those who do not obey the gospel of God' (4:17). Peter saw himself and his readers ('us') as the 'house of God'. Yet, as in 2:5, the use of οἶκος plainly refers in the first instance to the Jerusalem Temple, not to God's 'household' or 'family'.[7] The imagery is drawn from two Old Testament passages which speak of God's work of judgement beginning in the Jerusalem Temple (Ezek. 9; Mal. 3:1-5).[8] Peter now takes this scriptural teaching and applies it without apology to the Church. The Christian community thus inherits not just the privileges but also the demanding responsibilities of the Jerusalem Temple (the first place to witness God's judgement). This was a clear example of how the Church needed to eschew triumphalism and always apply the biblical theme of judgement in the first instance to itself.[9] It also made it quite plain that the Church had the right to see itself as the true inheritor of these Old Testament realities. Christians were the new Temple.

Secondly there is a new understanding of Jerusalem. This may be seen through noting the consequences of Peter's emphasis on his readers being in 'exile' (1:1, 17). Although this initially suggests a distance from the physical Jerusalem, it becomes clear that Peter is using this biblical imagery to make a new point about Christian experience. He immediately speaks about their 'inheritance that is imperishable, undefiled and unfading, kept in heaven' (v. 4); this is what they are hoping will be 'revealed' (v. 5), and from which they are currently in 'exile'. Christians live in the 'in-between' period, marked by faith and not by sight (vv. 8-9). In the meantime they are in 'exile' (v. 17).

The Jerusalem from which they are exiled, therefore, is not the physical one. Jeremiah had written to the exiles that they were to maintain their hopes for the physical Jerusalem (Jer. 29:10), but Peter encouraged the 'exiles' of his day to 'set all their hope' on a different homeland, a different Jerusalem—the 'grace that Jesus Christ will bring you when he is revealed (1:13. Moreover, like the Old Testament people of God when in the wilderness *en route* to the promised land, so now these Christians are to respond to the God who has declared, 'You shall be holy, for I am holy' (Lev. 11:44-5 in 1 Peter 1:16). Although Peter does not develop it further, we may reasonably suppose that he would have had little difficulty with the parallel reasoning in Hebrews which saw the New Testament people of God being on a journey through the wilder-

---

[7] Johnson (1986); Grudem (1988) 181; *contra* J.H. Elliott (1981) 201 (and NRSV).

[8] This is well argued in Johnson (1986) and followed by Grudem (1988) 181-4.

[9] This understanding of divine judgement against God's 'house' would pave the way for (if it did not already reflect) a Christian evaluation of the destruction of the Jerusalem Temple in AD 70; see Michaels (1988) 271, who leaves it open as to whether 1 Peter should be dated before or after 70 (pp. lv-lxvii). The destruction of this 'house' was a warning both to the world and to the Church. *Cf.* above ch. 7 (n. 72ff), where in Rev. 11:1-2 the fall of the physical Temple similarly acts as a warning to the Church, the true Temple.

ness to the 'heavenly Jerusalem' (Heb. 12:22). If Peter's audience was in 'exile and diaspora' (1:1), then the Jerusalem from which they had been 'dispersed' was the heavenly one—the place of their 'imperishable inheritance' (v. 4). Their distance from the physical Jerusalem served only to pinpoint a far more significant alienation—their distance from that place where they would be united with Christ, the one whom they loved but had not seen. It was by reference to *this* home and 'inheritance' that they were in 'exile'.

Peter therefore endorses the new approach to Jerusalem and the Temple observed in the other New Testament writers and demonstrates the direction in which Christians in the first century were developing the biblical tradition. Although they were convinced that God had acted in a new way towards the world in Christ , they saw this as a continuation of his Old Testament purposes. Motifs could be taken from the scriptures and applied in ways which, though new, were in keeping with the underlying unity of the biblical tradition. It is essentially the same task of 'biblical theology' that presents us today.

Not unnaturally, such 'biblical theology' is dismissed as impossible in many quarters on the grounds that one could not expect the witness of the many biblical authors, writing over such a vast period of time, to manifest any such underlying unity or coherence. Yet, at least as far as the New Testament is concerned (admittedly composed within a much briefer span) our study has revealed a significant 'oneness of mind' on this issue. Though the landscapes of Jerusalem have been drawn from different vantage-points, it is possible to detect that the subject of their portrait is one and the same: a Jerusalem, changed by the coming of her King. The fact that we are presented with more than one picture provides cumulative evidence which is not easily dismissed, and only serves to bring about a view of Jerusalem which is multi-dimensional and therefore far richer than anything we could have gained had the New Testament been penned by a single author.

In the previous chapter it has been shown that the scepticism concerning the possibility of developing a New Testament theology of Jerusalem is unfounded. The same might hold true for an overall 'biblical theology' as well, though clearly it is beyond the scope of this study to engage with this important question in any detail.[10] The most important consequence, however, from our present study would be that anyone engaged in constructing a biblical theology of Jerusalem should read the Old Testament through the interpretative prism of the New. For it is not as though the New Testament writers were reflecting on Jerusalem *de novo* and without any reference to what had

---

[10] This was partially addressed in the various articles in my (1994a)—especially, J.G. McConville's, 'Jerusalem in the Old Testament' (pp. 21-52). *Cf.* also de Young (1961) and Ellul (1970).

gone before; none of their writings suggests an ignorance or 'Marcionite' disrespect for the Old Testament. On the contrary, they saw themselves as continuing (indeed completing) the story that had authentically been started
within the Old Testament. With a notable air of authority, they set about reworking the biblical tradition in order to do full justice to what they believed
God had done in the sending of Israel's Messiah. If they came to see Jerusalem
in a new light, this has to be seen, not as a dismissal, but rather as a conscious
adaptation of the Old Testament tradition—an 'apostolic' witness to how
these truths were now to be understood in the light of Christ.

Within Christian theology it is therefore illegitimate to approach the
Old Testament text as though the New Testament had not been written. Nor is
it possible to attempt a mediating position whereby the New Testament critique of Jerusalem is acknowledged, but the Old Testament understanding of
the city is somehow allowed to stand, unaltered and unscathed. Christians,
having accepted that the Christ has come, cannot ignore that reality when it
comes to interpreting the Old Testament scriptures. Needless to say, this has
implications for contemporary 'Christian' approaches to Jerusalem, many of
which seem to by-pass the New Testament in their elevation of the Old.

Again, this issue has been dealt with elsewhere.[11] One example, however, of what this means might be helpful. Many would see Ezekiel's expansive vision of the Temple (chs. 40-48) as encouraging a belief that there will
be an end-time Temple matching Ezekiel's prophetic description. Yet a biblical theologian cannot approach this prophecy without noting the way in which
this prophecy is understood by the New Testament writers. Ezekiel's imagery
of the river flowing from the Temple (Ezek. 47:1ff) reappears twice in the
New Testament. In John 7:37-9 the 'rivers of living water' flow from Jesus
himself;[12] meanwhile in Revelation the 'river of the water of life' flows
through the middle of the New Jerusalem (Rev. 22:1ff). These two writers
have consciously drawn upon Ezekiel's prophecy and applied it to Jesus and
the heavenly Jerusalem. As a result, they were presumably not expecting
Ezekiel's prophecy to be fulfilled literally at some future point in a physical
Temple. Instead this prophecy became a brilliant way of speaking pictorially
of what God had now achieved in and through Jesus. Paradoxically, therefore,
although Ezekiel's vision had focused so much upon the Temple, it found its
ultimate fulfilment in that city where there was 'no Temple', because 'its
Temple is the Lord God Almighty and the Lamb' (Rev. 21:22).[13]

---

[11] See *e.g.* C. Chapman (1989); Walker (1996a)

[12] Or possibly, from the Christian believer: see above ch. 5, n. 24.

[13] The same would apply equally to the passages in Isaiah which are also taken up in Rev.
21-22; *cf.* above ch. 7, n. 46ff.

Failure to note such New Testament interpretations will lead to theologies which can scarcely claim to be 'biblical' in any coherent sense. The paradox is that such theologies are often developed by those who desire to be 'biblical' and to acknowledge the authority of both Old and New Testaments; yet in practice, the normative authority of the New is denied.

A credible biblical theology of Jerusalem, therefore, will give great weight to the witness of the New Testament writers—both in their explicit statements, and also in their implicit understanding of the pattern of God's fulfilment in Christ. It will also reckon seriously with the evident contrast between the Old and New Testaments—on this issue, as on many others. There will be a frank acknowledgement that within the overall continuity of the biblical revelation, there are important elements of *dis*continuity. Thus, for example, the ethnocentricity of the Old Testament, whereby the 'people of God' was defined in ethnic and racial terms, gives way in the New to an emphasis on faith as the defining marker of the 'people of God' (*e.g.* Gal. 3; Rom. 4). Or again, the monotheistic thrust of the Old becomes the paradoxical base for the New Testament's witness to God as Trinity (1 Cor. 12:4-6; 2 Cor. 13:13). The struggles caused by these radical new insights can readily be discerned within the pages of the New Testament. Jerusalem needs to be seen in the same light—as an Old Testament reality which was affected by the revelation of God in the New. The Old Testament tradition about the Temple's sanctity and Jerusalem's central role within God's purposes had now been given a new twist—precisely because of what God had done in Jerusalem.

As with these other areas of seeming discontinuity between Old and New Testaments a biblical theology will also need to develop some explanation for this phenomenon. Can an intelligible, underlying continuity within God's purposes be discerned? Much of Paul's theology is concerned with explaining that the new defining marks of the people of God are consistent with God's intention to 'bless all nations' through the 'offspring' of Abraham (Gal. 3:6-18). God's purposes can be discerned to have moved into a new phase within the 'economy' of salvation, yet this novelty is compatible with an eternal purpose. Similar explanations will need to be forged for Jerusalem.

Here too the concept of the 'economy of salvation' proves useful. The author of Hebrews implicitly uses this category when he argues that the Temple's sacrificial system was a necessary and valuable institution, but ultimately temporary. It was indeed God-given and God-ordained, but God himself would take it away. It was part of the 'old covenant' which was soon to 'disappear' (Heb. 8:13), now that the 'new' had come. It was a 'shadow' (8:5) of the reality which had been revealed in Christ.

This can be developed further. Seen in this light Jerusalem and its Temple were always destined to be eclipsed by the revelation of the Messiah and his inauguration of the new covenant. Just as Paul saw the Torah as designed to point the way towards Christ (Gal. 3:24), so too Jerusalem's role was inherently preparatory. When the one came who would offer himself outside its walls as a sacrifice for sin, its sacrificial system would not be required. When the one came who would embody the incarnate presence of God, the true *shekinah* presence, then the Temple as the previous focused location of the divine name would need to be laid aside. When the Spirit came, Jerusalem's role as witnessing to the presence of God in the midst of his people would no longer be necessary. When the time came that the gospel could go out 'to all nations', then the previous particularity associated with Jerusalem would need to give way. When Gentiles could at last enter the 'people of God', then the necessary distinction between Jew and Gentile emblazoned within the Temple would have to be 'broken down'. Finally, when the full revelation of God in Christ was made known and the glories of his heavenly Jerusalem could be glimpsed, then the previous symbolic role of Jerusalem as encapsulating God's final purpose for his world could be seen to have truly fulfilled its purpose.

Such a model in no way denigrates Jerusalem or dismisses its vital role within salvation-history. While open to being pushed in a Marcionite direction, it in itself strongly affirms the value of Jerusalem within God's purposes. Without this divinely sanctioned 'preparation', the revelation of Christ and the Spirit would be largely unintelligible. Yet Jerusalem is more than just a helpful illustration for those who come after. Within this model, it can also be readily affirmed that God was truly at work, revealing himself and blessing people through the Old Testament period, and acting in a way which comports with his activity in the era of the New Covenant. There was a divine presence within Jerusalem, an appointed means of approach through sacrifice, a true vision of God's desire to dwell amongst his people and to form a community around himself. The Jerusalem-associated experiences of the faithful within the Old Testament were not invalid, but were simply localized in a way which now no longer pertains because of the coming of Christ and the Spirit.

This emphasis on the 'economic' transition within God's purposes, however, needs to be balanced in the case of Jerusalem with a theme of judgement. In other words, the critique of Jerusalem within the New Testament is not couched entirely in terms of the 'temporary' now being eclipsed by the 'eternal', or of the 'shadow' giving way to the reality. There is also a clear sense that Jerusalem has lost its sacred status as a result of an act of divine judgement. Indeed, if it were not for Hebrews and John's Gospel (where the focus is more on the 'economic' replacement of the Temple by Christ), this would be the predominant note. Jerusalem is no longer what it was because the time had come for God to reveal his judgement upon it.

It would no doubt be more tactful to ignore this New Testament theme. The fact that Jewish writings after AD 70 (such as 2 Baruch and 4 Ezra) also use this category to explain Jerusalem's fall somehow does not mitigate the fear that such concepts will be mis-applied today. Yet responsible applications can be made. In this respect the assumptions underlying 1 Peter 4:17 are important, where the author acknowledges the reality of divine judgement but insists that his audience must see *themselves* as those to whom it first applies.[14] If the subject is approached with such an attitude of humility and self-critique, then Jerusalem's history is able to impart some of its most valuable lessons.

The prophetic tradition within the Old Testament had frequently denounced Jerusalem's sin and understood its predicaments as being the result of divine judgement. This conceptual framework could hardly have been avoided by anyone, whether Jewish or Christian, when reflecting theologically on Jerusalem in the period before and after 70, and there is good reason for arguing that Jesus himself used it unambiguously and without apology. Just as before in 587 BC, so now Jerusalem was entering a time of judgement, a dramatic encounter with her God.

When analysing Jesus' critique of the city, various reasons were offered.[15] Beneath them all was the theme that Jerusalem was now in different ways working against God's purposes: instead of being a helpful pointer towards God it had become a hindrance; instead of being seen as a gracious gift from God, the gift was being turned against God and used for all-too-human purposes; instead of welcoming God, its attitude was hostile.

Thus the fall of Jerusalem, when set within a biblical theology and mindful of the parallels with 587 BC, speaks of the *divine removal of a divine gift due to human abuse*. The human presumption of God's blessing in the place associated with his promises has so twisted those promises as to render it necessary that they be finally revoked. On this view the story of Jerusalem becomes a pointed paradigm to all generations of the important principle that God's good gifts can be turned against him, that divine promises can be twisted by human pride and presumption, and that arenas of past blessing from God can become centres of human rebellion against him. The 'city of God' could turn against him. Jerusalem, yes even Jerusalem, could become not so distinct from a Babylon (Rev. 11:8; 14:6).

This sombre truth that Jerusalem could become the epitome of the 'world' in its hostility towards God has clearly been grasped by the New Testament writers. It is seen especially in John's Gospel and in Revelation; yet it is also rooted in the Apocalyptic Discourse, where there is a merging between

---

[14] See above p. 311.
[15] See above ch. 8 (2).

Jerusalem and the world and their respective fates. As a result, it becomes legitimate to deduce from the New Testament a further truth, that *the fall of Jerusalem functions theologically as an advance paradigm of the final judgement of the world.* It is a revelation in microcosm of what ultimately awaits us all. It is an event rooted in history which emblazons a truth that should make everyone in subsequent generations take serious note. Contemplation on this event, though located in one time and place, is thus meant to make all people aware of the awesome holiness and reality of the God with whom we have to do: 'it is a fearful thing to fall into the hands of the living God' (Heb. 10:31). If so, there is no cause for presumption or for a judgemental critique of that particular generation, but rather for repentance.

If this is a hard truth, the mystery of the Christian gospel presses us further to note that this divine judgement was borne in advance by the divine Son. As indicated above, Jesus so identified with Jerusalem and its forthcoming fate as to suffer that fate in advance.[16] The Roman soldiers would soon be coming against Jerusalem, but first they would nail Jerusalem's true King to a tree. If it is unpalatable in today's climate to mention the theme of judgement, reflection on Jesus' death may make it that much easier. For he who pronounced judgement was also he who bore it in his own person.

Recognizing the theme of judgement in the events of AD 70 thus opens up a new understanding of the Cross. Indeed, to ignore this context, is to make the crucifixion largely unintelligible at a historical level, and therefore puzzling at a theological level. It also throws an authentic light on the resurrection, which can now be seen as an advance paradigm of the way *through* that judgement. To follow Jerusalem's way was to go down to judgement; to follow Jesus' way was to experience resurrection, to 'pass from death to life' (*cf.* John 5:24). Once the resurrection had occurred, it was only a matter of time, before Jerusalem would be removed. The new chrysalis had been formed.

Jerusalem cannot therefore be understood biblically without a category of divine judgement. Important insights into Jerusalem's are also gained from emphasizing the notion of God's evolving purposes within the 'economy of salvation'. A biblical theology of Jerusalem must hold together in creative tension these twin explanations of its fall: Jerusalem's distinctive role comes to an end in the New Testament period *both* because of God's judgement *and* because of the necessary outworking of God's economy of salvation. Although this mysterious paradox is not easily explained, both these 'levels of causation' need to be affirmed if we are to be true to the New Testament witness.

It is in such ways that a biblical theology of Jerusalem could be developed. Some of the important questions to be addressed within such a theology

---

[16] Above ch. 8 (4).

would include: in the light of the gospel's going out to 'all nations', where is now the 'dwelling-place' of God's 'name'? Who are God's people, and what is the means of access into his presence? Where does 'holiness' truly reside? Even if such questions lead to the denial of the ongoing 'sanctity' of Jerusalem itself, there are still vital and enduring truths to be discovered through noting the city's unique role within salvation-history.

A recent example of this would be Ellul's characteristically perceptive analysis in his book, *The Meaning of the City*, in which the divine endorsement in the Old Testament of Jerusalem, the human city, speaks of God's involvement with, and re-shaping of, all human endeavours, even those which are 'counter-creations' motivated by the desire to escape from God or to rebel against him.[17] What then occurs in the New Testament bears witness to the final truths of God's judgement and her replacement by the heavenly Jerusalem.[18] Yet this does not mean that Jerusalem is unimportant. On the contrary,

> it is in Jerusalem and nowhere else that the final destiny of all mankind is to be decided and the immovable stone of reconstruction and resurrection is to be established. She is there only to disappear, her only truth is in her death. But in her is found the one thing necessary to pass victoriously through judgement and death. But she herself is not that thing. 'I am laying in Zion', says the Lord. It is an act of God.[19]

In this way Jerusalem indeed gains a new and important significance— though not the significance for which some might have hoped. In the era of the New Testament the city's *sign*ificance is at last revealed to be that, simply, of a *sign*. Not only was Jerusalem's fall a sign of God's judgement upon his world and upon human sin, but God's involvement in the city in times past could now be seen as having been pulsed with a forward intention, preparing the way as a sign for that day when the true presence of God would be revealed, the ultimate sacrifice paid, and the nature of the heavenly Jerusalem made clear. Jerusalem was a divine signal to the effect that more was yet in store. It pointed beyond itself to something which it could not by itself produce. When that time then came, though the memory of its history would be forever instructive, the sign would need to give way to the greater reality. The same is true of Jerusalem today.

---

[17] Ellul (1970). This is a most creative work, though clearly bound up with an 'urban theology' which is highly critical of the technological city, seeing it as 'mankind's principal fortress' (p. 132) and his 'bulwark against God' (p. 145).

[18] 'By her very presence she shows the world that there is a final judgement. . . . She must announce final truths, but by doing so she shows that her role is to be replaced. . . . She is nothing if she allows herself to be separated from her eschatological function' (pp. 107-9).

[19] Ellul (1970) 110.

AFTERWORD
Jerusalem in Christian reflection

The shockwaves did not cease with the completion of the New Testament. The question of Jerusalem and how it is to be understood in the light of the coming of Jesus has continued to be a key question within Christian theology and practice ever since.

On the one hand, Christian theology cannot deny the unique role that Jerusalem has played within salvation-history. For reasons both of its prominence within the Old Testament and of its role as the supreme focus of the events associated with the Incarnation, Jerusalem cannot be viewed simply as just another city. Christians are forever 'debtors to Zion'.[1] For as long as history is important, Christians will be in some sense 'tied' to Jerusalem and rooted in its soil. Any attitude which dismisses the physical Jerusalem in the name of 'spiritualisation', would be dangerous: in addition to encouraging a quasi-Marcionite dismissal of the Old Testament and a loss of historical 'rootage', it would lead to an effective denial of Christian belief in divine involvement within the real world. As far as Christians are concerned, the lesson of Jerusalem is precisely the opposite: that by grace God has indeed been involved in this all-too-human city, using it as an integral means of his self-revelation. If this conviction about divine involvement causes subsequent problems, as Christians (in ways not dissimilar to those of Jews and Muslims) have sought to evaluate Jerusalem in their own generation, this does not deny its fundamental importance within a Christian world-view.

On the other hand, the overall conclusion of our analysis of the New Testament is that in the strictest sense of the word, Jerusalem has lost whatever *theological* status it previously possessed. The way the Old Testament ascribes to Jerusalem a special, central and sacred status within the on-going purposes of God is not reaffirmed by the New Testament writers. Instead they see God's purposes as having moved forward into a new era in which the previous emphasis on the city (as well as on the Land and the Temple) is no long-

---

[1]   Chadwick (1966) 25.

er appropriate. The coming of Jesus has been its undoing. An event, which to outsiders might have appeared so minuscule within the long history of this famous city, has had a quite disproportionate effect upon the city. As a result, any subsequent Christian responses which seek to understand Jerusalem without reference to the enormity of Jesus' identity and mission will be significantly awry.

According to this interpretation, therefore, an authentically Christian evaluation of Jerusalem would need to work within these parameters: affirming the historical (and therefore the 'religious') significance of the city, but questioning the ascription to it of any distinctively theological role today. As such, in contrast to the more straightforwardly positive approaches to the city found within Judaism and Islam, there would be within the Christian tradition an inherent ambivalence and tension concerning Jerusalem—in large part, resulting from the tension which exists between the Old and New Testaments.

It would be easy to document that subsequent Christian reflection on Jerusalem has exhibited this tension, being either affirmative or critical of the city at different times.[2] Through the centuries, however, the situation has inevitably been yet further complicated by pragmatic and 'political' factors, as well as by the fact that, contrary to the position outlined here, some Christians have sought to re-invest Jerusalem with an important theological status. This has been done in two quite distinct ways: either by emphasizing the Incarnation, or through a theology of 'restoration'.

A strong case, however, can be made for saying that in the first three centuries of the Christian era the Church continued in the pattern set by the New Testament writers and espoused a predominantly negative approach to the physical Jerusalem of their own day. Thus, after the events of AD 70, and especially after the further destruction of Jerusalem in AD 135, the Church concluded that the functions previously associated with Jerusalem had come to an end. From that time on, Christian theologians agreed that the sacrifices commanded in the Law had been intended as temporary. Meanwhile the Church had spread far from its original home, and the church community in Aelia Capitolina (the new pagan name given to Jerusalem by Hadrian) was in no position to function as a centre or 'mother-church'. Inevitably, therefore, Jerusalem was seen as having little role to play in the present.

In emphasizing the validity of this new state of affairs, however, there was always the temptation to be overly-dismissive of Jerusalem, through discarding the validity of the Old Testament tradition. Even 'orthodox' Christian

---

[2]   Davies (1974), 367, concluded that, with regard to the parallel issues of the Land and holy space, there had been four different responses within the Christian tradition: 'rejection, spiritualisation, historical concern and sacramental concentration'. A full history of Christian involvement in Jerusalem would reveal the same prismatic spread of ideas.

writers in the second century seem to have questioned whether the Temple and its sacrifices had truly been instituted by God. This critical approach to Jerusalem's past was soon pushed to an unacceptable extreme by Marcion and the Gnostics. Within this sphere of thought, the physicality and particularity of Old Testament concerns with Jerusalem and the Temple were dismissed outright: they were the mark of a 'lesser god' than the God revealed in Jesus. Jerusalem thus lost even its historical role within God's purposes; its history was now to be dismissed as having had nothing to do with the Christian God.[3]

Not surprisingly, this led to a reaction. Nevertheless, the fact that the Christian Church in this earliest phase of its existence was prone to this kind of thought is highly significant. It is evidence, though of a negative kind, of how readily it was accepted that Jerusalem's status had been affected by New Testament events.

Orthodox theologians thus had to argue that this simplistic solution of the relationship between the Old and New Testaments (whereby the Old was straightforwardly discarded) was unacceptable. This may help to explain why Justin Martyr, Tertullian and Irenaeus all espoused a form of millenarianism (in which God's final purposes for his people after the 'resurrection of the just' would be focused upon a reign of Christ centred upon Jerusalem).[4] This belief, which perhaps could be traced back through Papias to an early interpretation of the book of Revelation, was a useful buttress against such Gnostic extremes. It affirmed the enduring validity of the Old Testament's prophetic teaching, as well as endorsing the biblical truth that God had good purposes for *this physical world*. Evidently their main concern was to affirm the Old Testament and the underlying consistency of God's purposes. Yet this had the consequence that, for these writers, Jerusalem came to be seen as having a significant role to play within God's purposes—at the end of time.

This is an important point. They were not thinking of Jerusalem in the present, but only of what would happen on the farther side of Christ's return. These writers maintained an essentially negative approach to the Jerusalem of their own day. Particularly instructive is Irenaeus' response to the Gnostic ar-

---

[3] See *e.g.* Norelli (1994), 160ff; C.P. Bammel (1991). *The Epistle of Barnabas* (2; 16) comes close to denying that God had truly ordained the Temple and its sacrifices at all. The Clementine *Recognitions* imply that the institution of sacrifice was a concession to the instinct revealed in the incident of the golden calf (1:36-8, 64). Within Gnostic theory the fall of Jerusalem signified the defeat of the god revealed in the Old Testament; according to Basilides (as recounted in Irenaeus *AH* 1.24.4), this god had sought to make other nations subject to the Jews but only succeeded in arousing their enmity, leading to the city's destruction. In one of the Nag Hammadi texts (NH. 6.4) Jerusalem's fall is even seen as the result of the angry response of angelic powers to the city where Jesus' victorious religion was founded.

[4] See further Wilken (1992), ch. 3.

gument that the fall of Jerusalem indicated that it had never truly been the 'city of the great King' (Matt. 5:35). This is incorrect, replies Irenaeus; Jerusalem *had* possessed this special status, but the contemporary city now must be likened to vine branches which, when they have borne fruit, are cut away.

> The fruit, therefore, having been sown throughout all the world, Jerusalem was deservedly forsaken, and those things which had formerly brought forth fruit abundantly were taken away. . . . Therefore Jerusalem taking its commencement from David and fulfilling its own times, must have an end of legislation, when the new covenant was revealed.[5]

Even if Jerusalem still had some role in the future 'resurrection of the just', this evidently did not give it any special role in the present.

How then could Christians affirm the consistency of the Old and New Testaments, while doing justice to the novelty of the latter? Scholars in the third century such as Origen (c.185-253) and Eusebius (c. 260-339) found ways of doing this which did not require millenarianism. In their treatment of the matter Jerusalem lost whatever eschatological role it might have had. Instead the negative approach concerning Jerusalem in the *present* came to the fore. This is especially interesting since both Origen and Eusebius lived in Caesarea Maritima, Palestine's administrative capital on the coast, and had visited the Jerusalem of their day. Yet for them the New Testament teaching made it clear that this physical Jerusalem was no longer to be regarded as a 'holy city'; its destruction by the Romans and its present sorry state as the refounded city of Aelia clearly manifested that its glory was a thing of the past. Drawing on the teaching of Paul and Hebrews, they asserted that Christian hope was to be focused instead on the 'heavenly Jerusalem'.

Compared with Origen, Eusebius (chiefly remembered for his *Ecclesiastical History*) was more interested in matters of history, and therefore showed a great interest in Jerusalem's past. At least until the coming of Constantine, however, there is no evidence that he allowed this historical concern to cause him to elevate Jerusalem's significance *theologically*.[6] There are thus significant and instructive parallels between his thought and that which, according to our argument here, is to be found in the New Testament.

This approach to Jerusalem came to an end after the year 324, when Constantine's coming to power in the eastern half of the empire opened up the possibility of a new, more positive approach to Jerusalem. An earlier study

---

[5]   Irenaeus, *AH* 4.4.2.

[6]   Thus, writing in the decade before Constantine, he says that any Christians visiting the Mount of Olives should reflect chiefly upon the tragedy and reality of the city's fall: *Demonstratio Evangelica* 6.18.

sought to show the effect of these events on Eusebius' thought in the last fifteen years of his life, and how his views still represent a significant contrast
with those of his younger contemporary, Cyril.[7] It was Cyril who, as bishop
of Jerusalem from 349 to 387, re-introduced the concept of Jerusalem as a 'holy city'. He endorsed Jerusalem's continuing significance on the basis of what
had taken place in the city during the biblical period—not least the Incarnation. Memory fuelled the city's sanctity. Though there were occasional critics
of this new development, such as Gregory of Nyssa,[8] who sensed that the universal nature of spiritual worship under the New Covenant was being compromised by this renewed emphasis on physical place, Cyril's approach left an
enduring legacy which would shape Christian approaches to Jerusalem for
centuries to come— through the era of the Crusades to the present day.[9]

In recent centuries, however, there has developed within the Christian
tradition a second, quite different way of emphasizing the significance of the
contemporary, physical Jerusalem: namely, restorationism. Within this
scheme the driving conviction is not incarnational memory but eschatological
hope: the restoration of Jerusalem according to Old Testament promise. At
first sight this might appear as a modern resurgence of the early 'restorationism' (if that is the proper term) of some of the Apostolic Fathers (see above).
Yet there are important differences. In that earlier period (in contrast to our
own day) the prophecies of 'return' were applied exclusively to Christians,
and then only to that eschatological period after the 'resurrection of the just'.
The argument of this present book is that the New Testament understands
these Old Testament promises of 'restoration' to have been fulfilled in Christ,
and that therefore fulfilments of a different kind are not in accordance with
New Testament expectation.

Thus in the long and varied history of Christian responses to Jerusalem,
one can discern three distinct strands: 1), the approach associated with the
New Testament and continued through the first centuries of the Church's life;
2), the 'incarnational' approach developed in the fourth century; and 3), the
'restorationist' approach of modern times.[10] There are clearly some irreconcilable differences between these view-points. For example, the second and
third approaches may be reactions to the first, as though it is unbearable for
Jerusalem to be passed by, and an overly-negative approach to the city must
be countered by finding some means of emphasizing its importance. Mean-

---

[7] See my (1990a), esp. chs. 2 and 11.
[8] Gregory of Nyssa, *Ep.* 2 (*PG*.46:1012).
[9] A summary presentation of the contrast between Eusebius and Cyril can also be found
in my (1990b), (1994a), 79-98 and (1995).
[10] I have explored further the inter-relation of these three strands in my (1994a), 188-202
and (1996b).

while, if the 'incarnational' approach is largely to be found within the spirituality of those identified with the Orthodox and Catholic traditions, the
'restorationism' approach is almost entirely to be found within the Protestant
wing of the Church. All branches of the Church have thus found ways of re-
affirming the importance of the physical Jerusalem, yet the means of doing so
prove to be quite divergent, if not mutually exclusive.

One of the consequences of this present study, therefore, when seen in
the light of Church history, is to highlight the contrast which exists between
these subsequent, more positive approaches to Jerusalem and the attitude of
the New Testament writers. Furthermore, the New Testament appears to have
an inherent critique of such developments. In other words, over against the
'incarnational' approach, the New Testament asserts that it is possible to have
a high christological doctrine which does not lead to a parallel elevation of Jerusalem (or its 'holy places'); on the contrary, the higher one's christology, the
greater the tragedy of what occurred in Jerusalem and the more logical the
conviction that this 'Christ' could indeed fulfil the previous functions of the
Temple and city in his own person. Meanwhile, over against the restorationist
position, the New Testament betrays clear signs that, contrary to the opinion
of many, this was a vital issue for the apostles, and that they were forced to
the unexpected conclusion that the longed-for 'restoration' of Israel had been
accomplished in Christ. The New Testament cannot therefore be dismissed as
irrelevant, as though it does not speak to these issues. Instead it affirms that to
believe in the enduring validity of the Old Testament or in the supreme truth
of the Incarnation need not necessarily lead to an elevation of Jerusalem in the
present.

The New Testament evidence is sometimes dismissed on other
grounds—because it is the contingent product of its time. Some might wish to
explain the New Testament's approach to Jerusalem as a form of theological
jaundice—a negativity borne of psychological hurt as its writers experienced
an increasing estrangement from the Jerusalem of their day. As such it would
need to be seen as an unfortunate historical 'accident' which in no way should
be treated as normative or be allowed to colour and contaminate subsequent
Christian reflection. This procedure of theological reductionism is always
tempting, and no more so than amongst the thorny issues raised by Jerusalem
today. While a full rebuttal to this approach is beyond the purview of this
present work, Jerusalem's own history may provide some of the strongest evidence against this view. For when one considers the religious and political
tensions which for centuries and to the present day have beset the city precisely because of its supposed theological importance, the still, small, voice of the
New Testament comes as a breath of fresh air.

In the light of the way Jerusalem's 'sanctity' has so often led instead to its seeming desecration, it may not be so sacrilegious to ask the question, together with the New Testament, whether the city is really 'holy' after all. Does this claim to holiness have any genuinely theological basis, or is it a merely human construct? If it was once valid, does that mean that it is always vaild? How much might the history of Jerusalem be understood instead as the chasing after a divine presence that has long since disappeared, a 'glory that has departed' (*cf.* 1 Sam. 4:21; Ezek. 11:23)?

Even though it belongs to antiquity, the New Testament should therefore be allowed to play its appropriate role, highlighting as it does some of the critical issues at stake in this debate. How can Christian spirituality combine an emphasis on its historical indebtedness to Jerusalem with an appropriate emphasis on the 'heavenly Jerusalem'? If there is an inherent contrast between Jesus and Jerusalem, is it possible to elevate both simultaneously? In what way can the city of the crucifixion ever be subsequently glorified? If Christians believe God did something unexpected and surprising in the first century, what should be an appropriate attitude in Jerusalem today towards this 'God of surprises'? Moreover, if Jerusalem's fate warns of how specialness can be abused and the 'holy' desecrated, what are the ways in which this same principle might be at work today—whether in contemporary Jerusalem, in the world-wide Church, or in individual lives? Such questions need to be asked in any generation, but they have a particular urgency now, as Jerusalem continues to be at the centre of so much religious and political debate.[11]

In keeping with the focus of this present study on New Testament issues, however, it is appropriate to close with two motifs, culled from the New Testament itself, which might colour our approaches to Jerusalem today. Reflecting on Jesus' love for Jerusalem and for his people as they experienced oppression under Rome, Tom Wright develops a poignant parallel between Jesus and the Homeric story of Odysseus passing the island of the Sirens. Others before Odysseus had found the exquisite song of the Sirens irresistible, but in then being lured to the island had met a terrible death. Odysseus orders his men to tie him to the crossbeam of his ship's mast and, if he ever appears to desire to be loosed, only to tie him tighter. Despite the agony, his prior decision prevents him from responding to the Sirens' song.

> And so Jesus hung outside his beloved Jerusalem, having listened to the sweet song of liberty that she had been singing to him these many years, and having set his face against it by his own act of obedient will. [For] he was mastered by a deeper love, that saw that political Messiahship would solve

---

[11] For a popular-level presentation of how some of these issues could be worked through in contemporary and practical terms, see my (1996a).

nothing. And now he looks on Jerusalem finally and loves her still, taking on himself in his innocent love the judgement she had merited, becoming in very truth the King of the Jews [and] revealing in the process that all earthly king-doms are as dust and ashes before the Kingdom of God.[12]

It is a powerful picture, which indicates that Jesus expressed his true love for Jerusalem, not by acceding to its agendas, but rather by denying them. Those who follow in his steps and who truly love Jerusalem may similarly have to resist some of the enticements which this city offers.

Yet if the earthly Jerusalem may prove to be a false lodestone by which to compass one's journey, the same is not true of the heavenly Jerusalem. This New Testament vision of God's ultimate future makes it clear that Christians have the task of helping to create societies in this world which will anticipate the 'new Jerusalem'—communities which, without a renewed emphasis on race or geographical pride, allow love, justice and *shalom* to flourish for all. This vision, applicable to societies throughout the world, must also pertain to Jerusalem itself. The old 'city of peace' is not exempt. The supposed sanctity of Jerusalem can be a snare, but the simple awareness that this city has never-theless played a key role within biblical history can only have a positive ef-fect; for it would be ironic if here, of all places, this biblical vision went unheeded.

The New Testament therefore proves to be rich indeed, even if in sur-prising ways, in its reflections on Jerusalem and the consequences of that mes-sage both for Jerusalem and for the Church today. If its authors distanced themselves from those who might eulogize the city, that did not indicate a lack of love for it. On the contrary, they were convinced that in Jerusalem, and no-where else, something radically new and unexpected had occurred, which re-quired all their former realities and loyalties to be re-evaluated and in some cases even to be laid aside. If, as a result, Jerusalem was to some extent de-moted in their thinking, it was only because something greater had now been revealed.

---

[12] Wright (1992b), 32-33.

Abbreviations

AUSS	*Andrews University Seminary Studies*
BETL	Bibliotheca ephemiderum theologicarum lovanensium
BJRL	*Bulletin of the John Rylands Library*
BNTC	Black's New Testament Commentary
BZNW	Beihefte zur Zeitschrift für neutestamentliche Wissenschaft
CBQ	*Catholic Biblical Quarterly*
CBQMS	Catholic Biblical Quarterly Monograph Series
EPTA	*European Pentecostal Theological Assocciation*
ExpT	*Expository Times*
FRLANT	Forschungen zur Religion und Literatur des Alten und Neuen Testaments
FS	Festschrift
GNS	Good News Studies
HTR	*Harvard Theological Review*
ICC	International Critical Commentary
JBL	*Journal of Biblical Literature*
JEH	*Journal of Ecclesiastical History*
JETS	*Journal of the Evangelical Theological Society*
JRS	*Journal of Roman Studies*
JSNT	*Journal for the Study of the New Testament*
JSNTSS	Journal for the Study of the New Testament Supplement Series
JTS	*Journal of Theological Studies*
NAC	New American Commentary
NCB	New Century Bible
NICNT	New International Commentary on the New Testament
NIGTC	New International Greek Testament Commentary
NIV	New International Version
NRSV	New Revised Standard Version
NovT	*Novum Testamentum*
NovT Supp.	Novum Testamentum Supplement
NTS	*New Testament Studies*
RB	*Revue Biblique*
SBT	Studies in Biblical Theology
SBL	Society of Biblical Literature
SBLDS	Society of Biblical Literature Dissertation Series
SNTSMS	Society for New Testament Studies Monograph Series
SNTW	Studies of the New Testament and its World
SJLA	Studies in Judaism in Late Antiquity

SP   Sacra Pagina
ST   *Studia Theologica*
TNTC   Tyndale New Testament Commentary
TPINTC   Trinity Press International New Testament Commentary
TynB   *Tyndale Bulletin*
WBC   Word Biblical Commentary
WUNT   Wissenschaftliche Untersuchungen zum Neuen Testament
ZNW   Zeitschrift für neutestamentliche Wissenschaft

Bibliography

Achtemeier, P.J. *Mark* (Philadelphia: Fortress, **1975**).
    'An Elusive Unity: Paul, Acts and the Early Church', *CBQ* 48 (**1986**) 1-26.
Allison, D.C. 'Matt. 23:39 = Luke 13:35b as a Conditional Prophecy', *JSNT* 18 (**1983**) 75-
    84.
    The New Moses (Edinburgh: T. & T. Clark, **1993**).
Ashton, J. 'The Identity and Function of the Ἰουδαῖοι in the Fourth Gospel', *NovT* 27
    (**1985**) 40-75.
    Understanding the Fourth Gospel (Oxford: OUP, **1991**).
Attridge, H.W. 'Let Us Strive to Enter That Rest: The Logic of Heb. 4:1-11', *HTR* 73
    (**1980**) 279-88.
    The Epistle to the Hebrews (Philadelphia: Fortress, **1989**).
Aus, R.D. 'Three Pillars and Three Patriarchs: A Proposal Concerning Gal. 2:9', *ZNW* 70
    (**1979a**) 252-61.
    'Paul's Travel Plans to Spain', *NovT* 21 (**1979b**) 232-62.
Bachmann, M. *Jerusalem und der Tempel: Die geographisch-theologischen Elemente in
    der lukanischen Sicht des jüdischen Kultzentrums* (Stuttgart: Kohlhammer,
    1980).
Bailey, K. 'The Fall of Jerusalem and Mark's Account of the Cross', *ExpT* 102 (**1990-1**)
    102-5.
Balfour, G. *Is John's Gospel Antisemitic? With Special Reference to Its Use of the Old Tes-
    tament* (unpub'd Ph.D.: Nottingham, **1995**).
Baltzer, K. 'The Meaning of the Temple in the Lukan Writings', *HTR* 58 (**1965**) 263-77.
Bammel, C.P. 'Law and Temple in Origen', in W. Horbury (ed.), *Templum Amicitiae* (FS
    E. Bammel, Sheffield: JSOT, **1991**) 464-476.
Bammel, E. 'Judenverfolgung und Naherwartung: Zur Eschatologie des Ersten Thessalon-
    icherbriefs', *Zeitschrift für Theologie und Kirche* 56 (**1959**) 294-315.
Barclay, J.M. *Obeying the Truth* (Edinburgh: T. & T. Clark, **1988**).
Barnett, P. *Apocalypse Now and Then: Reading Revelation Today* (Sydney: Anglican In-
    formation Office, **1989**).
Barrett, C.K. 'Paul and the "Pillar" Apostles', in J.N. Sevenster and W.C. van Unnik (eds.),
    Studia Paulina (FS J. de Zwaan, Haarlem: Bohn, **1953**) 1-19.
    'The Eschatology of the Epistle to the Hebrews', in W.D. Davies and D. Daube
    (eds.), *The Background of the New Testament and its Eschatology* (FS C.H.
    Dodd, Cambridge: CUP, **1956**) 363-93.
    'Paul's Opponents in 2 Corinthians', *NTS* 17 (**1971**) 233-54.
    'The House of Prayer and the Den of Thieves', in E.E. Ellis and E. Grässer (eds.),
    Jesus und Paulus (FS W.G. Kümmel, Göttingen: Vandenhoeck & Ruprecht,
    1975) 13-20.

'The Allegory of Abraham, Sarah and Hagar in the Argument of Galatians', in J.
    Friedrich, W. Pohlmann and P. Stuhlmacher (eds.), *Rechtfertigung* (FS E.
    Käsemann, Tübingen: Mohr, **1976**) 1-16.
The Gospel According to St John (2nd ed., London: SPCK, **1978**).
'Apostles in Council and in Conflict', *Australian Biblical Review* 31 (**1983**) 14-32.
'Faith and Eschatology in Acts 3', in E. Grässer and O. Merk (eds.), *Glaube und
    Eschatologie* (FS W.G. Kümmel, Tübingen: Mohr, **1985**) 1-17.
The Second Epistle to the Corinthians (BNTC, London: A. & C. Black, **1986**).
'Attitudes Towards the Temple in the Acts of the Apostles', in W. Horbury (ed.),
    Templum Amicitiae (FS E. Bammel, Sheffield: JSOT, **1991**) 345-67.
Barton, G.A. 'The Date of the Epistle to the Hebrews', *JBL* 57 (**1938**) 195-207.
Barton, S.C. *The Spirituality of the Gospels* (London: SPCK, **1992**).
    '"All things to all People": Paul and the Law in the Light of 1 Cor. 9:19-23', in
    J.D.G. Dunn (ed.), *Paul and the Jewish Law* (Tübingen: Mohr, forthcoming,
    1996).
Bassler, J.M. 'The Galatians: A Neglected Factor in Johannine Community Research',
    CBQ 43 (**1981**) 243-57.
Batdorf, I.W. 'Hebrews and Qumran: Old Methods and New Directions', in E.H. Barth &
    R.E. Cocroft (eds.), *Festschrift to Honor F. Wilbur Gingrich* (Leiden: Brill,
    1972) 16-35.
Bauckham, R.J. *Jude, 2 Peter* (WBC, Waco: Word Books, **1983**).
    'Jesus' Demonstration in the Temple', in B. Lindars (ed.), *Law and Religion* (Cam-
    bridge: CUP, **1988a**) 72-89.
'Pseudo-apostolic Letters', *JBL* 107 (**1988b**) 469-94.
Jude, 2 Peter (Word Biblical Themes, Dallas: Word, **1990a**).
Jude and the Relatives of Jesus (Edinburgh: T. & T. Clark, **1990b**).
'The List of the Tribes in Revelation 7 Again', *JSNT* 42 (**1991**) 99-115.
The Climax of Prophecy: Studies on the Book of Revelation (Edinburgh: T. & T.
    Clark, **1993a**).
The Theology of the Book of Revelation (NT Theology, Cambridge: CUP, **1993b**).
'The Parting of the Ways: What Happened and Why', *ST* 47 (**1993c**) 135-151.
'James and the Jerusalem Church', in R.J. Bauckham (ed.), *The Book of Acts in its
    Palestinian Setting* (Grand Rapids/Carlisle: Eerdmans/Paternoster, **1995a**)
    415-480.
'James at the Centre', *EPTA Bulletin* 14 (**1995b**) 23-33.
'For Whom Were the Gospels Written?', in R.J. Bauckham (ed.), *The Gospel for
    All Christians* (forthcoming, **1997**).
Bayer, H.F. 'Christ-Centred Eschatology in Acts 3:17-26', in J.B. Green and M. Turner
    (eds.), *Jesus of Nazareth, Lord and Christ* (FS I.H. Marshall, Grand Rapids/
    Carlisle: Eerdmans/Paternoster, **1994**) 236-50.
Beagley, A.J. *The 'Sitz im Leben' of the Apocalypse with Particular Reference to the Role
    of the Church's Enemies* (Berlin/New York: de Gruyter, **1987**).
Beale, G.K. 'The Use of Daniel in the Synoptic Eschatological Discourse and in the Book
    of Revelation', in D. Wenham (ed.), *Gospel Perspectives: The Jesus Tradi-
    tion Outside the Gospels* (Sheffield: JSOT, **1985**) 129-154.
'Revelation', in D.A. Carson and H.G.M. Williamson (eds.), *It is Written: Scripture
    Citing Scripture* (FS B. Lindars, Cambridge: CUP, **1988**) 318-336.
Beasley-Murray, G.R. *Jesus and the Future* (London: Macmillan, **1954**).
The Book of Revelation (NCB, London: Marshall, Morgan & Scott, **1974**).

John (WBC, Waco: Word, **1987**).

John (Word Biblical Themes, Dallas: Word, **1989**).

Beck, B.E. *'Imitatio Christi* and the Lucan Passion Narrative', in W. Horbury and B. Mc-Neil (eds.), *Suffering and Martyrdom in the New Testament* (FS: G. Styler, Cambridge: CUP, **1981**) 28-47.

Benoit, P. *L'Evangile selon Saint Matthieu* (Paris: Cerf, **1950**).

Berkouwer, G.C. *The Return of Christ* (ET, Grand Rapids: Eerdmans, **1972**).

Best, E. *Following Jesus: Discipleship in the Gospel of Mark* (JSNTSS 4, Sheffield: University of Sheffield, **1981**).

Mark the Gospel as Story (SNTW, Edinburgh: T. & T. Clark, **1983**).

Betori, G. 'Luke 24:47: Jerusalem and the Beginning of the Preaching to the Pagans in the Acts of the Apostles', in G. O'Collins and G. Marconi (eds.), *Luke and Acts* (ET, New York: Paulist, **1993**) 103-120.

Betz, O. '"To Worship God in Spirit and in Truth": Reflections on John 4:20-26', in A. Finkel and L. Frizzell (eds.), *Standing Before God* (FS J.M. Oesterreicher, New York: Ktav, **1981**) 53-72

Blair, E.P. 'Paul's Call to the Gentile Mission', *Biblical Research* 10 (**1965**) 19-33.

Blancehtière, F. and Pritz, R. 'La migration des nazaréens à Pella', in F. Blanchetière and M.D. Herr (eds.), *Aux Origines Juives du Christianisme* (Jerusalem, **1993**).

Blomberg, C.L. *Matthew* (NAC, Nashville: Broadman, **1992**).

Bock, D.L. *Proclamation from Prophecy and Pattern* (JSNTSS 12, Sheffield: JSOT, **1987**).

Boobyer, G.H. 'Galilee and Galileans in St Mark's Gospel', *BJRL* 35 (**1952**) 334-48.

Borg, M.J. 'A New Context for Romans 13', *NTS* 19 (**1972-73**) 205-18.

Conflict, Holiness and Politics in the Teaching of Jesus (Lewiston: Edward Mellen, **1984**).

'Luke 19:42-44 and Jesus as Prophet?', *Forum* 8 (**1992**) 99-112.

Borgen, P. 'Polemic in the Book of Revelation', in C.A. Evans and D.A. Hagner (eds.), *Anti-Semitism and Early Christianity: Issues of Polemic and Faith* (Minneapolis: Fortress, **1993**).

Bornkamm, G. 'The Authority to "Bind" and "Loose" in the Church in Matthew's Gospel', (**1970**) reprinted in Stanton (**1995**) 101-14.

'The Revelation of Christ to Paul', in R. Banks (ed.), *Reconciliation and Hope* (FS L.L. Morris, Exeter: Paternoster, **1974**) 90-103.

Brandon, S.G.F. *The Fall of Jerusalem and the Christian Church* (London: SPCK, **1951**).

Jesus and the Zealots: A Study of the Political Factor in Primitive Christianity (Manchester: MUP, **1967**).

Braumann, G. 'Die lukanische Interpretation der Zerstörung Jerusalems', *NovT* 6 (**1963**) 120-27.

Braun, M.A. 'James' Use of Amos at the Jerusalem Council', *JETS* 20 (**1977**) 113-121.

Braun, F.M. 'L'Evangile de Saint Jean et les grandes traditions d'Israel IV: Moise et l' Exode', *Rev. Thom.* 60 (**1960**) 165-84.

Brawley, R.L. 'Paul in Acts: Lucan Apology and Conciliation', in C. Talbert (ed.), *Luke-Acts: New Perspectives from the Society of Biblical Literature* (New York: Crossroad, **1984**) 129-47.

Luke-Acts and the Jews: Conflict, Apology and Conciliation (Atlanta: Scholars, **1987**).

Brodie, T.L. *The Gospel According to John* (Cambridge: CUP, **1993**).

Brooke, G.J. *Exegesis at Qumran: 4QFlorilegium it its Jewish Context* (Sheffield: JSOT, **1985**).
    'Isaiah 40:3 and the Wilderness Community', in G.J. Brooke (ed.), *New Qumran Texts and Studies* (Paris: Proceedings of the First Meeting of the International Organisations for Qumran Studies, **1992**) 113-132.
Brown, R.E. *The Gospel According to John* (Anchor Bible, 2 vols., Garden City: Double-day, **1966/70**).
    The Community of the Beloved Disciple (New York: Paulist, **1979**).
Bruce, F.F. *The Epistle to the Hebrews* (NICNT, London: Marshall, Morgan & Scott, **1964**).
    'Paul and Jerusalem', *TynB* 19 (**1968**) 3-25.
    1 & 2 Thessalonians (WBC, Waco: Word, 1982a).
    The Epistle to the Galatians (NIGTC, Grand Rapids: Eerdmans, **1982b**).
    'The Church of Jerusalem in the Acts of the Apostles', *BJRL* 67 (**1985**) 641-661.
    'The Apostolic Decree of Acts 15', in W. Schrage (ed.), *Studien zum Texte und zur Ethik des neuen Testaments* (Berlin: de Gruyter, **1986**) 115-24.
    'Hebrews: A Document of Roman Christianity', in W. Haase (ed.), *Aufstieg und Niedergang der römischen Welt* II 25.4 (Berlin: de Gruyter, **1987**) 3496-521.
    'Eschatology in Acts', in W.H. Gloer (ed.), *Eschatology and the New Testament* (FS G.R. Beasley-Murray, Peabody: Hendrickson, **1988**) 51-64.
    The Acts of the Apostles: Greek Text with Introduction and Commentary (revd. ed., Grand Rapids: Eerdmans, **1990**).
    'The Romans Debate—Continued', *BJRL* 64 (1981-2) 334-59, reprinted in K.P. Donfried (**1991**) 175-194.
Buchanan, G.W. 'The Present State of Scholarship on Hebrews', in J. Neusner (ed.), *Christianity, Judaism and Other Greco-Roman Cults* (SJLA 12, FS Morton Smith, Leiden: Brill, **1975**) 299-330.
    Hebrews (Anchor Bible, New York: Doubleday, **1972**).
    Revelation and Redemption (Dillsboro: Western North Carolina Press, **1978**).
Bultmann, R. *Theology of the New Testament* (ET, 2 vols., London: SCM, **1952/55**).
Burge, G.M. *The Anointed Community* (Grand Rapids: Eerdmans, **1987**).
    'Territorial Religion, Johannine Christology, and the Vineyard of John 15', in J.B. Green and M. Turner (eds.), *Jesus of Nazareth: Lord and Christ* (FS I.H. Marshall, Grand Rapids/Carlisle: Eerdmans/Paternoster, **1994**) 384-96.
Burkill, T.A. *Mysterious Revelation* (Cornell University: Ithaca, **1963**).
    New Light on the Earliest Gospel (Ithaca: Cornell, **1972**).
Cadbury, H.J. '"We" and "I" Passages in Luke-Acts', *NTS* 3 (**1956-7**) 128-32.
Caird, G. B. 'Review of Nairne's *The Epistle of Priesthood* (**1913**)', *ExpT* 72 (**1960-61**) 204-6.
    Luke (Pelican, London: A. & C. Black, **1963**).
    Jesus and the Jewish Nation (Ethel Wood Lecture, London: Athlone, **1965**).
    A Commentary on the Revelation of St John the Divine (BNTC, London: A. & C. Black, **1966**).
    'Jesus and Israel: the Starting-Point of New Testament Christology', in R.F. Berkey and S. Edwards (eds.), *Christological Perspectives* (FS H. McArthur, New York: Pilgrims, **1982**) 56-68.
Campbell, K.M. 'The New Jerusalem in Matthew 5:14', *SJT* 31 (**1978**) 335-63.

Carmignac, J. 'Pourquoi Jérémie est-il mentionné en Matthieu 16,14', in G. Jeremias (ed.), *Tradition und Glaube: Das frühe Christentum in seiner Umwelt* (FS K.G. Kuhn, Göttingen: Vandenhoeck & Ruprecht, **1971**) 283-298.

Carson, D.A. 'Matthew', in F. Gaebelein (ed.), *The Expositor's Bible Commentary* 8 (Grand Rapids: Zondervan, **1984**) 3-600.

'Pauline Inconsistency: Reflections on 1 Cor. 9:19-23 and Gal. 2:11-14', *Churchman* 100 (**1986**) 6-45.

'The Purpose of the Fourth Gospel: John 20:31 Reconsidered', *JBL* 106 (**1987**) 639-51.

The Gospel According to John (Leicester: IVP, **1991**).

Carter, W. 'The Crowds in Matthew's Gospel', *CBQ* 55 (**1993**) 54-67.

Catchpole, D.R. 'Paul, James and the Apostolic Decree', *NTS* 23 (**1977**) 428-44.

Chadwick, H. '"All Things to All Men"', *NTS* 1 (**1954-55**) 261.

'The Circle and the Ellipse', in H. Chadwick and H. van Campenhausen, *Jerusalem and Rome* (Philadelphia: Fortress, **1966**) 23-36.

Chance, J.B. *Jerusalem, the Temple and the New Age in Luke-Acts,* (Macon: Mercer University Press, **1988**).

Chapman, C. *Whose Promised Land?* (revd. ed., Tring: Lion, **1989**).

Chapman, D.W. *The Orphan Gospel: Mark's perspective on Jesus* (Sheffield: JSOT, **1993**).

Charles, R.H. *A Critical and Exegetical Commentary on the Revelation of St John* (ICC, 2 vols., Edinburgh: T. & T. Clark, **1920**).

Charlesworth, J.H. *The Beloved Disciple: Whose Witness Validates the Gospel of John?* (Valley Forge: Trinity Press International, **1995**).

Charette, B. *The Theme of Recompense in Matthew's Gospel* (JSNTSS 79, Sheffield: JSOT, **1992**).

Chilton, B. *The Temple of Jesus: His Sacrificial Program within a Cultic History of Sacrifice* (University Park: Pennsylvania State, **1992**).

Chilton, D. *The Days of Vengeance: an Exposition of the Book of Revelation* (Fort Worth: Dominion, **1987**).

Clark, K.W. 'The Gentile Bias in Matthew', *JBL* 66 (**1947**) 165-72.

Clarke, W.K.L. 'The Use of the Septuagint in Acts', in F.J. Foakes-Jackson and K. Lake (eds.), *The Beginnings of Christianity: Part 1* (London: Macmillan, **1922**) ii, 66-105.

Cody, A. *Heavenly Sanctuary and Liturgy in the Epistle to the Hebrews* (St Meinrad: Grail, **1960**).

Conzelmann, H. *The Theology of St. Luke* (ET, London: Faber and Faber, **1960**).

Court, J.M. *Revelation* (NT Guides, Sheffield: JSOT, **1994**).

Cranfield, C.E.B. *The Gospel According to St Mark* (Cambridge: CUP, **1959**).

Romans: A Shorter Commentary (Edinburgh: T. & T. Clark, **1985**).

Cullmann, O. 'A New Approach to the Interpretation of the Fourth Gospel, *ExpT* 71 (**1959-60**) 8-12, 39-43.

The Johannine Circle (ET, London/Philadelphia: SCM/Fortress, **1976**).

Culpepper, R.A. *The Johannine School* (SBLDS 26, Missoula: Scholars, **1975**).

Anatomy of the Fourth Gospel: A Study In Literary Design (Philadelphia: Fortress, **1983**).

John, the Son of Zebedee: the Life of a Legend (Columbia: University of South Carolina, **1994**).

Dahl, N.A. *Studies in Paul* (Minneapolis: Augsburg, **1977**).

Dahms, J. V. 'The First Readers of Hebrews', *JETS* 20 (**1977**) 365-75.

Davies, G.I. 'The Presence of God in the Second Temple and Rabbinic Doctrine', in W. Horbury (ed.), *Templum Amicitiae* (FS E. Bammel, Sheffield: JSOT, **1991**).

Davies, W.D. *The Setting of the Sermon on the Mount* (Cambridge: CUP, **1964**).

    The Gospel and the Land: Early Christianity and Jewish Territorial Doctrine (Berkeley: University of California, **1974**).

    'Paul and the People of Israel', *NTS* 24 (**1978**) 4-39.

    The Territorial Dimensions of Judaism (Minneapolis: Fortress, **1992**).

Davies, W.D. and Allison, D.C. *A Critical and Exegetical Commentary on the Gospel According to Saint Matthew* (ICC, vols. 1 and 2, Edinburgh: T. & T. Clark, **1988/1991**).

De la Potterie, I. 'Les deux noms de Jérusalem dans les Actes des Apôtres', *Biblica* 63 (**1982**) 153-87.

De Young, J.C. *Jerusalem in the New Testament* (Amsterdam: J.H. Kok/N.V. Kampen, **1960**).

Delitzsch, F. *Commentary on the Epistle to the Hebrews* (2 vols., Edinburgh: T. & T. Clark, **1871**).

Derrett, J.D.M., 'The Zeal of the House and the Cleansing of the Temple', *Downside Review* 95 (**1977**) 79-94.

Dodd, C.H. 'The Fall of Jerusalem and the Abomination of Desolation', *JRS* 37 (**1947**) 47-5, reprinted in his *More New Testament Studies* (Manchester: MUP, **1968**) 69-83.

    According to the Scriptures (London: Nisbet & Co., **1952**).

    Historical Tradition in the Fourth Gospel (Cambridge: CUP, **1963**).

Donaldson, T.L. 'Moses Typology and the Sectarian Nature of Early Christian Anti-Judaism: A Study in Acts 7', *JSNT* 12 (**1981**) 27-52.

    Jesus on the Mountain: A Study in Matthean Theology (JSNTSS 8, Sheffield: JSOT, **1985**).

    '"Riches for the Gentiles" (Rom. 11:12): Israel's Rejection and Paul's Gentile Mission', *JBL* 112 (**1993**) 81-98.

Donfried, K.P. 'Paul and Judaism: 1 Thess 2:13-16 as a Test Case', *Interpretation* 38 (**1984**) 242-53.

    (ed.) *The Romans Debate* (revd. ed., Edinburgh: T. & T. Clark, **1991**).

Drury, J. *Tradition and Design in Luke's Gospel: A Study in Early Christian Historiography* (London: DLT, **1976**).

Dumbrell, W.J. *The End of the Beginning: Revelation 21-22 and the Old Testament* (Grand Rapids: Baker, **1985**).

Dungan, D. *The Sayings of Jesus in the Churches of Paul* (Oxford: Basil Blackwell, **1971**).

Dunn, J.D.G. *Unity and Diversity in the New Testament* (London: SCM, **1977**).

    'Paul and Jerusalem according to Galatians 1 and 2', *NTS* 28 (**1982**) 461-78.

    Romans (WBC, 2 vols., Waco: Word, **1988**).

    Jesus, Paul and the Law (London: SPCK, **1990**).

    The Partings of the Ways (London: SCM, **1991a**).

    'Let John be John: A Gospel for its Time', in P. Stuhlmacher (ed.), *The Gospel and the Gospels* (ET, Grand Rapids: Eerdmans, **1991b**).

    The Epistle to the Galatians (BNTC, London: A. & C. Black, **1993a**).

    Theology of Paul's Letter to the Galatians (NT Theology, Cambridge: CUP, **1993b**).

Edmundson, G. *The Church in Rome in the First Century* (Bampton Lectures, London: Longmans, **1913**).

Edwards, J.R. 'Markan Sandwiches: The Significance of Interpolations in Markan Narratives', *NovT* 31 (**1989**) 193-216.

Egelkraut, H.L. *Jesus' Mission to Jerusalem : A Redactional-Critical Study of the Travel Narrative in the Gospel of Luke* (Bern/Frankfurt: H. & P. Lang, **1976**).

Ellingworth, P. *The Epistle to the Hebrews* (London: Epworth, **1991**).

    Commentary on Hebrews (NIGTC, Grand Rapids/Carlisle: Eerdmans/Paternoster, **1993**).

Elliott, J.H. *A Home for the Homeless: A Sociological Exegesis of 1 Peter, Its Situation and Strategy* (Philadelphia: Fortress, **1981**).

Elliott, J.K. 'Jerusalem in Acts and the Gospels', *NTS* 23 (**1977**) 462-69.

Ellis, E.E. *The Gospel of Luke* (NCB, Greenwood: Attic, **1974**).

Ellul, J. *The Meaning of the City* (Grand Rapids: Eerdmans, **1970**).

Emerton, J.A. 'The Hundred and Fifty-Three Fishes in John xxi.11', *JTS* 9 (**1958**) 86-9.

Enz, J.J. 'The Book of Exodus as a Literary Type of the Gospel of John', *JBL* 76 (**1957**) 208-15.

Esler, P.F. *The Community and the Gospel in Luke-Acts* (Cambridge: CUP, **1987**).

Evans, C.A. '"He Set His Face": A Note on Luke 9:51', *Biblica* 63 (**1982**) 544-8.

    '"He Set His Face": Luke 9:51 Once Again', *Biblica* 68 (**1987**) 80-84.

    'Jesus' Action in the Temple: Cleansing or Portent of Destruction?', *CBQ* 51 (**1989**) 237-270.

    Word and Glory: On the Exegetical and Theological Background of John's Prologue (JSNTS 89, Sheffield: JSOT, **1993a**).

    'Jesus and the "Cave of Robbers": Towards a Jewish Context for the Temple Action', *Bulletin of Biblical Research* 3 (**1993b**) 93-110.

Evans, C.A. and Sanders, J.A. *Paul and the Scriptures of Israel* (JSNTSS 83, Sheffield: JSOT, **1993**).

Evans, C.F. '"I Will Go Before You Into Galilee"', *JTS* 5 (**1954**) 3-18.

    'The Central Section of St. Luke's Gospel', in D.E. Nineham (ed.), *Studies in the Gospels* (FS R.H. Lightfoot, Oxford: Blackwell, **1955**) 37-53.

Fee, G.D. 'On the Text and Meaning of John 20:30-31', in F. van Segbroech *et al* (eds.), *The Four Gospels* (FS F. Neirynck, Leuven: LUP, **1992**) 2193-2206.

Filson, F.V. *A Commentary on the Gospel according to St Matthew* (BNTC, London: A. & C. Black, **1960**).

    Yesterday: A Study of Hebrews in the Light of Chapter 13 (SBT 4, London: SCM, **1967**).

    'The Journey-Motif in Luke Acts', in W.W. Gasque & R.P. Martin (eds.), *Apostolic History and the Gospel* (FS F.F. Bruce, Grand Rapids: Eerdmans, **1970**) 68-77.

Fitzmyer, J.A. *The Gospel According to Luke* (Anchor Bible, 2 vols., Garden City: Doubleday, **1981/1985**).

    Luke the Theologian (London: G. Chapman, **1989**).

Flender, H. *St. Luke: Theologian of Redemptive History* (ET, London: SPCK, **1967**).

Flusser, D. *Jesus* (Jerusalem: Magnes, **1996**).

Ford, J.M. *Revelation* (Anchor Bible, Garden City: Doubleday, **1975**).

    'The Heavenly Jerusalem and Orthodox Judaism', in E. Bammel, C.K. Barrett and W.D. Davies (eds.), *Donum Gentilicium* (FS D. Daube, Oxford: Clarendon, **1978**) 215-226.

Fortna, R.T. 'Theological Use of Locale in the Fourth Gospel', in M. Shepherd and E.C. Hobbs (eds.), *Anglican Theology Review* (Supp. Ser. 3, FS S.E. Johnson, **1974**) 58-95.

 The Fourth Gospel and Its Predecessors (Philadelphia: Fortress, **1988**).

France, R.T. *Jesus and the Old Testament: His Application of Old Testament Passages to Himself and his Mission* (London: Tyndale, **1971**).

 'Old Testament Prophecy and the Future of Israel', *TynB* 26 (**1975**) 53-78.

 'The Formula Quotations of Matthew 2 and the Problem of Communication', *NTS* 27 (**1980-1**) 233-51.

 The Gospel According to Matthew (TNTC, Leicester: IVP, **1985**).

 Matthew: Evangelist and Teacher (Exeter: Paternoster, **1992**).

Franklin, E. *Christ the Lord* (Philadelphia: Westminster, **1975**).

Freedman, H. and Simon, M. (ed.), *Midrash Rabba* (London: Soncino, **1939**).

Freudmann, L.C. *Anti-Semitism in the New Testament* (Lanham: University Press of America, **1994**).

Freyne, S. 'Locality and Doctrine: Mark and John Revisited', in F. van Segboech *et al* (eds.), *The Four Gospels* (FS F. Neirynck, Leuven: LUP, **1992**) 1889-1900.

Fuller, R.H. *A Critical Introduction to the New Testament* (London: Duckworth, **1966**).

Furnish, V.P. *Jesus According to Paul* (Cambridge: CUP, **1993**).

Fusco, V. 'Luke-Acts and the Future of Israel', *NovT* 38 (**1996**) 1-17.

Garland, D.E. *The Intention of Matthew 23* (NovT Supp. 52, Leiden: Brill, **1979**).

Garrow, A.J.P. *'What Is and What Is to Come': The Serialized Story in the Book of Revelation* (unpub'd M. Phil. thesis: Coventry University, **1994**).

 Revelation (NT Readings, London: Routledge, forthcoming, **1997**).

Gärtner, B. *The Temple and the Community in Qumran and the New Testament* (Cambridge: CUP, **1965**)

Gasque, W.W. 'A Fruitful Field: Recent Study of the Acts of the Apostles', *Interpretation* 42 (**1988**) 117-31.

Gaston, L. *No Stone on Another: Studies in the Significance of the Fall of Jerusalem in the Synoptic Gospels* (NovT Supp. 23, Leiden: Brill, **1970**).

 'Paul and Jerusalem', in P. Richardson and J.C. Hurd (eds.), *From Jesus to Paul* (FS F.W. Beare, Waterloo: Wilfrid Laurier University, **1984**) 61-72.

Geddert, T.J. *Watchwords: Mark 13 in Markan Eschatology* (Sheffield: JSOT, **1989**).

Gentry, K.L. *Before Jerusalem Fell: Dating the Book of Revelation* (Texas: Tyler, **1989**).

George, T. *Galatians* (NAC, Nashville: Broadman, **1994**).

Georgi, D. *The Opponents of Paul in Second Corinthians* (Philadelphia: Fortress, **1986**).

 Remembering the Poor (ET, Nashville: Abingdon, **1992**).

Gerhardsson, B. *Memory and Manuscript* (Lund: Gleerup, **1961**).

 The Testing of God's Son (Lund: Gleerup, **1966**).

Giblin, C.H. *The Destruction of Jerusalem According to Luke's Gospel*, (Analecta Biblica 107, Rome: Biblical Institute, **1985**).

Giesbrecht, H. 'The Evangelist John's Concept of the Church', *EQ* 58 (**1986**) 101-119.

Gill, D. 'Observations on the Lukan Travel Narrative and Some Related Passages', *HTR* 63 (**1970**) 199-221.

Glasson, T.F. *Moses in the Fourth Gospel* (SBT 40; London: SCM, **1963**).

Gordon, R.P. 'Better Promise', in W. Horbury (ed.), *Templum Amicitiae* (JSNTSS 48, Sheffield: JSOT, **1991**) 434-49.

Goulder, M. *A Tale of Two Missions* (London: SCM, **1994**).

Grappe, C. *D'un Temple à l'autre* (Paris: Presses universitaires de France, **1992**).

Green, J.B. 'The Death of Jesus and the Rending of the Temple Veil (Luke 23: 44-49): A Window into Luke's Understanding of Jesus and the Temple', *SBL 1991 Seminar Papers* (Atlanta: Scholars, **1991**) 543-57.

    The Theology of the Gospel of Luke (NT Theology, Cambridge: CUP, **1995**).

Grigsby, B. '*Gematria* and John 21—Another Look at Ezekiel 47:10', *ExpT* 95 (**1993-4**) 177-8.

Grudem, W.A. *1 Peter* (TNTC, Leicester: IVP, **1988**).

Guelich, R.A. *Mark 1-8:26* (WBC, Dallas: Word Books, **1989**).

Guilding, A. *The Fourth Gospel and Jewish Worship* (Oxford: Clarendon, **1960**).

Gundry, R.H. '"In My Father's House Are Many Μοναί"' (John 14:2)', *ZNW* 58 (**1967**) 68-72.

    'The New Jerusalem: People as Place, not Place for People', *NovT* 29 (**1987**) 254-264.

    Matthew: A Commentary on His Handbook for a Mixed Church under Persecution (2nd ed., Grand Rapids: Eerdmans, **1994**).

    Mark: A Commentary on His Apology for the Cross (Eerdmans: Grand Rapids, **1993**).

Guthrie, D. *Galatians* (NCB, revd. ed., London: Oliphants, **1974**).

    Hebrews (TNTC, Leicester: IVP, **1983**).

Haenchen, E. *The Acts of the Apostles* (ET, Philadelphia: Westminster, **1971**).

    John (ET, 2 vols., Philadelphia: Fortress, **1984**).

Hagner, D.A. 'Interpreting the Epistle to the Hebrews', in M.A. Inch and C.H. Bullock (eds.), *The Literature and Meaning of Scripture* (Grand Rapids: Baker, **1981**) 217-42.

    Hebrews (NIBC, Peabody: Hendrickson, **1983**).

    'Paul's Quarrel with Judaism', in C.A. Evans and D.A. Hagner (eds.), *Anti-Semitism and Early Christianity: Issues of Polemic and Faith* (Minneapolis: Fortress, **1993**) 128-50.

    Matthew (WBC, 2 vols., Dallas: Word, **1993/5**).

Hammerton-Kelly, R.G. *The Gospel and the Sacred: Poetics of Violence in Mark* (Minneapolis: Fortress, **1994**).

Hansen, G.W. *Galatians* (Downers Grove: IVP, **1994**).

Hare, D.R.A. *The Theme of Jewish Persecution of Christians in the Gospel According to St. Matthew* (SNTSMS 6, Cambridge: CUP, **1967**).

Hare, D.R.A. and Harrington, D.J. '"Make Disciples of All the Gentiles" (Matt. 28:19)', *CBQ* 37 (**1975**) 359-69.

Harrington, D.J. *Paul on the Mystery of Israel* (Collegeville: Michael Glazier, **1992**).

Harrington, W.J. *The Apocalypse of St John: A Commentary* (Washington: Corpus, **1969**).

    Revelation (SP, Collegeville: Liturgical, **1993**).

Hartman, L. 'He Spoke of the Temple of His Body', *Svensk Exegetisk Årsbok* 54 (**1989**) 70-79.

Hastings, A. *Prophet and Witness in Jerusalem* (London: Longmans, **1958**).

Hawthorne, G.F. *Philippians* (WBC, Waco: Word, **1987**).

Hays, R.B. *Echoes of Scripture in the Letters of Paul* (New Haven: Yale University, **1989**).

Head, P.M. 'Restoration Prophecies and New Testament Fulfilment: A Case Study in Matt. 1-4', unpublished paper delivered at Tyndale Fellowship Conference (**1994**).

Helyer, L.R. 'Luke and the Restoration of Israel', *JETS* 36.3 (**1993**) 317-29.

Hemer, C.J. *The Letters to the Seven Churches of Asia in Their Local Setting* (JSNTSS 11, Sheffield; JSOT, **1986**).

The Book of Acts in the Setting of Hellenistic History (ed. C.H. Gempf, Tübingen: Mohr, **1989**).

Hengel, M. *Victory Over Violence* (ET, London: SPCK, **1975**).

Studies in the Gospel of Mark (ET, Philadelphia: Fortress, **1985**).

The Johannine Question (ET, London: SCM, **1989a**).

The Zealots: Investigations into the Jewish Freedom Movement in the Period from Herod I until 70 AD (ET, Edinburgh: T. & T. Clark, **1989b**).

The Pre-Christian Paul (ET, London: SCM, **1991**).

'The Geography of Palestine in Acts', in R.J. Bauckham (ed.), *The Book of Acts in its Palestinian Setting* (Grand Rapids/Carlisle: Eerdmans/Paternoster, **1995**) 27-78.

Héring, J. *The Epistle to the Hebrews* (London: Epworth, **1970**).

Hill, C.C. *Hellenists and Hebrews: Reappraising Division within the Earliest Church* (Minneapolis: Fortress, **1992**).

Holl, K. 'Der Kirchenbegriff des Paulus in seinem Verhältnis zu dem der Urgemeinde', in K. Holl (ed.), *Gesammelte Aufsätze zur Kirchengeschichte* (Tübingen: Mohr, **1928**) ii, 44-67.

Holmberg, B. *Paul and Power: The Structure of Authority in the Primitive Church as Reflected in the Pauline Epistles* (Lund: Gleerup, **1978**).

Holwerda, D.E. *Jesus and Israel: One Covenant or Two?* (Grand Rapids/Leicester: Eerdmans/Apollos, **1995**).

Hooker, M.D. 'Traditions about the Temple in the Sayings of Jesus', *BJRL* 70 (**1988**) 7-19.

St Mark (BNTC, London: A. & C. Black, **1991**).

Horbury, W. 'Land, Sanctuary and Worship', in J.M. Barclay and J.P.M. Sweet (eds.), *Early Christian Thought in Its Jewish Context* (Cambridge: CUP, **1996**) 207-224.

Horsley, R.A. *Jesus and the Spiral of Violence: Popular Jewish Resistance in Roman Palestine* (Harper & Row: San Francisco, **1987**).

Horton, F.L. *The MelchizedekTradition* (SNTSMS 30, Cambridge: CUP, **1976**).

Hoskyns, E.C. *The Fourth Gospel* (ed. F.N. Davey, 2 vols., London: Faber and Faber, **1940**).

Howard, G. *Paul's Crisis in Galatia* (SNTSMS 35, Cambridge: CUP, **1979**).

Hughes, P.E. *A Commentary on the Epistle to the Hebrews* (Grand Rapids: Eerdmans, **1977**).

The Book of the Revelation (Grand Rapids/Leicester: Eerdmans/IVP, **1990**).

Hurst, L.D. *The Epistle to the Hebrews: Its Background of Thought* (Cambridge: CUP, **1990**).

Hurtado, L.W. 'The Jerusalem Collection and the Book of Galatians', *JSNT* 5 (**1979**) 46-62.

Isaacs, M.E. *Sacred Space: An Approach to the Theology of the Epistle to the Hebrews* (JSNTSS 7, Sheffield: JSOT, **1992**).

Jansen, H.L. 'Typology in the Gospel of John', in P. Borgen (ed.), *The Many and the One* (FS H.L. Jansen, Trondheim: Tapir, **1985**) 125-43.

Jeremias, J. *Jerusalem in the Time of Jesus* (ET, London: SCM, **1969**).

Jervell, J. *Luke and the People of God* (Minneapolis: Augsburg, **1972**).

Jewett, R. 'Agitators and the Galatian Congregation', *NTS* 17 (**1970-1**) 198-212.

Johnson, L.T. 'The Lukan Kingship Parable (Luke 19:11-27)', *NovT* 24 (**1982**) 139-159.

Luke (SP, Collegeville: Liturgical, **1991**).

Acts (SP, Collegeville: Liturgical, **1992**).

Johnsson, W.G. 'The Pilgrimage: A Motif in the Book of Hebrews', *JBL* 97 (**1978**) 239-51.

Jones, P.R. 'The Figure of Moses as a Heuristic Device for Understanding the Pastoral Intent of Hebrews', *Review and Expositor* 76 (**1979**) 95-102.

Juel, D. *Messiah and Temple: The Trial of Jesus in the Gospel of Mark* (SBLDS 31, Missoula: Scholars, **1977**).

Kaiser, W.C. 'The Davidic Promise and the Inclusion of the Gentiles (Amos 9:9-15 and Acts 15:13-18)', *JETS* 20 (**1977**) 97-111.

Käsemann, E. *The Wandering People of God* (ET, Minneapolis: Augsburg, **1984**).

Kazmierski, C.R. *Jesus, the Son of God: A Study of the Markan Tradition and Its Redaction by the Evangelist* (Würzburg: Echter Verlag, **1979**).

Keathley, N.A. 'The Temple in Luke-Acts', in N.A. Keathley (ed.), *With Steadfast Purpose* (FS H.J. Flanders, Waco: Baylor University, **1990**) 77-105.

Keck, L.E. 'The Poor Among the Saints in the New Testament', *ZNW* 56 (**1965**) 100-29.

Kee, H.C. 'The Function of Scriptural Quotations and Allusions in Mark 11-16', in E.E. Ellis (ed.), *Jesus und Paulus* (FS W.G. Kümmel, Göttingen: Vandenhoeck & Ruprecht, **1975**) 165-187.

　Community of the New Age: Studies in Mark's Gospel (Philadelphia: Westminister, **1977**).

Kelber, W.H. *The Kingdom in Mark: A New Place and a New Time* (Philadelphia: Fortress, **1974**).

　'Conclusion: From Passion Narrative to Gospel', in W.H. Kelber (ed.), *The Passion in Mark: Studies on Mark 14-16* (Philadelphia: Fortress, **1976**) 153-180.

Kiddle, M. *The Revelation of St. John* (Moffatts, London: Hodder and Stoughton, **1940**).

Kilgallen, J. *The Stephen Speech* (Analecta Biblica 67, Rome: Biblical Institute, **1976**).

Kim, S. *The Origin of Paul's Gospel* (2nd ed., Tübingen: Mohr, **1984**).

Kingsbury, J.D. *The Christology of Mark's Gospel* (Philadelphia: Fortress, **1983**).

　Matthew as Story (2nd ed., Philadelphia: Fortress, **1988**).

Klassen, W. 'To the Hebrews or Against the Hebrews? Anti-Jewishness and the Epistle to the Hebrews', in S.G. Wilson (ed.), *Anti-Judaism in Early Christianity* (Waterloo: Wilfrid Laurier University, **1986**) 1-16.

Klijn, A.F.J. *De Brief aan de Hebreeën* (Nijkerk: Callenbach, **1975**).

Knibb, M.A. 'The Exile in the Literature of the Intertestamental Period', *Heythrop Journal* 17 (**1976**) 253-272.

Knowles, M. *Jeremiah in Matthew's Gospel* (JSNTSS 68, Sheffield: JSOT, **1993**).

Knox, J. *Chapters in a Life of Paul* (revd. ed., London: SCM, **1987**).

Knox, W.L. *St Paul and the Church of Jerusalem* (Cambridge: CUP, **1925**).

Kodell, J. '"The Word of God grew." The Ecclesial Tendency of Λόγος in Acts 6:7, 12:24; 19:20', *Biblica* 55 (**1974**) 505-19.

Koester, C.R. *The Dwelling of God: The Tabernacle in the Old Testament, Intertestamental Jewish Literature, and the New Testament* (CBQMS 22, Washington: Catholic Biblical Association of America, **1989**).

　Symbolism in the Fourth Gospel (Minneapolis: Fortress, **1995**).

Koester, H. 'Outside the Camp: Hebrews 13:9-14', *HTR* 53 (**1962**) 300.

　Introduction to the New Testament (Philadelphia, Fortress, **1982**).

Kümmel, W.G. *Introduction to the New Testament* (ET, London: SCM, **1975**).

Kynes, W.L. *A Christology of Solidarity: Jesus as the Representative of His People in Matthew* (Lanham: University Press of America, **1991**).

Kysar, R. *The Fourth Evangelist and His Gospel: An Examination of Contemporary Scholarship* (Minneapolis: Augsburg, **1975**).

'The Fourth Gospel: A Report on Recent Research', in H. Temporini and W. Haase (eds.), *Aufstieg und Niedergang der römischen Welt* II 25.3 (Berlin: de Gruyter, **1985**) 2389-2480.

'Antisemitism in the Gospel of John', in C.A. Evans and D.A. Hagner (eds.), *Antisemitism and Early Christianity: Issues of Polemic and Faith* (Minneapolis: Fortress, **1993**) 113-27.

Lacomara, A. 'Deuteronomy and the Farewell Discourse', *CBQ* 36 (**1974**) 65-84.

Lampe, G.W.H. *St Luke and the Church of Jerusalem* (London: Athlone, **1969**).

'AD 70 in Christian Reflection', in E. Bammel and C.F.D. Moule (eds.), *Jesus and the Politics of His Day* (Cambridge: CUP, **1984**) 153-172.

Lane, W.L. *The Gospel According to St Mark* (NICNT, Eerdmans: Grand Rapids, **1974**).

Hebrews: A Call to Commitment (Peabody: Hendrickson, **1985**).

Hebrews (WBC, 2 vols., Dallas: Word, **1991**).

Lane, W.L. and Wall, R.W. 'Polemic in Hebrews and the Catholic Epistles', in C.A. Evans and D.A. Hagner (eds.), *Anti-Semitism and Early Christianity: Issues of Polemic and Faith* (Minneapolis: Fortress, **1993**) 166-98.

Larsson, E. 'Temple-Criticism and the Jewish Heritage', *NTS* 39 (**1993**) 379-95.

Légasse, S. 'L'antijudaïsme dans l'Evangile selon Matthieu', in M. Didier (ed.), *L'Evangile selon Matthieu: Rédaction et théologie* (BETL, Gembloux: Duculot, **1972**) 417-28.

Lehne, S. *The New Covenant in Hebrews* (JSNTSS 44, Sheffield: JSOT, **1990**).

Lemcio, E.E. *The Past of Jesus in the Gospels* (SNTSMS 68, Cambridge: CUP, **1991**).

Levenson, J.D. *Sinai and Zion* (Minneapolis: Winston, **1985**).

Levine, A-J. *The Social and Ethnic Dimensions of Matthean Salvation History* (Lewiston: Edward Mellen, **1988**).

Lightfoot, J.B. *Biblical Essays* (London: Macmillan, **1893**).

Lightfoot, R.H. *Locality and Doctrine in the Gospels* (London: Hodder and Stoughton, **1938**).

St. John's Gospel: A Commentary (Oxford: Clarendon, **1956**).

Lincoln, A.T. *Paradise Now and Not Yet* (SNTSMS 43, Cambridge: CUP, **1981**).

Ephesians (WBC, Dallas: Word, **1990**).

Lindars, B. *The Gospel of John* (NCB, London: Oliphants, **1972**).

'The Rhetorical Structure of Hebrews', *NTS* 35 (**1989**) 382-406.

The Theology of the Letter to the Hebrews (NT Theology, Cambridge: CUP, **1991a**).

'Hebrews and the Second Temple', in W. Horbury (ed.), *Templum Amicitiae* (JSNTSS 48, Sheffield: JSOT, **1991b**) 410-33.

Loader, W.G. *Sohn und Hoherpriester* (Neukirchen-Vluyn: Neukirchener, **1981**).

Lohmeyer, E. *Galiläa und Jerusalem* (FRLANT 34, Göttingen: Vandenhoeck & Ruprecht, **1936**).

Lohse, E. 'Zion-Jerusalem in the New Testament', in G.W. Bromiley (ed.), *Theological Dictionary of the New Testament* (vol. 7., ET, Grand Rapids: Eerdmans, **1971**) 327-338.

Longenecker, B. 'Different Answers to Different Issues: Israel, Gentiles, and Salvation History in Romans 9-11', *JSNT* 36 (**1989**) 95-123.

2 Esdras (Sheffield: SAP, **1995**).

Longenecker, R.N. *Paul, Apostle of Liberty* (New York: Harper & Row, **1964**).

'On the Concept of Development in Pauline Thought', in K.S. Kantzer and S.N. Gundry (eds.), *Perspectives in Evangelical Theology* (Grand Rapids: Baker, **1979**) 179-207.

'The Nature of Paul's Early Eschatology', *NTS* 31 (**1985**) 85-95.

Galatians (WBC, Dallas: Word, **1990**).

Lowe, M. 'Who Were the Ἰουδαῖοι?', *NovT* 18 (**1976**) 101-30.

Lüdemann, G. *Opposition to Paul in Jewish Christianity* (Minneapolis: Fortress, **1989**).

Lupieri, E. 'Dalla Storia al mito la Distruzione di Gerusalamme in alcune apocalissi degli anni 70-135', in P. Sacchi (ed.,) *Il Guidaismo Palestinese: dal 1 secolo a.C. a 1 secolo d.C.* (Rome: Associazone Italiana per lo Studio del Guidaismo, **1993**).

Luz, U. *Matthew 1-7: A Commentary* (ET, Minneapolis: Augsburg, **1989**).

Maddox, R. *The Purpose of Luke-Acts* (Edinburgh: T. & T. Clark, **1982**).

Maile, J. 'The Ascension in Luke-Acts', *TynB* 37 (**1986**) 29-60.

Mánek, J. 'The New Exodus in the Book of Luke', *NovT* 2 (**1957**) 8-23.

Manson, W. *The Epistle to the Hebrews* (London: Hodder & Stoughton, **1951**).

Marcus, J. 'The Jewish War and the *Sitz im Leben* of Mark', *JBL* 111 (**1992**) 441-62.

The Way of the Lord: Christological Exegesis of the Old Testament in the Gospel of Mark (Edinburgh: T. & T. Clark, **1993**).

Marshall, I.H. *The Epistles of John* (NICNT, Grand Rapids: Eerdmans, **1978**).

Acts (TNTC, Leicester: IVP, 1980).

1 & 2 Thessalonians (NCB, London: Marshall, Morgan & Scott, **1983**).

'The Church and the Temple in the New Testament', *TynB* 40 (**1989**) 203-22.

An Introduction to Acts (Sheffield: JSOT, **1992**).

'Acts and the "Former Treatise"', in B.W. Winter and A.D. Clarke (eds.), *The Book of Acts in its Ancient Literary Setting* (Grand Rapids/Carlisle: Eerdmans/Paternoster, **1993**) 163-82.

Martin, R.P. *2 Corinthians* (WBC, Waco: Word, **1986**).

New Testament Foundations (Grand Rapids: Eerdmans, **1978**).

Martinez, F.G. *The Dead Sea Scrolls Translated* (ET, Leiden: Brill, **1994**).

Marxsen, W. *Mark the Evangelist: Studies on the Redaction History of the Gospel* (Abingdon: Nashville, **1969**).

Mason, S. *Josephus and the New Testament* (Peabody: Hendrickson, **1992**).

Matera, F.J. *What Are They Saying About Mark?* (New York: Paulist, **1987**).

'The Prologue as the Interpretative Key to Mark's Gospel', *JSNT* 34 (**1988**) 3-20.

Mauser, U. *Christ in the Wilderness: The Wilderness Theme in the Second Gospel and its Basis in the Biblical Tradition* (SBT 39, Naperville: Allenson, **1963**).

Mazzaferri, F.D. *The Genre of the Book of Revelation from a Source-Critical Perspective* (BZNW 54, Berlin/New York: de Gruyter, **1989**).

McCaffrey, J. *The House with Many Rooms: The Temple Theme of Jn. 14, 2-3* (Rome: Pontifical Biblical Institute, **1988**).

McHugh, J. 'In Him Was Life: John's Gospel and the Parting of Ways', in J.D.G. Dunn (ed.), *Jews and Christians* (WUNT 66, Tübingen: Mohr, **1992**) 123-58.

McKelvey, R.J. *The New Temple: The Church in the New Testament* (Oxford: OUP, **1969**).

McKnight, S. 'A Loyal Critic: Matthew's Polemic with Judaism in Theological Perspective', in C.A. Evans and D.A. Hagner (eds.), *Anti-Semitism and Early Christianity: Issues of Polemic and Faith* (Minneapolis: Fortress, **1993**) 55-79.

Meeks, W.A. 'Galatia and Judea in the Fourth Gospel', *JBL* 85 (**1966**) 159-69.

The Prophet-King: Moses Traditions and the Johannine Christology (NovT Supp. 14, Leiden: Brill, **1967**).

Meier, J.P. 'Nations or Gentiles in Matthew 28:19?', *CBQ* 39 (**1977**) 94-102.

The Vision of Matthew: Christ, Church and Morality in the First Gospel (New York: Paulist, **1979**).

Menken, M. 'The Quotations from Zechariah 9:9 in Matthew 21:5 and in John 12:18', in A. Denaux (ed.), *John and the Synoptics* (Leuven: LUP, **1992**).

Merkel, H. 'Israel im lukanischen Werk', *NTS* 40 (**1994**) 371-98.

Meyer, B.F. *The Aims of Jesus* (London: SCM, **1979**).

Michaels, J.R. *1 Peter* (WBC, Waco: Word, **1988**).

Minear, P.S. 'The Original Functions of John 21', *JBL* 102 (**1983**) 85-98.

Moessner, D.P. 'The Christ Must Suffer: New Light on the Jesus-Peter, Stephen, Paul Parallels in Luke-Acts', *NovT* 28 (**1986**) 220-56.

'Paul in Acts: Preacher of Eschatological Repentance to Israel', *NTS* 34 (**1988**) 96-104.

Lord of the Banquet (Minneapolis: Fortress, **1989**).

Moffatt, J. *A Critical and Exegetical Commentary on the Epistle to the Hebrews* (ICC, Edinburgh: T. & T. Clark, **1924**).

An Introduction to the Literature of the New Testament (Edinburgh: T. & T. Clark, **1927**).

Mollat, D.M. 'Remarques sur le vocabulaire spatial du quatrième évangile', in K. Aland (ed.), *Studia Evangelica* I (TU 73, **1959**) 321-8.

Moloney, F.J. 'Reading John 2:13-22: Purification of the Temple', *RB* 97 (**1990**) 432-52.

Montefiore, H. *A Commentary on the Epistle to the Hebrews* (London: A. & C. Black, **1964**).

Morgado, J. 'Paul in Jerusalem: A Comparison of His Visits in Acts and Galatians', *JETS* 37 (**1994**) 55-68.

Morgan, R. 'Fulfillment in the Fourth Gospel', *Interpretation* 11 (**1957**) 155-165.

Morris, L.L. *Studies in the Fourth Gospel* (Grand Rapids: Eerdmans, **1969**).

The Gospel According to John (Grand Rapids: Eerdmans, **1971**).

The Book of Revelation: An Introduction and Commentary (TNTC, revd. ed., Grand Rapids/Leicester: Eerdmans/IVP, **1987**).

Luke (TNTC, revd. ed., Leicester: IVP, **1988**).

Morton, A.Q. and Macgregor, G.H.C. *The Structure of Luke-Acts* (London: Hodder and Stoughton, **1964**).

Moscato, M.A. 'Current Theories Regarding the Audience of Luke-Acts', *Currents in Theology and Mission* 3 (**1976**) 355-361.

Motyer, S. *Israel in the Plan of God: Light on Today's Debate* (Leicester: IVP, **1989**).

John 8:31-59 and the Rhetoric of Persuasion in the Fourth Gospel (unpub'd PhD thesis, King's College, London, **1992**).

Moule, C.F.D. 'Sanctuary and Sacrifice in the Church of the New Testament', *JTS* n.s. 1 (**1950**) 29-41.

The Birth of the New Testament (2nd ed., London: A. & C. Black, **1966**).

'The Christology of Acts', in L.E. Keck and J.L. Martyn (eds.), *Studies in Luke-Acts* (FS P. Schubert, London: SPCK, **1980**) 159-185.

Mounce, R.H. *The Book of Revelation* (NICNT, Grand Rapids: Eerdmans, **1977**).

Mouw, R.J. *When the Kings Come Marching In: Isaiah and the New Jerusalem* (Grand Rapids: Eerdmans, **1983**).

Munck, J. *Paul and the Salvation of Mankind* (ET, London: SCM, **1959**).

Christ and Israel: An Interpretation of Romans 9-11 (Philadelphia: Fortress, 1967).

Murphy O'Connor, J. 'Paul in Arabia', *CBQ* 55 (**1993**) 732-37.

'Pre-Constantinian Christian Jerusalem', in A. O'Mahoney *et al.* (eds.), *The Christian Heritage in the Holy Land* (London: Scorpion Cavendish, **1995**) 13-21.

Murray, R. 'Jews, Hebrews and Christians: Some Needed Distinctions', *NovT* 24 (**1982**) 194-208.

Myers, C. *Binding the Strong Man : A Political Reading of Mark's Story of Jesus* (New York: Orbis, **1988**).

Nairne, A. *The Epistle of Priesthood* (Edinburgh: T. & T. Clark, **1913**).

Nereparampil, L. *"Destroy This Temple, and in Three Days I Will Raise It Up" (John 2:19). An Exegetico-Theological Study on the Meaning of Jesus' Temple-Logion in Its Johannine Presentation* (Rome: Pontificia Universitas Gregoriana, **1972-3**).

Neyrey, J.H. 'Jesus' Address to the Women of Jerusalem (Luke 23:27-31)', *NTS* 29 (**1983**) 74-86.

(ed.), *The Social World of Luke-Acts: Models for Interpretation* (Peabody: Hendrickson, **1991**).

Nickle, K.F. *The Collection* (SBT 48, London: SCM, **1966**).

Niedner, F.A. 'Rereading Matthew on Jerusalem and Judaism', *Biblical Theology Bulletin* 19 (**1989**) 43-46.

Nolland, J. *Luke* (WBC, 3 vols., Dallas: Word, **1989/93**).

Norelli, E. 'Fin d'un Temple, Fin d'un Dieu? La Réflexion suscitée par la Destruction du Temple de Jérusalem chez les Auteurs Chrétiens du Deuxième Siècle', in P. Borgeaud *et. al.* (eds.), *Le Temple, Lieu de Conflit* (Leuven: LUP, **1994**) 151-169.

O'Neill, J.C. *The Theology of Acts in its Historical Setting* (London: SPCK, **1961**).

O'Toole, R.F. *The Unity of Luke's Theology: An Analysis of Luke-Acts* (GNS, Wilmington: M. Glazier, **1984**).

Oepke, A. *Das neue Gottesvolk* (Gütersloh: Bertelsmann, **1950**).

Okeke, G.E. '1 Thess. 2:13-16: The Fate of Unbelieving Jews', *NTS* 27 (**1980-81**) 127-36.

Osborne, R.E. 'St Paul's Silent Years', *JBL* 84 (**1965**) 59-65.

Overman, J.A. *Matthew's Gospel and Formative Judaism: The Social World of the Matthean Community* (Minneapolis: Augsburg-Fortress, **1990**).

Pancaro, S. 'The Relationship of the Church to Israel in the Gospel of John', *NTS* 16 (**1969-70**) 114-29.

The Law in the Fourth Gospel (NovT Supp. 42, Leiden: Brill, **1975**).

Parker, P. 'The "Former Treatise" and the Date of Acts', *JBL* 84 (**1965**) 52-58.

Parsons, M.C. *The Departure of Jesus in Luke-Acts* (JSNTSS 21, Sheffield: JSOT, **1987**).

Peake, A.S. 'Paul and the Jewish Christians', *BJRL* 13 (**1929**) 31-62.

Pearson, B.A. '1 Thessalonians 2:13-16: A Deutero-Pauline Interpolation', *HTR* 64 (**1971**) 79-94.

Pedersen, S. 'Zum Problem der vaticinia ex eventu', *ST* 19 (**1965**) 167-88.

Pervo, R.I. *Luke's Story of Paul* (Minneapolis: Fortress, **1990**).

Petersen, N.R. *Literary Criticism for New Testament Critics* (Philadelphia: Fortress, **1978**).

Peterson, D. 'The Motif of Fulfilment and the Purpose of Luke-Acts', in B.W. Winter and A.D. Clarke (eds.), *The Book of Acts in Its Ancient Literary Setting* (Grand Rapids/Carlisle: Eerdmans/Paternoster, **1993**) 83-104.

Plummer, A. *The Second Epistle of Paul to the Corinthians* (ICC, Edinburgh: T. & T. Clark, **1915**).

Polhill, J.B. *Acts* (NAC, Nashville: Broadman, **1992**).

Porter, R.J. 'What Did Philip Say to the Eunuch?', *ExpT* 100 (**1988-89**) 54-55.

Porter, S.E. 'The "We" Passages', in D.W.J. Gill and C.H. Gempf (eds.), *The Book of Acts in its Graeco-Roman Setting* (Grand Rapids/Carlisle: Eerdmans/Paternoster, **1994**) 545-574.

Powell, M.A. *What Are They Saying About Luke?* (New York: Paulist, **1989**).

——— *What Are They Saying About Acts?* (New York: Paulist, **1991**).

Praeder, S.M. 'Jesus-Paul, Peter-Paul, and Jesus-Peter Parallelisms in Luke-Acts: A History of Reader Response', *SBL 1984 Seminar Papers* (Atlanta: Scholars, **1984**) 23-40.

Pritz, R.A. *Nazarene Jewish Christianity: From the End of the New Testament Period until Its Disappearance in the Fourth Century* (Leiden: Brill, **1988**).

Pryor, J.W. 'John 4:44 and the *Patris* of Jesus', *CBQ* 49 (**1987**) 254-63.

——— 'Jesus and Israel in the Fourth Gospel—John 1:11', *NovT* 32 (1990) 201-18.

——— *John: Evangelist of the Covenant People* (Leicester: IVP, **1992**).

Radl, W. *Paulus und Jesus im lukanischen Doppelwerk: Untersuchungen zu Parallelmotiven im Lukasevangelium und in der Apostelgeschichte* (Bern/Frankfurt: H.& P. Lang, **1975**).

Räisänen, H. 'The Redemption of Israel: A Salvation-Historical Problem in Luke-Acts', in P. Luomanen (ed.), *Luke-Acts: Scandinavian Papers* (Göttingen: Vandenhoeck & Ruprecht, **1991**) 94-114.

Ramsay, W.M. 'The Date and Authorship of the Epistle to the Hebrews', in *Luke the Physician* (London: Hodder & Stoughton, **1908**).

Ravens, D. *Luke and the Restoration of Israel* (JSNTSS 119, Sheffield: SAP, **1995**).

Reicke, B. 'Caesarea, Rome and the Captivity Epistles', in W.W. Gasque and R.P. Martin *Apostolic History and the Gospel* (FS F.F. Bruce, Grand Rapids: Eerdmans, **1970**) 277-86.

——— 'Synoptic Prophecies and the Destruction of Jerusalem', in D. Aune (ed.), *Studies in the New Testament and Early Christian Literature* (NovT Supp. 33, FS A.P. Wikgren, Leiden: Brill, **1972**) 121-34.

——— 'Judaeo-Christianity and the Jewish Establishment, A.D. 33-66', in E. Bammel and C.F.D. Moule (eds.), *Jesus and the Politics of His Day* (Cambridge: CUP, **1984**) 145-152.

Rengstorf, K.H. 'Die Stadt der Mörder (Mt. 22:7)', in W. Eltester (ed.), *Judentum, Urchristentum, Kirche* (FS J. Jeremias, Berlin: de Gruyter, **1960**) 106-29.

Rhoads, D. and Michie, D. *Mark as Story: An Introduction to the Narrative of a Gospel* (Philadelphia: Fortress, **1982**).

Richardson, A. *The Miracle Stories of the Gospels* (London: SCM, **1941**).

Richardson, P. *Israel in the Apostolic Church* (SNTSMS 10, Cambridge: CUP, **1969**).

——— 'Pauline Inconsistency: 1 Cor 9:19-23 and Galatians 2:11-16', *NTS* 26 (**1979-80**) 347-62.

Robinson, J.A.T. *Jesus and His Coming: The Emergence of a Doctrine* (London: SCM, **1957**).

——— *Redating the New Testament* (London: SCM, **1976**).

——— *The Priority of John* (London: SCM, **1985**).

Rosner, B.S. 'Acts and Biblical History', in B.W. Winter and A.D. Clarke (eds.), *The Book of Acts in its Ancient Literary Setting* (Grand Rapids/Carlisle: Eerdmans/Paternoster, **1993**) 65-82.

Ross, J.M. 'The Spelling of Jerusalem in Acts', *NTS* 38 (**1992**) 474-6.

Rowland. C. *Revelation* (London: Epworth, **1993**).

Rubinstein, R. *My Brother Paul* (New York: Ktav, **1972**).

Russell, H.G. 'Which Was Written First, Luke or Acts?', *HTR* 48 (**1955**) 167-74.

Sabourin, L. *L'Evangile selon St Matthieu et ses Principaux Parallèles* (Rome: Biblical Institute, **1978**).

Safrai, S. 'Relations Between the Diaspora and the Land of Israel', in S. Safrai and M. Stern (eds.), *Compendia Rerum Iudaicarum ad Novum Testamentum* (Assen: Van Gorcum, **1974**) i, 184-215.

Saldarini, A.J. *Matthew's Christian-Jewish Community* (Chicago: University of Chicago, **1994**).

Sanders, E.P. *Jesus and Judaism* (Philadelphia: Fortress, **1985**).

    The Historical Figure of Jesus (London: Penguin, **1993**).

Sanders, J.A. and Evans, C.A. *Luke and Scripture* (Minneapolis: Fortress, **1993**).

Scharlemann, M. *St Stephen: A Singular Saint* (Analecta Biblica 34, Rome: Pontifical Biblical Institute, **1968**).

Schein, B.E. *Following the Way: The Setting of John's Gospel* (Minneapolis: Augsburg, **1980**).

Schillebeeckx, E. *Christ: The Christian Experience in the Modern World* (ET, London: SCM, **1980**).

Schlatter, A. *Der Evangelist Matthäus* (6th ed., Stuttgart: Calwer Verlag, **1963**).

Schlueter, C.J. *Filling Up the Measure: Polemical Hyperbole in 1 Thess 2:14-16* (JSNTSS 98, Sheffield: JSOT, **1994**).

Schmidt, D. '1 Thess. 2:13-16: Linguistic Evidence for an Interpolation', *JBL* 102 (**1983**) 269-79.

Schmithals, W. *Paul and James* (SBT 46, London: SCM, **1965**).

Schnackenburg, R. *The Gospel According to John* (ET, 3 vols., London: Burns & Oates, 1980/82).

Schnellbächer, E.L. 'The Temple as Focus of Mark's Theology', *Horizons in Biblical Theology* 5 (**1983**) 95-112.

Schürer, E. *The History of the Jewish People in the Age of Jesus Christ [175BC-AD 135]* (revd. ed. G. Vermes *et al*, 4 vols., Edinburgh: T. & T. Clark, **1973-87**).

Schüssler Fiorenza, E. *The Book of Revelation: Justice and Judgment* (Philadelphia: Fortress, **1985**).

    Revelation: Vision of a Just World (Proclamation Commentaries, Minneapolis: Fortress, **1991**).

Schwartz, D.R. '"The End of the ΓΗ" (Acts 1:8): Beginning or End of the Christian Vision?', *JBL* 105 (**1986**) 669-76.

    'Temple and Desert: On Religion and State in the Second Temple Period Judaism', in his *Studies in the Jewish Background of Christianity* (WUNT 60, Tübingen: Mohr, **1992a**) 29-43.

    'On Sacrifices by Gentiles in the Temple of Jerusalem', in his *Studies in the Jewish Background of Christianity* (WUNT 60, Tübingen: Mohr, **1992b**) 102-16.

Scott, J.J. 'Parties in the Church of Jerusalem as Seen in the Book of Acts', *JETS* 18 (**1975**) 217-27.

Scott, J.M. 'Luke's Geographical Horizon', in D.W.J. Gill and C.H. Gempf (eds.) *The Book of Acts in its Graeco-Roman Setting* (Grand Rapids/Carlisle: Eerdmans/Paternoster, **1994**) 483-544.

Seccombe, D. 'Luke and Isaiah', *NTS* 27 (**1980-1**) 252-9.

Segal, A. 'Matthew's Jewish Voice', in D.L. Balch (ed.), *The Social History of the Mat-
    thean Community: Cross Disciplinary Approaches* (Minneapolis: Fortress,
    1991) 3-37.
Senior, D. *The Passion Narrative According to Matthew: A Redactional Study* (Leuven:
    LUP, **1982**).
Simon, M. 'Saint Stephen and the Jerusalem Temple', *JEH* 2 (**1951**) 127-42.
    St. Stephen and the Hellenists in the Primitive Church (London: Longmans, Green
    & Co., **1958**).
Simpson, J.W. 'Problems Posed by 1 Thessalonians 2:15-16', *Horizons in Biblical Theol-
    ogy* 12 (**1990**) 42-72.
Simson, P. 'The Drama of the City of God: Jerusalem in Luke's Gospel', in M. Rosalie
    Ryan (ed.), *Contemporary New Testament Studies* (Minnesota: ?? **1965**) 224-
    37.
Slingerland, H.D. 'The Transjordanian Origin of Matthew's Gospel', *JSNT* 3 (**1979**) 18-28.
Smalley, S.S. 'John's Revelation and John's Community', *BJRL* 69 (**1987**) 549-571.
    Thunder and Love: John's Revelation and John's Community (Milton Keynes: Nel-
    son Word, **1994**).
Smith, C.R. 'The Portrayal of the Church as the New Israel in the Names and Order of the
    Tribes in Revelation 7:5-8', *JSNT* 39 (**1990**) 111-118.
Smith, C.W.F. 'Tabernacles in the Fourth Gospel and Mark', *NTS* 9 (**1962-3**) 130-46.
Smith, R.H. 'Exodus Typology in the Fourth Gospel', *JBL* 81 (**1962**) 329-42.
Snell, A. *New and Living Way* (London: Faith Press, **1959**).
Songer, R.H.S. 'Paul's Mission to Jerusalem: Acts 20-28', *Review and Expositor* 71 (**1974**)
    499-510.
Spicq, C. *L'Epître aux Hébreux* (2 vols., Paris: Gabalda, **1953**).
Stagg, F. 'Paul's Final Mission to Jerusalem', in N.A. Keathley (ed.), *With Steadfast Pur-
    pose* (FS H.J. Flanders, Waco: Baylor University, **1990**) 259-77.
Standaert, B. *L'Evangile selon Marc: Commentaire* (Paris: Cerf, **1978**).
Stanley, C.D. *Paul and the Language of Scripture: Citation Technique in the Pauline Epis-
    tles and Contemporary Literature* (SNTSMS 69, Cambridge: CUP, **1992**).
Stanton, G. 'The Origin and Purpose of Matthew's Gospel: Matthean Scholarship from
    1945-1980', in H. Temporini and W. Haase (eds.), *Aufstieg und Niedergang
    der römischen Welt* II 25.3 (Berlin: de Gruyter, **1985**) 1889-1951.
    A Gospel for a New People (Edinburgh: T. & T. Clark, **1992**).
    'Revisiting Matthew's Communitites', *SBL 1994 Seminar Papers* (Atlanta: Schol-
    ars, **1994**) 9-23.
    (ed.), *The Interpretation of Matthew* (2nd ed., Edinburgh: T. & T. Clark, **1995**).
Stedman, R.C. *Hebrews* (Leicester, IVP, **1992**).
Steichele, HJ. *Der Leidende Sohn Gottes* (Regensburg: Friedrich Pustet, **1980**).
Stemberger, G. 'Galilee—Land of Salvation', in W.D. Davies, *The Gospel and the Land:
    Early Christianity and Jewish Territorial Doctrine* (Berkeley: University of
    California, **1974**) 409-438.
Stendahl, K. 'Quis et unde? An Analysis of Matthew 1-2', in W. Eltester (ed.), *Judentum,
    Urchristentum, Kirche* (FS J. Jeremias, Berlin: de Gruyter, **1960**) 94-105.
Stibbe, M.W.G. *John* (Sheffield: JSOT, **1993**).
Stonehouse, N.B. *The Witness of Matthew and Mark to Christ* (London: Tyndale, **1944**).
Strack, H.L. and Stemberger, G. *Introduction to the Talmud and Midrash* (ET by M.N.A.
    Bockmuehl, Edinburgh: T. & T. Clark, **1991**).

Strecker, G. *Der Weg der Gerechtigkeit: Untersuchungen zur Theologie des Matthäus* (FR-LANT 82, Göttingen: Vandenhoeck & Ruprecht, **1971**).

Streeter, B.H. *The Four Gospels* (London: Macmillan, **1936**).

Strobel, A. *Der Brief an die Hebräer* (Göttingen: Vandenhoeck & Ruprecht, **1991**).

Struthers Malbon, E. 'Galilee and Jerusalem: History and Literature in Marcan Interpretation', *CBQ* 44 (**1982**) 242-55.

'The Jesus of Mark and the Sea of Galilee', *JBL* 103 (**1984**) 363-377.

Narrative Space and Mythic Meaning in Mark (2nd ed., Sheffield: JSOT, **1991**).

Stuhlmacher, P. 'The Purpose of Romans', in K.P. Donfried (ed.), *The Romans Debate* (revd. ed., Edinburgh: T. & T. Clark, **1991**) 231-244.

Sumney, J.L. *Identifying Paul's Opponents: The Question of Method in 2 Corinthians* (JS-NTSS 40, Sheffield: JSOT, **1990**).

Sweet, J.P.M. 'A house not made with hands', in W. Horbury (ed.), *Templum Amicitiae* (FS E. Bammel, Sheffield: JSOT, **1991**) 368-390.

Revelation (TPINTC, revd ed., Philadelphia/London: Trinity Press International/ SCM, **1990**).

Sylva, D.D. 'Ierousalem and Hierosoluma in Luke-Acts', *ZNW* 74 (**1983**) 207-21.

'The Temple Curtain and Jesus' Death in the Gospel of Luke', *JBL* 105 (**1986**) 239-50.

Talbert, C.H. *Literary Patterns, Theological Themes, and the Genre of Luke-Acts*, (SBLMS 20, Missoula: Scholars, **1974**).

(ed.), *Luke-Acts: New Perspectives from the SBL Seminar* (New York: Crossroad, 1984).

Tannehill, R.C. 'Israel in Luke-Acts: A Tragic Story', *JBL* 104 (**1985**) 69-85.

The Narrative Unity of Luke-Acts: A Literary Interpretation (2 vols., Philadelphia and Minneapolis: Fortress, **1986/90**).

Taylor J. 'Why Did Paul Persecute the Church?', in G. Stanton and G. Stroumsa (eds.), *Tolerance and Intolerance in Early Judaism and Early Christianity* (Cambridge: CUP, **1996**).

Taylor, N. *Paul, Antioch and Jerusalem* (JSNTSS 66, Sheffield: JSOT, **1992**).

Telford, W.R. *The Barren Temple and the Withered Tree* (JSNTSS 1, Sheffield: JSOT, **1980**).

(ed.), *The Interpretation of Mark* (2nd ed., Edinburgh: T. & T. Clark, **1995**).

Temple, W. *Readings in St John's Gospel* (2 vols., London: Macmillan, **1943**).

Theissen, G. *The Social Setting of Pauline Christianity: Essays on Corinth* (ET, Philadelphia: Fortress, **1982**).

Social Reality and the Early Christians (ET, Edinburgh: T. & T. Clark, **1993**).

Therath, A. *Jerusalem in the Gospel of John* (Rome: Pontifical Biblical Institute: **1994**).

Thomas, J.C. *Footwashing in John 13 and the Johannine Community* (JSNTSS 61, Sheffield: JSOT, **1991**).

Thompson, J. W. '"Outside the Camp": A Study of Hebrews 13:9-14', *CBQ* (**1978**) 53-63.

The Beginnings of Christian Philosophy: The Epistle to the Hebrews (CBQMS 13; Washington: Catholic Biblical Association of America, **1981**).

Tiede, D.L. *Prophecy and History in Luke-Acts*, (Philadelphia: Fortress, **1980**).

'The Exaltation of Jesus and the Restoration of Israel in Acts 1', *HTR* 79 (**1986**) 278-86.

'The Death of Jesus and the Trial of Israel in Luke-Acts', *SBL 1990 Seminar Papers* (Atlanta: Scholars, **1990**) 158-64.

'Fighting Against God: Luke's Interpretation of the Jewish Rejection of the Messiah Jesus', in C.A. Evans and D.A. Hagner (eds.), *Anti-Semitism and Early Christianity: Issues of Polemic and Faith* (Minneapolis: Fortress, **1993**) 102-112.

Trilling, W. *Das wahre Israel: Studien zur Theologie des Matthäus Evangeliums* (München: Kösel-Verlag, **1964**).

Trocmé, E. *The Formation of the Gospel According to Mark* (Philadelphia: Westminster, **1975**).

Trudinger, L.P. 'The Gospel Meaning of the Secular (Hebrews 13:10-13)', *EQ* 54 (**1982**) 235-37.

Turner, M.B. *Power From on High: The Spirit in Israel's Restoration and Witness in Luke-Acts* (Sheffield: SAP, **1996**).

Tyson, J.B. *The Death of Jesus in Luke-Acts* (Columbia: University of South Carolina, **1986**).

—(ed.), *Luke-Acts and the Jewish People* (Minneapolis: Augsburg, **1988**).

—*Images of Judaism in Luke-Acts* (Columbia: University of South Carolina, **1992**).

—'Jews and Judaism in Luke-Acts: Reading as a God-Fearer', *NTS* 41 (**1995**) 19-38.

Van der Waal, C. 'The Temple in the Gospel According to Luke', *Neotestamentica* 7 (**1973**) 49-59.

Vanhoye, A. 'L'utilisation du livre d'Ezéchiel dans l'Apocalypse', *Biblica* 43 (**1962**) 436-77.

—*The Structure and Message of the Epistle to the Hebrews* (Rome: Pontifical Biblical Institute, **1989**).

Van Tilborg, S. *The Jewish Leaders in Matthew* (Leiden: Brill, **1972**).

Van Unnik, W.C. *Tarsus or Jerusalem: The City of Paul's Youth* (ET, London: Epworth, **1962**).

Vesco, J.L. *Jérusalem et son prophète* (Paris: Cerf, **1988**).

Vielhauer, P. 'On the "Paulinism" of Acts', in L.E. Keck and J.L. Martyn (eds.), *Studies in Luke-Acts* (FS P. Schubert, London: SPCK, **1980**) 33-50.

Viviano, B.T. 'Where was the Gospel According to St. Matthew Written?', *CBQ* 41 (**1979**), 533-546.

Von Wahlde, U.C. 'The Johannine "Jews": A Critical Survey', *NTS* 28 (**1982**) 33-60.

Wainwright, A.W. 'Luke and the Restoration of the Kingdom to Israel', *ExpT* 139 (**1977-8**) 76-9.

Walaskay, P.W. *'And So We Came to Rome'* (Cambridge: CUP, **1983**).

Walker, P.W.L. *Holy City, Holy Places? Christian Attitides to Jerusalem and Holy Land in the Fourth Century* (Oxford: OUP, **1990a**).

—'Gospel Sites and "Holy Places": The Contrasting Attitudes of Eusebius and Cyril', *TynB* 41 (**1990b**) 89-108.

—(ed.), *Jerusalem Past and Present in the Purposes of God* (revd. ed., Carlisle/Grand Rapids: Paternoster/Baker, **1994a**).

—'Jerusalem in Hebrews 13:9-14 and the Dating of the Epistle', *TynB* 45.1 (**1994b**) 39-71.

—'Jerusalem and the Holy Land in the Fourth Century', in A. O'Mahoney *et al* (eds.), *The Christian Heritage in the Holy Land* (London: Scorpion Cavendish, **1995**) 22-34.

—'Centre Stage: Jerusalem or Jesus?', *Cambridge Papers* 5.1 (**1996a**).

—'Christians and Jerusalem, Past and Present', in *The Mountain of the Lord: Israel and the Churches* (London: Council of Christians and Jews, **1996b**).

Wanamaker, C.A. *1 and 2 Thessalonians* (NIGTC, Grand Rapids: Eerdmans, **1990**).

Watson, F.B. *Paul, Judaism and the Gentiles* (SNTSMS 56, Cambridge: CUP, **1986**).

Wead, D.W. *The Literary Devices in John's Gospel* (Basel: Friedrich Reinhardt Kommissionsverlag, **1970**).

Weatherly, J.A. 'The Jews in Luke-Acts', *TynB* 40 (**1989**) 107-17.

    'The Authenticity of 1 Thessalonians 2:13-16', *JSNT* 42 (**1991**) 79-98.

    Jewish Responsibility for the Death of Jesus in Luke-Acts (JSNTSS 106, Sheffield: SAP, **1994**).

Weinert, F.D. 'The Meaning of the Temple in Luke-Acts', *Biblical Theology Bulletin* 11 (**1981**) 85-89.

    'Jesus' Saying About Jerusalem's Abandoned House', *CBQ* 44 (**1982**) 68-76.

    'Luke, Stephen and the Temple in Luke-Acts', *Biblical Theology Bulletin* 17 (**1987**) 88-91.

Wengst, K. *Bedrängte Gemeinde und verherrlichter Christus* (Neukirchen-Vluyn: Neukirchener, **1981**).

Wenham, D. *The Rediscovery of Jesus' Eschatological Discourse* (Sheffield: JSOT, **1984**).

    'Acts and the Pauline Corpus: The Evidence of Parallels', in B.W. Winter and A.D. Clarke (eds.), *The Book of Acts in Its Ancient Literary Setting* (Grand Rapids/Carlisle: Eerdmans/Paternoster, **1993**) 215-258.

    Paul: Follower of Jesus or Founder of Christianity? (Cambridge/Grand Rapids: Eerdmans, **1995**).

Wenham, D. and A.D.A. Moses '"There are Some Standing Here . . ." Did they become the "Reputed Pillars" of the Jerusalem Church? Some Reflections on Mark 9:1, Galatians 2:9 and the Transfiguration', *NovT* 36 (**1994**) 146-63.

Wenham, J. 'When Were the Saints Raised?', *JTS* 32 (**1981**) 150-2.

Wescott, B.F. *The Epistle to the Hebrews* (3rd ed., London/New York: Macmillan, **1903**).

    The Gospel According to St. John (London: John Murray, **1908**).

Wiefel, W. 'The Jewish Community in Ancient Rome and the Origins of Roman Christianity', in K.P. Donfried (ed.), *The Romans Debate* (revd. ed., Edinburgh: T. & T. Clark, **1991**) 85-101.

Wilken, R.L. *The Land Called Holy: Palestine in Christian History and Thought* (New Haven/London: Yale University Press, **1992**).

Williams, C.S.C. 'The Date of Luke-Acts', *ExpT* 64 (**1952-3**) 283-4.

Wilson, R.M. *Hebrews* (NCB, Basingstoke: Marshall, Morgan and Scott, **1987**).

Wilson, S.G. *The Gentiles and the Gentile Mission in Luke-Acts* (SNTMS 23, Cambridge: CUP, **1973**).

Windisch, H. *Der Hebräerbrief* (2nd ed., Tübingen: Mohr, **1931**).

Winkle, R.E. 'The Jeremiah Model for Jesus in the Temple', *AUSS* 24 (**1986**) 155-72.

Witherington, B. *The Christology of Jesus* (Minneapolis: Fortress, **1990**).

    'The Influence of Galatians on Hebrews', *NTS* 37 (**1991**) 146-52.

    'Not So Idle Thoughts About *eidolothuton*'', *TynB* 44.2 (**1993**) 237-54.

Witherup, R.D. 'The Death of Jesus and the Raising of the Saints in Matthew 27:51-4 in Context', *SBL 1987 Seminar Papers* (Atlanta: Scholars, **1987**) 574-85.

Wright, A.G. 'The Widow's Mites: Praise or Lament? A Matter of Context', *CBQ* 44 (**1982**) 256-65.

Wright, C.J.H. 'A Christian Approach to Old Testament Prophecy Concerning Israel', in P.W.L. Walker (ed.), *Jerusalem Past and Present in the Purposes of God* (revd. ed., Carlisle/Grand Rapids: Paternoster/Baker, **1994**) 1-20.

Wright, N.T. 'The Paul of History and the Apostle of Faith', *TynB* 29 (**1978**) 61-88.

'Jesus, Israel, and the Cross', *SBL 1985 Seminar Papers* (Atlanta: Scholars, **1985**) 77-95.

The Climax of the Covenant (Edinburgh: T. & T. Clark, **1991**).

The New Testament and the People of God: Christian Origins and the Question of God (London: SPCK, **1992a**).

The Crown and the Fire: Meditations on the Cross and the Life of the Spirit (London: SPCK, **1992b**).

'Romans and the Theology of Paul', *SBL 1992 Seminar Papers* (Atlanta: Scholars, **1992c**) 184-213.

'Jerusalem in the New Testament', in P.W.L. Walker (ed.), *Jerusalem Past and Present in the Purposes of God* (revd. ed., Carlisle/Grand Rapids: Paternoster/ Baker, **1994a**) 53-78.

'Gospel and Theology in Galatians', in L.A. Jervis and P. Richardson (eds.), *Gospel in Paul* (FS R.N. Longenecker, JSNTSS 108, Sheffield: SAP, **1994b**) 222-239.

Jesus and the Victory of God (London: SPCK, forthcoming, **1996**).

Yarbro Collins, A. *Crisis and Catharsis: The Power of the Apocalypse* (Philadelphia: Westminster, **1984**).

Zahn, T. *Introduction to the New Testament* (ET, 3 vols., Edinburgh: T. & T. Clark, **1909**).

Ziesler, J. *Paul's Letter to the Romans* (TPINTC, London: SCM, **1989**).

INDEX OF BIBLICAL REFERENCES

OLD TESTAMENT

351

INDEX OF MODERN AUTHORS

INDEX OF SUBJECTS